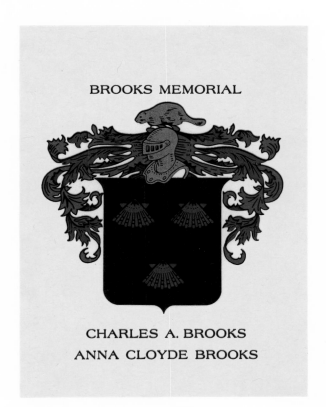

BROOKS MEMORIAL

CHARLES A. BROOKS

ANNA CLOYDE BROOKS

HISTORY OF WORLD ARCHITECTURE

Pier Luigi Nervi, General Editor

GRACE LIBRARY, CARLOW COLLEGE
PITTSBURGH, PA. 15213

NEOCLASSICAL AND 19TH CENTURY ARCHITECTURE

Robin Middleton and David Watkin

NA
600
M513

Harry N. Abrams, Inc., Publishers, New York

CATALOGUED

Series Coordinator: Giuseppe Positano de Vincentiis

Produced under the supervision of Carlo Pirovano,
editorial director of Electa Editrice

Designed by Diego Birelli, art director of Electa Editrice
Italian edition edited by Enzo Fiano and Angelo Salvioni

American edition edited by Ellyn Childs Allison

Library of Congress Cataloging in Publication Data

Middleton, Robin.
    Neoclassical and 19th century architecture.

    (History of world architecture)
    Bibliography: p.
    Includes indexes.
    1. Neoclassicism (Architecture) 2. Architecture,
Modern—19th century. I. Watkin, David, 1941–
joint author. II. Title.
NA600. M513   724   79–18099

ISBN 0-8109-1014-4

Library of Congress Catalog Card Number: 79–18099
© Electa Editrice® 1977—Gruppo Editoriale Electa S.p.A.
Published in 1980 by Harry N. Abrams, Incorporated, New York
All rights reserved. No part of the contents of this book may be
reproduced without the written permission of the publishers

Printed and bound in Japan

FOREWORD

Architectural criticism has nearly always been concerned with the visible aspect of individual buildings, taking this to be the decisive factor in the formulation of value judgments and in the classification of those "styles" which appear in textbooks, and which have thus become common knowledge. But once it is recognized that every building is, by definition, a work subject to the limitations imposed by the materials and building techniques at hand, and that every building must prove its stability, as well as its capacity to endure and serve the needs it was built for, it becomes clear that the aesthetic aspect alone is inadequate when we come to appraise a creative activity, difficult enough to judge in the past, rapidly becoming more complex in our own day, and destined to become more so in the foreseeable future.

Nevertheless, what has struck me most, on studying the architecture of the past and present, is the fact that the works which are generally regarded by the critics and the general public as examples of pure beauty are also the fruit of exemplary building techniques, once one has taken into account the quality of the materials and the technical knowledge available. And it is natural to suspect that such a coincidence is not entirely casual.

Building in the past was wholly a matter of following static intuitions, which were, in turn, the result of meditation, experience, and above all of an understanding of the capacity of certain structures and materials to resist external forces. Meditation upon structural patterns and the characteristics of various materials, together with the appraisal of one's own experiences and those of others, is an act of love toward the process of construction for its own sake, both on the part of the architect and his collaborators and assistants. Indeed, we may wonder whether this is not the hidden bond which unites the appearance and substance of the finest buildings of the past, distant though that past may be, into a single "thing of beauty."

One might even think that the quality of the materials available not only determined architectural patterns but also the decorative detail with which the first simple construction was gradually enriched.

One might find a justification for the difference in refinement and elegance between Greek architecture, with its basic use of marble—a highly resistant material, upon which the most delicate carvings can be carried out—and the majestic concrete structures of Roman architecture, built out of a mixture of lime and pozzolana, and supported by massive walls, to compensate for their intrinsic weaknesses.

Would it be too rash to connect these objective architectural characteristics with the different artistic sensibilities of the two peoples?

One must recognize, therefore, the importance of completing the description of the examples illustrated with an interpretation of their constructional and aesthetic characteristics, so that the connection between the twin aspects of building emerges as a natural, logical consequence.

This consequence, if understood and accepted in good faith by certain avant-garde circles, could put an end to the disastrous haste with which our architecture is rushing toward an empty, costly, and at times impractical formalism. It might also recall architects and men of culture to a more serene appraisal of the objective elements of building and to the respect that is due to a morality of architecture. For this is just as important for the future of our cities as is morality, understood as a rule of life, for an orderly civil existence.

PIER LUIGI NERVI

PREFACE

The chronological span of this book is 1750 to 1870. We have avoided reliance on the misleading descriptive term neoclassicism *and have emphasized the importance of both the rationalist theory developed in France and the Picturesque movement in England. The book is primarily a history of architecture and thus does not cover many of the important developments that took place during the years in question in town planning, transport, and engineering. We also felt it impossible, in a single volume, to give equal attention to each period and country. Thus, the reader will find less on England than on France, for English architecture has been examined by such historians as John Summerson, Henry-Russell Hitchcock, and Nikolaus Pevsner, whereas French architecture—particularly of the nineteenth century—has been much less extensively investigated. Architecture rests on intellectual as well as material foundations, and we hope that fresh light will be shed on the period by our emphasis on the theories and ideas that so often lay behind the new movements.*

ROBIN MIDDLETON
DAVID WATKIN

Cambridge, 1976

TABLE OF CONTENTS

Chapter One

THE RATIONAL TRADITION IN FRANCE

The architecture of the eighteenth and nineteenth centuries was conditioned largely by two traditions of thought, the French rationalist tradition emerging from a Cartesian delight in clarity and mathematical certainty, and the English or rather British Empirical tradition that was to suggest another system of ordering, ultimately to be popularized as the Picturesque. The two phenomena were quite distinct and were independently developed, though by the late eighteenth century their particular qualities were clear enough for them to be taken up and adapted to new situations. The impact of Marc-Antoine Laugier's somewhat simplistic rationale of architecture, the primitive hut, was felt throughout Europe, in England no less than in Italy and Germany, while that particular expression of the Picturesque, the *jardin anglais*, was to be taken up not only in Italy and Germany and the outer states of Europe but in the home of rational enlightenment itself—not that the French ever understood the subtleties of Picturesque composition or grappled long with the problems. Likewise, the geometrical ordering principles evolved by Jean-Nicolas-Louis Durand at the turn of the century were to be adopted by architects throughout Europe, but in England with noticeably less enthusiasm and effect than anywhere else. But the rational interpretation of Gothic that the French had evolved from the sixteenth century onward was to be introduced into England in the early nineteenth century by A. W. N. Pugin with the most profound and dramatic results. Even John Ruskin, that man of sensitivity and feeling who cared little enough for the way in which a building was organized or the techniques of its construction, was conditioned to the deepest respect for the rigidly deterministic analyses of Gothic made by the Frenchman Eugène-Emmanuel Viollet-le-Duc.

There was thus much exchange of thought and opinion and no little interaction of opposed ideas, but the main development of the two traditions of thought remained separate and distinct, and they are best dealt with independently.

The French rationalist ideal demands the first attention, for it provided the framework of thought for the whole of the Enlightenment. The beginnings, for our purposes, lie in the works of Claude Perrault (1613–1688), a doctor, anatomist, and experimenter in all kinds of devices, mostly mechanical, who turned unaccountably to architecture when he was already over fifty. His chief architectural works were the Observatoire in the Faubourg Saint-Jacques, Paris, a decidedly gaunt and singular building, dating from 1667 to 1672; the east facade of the Louvre, begun in the same year and more or less completed by 1674; and a triumphal arch for the Porte Saint-Antoine, also in Paris, designed in 1668 (started at once, mocked up in lath and plaster, which deteriorated, it was torn down in 1716). The key work is the Louvre facade, which may or may not be Perrault's own composition. It was the outcome of a combined effort by a committee composed of Louis Le Vau, *Premier Architecte du Roi*; Charles Le Brun, *Premier Peintre du Roi*; Perrault himself; and his brother, Charles, who acted as secretary and stand-in for his master, Jean Baptiste Colbert, the king's chief adviser. Claude Perrault's contribution has often been called in question, first by Nicolas Boileau soon after his death, but those who saw the relevant documents and drawings before they were destroyed in the fire at the Hôtel de Ville in 1870 found no evidence to dispute his claim to authorship.

The whole enterprise was an occasion, almost, of national importance. Le Vau had done the first project, but this was little admired by Colbert, who submitted it to the judgment of an array of Italian architects, among them the great Bernini, who was induced to journey to Paris to undertake the design himself. The pope's release of his favorite architect was a triumph for French diplomacy. But having gotten Bernini to Paris, they feared that national prestige might suffer should an Italian complete the royal palace. Bernini's robust, grandiose designs were not, in any case, to French taste. He was sent home, richly rewarded with gold but enraged. Instead, the committee set up by Colbert built the majestic, calm, and rhythmical facade that stands today and that has been regarded always as a model of excellence by architects and connoisseurs of French architecture. Le Corbusier himself found it in him to admire it. Its particular qualities may seem to us negative rather than positive, but they have nonetheless been potent influences. There is very little emphasis in the facade. The traditional French composition of a central feature with outlying pavilions is still in evidence, but there is scarcely a break in the plan, scarcely a break in the outline. The composition is neat and rectangular. The pediment in the center is low and unobtrusive. The essence of the architecture seems to reside in the rows of coupled freestanding columns that link the main elements, a curious paradox but one that evidently embodied Perrault's intentions. He aimed that the column should resume its antique role as a supporting element, thus constituting the architecture and no longer appearing as an applied decorative device. This clear and honest expression of the role and the form of the main elements in the architecture was a quality he thought to discern not only in ancient Greek temples but also, it may be surprising to learn, in Gothic cathedrals. He defended his arrangement of columns on the Louvre facade with reference to the clustered shafts of Notre-Dame in Paris.

In consciously renewing the French tradition by a return to sources, he referred thus to both classical and national prototypes.

1. *Claude Perrault, Observatoire, Paris, 1667–72.*
2. *Frontispiece of Claude Perrault's translation of Vitruvius, 1673. Represented are three of Perrault's principal works: in the background, the Observatoire; in the middleground, the east façade of the Louvre; to the left, the triumphal arch for the Porte Saint-Antoine (now the Place de la Nation).*
3. *Claude Perrault and others, east façade of the Louvre, Paris, 1667–74.*

But he pleaded for no simpleminded return to the past. He was trained as a doctor and a scientist and took it for granted that the contemporary endeavor would be in advance of that of the past. He looked to the past only as a point of departure in the establishment of principles. His most earnest achievement in this respect was the translation of the ten books of architecture ascribed to Vitruvius, the only architectural treatise to survive from antiquity. This was another venture abetted by Colbert. Jean Martin and Jean Goujon had published a French translation in 1547, but the text was unsatisfactory and the plates were culled for the most part from earlier Italian editions. Perrault's professional grounding in Latin and Greek stood him in good stead. In 1673 he issued the first edition of his scholarly and altogether competent text. It was not an antiquarian exercise but rather a polemical work. It was illustrated with magnificent plates—the finest by Sébastien Le Clerc, who was later to attempt an architectural treatise on his own account—featuring all of Perrault's own works and an array of suggested reconstructions of antique buildings intended to set a new standard for contemporary architecture. The forms are precisely defined and rectangular; freestanding columns are in evidence everywhere. A revised edition appeared in 1684 with a great many footnotes that make more clear Perrault's theoretical standpoint, though this had been expressed clearly enough the year before in his *Ordonnance des cinq espèces de colonnes selon la méthode des anciens*. This was, as the name implies, largely concerned with the orders. But in it Perrault was to introduce his theory of beauty that served to shatter the Renaissance and post-Renaissance belief in the transcendental role of the orders. There were, Perrault declared, two types of beauty in architecture, positive and arbitrary. Positive beauty was based quite simply on the quality of materials, on precision and neatness of execution, on size, on sheer magnificence, and on symmetry—values that must have seemed obvious enough in the reign of Louis XIV. Arbitrary beauty resided in such qualities as proportional relationships, form, and shape. It was in his ability to manipulate these and compose his designs that the real talent of the architect rested. For there were no sure guides, no fixed rules, only custom. Perrault rejected quite rudely the idea that there was an absolute criterion for architectural proportions. The architectural proportions derived from the orders, he said, were not related to the scale of musical harmonies as was commonly thought; they were in no sense a feature of a divine or universal order; they were simply a matter of custom. The cultivated eye had grown used to certain proportions and was thus shocked by any departure from the norm. Perrault himself respected the norm—like Descartes and even Pascal he upheld an ideal of "médiocrité." He thus determined to investigate the welter

of proportional systems that had been proposed by theorists from the Renaissance onward and to find a workable mean. Antoine Desgodets's carefully measured drawings of forty-nine buildings in Rome, to be published in 1682 as *Les édifices antiques de Rome*, confirmed his belief that there was no consistency in antique proportions. His own system was based on a single module, readily applicable to all parts of each of the five orders.

Perrault does not appear to have been a member of the Académie Royale d'Architecture that Colbert established in 1671—one year after Le Vau's death—but he nonetheless attended some of its meetings and proposed that the Académie take up his system of proportioning and adopt it as its own. The members were shocked by his rude disregard for the Renaissance system of belief and were confused, moreover, by his suggestion that a new set of rules be substituted for the old. They did not grasp clearly his determination, like that of Colbert in all his undertakings, to establish a common and sensible working standard. To what extent Perrault's system was adopted is impossible to judge until the buildings of the period have been measured. We can be sure, though, that his published works were widely read. He was staunchly upheld during the eighteenth century by that most respected, and indeed academic, of teachers, Jacques-François Blondel (1705–1774). In England his architectural works had been translated and issued by the end of the first decade of the century, and, perhaps more significant, they were embodied in Isaac Ware's *Complete Body of Architecture* in 1756.

Though he offered a more reticent and rational architecture as a model and radically reinterpreted and reassessed accepted assumptions, it is clear that Perrault did not provide a coherent body of theory. His commonsensical approach, however, was to be followed up and rendered more useful in two small books published early in the eighteenth century, Michel de Frémin's *Mémoires critiques d'architecture*, of 1702, and Jean-Louis de Cordemoy's *Nouveau traité de toute l'architecture; ou, l'art de bastir: utile aux entrepreneurs et aux ouvriers*, of 1706. Neither of these men was an architect. Frémin appears to have been a tax collector; Cordemoy (1631–1713) was settled in the church, a cousin, or brother even, of Gerauld de Cordemoy, upholder of Descartes, author of that pioneering study of language the *Discours physique de la parole*, of 1668. Frémin's book is a plea for a reasoned approach to design, expressing a concern for the restrictions imposed by the site, the qualities of materials, the cost, and the needs of the client. The orders and the classical measures were of no real importance in architecture, he said, and in demonstrating his convictions he compared St.-Eustache and Le Vau's church of St.-Sulpice with Notre-Dame and the Ste.-Chapelle and concluded force-

4. *Claude Perrault and others, east façade of the Louvre, Paris, detail of the colonnade, 1667–74.*

5. *Interior perspective of a basilica, illustrated in Claude Perrault's translation of Vitruvius, 1673. Engraved by Sébastien Le Clerc.*

fully that the Gothic buildings were more rationally designed and thus preferable as architecture. This sympathy for Gothic arrangements and, in particular, structural manipulations is a feature also of Cordemoy's treatise, though the latter was intent to show that the qualities he admired in Gothic architecture could be interpreted in classical terms. Cordemoy required an architecture that was made up of rectangular forms, largely unadorned, with plain masonry walls or series of columns supporting lintels. He disliked arches and all acute angles, including those of the classical pediment. The ancients, he said, would have preferred the mansard roof to the pitched roof, had they known it, because it more nearly approximated to the rectangle. He proposed a model church with freestanding columns between the nave and aisles, supporting horizontal entablatures (absolutely not arches, he insisted) and, above, a barrel vault. For the west front he suggested a portico of columns with a balustrade over them, not unlike that built many years before by Inigo Jones at St. Paul's in London. He was consciously emulating both Gothic and, he fancied, Early Christian and Greek models. The structural supports, indeed, the whole structural system, were to be expressed and made evident so as to constitute the architecture, as in pre-Renaissance times. He wanted a trabeated architecture. Michelangelo's work at St. Peter's, Rome, was to be dismissed in the second edition of the *Nouveau traité*, published in 1714, though Bernini's colonnade on the piazza was to be admired. The real source of inspiration for Cordemoy's model church, however, was a design made about 1680 by Claude and Charles Perrault for the new church of Ste.-Geneviève in Paris. Freestanding columns line the long nave, carrying a horizontal entablature with a curved vault above. There was at that time no church like this, though the genesis of the arrangement can be traced back to the plan of an entranceway in Fra Giocondo's edition of Vitruvius, of 1511, and then to the work of Raphael and his pupils on the entrance of the Palazzo Farnese and its imitation in France by Le Vau, on the south side of the Louvre. An antique precedent was concocted also at this time by the engraver Jean Marot, who inaccurately illustrated the interior of the Temple of Bacchus at Baalbek in this form, perhaps at the behest of the Perraults. It was Charles Perrault who, as Colbert's secretary, was responsible for issuing instructions and payments to travelers to the east who went in search, for the most part, of manuscripts for Colbert's collections. Claude Perrault himself acknowledged the use of some drawings done by one such traveler, M. de Monceaux, who was to visit Baalbek in 1668; however, it is possible that the reconstruction was based on the observations of Balthasar de Monconys, who was there in 1647.

But even as Cordemoy was writing, a church was being put up

plus petites que celle
d'embas, comme il
esté dit.[8] La cloiso
qui est entre les co
lonnes d'enhaut n
doit avoir de hauteu
que les trois quarts d
ces mesmes colonnes
afin que ceux qui s
promenent sur cette

8. LA CLOISON. Vitruv
met icy *Pluteum* pour *Pluteu*
ainsi qu'il fait en plusieurs a
tres endroits. Philander & Bar
baro ont pris ce *Pluteum* o
Pluteus pour l'espace qui est en
tre les colonnes d'embas &
celles d'enhaut, & ils ont cr
que Vitruve ayant dit *Spatium*
quod est inter superiores colum
nas, il falloit suppléer & infe
riores, mais il n'est parlé dan
le texte que de la *cloison* qui es
entre les colonnes d'enhaut, ce
qui peut avoir un fort bon sens
pourveu qu'on entende que Vi
truve a conçû que cette cloi
son qui étoit comme un pie
destail continu sous toutes le
colonnes d'enhaut, ne devoi
passer pour cloison qu'à l'en
droit qui répondoit entre le
colonnes : parce que l'endroi
de ce piedestail continu qu
estoit immediatement sous le
colonnes, devoit estre pris pou
leur piedestail. Il est plus am
plement prouvé sur le 7. chapi
tre de ce Livre, que *Pluteus* n
sçauroit signifier icy que Cloi
son, Balustrade ou Appuy.

EXPLICATION

DE LA PLANCHE

XXXVIII.

Cette Planche contient
l'élevation perspective de
la Basilique. Il faut en
tendre que de mesme que
l'on a fait servir un seu
Plan pour les deux éta
ges de la Basilique ; o
n'a aussi mis icy qu'un
partie de son élevation
supposant que l'on com
prendra aisément que ce
qui est icy ne represente
qu'environ un quart de
tout l'Edifice, represente
dans le plan par ce qui es
renfermé dans des li
gnes ponctuées.

6. *Claude and Charles Perrault, project for Ste.-Geneviève, Paris, c. 1680.*

7. *Jean Marot, reconstruction of the Temple of Bacchus at Baalbek, c. 1680, based on plans made at the site by either M. de Monceaux or Balthasar de Monconys.*

8,9. *Interior of the royal chapel at Versailles, designed by Jules Hardouin Mansart and begun in 1698, finished by Robert de Cotte in 1710.*

The play of Gothic that is so curious a part of the architectural theory of Perrault, Frémin, and Cordemoy requires, perhaps, further explanation. It was not an isolated and idiosyncratic excursion into thought, but part of a long-standing French tradition, upheld, as a rule, by adventurous thinkers. Gilles Corrozet, a humanist scholar, translator of the works of Leon Battista Alberti and Trissino (Palladio's patron), and author of one of the first guidebooks to Paris, issued first in 1532, chose, surprisingly, to study Gothic buildings and to praise their manner of construction. His lead was taken up, in the years that followed, by other such authors, many of them associated with the Benedictine congregation of St.-Maur, the founders of French historical study. Terms such as "hardiesse," "légèreté," and "délicatesse" are invariably encountered in descriptions of Gothic buildings in these popular guidebooks or histories—of which there were many. In the more restricted field of architectural theory there was a similar emphasis on the structural finesse of Gothic architecture. Philibert de l'Orme, who thought of himself as the first architect to introduce classical refinements into France, nevertheless described and illustrated the construction of a Gothic vault in his *Architecture*, of 1567. And it is evident that he thought of the columns and ribs as an independent and clearly expressed structural scaffold supporting the webs of the vault above. This separation of the structural features from the enclosing elements was to assume great importance in the years to come. François Derand, the Jesuit mathematician and architect, author of *L'architecture des voûtes; ou, l'art des traits et coupe des voûtes*, a standard work on building construction published first in 1643, but issued again in 1743 and yet again in 1755, emphasized not only the structural elegance of the Gothic columns and ribs but also the role of the flying buttress and the outer buttress. He saw Gothic architecture as the solution to a problem in equilibrium.

A great deal more evidence could be adduced to show the vitality of this tradition of thought in France, in particular, the works of Amédée-François Frézier (1682–1773), who, in a lively exchange of letters in the *Mémoires de Trévoux* early in the eighteenth century, was to disparage Cordemoy's conception of a trabeated architecture, noting correctly that with the small stones available in France it was sounder to put arches rather than lintels over columns. Frézier attacked Cordemoy on many other points, but he proved himself equally sympathetic as an interpreter of Gothic, and far more knowledgeable than his predecessors. In his *Théorie et pratique de la coupe des pierres et des bois pour la construction des voûtes . . . ; ou, traité de stéréotomie à l'usage de l'architecture*, published first between 1738 and 1739, he described Gothic architecture as a precisely calculated affair, dependent on a carefully worked out system of vaulting. And he ex-

in France that embodied some of the qualities he demanded—the royal chapel at Versailles. Once again, Claude Perrault appears to have been involved in the early design, though the building begun in 1698 is generally attributed to Jules Hardouin Mansart, with Robert de Cotte responsible for its completion. The lower level of the chapel has heavy piers and arcades between the nave and aisles, but at the upper level, from which the king was to follow the service, there are majestic, widely spaced Corinthian columns with a horizontal entablature and vault above. The details are all classical, but the effect is of the spacious Gothic kind, with flying buttresses outside to confirm the hybrid basis of the inspiration.

tended the usual structural analysis to show that the webs of the vaults were particularly light and strong because they were slightly concave. His analysis was more subtle and penetrating than any yet made. He was not, however, an admirer of Gothic architecture. Like most interested Frenchmen he intended to analyze Gothic architecture and to infuse its principles of organization and construction, not its forms, into contemporary building. The detailed study of Gothic in France was thus in no way a preliminary to a revival of the style, though it is noteworthy that the Benedictines of the congregation of St.-Maur did uphold the Gothic style as such: St.-Wandrille, for example, was constructed in the Gothic manner between 1636 and 1656, and at their center, St.-Germain-des-Prés, in Paris, the Benedictines introduced Gothic vaults of stone over the nave and transepts, in 1644. When they came to build the west front of St.-Pierre at Corbie, in the first decade of the eighteenth century, they substituted a design in the Gothic mode for the proposed classical facade that was submitted earlier, a decision parallel to that made at the same time for the west front of Orléans cathedral, where the king, possibly under the influence of the Maurist scholar Bernard de Montfaucon, demanded that "l'ordre gothique" be adhered to. These, though, may all be interpreted as examples of Gothic survival.

More problematical and far more challenging was the design prepared in 1718 by the master mason of Orléans cathedral, Guillaume Hénault, for a Maurist chapel in the same town. For the interior he adapted the chapel at Versailles, for the exterior he provided a Gothic pastiche, complete with pointed windows, finials, and flying buttresses. This was not built. And nothing like it was to be designed in France until the end of the century, when the introduction of a playful Gothic mode in garden architecture resulted in something of a Gothic revival. But this was an English intrusion.

Cordemoy's ideas were not to be taken up immediately in France; the columnar screen around the forecourt of Pierre-Alexis Delamair's Hôtel de Soubise, of 1705-9, may owe something to his suggestions, as may the columnar episodes that appear so frequently in Germain Boffrand's early works, but only the chapel that Boffrand designed for the château at Lunéville in 1709—to be completed several years later—demonstrably fulfilled Cordemoy's program. The first architect to develop Cordemoy's ideas with any real consistency was the Parisian Pierre Contant d'Ivry (1698-1777), who designed the church of St.-Vasnon at Condé-sur-l'Escaut, in 1751, and that of St.-Vaast at Arras a year or two later, both with freestanding columns supporting horizontal lintels of stone and, above, barrel vaults. But by then another propagandist and interpreter of the ideas of both Perrault and Cordemoy had emerged, the Abbé Marc-Antoine Lau-

12. *Guillaume Hénault, design for Notre-Dame-de-Bonne-Nouvelle, Orléans, a chapel for a Benedictine Congregation of St.-Maur, 1718.*
13. *Pierre Contant d'Ivry, St.-Vasnon, Condé-sur-l'Escaut, interior, 1751.*

gier (1713–1769). His startling manifesto, the *Essai sur l'architecture,* was first issued anonymously in 1753.

Laugier dutifully paid his respects to Perrault, praising highly the Louvre facade—though he noted that it would have been improved if the central pediment had not broken the line of the balustrade—and was careful to acknowledge his debt to Cordemoy, but he was more radical than either of his predecessors. In his determination to purge and invigorate the tradition of architecture by a return to sources, he was led to entertain the idea that the basis of all architecture should be envisaged as the rustic hut, a hut stark and almost natural in its forms. It consisted of four tree trunks, still growing, as supports, with logs as lintels, and smaller branches above making up a pitched roof. This was to be illustrated as the frontispiece in the second edition of the *Essai,* in 1755. The concept was not new. Commentators of Vitruvius, including Perrault, had illustrated the origins of architecture in the guise of the rustic hut, but none had proposed that it be taken as the model of excellence in architecture. The essential elements in architecture, in Laugier's analogy, were, thus, the freestanding column, acting as a support, the attendant lintel, as a beam, and the pediment, as an expression of the pitched roof. Everything else was to be regarded as secondary. The rich heritage of Renaissance forms and ornamentation was to be disregarded. Inevitably, for practical design purposes, walls were to be provided, doors and windows accepted. But there was to be nothing superfluous to necessity.

Laugier's ideal, as may be imagined, was best adapted to the design of churches, and, like Cordemoy, he proposed one made up with single or coupled freestanding columns in one or two tiers along the aisles, all supporting horizontal entablatures without cornices, and a barrel vault above. As before, the arrangement was related to both the temples of ancient Greece and the cathedrals of Gothic France. But Laugier's moving descriptions of the interior of Notre-Dame show that new emotions, new feelings, had come into play. He admired the lightness and the structural strength of Gothic architecture and hoped to incorporate these qualities into contemporary design in the most rational way possible. But he was susceptible also to those more intangible qualities of mystery and sublime grandeur of the Gothic. That he was influenced by these tastes beyond the bounds of restraint usually accepted in France was particularly evident in 1765, when he published his *Observations sur l'architecture.* Therein he proposed churches no longer based on Latin- or Greek-cross plans, but of a variety of shapes, ordered internally with soaring columns bursting at their tops into formalized palm fronds and an array of richly decorated vaults. Gone were the lintels and entablatures, gone were the classi-

1731 to 1738, during which time he measured St. Peter's and other Italian churches, including the Milan cathedral. He then returned to his native Burgundy, settling in Lyons, where he was to build the great Hôtel-Dieu, a grand if unlovely building, stretching over two hundred fifty meters (eight hundred twenty feet) along the banks of the Rhône. The prestige it brought him prompted Mme. de Pompadour to select him as companion to her brother, soon to become the Marquis de Vandières (later the Marquis de Marigny), on his grand tour of Italy, in preparation for the young man's assumption of the position of *Directeur Général des Bâtiments.* Their journey was begun in December 1749; by February 1751 Soufflot was back in Lyons. But in the following year he was installed in an apartment in the Louvre and in January 1755 was made *Contrôleur des Bâtiments du Roi au Département de Paris* and commissioned to design the church of Ste.-Geneviève. This was intended to initiate a new departure in architecture. The plan was a Greek cross, to which Soufflot was forced by the clergy to add two bays and flanking towers at the east end, making the geometry less pure. Inside, the nave and aisles were divided by rows of giant Corinthian columns, supporting a continuous entablature from which sprang an array of lightly constructed and cut-away vaults and domes. The spatial elegance of the whole was extraordinary. But even more extraordinary was the structural finesse of the whole undertaking. "Le principal objet de M. Soufflot en bâtissant son église," his pupil Maximilien Brebion wrote later, "a été de réunir, sous une des plus belles formes, la légèreté de la construction des églises gothiques avec la pureté et la magnificence de l'architecture grecque" (Brebion to Ch. Cl. de Flahaut de la Billarderie, Comte d'Angiviller, October 20, 1780, Paris, Archives Nationales, 0¹ 1694-[43]).

During the long period of construction, Soufflot and his friends the engineer Jean-Rodolphe Perronet (1708–1794), *Inspecteur Général des Ponts et Chaussées,* and founder in 1747 of the École des Ponts et Chaussées, and his pupil Émiliand-Marie Gauthey (1732–1808), scoured France for stones, building machines to test their compressive strengths in a laboratory set up in the Louvre, coordinating and interpreting their results, and arriving at formulas and equations that they applied to the design of Ste.-Geneviève. They continued to refine the structure and whittle away the masonry mass but were forced to justify their procedures to the members of the Académie, particularly when the main piers were found to be cracking. They might be said to have mounted a campaign, presenting drawings of a whole range of lightly constructed churches for inspection: S. Agostino in Piacenza, the Cappella della SS. Sindone in Turin, S. Maria della Salute in Venice, and a number of French Gothic churches. The Gothic

cal measures, though for the exterior, he insisted, classical forms were to be retained. But for domestic architecture, he suggested, Gothic effects might be conjured up exteranlly by introducing turrets and broken roof lines. In compensation, perhaps, the ideal system of proportioning that he proposed in the *Observations* was more limited and restrictive than ever before. The ideal ratio was 1:1; the best figure the square; the best volume the cube. Not surprisingly, his second book was regarded as quirky and highly idiosyncratic. His first book, however, was acclaimed and eagerly read throughout Europe; it was considered a revolutionary tract.

The first major building that might be seen as an illustration of Laugier's ideal, and one that Laugier himself was to praise as "le premier modèle de la parfaite architecture, le véritable chef-d'oeuvre de l'architecture française" ("Discours sur le rétablissement de l'architecture antique," Lyons, Académie des Sciences, MS 194), was the church of Ste.-Geneviève, now known as the Panthéon. The architect was Jacques-Germain Soufflot (1713–1780). Soufflot had been to Rome as a young man and had spent seven years there, from

17. *Jacques-Germain Soufflot, final plan of Ste.-Geneviève, Paris. Engraved by F. N. Sellier.*

18. *Jacques-Germain Soufflot, Ste.-Geneviève, Paris, detail of the internal iron framework proposed for the pediment.*

19. *Jacques-Germain Soufflot, Ste.-Geneviève, Paris, 1756–90, as it appears today after its transformation into the Panthéon by Antoine-Chrysostome Quatremère de Quincy.*

20. *Jacques-Germain Soufflot, Ste.-Geneviève, Paris, detail of the vaults, 1756–90.*

21. *Jacques-Germain Soufflot, Ste.-Geneviève, Paris, interior.*

parallel remained of paramount importance in the justification of Ste.-Geneviève. Soufflot's pupil Jallier sent painstaking measured drawings of Notre-Dame in Dijon, in 1762, the first such drawings of a Gothic church to be made. Soufflot himself read a paper on Gothic architecture, chiefly on the proportional system involved, that he had delivered first to the Académie des Sciences in Lyons in 1741, when it was probably heard—or heard of—by Laugier, then at the Jesuit college there.

The discussion occasioned by the building of Ste.-Geneviève was of the highest importance in furthering theories of construction in France. Soufflot and his associates stressed the development of abstract theories based on experiment and mathematical calculation; their adversaries, chief among them the architect Pierre Patte (1723–1814), relied rather on empirical knowledge alone. But even Patte was to extend greatly the common understanding of structure, especially Gothic structure. He planned a treatise on this subject that he was never to finish, but when that great pedagogue Jacques-François Blondel died in 1774, Patte took over and completed the last two volumes of Blondel's *Cours d'architecture*, devoted to building materials and construction. These were issued in 1777. Blondel's *Cours d'architecture*, the issue of a lifetime's teaching—first at an independent school that he started in 1743, then from 1762 onward as an authorized professor of the Académie—served to consolidate and disseminate French doctrine at its most sound and most sensible. His judgments were always cautious and carefully explained. He could scarcely be thought intolerant, though he was not too adventurous. Tradition and reason conditioned all his attitudes. He did, however, take up the idea of designing churches with freestanding columns along their naves—but with arches above, as Frézier had shown that they were more sensible in France—and was fully aware of the Gothic sympathies thus involved, defending them in terms that were to be taken up by A.W. N. Pugin and the Ecclesiologists in nineteenth-century England, on the grounds of religious tradition.

Blondel was in no sense a connoisseur of construction. "La magie de l'art," he wrote, "veut des bornes; trop de hardiesse étonne plus qu'elle ne satisfait" (*Cours*, vol. 4, p. 315). He lagged in completing the last two volumes of the *Cours* through lack of vital interest. But Patte had a long-sustained and inquisitive concern with the techniques of building. He had already written several memoirs on the subject, and he returned in the *Cours* to his attack on Soufflot's great church and to the intricacies of Gothic engineering. To illustrate his text, Patte chose drawings of Notre-Dame in Dijon that Jallier had prepared for Soufflot, and, in analyzing the section, he showed that not only were the ribs of the vaults, the flying but-

22. *Drawings by Jallier of Notre-Dame, Dijon, 1762, illustrated in Jacques-François Blondel's and Pierre Patte's* Cours d'architecture, *1777. Engraved by Le Jolivet.*

tresses, and the outer buttresses essential structural features—nothing more—but so also were the finials, which acted as counterthrusts to the forces directed through the flying buttresses. He thought that even the timber trusses over the aisles were designed as buttresses. His ingenuity in isolating what he recognized as the Gothic principle never deserted him. He discerned it even in the Augustinian church at Lille, where iron tie-rods rather than buttresses were used to restrain the thrust of the vaults. Whatever their basic disagreements, like Soufflot he sought an architecture that was altogether economical and honest in its expression.

Something of this spirit, it should be noted, was developed independently in Venice, during the first half of the eighteenth century, by Carlo Lodoli (1690–1761). Lodoli was not an architect; he was a brilliant, radical polymath, a Franciscan friar, who started a small academy about 1720 for the sons of Venetian noblemen, teaching them languages, mathematics, law, and statesmanship for a few hours each day. He also taught them something of architecture, his favorite subject. He evolved no fully worked-out theory of architecture but some highly original notions, based in part on the experiments and mathematical theories of a succession of Scottish engineers active in Padua, among them James Gregory and James Stirling. Lodoli's ideas were to be recorded by two of his disciples, the fashionable gadabout Francesco Algarotti (1712–1764), whose ironical commentary, the *Saggio sopra l'architettura,* was to be published in 1757, and the more staid but dreadfully muddled Andrea Memmo (1729–1793), who did not start to write his account until 1784. It was published in two parts: the first, *Elementi dell' architettura Lodoliana; ossia, l'arte del fabbricare con solidità scientifica e con eleganza non capricciosa,* in 1786, reprinted together with the second in 1833 and 1834. It was once thought that Laugier—who published the *Histoire de la République de Venise* between 1759 and 1768, and is known to have been in Venice in 1757, and perhaps in 1752, to collect material for this work—was directly influenced by Lodoli when he came to write the *Essai sur l'architecture.* But this has been disproved. To judge by the references made to French architects and ideas in both Algarotti's and Memmo's accounts, the Venetian was strongly influenced rather by the works of Perrault, Cordemoy, Frézier, and others. But Lodoli was more extreme in his views; he held that architecture should derive entirely from the nature of materials and the laws of statics. Ornament or decoration might be applied, provided that it did not disrupt the basic forms and shapes. But he rejected outright the whole range of forms, moldings, and details belonging to the classical language of architecture, for they had been evolved originally, he said, in timber. The temples of ancient Greece were made first of timber. They were therefore unsuitable as models for buildings in stone. All the architecture of the Romans and by the men of the Renaissance was thus lacking in honesty; it was to be dismissed. The only true architecture of stone, Algarotti noted, was that of Egypt and Stonehenge.

Neither the niceties of argument offered by Lodoli nor the refinements of structure proposed by Soufflot and his friends were to be greatly favored in late eighteenth-century France. Architects were no longer interested in structural elegance and lightness of form; they had learned by then to appreciate the strong sculptural qualities of the architecture of antiquity, Greek no less than Roman, and had begun to cherish in their own work large and simplified mass. Those uncomplicated proportional relationships that Laugier had so much admired had come into their own. The square and the cube had passed into favor, and with them the sphere. But whatever the mathematical certainties relied upon to produce this purified geometry, there was a delight in large-scale elementary forms for their visual effects alone. Explanations offered were often, as we shall see, of a sophisticated kind. Étienne-Louis Boullée (1728–1799), the greatest of the visionary architects, who had intended at first to pursue a career as a painter, saw embodied in the sphere all manner of marvelous qualities.

The irrational, emotive streak that appears in architectural theory in the late eighteenth century was no doubt conditioned by the complete break in building activity during the French Revolution, so that the practicalities of architecture could be set aside for a time in favor of the production of grand and ever more vast imaginative projects. But this tendency was evident even before 1789, when the less restrictive, sensational English attitudes toward beauty—and, in particular, Edmund Burke's concept of the Sublime—were introduced into France in the form of Picturesque gardening theory. The first significant book on the subject to appear in France was the translation and extension of Thomas Whately's *Observations on Modern Gardening*, itself the first coherent attempt to systematize Picturesque theory. This was issued in 1771, only a year after its publication in England. The translator was François de Paule Latapie, a protégé of Montesquieu, who is often credited with having laid out the earliest *jardin anglais* in France, at his estate at La Brède, soon after his return from England in 1750. No record or trace of this survives. A better-known and certainly more influential exemplar of the natural garden in something of an English manner was that begun soon after 1754 at Moulin-Joli near Bezons, by Claude-Henri Watelet, who was to record his experiences and all his intentions in his *Essai sur les jardins*, of 1774. This was intended as only a part of a general treatise on taste and beauty. Its influence was considerable. The fashion for Picturesque gardens in France dates from its publication. More important, it introduced a whole new range of ideas and notions into artistic theory. *Le génie de l'architecture; ou, l'analogie de cet art avec nos sensations*, issued in 1780 by Nicolas Le Camus de Mézières (1721–1789)—the architect of the great circular Halle aux Blés in Paris, who was to dedicate his work to Watelet—marks a new departure in French architectural thought. For the first time, a major part of an architectural treatise was devoted to the idea that architecture should be pleasing to the senses and that it should, in addition, induce elevating impressions on the spirit and soul. This heady, speculative venture was to be balanced in the second part of the book by a detailed discussion of the matter-of-fact problems of planning. In the following year Le Camus was to publish an even more practical manual on building construction, *Le guide de ceux qui veulent bâtir*. But it was his more rarefied notions that were to appeal to such architects as Boullée. Boullée virtually gave up building at this time and turned instead to that sublime abstract architecture of monuments without practical function, for which he is famous, and to the composition of his *Essai sur l'art*. A measure of how far he had moved from any acceptance of the standard French criteria for architectural excellence is evident in his opening lines:

> Qu'est-ce que l'architecture? La définirai-je avec Vitruve l'art de bâtir? Non. Il y a dans cette définition une erreur grossière. Vitruve prend l'effet pour la cause. Il faut concevoir pour effectuer. Nos premiers pères n'ont bâti leurs cabanes qu'après en avoir conçu l'image. C'est cette production de l'esprit, c'est cette création qui constitue l'architecture, que nous pouvons, en conséquence, définir l'art de produire et de porter à la perfection tout édifice quelconque. L'art de bâtir n'est donc qu'un art secondaire, qu'il nous paraît convenable de nommer la partie scientifique de l'architecture (J. M. Pérouse de Montclos, ed., *E. L. Boullée: Architecture, essai sur l'art*, 1968, p. 49).

There is nothing in his essay on that scientific aspect of architecture, nothing on those practical, rational notions that had occupied architectural theorists in France from Perrault onward, though there was a great deal on Perrault's proposition that beauty be regarded as both positive and arbitrary, with interest directed in particular to the arbitrary, fantastical forms. Not that Boullée's architecture was ever wayward or disorderly. Though he and most of his contemporaries were sympathetic to the theories that sustained the Picturesque movement, they were intent to interpret them always in compositions of a rigid symmetry and pure geometrical form. Clear-cut geometry for the French (Jean-Jacques Lequeu apart) remained all.

The legacy of eighteenth-century architectural thought in France was to be contained and summed up in two books, the *Traité théorique et pratique de l'art de bâtir*, issued between 1802 and 1803, and the *Précis des leçons d'architecture données à l'École royale polytechnique*, published between 1802 and 1805. They were to remain standard texts for fifty years and more. The first was written by Jean-Baptiste Rondelet (1734–1829), a pupil of Soufflot, who had been responsible for the completion of Ste.-Geneviève and had later reinforced the main piers with inestimable tact and skill when they were found, for the second time, to be collapsing. Rondelet's knowledge of building construction was unsurpassed. The second book was the work of Boullée's favorite pupil, Jean-Nicolas-Louis Durand (1760–1834), who was made professor of architecture at the École Polytechnique in 1795 and was to teach there for the rest of his life, mainly instructing surveyors and engineers. The only architects of note who passed through the school were Hubert Rohault de Fleury and his son Charles and Émile-Jacques Gilbert. But Durand exerted his enormous influence on architects through the medium of books: In addition to the *Précis*, he wrote the *Recueil et parallèle des édifices de tout genre anciens et modernes*, of 1800, and an appendix to the *Précis*, the *Partie graphique des cours d'architecture faits à l'École royale polytechnique*, of 1821. His works propounded the strictest standards of formal geometry and design.

Rondelet's book is probably unique among architectural treatises in that it contains no—or almost no—general discussion of architecture, apart from a few pages at the beginning (published twice, separately) that make it clear nonetheless that his treatise was to be regarded as a comprehensive foundation for the study and practice of architecture. Architecture was constituted entirely in "l'art de bâtir." "La théorie," he wrote,

> est une science qui dirige toutes les opérations de la pratique. Cette science est le résultat de l'expérience et du raisonnement fondé sur les principes de mathématique et de physique appliquées aux différentes operations de l'art. C'est par le moyen de la théorie qu'un habile constructeur parvient à déterminer les formes et les justes dimensions qu'il faut donner à chaque partie d'un édifice en raison de sa situation et des efforts qu'elle peut avoir à soutenir, pour qu'il résulte perfection, solidité et économie (vol. 1, p. v).

Architecture, Rondelet insisted, was not an imaginative art but a science, controlled by need and necessity. The five volumes of his treatise were therefore devoted to lengthy accounts of building materials, their properties and their strengths, the techniques of all manner of building, and the most efficient means of estimating and calculating costs. There was much challenging reinterpretation of Gothic construction, as one might expect from a pupil of Soufflot, and much more up-to-date information on the latest experiments in building in iron, once again reflecting an interest of Soufflot. Most of the new bridges in iron in both England and France were illustrated, with suggestions as to how their design might have been improved. French theorists, whether they looked to the architecture of the past or the present, sought always to refashion it in terms of their own ideals.

Durand took as part of the frontispiece of his *Recueil et parallèle* that view of the Propylaea in Athens that had first appeared in Julien-David Le Roy's *Ruines des plus beaux monuments de la Grèce* (1758) in which all the elements are rearranged in axial symmetry around a monumental flight of stairs. Throughout, Durand redrew the buildings in the illustrations so that they might appear more neat and orderly, for though he selected his examples from all periods of history—from Egyptian, Greek, Roman, Gothic, or Renaissance times—he was intent to disregard their oddities and stylistic characteristics and to present them all drawn to the same scale and arranged for comparison, as particular building types. Temples are grouped together on one page, churches on another, theaters on yet another, and so on. Once again the initial idea can be traced back to Le Roy, who illustrated a set of plans thus in the second edition of his book on Greek architecture, though the idea was initiated by Soufflot's pupil Gabriel-Pierre-Martin Dumont (1720–1791), who issued two such plates illustrating theaters in 1764 or 1765.

Durand's theoretical approach to architecture is contained in the *Précis* and the *Partie graphique*. He refused to consider Laugier's rustic cabin as the model for all architecture; it was no more, he said, than a rude beginning. Architecture was a reasoned affair, a considered and evolving solution to practical problems. "Soit que l'on consulte la raison," he wrote, "soit que l'on examine les monuments, il est évident que plaire n'a jamais pu être son objet. L'utilité publique et particulière, le bonheur et la conservation des individus et de la société, tel est le but de l'architecture" (*Précis*, vol. 1, p. 18).

Such high-minded sentiments, however, cannot be taken as grounds for considering Durand as a strict utilitarian; his language is only an aspect of post-Revolutionary cant. Though he proposed that architecture be conditioned by social demands, convenience, and economy, his criteria in designing were symmetry—at best, true symmetry—and a simplified geometry, which happened to be his aesthetic preferences. He developed his themes with logic, but it is a logic not free from naivety. He argued that symmetry and regularity resulted in economy of means and were thus ideals. The circle and the sphere were the finest figures because they enclosed the maximum area—or volume, in the case of the sphere—for the minimum circumference or surface area. He accepted, though, that these figures might be impractical in building design and chose, therefore, as the next best, the square and the cube. To learn to be an architect, he said, one had only to learn to divide a square into a regular grid. Architecture, he claimed, was a graphic formula. His method of composition was to start with the plan (almost invariably a square), to transform this into a grid, to draw on the main and subsidiary axes required to link the rooms, and then to impose upon this grid what he recognized to be the elements of architecture: the walls and columnar supports, together with such "negative" elements as doors and window openings. To arrive at the section and form of the building, the established grid was projected vertically. Durand had no feeling for form and volume. Even his plans were altogether unsatisfactory from the point of view of human requirements, though as geometrical patterns they are undeniably impressive. Certainly they were to impress architects throughout Europe, and in Germany in particular. It is of some significance, perhaps, that the one building he was to approve without restraint, the vast circular Hôpital Ste.-Anne in Paris, begun in 1788 by Bernard Poyet (1742–1824), was stopped soon after on grounds of inefficient planning and inordinate cost. But there was more to Durand's theory than grid planning; he wished to do away with all unnecessary extravagance and decoration in architecture (the normally accepted forms of expression), and he proposed therefore that the style of a building be the visible expression of its functioning parts. The walls were to appear as plain masonry surfaces. The independent supports were to be in the form of piers or columns, equally spaced and made of materials that were demonstrably stronger than those used for the rest of the structure. There was to be a minimum of adornment and molding, and what there was had to present a palpable argument to the spectator of the role of the form to which it was applied. For richness or variety architects were to turn to plants, and many of Durand's stark and barren buildings were relieved with vines and creepers.

Rondelet and Durand together reduced architecture to two of its component parts, structure and formal geometry, and though Rondelet cared little for formal planning and Durand knew next to nothing of the art of construction (he had relegated it to a few notes at the back of the *Précis*, he was to explain in a later edition, lest it disrupt the thread of his argument), their books were by no means opposed in spirit; indeed, most architects regard them as complementary studies summarizing and reformulating the chief interests of the architects of the eighteenth century. Architecture entered a period of doctrinaire orthodoxy in the early years of the nineteenth century, and these

23. Plate from Jean-Baptiste Rondelet's Traité théorique et pratique de l'art de bâtir, *1802–3, illustrating the internal iron framework of the Louvre colonnade, the pediment of Ste.-Geneviève, and other building projects, some by Rondelet himself.*

24. Julien-David Le Roy, reconstruction of the Propylaea, Athens, from his Ruines des plus beaux monuments de la Grèce, *1758.*

books were to provide suitable formulas for building countless *mairies*, *palais de justice*, hospitals, prisons, and barracks throughout France. Émile-Jacques Gilbert, Durand's most enlightened pupil, was to make a sustained and serious attempt to reinvigorate architecture by introducing into it those humanitarian and social concerns of the early penal and health reformers, and later the ideas of Claude-Henri, Comte de Saint-Simon himself. Gilbert devoted his life to building no more than a prison, an asylum, a hospital, and a police barracks—and also, one might note, a morgue—yet he reflected faithfully in all his work and in all his teachings the ideals of Durand and Rondelet. The only other attempt to disrupt the torpor of architecture in France in the early decades of the century was the desperate bid by Jacques-Ignace Hittorff (1792–1867)—born in Cologne, but trained in France under François-Joseph Bélanger—to justify the application of riotous surface coloring to architecture. He fought bitterly to prove that the ancient temples of Greece had been richly colored. He recorded and publicized the murals and decorations of Pompeii and Herculaneum and even Raphael's grotesques. He sought to decorate his own buildings with enameled plaques, but such was not the means to renew architecture. Yet there can be no doubt that Gilbert and Hittorff prepared the way for those reformers of the middle years of the century Guillaume-Abel Blouet, Félix-Jacques Duban, Pierre-François-Henri Labrouste, Louis-Joseph Duc, and Léon Vaudoyer. Only the eldest of these, Blouet, was to attempt a full-scale exposition of his theory, and it is scarcely surprising to find that as his architectural activity was close in its range to that of Gilbert (he designed prisons and built a penal colony), his ideas were no more than an extension of those expounded many years before by Rondelet. Indeed, Blouet's treatise took the form of a *Supplément à la traité théorique et pratique de l'art de bâtir de Jean Rondelet*, issued in two volumes in 1847 and 1848. This is essentially a catalogue of nineteenth-century engineering achievements, though there is a clear enough exposition of the theoretical underpinnings of such structures. Blouet's arguments are based on two tenets, which are worth quoting at length, for they served to reaffirm and reestablish the rationalist position worked out half a century before.

> 1°—à concevoir ce qu'il faut, rien de plus, et à le réaliser le plus simplement possible, ce qui ne peût être obtenu qu'en subordonnant d'abord ses conceptions, qui doivent devenir des réalités, aux moyens d'exécution et aux propriétés des materiaux dont on dispose.
>
> 2°—à n'employer la décoration que pour compléter l'expression en ébauché dans la disposition et la construction, accentuer les par-

ties en raison de leurs fonctions relatives et déterminer par suite, avec plus de précision, le caractère de l'édifice à l'aide des moyens qui favorisent les matériaux auxquels ils sont appliqués, de moyens, en un mot, rendant sensible à la fois le but de l'édifice et sa construction, tant sous le rapport du mode de l'exécution que sous celui de la nature des matières employées (vol. 2, pp. ix, 227).

There is scarcely any need to comment on this program, though it is worth noting that it served from 1846 until 1853, when Blouet was *Professeur de Théorie* at the École des Beaux-Arts, as the official doctrine. At the École Polytechnique itself, oddly enough, a rationalist doctrine of considerably less intellectual rigor and restrictiveness was being propounded from 1837 onward by François-Léonce Reynaud (1803–1880), the engineer, who was to publish his *Traité d'architecture* in two volumes in 1850 and 1858. This is devoted largely to building materials, methods of construction, and various building types, but the seventeen pages of theoretical text and the introduction make the guiding principles disarmingly clear. The aim of architecture, Reynaud declared, was beauty, not utility, though practical requirements must always be carefully fulfilled. Taste was to be the ultimate arbiter of architectural harmony and expression. Ornament and decorative forms, though certainly not to be regarded as essential, were vital to such expression and might give value to architecture. But in other respects Reynaud was far less lax and tolerant than Blouet; whereas Blouet extolled the economy of Gothic construction and was even prepared to set up programs for his students for churches in the Gothic style, Reynaud disliked all aspects of the Gothic and dreaded lest there be a Gothic revival. "L'art du moyen âge est mort," he wrote, "aussi bien que son esprit et ses institutions, et leur résurrection est impossible. On peut galvaniser un cadavre, mais non le rappeler à la vie" (vol. 2, p. 270).

It was precisely those men of Gothic inclination who were to take up the rationalist doctrine of Blouet and his circle—in particular, that transmitted by Henri Labrouste—and who were to demonstrate that, by a renewed and more thorough analysis of Gothic architecture, more stringent principles yet might be adduced that could even lead to an architecture with style, but one that owed nothing to any styles of the past. Eugène-Emmanuel Viollet-le-Duc (1814–1879) was the chief exponent of this brand of rationalism. He was the bugbear of the École des Beaux-Arts. And it is not without irony that Jean-Louis-Charles Garnier, architect of the Paris Opéra—who was to destroy, almost, the intellectual tradition of architecture in France, and to show that by conjuring up a whole medley of styles, forms, and motifs a vigorous architecture could be produced—should have been asked, as a student, to swear "Haine à Viollet-le-Duc" on the

"Grand Durand," the *Recueil et parallèle des édifices de tout genre anciens et modernes.*

The Gothic movement in nineteenth-century France sprang from romantic beginnings, from Alexandre Lenoir's atmospheric museum in the Couvent des Petits Augustins, later to become part of the École des Beaux-Arts, where fragments from the past were reassembled after the Revolution and imbued with an aura of poetry and mystery. Chateaubriand's Gothic leanings were first nurtured there; so also were those of the historian Jules Michelet. But though Michelet's brilliant *Introduction à l'histoire universelle*, of 1831, and the six volumes on French medieval history that followed were to arouse a popular passion for the Gothic past—particularly in Catholic circles—he was to find that his ideal image had little relation to reality and he was to become the leader of an anticlerical coterie of historians who despised the Middle Ages. The Catholic national credo and the manifesto for the restoration, if not the revival, of Gothic architecture was, in fact, a novel, Victor Hugo's *Notre-Dame de Paris*, issued first in February 1831, but republished in the following year with three additional chapters that made quite explicit Hugo's aims: "Inspirons," he wrote, "s'il est possible à la nation l'amour de l'architecture nationale. C'est là, l'auteur le déclare, un des buts principaux de ce livre; c'est là un des buts principaux de sa vie" (1832 ed., preface).

Viollet-le-Duc was inspired by such works, and he was to retain always a romantic, emotional sympathy for the Gothic, but it was rather those self-sure Protestant historians of the Middle Agees grouped around François-Pierre-Guillaume Guizot—and, in particular, Guizot himself—who were to supply his knowledge of the national past and to give him the opportunity to develop his inclinations. When Guizot assumed political power, he at once established the Commission des Monuments Historiques and began to provide money for the restoration of historical buildings. Viollet-le-Duc was drawn early into this orbit by Prosper Mérimée, *Inspecteur Général des Monuments Historiques*. In 1840, at the age of twenty-six, he was appointed to restore Ste.-Madeleine at Vézelay; later in the same year he joined Labrouste's pupil Jean-Baptiste-Antoine Lassus (1807–1857) on the restoration of the Ste.-Chapelle; and in another four years they began the restoration of Notre-Dame. His career was to be largely concerned with restoration. This was the source of his immense knowledge and understanding of Gothic architecture and the basis of those two great works for which he is famous, the *Dictionnaire raisonné de l'architecture française du XIe au XVIe siècle*, published between 1854 and 1868, and the *Dictionnaire raisonné du mobilier français de l'époque carlovingienne à la renaissance*, issued from 1858 to 1875.

In his early years Viollet-le-Duc's energies were directed not only to the restoration of Gothic architecture but also to a revival of the style itself. Lassus, together with a group of Gothic enthusiasts and archaeologists, chief among them Adolphe-Napoléon Didron, was then busy restoring the church of St.-Germain-l'Auxerrois, and was showing both there and at the Ste.-Chapelle that an image of the Middle Ages could be conjured up that was quite as colorful and rich as that proposed at the same time by Hittorff for Greek architecture. They all propagated their ideas in Didron's *Annales archéologiques,* begun in 1844. But from Lassus Viollet-le-Duc also learned something of that rationalist doctrine of the Gothic that was contained in the works of Rondelet and that had been transmitted by Lassus's master, Labrouste. Already, in his first major series of articles, "De la construction des édifices religieux en France depuis le commencement du Christianisme jusqu'au XVIe siècle," published in the *Annales* between 1844 and 1847, Viollet-le-Duc indicated that he had absorbed all that his predecessors could teach him on the structure and the rational nature of the Gothic. Soon after, he was to reject the idea of a revival of the style and to turn his attention instead to the most rigorous analysis of every form, every detail, of Gothic, to arrive at a set of principles for design that he hoped might be applicable to the nineteenth century. The architecture of the nineteenth century was thus to be analogous to, though distinct from, that of the thirteenth century; it was to be the visible expression in contemporary terms, using contemporary materials such as iron, of a system evolved in the thirteenth century. In the *Dictionnaire raisonné de l'architecture française* he illustrated a section through the aisle and nave of a church showing how timber props might be substituted for the stone of the flying buttresses, and cast-iron columns used in place of the piers of the nave; this, in its most elementary form, was the way in which he thought Gothic structural principles might begin to be reinterpreted. His analyses were to become far more complex and subtle than this, for he was led to believe that every feature, every molding, of a Gothic building could be interpreted as a functional device, whether as part of a supporting system or to throw off rainwater. He was convinced that architecture was a clear expression of function, a function that embodied political and social aspirations, material limitations and needs. His analyses of medieval social organizations were marvelously distorted so that they might accord with his architectural theories.

Later, he assaulted the citadel of classical rationalism, the École des Beaux-Arts itself, first, in 1857, by opening an independent *atelier* of his own in the Rue Bonaparte, taking over some of Labrouste's students, and then, in 1863, by intriguing with Prosper Mérimée, a long-standing friend of the Empress Eugénie, to have himself ap-

28. *Eugène-Emmanuel Viollet-le-Duc and Félix Narjoux, gallery in the Château de Pregny (near Geneva), 1875.*

29. *Eugène-Emmanuel Viollet-le-Duc, house built between 1860 and 1863 in the valley below the Château de Pierrefonds (now École Secondaire d'Agriculture du Prieuré).*

pointed *Professeur d'Histoire de l'Art et Esthétique* at that venerable institution. He retired soon after, rudely rebuffed by the students. He had attempted to show that the rational theories he had evolved in relation to the Gothic style were applicable also to all great architecture—among which he ranked Greek and Byzantine architecture, with some reservations as to the quality of Roman buildings. Roman structure was sound enough, he thought, but the decorative overlay adopted had been evolved in relation to Greek architectural forms and was altogether inappropriate. His exposition of these ideas took the form of the *Entretiens sur l'architecture*, appearing in chapters from 1858 onward; the first volume was completed in 1863, the second in 1872. The second volume reveals Viollet-le-Duc at his most adventurous. He was a dogged theoretician who argued his way through even the knottiest problems with determination and an air of success, but he was never able to give convincing form to his ideas. His restorations apart, he designed almost one hundred buildings on his own account (often credited to his students and associates), but he never once built anything that accords successfully with his theories. His buildings, individual houses for the most part, are lackluster and commonplace, conceived in a range of styles from Gothic to late Renaissance. The ultimate disappointment was his gallery, of 1875 in the Château de Pregny, on the outskirts of Geneva—built in 1860–64 for the Baron de Rothschild by none other than Sir Joseph Paxton, designer of the Crystal Palace of 1851. The gallery is a fussily decorated period pastiche.

Yet in a handful of plates in the twelfth *Entretien*, issued about 1867, he showed that with dogged determination he could produce a visual embodiment of his theories that was to be almost as memorable to twentieth-century architects as the Crystal Palace itself. Viollet-le-Duc's designs are awkward and ungainly, but the system of angled iron struts that he indicated first for a town hall, then in increasing complexity for a series of large covered spaces, and finally for a concert hall for three thousand people, provided just that liberating stimulus required by architects trained in a rational functionalist ideal but encumbered always by a range of historical styles. Viollet-le-Duc suggested how they might abandon these and evolve a new style for the future. This not only was to be an expression of a solution to a problem in structure but was to embody also an absolute geometrical ideal based on the form of the equilateral triangle. Viollet-le-Duc's giant concert hall is an illustration of his belief that everything in nature, indeed the whole universe, was built up of polyhedra based on the equilateral triangle. This was, to him, the essence of style.

Chapter Two

THE PICTURESQUE TRADITION IN ENGLAND

Perhaps the most striking architectural impact of the Picturesque was the new emphasis it placed on architecture as part of an environment. We may interpret the word *environment*, so fashionable today, in a rather broad way so as to refer not merely to the physical setting, whether rural or urban, but also to the historical setting. Architecture, in other words, came to be regarded as possessing evocative narrative or literary powers. This emphasis on architecture as part of something else, as an incident in history or in a landscape, encouraged the concept of growth, of flexibility, in architecture; thus, buildings were thought to have a special merit if one could read in them the process of their alteration during the years or even centuries of their existence.

One of the clearest ways in which this new approach to architecture was expressed in the eighteenth century was, perhaps ironically, in the obsession with the ruin. Admiration for ruins is an obvious indication of a belief that there are more important aspects to a building than the functional and visual roles its designer intended it to fulfill. Thus some architects, at once frustrated and excited by this implied shift in their role, began to imagine what their own buildings would look like when change and decay had reduced them to ruin. Perhaps the first English design that is clearly part of the international neoclassicism developed in Franco-Italian circles in the 1740s is the one for a mausoleum for the Prince of Wales, of 1751–52, by Sir William Chambers. Yet its monumental neoclassicism, doubtless derived from designs by such architects as Louis-Joseph Le Lorrain for the Festa della Chinea in Rome, is dissolved by Chambers's unexpectedly Romantic decision to show the mausoleum not merely in a landscaped setting but also as it would appear when ruined. Few went so far as Racine de Monville, who, with help from the architect François Barbier, in 1780 built a house for himself in the form of a ruined column, at the Désert de Retz, not far from Paris. The essentially pictorial character of this enterprise is emphasized by the fact that the *jardin anglais* that surrounded this bizarre dwelling was designed with assistance from the painter Hubert Robert. The continual dissolution of neoclassicism by the Picturesque is a particularly English phenomenon, and it reached a climax with Sir John Soane (1753–1837), who commissioned Joseph Michael Gandy (1771–1843) to depict his vast rotunda at the Bank of England, London, at a point when it could be said to possess the status of a Piranesian ruin.

Sir John Vanbrugh's memorandum of June 11, 1709, arguing for the preservation of the ruins of Woodstock Manor in the park at Blenheim is a key document in the history of eighteenth-century ruin mania. Vanbrugh (1664–1726) urged the upkeep of buildings of distant times because "they move [inspire] more lively and pleasing Reflections (than History without their aid can do) on the Persons who

30. *Sir William Chambers, project for the mausoleum of Frederick, Prince of Wales, section, 1751–52. London, Victoria and Albert Museum.*

31. *Joseph Michael Gandy,* The Bank of England, *watercolor, c. 1830. The building is shown in cutaway perspective, making it look ruinous. London, Sir John Soane's Museum.*

32. *Anthony Salvin, Scotney Castle, Kent, 1835–43.*

have inhabited them; on the remarkable things which have been transacted in them, or the extraordinary occasions of erecting them." Vanbrugh went on to argue that because the park at Blenheim "has little variety of objects" it "stands in need of all the helps that can be given . . . Buildings and Plantations." These, in his opinion, "rightly dispos'd will indeed supply all the wants of Nature in that place. And the most agreeable disposition is to mix them in which this old Manour gives so happy an occasion for; that were the enclosure filled with Trees (principally fine Yews and Hollys) promiscuously set to grow up in a wild thicket, so that all the buildings left might appear in two risings amongst'em, it would make one of the most agreeable objects that the best of Landskip painters can invent" (*The Complete Works of Sir John Vanbrugh*, ed. B. Dobrée and G.Webb, 4 vols., 1928, vol. 4, pp. 29–30). This quotation encapsulates the Picturesque tendency to dethrone architecture, to replace the traditional Renaissance architect with historians, Romantics, painters—people who see a building as an incident in an environment, whether natural or historical. We can usefully tabulate the three principal points of Vanbrugh's thesis as follows:

1. Buildings can bring the past to life more vividly than written history
2. Buildings can be composed as an integral part of a landscape
3. In mingling buildings and trees in a designed landscape we should take seventeenth-century landscape paintings as a model if we want the result to be authentically "Picturesque"

From Vanbrugh in the early eighteenth century to Edwin Lutyens in the early twentieth we can trace the development of the ideas contained in these three points. An intense emphasis on architecture as part of a landscape or of a natural setting, which was so much to characterize the work of John Nash, led in time to an emphasis on local materials and local techniques, which marks the work of Philip Webb and Lutyens.

Vanbrugh lost his battle with the forceful duchess of Marlborough over the preservation of Woodstock Manor, but the victory was ultimately his since his ideas were adopted later in the eighteenth and nineteenth centuries. Thus the ruins of medieval houses or castles were preserved as Picturesque objects in the landscaped parks of many new houses: in the 1760s, at Tabley House, Cheshire, by John Carr (1723–1807); in the 1770s, at Wardour Castle, Wiltshire, by James Paine; in 1807, at Belsay Castle, Northumberland, by Sir Charles Monck; and, most strikingly of all, in 1835, at Scotney Castle, Kent, by Edward Hussey, Anthony Salvin (1799–1881), and William Sawrey Gilpin. At Scotney, Salvin's new house is, in a sense, a mere window

placed to catch a view of the Picturesque ruins of the moated castle in the valley below. Hussey and Salvin made these ruins even more "Picturesque" by eliminating most of the additions made to them in the seventeenth century.With further help from the landscape gardener Gilpin, son of the celebrated Picturesque theorist, the castle was linked visually to the house by a landscaped garden of dreamlike quality and intense beauty. At Peckforton Castle, Cheshire, Salvin provided a different interpertation to a similar theme. Here, from 1844 to 1850, he created a vast new castle on a hill adjacent to the thirteenth-century Beeston Castle. As at Scotney, the principal rooms commanded views of the nearby ruins, but the parallel ends there since Beeston Castle plays only a very minor role in the whole composition. It is the expansive new castle of Peckforton and not the landscape or the ruins that is the center of attention.

The story of the Picturesque begins not with architecture but with gardens. The Romantic "natural" garden, or park, developed in England in the eighteenth century, had undoubtedly been anticipated in Renaissance Italy. So far, research into either the Italian gardens themselves or English knowledge of them has been insufficient to enable us to assess the measure of their influence. The groves, grottoes, nymphaea, and irregular areas of Italian gardens were as rich with antique literary and mythological symbolism as Stourhead was to be in the eighteenth century. In the Vatican gardens, the early sixteenth-century Fontana dello Scoglio was a cross between a grotto and a ruin that would have delighted the poet Alexander Pope, while the largest of the four sections of the grounds of the Villa Borghese was laid out as a park at the beginning of the seventeenth century in a way that might similarly have pleased the designer William Kent (1685–1748). A description of the Villa Borghese written in 1700 claims that the inspiration for this part of the garden was antique and that it "seems irregular but art and industry have so well regulated it that it alternates from hill to plain and from wild to domesticated valleys" (see G. Masson, *Italian Gardens*, 1961, p. 154).

Among the first English landscaped parks and gardens were Pope's own at Twickenham, Middlesex (begun 1719), with its little wilderness, shell temple, and grotto. The new movement had strong literary and philosophical overtones, not only in the writings of Pope but in those of the first earl of Shaftesbury and Joseph Addison as well. The gardens of Stephen Switzer and the writings of Batty Langley (*New Principles of Gardening*, 1728) lent support to a movement that reached a climax in William Kent's garden at Rousham, Oxfordshire, in the 1730s. The second phase in the history of the Picturesque is represented by Lancelot "Capability" Brown (1716–1783), whose work from about 1750 to about 1780 is an extension and populariza-

33. *Plan of the garden at Alexander Pope's villa at Twickenham, Mid-dlesex, begun 1719.*

34. *William Kent, Temple of Ancient Virtue, Stowe, Buckinghamshire, 1734.*

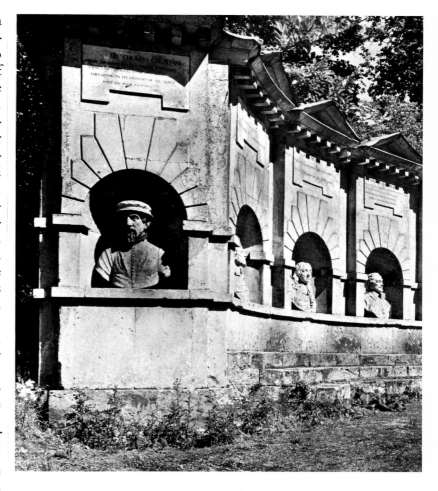

tion not so much of what Kent had achieved at Rousham—which is still essentially a *garden*—but of the bigger, barer *parks* he had projected at Euston and Holkham Hall. Reaction quickly set in to Brown's rather bland landscapes, thus producing the third phase of the Picturesque, associated with the writings of Sir Uvedale Price (1747–1829) and Richard Payne Knight (1750–1824) in the 1790s. For our purposes at the moment this third phase is the most significant, since it had more impact on architectural design than the other two phases. Nonetheless, we should look at some of the great landscaped parks of the mid-eighteenth century with their pictorial treatment of nature and architecture.

A contemporary described the Elysian Fields at Stowe, Buckinghamshire, as "the painting part" of the gardens. In this "sacred landscape," with its complex mythological and political iconography, Kent designed the circular Temple of Ancient Virtue (1734), based on Palladio's drawing of the Temple of Vesta at Tivoli. The antique source makes both the building and the pastoral scene of which it is part important in the history of neoclassicism since the temple and gorge at Tivoli are the only Roman "sacred landscape" to survive. However, Kent was equally susceptible to Italian Renaissance sources, as is shown in the remarkable Temple of British Worthies on the other side of the Elysian Fields. This may have been inspired by the exedra, or circus, on the grounds of the Villa Mattei in Rome. Thus it is probably not quite accurate to say that Kent was attempting to re-create paintings by Claude Lorrain or Poussin, though such an attempt may be seen in the Grecian Valley, which extends from the upper end of the Elysian Fields. Laid out in the 1740s—probably from designs by Lord Cobham, after Kent had left Stowe—and dominated by the imposing Temple of Concord and Victory, designed by Cobham's nephew, Lord Grenville, about 1748, it is a landmark in the history of British neoclassicism. On another part of the grounds, Kent had designed a temple perhaps as early as 1731 that is also unique for its time in Europe. This is the Temple of Venus, in which a Palladian quadrant theme is handled with a neoclassical austerity. The open screen of columns before a coffered apse was to recur more than thirty years later in the work of Robert Adam and Claude-Nicolas Ledoux. At Rousham, Oxfordshire, in the 1730s, Kent laid out a garden that had much in common with the Elysian Fields at Stowe but that was at once more varied and more unified. It is approached from a remarkable balustraded terrace called the Praeneste, which may have been based on the pedimented arcades of the Roman Baths as illustrated by Palladio in the *Fabbriche antiche disegnate da Andrea Palladio Vicentino*, published by Lord Burlington in 1730. The source of the Praeneste itself is the Roman Temple of Virtue; with its ramped terraces com-

manding distant views, it is itself the prototype of continental garden design from the Villa d'Este to Versailles. From the Praeneste a path leads to the small valley originally laid out by Charles Bridgeman as a wilderness with tortuous paths. This was opened out by Kent so as to become Venus's Vale, with "the opening and retiring shades" admired by Horace Walpole. Kent remodeled Bridgeman's uncompromisingly square pool into an octagon, which, though perhaps softer on the eye than the square, was still a long way from the dreamy undulations of Capability Brown. The pool is flanked by an Upper and Lower Cascade in the form of grottoes, perhaps based on the Fontana Rustica at the Villa Aldobrandini, Frascati.

The type of garden represented by the development from Twickenham to Rousham was popularized much later in France as

36. *Charles Bridgeman, the gardens at Rousham, Oxfordshire, before William Kent's alterations, plan, 1715–20.*

37. *William Kent, the gardens at Rousham, Oxfordshire, plan, 1730 and later.*

38. *William Kent, Venus's Vale, Rousham, Oxfordshire, after 1730.*

the *jardin anglais*. Characteristic examples, crowded with naive architectural incident, are the gardens at Ermenonville (1766–76) and Louis Carrogis de Carmontelle's Jardin de Monceau, Paris (1773–78).

Stowe and Rousham are essential preliminaries to an appreciation of the work carried out at Stourhead, Wiltshire, in the 1740s and 1750s. At Stourhead, more than anywhere else in Europe, one can admire the way in which poetry, painting, gardening, architecture, travel, the study of antiquity, and topography blend to form the single art of Picturesque landscape. Both the house and its contents—pictures, books, and furniture—and the grounds and their contents—trees, water, and temples—merge to form an idyllic, narrative, cultural picture dominated by a profound sense of place. That sense of place, that *genius loci*, was perhaps the particular legacy to Europe of the English Picturesque movement. What Alexander Pope had written in his "Epistle to Lord Burlington on the Use of Riches," in the 1730s, sums up the spirit that created Stourhead:

> Consult the Genius of the Place in all
> That tells theWaters or to rise or fall
> Or helps th'ambitious Hill the heav'n to scale,
> Or Scoops in circling theatres the vale,
> Calls in the Country, catches opening glades,
> Joins willing woods, and carries shades from shades,
> Now breaks or now directs th'intending Lines,
> Paints as you plant, and, as you work, designs.

Stourhead lies at the center of a historic and beautiful part of English geography and history, at the point between Salisbury Plain and Glastonbury where myth and history have been intertwined for centuries. There, at the remote meeting point of three counties—Somerset, Dorset, and Wiltshire—Henry Hoare, a rich city banker, built a large, bleak Palladian villa, designed by Colen Campbell (1676–1729), in 1718. Situated on a height, the house faces east across the bare plain. But just three hundred yards to the west, the ground drops sharply into a lush, almost tropical, hidden valley, long known as "Paradise," which contains the tiny village of Stourton. In 1743 Hoare's son, also Henry, began to plan a Picturesque circuit tour around the sides of the valley, in the manner of Stowe and Rousham. In August 1744, in a letter to Henry Hoare, Henry Flitcroft (1697–1769), who was completing the interiors of the house, referred to his designs for a "Circular Open Temple of the Ionic order, Antique." He also sent "a sketch of how I conceive the head of the lake should be formed. Twill make a most agreeable scene with the solemn shade about it and the variety of other agreeable circumstances." The letter establishes that as early as 1744 Hoare envisaged uniting his garden buildings within the valley by means of a lake. In fact, the dam that made the lake possible was not formed until ten years later. Flitcroft's Temple of Ceres (or Flora) contains altars designed by Flitcroft as well as an inscription over the door from the sixth book of Virgil's *Aeneid*: "Procul, o procul este profani" ("Begone all you who are uninitiated"). The lakeside Virgilian overtones were thus established from the first, though it is possible that in creating his lake landscape—which is what distinguishes Stourhead from Stowe and Rousham—Hoare may also have had in mind Pliny's description of the Source of the Clitumnus (*Letters*, book 8, chapter 8).

On the other side of the lake from the Temple of Flora an elaborate grotto was created, in 1748, containing a statue of the Nymph of the Grot carved in white lead by John Cheere, after the antique. The grotto is very much in the style of Italian Mannerist gardens and would have appealed to Pope. Indeed, a suitable quotation from Pope is carved in the marble bath within the grotto. Hoare wrote in 1765: "I have made the passage up from the souterrain serpentine & will make it easier of access *facilis descensus Averno*," thus confirming the notion that the path around the lake is an allegory of Aeneas's journey through the underworld.

From the grotto we reach the Claudian and Virgilian Pantheon, a remarkable neoclassical building completed in 1756 from designs by Flitcroft. Its impressively austere interior contains statues of Hercules and Flora by John Rysbrack, and an antique marble figure of Livia Augusta as Ceres, brought from Herculaneum. Here the analogy with landscape painting, adumbrated by Vanbrugh, becomes more relevant than ever, for the form, position, and iconographical significance of the Pantheon seem to have been inspired by Claude's *Coast View of Delos with Aeneas*. We know that Hoare owned a version by Andrea Locatelli of Claude's *View of Delphi with a Procession*, which contains just such a pantheon temple. Higher up on the other side of the lake is a companion piece to Flitcroft's Pantheon, another "antique" temple, which was completed in 1765. Flitcroft took its design from the late Roman Temple of Venus at Baalbek, which had been included in Robert Wood's *The Ruins of Balbec*, published in 1757. This wholesale incorporation of antique monuments into a landscaped scene is significant enough, but the deliberate inclusion of views of the village of Stourton into the composition is equally worthy of comment. Whereas at Stowe the medieval parish church was deliberately planted out, at Stourhead one of the great composed vistas is of the medieval church tower rising above cottage roofs and a village cross. This incorporation of the quintessence of the English rural scene into the Picturesque elegiac idyll is, of course, a make-believe in every possible way. The village cross is not the village cross

39. *Stourhead, Wiltshire, plan, 1743 and later.*

40. *Henry Flitcroft, Temple of the Sun, Stourhead, Wiltshire, 1765.*

41. *Stourhead, Wiltshire, view toward the Pantheon, completed 1756.*

42. *Henry Flitcroft, the Pantheon, Stourhead, Wiltshire, interior, 1754–56.*

43. *Robert Adam, Culzean Castle, Ayrshire, aerial view, 1777–90.*

but a sophisticated urban market cross of 1373 brought to Stourton from Bristol High Street in 1768. Moreover, it is not even in the village at all—though it appears to be, from the Pantheon—and the triangle of grass behind it, which looks like the village green, is also within the park boundary. The Picturesque make-believe is exposed in a letter written by Hoare to his daughter, in 1762, about the bridge that he constructed in front of the cross: "I took it from Palladio's Bridge at Vicenza, 5 arches, & when you stand at the Pantheon the Water will be seen thro the arches & it will look as if the River came down thro the Village & that this was the Village Bridge for the Public use; the view of the Bridge, Village and Church altogether will be a charming Gaspard view at the end of that Water." Hoare's words remind one forcibly of Vanbrugh's claim half a century earlier that if architecture and trees were combined at Woodstock Manor "so that all the buildings left might appear in two risings amongst'em, it would make one of the most agreeable objects that the best of Landskip painters can invent."

Robert Adam's Culzean Castle, Ayrshire (1777 onward), towering dramatically above the rocky coastline, is a realization in stone of the imaginary landscape architecture Adam (1728–1792) spent so much of his spare time painting. A celebrated example of an architect's deliberately designing a building that appears to have strayed from a painting by Claude is Nash's Cronkhill, Shropshire (c. 1802). The undoubted source for this round-towered villa is the buildings that appear in the backgrounds of such paintings as Claude's *Landscape with the Ponte Molle*. Moreover, the Ponte Molle is very close in form to the bridge at Stourhead. A curious example of the pictorial approach to architecture and landscape is afforded by an aquatint of the front door of Sezincote House, Gloucestershire, of 1810, by John Martin, showing the Picturesque park reflected in the glass. As soon as this remarkable Indian-style country house was completed, its owner commissioned the aquatints from Martin—which suggests that a house that came into being as a realization in architecture of Picturesque drawings and views of India could only be fully appreciated once it had been translated back into pictorial imagery.

Even an architect so imbued with classical archaeology as Charles Robert Cockerell (1788–1863) found it impossible to look at William Wilkins's Grange Park, Hampshire (1809), without immediately recalling landscape paintings by Claude and Poussin. It is not clear whether Wilkins (1778–1839) had such analogies in mind when designing the great temple-like house, but to Cockerell, in a now-celebrated passage in his diary for 1823, "nothing [could] be finer, more classical or like the finest Poussino. It realises the most fanciful representations of the painters pencil or the poets description . . . there is noth-

ing like it on this side of Arcadia." More surprisingly, it occurred to Cockerell only *after* he had designed the Hanover Chapel in Regent Street, in 1821, that its source lay in a painting by Claude. Looking at some of Claude's seaport scenes in the collection of J. J. Angerstein, in 1823, Cockerell noted in his diary: "much flattered at Claude's pictures & finding in 2 of the 5 pictures in this collection the idea of the two turrets at the entrance of a building as in my chapel. I have little doubt that the idea of this adoption arose in my mind from having seen these pictures and engravings. In these wonderful pictures one feels the balmy rosy atmosphere of the Mediterranean, that agreeable air . . . which I so well remember in those parts." Rather unexpectedly, Cockerell also found that his twin-towered chapel reminded him of Vanbrugh's Morpeth Town Hall, Northumberland (1716). After passing through Morpeth, in July 1822, he noted in his diary that the town hall was "picturesque *like my chapel*."

There can be no doubt that the heroic romance of Vanbrugh's buildings, of his "Castle style" in particular, was a source of inspiration to his successors from Adam to Cockerell, even though they worked in a style different from his. Adam's eulogy of Vanbrugh in the preface to his *Works in Architecture of Robert and James Adam, Esquires* (1773) is well known, but as a central and beautiful text in eighteenth-century aesthetics it must be quoted here. He begins by describing the revolution his own architecture had achieved in defeating neo-Palladianism: "The massive entablature, the ponderous compartment ceiling, the heavy frames . . . are now universally exploded." In their place he had established what he called "movement," a quality he defined as follows:

> *Movement* is meant to express, the rise and fall, the advance and recess, with other diversity of form, in the different parts of a building, so as to add greatly to the picturesque of the composition. For the rising and falling, advancing and receding, with the convexity and concavity, and other forms of the great parts, have the same effect in architecture, that hill and dale, fore-ground and distance, swelling and sinking have in landscape: That is, they serve to produce an agreeable and diversified contour, that groups and contrasts like a picture, and creates a variety of light and shade, which gives great spirit, beauty and effect to the composition. . . .
>
> We cannot however allow ourselves to close this note without doing justice to the memory of a great man, whose reputation as an architect has been long carried down the stream by a torrent of undistinguishing prejudice and abuse.
>
> Sir John Vanbrugh's genius was of the first class; and, in point of movement, novelty and ingenuity, his works have not been

44. *John Nash, Cronkhill, Shropshire, c. 1802.*
45. *Robert Adam, Seton Castle, East Lothian, 1789–91.*
46. *William Wilkins, Grange Park, Hampshire, 1809, with the conservatory wing added on (left) by Charles Robert Cockerell in 1823.*

47. *Richard Payne Knight, Downton Castle, Herefordshire, entrance facade, 1772–78.*

exceeded by anything in modern times (*The Works in Architecture of Robert and James Adam, Esquires*, vol. 1, 1773, p. [4]).

How far Adam achieved this movement in his own architecture is a matter for debate. One distinctly Vanbrughian building by him is his last work, Seton Castle, East Lothian (1789–91), which seems to have been inspired by Vanbrugh's own house at Greenwich, Vanbrugh Castle (1718, with later additions). The combination at Vanbrugh Castle of symmetrical with consciously asymmetrical forms in the disposition of both the house and its linked outbuildings was fraught with consequences for the future. However, it was not this aspect of Vanbrugh's work that, on the whole, was to influence Adam. It was in the subtle variety of the volumes of his rooms and in his internal planning that Adam sought to recapture the "movement" that had marked Vanbrugh's handling of exterior forms. A characteristically beautiful example of this is Adam's Syon House, Middlesex (1762–69), of which he claimed, in 1773, that "the inequality of the levels has been managed in such a manner as to increase the scenery and add to the movement so that an apparent defect has been converted into a real beauty" (ibid., p. 9). Here, another central tenet of Picturesque theory is stated: that the architect should make use of, not ignore or conceal, natural accidents.

A quintessentially Picturesque environment was created at Strawberry Hill, Middlesex, from 1749 onward, by Horace Walpole (1717–1797). The slow growth of his villa was emphasized, not concealed, so that one could follow its development northward from the simple cottage he found on the site. Strawberry Hill was consciously asymmetrical, and the architect's choice of the Gothic style consciously associational. Its principles were further elaborated upon in a brilliant, asymmetrical house created by the greatest theorist of the Picturesque movement, Richard Payne Knight. Knight's own house, Downton Castle, Herefordshire (1772–78), superbly sited above the deep valley of the Teme River, with views to the Welsh hills beyond, is the first and most influential of those houses that rely for their effect on painterly and asymmetrical massing and grouping. Fortunately, Knight gave a clear account of his intentions at Downton in his distinguished and stimulating book, *An Analytical Inquiry into the Principles of Taste* (1805):

> It is now more than thirty years since the author of this inquiry ventured to build a house, ornamented with what are called Gothic towers and battlements without, and with Grecian ceilings, columns, and entablatures within. . . . It has, however, the advantage of being capable of receiving alterations and additions in almost any direction, without any injury to its genuine and original character.

The best style of architecture for irregular and picturesque houses, which can not be adopted, is that mixed style, which characterizes the buildings of Claude and the Poussins: for as it is taken from models, which were built piece-meal, during many successive ages; and by several different nations, it is distinguished by no particular manner of execution, or class of ornaments; but admits of all promiscuously, from a plain wall or buttress, of the roughest masonry, to the most highly wrought Corinthian capital. . . .

In choosing a situation for a house of this kind, which is to be a principal feature of a place, more consideration ought to be had of the views towards it, than of those fromwards it: for, consistently with comfort, which ought to be the first object in every dwelling, it very rarely happens that a perfect composition of landscape scenery can be obtained from a door or window; nor does it appear to me particularly desirable that it should be: for few persons ever look for such compositions, or pay much attention to them, while within doors. It is in walks or rides through parks, gardens or pleasure grounds that they are attended to and examined, and become subjects of conversation. . . .

Sir John Vanbrugh is the only architect, I know of, who has either planned or placed his houses according to the principle here recommended; and, in his two chief works, Blenheim and Castle Howard. . . . The views from the principal fronts of both are bad . . . but the situations of both, as objects to the surrounding scenery, are the best that could have been chosen (4th ed., 1808, pp. 225–27).

This passage makes clear the revolutionary way in which the Picturesque dissolved the compositional techniques that were traditional in Palladian and Baroque architecture in favor of an architecture of growth and change, designed pictorially so as to be absorbed into its landscape setting. In emphasizing this point Knight found it necessary to censure the great Capability Brown, whose landscaped parks, which seem so beautiful to us today, were too smoothly artificial for Knight's tastes, and whose designs for country houses were for the most part conventionally Palladian. Less fairly, Knight associated Humphry Repton (1752–1818) with his attacks on Capability Brown. Yet it is the executed work of Repton and his partner John Nash (1752–1835) that most closely approximates the ideals laid down by Knight, Uvedale Price, and William Gilpin. It was Gilpin (1724–1804) who had first popularized the term Picturesque in a book called *Observations Relative Chiefly to Picturesque Beauty* (1789). This was quickly followed by three important publications, of 1794: his own *Three Essays on Picturesque Beauty*, Knight's *The Landscape, a Didactic Poem* (dedicated to Uvedale Price), and Price's *Essay on the Picturesque*. In 1795 Humphry Repton produced his own contribution to the corpus of Picturesque theory, *Sketches and Hints on Landscape Gardening*, which was, of course, more practical and less theoretical than the work of Price and Knight. Indeed, in the next year, 1796, Repton formed an alliance with John Nash, a practicing architect, to show how architecture and landscape could be designed according to the same principles.

Perhaps the principal achievement of the partnership between Repton and Nash was Luscombe Castle, Devon (1799–1804), built for Charles Hoare, great-nephew of Henry Hoare of Stourhead. The *Red Book* in which Repton presented his proposals to Mrs. Hoare contains a view of Luscombe as developed according to Capability Brown's ideas, contrasted with a view showing Nash's and Repton's proposals for a more dramatic and Picturesque scheme in accordance with the ideas of Price and Knight. Derived from the asymmetrical composition of Downton Castle, the smaller Luscombe pivots on an octagonal tower containing a drawing room leading into a large conservatory. Varied, compact, and practical, with all the ground-floor windows coming down to floor level so as to make the most of the views across the park and valley to the sea, the plan is totally original. Such planning anticipates the "organic" sophistication of Frank Lloyd Wright's so-called Prairie Houses. Certainly no other European country could produce plans as revolutionary as this as early as 1799.

Other architects adopted Nash's daring and delectable asymmetry, notably Sir Jeffry Wyatville (1766–1840), who, at Endsleigh, Devon (1810–11), created one of the most striking houses of the nineteenth century. With a view to the erection of a large cottage orné, the duke of Bedford had selected a superb site in the wooded hills above the Tamar River already occupied by a simple cottage. Repton was called in to landscape the grounds while Wyatville provided a long, low house of astonishing freedom of plan in a mixed vernacular style, the whole anticipating the Shingle style of later nineteenth-century America. With the strange diagonal articulation of its plan, the rustic verandas and bay windows, Endsleigh, like Salvin's Scotney, is a perfect visual expression of the essential Picturesque idea so clearly stated by Uvedale Price: "If the owner of such a spot, instead of making a regular front and sides were to insist on having the windows turned towards the points where objects were most happily arranged, the architect would be forced into inventing a number of picturesque forms and combinations which otherwise might never have occurred to him; and would be obliged to do what has so seldom been done—accommodate his building to the scenery, not make that give way to the building" (*Essays on the Picturesque*, 2d ed., vol. 11, 1810, p. 268).

Another Picturesque extravaganza, with a plan as bizarre and

unprecedented as that of Endsleigh, is Highcliffe Castle, Hampshire (1830–34), by W. J. Donthorn (1799–1859). The first Lord Stuart de Rothesay employed Donthorn to blend the transported fragments of an early sixteenth-century French Flamboyant Gothic mansion into a sympathetic modern re-creation. The deliberate blurring of the visual boundary between what twentieth-century man would call "original," on the one hand, and "fake," on the other, must be regarded as characteristic of neoclassical and Picturesque taste. Lord Stuart's daughter complained that Donthorn "was ambitious of his own fame and wanted to emulate Fonthill and Ashridge"—and certainly the astonishing composition of Highcliffe, with its aspiring verticality and its tangential wings thrusting forward along the cliff top, owes much to the planning revolution effected by the practitioners of the Picturesque in late eighteenth-century England. Highcliffe was also Picturesque in the literal sense in that, in reconstructing this Normandy château, Donthorn relied on views of it *in situ*, by J. S. Cotman, made before Lord Stuart de Rothesay brought the house to England in 1830.

A very different house built at about the same time as Endsleigh shows that an irregular building could be designed in a style other than Gothic or Tudor and still fit appropriately into a dramatic or Picturesque landscape. This is Dunglass, Haddingtonshire, executed from 1807 to 1813 for the architectural historian Sir James Hall (1761–1832), from designs by Richard Crichton (1771–1817). Pivoting on a tower perched at the head of a rocky glen, Dunglass has some stylistic affinities with the Vanbrugh/Nicholas Hawksmoor approach and recalls the enthusiasm for Vanbrugh shared by Price and Knight. Hall went so far in following Price's recommendations as to employ the services of a landscape painter, Alexander Nasmyth, to settle the site of the house, before calling in the architects.

Another rather later Picturesque house which seems to owe something to Vanbrughian composition is Beaufront Castle, Northumberland (1836–42), by John Dobson (1787–1865). A prolific north-country architect, Dobson is today best remembered for his austere, late neoclassical country houses, but the pictorial massing of Beaufront reminds us that he had been a pupil of the watercolorist John Varley, and that one of his first commissions had been to carry out alterations at Vanbrugh's powerfully romantic Seaton Delaval, also in Northumberland.

Dodington Park, Gloucestershire (1798–1808), by James Wyatt (1746–1813), and Sezincote House, Gloucestershire (c. 1805), by Samuel Pepys Cockerell (1753–1827)—though one is neoclassical and the other neo-Mogul—are among the most successful examples of pictorially composed houses, blending nature and architecture by

55. *James Wyatt, Dodington Park, Gloucestershire, 1798–1813.*
56. *Samuel Pepys Cockerell, Sezincote House, Gloucestershire, c. 1805.*

57. *Thomas Hope and William Atkinson, The Deepdene, Surrey, plan, 1818–23.*

58. *Thomas Hope and William Atkinson, The Deepdene, Surrey, conservatory wing, 1818–23. Watercolor. British Architectural Library Drawings Collection.*

means of long quadrant greenhouses. Equally significant, though now demolished, was Thomas Hope's remarkable country house, The Deepdene, near Dorking, in Surrey. This was a late eighteenth-century house that Hope (1769–1831) bought in 1807 and to which he made a series of irregular Picturesque additions in 1818–19 and 1823. First of all came a new entrance front and private wing, with exteriors ranging stylistically from Gothic to Pompeian and culminating in an asymmetrically placed, loggia-topped tower of Lombard or Tuscan origin. With this striking object Hope had created, at a stroke, the language in which so many Italianate villas of the first half of the nineteenth century—by such architects as Sir Charles Barry (1795–1860) and Thomas Cubitt (1788–1855), and their many followers—were to be composed. In April 1819 Hope's friend, the novelist Maria Edgeworth, recorded in a letter that the house appeared "grotesque and confused among trees in no one particular taste." Had she been more familiar with the writings of Knight she might have welcomed the blending of styles as a realization of his recommendations concerning "that mixed style, which characterizes the buildings of Claude and the Poussins." The irregular skyline of The Deepdene, the tower and the detached group of kitchen offices placed among trees on sloping ground and sporting a belvedere and spire, similarly followed advice given by Sir Uvedale Price.

Thomas Hope was, of course, himself a Picturesque theorist. In 1808 he published an article, "On the Art of Gardening," which was reprinted in Mrs. Hofland's *A Descriptive Account of . . . White-Knights* (1819). Here Hope developed further the occasional expressions of regret made by Price and Knight at the way in which Capability Brown swept away all survivals of formal gardens, terraces, and balustrades, so as to bring his shaven lawns right up to the house. Thus Hope felt able to speak warmly of "the suspended gardens within Genoa, and of the splendid villas about Rome . . . those striking oppositions of the rarest marbles to the richest verdure; those mixtures of statues, and vases, and balustrades, with cypresses, and pinasters, and bays; those distant hills seen through the converging lines of lengthened colonnades . . ." (pp. 11–13).

By developing ideas outlined by Price and Knight, Hope anticipated, as with his loggia-topped tower, later nineteenth-century practice: in this case the vast, formal Italianate gardens laid out by Barry and William Eden Nesfield (1835–1888). In the same essay he wrote of the new Picturesque architecture; he wished to establish that "the cluster of highly adorned and sheltered apartments that form the mansion . . . should shoot out, as it were, into . . . ramifications of arcades, porticos, terraces, parterres, treillages, avenues. . . ." He gave a striking demonstration of this in the additions he made to The

59, 60.   *Karl Friedrich Schinkel, Schloss Charlottenhof, Potsdam, 1826.*
61.   *Karl Friedrich Schinkel and Ludwig Persius, court gardener's house, Schloss Charlottenhof, Potsdam, 1829–36.*

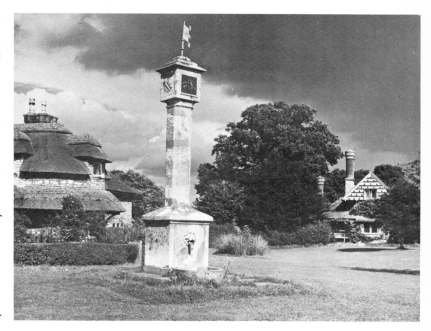

Deepdene, in 1823: a bizarre complex of conservatories, sculpture galleries, and orangeries extended from the house down the hill at an angle of about forty-five degrees. This represented the height of the Picturesque ambition to break down the barriers between nature and architecture. In general, this ambition was, in these years, a particularly English one—indeed, it was England's gift to Europe and North America—but we can also find it clearly stated in the work of the German Karl Friedrich Schinkel (1781–1841).

In 1824 work began on Schloss Glienicke, a villa near Berlin, by the side of the Potsdam Bridge over the Havel River. Schinkel built it for the twenty-five-year-old Prince Karl, one of the sons of King Friedrich Wilhelm III of Prussia. The house is simple, asymmetrical, and low-spreading and pivots around a tower. It forms a courtyard of simplified Italianate architecture on the walls of which are displayed antique Roman sculpture and casts acquired by Prince Karl in Italy. The small, undulating park, prettily landscaped by P. J. Lenné (1789–1866), contains numerous garden buildings by Schinkel as well as the remarkable Klosterhaus, a small cloister in a rich Byzantine style, built shortly after Schinkel's death in order to house the collection of Byzantine sculptures that the prince brought back from Venice, Padua, and elsewhere. Near the edge of the river are two additional buildings by Schinkel, the gardener's house and the Kasino (1826). With its vine-clad loggias looking out across the water, the elegant Italianate Kasino reminds one how much Berliners must have wished to forget the forbidding Prussian climate and imagine themselves on the shores of Italian lakes.

Also from 1826 is the Schloss Charlottenhof at Potsdam, designed by Schinkel on his return from an important visit to England. This was a pleasure pavilion for Prince Karl's brother, the crown prince, an architect manqué to whom the general disposition of the building is due. The relationship of the low, Italianate house with its Greek Doric portico to the gardens, loggias, canals, and pavilions, is masterly. In 1829–36 Schinkel and Ludwig Persius (1803–1845) greatly heightened the Picturesque charms of Charlottenhof by laying out a water garden punctuated by irregularly placed buildings such as the court gardener's house, the Tea House, and Roman Bath. The subtle and delectable blending of nature and architecture, though developed from hints in the writings of J.-N.-L. Durand, J. K. Krafft, and Pierre-Nicolas Ransonnette, closely parallels both what Thomas Hope had achieved at The Deepdene from 1818 to 1823, and the remarkable village of Clisson in the Vendée, built from 1805 to 1820 in an Italianate vernacular style.

For yet another of King Friedrich Wilhelm's sons, Prince Wilhelm, Schinkel designed the extensive Schloss Babelsberg near

64. *John Nash, Regent Street and Regent's Park, London, plan, 1811–30.*
1. *Regent's Park | 2. Cumberland Terrace |3. Chester Terrace | 4. Portland Place | 5. Grosvenor Square | 6. Regent Street |7. Hyde Park | 8. Green Park | 9. National Gallery | 10. Buckingham Palace | 11. St. James's Park | 12. Whitehall | 13. All Souls' church, Langham Place | 14. Carlton House Terrace*
65. *John Nash, the Regent Street quadrant, London, 1818–20.*

66. *John Nash, Chester Terrace, Regent's Park, London, 1820 and later.*

Potsdam (1833) in Nash's castellated style; its turrets can be glimpsed through the trees from Schloss Glienicke. The crown prince certainly had a hand in selecting the style of Schloss Babelsberg, which is so closely based on such castles by Nash as Luscombe, Caerhayes, and East Cowes that it must be one of the most English buildings in Germany.

So far, we have spoken as though the Picturesque could be realized only in the country, but John Nash showed brilliantly its suitability for urban design. In 1811 his Blaise Hamlet near Bristol, curiously similar to Richard Mique's *hameau* at Versailles, of 1778–82, was a foretaste of subsequent garden suburbs from Richard Norman Shaw's Bedford Park onward, but it is Nash's redevelopment of central London, also initiated in 1811, to which we should now turn our attention.

John Fordyce, Surveyor-General of the Office of Woods and Forests, was a great believer in comprehensive town planning. Seeing that the king's largely rural Marylebone estate, which was leased to the duke of Portland, was to revert to the Crown in 1811, Fordyce argued for the creation of a new major road leading to the estate from Charing Cross. In 1806 he appointed Nash as one of the two architects in the Office of Woods and Forests, and in October 1810 the department commissioned two alternative schemes for the development of the Marylebone estate and the new road. The architects invited to submit designs were Thomas Leverton and Thomas Chawner, the department's surveyors, and Nash and James Morgan. When Nash's plans were accepted in July 1811 the Prince of Wales was so pleased with their magnificence that he exclaimed: "It will quite eclipse Napoleon." If he had in mind such schemes as the Rue de Rivoli by Charles Percier and Pierre-François-Léonard Fontaine he was quite right in supposing that Nash's genius in town planning was of an altogether different order. Instead of covering Marylebone with a grid of streets and squares, as Leverton and Chawner envisaged, Nash realized that since many people living in London would prefer to live in the country, the most popular way of developing the Marylebone estate would be to turn it into a Picturesque rural park dotted with villas and flanked by broken runs of terraced houses glimpsed irregularly through trees. In fact, Nash's first plan of 1811 was rather more stilted than the final proposals. Nevertheless, in 1812 a part of the 1811 plan was begun, the southern half of the circus at the north end of Portland Place, but the builder went bankrupt so that the northern half was never built. The result is more in keeping with Nash's eventual proposals since it enables the greenery of the park to be seen from Portland Place. In 1812 Nash also presented his scheme for linking

68. *George Devey, cottages, Penshurst, Kent, 1850.*
69. *George Devey, Betteshanger, Kent, 1856–61.*

the new buildings in the park with the prince's dwelling at Carlton House, and from there, by implication, to the seat of government at Westminster. Nash saw immediately what no one else had thought of, that the line of his new road should follow that curious division between the sleaziness of Soho to the east and the elegance of Mayfair to the west. Thus he could buy up property fairly cheaply at Soho prices and sell it at Mayfair prices. Henry Holland's impressive colonnaded screen in front of Carlton House provided the visual climax at the southern end of Nash's scheme, but, since Portland Place and the entrance to the Marylebone estate lay to the northwest of this, the new processional route would necessarily have to follow a convoluted course. Here Nash heeded the advice of the Picturesque theorists—to make use of, rather than to conceal, natural accidents. Hence the celebrated Picturesque curve of the Regent Street quadrant, which he justified as "resembling in that respect the High Street at Oxford." Hence also the scenically placed if eccentrically planned All Souls' church, Langham Place, which subtly and seductively directed one's glance around an awkward shift in axis.

Behind the sweeping terraces surrounding Regent's Park, Nash developed a Picturesque enclave of Italianate villas and cottages ornés known as Park Village East and Park Village West. An outgrowth of his Blaise Hamlet theme, these were the prototypes of subsequent garden suburbs.

The strong emphasis that the Picturesque theory of the eighteenth century placed on domestic architecture led, in the nineteenth century, to a not unhealthy preoccupation with the house as a building type. This preoccupation survived the Gothic Revival of the first half of the century and its concern with church building and reemerged in the so-called Queen Anne movement, or Domestic Revival, of the 1870s, which had been created by Nesfield and Shaw in the 1860s. Indeed, there was an almost moral seriousness in the approach to house design after 1850. It became a kind of sacred task. We can sense something of this in the lectures on architecture that Ruskin delivered at Edinburgh in 1853. His lecture on domestic architecture proclaimed a belief in the value of vernacular buildings and the country cottage, which linked him, ironically, with the Picturesque movement and the Regency pattern-books of rural architecture. What distinguished such cottages from the boxlike neoclassicism he so much despised was their roofs. These, he felt, were not merely Picturesque in themselves but deeply expressive of the human need for shelter. He argued that the cottage was "really more roof than anything else." For him, "The very soul of the cottage—the essence and meaning of it—are in its roof; it is that, mainly, wherein consists its shelter; that, wherein it differs most completely from a cleft in rocks or bower in woods. It is in its thick impenetrable coverlid of close thatch that its whole heart and hospitality are concentrated. Consider the difference, in sound, of the expression 'beneath my roof' and 'within my walls.'" Ruskin went on to ask: "Do you suppose that which is so important in a cottage can be of small importance in your own dwelling-house? . . . It is vain to say you take the roof for granted. You may as well say you take a man's kindness for granted." Second only to the roof in architectural and spiritual significance was the bay window: "You surely must all of you feel and admit the delightfulness of a bow-window; I can hardly fancy a room can be perfect without one."

In fact, there were a good many architects who shared Ruskin's fancies and, from George Devey (1820–1886) in the 1850s to Edwin Lutyens (1869–1944) in the 1890s, they put them unceasingly into practice. At Penshurst, Kent, in 1850, Devey designed cottages for Lord de l'Isle that are narrative statements about the Old English rural way of life. They are Picturesque not only for that reason but also because they remind one of both old country cottages and *pictures* of such cottages. Devey had been trained as a watercolorist under J. D. Harding, and Penshurst in the 1840s and 1850s became something of an artists' colony. Devey's patrons at two of his major country houses in Kent, Sir Walter James at Betteshanger and W. O. Hammond at St. Alban's Court, were both keen watercolorists and appreciators of Old English rural traditions. At Betteshanger, from 1856 to 1861 and in 1882, Devey created "instant history" by echoing the enthusiasm of eighteenth-century Picturesque theorists for buildings in which one could read a process of growth and change. The historical and pictorial fantasy which Devey created at Betteshanger is that of a late-medieval house, successively altered, extended, and patched with different materials in the Elizabethan period and in the seventeenth and eighteenth centuries. A lazy, spreading plan of the type pioneered by Wyatville at Endsleigh, in 1810, heightens the impression of informal growth. St. Alban's Court (1874–78) is a more unified design, but even here the lower parts of the walls are of stone, ending in a ragged, uneven line, and the upper parts are of brick, so as to suggest, falsely, the re-use of an earlier house on the site. In fact, the earlier house lay in the valley below, and its remains, suitably restored and romanticized by Devey, form a Picturesque object much as the old Scotney Castle does on the grounds of Salvin's new Scotney.

70. *Jacob Spon, engraving of the Parthenon, Athens, from his* Voyage d'Italie, de Dalmatie, de Grèce, et du Levant, *1676.*

71. *Johann Fischer von Erlach, reconstruction of the Temple of Zeus at Olympia, from his* Entwurff einer historischen Architektur, *1721.*

72. *Jacques Carrey (attributed),* The Expedition of the Marquis de Nointel to Athens. *Chartres, Musée des Beaux-Arts.*

Greece was described in 1650 by Roland Fréart de Chambray as "the divine country." Claude Perrault declared that he aimed to renew architecture by reverting to the purity of the temples of ancient Greece, and in his translation of Vitruvius's works he illustrated a baseless and fluted Doric column, a concept that had been illustrated also by Renaissance commentators, though never as accurately. But though Greek architecture was long regarded as the basis of all excellence, and though there were attempts to conjure up and explore its visual forms, almost nothing was known about it. It remained, largely, a literary ideal. Not until 1750, when J.-G. Soufflot and his pupil G.-P.-M. Dumont measured the Doric temples of Paestum, were French architects to begin to make any serious inspection of the ruins of Greek antiquity. They were not quick, however, to use this information. Soufflot introduced an engaged version of the Paestum Doric column, with a base and pedestal, into the crypt of Ste.-Geneviève about 1758, but not until 1764 was Dumont to publish the results of their fieldwork in *Suite de plans . . . de trois temples . . . de Paestum*, and even then it was the first publication of its sort. One may wonder at their lack of response. The answer lies in their aesthetic preferences. Not until the late eighteenth century did architects in Europe learn to respond to the bold sculptural qualities of the Doric. They followed their Renaissance predecessors in finding their inspiration rather in the forms of Roman antiquity. When Colbert thought to ensure that his architects might have the correct antique models, he sent Antoine Desgodets to Rome, where he measured no less than forty-nine Roman monuments; engravings of these were published in 1682 in the sumptuous *Les édifices antiques de Rome*. This was to remain the standard reference for two hundred years. Colbert made no attempt to sponsor a similar publication on the monuments of Greece. Yet for twenty years and more, at considerable expense, he sent out agents to the mainland of Greece, to the islands, to Turkey, Palestine, Syria, and even to Persia and beyond to collect manuscripts, medallions, and coins for his extensive collections. And though these agents were instructed by Claude Perrault's brother, Charles, and told to take their copies of Pausanias with them and to visit all possible ancient sites, they can scarcely be said to have enhanced existing knowledge of Greek architecture. Early travelers to Greece—and there were many who went on trade and diplomatic missions—stopped at Athens and penetrated to the Parthenon, then more or less intact, and recorded their wonder. Robert de Dreux, for instance, who was there in 1668, said that it appeared so magnificent that, having seen it, there was no need to look further for architectural perfection.

That most enlightened of early ambassadors, the Marquis de Nointel, explored Athens and several of the islands in 1674 with a

73. *Johann Fischer von Erlach, plate from his* Entwurff einer historischen Architektur, *1721, showing Chinese buildings, artificial rock mounds,
and a suspension bridge.*

74. *Johann Fischer von Erlach, plate from his* Entwurff einer historischen Architektur, *1721, showing the Egyptian pyramids.*
75. *Julien-David Le Roy, view of the Parthenon, Athens, illustrated in his* Ruines des plus beaux monuments de la Grèce, *1758.*

carefully chosen and extremely costly retinue, including the author of *Les mille et une nuits*, Antoine Galland, and two artists, Rombaut Faydherbe and Jacques Carrey, who were to record the sculptures of the Parthenon, but they did very little, indeed, to publicize the results of their investigations. Nointel did, however, send back to France some notes and observations made by the Jesuit missionary J.-P. Babin, which were published at once by the scholar and doctor Jacob Spon. Spon himself was inspired to travel to Greece and—financed by Colbert—he set out; in Venice he encountered the English botanist George Wheler, whom he took with him. By 1676 he was back in his native Lyons, where he published his *Voyage d'Italie, de Dalmatie, de Grèce, et du Levant*. This was to remain for almost seventy years the most reliable and, from an architectural standpoint, most illuminating account of the buildings of Athens. It contained a miserable engraving of the Parthenon, showing that the columns were heavily proportioned, fluted, and baseless. Although the illustration was not of the sort to inspire architects, it nonetheless became famous, having been reproduced by Wheler in his plagiarized account of the journey with Spon, published in England in 1682, and in a description of Athens by Cornelio Magni, issued in Italy from 1679 to 1692. When Bernard de Montfaucon published his monumental compilation of all the known artifacts of antiquity, *L'antiquité expliquée*, issued in fifteen folio volumes, from 1719 to 1724, he was still forced to rely on Spon's record of the Doric temple. Similarly, for the temples of Baalbek, the only ones in Palestine that he was able to illustrate, Montfaucon was compelled to turn to seventeenth-century engravings, those made about 1680 by Jean Marot, probably on the basis of drawings provided by another of Colbert's agents, M. de Monceaux, who visited the site in 1668. The Perrault brothers, as we have seen, may have had a hand in Marot's distorted reconstruction of the Temple of Bacchus at Baalbek, endowing it with a nave and aisles separated by columns, and a coffered barrel vault above. This variant, however incorrect, had its appeal, and soon after its appearance in Montfaucon's work it became the basis for the reconstruction drawings of the temples at Palmyra and Olympia by Johann Fischer von Erlach (1656–1723), author of that first extensively illustrated history of architecture *Entwurff einer historischen Architektur*, issued first in 1721, and then in 1725, 1730, 1737, and 1742. This was a book to which architects could respond; the text was limited to a few lines underneath each engraving.

The plates depicted an extraordinary and breathtaking array of buildings, real and imaginary, including the wonders of the ancient world, the mosques of Constantinople, the palaces and bridges of

China, and also a sheaf of Fischer von Erlach's own designs. At the end of the eighteenth century Boullée was basing his pyramids on those reconstructions by Fischer von Erlach, while in the early years of the next century Fischer's naumachia was being adapted for an arena in Milan by Luigi Canonica. Fischer's imagery was to remain potent for almost one hundred years, although there was no great accuracy of observation in his views.

A more informed knowledge of Greek architecture became possible only in the middle years of the eighteenth century when measured drawings of the temples of Athens were included in the third volume of Richard Pococke's *Description of the East and Some Other Countries*, of 1745, to be followed in 1752 by the work of another Irishman, Richard Dalton's *Antiquities of Greece and Egypt*. Something of the nature of the Doric temples of Sicily was made known also at exactly the same time with the appearance of the second volume of G. M. Pancrazi's *Antichità siciliane*. However, there was nothing either reliable or captivating in these works. Among the first of that succession of scholarly studies that were to open up a real knowledge of antique architecture and provide models for emulation and even imitation were *The Ruins of Palmyra*, of 1753, and *The Ruins of Balbec*, of 1757, the results of an expedition undertaken in 1750 by James Dawkins and Robert Wood (1716–1771) together with John Bouverie and the draftsman Giovanni Battista Borra. These books marked the ascendancy of the British, and in particular the Society of Dilettanti, as patrons and explorers of antiquity. All the important archaeological publications to follow emanated from the British Isles. In France—Dumont's publication of the temples of Paestum apart (and he was to issue a revised edition in 1769)—only Julien-David Le Roy's *Ruines des plus beaux monuments de la Grèce*, of 1758, may be said to have provided hard archaeological information of the sort required by practicing architects. The information contained there, however, was soon shown to be less hard than might have been expected. In the first volume of their *Antiquities of Athens*, of 1762, Le Roy's rivals James Stuart and Nicholas Revett were to remark that his errors "have most of them been made before, tho' in fewer words by Wheler and Spon" (vol. 1, p. 35). Le Roy's work was, in fact, inspired by Stuart's and Revett's; in 1751 they published two detailed proposals for their work and began their protracted studies in Greece. By the beginning of 1754 Le Roy was in Greece and, soon after, he published a proposal of his own, based on one of Stuart's and Revett's; by 1758 he had published his own book. This in turn was to be plagiarized when Robert Sayer issued his *Ruins of Athens and Other Valuable Antiquities in Greece*, in 1759. Le Roy's publication, for all its haste

and inaccuracy, offered a most seductive array of views and measured drawings of the antiquities of Athens, Attica, and Corinth. Its impact in France, at least, was considerable. When he issued a second edition in 1770, he rearranged all his plates as a rebuke to Stuart and Revett, demonstrating that the monuments included in their first volume—the Temple on the Ilissus, the Choragic Monument of Lysicrates, the Tower of the Winds, and the Stoa at Athens—were all post-Periclean works, and thus somewhat lax in style. And he answered their gibes at his errors by pointing out that he was in no way interested in the minutiae of measurements. He did not wish to provide models for imitation. He was intent to conjure up only the effects and the qualities of architecture. And this statement might be taken as a hint as to why the French, though they continued to visit classical ruins with great eagerness—witness the studies of the French *pensionnaires* (students, usually winners of the Grand Prix, sent to study at the Académie de France in Rome) and the magnificent volumes of the Abbé Richard de Saint-Non's *Voyage pittoresque; ou, description des royaumes de Naples et de Sicile*, issued between 1781 and 1786, Jean-Pierre Houel's *Voyage pittoresque des isles de Sicile, de Malte, et de Lipari*, of 1782 to 1787, and the Comte de Choiseul-Gouffier's *Voyage pittoresque de la Grèce*, of 1782 and 1809—did not at any time instigate a Greek or even a doctrinaire Roman revival. The French were not interested in copying Greek and Roman forms. As with their study of Gothic architecture, they were concerned only to discover principles, methods of grouping and composing, means of handling scale and proportion, and techniques of building. They sought the spirit of antiquity—and also of Gothic architecture—not the detail.

Yet there was something of a minor Greek revival in France in the 1760s known as the *goût grec*, and also a fierce polemic waged against the fiery Piranesi in Rome as to the merits of Greek architecture.

The *goût grec* was the creation of the Comte de Caylus (1692–1765). He had, in fact, set out in 1716 to search for the site of Troy and had spent almost a year wandering in Asia Minor, visiting the Temple of Diana at Ephesus, but he returned home when recalled by his mother without having explored Athens itself. He was to become a connoisseur and antiquarian, and in 1729 he began to form a mixed collection of antiquities similar to that begun by Montfaucon in 1693. This was to become the focus of his salon and to serve as the basis for the seven volumes of his *Recueil d'antiquités* that appeared between 1752 and 1767. There was not much in these on architecture, though the later volumes did include the Gallo-Roman antiquities

76, 77. *Louis-Joseph Le Lorrain, designs for the first Festa della Chinea, Rome: Temple of Minerva, 1746, and Temple of Venus Genetrix, 1747.*

78. *Louis-Joseph Le Lorrain, writing desk, cabinet, and clock designed for Ange-Laurent La Live de Jully, 1756. Chantilly, Musée Condé.*

of southern France. His influence was exerted rather through his friends, the collector and publisher Pierre-Jean Mariette, the critic Abbé Jean-Baptiste Leblanc, and the Abbé Jean-Jacques Barthélemy, and through his personal efforts.

The young painter Louis-Joseph Le Lorrain (1715–1759) was a *pensionnaire* in Rome who had made something of a name for himself with three designs for the Festa della Chinea of 1745, 1746, and 1747 that may be said to have taken up where Perrault left off. He was warmly recommended by Caylus to Ange-Laurent La Live de Jully, master of ceremonies at court, for whom, in 1756, he designed a suite of furniture, in ebony and gilt-bronze, a writing table, cabinet, and clock that were regarded as startlingly Greek in inspiration and form. Each object was decidedly heavier and clumsier than contemporary French furniture, recalling that of Louis XIV's reign, but was in no sense antique. Yet this furniture led, at once, to a wide if ineffectual fashion for things *à la grec*—fans, snuffboxes, occasional chairs or tables, and a handful of houses. Details for the more authentically antique works were taken from such early publications on the ruins of Herculaneum—where excavations had started in 1738—as that produced in 1751 by Soufflot's companion on his voyage C.-N. Cochin. Even in its revised form of 1754, this was not particularly informative. Revelation had to await the appearance of the nine large volumes of the *Antichità d'Ercolano*, which appeared from 1755 until 1792. But the disclosures they contained were taken up by painters rather than by designers and architects. Joseph-Marie Vien, a protégé of Caylus, introduced an authentic-looking antique tripod into his insipid Grecian study *Une prêtresse qui brûle de l'encens sur un trépied*, of 1763 (later to become known as *La vertueuse athénienne*). In Rome, it should be noted, such attempts to depict antique furniture had already been made in 1761 in Gavin Hamilton's *Andromache Bewailing the Death of Hector*, and, in the same year, in Anton Raphael Mengs's *Augustus and Cleopatra*. But the French, as we have seen, were not greatly interested in archaeological accuracy.

The Abbé Laugier acclaimed the Hôtel de Chavannes on the Boulevard du Temple, in Paris, built between 1756 and 1758 by Pierre-Louis Moreau-Desproux (1727–1793), as an exemplar of the new Greek mode, but the surviving drawing of the elevation shows that the only features that might connect it to Greek architecture were some bands of fretwork—and they were probably derived from Renaissance buildings—and an unusual largeness of scale conveyed by the use of giant pilasters. The fashion was soon ridiculed both by that spry entertainer Louis Carrogis, known as Carmontelle (1717–1806), in some masquerade costumes, and later, in 1771, in a similar

81, 82. Ennemond–Alexandre Petitot, Berger et bergère à la grecque, *costumes for a masked ball at the court of Parma, 1771.*

set of costumes designed by Ennemond-Alexandre Petitot (1727–1801), who had been a student in Rome with Le Lorrain but had been sent as architect to the court of Parma in 1753 at the instigation of Caylus himself. On Caylus's recommendation Le Lorrain was employed to tidy up Le Roy's drawings for *Les ruines des plus beaux monuments de la Grèce* and was then given a post in Russia, where he died in 1759.

The *goût grec* was an ephemeral fashion, but it cannot be overlooked. Yet another of Caylus's protégés, the Belgian-born architect and engraver Jean-François de Neufforge (1714–1791), who was to engrave more than half the plates for Le Roy's publication, began to issue his *Recueil élémentaire d'architecture* in 1757. It comprised nine volumes and a total of nine hundred illustrations by 1772. Because these diffused and popularized a coarsened and heavy geometrical style thought to be antique in manner, they may be held to have prepared the ground for the more considered classicism of Louis XVI's reign. The first full-scale example of the new taste was the Hôtel de Varey, in Lyons, designed about 1758 by Toussaint-Noël Loyer (1724–1807), a pupil of Soufflot. There is no feeling for the refinements of classical architecture either in the facades on the Rue Auguste-Comte or on the Place Bellecour, or in the moldings of the salons of this *hôtel*, although they very convincingly reflect the coarsened taste inspired by Caylus and his associates.

Piranesi's quarrel over the merits of Greek architecture, instigated in 1761 with Le Roy and then with Mariette, was prompted more by nationalistic pride and a very real concern for his own livelihood than by any scholarly convictions. Giambattista Piranesi (1720–1778) arrived in Rome at the age of nineteen; he came from Venice, where he had learned etching and may have absorbed some of Carlo Lodoli's radical notions. In Rome he was stunned and then stirred by the sight of the ruins and influenced by a whole range of artists and stage designers such as the Bibienas and the Valeriani brothers, by the architect Filippo Juvarra, and, in particular, by the painter Gian Paolo Panini, who, in 1711, had himself come south from Piacenza to Rome, where he had established himself as the most prolific painter of scenes of ruins, both real and imaginary. Panini was to teach perspective drawing at the Académie de France and to open the eyes of a whole generation of French architects to the picturesque qualities of ruins—and thus to a more atmospheric view of architecture. He taught them to see architecture in painterly terms. Jean-Laurent Legeay (c. 1710–c. 1788), G.-P.-M. Dumont, Nicolas-Henri Jardin, Charles-Louis Clérisseau, Jérôme-Charles Bellicard (1726–1786), and Petitot, all of whom were in Rome in the 1740s, learned to present their projects in an atmospheric and painterly manner—a manner that conferred more interest on their works than they sometimes merited. Piranesi was in close contact with all these architects, and also with those French painters and sculptors studying in Rome—Jean-Baptiste Lallemand, Le Lorrain, the Challe brothers, Jacques Saly, Claude-Joseph Vernet, Vien, and, later, Hubert Robert. One of the first works to which Piranesi contributed, Fausto Amidei's *Varie vedute di Roma antica e moderna*, issued in 1745, also contained plates by Legeay, and in later editions views of Bellicard were to be added.

But Piranesi soon established himself on his own merit. Already in July 1743, he had published his first suite of etchings, the *Prima parte di architetture e prospettive*, which, though influenced by the works of Fischer von Erlach and the Bibienas, was to influence, in turn, Le Lorrain's designs for the Festa della Chinea of 1746 and 1747. Then in 1748 came the *Antichità romane de tempi della repubblica, e de primi imperatori*, which established his style and his reputation as a recorder of buildings old and new, in and around Rome. Some more idiosyncratic works followed, the four plates of the *Grotteschi*, mysterious rococo confections influenced by his contact with G. B. Tiepolo in 1744, and the fourteen plates of the *Invenzioni capric. de carceri*, the initial version of his theatrical prison designs. All these works were combined and published together in various combinations, for they were not equally successful. What the connoisseurs and cognoscenti who visited Rome wanted, above all, were renderings of the monuments of the city. For four years Piranesi worked feverishly, excavating and measuring ruins, using his imagination for what he could not inspect for himself. In 1756 he began to issue the grandest and most stunning of all his works, the *Antichità romane*, to run eventually to two hundred plates, each two feet across. He had used his wife's dowry to pay for the plates and his strongest influence to secure a tax exemption to cut the cost of the paper. His future was thus tied up in the enterprise. When Le Roy's volume of Grecian antiquities appeared in 1758, with the threat of Stuart's and Revett's to follow, Piranesi determined to shatter all rival claims to originality and magnificence in architecture. With the aid of several local scholars he concocted the long and muddled text and the thirty-eight plates of *Della magnificenza ed architettura de' Romani*, which appeared in 1761. Refuting both Le Roy's claim that Roman architecture was derived from that of the Greeks—whose architecture was based, in turn, on that of the Egyptians—and a similar historical analysis made in a *Dialogue on Taste*, published as far back as 1755 by the Scottish painter Allan Ramsay, he sought to prove that Roman architecture owed nothing to Greece, that it developed rather from ancient Etruscan architecture, and that if there was not much of

86. *Plate from Giambattista Piranesi's* Prima parte di architetture e prospettive, *1743, showing the vestibule of a temple.*

87. *Plate from Giambattista Piranesi's* Antichità romane, *1756 onward, showing the foundations of the Theater of Marcellus.*

88. *Plate from Giambattista Piranesi's* Antichità romane, *1756 onward, showing visitors in the Tomb of Arruntius.*

89. *Plate from Giambattista Piranesi's* Prima parte di architetture e prospettive, *1743, showing the forum in the ancient Campidoglio.*

that at hand to prove his point, there were at least stupendous engineering works such as the Cloaca Maxima, substructures, aqueducts, and roadways extant. Greek architecture had no such logic and splendor of engineering. Roman architecture, moreover, was richer and far more varied than that of the Greeks, and thus infinitely to be preferred. Reason played small part in Piranesi's propaganda. Caylus's friend Mariette responded succinctly to this outburst in November 1764, in the *Gazette littéraire de l'Europe*, adding to Le Roy's summary history the suggestion that not only was Roman architecture altogether dependent on that of the Greeks, but that it owed whatever finesse it might possess to the labors of Greek slaves. Incensed, Piranesi rushed into print in 1765 his rebuttal of Mariette's arguments, the *Osservazioni . . . sopra la lettre de M. Mariette*, and the related *Parere su l'architettura* with its handful of extraordinary compositions, in which he abandoned all archaeological verisimilitude in favor of original composition. This was followed in 1769 by his equally outrageous, altogether shocking designs for the *Diverse maniere d'adornare i cammini*. "Je pense absolument comme vous," Caylus wrote to the archaeologist Paolo Maria Paciaudi, in 1765, "sur l'excès de l'encre et du foin de Piranesi, mais que voulez-vous? C'est sa manière . . ." (*Correspondance*, 1877, vol. 2, p. 95). Caylus could admire only the early works. But by then Pierre Patte was selling copies of Piranesi's etchings in Paris. Piranesi's reputation remained strong and his works continued to sell. The feud with the French was soon forgotten. Just before he died, in 1778, he produced the boldest, most somber of his works, a sheaf of etchings of the temples at Paestum, the title in French, *Différentes vues de quelques restes de trois grands édifices qui subsistent encore dans le milieu de l'ancienne ville de Pesto*. The solemn magic of these plates, more than anything else, perhaps, was to reveal to architects the solid splendor of Greek antiquity.

There were other propagandists, however, the greatest of them Johann Joachim Winckelmann (1717–1768), with whom we still associate the ideal of the "noble simplicity and quiet grandeur" of Greek art. Like Caylus, Winckelmann never visited the temples of Greece itself, though he was invited on three occasions to do so. He preferred that Greece remain a remote landscape. He wanted an ideal image, not reality. When he wrote his first invocation to Greek art, the *Gedanken über die Nachahmung der griechischen Werke in der Malerei und Bildhauerkunst*, in Dresden, in 1755, he had not even traveled to Rome. For his ideas on Greek art he relied on the writings of Pliny the Elder and Pausanias. He visualized Greek art entirely in terms of that of Raphael—in particular, the *Sistine Madonna*, with which he was familiar in Dresden. Raphael's smooth and rounded forms established Winckelmann's ideal. This was sapless and colorless. "Color,"

90. Plate from Giambattista Piranesi's Différentes vues de quelques restes . . . de l'ancienne ville de Pesto, *1778, showing the Temple of Neptune.*

Winckelmann wrote in the second chapter of his *Geschichte der Kunst,* "should have but little share in our consideration of beauty, because the essence of beauty consists not in color but shape, and on this point enlightened minds will at once agree." Elsewhere he wrote that great art should have no flavor, but should be like pure water.

Winckelmann's interest, as one might expect, was focused on sculpture, on the *Apollo Belvedere* and on the *Laocoön.* He did not know the works of Phidias, never saw a statue dating from before the fifth century B.C., and never really experienced the noble simplicity of the Greek art that he extolled. His concern for architecture was strictly limited. He described the temples of Agrigento, but summarily, in 1759, in *Anmerkungen über die Baukunst der alten Tempel zu Girgenti in Sizilien,* relying on the observations of the Scottish architect Robert Mylne (1734–1811), and, for the rest, limiting himself to general remarks on the subject of Greek and Roman architecture. He lauded rather the works of Michelangelo, as represented at St. Peter's. None of his writings was illustrated in a way calculated to stir architects. His direct influence on architecture may thus be dismissed. Yet he did prompt a reassessment of Greek art among connoisseurs that was to affect architecture. For however shaky his premises, however personal his interpretations, his accounts of the stylistic evolution of Greek and Roman art, couched in elevated and rapturous language, riveted the attention of his contemporaries (and even his successors, as late as the end of the nineteenth century, when Walter Pater was still quoting him with the highest admiration). There can be no denying the dramatic impact of Winckelmann's writings, in particular the *Geschichte der Kunst des Altertums,* of 1764, the first systematic account of the evolving forms of antique art. He was the most important propagator of the Greek myth in the late eighteenth century. His books were translated into French almost immediately on publication, though they were less quick to appear in English. The Swiss painter Henry Fuseli translated some of Winckelmann's earlier works in the late 1760s but the *History of Ancient Art Among the Greeks* did not appear until 1849, and then in America.

Winckelmann's life, one may note, also had its dramatic side, not uninteresting to his contemporaries. Son of a Prussian cobbler, he rose rapidly from schoolmaster, to reader, to librarian; then, like Jean-Jacques Rousseau, he turned to Catholicism to further his career. In 1755, at the age of thirty-eight, he moved to Rome to become librarian to Cardinal Archinto. Archinto died, and three years later Winckelmann graduated to the library of Cardinal Albani, where he may have advised Anton Raphael Mengs on the famous ceiling fresco *Parnassus,* of 1760, and the architect Carlo Marchionni on the three *tempietti greci* just being completed outside the cardinal's villa.

Temple de Neptune à Pesto, vu de côté, et dessiné plus

In 1763 Winckelmann moved to the Vatican itself, where he became Keeper of Antiquities. He was an active and influential propagandist, regarded as a man of the highest sensibility, but on occasion his perception failed him. His friend Mengs, whom he had even known in Dresden, painted a fresco of Jupiter and Ganymede in the antique style in imitation of one from Herculaneum. Winckelmann acclaimed it as an antique original. He liked the cupbearer. "Jove's paramour," he wrote to his friend Friedrich Reinbolt von Berg, "is certainly one of the most extraordinarily beautiful figures that has come down to us from antiquity, and I could not hope to find anything to compare with his face, it breathes so great a voluptuousness that his whole soul seems to be drawn into this kiss." Goethe, too, liked this Ganymede.

There were shadows in Winckelmann's life. In 1768 he was brutally murdered by a hustler in Trieste. Such scandalous incidents served, however, to attract more than usual attention not only to the man, but also to his work and all that he upheld. The French were particularly intrigued, but they were not to be spurred to the extent of initiating a Greek Revival.

England made the most determined effort to apply the new archaeological information to the creation of a new architecture directly inspired by the antique. English architects were less troubled by theory and ideas than their French counterparts and their powers of invention were further stimulated by the growth of the Picturesque tradition.

The new wave of enthusiasm for the antique, which enables us to see the middle of the eighteenth century as a turning point in British architecture, had been anticipated by Lord Burlington (Richard Boyle; 1694–1753) and his neo-Palladian circle. Thus, although England could scarcely parallel the long French tradition of theorists proposing a new rational architecture shorn of Baroque trimmings, many of the forms that were to be characteristic of neoclassical architecture had already been exploited by the Burlingtonians—in particular, the sequences of domed and apsed spaces derived from the Roman Baths. Lord Burlington was determined to purify British architecture of Baroque extravagance by recapturing that classical harmony which, he believed, had been codified and enshrined in the architecture and theory of Palladio. This obsession with the antique, if only at second hand through the eyes and researches of Palladio, made England unique in Europe at the beginning of the eighteenth century and helps explain why English architecture was out of step with, and, in some ways, stylistically in advance of, that of the rest of Europe.

One of the most influential products of Burlington's ruthless and doctrinaire classicism was the Assembly Rooms at York, which he designed in 1730. In his search to discover how the ancients would have designed a festival hall he was directed, probably by Giacomo Leoni (1686–1746), to Palladio's reconstructions of a hall in the "manner of the Egyptians," based on a description in Vitruvius, and of the courtyard of a Greek house. Leoni himself had published a similar design in his *Designs for Buildings both Publick and Private*, which appeared in 1726–29. However, the credit for realizing the idea for the first time in an actual building must go to Burlington, since not even Palladio had been able to carry his scheme into execution. Similarly, at Holkham Hall, William Kent and Lord Burlington were able to realize a plan type invented though never fully executed by Palladio. Burlington's chill hall at York, with its insistent freestanding columns carrying an unbroken horizontal entablature, set a precedent that was to be followed throughout the eighteenth century and later, from Mereworth church, Kent (1744–46; anonymous), via Adam's hall at Kedleston, Derbyshire (1760–70), to Leo von Klenze's throne room at the Munich Residenz (1832).

In the same year as his York design, 1730, Burlington printed for private circulation an edition of Palladio's original drawings for the restoration of the Roman Baths that Burlington had bought from the Bishop of Verona. Entitled *Fabbriche antiche disegnate da Andrea Palladio Vicentino*, this important contribution to archaeology gave Burlington the inspiration for the round and apsidal rooms that flank the great colonnaded hall at York and also for the remarkable entrance facade (now destroyed) with its curved portico containing windows similar to those of the Baths of Diocletian.

Burlington was an important forerunner of the architect as archaeologist, as exemplified during the next hundred years in England by Stuart and Revett, Adam, William Wilkins, C. R. Cockerell, and Henry W. Inwood. Another architect who had been interested in Palladio's reconstruction of Vitruvius' Egyptian Hall was Inigo Jones's pupil John Webb (1611–1672). We should not forget that the seventeenth century in England had enjoyed its own Palladian Revival. In the 1630s Jones added a colossal Corinthian portico to Old St. Paul's cathedral on a scale that still impressed Cockerell two centuries later, and about 1655 Webb provided The Vyne, Hampshire, with a giant Corinthian portico probably inspired by Palladio's chapel at the Villa Barbaro, Maser. Webb's was the first portico ever to adorn an English country house and is thus the father of the countless examples erected in Europe and North America during the following century.

Burlington was a learned and influential architect but he lacked flare and panache as a designer. Those qualities were possessed in

95. Robert Adam, Kedleston Hall, Derbyshire, hall, 1760–70.
96. William Kent, Holkham Hall, Norfolk, hall, c. 1734.

abundance by his intimate friend and follower, William Kent. Burlington and Kent's collaboration on the design of Holkham Hall, Norfolk, for Lord Leicester, produced one of the most spectacular interiors of eighteenth-century Europe: the entrance hall of about 1734. To the basic theme of Palladio's Vitruvian Hall, as revived at York, has been added a great apse partly inspired by Palladio's reconstruction of the antique basilica and partly by his own Venetian churches. The rich frieze, the coffered cove, and the details of the eighteen fluted Ionic columns from the Temple of Fortuna Virilis in Rome are based on plates in that popular work of archaeology Desgodets's *Édifices antiques de Rome* (1682). The light coloring of the Derbyshire alabaster and the prominent Greek-key and Vitruvian-scroll friezes also help to create a thoroughly classical effect in a room whose disposition obviously has a certain Baroque or theatrical drama.

Of the many sides to Kent's genius that cannot be fully explored here, one of the most significant is his interest in the Etruscan or Pompeian type of interior decoration that had been revived by Raphael and Giovanni da Udine in Renaissance Rome and that was to be given prominent emphasis in a number of celebrated interiors by Robert Adam. Kent painted ceilings in this festive classical taste in the Audience and Council chambers at Kensington Palace, London (1724), and in the parlor at Rousham, Oxfordshire (1738–40). The Rousham ceiling, framed within a striking Greek-key border, is especially noteworthy since it contains two Romantic landscape paintings by Kent, which also point the way to future developments in painting.

From Kent's revolutionary interiors of the 1720s and 1730s it is but a step to what is sometimes regarded as the first neoclassical interior in England, James Stuart's Painted Room at Spencer House, London (1759), and to Clérisseau's celebrated room in the Hôtel Grimod de la Reynière, Paris (1774 or 1775). To mention the name of James Stuart is to recall the Society of Dilettanti. Founded in 1733–34, this remarkable institution may justly be regarded as the fountainhead of English neoclassical architecture. A group of about forty rich young noblemen and gentlemen, mostly in their late twenties and in the process of making their *grands tours*, got together to form a club to promote what they called "Greek taste and Roman spirit." Their aim was to institutionalize, as it were, the interest in the antique expressed more indirectly by Burlington and his circle, and for the next century successive members of the society, by acting as patrons of designers and architects and by financing archaeologists and scholars, were able to exercise great influence over the development of taste. In some ways the most characteristic members were the architects Stuart and Revett in the mid-eighteenth century, and Wilkins and Cockerell in the early nineteenth, for all four combined the roles of archaeologist and architect. But the patrons, following in the footsteps of Lord Burlington, were almost as important: such men as Sir George Beaumont, elected in 1784, and Thomas Hope, elected in 1800. Though the Society of Dilettanti was aristocratic in impetus, its membership reflected both the social mobility of England and the strength of the Whig oligarchy. Nothing like it could have existed in any other European country.

James Stuart (1713–1788) was born into humble circumstances. He first found employment with Louis Goupy, a fan painter who had accompanied Lord Burlington on an Italian tour. Goupy's fans were decorated with views of classical buildings. Stuart set out for Rome in 1742; there, he acquired a reputation as a connoisseur of pictures and probably acted as *cicerone* to Englishmen on the *grand tour*. In 1748 he accompanied Gavin Hamilton, Matthew Brettingham, and his future partner, Nicholas Revett, on an expedition to Naples, during which the plan to visit Athens was first discussed. Revett (1720–1804), the son of a Suffolk squire, was very different in background from Stuart. In 1742 he traveled to Rome to study painting with Cavaliere Benefiale. The friendship of these four widely different men—Hamilton, Brettingham, Stuart, and Revett—led to their decision to measure the buildings of Athens, and they were encouraged by such English dilettanti in Rome as Lord Malton, Lord Charlemont, James Dawkins, and Robert Wood. Money was raised to finance the expedition, though in the end Brettingham and Hamilton were unable to take part. In 1748 Stuart and Revett issued their "Proposals for Publishing an Accurate Description of the Antiquities of Athens." Their aim was to parallel the way in which "Rome, who borrowed her Arts, and frequently her Artificers, from Greece, has by means of Serlio, Palladio, Santo Bartoli, and other ingenious men, preserved the memory of the most excellent sculptures and Magnificent Edifices which once adorned her." They also pointed out that "A work so much wanted will meet with the approbation of all those Gentlemen who are lovers of Antiquity, or have a taste for what is Excellent in these Arts, as we are assured that those Artists who aim at perfection must be infinitely more pleased and better instructed the nearer they can draw their Examples from the Fountain-head."

This clear statement of a neoclassical aesthetic in 1748 emphasizes the close connection between the study of archaeology and the practice of architecture. Stuart and Revett left Rome for Greece in 1750. They spent some time on the way in Venice, where the British Resident, Sir James Gray, procured their election to the Society of Dilettanti. They arrived in Athens in March 1751 and returned to England four years later to prepare their drawings for publication. Naturally, those members of the Society of Dilettanti who had helped finance the expedition were impatient for the results. In Germany Winckelmann himself shared their impatience as we know from the preface to his *Anmerkungen über die Baukunst der Alten* (1762), written in 1760, two years before Stuart and Revett's first volume was published.

Between 1748 and 1762 Stuart and Revett changed their ideas as to the contents of the first volume, so that it eventually contained not the major buildings of the Acropolis but the smaller, later, and minor buildings in the city of Athens. These, they modestly hoped, might furnish hints concerning "the different Grecian modes of decorating buildings." Indeed, the buildings they chose to illustrate, such as the Choragic Monument of Lysicrates, the Tower of the Winds, and the Gateway to the Agora, were Hellenistic, not Greek, and lent themselves particularly to a process of transformation into garden ornaments for English parks. This is an early instance of the way in which, in England, the tradition of the Picturesque tended to dissolve any expression of pure neoclassicism. Stuart himself had contributed to this process even before the first volume of his *Antiquities of Athens* appeared in 1762, so that the first Greek Revival building in Europe is, characteristically, a garden ornament in an English landscaped park. This is the temple at Hagley Park, Worcestershire, designed by Stuart for Lord Lyttelton in 1758. Built of red sandstone originally covered with stucco, it is not an exact copy of any Greek building but, being Doric hexastyle with a column at each side of the cella entrance, it was perhaps inspired by the Theseum in Athens. In October 1758 Lord Lyttelton wrote to Mrs. Elizabeth Montagu: "Stuart is going to embellish one of my little hills with a true Attic building, a Portico of six pillars, which will make a fine effect to my new house, and command a most beautiful view of the country." Thus, the Greek Revival was conceived from the start as part of the Picturesque impact of contrived landscape scenery.

Six years after Hagley, Stuart began to develop in a quite extraordinary way this theme of reducing Greek architecture to garden ornaments. From 1764 on, at Shugborough, in Staffordshire, for another Whig landowner, Thomas Anson (a founder-member of the Society of Dilettanti), Stuart dropped a succession of Picturesque buildings based on the minor architecture of Athens into a park that had long been adorned with garden ornaments and ruins of different shapes and sizes, including Chinese.

In some ways Stuart was more successful at adapting his archaeological knowledge to modern design in furniture and interior decoration than to architecture. Soon after his return to England from Greece he was invited to design interiors for two Whig landowners who were to subscribe to the first volume of *Antiquities of Athens*. Stuart's tripod stands of about 1757 for Lord Scarsdale at Kedleston, Derbyshire, and a related pair of candelabra for Lord Spencer at Spencer House, London, of 1759–60, are based upon the tripod at the top of the Choragic Monument of Lysicrates, but develop it in a novel, beautiful, and functional way. Stuart's interiors for Kedleston were not executed, but his Painted Room of 1759 at Spencer House survives as the first "Etruscan" Revival room in Europe. It was conceived as a unity with its furniture, which included a set of four fantastic sofas and six armchairs with side pieces made up of gilt griffins. These derive from antique Roman marble seat furniture Stuart may have seen in the Vatican or in other Italian collections. Their flashy drama anticipates Regency and Empire style furniture and is astonishing for 1760.

Stuart's only remaining work of real consequence was his rebuilding and redecoration, after a fire, of Christopher Wren's chapel at the Royal Hospital, Greenwich. This was carried out with the assistance of Stuart's very talented Clerk of the Works, William Newton, between 1779 and 1788. Reflecting the impact of the mature Adam style, it is dominated by a rich but filigreed ornament, the details of which are Greek in origin though the overall impression is certainly not. The most imaginative feature of the chapel is the pulpit, obviously inspired by Stuart's favorite building, the Choragic Monument of Lysicrates.

It will have become clear that Stuart's career was marked by a certain failure of nerve and that he never created the new architecture for which his contemporaries were waiting. His procrastination delayed until 1789 the publication of the important second volume of the *Antiquities of Athens*, which illustrated the Parthenon. Nicholas Revett had in fact resigned his interest in the joint publishing venture even before the publication of the first volume. As a gentleman of leisure he certainly maintained his interest in Greek architecture and archaeology, and in 1764 was chosen by the Society of Dilettanti to go on an expedition to the coast of Asia Minor with Richard Chandler and William Pars. This resulted in his editorship of the *Antiquities of Ionia*, which appeared in two volumes in 1769 and 1797. The buildings depicted were of equal interest to those in the first volume of the *Antiquities of Athens*—in particular, the splendid Temple of Apollo at Didyma, near Miletus—but, rather unaccountably, they did not influence contemporary architecture as they could and perhaps ought to have done. One reason why they did not was that Revett himself used them in only one of his own buildings. His name can be con-

nected with the design of only three important buildings, and in two of these he used the order based on the Temple of Apollo at Delos, which he had illustrated in the first volume of the *Antiquities of Athens*. Revett adapted this late fourth-century Delian Doric style at Standlynch (now Trafalgar) House, Wiltshire (c. 1766), for his friend Henry Dawkins, and at the church at Ayot St. Lawrence, Hertfordshire (1778). At Standlynch the composition of the Doric portico is still basically Baroque and at Ayot St. Lawrence the whole composition, with a central pavilion linked to side wings by colonnades, is of Palladian origin. Evidently Revett could not think in a really Greek way, though at West Wycombe Park, Buckinghamshire, in 1770, he provided for Sir Francis Dashwood, a founder-member of the Society of Dilettanti, an undeniably impressive western portico, based on the Temple of Dionysus at Teos, of the second century B.C., which he had included the year before in the *Antiquities of Ionia*.

Other important archaeological publications that influenced taste were Robert Wood's *Ruins of Palmyra* and *Ruins of Balbec*. Thus, a late-Palladian building such as Henry Flitcroft's west front of Woburn Abbey, Bedfordshire (1757–61), incorporates in the State Bedroom a version of the ceiling of the vestibule at the south end of the cella of the Temple of the Sun at Palmyra of the early first century A.D., as illustrated in Wood's book. It is interesting to compare Flitcroft's straightforward imitation of antiquity with Adam's more fanciful adaptation in the drawing room at Osterly Park, begun in the 1760s and completed in 1773. The ceiling of Adam's Great Drawing Room at Syon House of the 1760s is an imaginative mingling of Wood's illustrations with Raphael's and Giovanni da Udine's decorations in the vaulting of the loggia of Villa Madama, Rome.

The engravings for Wood's *Ruins of Palmyra* were prepared in London in 1751 by Giovanni Battista Borra, a Piedmontese architect, after drawings he had made at Palmyra. From 1752 to 1755 he incorporated Palmyrene themes in the ceiling of his State Bedchamber at Stowe House, Buckinghamshire. In 1775 the painter-architect Vincenzo Valdrè (c. 1742–1814), of Faenza, created the magnificent oval saloon at Stowe, flanked by sixteen freestanding columns supporting a full Doric entablature and a crowded frieze depicting a Roman triumphal procession. This hermetic, monumental interior, windowless, domed, top-lit, leads into a richly Pompeian music room of 1777, also by Valdrè. In the drawing room the Greek Corinthian order was adapted by Valdrè from that of the Choragic Monument of Lysicrates as illustrated in Stuart and Revett; the Bacchic frieze in the south portico was also taken from Stuart and Revett.

A decade after the Pompeian music room at Stowe another Italian-born architect working in England produced a room of greater

98. *Joseph Bonomi, Packington Hall, Warwickshire, Pompeian Gallery,*
c. 1786.

99.   *Joseph Bonomi, church in the park at Packington, Warwickshire, 1789.*

100. Joseph Bonomi, church in the park at Packington, Warwickshire, interior, 1789.

101. James Wyatt, chapel at Dodington Park, Gloucestershire, interior, c. 1805.

archaeological accuracy. This was the Pompeian Gallery at Packington Hall, Warwickshire, designed for Lord Aylesford by the eccentric Joseph Bonomi (1739–1808). Bonomi, a Roman, was a pupil of Clérisseau who had been engaged in 1765 by Robert Adam as tutor, guide, and companion. In 1767 Bonomi came to England to work for Adam and married the niece of Angelica Kauffmann, one of Adam's decorative painters. On the collapse of the Adam brothers' Adelphi speculation (a development of terraced houses on the Thames), Bonomi left their office, possibly in 1774, for that of Thomas Leverton (1743–1824). The project for decorating the Long Gallery at Packington, initiated in 1782, seems to have been Bonomi's first independent commission. Lord Aylesford was a remarkable figure, a gifted painter, an architect manqué, a traveler and connoisseur, a friend of the Picturesque theorist Sir Uvedale Price and of the collector Sir George Beaumont. He was the dream patron for any neoclassical architect. The Pompeian Gallery that Bonomi created for him at Packington was the work of one English and three Italian craftsmen: Benedetto Pastorini, a painter and engraver who had been employed by Robert and James Adam to make the plates for their *Works in Architecture*; Domenico Bartoli, a scagliola manufacturer; Joseph Rose, Jr., Adam's plasterworker; Giovanni Borgnis, a fresco painter; and, perhaps most important, John Francis Rigaud, a painter from Turin who came to England by way of Paris in 1771. The lower part of the walls up to the shelf of the chimneypiece was of scagliola, imitating panels of porphyry surrounded by borders of Siena marble: This arrangement corresponds with what had been discovered at Pompeii. The strong black and terra-cotta coloring recalls the Greek vases that Lord Aylesford enthusiastically collected, although the real source for the decoration was neither Greek nor Pompeian but Roman. It was taken from the plates either in Ludovico Mirri's and Giuseppe Carletti's *Antiche camere delle terme di Tito e loro pitture* (1776) or in Vicenzo Brenna's, Ludovico Mirri's, and Franiszek Smuglewicz's *Vestigia delle terme di Tito* (c. 1780), which were both later used by Nicolas Ponce in his *Description des bains de Titus; ou, collection des peintures trouvées dans les ruines des thermes de cet empereur* (1786). As interesting as the bold archaeological decoration of the gallery is the design of a set of eight Greek Revival chairs that still adorn it. Bonomi based the klismos form of these—a type subsequently popularized by Thomas Hope—not on Roman furniture but on the chairs depicted in Greek vase paintings.

After his tour de force in the gallery Bonomi turned his attention to the design of a new church in the park at Packington. The plans were prepared in 1788 with the active assistance of Lord Aylesford, and the foundation stone was laid in April 1789. This grim,

102. *William Wilkins, project for the entrance to Downing College, Cambridge, 1806.*
103. *Thomas Harrison, Chester Castle, gateway, 1810–22.*

gaunt building is Revolutionary in the manner of Ledoux's *barrières*, which Bonomi presumably knew. Its interior is no less remarkable for its confident use of the still-revolutionary Greek Doric order. It seems to be based on the Temple of Neptune at Paestum, which had been illustrated in T. Major's *The Ruins of Paestum* (1768), though without the entasis so prominent at Packington. Lord Aylesford's etchings of Greek ruins can be seen in the fourth volume of Henry Swinburne's *Travels in the Two Sicilies* (1783), and it may be that the addition of entasis is due to him rather than to Bonomi. The Doric groin-vaulted interior seems to have influenced several interiors by Sir John Soane and James Wyatt in the 1790s: Soane's Tyringham Hall, Buckinghamshire; Bentley Priory, Middlesex; an unexecuted House of Lords project; and Wyatt's remarkable chapel at Dodington Park, Gloucestershire, designed some time between 1798 and 1805.

The stark and deliberately unprecedented air of the exterior of the Packington church is also echoed in the Berlin Mint (1798–1800; demolished 1886), by Heinrich Gentz (1766–1811). Gentz was a pioneer in the introduction of the Greek Doric style to Germany. He visited Paestum and Sicily, and also traveled in England, Holland, and France. He was a friend of the artist Asmus Jakob Carstens and the publisher Wilhelm Tischbein and he married the sister of Friedrich Gilly (1772–1800), the most original architect of late eighteenth-century Germany. Although so many German architects looked to the Paris of Ledoux for inspiration at this time, it was English neoclassical architecture, with its archaeological interest in the revival of the Greek Doric, that was closest in spirit to German architecture at the end of the century. Indeed, it was in Germany—not in England, and least of all in France—that the first building based on the Athenian Propylaea was erected. This was the Brandenburg Gate (1789–91) by Carl Gotthard Langhans (1732–1808), the gateway not only to Berlin but also, in a sense, to German neoclassicism itself. It was probably inspired by Le Roy's striking reconstruction of the Athenian Propylaea published in his *Ruines des plus beaux monuments de la Grèce*. Langhans had visited Italy in 1768–69, and Holland, France, and England in 1775. He became director of the Royal Office of Public Buildings in Berlin in 1788, and his striking Greek Revival gateway has always impressed visitors to that city. In December 1794, for example the influential connoisseur, patron, and designer Thomas Hope was so much affected by the gateway when he saw it that ten years later, when he came to write a pamphlet on the style he believed ought to be adopted at Downing College, Cambridge, he recommended it as a model for the entrance to the college. And sure enough, Hope's protégé, the dutiful William Wilkins, provided designs in 1806 for a more than usually extensive porter's lodge à la Propylaea.

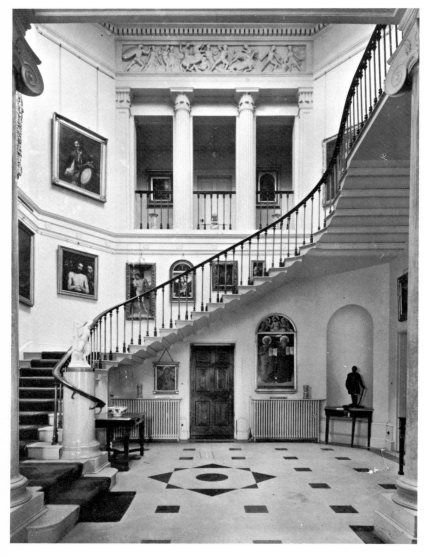

Whereas Wilkins's Greek Doric style was accurate and based on firsthand study of the originals in Greece—his *Antiquities of Magna Graecia* was published at Cambridge in 1807—Langhans had merely employed a sort of stripped Roman Doric style. His overattenuated columns have bases, unlike the Greek Doric order, and are unequally spaced in the side pavilions; also, there are demi-metopes at the ends of the frieze, whereas the Greeks ended their friezes firmly with a triglyph.

The examples of Langhans and Wilkins were followed by the architect Thomas Harrison (1744–1829) in his gateway at Chester Castle (1810–22), the design of which he had been cogitating since the 1780s. The theme was brought to a triumphant and imaginative conclusion by Leo von Klenze (1784–1864) in his Propylaeon, of 1846–60, on the west side of the Königsplatz in Munich. The project was first proposed in 1817, and Klenze's early sketches followed the Athenian prototype more closely than his final scheme with its powerful pylons.

Greek Doric was employed with varying degrees of accuracy by Benjamin Latrobe, James Wyatt, and Joseph Gandy. Shortly before embarking on his successful career in North America in 1796, Latrobe designed Hammerwood Lodge, Sussex, with Paestum-style Doric capitals. In the 1790s Wyatt transformed an unremarkable house, Stoke Poges Park, Buckinghamshire, into a neoclassical fantasy by surrounding it with stocky Greek Doric colonnades; similar stylistically was Storrs Hall, Westmorland, of 1808, by the eccentric Joseph Gandy, who later turned a temple inside out for the design of Doric House, Sion Hill, Bath (c. 1810). One of the noblest of all antique-inspired English houses is Belsay Hall, Northumberland. An austere product of the collaboration between 1806 and 1817 of three men—its owner Sir Charles Monck, the connoisseur Sir William Gell, and the architect John Dobson—Belsay Hall is the quintessence of what everyone in Europe had learned to feel about Greek art since Winckelmann first praised its noble simplicity and calm grandeur. The striking Villa Giulia at Palermo, Sicily (1789–92), by the French architect Léon Dufourny (1754–1818), is close in form to Belsay, but Dobson's building has a quality and an air of absolute authority that made it unique in Europe for its time. Karl Friedrich Schinkel gave his buildings the same stamp of conviction, as can be seen in his first important commission, the Royal Guard House in Unter den Linden, Berlin (1816). Two years later came an even greater masterpiece in the center of Berlin, the State Theater, of which Schinkel wrote: "I tried to emulate Greek forms and methods of construction insofar as this is possible in such a complex work." Apart from the Greek Ionic portico, the most memorable feature of the building is the frequent use of a kind of functionalist pilaster strip. For these Schinkel cited a Greek source, the Choragic Monument of Thrasyllus (illustrated in the second volume of Stuart's and Revett's *Antiquities of Athens*, 1789, and since destroyed), and also argued that, when used in windows, these pilasters admitted the maximum amount of light. Schinkel's theater was imitated by Sir Charles Barry in his Royal Institution, Manchester, now the City Art Gallery (1823–35).

C. R. Cockerell is in some ways the most characteristic of archaeologist-architects. His staggeringly successful seven-year tour of Greece, Turkey, and Italy resulted in the discovery of the pediment sculpture at Aegina, the Bassae frieze, and the use of entasis at the Parthenon. His early buildings show the difficulty he experienced in trying to incorporate this new knowledge of what Greek architecture was like into the classical tradition as practiced then in England. His staircase hall, of 1823, at Oakly Park, Shropshire, includes casts of the Bassae frieze with a version of the unique Ionic order from Bassae and details taken from the capitals of the Tower of the Winds in Athens. (However, Cockerell increasingly relied on Italian Renaissance and Mannerist sources to enliven his classical vocabulary, and will thus be considered later in the book.)

Two buildings of the greatest archaeological interest are Wilkins's Grange Park, Hampshire (1809), and, exactly contemporary with Oakly Park, St. Pancras church, London (1819–22), by William Inwood (c. 1771–1843) and his son Henry William (1794–1843). Henry Inwood had traveled to Greece to study Athenian architecture in 1819 and had formed a small collection of Greek antiquities which was later given to the British Museum. In 1827 he published *The Erechtheion at Athens, Fragments of Athenian Architecture and a Few Remains in Attica, Megara and Epirus*. Meanwhile, at immense expense, he and his father produced their own version of the Erechtheum—St. Pancras church, which, with its astonishing caryatid-flanked porches, has never failed to surprise generations of visitors.

Equally surprising is Wilkins's Grange Park, the grandest temple-like house in Europe. Its vast portico, alas only of brick and plaster, was based on the Theseum in Athens, and the monumental piers on the sides of the building are developed from those on the Choragic Monument of Thrasyllus. The effect was rather like a stage set, although beneath the Athenian drama Wilkins left the original seventeenth-century red-brick house more or less intact. Blending into its beautiful Hampshire landscape, richly wooded and watered, Grange Park epitomizes the archaeological and the Picturesque side of English neoclassicism. It is thus a fulfillment of what Stuart initiated at Hagley Park fifty years earlier with his little Greek garden temple described by Lord Lyttelton as "a true Attic building . . . which will . . .

112. *Antoine-Chrysostome Quatremère de Quincy, reconstruction in gold, ivory, and lapis lazuli of the Throne of Apollo, from his* Jupiter Olympien, *1815.*

command a most beautiful view of the country." That image of a Greek temple set in a high place remained powerfully in men's minds from the mid-eighteenth to the early nineteenth century. Nowhere was it more powerful than in Germany. Friedrich Gilly's entry of 1797 in the first of the many competitions for a monument to Frederick the Great in Berlin, though it departed from the terms of the competition, inspired a whole generation of architects with its solemn Doric temple set in a sacred precinct. The passionate desire to erect an adequate monument to Frederick's glory was linked to the process of establishing German national unity and self-identity, so that, in a sense, the real monument to Frederick was the foundation of the German Empire in 1871.

The competition for the monument to Frederick the Great did not, in fact, result in the erection of any single building. Curiously, something of the mood of Gilly's influential design can perhaps best be sensed in Scotland and in the north of England. In Edinburgh, for example, there are the Royal High School (1825–29) by Thomas Hamilton (1784–1858), the Royal Scottish Academy (1822–35) by W. H. Playfair (1789–1857), and Cockerell's and Playfair's uncompleted National Monument, or Walhalla, of 1821. The grim but dramatic Penshaw Monument in County Durham, modeled on the Parthenon (as was the Scottish National Monument), was erected in 1830 from designs by Benjamin Green (died 1858). As a bizarre but undoubtedly impressive footnote we should add that hybrid combination of Parthenon and Pantheon situated high up in the mountains above the village of Possagno, the Tempio del Canova (1819–33), designed by Antonio Canova (1757–1822) himself, possibly with help from Giannantonio Selva. The Walhalla near Regensburg in Bavaria (1830–42) is surely the culmination of the Picturesque vision of setting a temple on high and endowing it with that ennobling power with which Winckelmann had credited Greek art. But before examining this masterpiece by Leo von Klenze, we will turn again to France, since the design of the Walhalla was influenced by a new wave of archaeological discovery and debate, largely about polychromy, that was emanating from Paris.

During the early years of the nineteenth century a doctrinaire classicism was fostered in France, in particular by Antoine-Chrysostome Quatremère de Quincy (1755–1849), an unsuccessful sculptor who became *Secrétaire Perpétuel de l'Académie des Beaux-Arts* in 1816, a position he was to retain for twenty-three years, to be succeeded by a classicist of almost equally limited outlook, Désirée-Raoul Rochette (1790–1854).

Quatremère de Quincy upheld Winckelmann's ideals, though he was prepared to adapt them at times to accommodate new discoveries as they occurred. When he traveled to London in 1816 to see the Elgin Marbles, which he viewed with C. R. Cockerell, he was greatly moved, and thereafter altered his canons somewhat. But such small flexibility in his outlook was to destroy almost the image of classical rectitude for which he labored throughout his life. Already in 1815 he had produced a major study, *Le Jupiter Olympien; ou, l'art de la sculpture antique*, in which he had indicated that the great cult statues of the Greeks might not be of pure white marble, but might incorporate gold and ivory, lapis lazuli and semiprecious stones. He scarcely intended to evoke a colorful image of antiquity, but was following, rather, the scholarly lead of such men as Edward Dodwell—who had noticed traces of color on Greek fragments in Sicily in the early years of the century—and, more important, of that great French scholar and enthusiast of the Doric, Léon Dufourny—architect of the marvelously robust early essay in the Greek Revival, the Villa Giulia, in the Orto Botanico, Palermo. Dufourny had reported his findings directly to Quatremère de Quincy, whose rash interpretation of this discovery was to be taken up many years later by Jacques-Ignace Hittorff, who, as we have already seen, would attempt to revise totally the accepted image of antique architecture, to present it in the most vivid array of colors, as a basis for a livelier and more colorful contemporary style. This was the last occasion on which archaeological study was to make a fresh and vital impact on current design.

In Rome, in 1823, Hittorff encountered Thomas Leverton Donaldson (1795–1885), later to become president of the Royal Institute of British Architects, who had just written a brief essay on the discoveries of a group of young English scholars and architects—William Kinnaird, Joseph Woods, C. R. Cockerell, and Charles Barry—who had noticed traces of color on Greek buildings. Hittorff was hoping to make an archaeological discovery on his own account, and when he heard that William Harris and Samuel Angell had made similar observations in Sicily, he dashed there at once, overtaking Leo von Klenze, who was on the same trail. At Selinunte and at Agrigento Hittorff put eighteen excavators to work. He found what he wanted there and wrote at once to the editors of learned journals to stake his claim. When Hittorff returned to France, in 1824, he started a campaign to publicize his notions of a colorful image of antiquity. He believed that Greek temples had been covered completely with yellow paint, the sculpture and moldings heightened with lively patterns of bright blue, green, red, and gold paint. His short manifesto *De l'architecture polychrome chez les grecs; ou, restitution complète du temple d'Empédocle dans l'Acropolis d'Empédocle* was printed both in Italy and in France in 1830, starting an active and most acrimonious

TRÔNE ET SIMULACRE D'APOLLON À AMYCLÉE

113. *A. A. Jal, Jollivet House, 11. Cité Malesherbes, Paris, 1858. Majolica decoration.*
114. *Leo von Klenze, Walhalla, near Regensburg, 1830–42.*

115. *Leo von Klenze, Walhalla, near Regensburg.*

debate. Rochette defended the orthodox position; Antoine-Jean Letronne, professor of classical archaeology at the Collège de France, argued on Hittorff's behalf. Soon the debate became widespread. In 1834 Gottfried Semper voiced his theory that vapory red, rather than yellow, had served as the base color, and Franz Kugler produced his less fanciful reconstructions in the following year. In England a select committee was set up in 1837 to inspect the Elgin Marbles for traces of color, and Donaldson, Francis Cranmer Penrose, and Cockerell were to continue afterward to take a very active interest in the subject, though it was not until 1854 that Owen Jones and Sir Matthew Digby Wyatt erected the highly colored Greek court at the Crystal Palace at Sydenham. The influence of their ideas was enormous, especially in the field of decorative design. In France Hittorff, too, had attempted to infuse his ideas into contemporary design: His colorful portico for the Cirque Nationale, set up on the Champs-Élysées, Paris, in 1840, was one such experiment. Later, in 1852, he was to build another at the Cirque d'Hiver; it still stands in the Boulevard des Filles-du-Calvaire, though its present appearance is now toned down. His most important demonstration of architectural coloring, however, was the church of St.-Vincent-de-Paul, Place Lafayette, Paris, which was begun in 1824, though Hittorff took over only in 1830. Sixteen years later he began to cover the external portico wall with brightly colored enamel plaques depicting scenes from the Bible, but they were soon removed at the request of the clergy, who were incensed by the color and by the nudity of Adam and Eve.

The internal decorative scheme—a variant of that of the Norman cathedral in Monreale, Sicily—was also not begun until the 1840s. Something of Hittorff's intentions, though in muted form, was realized in the house built in 1858 by the architect A. A. Jal for the artist Pierre-Jules Jollivet at 11 Cité Malesherbes. But though Hittorff's own attempts to give expression to his ideas were of no great consequence, and though his final summation of his theories, the *Restitution du temple d'Empédocle à Selinonte; ou, l'architecture polychrome chez les grecs*, was probably not much read when it finally came out, between 1846 and 1851, there can be no doubt that he vitally influenced a whole range of architects, as disparate as Henri Labrouste and Charles Garnier, and showed them that a reassessment of antiquity was possible and most desirable. Hittorff was an indifferent archaeologist and an awkward, lackluster designer, but, almost unaided, he broke the spell of the doctrinaire classicists in France and prepared the way for the exuberance of the architecture of the Second Empire.

Leo von Klenze, Hittorff's rival in Sicily, was also influenced by the debate about polychromy, as is clear from the rich use of color,

particularly colored marbles, in his Walhalla near Regensburg, and from its elaborate openwork roof, which resembles that of Hittorff's St.-Vincent-de-Paul. In 1833 Klenze designed the temple in the English Garden in Munich, which was described at the time as the "first example of lithochromy in the present day." The notion of the Walhalla was initially suggested to Crown Prince Ludwig of Bavaria by the defeat of Napoleon at Leipzig in 1813. The competition was announced in 1814 and its terms demanded Greek forms because, it was argued, the Parthenon had been closely linked to the Greek victory over the Persians from which Greek unity derived. In 1815 the architect Haller von Hallerstein (1774–1817) submitted a project from Athens, where he was visiting Greek sites in the company of C. R. Cockerell. In 1829 the competition was reframed and Klenze's plan for a monumental temple on an enormous substructure was chosen. What exactly is the Walhalla? In Norse mythology it is the place in which the souls of slain heroes feast, having been brought there by the Valkyrie. For Ludwig it was also to be "to excellent Germans a monument, hence a Walhalla," and he emphasized that one was intended to be more German on leaving it than upon entering. It was a pantheon of political and intellectual portrait busts of, for example, Leibnitz, Schiller, Gluck, Mozart, Mengs, Thomas à Kempis, and Blücher. The Valkyrie also appear inside, but in the form of Greek caryatids wearing Nordic bearskins! Outside, one sculptured tympanum shows the defeat of Napoleon at Leipzig, the other the defeat in A.D. 9 of Augustus's legions by the united tribes of central and northwestern Germany, who thereby saved the country from Roman domination.

Faced with such a building, so classical yet so Romantic, so archaeological yet so much a part of nineteenth-century Germany, we are reminded forcibly of the paradox that neoclassicism can justly be regarded as one aspect of the Romantic movement. That point is neatly underlined by the fact that the painter J. M. W. Turner chose as the subject of and entitled one of his most remarkable paintings *The Opening of the Walhalla* (1842).

Chapter Four

THE FLOWERING OF NEOCLASSICISM

FRANCE: *From Gabriel to Ledoux*

The ideas that were to condition the changes in the form of architecture in late eighteenth-century France were generated early, by Perrault, Frémin, Cordemoy, and others; by 1753 these had been encapsulated and expressed with the utmost lucidity in the Abbé Laugier's *Essai sur l'architecture*. But the vital visual inspiration that was to make precise and alive the new style emerged but fitfully. L.-J. Le Lorrain's three designs for the Festa della Chinea of 1745, 1746, and 1747—borrowing motifs from Perrault's Louvre facade and also from Piranesi's *Prima parte*—provided the key for much that was to follow. Many formal devices and details can be traced to Le Lorrain's designs, but for a new boldness of massing, sudden changes of scale, contrasts of richness and stark wall surfaces, architects were to be indebted directly to Piranesi. His vision was to dominate architecture. The ruins of Rome, or rather an interpretation of them, were the mainspring of the new style.

Fittingly, the first architect who was to capture something of the new spirit, Giovanni Niccolò Servandoni (1695–1766), was trained in Rome by Piranesi's own forerunner G. P. Panini, and also by the Florentine architect Giuseppe Ignazio Rossi; he began his career as a stage designer, and he traveled in this capacity throughout Europe to Lisbon and London, Brussels, Stuttgart, and Vienna. Far too little is known of his designs, but he appears to have made his debut in France (whence came his father, coachman from Lyons) in 1726, with lavish sets for *Pyramus and Thisbe*. By 1732 he had won a competition for the west front of the church of St.-Sulpice in Paris. His design was not advanced—indeed, it had less to recommend it in the way of geometrical clarity than one drawn up six years earlier by Gilles-Marie Oppenordt—and was evidently derived from the west front of St. Paul's in London. But as work went slowly ahead the detail was modified and changed. In 1742 Servandoni engraved a variant that showed the entablature above the first order extending unbroken across the facade; by 1752 the entablature at the second level had also become an unbroken line across the facade. At this stage a third order was erected between the towers and a square planned in front of the church. Only the robust house that Servandoni designed and built for himself on the square from 1752 to 1757, on the corner of the Rue des Canettes, Paris, survives. The third order was taken down after Servandoni's death in 1766 and a giant pediment put in its place; this was struck by lightning in 1770 and replaced in turn by the simple balustrade that stands today—a reversion to the initial project by Oppenordt.

The north tower was then finished off by Jean-François-Thérèse Chalgrin, a pupil of Servandoni. "Plein des beautés de l'antique,"

Blondel wrote of Servandoni in his *Cours d'architecture*, "il a su soutenir le style grec dans toutes ses productions, tandis que Paris, de son temps, n'enfantoit guère que des chimères" (vol. 3, p. 351). No exaggeration surely was intended, for when it was finished in 1777 the west front of St.-Sulpice seemed to contemporaries to have the firmness of geometry, the regularity, and the columnar rhythms of a Greek temple. Certainly it was one of the starkest and most startling buildings in Paris. But its design had been evolved over a long period and by many architects, Chalgrin no less than Servandoni.

The chief architects of the years of transition were Pierre Contant d'Ivry and J.-G. Soufflot, whose designs for churches—especially Soufflot's Ste.-Geneviève—first suggested the form that the new architecture might take. But Contant d'Ivry did not visit Rome, and Soufflot was first there in the 1730s, before that interlude of enterprise and interaction between the French *pensionnaires* and the Italian painters of views, the *vedutisti*. In consequence, Soufflot's vision was to include little of novelty. The two architects took over an established tradition: Contant d'Ivry one that was French, Soufflot a late Renaissance formula. Neither was in any case greatly interested in novel formal devices. The spur to their architecture was structural finesse. The focus of interest in Contant d'Ivry's churches—at Condé-sur-l'Escaut, Arras, and, even more, the Abbaye Royale de Penthémont (106 Rue de Grenelle, Paris), of 1747 to 1756, and his unfinished project for the Madeleine, designed in 1761—is the refinement of construction. He experimented continually to reduce the mass of his structures and to make more daring his vaulting techniques.

Soufflot's concern for the way in which a building was made and how it might operate efficiently was evident from the start in the theater he began in 1754 in Lyons, in which the shape of the auditorium was conditioned by the sight lines and acoustics already tested in the theaters of Italy—though he went further than the Italians in introducing heating systems, tanks of water for fire fighting, and new lighting devices. His facades were creditable but dull. And at Ste.-Geneviève itself, as we have seen, though he was greatly concerned with the formal geometry, building the whole up from a regular grid, and slowly developing the design of the dome so that it became more and more pure in form, it was the manipulations of structure that drew forth his best energies and his delight—and led also, it was said, to his death (from worry). Considering that he presented himself as a reformer of architecture, and operated with the fullest support of the Marquis de Marigny, how disappointing is his output—in particular, those buildings in which structural experiment could play but a small part: the sacristy of Notre-Dame, of 1756; the École de Droit, facing Ste.-Geneviève, of 1771–83; and the buildings for Marigny himself,

117. *Giovanni Niccolò Servandoni, design for the west front of St.-Sulpice, Paris, 1732.*

118. *Giovanni Niccolò Servandoni, design for the west front of St.-Sulpice, Paris, with the addition of a third order, c. 1752.*

119. *Giovanni Niccolò Servandoni, St.-Sulpice, Paris, west front, 1732–77.*

120. *Pierre Contant d'Ivry, Abbaye Royale de Penthémont, Paris, interior of the dome and vaults, 1747–56.*

121. *Pierre Contant d'Ivry, Palais-Royal, Paris, grand staircase, 1756–70.*

122. *Pierre Contant d'Ivry, St.-Vaast, Arras, interior, designed 1754.*

which included a house in the Faubourg du Roule, of 1769, notable for its Palladian window, and the orangery and nymphaeum at the Château de Ménars. Soufflot relied too readily on what he had learned in Italy.

The first architect to provide a model for a new and reformed classical style and to infuse into it the well-considered grace and decorum of the French tradition, which—despite the rococo irruption—had continued strong from the reign of Louis XIV onward, was Ange-Jacques Gabriel (1698–1782). He did not go to Italy, but trained with his father, *Premier Architecte du Roi*, and succeeded to that title (as well as to *Directeur de l'Académie d'Architecture*) with the fullest confidence in his ability, in 1742; he retained the title until he retired, in 1774. He worked only at the king's command: Far too much of his time and energy was to be taken up with complex and futile schemes of alteration and extension to the royal palaces at Versailles, Fontainebleau, Compiègne, and Choisy. His *grands projets* no less than his *petits appartements*—and certainly the splendid and now beautifully restored theater that he built at Versailles for the dauphin's wedding in May 1770—are all deserving of study, and no doubt served to influence the course of architecture, but it was rather the succession of small and comparatively simple buildings that he erected for the court in the 1750s that was to indicate to his contemporaries how architecture might be reformed—Mme. de Pompadour's Pavillon Français (1749–50) at the Petit Trianon, Versailles, and her Ermitage (1749) at Fontainebleau, and the hunting lodges of Le Butard (1750), St.-Hubert (1755–57), Les Fausses-Reposes (1756; virtually unrecorded), and La Muette (1764), in the forests around Versailles. They were all neat and restrained in treatment. The culmination of his career was the Petit Trianon itself, promised to Mme. de Pompadour in 1761, begun in 1762, but not taken up in earnest until 1764, one year after the Seven Years' War, and the year of her death. The interiors, with paneling by Honoré Guibert, were not completed until 1769. This is a perfect example of the most refined taste of the period, the forerunner of the architecture of Boullée, Ledoux, and others. All admired Gabriel's work, but it was in Paris that its impact was to be most forcibly felt, once again on the initiative of Mme. de Pompadour. Even before her brother became *Directeur Général des Bâtiments*, in 1751, Gabriel had been called upon to design the imposing École Militaire, begun that year, greatly revised in 1765, and continued by a succession of architects until 1788.

In 1748 architects had been asked to submit proposals for a town-planning venture to frame a commemorative statue of the king. About one hundred fifty projects were sent in for sites all over Paris. But the king, alarmed at the cost of acquiring the sites proposed, ceded

124. *Pierre Contant d'Ivry, the Madeleine, Paris, interior, begun 1764. Drawing by P. A. Demachy.*

125. *Jacques-Germain Soufflot, design for the Hôtel de Marigny, Faubourg du Roule, Paris, 1769.*

126. *Jacques-Germain Soufflot, nymphaeum for the Marquis de Marigny, Château de Ménars (Loire), 1764.*

127, 128.   *Ange-Jacques Gabriel, Salle de l'Opéra, Versailles, 1748–70.*
129.   *Ange-Jacques Gabriel, Pavillon Français, garden of the Petit Tri-anon, Versailles, 1749–50.*
130.   *Ange-Jacques Gabriel, Le Butard, a hunting lodge near Marly, 1750.*

131–133. *Ange-Jacques Gabriel, Petit Trianon, Versailles, garden facade, courtyard facade, entry staircase, 1763, 1764–68.*

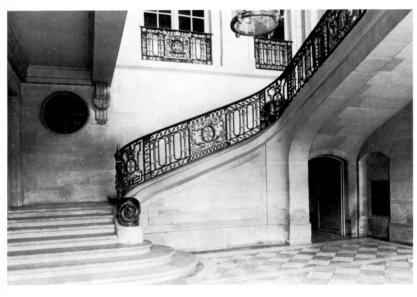

a large area of ground at the end of the Tuileries gardens and ordered another competition in 1753. Only nineteen architects submitted on this occasion. Gabriel's design was finally chosen in 1755 and work was begun—and continued until 1775—to provide Paris with the noblest and also the most unusual square in Europe, the Place Louis XV (today the Place de la Concorde). The rectangular space was defined by ditches and balustrades, with small pavilions, topped with statues, to mark the cutoff corners. The whole was dominated by two majestic colonnaded buildings, fittingly commemorating Perrault's example at the Louvre. "On aurait beaucoup mieux fait," Laugier carped in his *Observations*, of 1765, "de retrancher l'énorme soubassement de ces deux façades, d'établir le péristile au rez-de-chaussée sur un perron, élevé de plusieurs marches, et de lui donner toute la hauteur du bâtiment" (p. 35). But Ledoux, less intractable, wrote in his *L'architecture,* "Voyez les colonnes de la place Louis XV . . . on les aperçoit du quai du nord, à plus de trois cent toises; elles sont si bien conçues qu'elles s'effacent aux yeux, pour laisser à la pensée sublime idéal qui tient du prodige. C'est là, c'est dans ce fastueux édifice que brille le sentiment inépuisable de l'architecture française" (vol. 1, 1804, p. 108). One cannot be altogether sure that no sarcasm was intended here, for, like Laugier, Ledoux ridiculed the fussiness of the detail. Yet Gabriel's influence on later generations of architects was enormous. He was the exact counterpart of Jacques-François Blondel, a man of moderation and common sense in all things, wanting restraint and no great novelty, balance without violent movement or contrast. Together they provided a sound basis for the future.

With the signing of the Treaty of Paris in 1763 and the ending of the Seven Years' War, building activity began once again in Paris on an unprecedented scale. Whole new quarters sprang up within a few years on the site of the northern ramparts, where the new boulevards were laid out. Farther to the north toward Montmartre, to the west bordering the Champs-Élysées, and in scattered pockets to the south, a succession of small and elegant villas was built in imitation of Italian casinas, Vitruvius's *aedes pseudourbanae.* These marked the beginnings of a suburban development and were termed *folies,* not to account for any whimsicality—though many were bizarre enough —but because they were intended as retreats, hidden by foliage and trees. A new generation of architects emerged, then, to take control and impose their ideas, a generation inspired by Blondel, Gabriel, and Soufflot, but aiming at something different, something more severely classical, more starkly monumental and large in scale.

"La plupart de nos élèves s'y trompent-ils tous les jours," Blondel wrote in the fourth volume of his *Cours d'architecture,* in 1773, "il leur paroit plus aisé d'arriver aux compositions gigantesques, qu'aux

134. *Ange-Jacques Gabriel, Place Louis XV (now Place de la Concorde),*
Paris, designed 1753, executed 1755–75. Engraving by G. L. Le Rouge.
135. *Ange-Jacques Gabriel, Place de la Concorde, Paris.*

136. *Ange-Jacques Gabriel, building on the north side of the Place de la Concorde, Paris, 1758–75.*

137, 138. *Nicolas Le Camus de Mézières, Halle aux Blés, Paris, exterior and interior, 1763–67. Drawings by Maréchal.*

proportions de la belle architecture" (p. lxx). Yet he was able to appreciate the largeness of scale and the simple geometry of the circular Halle aux Blés that Nicolas Le Camus de Mézières was to build right in the heart of the Marais, on the site of the old Hôtel de Soissons, between 1763 and 1767. This was not, strictly, a classically inspired work, though contemporaries did liken it to an antique amphitheater and Laugier himself was moved to write, in 1765, even before its completion, that it was likely to become the finest building in Paris. When, in 1782 and 1783, Jacques-Guillaume Legrand (1743–1808) and Jacques Molinos (1743–1831) covered the circular central court with a giant dome, thirty-nine meters (one hundred twenty-nine feet) in diameter, of a light timber construction—similar to that proposed by Philibert de l'Orme for a nun's dormitory at Montmartre—the building appeared the most complete expression in France of the current liking for bold geometrical form. It was referred to as an equivalent of the Panthéon, which it almost equaled in size, and was to be inordinately admired by architects of the new generation.

The architects with whom we will deal first, Peyre, de Wailly, and Moreau-Desproux, had all been to Rome, though only two had won the Grand Prix. The most advanced was Marie-Joseph Peyre (1730–1785), an innovator of great power. His influence flashed suddenly into the international sphere with the publication, in 1765, of his *Oeuvres d'architecture*, dedicated to the Marquis de Marigny, and was instantly absorbed and lasted longer than that of most of his contemporaries. He was a pupil of Blondel, Denis Jossenay, and Louis-Adam Loriot. In 1751 he won the Grand Prix with a design for a public fountain, a grand affair with projecting side pavilions made up of Doric columns *in antis* supporting unadorned entablatures and pediments. The skyline is enlivened with statues and a dome, topped with a feature that looks something like an antique sarcophagus. But it is in no sense a design in the antique spirit; it is very characteristically a product of Blondel's school. In the spring of 1753 Peyre reached Rome, where he was to find at least one fellow pupil, William Chambers, and was to be joined within eighteen months by two more, Charles de Wailly (1730–1798) and Pierre-Louis Moreau-Desproux. Together with them Peyre was to explore the monuments of the city and measure the thermae, the circuses, and, in particular, Hadrian's Villa.

He soon put these studies to use. Not long after his arrival in Rome he entered and won a competition at the Accademia di San Luca for a cathedral and two related palaces, one for an archbishop and the other for the canons. His designs show that, though he had studied carefully both Michelangelo's and Bernini's work at St.

Peter's, he was also incorporating aspects of antique architecture into his work. From this period dates his extraordinary fondness for freestanding columns. His cathedral, a Greek cross surmounted by a great dome with four subsidiary cupolas, is set in a circular colonnade circumscribed by a circular space and an even larger colonnade, copied directly from Bernini. The two palaces, square buildings planned around open courtyards, are set laterally on either side of the circle thus formed. The scheme is vast. But it is no less vast, though perhaps less advanced, than that for an academic center he prepared a few years later, in 1756. The main building this time is square in plan, though diminished in area by the inclusion of two grand semicircular courts. It is far more overtly antique in conception in that it contains a variety of rooms and halls of different geometrical shapes, all top-lit, cleverly counterpointing one another and derived for the most part from Hadrian's Villa, but also no doubt from Piranesi's own variations on this theme. The main building, topped by a colonnaded drum, is again encompassed by columns, and is placed in a square court delimited by a range of buildings screened by more freestanding columns. This court is flanked by a "cirque . . . pour les révolutions militaires" and a naumachia, modeled, naturally, on Roman circuses, but terminating in hemicycles of serried columns.

The giant formality of these designs—though not at all unusual within the context of the competitions of the Accademia di San Luca—profoundly affected the future of architecture when they were published, together with a similar though slightly more commonplace project for a sovereign's palace, in the *Oeuvres d'architecture*, in 1765. They had no doubt exercised their potent influence on a number of architects even before their publication. Certainly their sheer magnificence of scale finds its parallel in the drawings of the Grand Prix winners of the early 1760s. And Peyre's insistence on the use of columns, so that all architecture appears as a sequence of columnar episodes (calling to mind Frézier's horrified comment on Cordemoy, "Il ne voulait partout que des colonnes, isolées et dégagées"; *Mémoires de Trévoux*, 1704, p. 161), can be traced in the works of such architects as Jacques Gondoin and Robert Adam long before it served to transform the late eighteenth-century architecture of France and England. Peyre's strong liking for toplighting was also to be echoed in the undertakings of Gondoin, Adam, and George Dance, the younger, before the end of the 1760s. Peyre wrote several articles at this time for the *Mercure de France* (reprinted in the second edition of his *Oeuvres d'architecture*, in 1795), one of which dealt with the planning arrangements of the ancient Romans, upholding for imitation their single-story buildings, with service areas below, made up of rooms of different shapes and sizes packed together and lit from above. "Les

139.   Marie-Joseph Peyre, competition project for a cathedral submitted to the Accademia di San Luca, Rome, 1753.

140.   Marie-Joseph Peyre, project for an academy, designed at Rome in 1756.

141, 142.   Marie-Joseph Peyre, project for the main building of an academy, section and elevation, designed at Rome in 1756.

143. *Louis-Denis Le Camus, Colisée, Champs-Élysées, Paris, plan,*
1769–71.

144. *Gabriel de Saint-Aubin,* La Fête du Colisée. *London, Wallace*
Collection.

145. *Henri Pètre with Alexandre-Théodore Brongniart, or, more likely,*
Brongniart alone, Pavillon d'Orléans, Paris, elevation and plan, 1774.

toujours quelques salles principales dans ce genre" (p. 11).

In only a handful of buildings in Paris, however, all of a fanciful kind, were the vastness of scale, the complexity of planning, and the experimental lighting effects to be realized. The most ambitious was the Colisée, built between 1769 and 1771 to the designs of Louis-Denis Le Camus, at the top end of the Champs-Élysées. This pleasure dome soon deteriorated and was demolished within fifteen years, though its spectacular effects were recorded in sketches by Gabriel de Saint-Aubin. In 1770 Victor Louis proposed a similar, if less elaborate, layout for a vauxhall in the Bois de Boulogne, which was never built, although a related enterprise, the Cirque Royal, designed by Nicolas Lenoir le Romain or Jacques Cellerier (1742–1814), was opened on the boulevards in 1775. Between 1774 and 1785 Henri Piètre (c. 1725–after 1785), a pupil of Jean-Silvain Cartaud, together with A.-T. Brongniart, completed a smaller, though private and permanent and thus more remarkable, pavilion for the Duc d'Orléans in the Rue de Provence, adjoining the house that Brongniart had built for the duke's morganatic wife, Mme. de Montesson. The Pavillon d'Orléans, an altogether charming work, was closest in appearance to Peyre's ideal, especially as illustrated—no doubt inaccurately—by J. K. Krafft and P.-N. Ransonnette in the *Plans, coupes, élévations des plus belles maisons et des hôtels construits à Paris et dans les environs*, in 1802.

Although Peyre had returned to Paris from Rome in 1756, it was not until 1762 that he was called upon to build his first—but very remarkable—work, a *folie*, the Hôtel Leprêtre de Neubourg, at Clos Payen ,south of Paris. This was built in the same year in which Gabriel produced the revised design for the equally remarkable but more elegant and less reserved Petit Trianon, and four years after Stuart's Doric temple at Hagley Park in Worcestershire was completed. Unlike Stuart, however, Peyre was not concerned with imitating antique architecture, but, following Palladio, he wished to distill its effects and infuse them into his work. The Hôtel Leprêtre de Neubourg is, in essence, neoclassical. It is, perhaps, the first strictly neoclassical building in France (though in appearance it is not at all unlike William Kent's Wakefield Lodge, at Potterspury in Northamptonshire, built about 1745 or soon after). Like many of Jules Hardouin Mansart's houses, it rests on a stylobate and consists broadly of two pedimented blocks joined by a rectangular mass to which a portico of six Doric columns, carrying a horizontal entablature, is appended. Leading up to the portico is a divided flight of stairs. The composition is compact, with unadorned wall surfaces—apart from a few niches—and well-spaced door and window openings, without surrounds; despite all its symmetry, there is a true neoclassical reluctance to emphasize the center. The principal entrance itself is placed not on the main axis of

romaines," he wrote, "étaient si persuadés de l'effet et de la beauté des grandes pièces éclairées par les voûtes, que, non seulement ils les pratiquaient dans les palais de leurs empereurs et dans les monuments publics, mais aussi dans les maisons des particuliers, et on y voyait the house but at the side, and the planning reflects this fondness for underemphasis. The stair is enclosed and played down, as Peyre had noted was usually the case in antique architecture. The entrance and stair hall, decorated with columns, lead to the dining room, which opens in turn on to the salon and then to the principal bedchambers and dressing rooms. There are no passages. Gone is the marvelous complexity and refinement of arrangement that Blondel had lauded as the great French contribution to architecture. Here is a baldly empirical arrangement, almost antique in character, suggesting that Peyre's innovations were applicable on even the smallest of domestic scales.

Peyre's next design was less severe. In April 1763 he drew up the plans of a house for the Prince de Condé, intended for a site opposite the Palais du Luxembourg, delimited today by the Rue de Condé, the Rue Monsieur-le-Prince, and the Rue de Vaugirard. The exaggerated aspect of his Roman projects is at once apparent in the perspective sketch (illustrated in the *Oeuvres d'architecture*), though the plan has none of that novelty. It is, indeed, not unlike that for an ideal château that Blondel drew for his pupils, though the central feature of Peyre's design—a low-domed rotunda containing a freestanding circle of columns behind which four symmetrical flights of stairs rise, preceded by a flat-topped portico—is an updated and purified version of the Panthéon. The most striking feature, however, is a columnar screen, with a triumphal arch enclosing the entrance court. This theme can be traced back to Cordemoy, and to Delamair's Hôtel de Soubise of the same period, and it was to be illustrated with flourishes by both Blondel and Neufforge in the 1750s. It was taken up in 1764 by Gabriel for the château at Compiègne, and a few years later suitably flattened, by Gondoin at the École de Chirurgie, Paris. The most direct transcription from Peyre, however, was the derivative masterpiece of Nicolas-Marie Potain's son-in-law, Pierre Rousseau (1751–1810), the Hôtel de Salm (now the Palais de la Légion d'Honneur), at 64 Rue de Lille, Paris, built between 1782 and 1785. In England, Robert Adam introduced the idea for the Admiralty Screen at Whitehall in 1759, soon after his return from Italy, but missed the point in placing a blank screen-wall immediately behind the colonnade.

From the first, Peyre was conscious of himself as an innovator. His purpose, he declared in the *Oeuvres d'architecture*, was to show how the works of the ancient Romans might be imitated to counteract the established French tradition, yet after the publication of his book he did very little work of importance. He became *Contrôleur* at Choisy. In 1767 he was admitted to the Académie, and throughout the rest of his life he submitted a number of schemes for reconstructions and new buildings (at least two of his houses in Paris survive today: the Hôtel de

147. *Marie-Joseph Peyre, Hôtel Leprêtre de Neubourg, Clos Payen, near Paris. Engraving by Durand.*

Nivernais, 10 Rue de Tournon, and the adjoining 11 Rue Garancière). But his only significant work was the Théâtre-Français (later Théâtre de l'Odéon, new Théâtre de France), designed in collaboration with his friend Charles de Wailly.

A pupil of Legeay and Blondel, de Wailly won the Grand Prix in 1752 with a design for a facade for a vast palace with a concave central feature screened with giant Corinthian columns, the whole preceded by a triumphal arch and a much lower curved colonnaded screen adapted from Bernini's at St. Peter's. Clearly, Peyre was to be indebted to this design for his *grands projets*. De Wailly generously offered to share his prize with his friend Pierre-Louis Moreau-Desproux, who, for three successive years, had come in second. Together they traveled to Rome, where they found Peyre. Moreau-Desproux was a man of no great talent: He built, as we have seen, the Hôtel de Chavannes (1756–58), the Théâtre de l'Opéra at the Palais-Royal (1763–70), and the Pavillon Carré de Beaudouin, on the heights of Ménilmontant (1770). All these works are of interest, and show promise, but all are unsatisfactory in that they lack tension of design. Moreau-Desproux was sustained

148. *Marie-Joseph Peyre, Hôtel de Condé, Paris, 1763.*
149. *Pierre Rousseau, Hôtel de Salm (now Palais de la Légion d'Honneur), Paris, entry colonnade, 1782–85.*

150. *Pierre Rousseau, Hôtel de Salm, facade on the Quai Anatole France, Paris.*

151. *Charles de Wailly, Grand Prix design for a palace, 1752.*

152. *Charles-Louis Clérisseau, design for the Ruin Room in the monastery of S. Trinità dei Monti, Rome, c. 1765.*

153. *Charles-Louis Clérisseau, decorative panels for the salon of the Hôtel Grimod de la Reynière, Paris, 1774 or 1775. London, Victoria and Albert Museum.*

154. *Charles-Louis Clérisseau, design for the wall of the salon of the Hôtel Grimod de la Reynière, Paris, 1774 or 1775. Drawing by J. C. Kamsetzera, 1782.*

155, 156. *Charles-Louis Clérisseau, Palais de Justice, Metz, facade and courtyard, 1776–89.*

by the family post he inherited in 1763, the *Maître des Bâtiments de la Ville de Paris*. He was the last to hold that title. De Wailly, however, was a challenging man. On his return from Rome he opened an *atelier* where he taught a number of architects—among them the Russians Vasili Ivanovich Bazhenov (1737–1799), Ivan Yegorovich Starov (1743–1808), and Fiodor Ivanovich Volkhov (1755–1803). In 1767 de Wailly became *Contrôleur* at Versailles under Gabriel, and in the same year he was literally forced into the *première classe* of the Académie Royale de Peinture et de Sculpture by Marigny, who greatly admired his work. Four years later he was elected to the Académie Royale de Peinture et de Sculpture, the only architect to achieve this distinction apart from that maverick recorder of ruins Clérisseau. Charles-Louis Clérisseau (1722–1820) was the painter of the Ruin Room at S. Trinità dei Monti, in Rome, that was so admired by Piranesi, designer of the early arabesque decorations for Grimod de la Reynière's salon in the Rue Boissy-d'Anglas (1774/75), and architect of the Palais du Gouverneur (now the Palais de Justice), in Metz (built between 1776 and 1789). De Wailly's activity was almost as diverse but his development was less consistent. Indeed, his output is baffling. In Rome, for instance, he made drawings of the ceiling of Il Gesù and of Bernini's *Throne of Saint Peter* with an obvious interest in the richness of form and the atmospheric qualities of lighting. Many of his interiors, such as the *salone* of the Palazzo Spinola in Genoa (1772–73), the Chapelle de la Vierge in St.-Sulpice (1777–78), and even the rooms of the old Hôtel d'Argenson (redecorated in 1784), are overabundant and exuberant in a Baroque sort of way. For the Marquis d'Argenson's country house, Les Ormes, he designed an elaborate stair in about 1771 (with which Sir William Chambers was in some way involved), derived from that by G. B. Piacentini, built in 1695 into the Palazzo dei Ranuzzi (now di Giustizia) in Bologna, where de Wailly had been made a member of the Academy in 1755. For the Marquis de Marigny, at the Château de Ménars, he designed a garden pavilion in 1768 or 1769, with partially fluted Doric columns like those of the Temple of Apollo at Delos, the only direct imitation of the Greek Doric in France, and for the crypt of St.-Leu–St.-Gilles, in Paris (1773–80), he used columns derived from the temples at Paestum, but with a square base and reeding rather than concave fluting—Gothic in effect rather than classical. In his whole manner of composing buildings there is this same discordance of vision: Some are made up of small, contrasting elements of divergent shapes and scale; others consist of large, simplified geometrical masses. Yet his major works, if not always as hard and stark as those of his contemporaries, are undeniably neoclassical.

The first and boldest of de Wailly's country houses, Montmusard,

159. *Charles de Wailly, crypt, St.-Leu–St.-Gilles, Paris, 1773–80.*

160. *Charles de Wailly, Château de Montmusard, Dijon, elevation and ground-floor plan as illustrated by J. K. Krafft, 1812.*

161. *Charles de Wailly, Château de Montmusard (now part of the École St.-Dominique), Dijon, 1764–72.*

162. *Detail of a painting of c. 1770 by Jean-Baptiste Lallemand, showing the Château de Montmusard as Charles de Wailly designed it in 1764. Dijon, Musée des Beaux-Arts.*

163. *Charles de Wailly, the architect's house in the Rue de la Pépinière, Paris, section, 1778.*

164. *Charles de Wailly, houses in the Rue de la Pépinière, Paris, elevation and plan. The house on the left, for the sculptor Augustin Pajou, was begun in 1776.*

on the outskirts of Dijon, was designed in 1764 for Olivier Fyot de la Marche, first president of the Parlement of Burgundy. The plan was marked by a complex yet wonderfully lucid geometry and was consciously antique in spirit; it was to be the first secular building in eighteenth-century France to be dedicated as a temple, a temple to the muses. This was clearly expressed in its arrangement. Only a fragment was built, but de Wailly's original plan survives, as does a painting by Panini's pupil Jean-Baptiste Lallemand (1716–1803), to convey the architect's intention. The plan is rectangular, almost square, with just the suggestion in the articulation of four corner pavilions. On the garden side a domed circular salon projects to form a semicircle; at the entrance front an open colonnaded temple is formed, cutting into the mass of the building. The detailed planning was more intricate than usual. The facades, though, were treated as a single story, with an attic above and a balustrade over, the whole unified by an overall pattern of rustication. There were no moldings around the window and door openings. Had it been completed in this form, the house would have been the most daring yet noble in France. But money ran out in 1772, long before the building was finished. In the following year de Wailly exhibited a design at the Salon for an even grander variant on the theme for Catherine the Great, dedicated this time to Minerva. Much later, in 1812, J. K. Krafft was to publish an altogether different design for the Château de Montmusard, consisting of a cylinder linked to two cubic blocks. The *raison d'être* of this arrangement was the domed open circular *salon d'été* at first-floor level, surrounded by two rows of columns with the staircase rising between them. This, no doubt, was derived from Peyre's stair hall for the Hôtel de Condé, though it may be distantly linked also to Balthasar Neumann's oval stair at the Episcopal Palace at Bruchsal, in Baden-Württemberg, built in 1731. Such central focus on the stair hall is unusual in France. In England experiments with a circular domed and colonnaded stair hall began with a design of 1759 for York House, Pall Mall, by Sir William Chambers; he, as we have seen, seems to have collaborated in 1774 with de Wailly on the latter's more complex variation at the Château d'Ormes. The most notable of these stair halls, however, was that designed in 1770 by James Paine for Wardour Castle, in Wiltshire.

The five town houses that de Wailly planned for the Rue de la Pépinière, Paris (only two were built—the sculptor Augustin Pajou's, in 1776, and his own, in 1778—and a third was begun in 1779), consist of an array of simple blocks, some of them surmounted by small pediments, others by rounded gables; they were evidently intended to form a unified architectural panorama of lively interest. The handling of the forms is wonderfully resourceful, if we are to judge by the illustrations in Krafft's and Ransonnette's *Plans . . . des plus belles maisons . . . à Paris*. Another circular colonnaded stair hall is introduced to give a central focus. But the constant setbacks in the composition, made up of small and varied elements, would have weakened the total effect.

In 1767 de Wailly was called upon with Peyre to design his greatest work, the Théâtre-Français (later Théâtre de l'Odéon, today Théâtre de France), on the site of the Hôtel de Condé. In the following years he traveled to England, Germany, and twice to Italy in order to study theaters. The history of the building is complex, with many changes of site and client and much rivalry involving a takeover at one stage by Moreau Desproux, who had not only benefited from de Wailly's friendship, as a student, but was by then the brother-

165, 166. Marie-Joseph Peyre and Charles de Wailly, Théâtre-Français (later Théâtre de l'Odéon, now Théâtre de France), Paris. Section and view of the foyer and staircase showing the design of 1770.

167. Marie-Joseph Peyre and Charles de Wailly, Théâtre-Français, Paris, 1779–82, rebuilt under thedirection of J.-F.-T. Chalgrin after a fire in 1799.

INTERIEUR DE LA NOUVELLE SALLE DE COMEDIE FRANÇAISE DE L'ANCIEN PROJET.

in-law of Peyre. But the building that was started in May 1779 on the foundations set down by Moreau-Desproux (to be completed in 1782) was in most respects similar to his and de Wailly's joint project approved in 1770. The circular auditorium is contained entirely within a rectangular block, rusticated all over, with arcades on the ground floor along the sides and the rear, rectangular windows on the second floor, and circular openings in the attic story. The whole is surmounted by a high pyramid roof. In front of the building is a Doric portico with a horizontal entablature, at one time intended to carry two reclining figures and a lyre, a symbolic dedication to Apollo. Later, in 1786, when the theater was to be converted into an opera house, de Wailly prepared a design in which two lodges and, further back, a pavilion with a Venetian window, niches, and sculptural decorations were to be set above the portico, providing a trinity of features in a different key from the rest. But the building that was erected, sober and severe in form, was made only marginally more severe when, after a fire in 1799, it was rebuilt by Chalgrin.

The bare account offered of the careers of Peyre and de Wailly gives some indication of the dramatic changes that took place in domestic architecture after 1763: changes in massing and the treatment of wall surfaces; changes in planning, from reliance on the simple *enfilade* to a complexity of interlocking rooms of different shapes and sizes; and changes also of detail. In the whole range of building types there were similar significant developments. More public buildings were erected than ever before. Theaters, which multiplied throughout France in this period, provide a particularly fruitful field for study. The practical demands of acoustics, sight lines, lighting, fire precaution, and construction resulted in notable departures from the norm. A progression—indeed, a progress—may be traced, starting with the new theater at Metz, or, more properly, with Soufflot's theater in Lyons begun in 1754, and including no less than twenty in Paris, dominated by Peyre's and de Wailly's designs for the Théâtre-Français. The building of theaters extended also to the provincial centers: to Amiens, where Jean Rousseau built a theater in 1778; to Besançon, where Ledoux was active from 1775 to 1784; and especially to Bordeaux, where the most magnificent theater in all of France, a great rectangular block preceded by a portico of twelve giant Corinthian columns, was erected between 1773 and 1780. This, containing a stair hall that is one of the splendors of eighteenth-century architecture, is still virtually intact. The designer was Louis-Nicolas-Victoire Louis (1731–c. 1807), a pupil of L.-A. Loriot, who called himself Victor Louis after he won the equivalent of the Grand Prix in 1755 and went to Rome for three years. Upon his return to France he established an extremely fashionable practice, first under the protection of Mme. Geoffrin, as

172. *Victor Louis, Grand Théâtre, Bordeaux, cross section.*
173. *Victor Louis, Grand Théâtre, Bordeaux, view of the auditorium.*
174. *Victor Louis, Grand Théâtre, Bordeaux, exterior.*
175. *Victor Louis, Grand Théâtre, Bordeaux, staircase.*

architect to the king of Poland, then as designer of a majestic temporary ballroom for the Spanish ambassador's reception in honor of the dauphin's marriage in 1770 (Chalgrin set up an equally noble ballroom for the Austrian ambassador). But Louis made a name and a living for himself chiefly in Bordeaux, where he built a number of *hôtels* in the new quarters adjoining his theater—the Hôtels Saige (1774–80), Fontfrède (1774–76), Legrix, de la Molère, de Rolly, and de Nairac (begun 1775). He was also responsible for several country houses, such as the Château de Virasel, near Marmande. The most ambitious by far was the Château de Bouilh, at St.-André-de-Cubzac, for the Marquis de la Tour du Pin, begun in 1786 but realized only in part. Even the unfinished fragment reveals it as one of the grandest country houses of the century. Louis's project of 1785 for the Place Louis XVI, on the site of the Château Trompette (now the Place des Quinconces), Bordeaux was of an equivalent heightened scale: a hemicycle of linked houses, 400 meters (1,320 feet) in diameter, was to open on to and extend along the Garonne River, but they were never begun. In 1772, while still busy in Bordeaux, he planned the Hôtel de l'Intendance (now the Préfecture) in Besançon, to be carried out faithfully during the next four years by a pupil of Blondel, Nicolas Nicole (1702–1784). Later, Louis was to return to Paris, upon which he conferred his expansive vision in 1781 in the form of the Galeries du Palais-Royal and a related theater, rebuilt by Julien Guadet in 1902, after a fire. The theater was notable for its cast-iron trusses and reinforcements, all lovingly photographed by Guadet's son Paul in their ruined state.

One of Louis's earliest works, the Chapelle des Âmes du Purgatoire in the church of Ste.-Marguerite-de-Charonne, Paris, designed in 1763, was no less distinctive a contribution to the evolution of church design than his theaters. The chapel—seemingly flanked by rows of Ionic columns supporting a horizontal entablature, without a projecting cornice, designed in imitation of a frieze from a sarcophagus, and carrying a coffered barrel vault—was, in fact, a *trompe l'oeil* painting by Paolo Antonio Brunetti, who, together with his father, Gaetano, and Charles-Joseph Natoire, had painted the scene of ruins on the walls of the chapel in Boffrand's Enfants-Trouvés (1746–51). It was a startling novelty, hailed by the Abbé Laugier in his *Observations* as "un des plus beaux dessins d'architecture que nous ayons à Paris" (p. 115). The revolution in church design that Louis thus acknowledged, proclaimed first by the Perraults with their project for Ste.-Geneviève and later by Cordemoy and Laugier, and culminating at just this time *en grand* with Soufflot's Ste.-Geneviève and Contant d'Ivry's Madeleine, was given convincing form a year or two later in the designs of three basilican churches: St.-Philippe-du-

Roule, in Paris; St.-Symphorien, at Versailles; and St.-Louis, at St.-Germain-en-Laye. These, one should note, were preceded by St.-Vincent-des-Augustins, in Lyons—built in 1759 by Léonard Roux (1725–c. 1794), an associate of Soufflot—which was finished only in 1789 and was thus not to achieve the fame or the influence of the Parisian exemplars of the genre.

The most famous of these, of course, is St.-Philippe-du-Roule,

the work of another pupil of Loriot and also of Boullée, Jean-François-Thérèse Chalgrin (1739–1811). He won the Grand Prix at the age of nineteen, and traveled to Rome the following year. From Rome, he corresponded with Soufflot. On his return to France he became *Inspecteur des Travaux de la Ville de Paris*, under Moreau-Desproux, and in this capacity supervised the building of the Hôtel de Saint-Florentin, just off the Place Louis XV, according to the designs of Gabriel. Chalgrin himself designed the gateway and entrance door. He was commissioned in 1764 by the Comte de Saint-Florentin, as *Ministre de la Maison du Roi*, to design a new church. But the site was not acquired until May 1767, the plans approved by the Académie only in August 1768, and work finally begun in 1772, to be completed in 1784. The arrogant novelty of the design—with its freestanding Ionic columns ranged down the nave and continuing around the curve of the apse, a coffered barrel vault above, and a squat Tuscan portico outside—was thus not to be appreciated until very late in the century. Today the church has lost the coherency and the feeling for classical unity so evident in old engravings, for it has twice been altered, once in 1846 by Étienne-Hippolyte Godde—who introduced windows into the vaults and built the Chapelle de la Vierge at the east end, opening up a vista through the screen of the apse—and in 1853 by Victor Baltard, who added the Chapelle des Catéchismes. Some of the initial quality was captured, however, by Chalgrin's pupil Jean-Baptiste Kléber (1753–1800), the future general, who copied the arrangement in 1774 for the Capuchin chapel at Strasbourg. Indeed, Kléber's version was even closer to Chalgrin's original intentions, for he retained the vault of stone complete with its flying buttresses that was omitted at St.-Philippe-du-Roule when a timber and plaster vault was built instead for economy.

Long before Chalgrin's church was complete, a similar basilica, designed in 1764 with partially fluted Doric columns supporting a horizontal entablature and surmounted by a coffered barrel vault (broken to accommodate windows), and preceded by a portico with freestanding Tuscan columns, was erected at Versailles. This was the church of St.-Symphorien de Montreuil, consecrated in 1770. The architect was Louis-François Trouard (1729–1794), once again a pupil of Loriot, who won the Grand Prix in 1753, arrived in Rome in the autumn of 1754, and spent three years there before returning to work at Versailles, where he was responsible for the barracks of the Gardes-françaises and other large and unremarkable buildings. He became architect at Orléans cathedral and at the Économats Royaux (an administration that spent the income from vacant bishoprics and estates confiscated from Protestants). In this capacity he was to design both St.-Symphorien and the Chapelle des Catéchismes at the east end of St.-Louis, in Versailles, in 1764–70. This chapel, divided with screens of columns, appears to have been derived directly from a plate in Piranesi's *Prima parte*. Another Italian-inspired church once attributed to Trouard but now more convincingly shown to be the work of Étienne-François Legrand—Trouard's successor at both the Économats Royaux and Orléans cathedral—is St.-Louis, in Port Marly (Yvelines), dating from 1778, the year in which Nicholas Revett built a comparable church at Ayot St. Lawrence, in England.

Legrand's successor at Orléans, in turn, was Trouard's pupil Pierre-Adrien Pâris (1747–1819). Pâris did not win the Grand Prix, but nonetheless traveled to Rome in 1770–71, in the company of Trouard's son; he returned to France in 1774 and four years later joined the Menus-Plaisirs, the administration responsible for royal fêtes, festivities, and spectacles, and to serve the world of fashion as well, with designs for neat, precise, and altogether charming town and country houses. Pâris's chief claim to distinction, though, derives from his larger works—a vast Italianate palace at Porrentruy, for the Prince Bishop of Basel, begun in 1776 but never completed; the town hall at Neuchâtel, erected between 1784 and 1790 by the local builder Raimond; and the hospital at Bourg-en-Bresse. When he died in 1819 he left to his native Besançon an unrivaled collection of drawings by such artists as François Boucher, Jean-Honoré Fragonard, and Hubert Robert, together with an even more extensive array of his own drawings done on his early visit to Italy. He made other drawings during later visits to Rome in 1783, and with his students, after 1806, when he became director of the Académie de France à Rome. These illustrate all the buildings he studied, whether antique, Renaissance, or later, and include not only Palladio's works and those of Giulio Romano and the Sangallos but also Pirro Ligorio's buildings and other oddities such as the Collegio Elvetico, in Milan (so admired by Gondoin), and the Certosa, at Ema (which would prove so exciting to Le Corbusier). All Pâris's original designs are still in Besançon, demonstrations of the exotic range of his sources, and, as such, urgently requiring investigation.

The third of the basilican churches being considered here, St.-Louis, in St.-Germain-en-Laye, was, like St.-Symphorien, also designed in 1764, though work was not begun for two years; it was interrupted and resumed only in 1787, just before the Revolution, and was finally built in 1823–24 by Alexandre-Jacques Malpièce and A.-J. Moutier. The original architect was Nicolas-Marie Potain (1713–1796), a man of Soufflot's generation, who had won the Grand Prix in 1738 and had remained in Rome until 1744, where, like Soufflot, he measured St. Peter's, and then traveled through Italy studying theaters. The result, in 1763, was an unusual project for a theater on

182. *Jean-François-Thérèse Chalgrin, St.-Philippe-du-Roule, Paris, approved 1768, built 1772–84.*

183. *Louis-François Trouard, St.-Symphorien de Montreuil, Versailles, east facade, 1764–70.*

184. *Louis-François Trouard, St- Symphorien de Montreuil, Versailles, west facade.*

185. *Louis-François Trouard, St.-Symphorien de Montreuil, Versailles, interior.*

186. *Jean-Baptiste Kléber, design for the Chapelle des Capucins, Strasbourg, 1774.*

187. *Louis-François Trouard, Chapelle des Catéchismes, St.-Louis, Versailles, 1764–70. Drawing by P. A. Demachy.*

188. *Plate from Giambattista Piranesi's* Prima parte di architetture e prospettive, *1743, showing a Doric atrium.*

189. *Étienne-François Legrand, St.-Louis, Port Marly, west facade, 1778.*

190–194. *Pierre-Adrien Pâris, design for a palace for the Prince Bishop of Basel, Porrentruy, plan of the ground floor, section, elevation, and section of a garden terrace, 1776. Besançon, Bibliothèque de la Ville.*

a corner site. The auditorium, with its axes on the diagonals, was elliptical in plan, with receding tiers of seats. The wide proscenium opening, divided up by columns, was to be recalled by Peyre and de Wailly. The elevations, however, are less striking: Two prostyle porticos of Ionic columns with balustrades above give the building an air of boldness, but the pattern of window openings and the decoration betray a fondness rather for Gabriel's brand of classicism. Potain was to work as Gabriel's assistant on the Place Louis XV from 1754 to 1770. His work was, not altogether surprisingly, much admired by Marigny. When, therefore, in 1762, Soufflot's fullest energies were required in Paris on Ste.-Geneviève, Marigny decided on Potain to replace him as architect of the new cathedral in Rennes. Soufflot's appointment dates from 1754; Potain's designs for the cathedral, based on those of Soufflot, were submitted to the Académie on July 26, 1762. They were revised the following year, and approved by the king on May 9, 1764. The surviving plan shows freestanding columns along the nave, on the foundations of a destroyed Gothic church. The nature of the vaulting is not indicated. Construction was started in 1786, to be stopped by the Revolution. Although the cathedral as it stands today was built between 1811 and 1844, it is tempting to think that this exemplary basilica, with its Ionic columns alongside the nave and continuing around the apse, its horizontal entablatures, and its coffered barrel vault, reflects Potain's early designs and thus, indirectly, Soufflot's first project (1754). Certainly this plan would have provided a prototype for all three basilicas designed about 1764, and would in some measure account for their simultaneous conception.

A number of churches of this type were to be built in the years that followed. One of the least visited, but the most elegant, is St.-Symphorien, at Gy, by the engineer Henri Frignet and the local architect Charles Colombot, constructed between 1769 and 1785 for the Bishop of Besançon. By the early nineteenth century the pattern was ubiquitous, accepted as a trite and well-tried formula; no one then cared about, or was aware of, the play of Gothic that had been so important an aspect of the eighteenth-century experiment.

Peyre, de Wailly, Louis, and Chalgrin have been presented as the first true representatives of the revised classical style of late eighteenth-century France, but no less important are Boullée, Jacques-Denis Antoine, Ledoux, Gondoin, Brongniart, and Bélanger—not one of whom was to win the Grand Prix, though Gondoin did travel to Italy. They made their debuts in the 1760s. Not all, though, were innovators. The youngest members of the group, Alexandre-Théodore Brongniart (1739–1813) and François-Joseph Bélanger (1744–1818), were indeed fashionable exponents rather than precursors of the new style. Heirs to Gabriel, excellent planners, and designers of

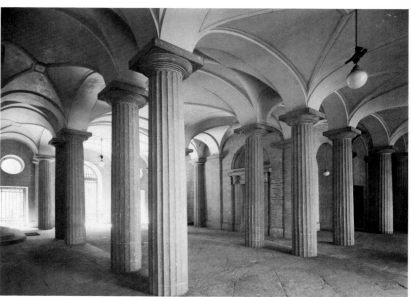

taste, they managed to capture much of the elegance and grace of his best mid-century work and to infuse it into their new, more sober—if sometimes even grander—Parisian manner.

Brongniart, a pupil of Blondel and Boullée, began his career in 1765, when he built the theater at Caen, a building of little enough merit, which shows a liking for the works of Soufflot and, naturally, Blondel. The numerous houses that he built in Paris in the years fol-

197. Nicolas-Marie Potain, St.-Louis, St.-Germain-en-Laye, interior, designed 1764. Drawing by P. A. Demachy.
198. Henri Frignet and Charles Colombot, St.-Symphorien, Gy, interior, 1769–85.

lowing, however, reflect the influence of de Wailly and the smooth and flattening tastes of advanced classicism. All his *hôtels* are restrained in outline and pure in form, beautifully planned, with most of the rooms rectangular or square but a few of a circular or other geometrical shape to provide a degree of variety. The facades of the houses are, almost invariably, composed with regular roundheaded openings on the ground floor and rectangular bas-relief panels or windows above, each unit separated by giant pilasters. The roof line is always horizontal. Later he was to forego the pilasters, retaining only the most restrained and even rustication. His first mature work, the Hôtel de Montesson, of 1770 to 1771, in the Chaussée-d'Antin, thus has affinities with the late buildings of Gabriel, though it is understandably more reserved and crisply geometrical. This has now been demolished, along with his most ambitious work, the Hôtel de Sainte-Foix, of 1775, on the Rue Basse-du-Rempart, but many of his later *hôtels* survive, if only in part, and may easily be visited—the Hôtel de Monaco (now the Polish Embassy), of 1775–77, at 57 Rue St.-Dominique, and a nearby group: the Hôtel de Mlle. de Bourbon-Condé, of 1780–81, at 12 Rue Monsieur (now minus Clodion's relief panels); the Hôtel de Montesquiou, of the following year, at 20 Rue Monsieur; his own house, of the same date, at 49 Boulevard des Invalides; the Hôtel Chamblin, of about 1789, at 3–5 Rue Masseran; and the Hôtel Masserano, dating from 1787, at 11 Rue Masseran.

Before the Revolution Brongniart built only two important buildings outside the domestic range: the church of St.-Germain-l'Auxerrois, at Romainville, Paris, of 1785–87, recalling St.-Philippe-du-Roule in its internal arrangement but with far sturdier Doric columns in the nave, and the Couvent des Capucins de la Chaussée-d'Antin (now the Lycée Condorcet and the church of St.-Louis d'Antin), of 1780–83, where he showed for the first time an original temper of mind. In the courtyard he introduced columns of the Paestum type, but with smaller capitals and without fluting. The main facade is also more robust and geometrical. Two pedimented pavilions linked by a lower mass, each with its own doorway, are otherwise sparsely punctuated with no more than empty niches and two elongated bas-relief panels. The whole, however, is inclined to be precise rather than powerful.

His great post-Revolutionary work, the Bourse, designed in 1807 when he was sixty-eight, was likewise not the creation of a man fitted for design in the grand manner. Yet it seemed to contemporaries to embody many of their ideals, and even Perrault's and Cordemoy's theories find their fullest expression there. Giant Corinthian columns supporting a simple entablature and cornice surround the solid rectangle of a structure pierced by regularly spaced, arched rectangular openings. Even before it was transformed into a Greek cross in 1903, the building did not convey an impression of either magnitude or magnificence. It lacked the weight needed for success.

Bélanger, taught by Le Roy and Contant d'Ivry, began his career in 1767, when, at the age of twenty-three, he was appointed *Dessinateur aux Menus-Plaisirs*. The previous year he had perhaps traveled to England, recording some of his impressions in a notebook that is today in the library of the old École des Beaux-Arts. He was certainly in England in 1778, when he prepared a design—he was one of a succession of such designers, from Robert Adam in 1773 to Robert Smirke in 1819—for Lord Shelburne's gallery in Lansdowne House, off Berkeley Square. But, for the rest, his activity and work were to be concentrated in Versailles and Paris; through the Menus he came into contact with the Comte d'Artois, whose architect he became, and also with the great singer Sophie Arnould, whose lover and architect he became. During the next twenty years he designed almost exclusively for her distinguished group of admirers, thus earning the title "faiseur à la mode." But he was an architect of the highest competence and finesse. He established himself early, in 1769, with the Pavillon Lauraguais in the garden of the Hôtel de Brancas, in the Rue Taitbout—a dazzling temporary confection in which he was assisted by Clérisseau—but his most spectacular feat was the Pavillon de Bagatelle, designed, erected, and furnished between September 21 and November 26, 1777, the result of a wager between the Comte d'Artois and Marie Antoinette. The famous *jardin anglais* there was laid out from 1778 onward, with the advice of the Scotsman Thomas Blaikie, who had been employed first by the Comte de Lauraguais in Normandy. But Bélanger was soon to prove adept at this genre, too, notably at the Folie Saint-James in nearby Neuilly-sur-Seine (also begun with the help of Blaikie in 1778), and later, starting in 1784, on the grandest of scales, on the estate of the court banker Jean-Joseph de Laborde at Méréville, near Étampes. Here he would be succeeded by Hubert Robert, who was to claim the garden as his own.

Boullée, Ledoux, and Gondoin were not all as adept and as busy but they were innovators of influence and power. All three were pupils of Blondel, though Boullée intended a career as a painter and studied first with Jean-Baptiste Pierre and later with the architects Pierre-Étienne Lebon and Jean-Laurent Legeay; Ledoux worked also for Louis-François Trouard. Not one of them won the Grand Prix; Gondoin, however, the son of a skillful gardener at Choisy, was sent to Rome in 1761 at the instigation of the king, and during his stay of two years he became—and remained—a close friend of Piranesi. Rome, in the imaginations of Boullée and Ledoux, remained the pretentious place of Piranesi's assembled engravings, although the exag-

202. J. Métivier, Hôtel Gouthière, Paris, entrance on the courtyard, 1780.

203. François-Joseph Bélanger, Pavillon Lauraguais, in the garden of the Hôtel de Brancas (Hôtel de Lassay), Rue Taitbout, Paris, facade elevation, 1769.

204. François-Joseph Bélanger, project for the gallery of Lord Shelburne in Lansdowne House, London, longitudinal section, 1778.

gerated fantasies for which they are held today in such uncritical esteem were not done, as one might expect, in their young and student days when Piranesi's influence was at its highest, but in the years that immediately preceded the Revolution and, in particular, in the idle years that followed. Their early works were, in comparison, almost restrained.

Étienne-Louis Boullée, by far the oldest member of the group, built little of importance. He made his reputation and demonstrated his ability as a teacher. At the early age of nineteen, it seems, he began to teach at the École des Ponts et Chaussées. Later he opened an *atelier* of his own from which emerged such distinguished architects as Brongniart, Chalgrin, J.-N.-L. Durand, N.-C. Girardin, Jacques-Pierre de Gisors, Antoine-François Peyre, Pâris, and Jean-Thomas Thibault. Though he taught for over fifty years, Boullée was not merely a pedagogue. His career began in 1752, when, together with his master, J.-B. Pierre, and the sculptor Étienne-Maurice Falconet, he began work on a dramatic *trompe l'oeil* decoration, greatly admired by Soufflot, in the Chapelle du Calvaire at St.-Roch, in Paris. But the works that first served to establish his reputation were the redecoration of the Hôtel de Tourolle (some of his *boiserie* survives) and a design for the entrance to the Hôpital de Charité, in the Rue Jacob, both dating from 1762. Thereafter, in quick succession, came eight *hôtels* in Paris—the Hôtel Alexandre (1763–66), the two Hôtels de Monville (1764), the Hôtel de Pernon (1768–71), the Hôtel de Thun (1769–71), the redecoration of the Hôtel d'Évreux (1774–78), the Hôtel de Brunoy (1775–79), and a speculative venture in the Rue Royale (1777–78). He worked on four houses near Paris: the financier Nicolas Beaujon's house at Issy-les-Moulineaux (1760–73), the Château de Perreux (begun 1761), the Château de Chaville (1764–66), and an extension to the Château de Chauvry (1783). Of these, only the first, the Hôtel Alexandre, at 16 Rue de la Ville-l'Évêque, survives, but drawings for the larger Hôtel de Monville, the Château de Chaville, and the Hôtel de Brunoy enable us to imagine their effect. The planning is straightforward, consisting largely of rectangular rooms in *enfilade*. The compositions are of unusual rectangularity and compactness, the masses, packed tightly against each other, related by continuous cornices and stringcourses. The facades of the *corps de logis* (main building) are articulated, as a rule, with giant Ionic pilasters, each bay thus formed being punctuated with a rectangular or round-headed doorway and a bas-relief panel above. The result is a closely woven surface pattern, the grid of pilasters overlying the stringcourses and moldings—a theme to be taken up soon enough by Brongniart. The entrance fronts of the Hôtel Alexandre and the Château de Chaville offer a variation in the format of a portico with freestanding

207. *François-Joseph Bélanger and Thomas Blaikie, plan of the jardin anglais*, *Parc de Bagatelle, Paris, 1778–80. Engraving by Le Rouge.*

208. *François-Joseph Bélanger, Folie Saint-James, Neuilly-sur-Seine, 1778–84.*

209, 210. *Étienne-Louis Boullée, Hôtel Alexandre, Paris, elevation and ground-floor plan, 1763–66.*

211. *Étienne-Louis Boullée, Hôtel Alexandre, Paris.*

212, 213. *Étienne-Louis Boullée, Hôtel de Brunoy, Paris, plan and elevation of the garden-facade, 1775–79.*
214. *Jacques-Denis Antoine, Hôtel des Monnaies, Paris, principal facade, begun 1767.*

columns *in antis*, flanked by rectangular openings, each with a wreathed oval medallion above. But the effect is not much different. Only on the garden front of the Château de Chaville is something novel attempted, an overall pattern of rustication punctured by rectangular openings. The handling of the detail is not at all unlike that of de Wailly's exactly contemporary Château de Montmusard.

During the first phase of his career Boullée was also responsible for a series of projects for the Hôtel des Monnaies, starting in 1755 and continuing until 1767, when the commission was awarded to Jacques-Denis Antoine (1733–1801). Antoine, the son of a joiner who had gained his knowledge of architecture from a building contractor, was to take up Boullée's proposals with considerable success, to produce that noble structure, more than three hundred meters (almost one thousand feet) long, on the Quai de Conti, its regular pattern of close-set openings broken only by a slightly advancing central pavilion, with a giant Ionic order on an arcuated and rusticated ground floor, and, above, a heavy cornice with a high attic and statues in front. The effect, however, is one of monotony rather than monumentality. As Le Camus de Mézières was to remark, the architecture was too well-ordered to face the sunless north; it lacked movement. The only entirely satisfactory feature was the triple-arched vaulted entry, with coupled columns, and the great stair hall, which led from the entry to an equally magnificent salon above. In 1764 Boullée prepared a scheme for the conversion of Giovanni Giardini's Palais-Bourbon into an establishment for the Prince de Condé, a design that M.-J. Peyre, who also submitted a plan, was to describe to his nephew as "une machine immense," though today it does not seem particularly shocking but rather a suitably enlarged version of his early domestic projects. In 1775 Boullée became *Intendant des Bâtiments* to the Comte d'Artois, for whom he designed a sumptuous suite in the Enclos du Temple, including a room in the Turkish style. Two years later he resigned this position, but in 1780 he prepared drawings for the Comte d'Artois for a palace on the site of the Pépinières du Roule. This was an immense affair, whose giant formality and colonnaded vistas presaged the phantasmagoria to come. Yet it was the Hôtel de Brunoy rather that marked the change both in his approach and in his activity. Though his earlier works are clear and consistent in design, they are lacking in the vigor of this composition, where a raised central feature, screened by a portico of six Ionic columns, is integrated with perfect fluency and restraint with a lower arcaded range, and is topped with a curious stepped roof terminating in a statue of the goddess Flora, recalling Pliny's description of the Mausoleum at Halicarnassus. This was Boullée's self-conscious archaeological twist. The house was, of course, known as the Temple de Flore. Thereafter Boullée designed

215. Jacques-Denis Antoine, Hôtel des Monnaies, Paris, salon, begun 1767.

216, 217. Claude-Nicolas Ledoux, boiserie for the Café Godeau, 1762. Paris, Musée Carnavalet.

in a new key, overblown and arrogant. He decided, it seems, to become a genius, or, at very least, to resume his early interest in painting. He virtually forsook domestic work. In October 1778 he became *Contrôleur des Bâtiments à l'Hôtel Royal des Invalides*; two years later he was appointed to a similar post at the École Militaire. He thus embarked on an official career in architecture, the aim of most members of the profession. Unaccountably, however, he resigned both positions in 1782. He continued with other minor official commissions, but he was more intent to indulge his fantasies. Unfortunately, as we shall see, they were of the histrionic kind. They were to ensure that his influence was enormous—in particular, in post-Revolutionary France. Almost all architects of the period derived something of their style from his sophisticated and superbly rendered designs. No one, however, endowed his work with Boullée's spectacular spirit as successfully as Ledoux.

Yet the early buildings of Claude-Nicolas Ledoux (1736–1806) are not unconventional. A pupil of Blondel and an assistant to Trouard, he competed unsuccessfully for the Grand Prix and, like Boullée, he did not travel to Rome. In 1762, at the age of twenty-six, he started his career with the design of the *boiserie* for a military café, the Café Godeau, once in the Rue St.-Honoré (now in the Museé Carnavalet), made up of panels supporting trophies divided by wreathed clusters of spears topped with plumed helmets. The design and execution, though of a seventeenth-century kind, are exceptionally bold. For the next four years, however, Ledoux was to be active in the provinces, in Champagne, Franche-Comté, and Burgundy, working for the Service des Eaux et Forêts, building and supervising the execution of bridges, fountains, schools, and five small churches, none of particular distinction. By 1766 he was able to return to Paris to rebuild the Hôtel de Bouligneux, at 28 Rue Michel-le-Comte, for the Comte d'Hallwyl, a building of note—in particular, for the colonnades that flank the walls of the garden, and, in *trompe l'oeil* perspective, terminate the garden on the wall of a property beyond, thus imitating Jacques Rousseau's seventeenth-century perspective on the wall of the Hôtel de Dangeau—but one that, on the strength of engravings in the second, greatly enlarged edition of *L'architecture considérée sous le rapport de l'art, des moeurs et de la législation* (published only in 1847, as *L'architecture de Claude-Nicolas Ledoux*), has generally been thought to have been more advanced than it was. The heavy unbroken cornice shown in his engraving of the street facade gives an unusual coherence and tension to the architecture and reinforces the importance of the recessed central portion. But on the building as it stands today the cornice is more conventionally designed to follow the outline of the plan, which has two end pavilions with a setback in the center. The

218. *Claude-Nicolas Ledoux, Hôtel d'Hallwyl, Paris, elevations of the street and garden facades, 1766–67.*
219. *Claude-Nicolas Ledoux, Hôtel d'Hallwyl, Paris.*

220. *Claude-Nicolas Ledoux, Hôtel d'Uzès, Paris, cour d'honneur, 1767–68.*
221. *Claude-Nicolas Ledoux, boiserie for the Hôtel d'Uzès, Paris (panels carved by J.-B. Boistou and J. Métivier, 1769). Paris, Musée Carnavalet.*

effect is altogether unlike Ledoux's Hôtel d'Uzès, based once again on an existing structure and designed a few months later in competition with two other architects, Pierre-Noël Rousset and Mathurin Cherpitel, and similarly lacking in vigor. The building is composed of rectangular masses, but dramatic tension is lost with the use of close-set openings—some rectangular, some roundheaded, all in the same run—and an uneasy pattern of overall rustication. The forecourt, however, with its portico of four giant Corinthian columns supporting a far-projecting cornice and heavy balustrade, illustrates forcibly the boldness inherent in his powers of composition. These were more successfully displayed in the interior paneling, carved in 1769 by Jean-Baptiste Boistou and Joseph Métivier, some of which is now also in the Musée Carnavalet. Ledoux's first country house, the Château de Bénouville (Calvados), also a remodeling—begun in 1770 and completed in 1777—is once again similar in treatment. It consists of a number of rectangular elements broadly composed to create a horizontal mass. The whole is pierced with very narrowly proportioned windows and is screened in part by a portico of giant Ionic columns. His engraved design of the building, not published until 1804, is, as before, bolder in conception than the executed work. There is no doubt that Ledoux updated his designs for publication. The great stone stair hall within, however, even as it stands, compares favorably with Antoine's contemporary stair at the Hôtel des Monnaies.

Ledoux's maturity begins with his next group of Parisian *hôtels*, starting in 1770 with the Hôtel de Montmorency, entered, exceptionally, on a corner (Boulevard de Montmorency and Rue de la Chaussée-d'Antin). The building is a cubic mass reinforced with a screen of Ionic columns on each of the two street facades, which suggests an unusual derivation from Potain's theater project of 1763, though it relates rather to the equal claims to the Montmorency lineage of the prince and princess, whose independent suites of rooms are thus expressed on the facades. The interior contains a succession of spaces, circular, oval, and some less straightforwardly geometrical, all brilliantly planned around a diagonal. Ledoux surpassed this tour de force in the same year with a pavilion nearby for the dancer Marie Madeleine Guimard. Here he scored a triumph. The open, semi-domed apse of the porch, screened by four Ionic columns carrying an entablature, and, above, a statue of Terpsichore, provides an altogether successful and ingenious focus for the design. The conception was inspired, no doubt, by the measured studies of Roman Baths carried out by Peyre and de Wailly, but the parallel between the Temple of Venus at Stowe—dated as early as 1732 and usually ascribed to William Kent—and Robert Adam's similar themes in the interiors of Syon House, Kenwood, and Newby is suggested irresistibly, the more so

as Ledoux is known to have traveled to England, where he is said to have designed a house for Lord Clive. The attracting feature was used a year later, but in a slightly different form, for the pavilion Ledoux designed at Louveciennes for Mme. du Barry. The exedra of the entrance porch is screened as before by four Ionic columns, but the semi-dome rises up instead behind the entablature and balustrade of the

224.   Claude-Nicolas Ledoux, *Château de Bénouville (Calvados), facade,*
1770–77.
225.   Claude-Nicolas Ledoux, *Château de Bénouville, grand staircase.*

226.   Claude-Nicolas Ledoux, *Hôtel de Guimard, Paris, principal facade,*
designed 1770, built 1773–76.
227.   Claude-Nicolas Ledoux, *Hôtel de Guimard, Paris, plan.*
228.   Claude-Nicolas Ledoux, *Pavillon de Mme. du Barry, Louveciennes,*
1770–.
229.   Claude-Nicolas Ledoux, *Pavillon de Mme. du Barry, Louve-*
ciennes, plan.

230. *Claude-Nicolas Ledoux, Hôtel Tabary, Paris, elevation, 1771.*
231. *Claude-Nicolas Ledoux, Hôtel de Thélusson, Paris, facade and main entrance in the form of a triumphal arch, 1778–83.*
232. *Claude-Nicolas Ledoux, Hôtel de Thélusson, Paris, plan.*

facade. The planning here, though exemplary, is also less adventurous than in the Guimard pavilion.

From this period dates a whole succession of small and costly *hôtels*, wonderfully resourcefully planned, and with much variation in design, often of a Palladian sort, beginning with the Hôtel Tabary, in the Faubourg Poissonnière, in 1771—which may be compared with Soufflot's slightly earlier handling of the same themes for Marigny's house in the Faubourg du Roule—and culminating in the magnificent and altogether overindulgent Hôtel de Thélusson in the Rue de Provence, dating from 1778 to 1783. This was approached through a triumphal arch, designed as if half-buried, as in Piranesi's Roman views.

All Ledoux's great works date from his middle years. In 1771 he was appointed *Inspecteur des Salines de la Franche-Comté*, as adjunct to Perronet, and within three years had designed and started to build his famous project for the Salines d'Arc-et-Senans; both the remaining heavily rusticated buildings of the saltworks, completed in 1779, and the outlandish unexecuted designs that he was to evolve later show him to have been at once an admirer of the reserved and dignified architecture of Louis XV's reign and an unbridled experimentalist with a pronounced liking for a conglomeration of heavy simplified masses and unadorned wall surfaces. This aspect of his character was to find its fullest expression in the *barrières*, or tollhouses, for Paris, built between 1785 and 1789, which seem at first sight supremely monumental in the traditional French manner, though on inspection reveal that the characteristic forms and measures of classical architecture have been interpreted with a waywardness and a willful wrong-headedness peculiar to Ledoux. They are the most powerful architectural works of the century. The promise of Piranesi finds its fulfillment here. However, when Ledoux attempted something of the sort on a larger scale the result was less immediately successful. At Aix-en-Provence he began a Palais de Justice and related prison in 1786. Work progressed slowly, and was stopped altogether in 1790; the structure was replaced in the nineteenth century by M.-R. Penchaud's Maison d'Arrêt. But Ledoux's engraved drawings show one of the buildings, the prison, as a solid simplified mass that is deliberately top-heavy. The roofs of the four corner pavilions dominate the whole, and all the richness and incident in the architecture, the curious squat porticos apart, are concentrated at the eaves. Nothing quite like it was to be built in eighteenth-century France. Yet many of the remarkable and altogether surprising projects that Ledoux prepared from 1786 onward (in particular, in the idle years that followed his fourteen-month stay in the prison of La Force, beginning in December 1793, when he was suspected of undermining the Revolution),

Élévation de la maison de Mr. Tabary.
Rue Poissonnière.

233. *Jacques Gondoin, project for a square in front of the École de Chirurgie, Paris, 1769. Important features of the plan included a new facade for the church of St.-Côme and a fountain against the wall of the adjoining disused monastery.*

234. *Jacques Gondoin, École de Chirurgie (now École de Médecine), Paris, anatomy theater, 1769–75.*

235. *Jacques Gondoin, École de Chirurgie, Paris, plan.*

236. *Jacques Gondoin, École de Chirurgie, Paris, principal facade.*

237. *Jacques Gondoin, École de Chirurgie, Paris, courtyard facade, detail.*

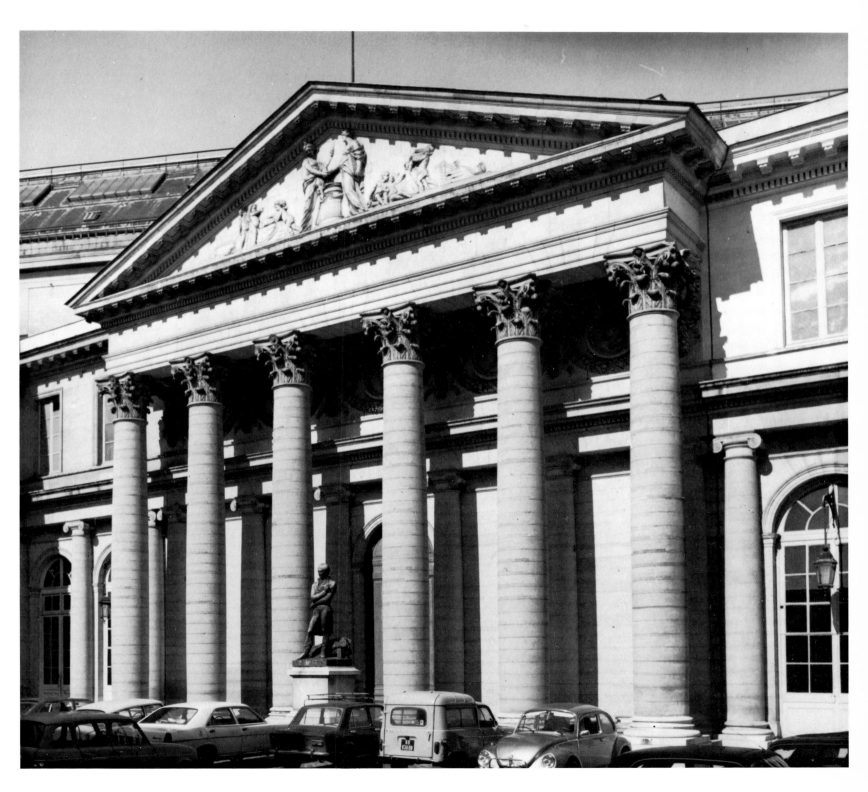

and that he published, in part, together with his equally idiosyncratic theories, in 1804, in *L'architecture*, all exemplify his notion of architectural beauty as something large in scale, simple and lumpish, enclosed and amplified by a clear-cut, if broken, outline. It was an ideal that many of his contemporaries shared and one that they derived, most probably, from Boullée; though more strictly classical in spirit, Ledoux tended to prefer continuous masses and unbroken outlines. Ledoux may thus have been the forerunner of much of the turgidity of nineteenth-century architecture.

Neither Boullée nor Ledoux, however, would have come to his early understanding of continuity and the unbroken line without Gondoin. Jacques Gondoin (1737–1818) was nine years younger than Boullée, one year younger than Ledoux, and he made his architectural debut about five years after the latter, yet he appears to have remained throughout his life a strict and consistent classicist. Indeed, he is remembered for one building and hardly any other, the École de Chirurgie in the Rue de l'École de Médecine in Paris, which might be said to epitomize the classical movement of the late eighteenth century: "Un seul mot doit faire l'éloge de ce monument," that upholder of classical orthodoxy, Quatremère de Quincy, was to write in the early nineteenth century. "Il est le monument classique du dix-huitième siècle" ("Notice sur . . . M. Gondoin," 1821, in *Recueil de notices historiques . . .*, Paris, 1834, p. 201).

Commissioned, designed, and begun in 1769, three years after Gondoin had returned from Italy—via Holland and England—the École de Chirurgie was finished by 1775. The problem of planning a surgical college in 1769 called for no great ingenuity, and the detailed arrangements are of little interest. But the semicircular lecture hall, with its rising tiers of seats, its blank curved wall, and its coffered half-dome and demi-oculus, was a creation of genius and not surprisingly was reflected in all the assembly halls of the Consulate and Empire periods—the Chambre des Députés, built between 1795 and 1797 by J.-P. de Gisors and Étienne-Chérubin Leconte; the Salle du Sénat at the Palais du Luxembourg, designed in 1804 by Chalgrin; and the Salle du Tribunat, installed a few years later by C.-E. de Beaumont in the Palais-Royal. Yet it was rather Gondoin's conception of a facade composed of a triumphal arch embedded in a continuous screen of Ionic columns, through which is glimpsed a court surrounded by similar columns, some engaged, some freestanding, and at the far end a giant Corinthian portico—in short, the dramatic interpenetration of continuous columnar screens—that makes the École de Chirurgie so remarkable and so stunning a work. The notion had been a part of French architectural thought from Perrault onward, and had recently been reinforced by Peyre, yet the liberating stimulus came from Italy,

from the arrangement of the Temple of Isis at Pompeii—the École de Chirurgie was conceived as a Temple of Aesculapius—and, more surprisingly, from the first court of the Collegio Elvetico in Milan, begun in 1608 by Fabio Mangone. There, freestanding columns are used with even greater uniformity and obsession, while the continuous, unbroken line of the cornice and the columns running the entire length of the facade, which seemed so rude a departure from the French tradition of composed elements, also came from Italian sources —perhaps from the Raphaelesque Palazzo Vidoni-Caffarelli, in Rome, begun in 1515 but greatly extended in the mid-eighteenth century, when it was engraved by Piranesi for his *Varie vedute di Roma*. But to Gondoin's contemporaries the design of the École, with its related yet contrasting square and fountain in front, was a revelation and altogether original. Many attacked it. Blondel reluctantly recognized its peculiar antique power and Peyre defended it with vigor. J.-G. Legrand wrote of it in C. P. Landon's *Annales du musée* in 1803: "Tout le système de la vieille architecture française fut renversé par cet exemple inattendu, et les partisans de la routine furent stupéfaits de voir une façade sans avant corps au milieu, sans arrière-corps, et dont la corniche suivant d'un bout à l'autre sans ressaut ni profil, contre l'usage reçu en France, et dont les Contant, les Gabriel, les Soufflot, venaient de donner de si récens et si dispendieux exemples dans l'École Militaire, dans la Madeleine, et dans la nouvelle Sainte-Geneviève. Cependant l'opinion publique se prononça en faveur du nouveau système, la critique se tut, et l'École de Chirurgie fut proclamée par tous les gens de goût, le chef-d'oeuvre de notre architecture moderne" (vol. 5, p. 127).

The success of this work won many commissions for Gondoin. In 1769 he became *Dessinateur du Mobilier de la Couronne* and started at once to design furniture for Marie Antoinette; he is said to have built a number of town and country houses, though only minor works such as the Hôtel Saint-Léonard, at 12 Rue Victor Hugo, Falaise (Calvados), and the Hôtel de Ville in the same town can yet be attributed to him. He also began a house for himself on the banks of the Seine, near Melun, in the late 1780s, and building continued in the years that followed the Revolution. He became wealthy. When, in 1775, he traveled to Italy for the second time, he sought to buy Hadrian's Villa at Tivoli. This proved impossible, as too many disputatious individual landowners were involved. He was thus forced to content himself with making measured drawings of the villa, which he gave to his friend Piranesi, who had been excavating there for several years with Gavin Hamilton and Clérisseau. Gondoin's drawings presumably served as the basis for the great site plan issued after Piranesi's death in 1781.

The classical movement of the eighteenth century was, as Quatremère de Quincy insisted, "une communauté d'instruction et de connaissance, une certaine égalité du goût et du savoir . . . entre toutes les contrées de l'Europe" (L. Hautecoeur, *Rome et la renaissance de l'antiquité à la fin du XVIIIᵉ siècle*, 1912, p. 224).

ENGLAND: *From Chambers to Wyatt*
The architects at whom we shall be looking in this section—principally Sir William Chambers, Robert Adam, James Wyatt, and Henry Holland—are more famous and were more prolific than those who figured in the earlier chapter on the influence of the antique. It is not that Chambers, Adam, Holland, and Wyatt were not interested in the antique—far from it—but they did not allow either archaeology or theory to interfere with their large and successful practices: They were ambitious, fashionable, popular, and stylistically omnivorous. Again we should begin by appreciating the pioneering achievements of the architects in the Palladian tradition, in particular of two second-generation Palladian architects, Sir Robert Taylor (1714–1788) and James Paine (1717–1789). Adhering basically to the Palladian canon, Paine created such powerful buildings as Stockeld Park, Yorkshire (1758–63), with its great arched facade and superb staircase, and Brocket Hall, Hertfordshire (1760s onward), where a dull exterior contains another remarkable staircase and a great saloon in which the painted historical and allegorical decoration by John Hamilton Mortimer offers a substantial alternative to the lighter Adam style. At Wardour Castle, Wiltshire, Paine created, in the 1770s, his most breathtaking interior—a centrally placed pantheon containing a circular staircase.

Sir Robert Taylor also created a pantheon at the Bank of England, in 1765, which he flanked by four identical transfer offices inspired by the Early Christian church of S. Costanza in Rome, believed in the eighteenth century to be an ancient Roman temple of Bacchus. In the late 1760s, at Purbrook, Hampshire, whose plan was similar to that of Paine's Kedleston Hall, Derbyshire (1757), he placed a Roman atrium in the center, perhaps the first reconstruction of its kind. But Taylor is particularly associated with the creation of a series of beautiful villas, of which the dramatically situated Sharpham, Devon (c. 1770), may stand as an example, where the Palladian tradition is enlivened by imaginative planning with interlocking rooms of contrasting shapes. Although Taylor had initiated this tradition at Harleyford Manor, Buckinghamshire, as early as 1755, it was not fully exploited until the end of the century by Sir John Soane, John Nash, and James Lewis.

Paine and Taylor scarcely traveled abroad, but the career of Sir

William Chambers (1723–1796) reveals the essentially cosmopolitan character of the style we call neoclassicism, which emerged in the 1740s and 1750s. As a pupil of J.-F. Blondel in Paris in 1749–50 he came into close contact with the brilliant group of designers who were developing a new Franco-Italian style, anti-rococo and neoclassical: men like L.-J. Le Lorrain and J.-L. Legeay, Charles de Wailly and M.-J. Peyre. From Paris Chambers moved naturally to Rome, where he spent the years 1750 to 1755, and learned much from Piranesi and Clérisseau. The outcome of all this learning and activity is clearly seen in the designs he made in Rome in 1751–52 for a mausoleum for Frederick, Prince of Wales. In some ways these designs, Chambers's first architectural production, constitute the beginnings of English neoclassical architecture, but they also represent a point from which Chambers subsequently retreated stylistically. Combining elements from such antique Roman buildings as the Tomb of Caecilia Metella and the Pantheon with features based on the Festa della Chinea designs of the 1740s by Frenchmen such as Le Lorrain and E.-A. Petitot, Chambers's mausoleum was too heady to be acceptable in England in the early 1750s. On his return from Rome in 1755 he prepared designs in an ill-digested Grand Prix manner for Harewood House, Yorkshire. When these were turned down by Edwin Lascelles in 1756 Chambers finally lost his nerve and retreated for the rest of his career into a safe, second-generation Palladianism inspired by Isaac Ware and enlivened with pretty motifs culled from the work of French architects ranging from A.-J. Gabriel (born 1698) to J.-G. Soufflot (born 1713) and J.-D. Antoine (born 1733). On a small scale, as at the Casina at Marino near Dublin (begun 1758), this was enchanting, but it was quite inadequate for a major public building such as Somerset House, London (1776–96). Like a number of English eighteenth-century architects, Chambers was perhaps at his best with staircase design. His *Treatise on Civil Architecture* (1759), expanded in a third edition to *A Treatise on the Decorative Part of Civil Architecture* (1791), was widely influential in England and France as a scholarly and broadly based survey of the use of the orders in antique and Renaissance architecture. Chambers's pupil James Gandon (1743–1823) was in some ways more successful than his master in creating a monumental architecture inspired by French neoclassical precedent. At the Four Courts in Dublin, which he took over from Thomas Cooley (1740–1784) in 1785, Gandon produced a powerful building, which, if it has Peyre for a father, has Sir Christopher Wren for a grandfather. Cooley, an assistant of Robert Mylne, was also a better architect than Chambers. His masterly and original Dublin Exchange (1769–79) reveals a close knowledge of contemporary French work and is one of the finest buildings of its date in Europe.

248. *James Gandon, Four Courts, Dublin, 1786–1802.*

249. *Thomas Cooley, Royal Exchange (now City Hall), Dublin, 1769–79.*

250. *Robert Adam, harbor elevation of the palace of Diocletian at Split (Spalato), Dalmatia, 1757.*

251. *Robert Adam, Kedleston Hall, Derbyshire, saloon, c. 1760–70.*▷

252. Robert Adam, Syon House, London, anteroom, 1762–69.

253. Robert Adam, Newby Hall, Yorkshire, sculpture gallery, begun 1767.

254. Robert Adam, Culzean Castle, Ayrshire, stair hall, 1779–90. ▷

Cooley and Gandon worked almost exclusively in Ireland, and their buildings had little impact in England. But if Chambers lacked the flair to create a new language out of the architectural experiments he had witnessed in Paris and Rome, there was one architect who was determined to achieve that very synthesis, Robert Adam. In 1754 he left his native Scotland for France and Italy, where, like Chambers, he became intimate with Piranesi and Clérisseau. With the assistance of Clérisseau and two other draftsmen in 1757 he prepared measured drawings of the great late Roman palace at Split in Dalmatia, which he published in sumptuous form in 1764 as *Ruins of the Palace of the Emperor Diocletian at Spalatro*. The speed with which Adam worked was characteristic of him—he spent only five weeks at Split—as also was an ability to rouse public interest in a Picturesque and arresting manner. The captivating engravings by Francesco Bartolozzi and others were in a rhetorical style inspired by Piranesi that Adam used again in the depiction of his own buildings, published in 1773 and 1779 as *The Works in Architecture of Robert and James Adam, Esquires*. This gift for self-advertisement, this determination to achieve success, explains much about his eye-catching, all-inclusive, yet individual style. He could not afford to be doctrinaire. Greek, Roman, Palladian, neo-Palladian, neoclassical, Picturesque, all were grist to his mill. He had a quick eye for everything that was going on around him and assimilated his observations into a style of unique loveliness, which matured rapidly from Harewood House, Yorkshire (begun 1759); Kedleston Hall, Derbyshire (1760 onward); Osterley Park, Middlesex (1761 onward); Syon House, Middlesex (1762–69); Luton Hoo, Bedfordshire (1766–70); Newby Hall, Yorkshire (1767–85); and Kenwood House, Hampstead (1767–69). The desire to please, which is so strong in the enchanting series of rooms contained in these houses, is frankly not an ambition that one particularly associates with the neoclassical movement, although those in search of the characteristically neoclassical interest in archaeology will find many hints from the Roman Baths, particularly at Syon. The essential adaptability of the Adam style is clearly conveyed in the preface to Part 2 of his *Works in Architecture*, where he writes of the orders, for example, that the Tuscan is needlessly austere, the Composite needlessly elaborate, the "great size of the volute of the Grecian Ionic [is] much too heavy," while those used by the Romans "border on the other extreme." "We have therefore," he concluded, "generally taken a mean between them." So perhaps the English *via media*, the comfortable compromise, must be taken into account in considering Adam's success. From the Grecian Ionic he adopted what he called the "double fillet" in the volute, which "far exceeds in grace and beauty that used by the Romans." Indeed, he claimed that he favored

255. *Robert Adam, No. 20 St. James's Square, London, second drawing room, 1772.*

256. *Robert Adam, Syon House, London, entrance hall, c. 1765.*

Greek profiles because Roman moldings were "considerably less curvilineal than those of the ancient monuments of Greece." An example of his empirical approach is his refusal to fix a definite entablature for each order: "A latitude in this respect is often productive of great novelty, variety and beauty."

What this meant in practice can be well appreciated in the celebrated anteroom at Syon of the mid-1760s. The volutes and moldings of the capitals here were taken from the Erechtheum as illustrated in J.-D. Le Roy's pioneering publication of 1758, *Les ruines des plus beaux monuments de la Grèce.* However, for the necking of the capitals he drew on a purely Roman source, familiar from the Baths and subsequently illustrated in Charles Cameron's *Description of the Baths of the Romans* (1772). The decoration of the Erechtheum necking he daringly and attractively transposed to the frieze of the entablature. Elsewhere in the room the gilded martial trophies anticipatory of the Empire style are derived from Piranesi's illustrations of the trophies of Octavian Augustus on the Campidoglio in Rome, which had already been imitated at the Villa Madama. The ceiling design, on the other hand, looks back to an English Palladian precedent established at Houghton Hall, Norfolk, by Colen Campbell in the 1720s. But the room recalls yet another period, for the twelve superb blue verde columns were antique Roman ones, said to have been excavated from the bed of the Tiber, and were dispatched by James Adam in April 1765 from Civitavecchia. In this one room, then, all the known historical boundaries are transcended by Adam's brilliant classical synthesis. This synthesis is not intellectual in origin but scenic and Picturesque, as we have already shown in Chapter 2.

The immediately recognizable style that Adam established in the 1760s, when remodeling the great Whig country houses put up by the first- and second-generation Palladian architects, was transferred in the 1770s to London, where, on a smaller scale, he created some of the most refined if rather mannered interiors of the century: No. 20 St. James's Square (1771–74); Derby House, No. 23 Grosvenor Square (1773–74; demolished 1862); and No. 20 Portman Square (1775). This exquisite style was not transported to the Continent, perhaps because it depended on a highly trained group of craftsmen, led by the plasterer Joseph Rose, Jr., who moved from house to house.

It should not be thought, however, that Adam's genius was limited to the creation of these pastel boudoirs. His colonnaded Admiralty Screen in Whitehall, of 1759, points forward to the bolder open screens of Jacques Gondoin at the École de Chirurgie, Paris (1769–75); Pierre Rousseau at the Hôtel de Salm, Paris (1782–85); Holland at Carlton House, London (c. 1794); and Karl Friedrich Schinkel at the palace for Prince Albrecht, Berlin (1829–33). At Bowood, Wiltshire,

257. *Robert Adam, mausoleum, Bowood, Wiltshire, 1761–64.*

258. Robert Adam, mausoleum, Bowood, Wiltshire, detail of the interior, 1761–64.

259. Robert Adam, Kedleston Hall, Derbyshire, south front, 1765–70.
260. Robert Adam, Register House, University, Edinburgh, 1774–92.

261. *James Wyatt, Pantheon, Oxford Street, London, plan, 1769.*
262. *William Hodges,* Interior of the Pantheon in Oxford Street, *c. 1771. Leeds City Art Galleries, Temple Newsam House.*
263. *James Wyatt, Heaton Hall, Lancashire, garden front, 1772.*

264. *Robert Adam, University, Edinburgh, 1789–93. Dome by Sir R. Anderson, 1887.*

265. *James Wyatt, Heaton Hall, Lancashire, Cupola Room, 1772.*
266. *Robert Adam, Osterley Park, Middlesex, dressing room in the Etruscan style, 1775–79.*
267. *James Wyatt, Heveningham Hall, Suffolk, hall, 1778–84.*▷

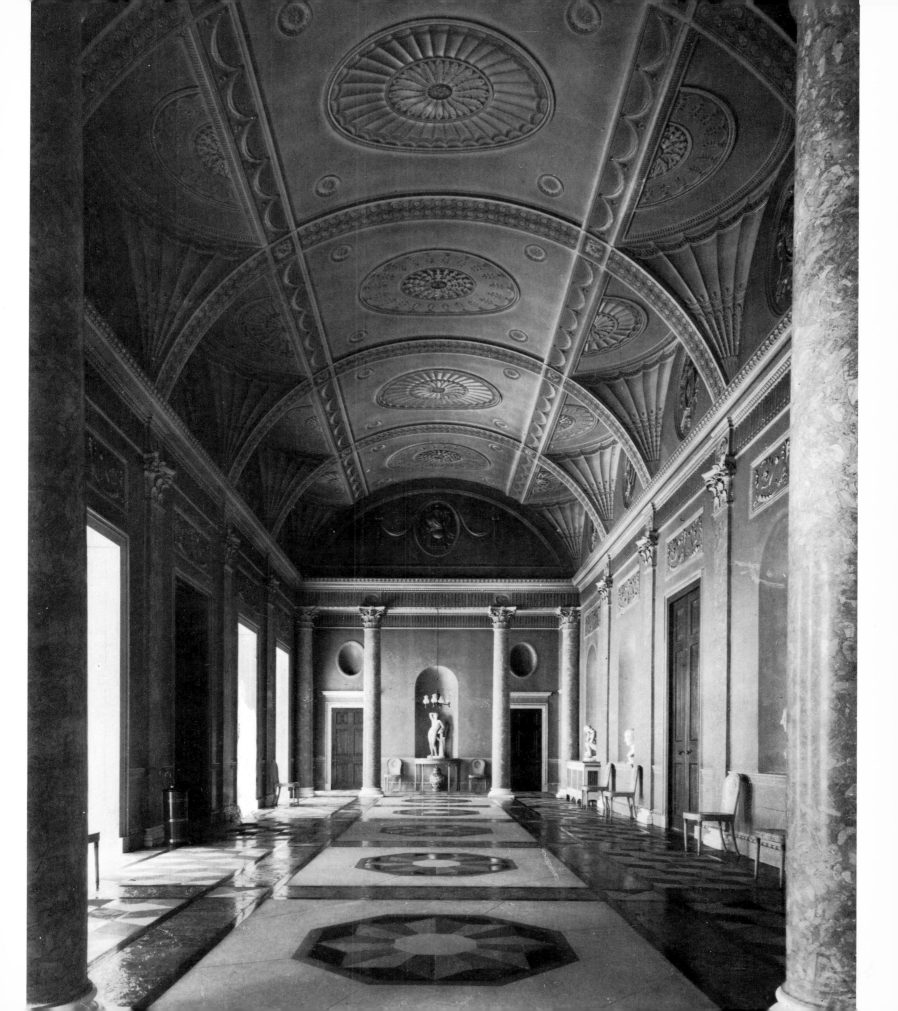

268. *Robert Adam, Kenwood House, Hampstead, London, library, 1767–69.*
269. *James Wyatt, Castle Coole, County Fermanagh, saloon, 1790–97.*

in 1761–64, he erected a chaste Tuscan mausoleum, domed and barrel-vaulted, which an architect like Gondoin might have envied. There is a ruthless originality about his twin-towered church at Mistley, Essex (1776; partially demolished 1870), which may have inspired Soane's Dulwich Gallery (1812). The garden front of Adam's Kedleston Hall, Derbyshire, takes its place in the long line of applications of the Roman triumphal-arch motif from Alberti to C. R. Cockerell, while at the Register House (1774–92) and University (1789–93) at Edinburgh, he created some of the most successful monumental public buildings of the century.

Adam was rarely short of commissions or publicity, though the flashy innovatory aspect of his style made him unpopular with Sir William Chambers, pillar of the academic tradition, who acquired for himself many of the official appointments of the day and prevented Adam from being elected to the Royal Academy. Adam also had to face difficulties of a different kind—imitation—by an architect very different from Chambers, James Wyatt. Nearly twenty years younger than Adam, Wyatt rocketed to fame as a very young man with his Pantheon in Oxford Street, designed in 1769 and opened in January 1772 as an unprecedented setting for entertainment. The brilliant and wholly unexpected plan led from a fairly simple street front past elegant but small vestibules and card rooms into the breathtaking rotunda. The disposition should be compared and contrasted with Lord Burlington's Assembly Rooms at York. Whereas Burlington's main room was an austere archaeological reconstruction based on Vitruvius and Palladio, Wyatt's was essentially a scenic composition modeled not on the all-too-familiar Pantheon in Rome (from which the building took its name) but on the less familiar and more exotic Hagia Sophia in Constantinople. This Byzantine source was somewhat unorthodox, but it lent itself to Picturesque adaptation that clearly caught the mood of the day. In any other country in Europe Burlington's Assembly Rooms would have been sufficiently novel if erected in 1769–72, but by then, England, having enjoyed a proto-neoclassicism during her Palladian Revival at the beginning of the century, needed something more hotly spiced to whet her jaded appetite. The feverishly excited reaction to Wyatt's display at the Pantheon is perfectly conveyed in Horace Walpole's account of his own impressions: "It amazed me myself. Imagine Balbec in all its glory! . . . There has been a Masquerade at the Pantheon, which was so glorious a vision that I thought I was in the old Pentheon, or in the Temple of Delphi or Ephesus. . . . All the friezes and niches were edged with alternate lamps of green and purple glass, that shed a most heathen light. . . ."

With this one building Wyatt shot to the top of the architectural profession and thereafter never wanted for commissions. The first fruit of the Pantheon success was the commission in 1772 for Heaton Hall, near Manchester. That year, when he was twenty-six, Wyatt exhibited a drawing for the house at the Royal Academy; his client, Sir Thomas Egerton, later first earl of Wilton, was only twenty-three. Like many of Adam's commissions this was essentially the remodeling and extending of an earlier house. To each side of the existing house Wyatt added long, colonnaded, one-storied wings, terminating in canted bays so as to produce a chaste but varied composition: the kind of movement that Adam had tried but often failed to achieve. This sophisticated composition has led to speculation as to whether James may not have been assisted by his brother Samuel Wyatt (1737–1807), for the Heaton manner was subsequently developed by Samuel at Hurstmonceux Place, Sussex; Winnington Hall, Cheshire; Shugborough, Staffordshire; Belmont, Kent; and elsewhere. The elegant semicircular projection in the middle of the south front at Heaton is French in feeling, though one should remember that Adam had provided just such a feature exactly ten years earlier at Mersham-le-Hatch, in Kent. On the first floor, Wyatt's projection contains the Cupola Room in the so-called Etruscan style, which was used on five occasions by Robert Adam, most notably in the only surviving example, at Osterley Park, Middlesex (1775–79). Adam's is an ordinary rectangular room to which has been applied spidery decoration probably inspired by the plates in Piranesi's *Diverse maniere d'adornare i cammini* (1769). Wyatt's room at Heaton, painted by Biagio Rebecca, is more imaginative in shape and the decoration more closely related to the structure. Another exquisite Etruscan room of the late 1770s is Thomas Leverton's at Woodhall Park, Hertfordshire. This style, which quickly found favor in France, was popular with those who, in the 1770s, had seen the arrival of Sir William Hamilton's first collection of Greek figured vases, then believed to be Etruscan.

Heaton was followed fairly quickly by Heveningham Hall, in Suffolk, where sometime between 1778 and 1784 Wyatt created a series of interiors that were probably the finest of his career. Just as Adam had been called to Kedleston to replace Paine, who was then regarded as old-fashioned, so Wyatt was called to Heveningham to replace Robert Taylor, who had designed the house in 1778 but was soon dismissed. Wyatt's patron, Sir Gerard Vanneck, was a merchant with no roots in the country. He wanted a house of display, a smart showpiece, and the result is, in a sense, a London mansion dropped down into remotest rural Suffolk. The entertaining rooms are one and a half stories high, so that, as in a London house of the period, there are few bedrooms and no state bedroom. Taylor had planned a large entrance hall with two tiers of columns, rather like his atrium at Purbrook, in Hampshire, but Wyatt decided that the height of the hall should speak for itself and allowed no columns to interfere with the flow upward into the wonderful barrel vault with its curious Gothic, concave fan vaults. It is instructive to compare the room with its ultimate source, Adam's library at Kenwood House, Hampstead, London (1767–69), whose plan and screen of columns based on the Roman Baths, and its remarkable curved vault decorated by the plasterer Joseph Rose, Jr., and the painter Antonio Zucchi, were revolutionary for their time. If anything, Wyatt's room is more of a unity. There is a logical relationship between the placing of the ribs of

the vault, the pilasters on the wall, and the red and black marble bands across the floor. The foundation color of the walls and ceiling is apple green, with pilasters of yellow Siena scagliola, and capitals and enrichments in white. The seating furniture was also designed by Wyatt *en suite* with the whole room. Though this hall is the tour de force of the house, there are also an Etruscan room, library, and drawing room, all of high quality.

At Castle Coole, County Fermanagh, Wyatt was once more called in at the beginning to modernize and make fashionable what another architect had begun. The plans for the house are by Richard

Johnston, dated Dublin, 1789, but before they could be executed Wyatt had waved the wand of London taste over them. On the facade, as executed by Wyatt, all superfluous ornament was eliminated, the unmolded window surrounds lack an entablature, and Johnston's Roman Doric was transformed into a bastardized Greek Doric of Wyatt's own invention. These Greek colonnades lead to pavilions inspired by Chambers's Casina at Marino. Inside Castle Coole, the two-storied entrance hall with its tiers of Doric columns was perhaps inspired by the interiors of Greek temples, but the most splendid interior is the great oval saloon in the middle of the garden front, with scagliola work by Domenico Bartoli and plasterwork by Joseph Rose, Jr. The whole production of the house was unusual, since it is doubtful that Wyatt ever saw it. His patron, Lord Belmore, was his own contractor and saw to it that Wyatt sent careful drawings for everything from ceilings to curtains and furniture. Once the joiners had finished the doors and windows they were set to work on Wyatt's furniture, which still survives in the rooms for which it was designed. The house cost more than double the original estimates, partly because of the decision to build it in Portland stone, necessarily imported from England. In June 1790 there was a total of sixty stonecutters and masons at work on the site. The whole house—design, materials, furniture, and plasterwork—is in every sense an importation from England. It was an extraordinary fantasy made reality, the quintessence of what one means by the Ascendancy in Ireland.

The Chambersian note, hinted at in Castle Coole and developed at Dodington Park, was frequently struck in Wyatt's works. In the mausoleum at Cobham Hall, Kent (1783), he was able to realize some of Chambers's early neoclassical ambitions. The canted corners with coupled columns are echoes of Chambers's design for a temple for the earl of Tylney, while the pyramid on top reminds one of designs by Neufforge. Wyatt's even more sumptuous mausoleum at Brocklesby Park, Lincolnshire (1787), recalls Chambers's mausoleum for the Prince of Wales, and also, interestingly enough, Nicholas Hawksmoor's at Castle Howard, Yorkshire (1728). Both are based ultimately on the Tomb of Caecilia Metella on the Appian Way, but whereas Hawksmoor's columns are set closer together than classical precedent allows, and thus create a crowded, restless, Baroque effect, Wyatt's intercolumniation is the correct one for the Doric order. He has further enlivened the building with references to the Temple of Vesta in Rome and the temple to the same deity at Tivoli. Inside, Hawksmoor placed his order on a tall pedestal; Wyatt's rests directly on the floor.

Of Wyatt's many country houses, the last at which we shall look is Dodington Park, Gloucestershire, commissioned in 1796. By this

date, however, he was far better known for his Gothic than his classical houses. He had made this style fashionable in the early 1780s with such buildings as Sheffield Place, Sussex; Sandleford Priory, Berkshire; Pishiobury Park, Hertfordshire; Lee Priory, Kent; and Slane Castle, County Meath. He continued to erect houses of this type right up until his death in 1813 but, with the exception of the astonishing Fonthill Abbey, Wiltshire, they do not rival in interest his classical work.

Dodington, designed after Adam's death, represents a new departure. Strikingly different from the tight symmetry of Castle Coole, the west front of Dodington is freely disposed like the elements in a Capability Brown landscape. The quadrant greenhouse, with a picture gallery following its curve behind it, stretches out lazily toward the remarkable domed cruciform church built by Wyatt on the site of the medieval church. In powerful contrast is the immense entrance portico on the west front of the house, Greek in spirit but Roman Corinthian in detail. Different again is the south front, which reverts to a Chambersian mode of composition, its pilasters and attic reminiscent of Somerset House. The east front is simple to the point of inadequacy, enlivened only by curved end bays. These three facades are completely different and unrelated; their seemingly casual asymmetry is continued on the east front by the office wing (demolished 1932), culminating in the elegant minor axis of the dairy with its Greek Doric tholos, or rotunda. Both the designing and the building of Dodington were slow processes. The plans were initiated in 1796 but the details of the facades were not settled until 1800 and building work was carried on until 1813. More than seven hundred drawings survive but few are signed or dated—this is typical of a certain slaphappy note about Wyatt's method of work.

The grandeur of the entrance portico is sustained by the scale of the interiors, particularly of the double-cube entrance hall, which runs its full length of twenty meters (sixty-five feet). In scale, originality, and quality this ranks with his hall at Heveningham as one of the best neoclassical interiors in England. Wyatt had now moved away from the Adam-inspired interpretation of the antique that characterized Heveningham to a more sober version of the Roman atrium. The heavily gilded, coffered ceiling of the central space is reflected in the patterning of the floor in black marble, red Scottish stone, and cream Painswick stone enriched with thin strips of brass between the flagstones. Porphyry scagliola columns, which have lighter lozenge-shaped coffering inspired by the Basilica of Maxentius in Rome, screen off raised areas at each end of the room. Visiting the house in the 1820s the young architect C. R. Cockerell could not help admiring the hall, but felt obliged to record in his diary: "I should say it is very injudicious to have scagliola oriental granite & gilt capital and ceilings in the Hall. If you begin thus, what can you end in? Nothing you can put in the drawing rooms & others can ever keep pace with such a commencement." In fact, Cockerell was too hard on Wyatt, for the staircase hall undoubtedly maintains the grandeur and drama of the entrance hall. In true Picturesque manner it is not approached axially but from one corner of the entrance hall, so that the first view of it is obliquely through the trio of arches in shadow. Behind them light flows down from the as-yet-concealed dome. The source for this magnificently architectural staircase hall and its arched

colonnade is Chambers's staircase at Gower (sometimes called Carrington) House, Whitehall (1765–74; demolished 1886), which had itself been inspired by Baldassare Longhena's staircase at S. Giorgio Maggiore, Venice (1643).

Dodington had a powerful influence on James Wyatt's nephew, Lewis William Wyatt (1777–1853), who was helping with the designs for it by 1801–2. In 1807 Lewis was called to Tatton Park, Cheshire, to complete the house begun about 1785 by another of his uncles, Samuel Wyatt. His proposals of 1807 included a giant, hexastyle, Corinthian portico identical to that at Dodington. This was not executed. The new entrance hall, carried out to Lewis Wyatt's designs with screens of porphyry Ionic columns carrying a segmental coffered vault, was also a variant of the hall at Dodington. The real fruit of Dodington, however, was not Tatton but Willey Park, Shropshire. Here in 1812 Lewis Wyatt produced the final synthesis of Burlingtonian Palladianism as successively developed by Paine and James Wyatt. As befits its late date, the house is both more Picturesque and more antique than would have been the case in the eighteenth century. It is superbly related to a Picturesque park and contains an interior more temple-like than that of any other English neoclassical house.

We should look finally at the work of an exact contemporary of James Wyatt's, Henry Holland (1745–1806). Though undoubtedly attracted stylistically to the Adam-Wyatt synthesis, which was the great achievement of the second half of the eighteenth century in England, he also pursued a calm, agreeable path, with one eye firmly fixed on the Louis XVI style in France, which gave most of his work a flavor of uncontroversial but elegant consistency unruffled by any real interest in the Greek Revival, the Picturesque, or antiquity.

His first significant commission was for Brooks's Club in St. James's Street, London, in 1776. Behind a yellow brick facade of still basically Palladian disposition, on the first floor, lies the Subscription Room, in which Holland kept the Adam-like decoration to a minimum. The commission was one of extreme importance for Holland since the club was one of the most fashionable in London, patronized by the Prince of Wales and his intimate circle. The discreetly elegant interiors were popular with the club's members, so that not only was Holland commissioned to design Carlton House for the Prince of Wales, but other members followed the prince's example by patronizing Holland: notably the duke of Bedford at Woburn Abbey, Lord Spencer at Althorp, Samuel Whitbread at Southill House, and R. B. Sheridan at the Drury Lane and Covent Garden theaters.

In 1778 Holland began work on Berrington Hall, Herefordshire, where his partner from 1771, and father-in-law from 1773, the cele-

brated landscape designer Capability Brown, had been engaged from 1775. The exterior of Berrington is memorable, with its gaunt, emphatic portico and its monumental office courtyard laid out geometrically behind the house. The magnificent staircase hall is the richest surviving interior by Holland since the destruction of Carlton House. Its mood is not, perhaps, one we tend to associate with Holland, but it helps us to understand what it was that the Prince of Wales saw in him. The hall at Berrington has a dramatic double or ambiguous axis, with a coffered, arched recess which, in fact, leads only to the back staircase. Thus, as one enters from the entrance hall one has a dramatic view in perspective of the underbelly of the segmental arch. This painterly, Piranesian atmosphere, which is sustained as one mounts the cantilevered staircase beneath its glazed dome, had affinities with the staircase of a year or so later at Woodhall Park, Hertfordshire, by Thomas Leverton. Holland's drawing room, library, and boudoir at Berrington are also extremely fine, though their debt to Adam is clearer. The increasing richness in the decoration of these rooms reflects the marriage of Mr. Harley's daughter and co-heir to the son and heir of Admiral Lord Rodney in 1781.

The commission for Holland's most important work, Carlton House, came in 1783, the year in which the Prince of Wales, whose London residence it was to be, came of age. The site was occupied by a muddle of buildings put up in 1709 for Lord Carleton and partially remodeled in 1733 by Henry Flitcroft. Holland's extensive transformations were not completed until 1789, though the celebrated north front with its entrance portico and open screen-wall to Pall Mall were not ready until 1794. In 1785 Holland had visited Paris, where he would have seen such buildings as Rousseau's Hôtel de Salm, Ledoux's Hôtel de Thélusson, the Palais-Royal, the Hôtel de Condé, and Godoin's École de Chirurgie, which would have given him a number of ideas, particularly for the open Ionic screen along the road. The complex, interlocking plan of smallish rooms is probably French in origin, though the idea of the central octagonal tribune on which the whole plan seems to pivot is perhaps derived from Adam—in particular, from his similarly placed circular tribune at Luton Hoo, Bedfordshire. To help him in the design of decoration and furniture, Holland employed a number of French craftsmen, of whom two are of special interest. They are Alexandre-Louis Delabrière and Dominique Daguerre, who in 1777 had been involved in the decoration of one of the most exquisite Parisian houses of the century, the Pavillon de Bagatelle in the Bois de Boulogne, designed for Louis XVI's brother, the Comte d'Artois, by F.-J. Bélanger. Contact between England and France reached a peak in exactly these years with the signing of the Anglo-French Treaty of Commerce in 1786. Moreover, after the Revolution many goods and much furniture were smuggled out of France and sold in England, with Daguerre acting as an important medium. The large scale of Carlton House and the enthusiasm of the Prince of Wales enabled Holland to develop a style of his own with the strong French influences that appealed to the Whig circle at the moment. We know the Carlton House interiors principally from the magnificent aquatints published in the second volume of William Henry Pyne's *Royal Residences* (1819), though by that time they had been considerably enlivened by the architect John Nash and the decorator Walsh Porter with rather flashy draperies and seating furniture. The granite-green entrance hall seems to have remained much as Holland left it, as did the lovely lavender and blue circular saloon flanked by Greek Ionic columns with silvered capitals.

In 1794–96 Holland employed the architect Charles Heathcote Tatham (1772–1842) to make sketches in Italy of antique decorative fragments, including antique furniture, which Holland could use as a model. Tatham shipped back numerous antique ornamental and architectural fragments, which were subsequently bought (about 1821) by Sir John Soane, who utilized them in a characteristically claustrophobic way in the tiny study and dressing room leading from the dining room of his house-*cum*-museum in Lincoln's Inn Fields. In this way Holland exercised an important influence over the development of Regency furniture styles.

For the immediate influence of Carlton House in the late 1780s we need look no further than Dover House, Whitehall. When, in his early twenties, Prince Frederick, younger brother of the Prince of Wales, needed a London house, it was natural to look to Holland. The house chosen for him had been built in the 1750s by James Paine and stood some way back from Whitehall. Holland increased its accommodation and its privacy by filling in the courtyard with a beautiful domed circular vestibule inspired by French plans such as those in Neufforge's *Recueil élémentaire d'architecture* (9 vols., 1757–72). He further concealed the house from public view behind a blank rusticated screen-wall. This was punctuated by Greek Ionic columns with an order based on that of the Temple on the Ilissus, as illustrated in Stuart and Revett, but engaged against the wall in a manner inspired by a Hellenistic building also illustrated in Stuart and Revett, the so-called Library of Hadrian in Athens.

In December 1786 Holland was called to Althorp, Northamptonshire, by the Whig grandee Lord Spencer. Holland's remodeling of this basically Elizabethan house resulted in one of the most convincing late Louis XVI interiors in England; the dressing room was painted in 1790–91 by the French artist T. H. Pernotin, whom Holland was at the time employing at Carlton House. Holland's work at

Woburn Abbey, Bedfordshire, for the duke of Bedford, was more eclectic. Apart from some characteristically restrained interiors in his Anglo-Parisian manner, he provided a deep porte cochere in a style verging on the Greek Doric (demolished 1950); a Chinese dairy, after plates in Sir William Chambers's *Chinese Designs* (1757); and, in 1801, an exquisite little Temple of Liberty at one end of the sculpture gallery. Based on the Greek Ionic order of the Temple on the Ilissus, it was built to contain busts of the duke's favorite political heroes and was presided over by Joseph Nollekens's bust of the arch-Whig Charles James Fox, whose bust also presides over Brooks's Club.

Holland's last major commission came in 1795 from the brewer Samuel Whitbread for the remodeling of his mid-eighteenth-century residence, Southill House, Bedfordshire. Mrs. Whitbread's drawing room and boudoir, painted by Delabrière with delicate white and gray coloring set off by a few chaste, Pompeian-style decorations, were finished by April 1800. The same artist painted some of the furniture, which still survives at Southill. The drawing room and dining room also contain furniture designed by Holland in a style moving away from Louis XVI to Regency. The large scale and rich gilding of this furniture create an opulent, almost royal, atmosphere, which contrasts with the refined and understated design of the rooms themselves. Holland's thoughtful Gallic manner separates him from his contemporaries, yet no one could deny that—like the better-known Adam and Wyatt—he formed a successful synthesis out of the myriad stylistic sources about which information had been accumulating so rapidly during the eighteenth century: Greek, Hellenistic, Roman, Renaissance, and neoclassical.

Chapter Five

VISIONARY ARCHITECTURE

FRANCE: *Boullée and Ledoux*

The largeness of scale, the delight in formal geometry that are associated, as a rule, with the visionary architecture of the late eighteenth century are evident even in the earliest years of the century in the drawings, in particular, submitted to the Accademia di San Luca in Rome. The annual competitions organized there were a vital feature of architectural activity, even before G. P. Panini became *Principe* of the Accademia in 1754, serving to focus all aspiration and experiment in architecture, international rather than local. Many young architects visiting Rome thought to establish a reputation for themselves by winning one of its prizes. Marie-Joseph Peyre, as we have seen, started off with a grandiose cathedral (and two related palaces) and went on to design his equally vast *envoi de Rome*, an academic center, both of which he illustrated in 1765 in his *Oeuvres d'architecture*. The impetus that these gave to students in France was considerable. But, already, if we are to judge by the entries for the Prix de Rome dating from the 1750s, the overblown, intoxicating visions of the Accademia had become an established part of the French academic tradition. Blondel, as we know, did not approve. Whatever his reservations, they were not heeded by the students. The designs of the Prix de Rome winners of the late eighteenth century became consistently more and more grand. Even the members of the Académie grew alarmed. In August 1787, in a letter signed by de Wailly, Pâris, and Boullée, they complained to the director of the Académie de France à Rome, "Les projets envoyés à l'Académie ont très rarement répondu à son attente; la pluspart étoient plutôt des compositions gigantesques d'une éxécution impossible, que les productions d'architectes qui, mettant le dernier sceau à leur instruction, sont prêts à revenir dans leur patrie réclamer la confiance de leurs concitoyens" (*Correspondance des directeurs*, vol. 15, p. 161). Boullée himself, somewhat compromised by this pronouncement, later found it necessary to draw a distinction between "gigantesque" and "colossale." After the Revolution this largeness of vision was to be regarded as a positive need of resurgent citizens, a means of asserting their rights and their very existence. In his *Discours sur les monuments publics* addressed to the Conseil du Département de Paris in December 1791, Armand-Guy Kersaint declared, "Affermissons la liberté et tout deviendra facile; pour y parvenir joignons aux instructions de la parole le langage énergique des monuments: la confiance qu'il est nécessaire d'inspirer sur la stabilité de nos nouvelles lois, s'établira, par une sorte d'instinct, sur la solidité des édifices destinés à les conserver et à en perpétuer la durée." Architects in the years that followed were to produce an endless series of projects for vast public buildings, but the successive administrations of the Revolution were to leave nothing tangible—even their *fêtes* to the *Être suprême* were ephemeral manifestations.

A great many architects may be adduced to give evidence of the visionary splendor in late eighteenth-century France—Jean-Nicolas Sobre, J.-P. de Gisors (1755–1818), Pierre-Jules-Nicolas Delespine (1756–1825), Antoine-Laurent-Thomas Vaudoyer (1756–1846), J.-T. Thibault (1757–1826), J.-N.-L. Durand, and Jean-Jacques Tardieu (1762–1833) are some of them—but the two men who were most inspired and inspiring were Boullée and Ledoux. Their work was quite distinct, though there was clearly some interaction between them. Boullée seems to have been the first to break from the traditional bonds of architecture to produce a new visionary style, though it is just possible that Ledoux initiated the genre; both, however, grounded their first experiments on actual projects, even commissions.

The completion of the Hôtel de Brunoy in 1779 marks the vital change in Boullée's style; it became at once more solemn and splendid, and also more pretentious. In 1780 he prepared a series of designs for the rebuilding of Versailles of which only the last, the *grand projet*, survives. This shows a vastly extended building of dreadful uniformity and dullness. Boullée cannot have expected that it would be built. Gabriel's work at Versailles had been in abeyance for five years, finances were low, and the king was not greatly interested in large architectural projects. Similarly, the theater and church that Boullée designed immediately after, though ostensibly based on definite programs, were not in any sense realistic. They were *exercices de style*. His theater of 1781 for the Place du Carrousel, Paris, though related to an earlier project by Soufflot, is fitted unconvincingly into a vast colonnaded drum with a flattened dome above. The church (in a series of projects of the same year) was intended, he said, to stand on the foundations of Contant d'Ivry's unfinished Madeleine, but successive drawings show that he was slowly transforming Soufflot's Ste.-Geneviève rather into a building of unearthly grandeur. Absolutely it is beyond the bounds of eighteenth-century resources. The vaults are empyreal, the colonnades unending. Three thousand columns would have been required in the interior alone. Boullée's project of 1783 for a museum is an even grander and more purified variation on the columnar theme. But the innumerable columns, the interminable steps, and the great barrel vaults are on this occasion conspicuously and ostentatiously useless; the whole serves only a symbolic purpose. Even his projected library, which was formally commissioned in 1784—first for the site of the Couvent des Capucines, then, when that scheme was found to be too expensive, for the old Palais Mazarin—was grossly impractical.

There is no evidence that Boullée considered how a library might

282. *Étienne-Louis Boullée, project for a theater for the Place du Carrousel,*
Paris, plan, 1781.

283. *Étienne-Louis Boullée, project for a theater for the Place du Carrousel, Paris.*
284. *Étienne-Louis Boullée, project for a large church, perspective view, after 1781.*

285. *Étienne-Louis Boullée, a large metropolitan church during Evensong, interior view, c. 1781.*
286. *Étienne-Louis Boullée, project for the new hall of the Bibliothèque Nationale, Paris, 1784.*
287. *Étienne-Louis Boullée, project for a large museum, 1783.*

288. *Étienne-Louis Boullée, project for a monument to Newton, 1784.*
289. *Étienne-Louis Boullée, project for a monument in the form of a truncated Egyptian pyramid.*
290. *Étienne-Louis Boullée, project for a funerary monument.*

work. The limitations imposed by the site were no less willfully ignored. The celebrated perspective of the interior of the library can only with the greatest difficulty be related to the courtyard of the Palais Mazarin, which it was to enclose. The figures, moreover, were shown in togas, recalling, Boullée explained, Raphael's *School of Athens*—a conceit in which de Wailly had first indulged in his perspective of the foyer of the Théâtre-Français, exhibited in 1771 (see illustration 166). The very meaning of the word *monument*, it is not surprising to find, was extended, at this time, from "a commemorative edifice" to a "public building of symbolic connotation." Boullée was, in effect, designing temples. His museum was manifestly inspired by Alexander Pope's *Temple of Fame*. The dreadful pretension of his designs became more marked. Human conditions had ceased to be relevant. People were mere decorative adjuncts. "Jaloux enfin d'offrir le tableau le plus agréable," he wrote of his theater (or temple of pleasure), "j'ai cru y parvenir en disposant les spectateurs tellement que ce fussent eux qui décorassent ma salle et en formassent le principal ornement" (J. M. Pérouse de Montclos, ed., *E. L. Boullée: Architecture, Essai sur l'art*, 1968, p. 107). Human figures served only to increase the apparent size of his architecture. By 1784 he was able to epitomize his ideals in a great empty sphere designed as a cenotaph to Newton. "O Newton! Si par l'étendue de tes lumières et la sublimité de ton génie, tu as déterminé la figure de la terre, moi j'ai conçu le projet de t'envelopper de ta découverte" (ibid., p. 137). Boullée seems to have confused Newton and Galileo, but it scarcely mattered. His aim was to conjure up a vision of the immensity of the universe, to indulge celestial sensations. Thereafter, and particularly after the Revolution, his designs for even more magnificent public buildings, triumphal arches, gateways, towers of light, tombs, and pyramids pass into the realm of the truly sublime. He had sacrificed all reality and had determined to approach architecture as a painter; his motto, "Ed io anche sono pittore," was borrowed from Correggio, but he had reduced architecture to pictorial representation—little more. Drawing was all.

Boullée published nothing during his lifetime. However, his random notes and his *Essai sur l'art*—begun about 1780, but set down, for the most part, between 1790 and 1793 when he retired, ill, to the country—serve to illuminate his drawings and indicate something of his teachings. He had studied the works of Perrault—"Étant jeune, je partageais l'opinion publique; j'admirais la façade du péristyle du Louvre et regardais cette production comme tout ce qu'il y avait de plus beau en architecture" (ibid., p. 154)—but he found, in time, that he could not accept Perrault's contention that architecture was based, even in part, on an arbitrary system of rules. Boullée wanted

an absolute, fixed and all-embracing. He sought to find it in nature: "Je ne saurais trop le répéter, l'architecte doit etre le metteur en oeuvre de la nature" (ibid., p. 73). Nature was not to be too clearly defined, but he saw at once that forms and shapes served to conjure up thoughts and ideas.

"C'est par les effets que produisent leurs masses sur nos sens que nous distinguons les corps légers des corps massifs et c'est par une juste application, qui ne peut provenir que de l'étude des corps, que l'artiste parvient à donner à ses productions le caractère qui leur est propre. Les corps circulaires nous sont agréables par la douceur de leurs contours; les corps anguleux nous sont désagréables par la dureté de leurs formes; les corps qui rampent sur la terre nous attristent; ceux qui s'élèvent dans les cieux nous ravissent et ceux qui s'étendent sur l'horizon sont nobles et majestueux" (ibid., p. 35).

There was thus a direct relationship between forms and the sensations they aroused. This was the basis of his theory—*la théorie des corps.* He chose for study the regular solids, for he despised irregularity in all things. He sought order desperately—not to be wondered at in the years of the Terror. Symmetry, his very image of order, was the inviolable rule. He built up his designs with cubes, cylinders, pyramids, and cones (always shown truncated, it should be remarked), but his ideal was the sphere, for not only was it the most regular of figures but, under the effects of light, it was capable of exhibiting the most infinite variety, from the darkest of shades to the sharpest brilliance. Light was an essential component in Boullée's ideal architecture.

"Le corps sphérique," he wrote, "sous tous les rapports, est l'image de la perfection. Il réunit l'exacte symétrie, la régularité la plus parfaite, la variété la plus grande; il a le plus grand développement; sa forme est la plus simple, sa figure est dessinée par le contour le plus agréable; enfin ce corps est favorisé par les effets de la lumière qui sont tels qu'il n'est pas possible que la dégradation en soit plus douce, plus agréable et plus variée. Voilà des avantages uniques qu'il tient de la nature et qui ont sur nos sens un pouvoir illimité" (ibid., p. 64).

In his design for a theater Boullée was already attempting to give form to this idea; in his monument to Newton he might be said to have achieved it. Ledoux, it is worth noting, was to outdo him in sheer boldness of conception in his shepherds' house for the park at Maupertuis, as was his pupil Sobre—using the device of a reflecting pool—in his Temple of Immortality. But Boullée was concerned not only with the finite beauty of forms; he saw that their effects might change under different conditions, at different times of the year, at different times of the day, in sunlight or in moonlight, and even in relation to the spectator's mood.

"Toutes nos idées, toutes nos perceptions," he remarked, quoting John Locke or his French disciple Étienne Bonnot de Condillac, "ne nous viennent que par les objects extérieurs. Les objets extérieurs font sur nous différentes impressions par le plus ou le moins d'analogie qu'ils ont avec notre organisation" (ibid., p. 61).

Symbolism was thus of the highest importance in suggesting the character of each of Boullée's monuments: Certainly it was more important than practical considerations. The techniques of fortification were irrelevant to military architecture, Boullée said; the aim was "l'image de la force." Often his symbolism was overt, as with his trophies and shields applied to town gateways, or the text of the Constitution chiseled into the walls of his Palais National; more often it was obscure. For though his architecture might seem bland and formal, it was a distillation of a teeming esoteric knowledge. Like most French architects of the period, he was a Freemason. He was also an avid reader of travelers' tales. In his library he had James Bruce's account of the search for the source of the Nile, William Patterson on the Kaffirs and Hottentots, William Robertson's stories of the ancient American civilizations, and other tales of journeys to Siberia, China, and the South Seas. He himself scarcely moved out of Paris. This taste for the exotic was not to be overtly displayed in his designs. Everything was sublimated and given its purest form, for he aspired to the poetry of architecture. He aimed to elevate it above mere building (he despised Vitruvius for his humdrum mechanical interests) to a point beyond even the bounds of reason. His architecture was to be that of the sublime.

"La seule manière dont les artistes doivent s'entretenir entre eux," he wrote, "c'est de rappeler avec force et énergie ce qui excite leur sensibilité; c'est par cet attrait qui leur est propre qu'ils peuvent se stimuler et échauffer leur génie. Qu'ils se gardent bien d'entrer dans des explications qui tiennent trop au raisonnement, car l'impression d'une image sur nos sens s'attiédit quand nous nous appesantissons sur la cause qui produit son effet. Commenter sur ses plaisirs, c'est cesser de vivre sous leur empire, c'est cesser d'en jouir, c'est cesser d'exister" (ibid., p. 164).

Boullée was no unbridled enthusiast. He founded his vision on study and careful thought. He worked beneath portraits of Copernicus and Newton. He possessed books on physics and astronomy. He read Francis Bacon and the Comte de Buffon and had clearly studied to advantage Condillac's *Traité des systèmes et des sensations* (1754). There are close links between his theory of forms and Jean-Baptiste-Louis Romé de l'Isle's *Cristallographie; ou, description des formes propres à tous les corps du regne minéral* (1783). Knowledge is at the root of his activities. Identifiable prototypes may be adduced for each of his visionary projects, giving evidence of a wide erudition. The most obvious are the buildings of the ancient Romans—the Colosseum, the Pantheon, the Pyramid of Cestius, the Tomb of Caecilia Metella, the mausoleums of Hadrian and Augustus, and that at Halicarnassus—all of which he stripped bare and rendered more noble and ethereal. He borrowed from Athanasius Kircher, from Fischer von Erlach, and even from Hubert Robert.

291. *Louis Carrogis de Carmontelle, Jardin de Monceau, Paris, plan, 1773–78.*

292. *Louis Carrogis de Carmontelle, Jardin de Monceau, Paris. The Tartar tent and the dromedary with its two keepers.*

293. *François Barbier, house and garden for Racine de Monville, Désert de Retz, near Chambourcy, 1774–84.*

The liberating stimulus for Boullée's excursus, as for many of his contemporaries, was Jean-Jacques Rousseau and even his disciple Jacques-Henri Bernardin de Saint-Pierre, but the specific factor that served to alter the pattern of thinking on architecture was the introduction into France of the *jardin anglais*. Boullée himself was among the first to design one of these, possibly at the Château de Chaville, in 1765, certainly at Issy-les-Moulineaux a few years later. But the frenzied fashion for Picturesque gardening in France dates rather from the 1770s, when a spate of wonderfully resourceful but largely frivolous gardens was designed in something of an English manner: Simon-Charles Boutin's Tivoli at Montmartre (completed by 1771); L.Carrogis de Carmontelle's Monceau (1773–78); François Barbier's Désert de Retz (1774–84), for Boullée's own client Racine de Monville, where for the first time the house itself became a garden ornament—a simulacrum of a ruined column; then the *hameau* at Chantilly (1775) by Jean-François Leroy, and that at the Petit Trianon (1778–82) by Richard Mique (1728–1794); and also F.-J. Bélanger's gardens at Bagatelle (1780), the Folie Saint-James (1778–84), and Méréville (1784), this last finished off by Hubert Robert, who worked also at Betz with the Duc d'Harcourt and at Rambouillet, after 1783. The success of these, from an English point of view, varied greatly. "There are three or four very high hills," Horace Walpole wrote to his friend John Chute about Tivoli, on August 5, 1771, "almost as high as, and exactly in the shape of a tansy pudding. You squeeze between these and a river, that is conducted at obtuse angles in a stone channel, and supplied by a pump; and when walnuts come in, I suppose it will be navigable" (*Letters*, vol. 8, p. 64). Carmontelle's garden at Monceau was so flagrantly frivolous—a succession of *tableaux vivants* designed to ensure a maximum of conversational stimulus with a minimum of fatigue—that even its designer sought to distinguish it from the more serious English attempts to give order to nature: "Ceci," he wrote on on the wall, "n'est point un jardin anglais" (F. A. de Frénilly, *Souvenirs*, 1909, p. 7).

But there were, of course, many gardens in which noble aims were pursued, moral and uplifting aims. The finest of these were the gardens at Ermenonville, belonging to the Marquis René de Girardin. The hermit here was no less a man than Rousseau. And it was from Girardin that one of the most important theoretical studies was to come, *De la composition des paysages*, of 1777. "Ce n'est donc ni en architecte ni en jardinier, c'est en poète ou en peintre qu'il faut composer des paysages," he counseled (p. 8). Within six years this work had been translated into English. However, the first book of this sort to appear in France was, as one might expect, English—Thomas Whately's pioneering study on the theory of the Picturesque garden,

294. *François Barbier, house for Racine de Monville, Désert de Retz, section, 1774–84.*
295. *Richard Mique, hameau, Petit Trianon, Versailles, 1778–82.*

296. *Richard Mique, hameau, Petit Trianon, Versailles, the mill.*
297. *François-Joseph Bélanger and Hubert Robert, the park at Méréville (near Étampes) 1784 onward.*
298. *François-Joseph Bélanger and Hubert Robert, the park and the château at Méréville. Painting by Hubert Robert (Sceaux, Musée de l'Île-de-France).*

299. *François-Joseph Bélanger, the dairy at Méréville, now in the park of the Château de Jeurre.*

300. *Chinese pavilion, Parc de Cassan, near L'Isle Adam.*

301. *Chinese pavilion, Parc de Cassan, detail showing the unfluted and baseless columns surrounding the pool at the basement level.*

302. *René de Girardin, the gardens at Ermenonville, with the tomb of Jean-Jacques Rousseau. Engraving by Mérigot.*
303. *René de Girardin, Temple of Fame, pavilion in the gardens at Ermenonville. Engraving by Mérigot.*

Observations on Modern Gardening, of 1770, which F.-P. de Latapie translated into French the following year. Walpole was quick to notice this, too: "They have translated Mr. Whateley's book," he told Chute in his same letter, "and lord knows what barbarism is to be laid at our door." This was followed by two French works, C.-H. Watelet's *Essai sur les jardins*, of 1774, and Jean-Marie Morel's *Théorie des jardins*, issued two years later. Walpole's own study, *The History of the Modern Taste in Gardening*, first printed in 1771, was translated into French in 1785 by the Duc de Nivernois.

Morel had worked with Girardin at Ermenonville as early as 1766, but they had quarreled furiously as to the propriety of littering a landscape garden with buildings. He departed, piqued, to design no fewer than forty other gardens to his own liking. His writings make it clear that he did not object to buildings as such; cottages and barns or sheds that served a useful purpose and were designed in the traditional manner were altogether acceptable, as were old and rambling manor houses, but he wanted nothing new, nothing that might obtrude in the landscape. He liked best nature unadorned, and he described at great length the way in which he composed by natural means, making open expanses or enclosures, solids and voids. There should be no great insistence on logic, he explained, for the aim was poetry. His raw materials were grass and trees, rock, and water—still or running; he was alive to the effects of running water, the rustle of wind, and, of course, the play of light. Four successive chapters in his book were devoted to the changing effects of the four seasons. His interests, it is evident, are much the same as Boullée's, though Morel, it must be stressed, unlike Boullée, did not care much for symmetry. The transposition of these ideas into architectural theory, however, was probably not made by Boullée himself. His *Essai* was preceded by Le Camus de Mézières's *Le génie de l'architecture; ou, l'analogie de cet art avec nos sensations,* issued in 1780. Le Camus was spurred on by the landscape gardeners; indeed, he dedicated his book to Watelet. "Mon zèle," he wrote, "s'est soutenu en fixant mon attention sur les ouvrages de la nature. Plus j'ai examiné, plus j'ai reconnu que chaque objet possède un caractère qui lui est propre, et que souvent une seule ligne, un simple contour suffisent pour l'exprimer" (p. 3). Le Camus's ideas are less well developed than those of Boullée, the language certainly less elevated; his dogged insistence on indicating at length how his analogies might be incorporated into the routines of planning and detail design serve to set his book in an altogether different category from that of the *Essai*. But throughout there are parallels and similarities, for the preoccupations of both men were the same: "Un édifice très éclairé," Le Camus writes, "bien aeré, lorsque tout le reste est parfaitement traité, devient agréable et riant. Moins ouvert, plus

306. *Jean-Nicolas Sobre, project for a Temple of Immortality.*
307. *Claude-Nicolas Ledoux, projects for* barrières, *Paris, 1785–89.*

abrité, il offre un caractère sérieux: la lumière encore plus interceptée, il est mystérieux ou triste" (p. 43). It is scarcely necessary to trace at further length the connection between the ideas of Boullée and ideas regarding composition introduced into France by gardening theorists in the 1770s. Even at the most humdrum level one can note his borrowings from gardeners: His biographer Jean-Marie Pérouse de Montclos has suggested that his great theater is no more than an enlarged Temple of Love, while the monument to Newton itself, though it accords with a description in Pope's *Temple of Fame*, may equally be an illustration of the Miau Ting, or the Halls of the Moon, described in Sir William Chambers's *Dissertation on Oriental Gardening* (1772), available in French by 1773. The French, inspired by the visions of Panini and Piranesi and then the English, were learning to accept visual criteria alone.

The authority of the Picturesque theorists and of such men as Boullée was enormous. For though Boullée published nothing, he was active as a teacher. Indeed, many of his designs seem to have been prepared as a direct result of his teaching; they are based on the Grand Prix programs and incorporate, moreover, ideas that appear first in his students' submissions: magisterial corrections, as it were, to their hesitant essays. Not that they were slow to learn. Even outside Boullée's classes his works must have been known. Antoine-Laurent-Thomas Vaudoyer, a pupil of A.-F. Peyre, claimed to have produced his design for a *maison d'un cosmopolite*, a house in the form of a globe, in 1785, the year after Boullée designed his monument to Newton. And Pierre-François-Léonard Fontaine, a student of Jean-François Heurtier and A.-F. Peyre, who was awarded the second Grand Prix in 1785—but only after the students rioted when they heard that he had failed to win because the Académie feared to recompense so fine a draftsman—showed in his proposed "Monument sépulcral pour les souverains d'un grand empire" that he was in all things a true follower of Boullée. Boullée's influence was paramount.

Ledoux's impact as a visionary architect was not, at first, made through the mediums of teaching, drawing, and writing. He had very few students, but he liked to build. The forty *barrières* encircling Paris that he began in 1785, when he was already fifty, and built rapidly during the following four years—in part, under the supervision of J.-D. Antoine and Jean-Arnaud Raymond—showed that by changing the scale and measures of traditional forms, and by assembling these simplified geometrical forms in a bolder, if more complex, arrangement than usual, applying ornament only sparingly and then in a new relation to the surface or mass, an architecture of extraordinary novelty and power could be fashioned. Ledoux was a potent innovator. Most of the *barrières*, which continued to be built even after the Revolution, were torn down in the mid-nineteenth century, but four remain—the Barrière d'Enfer, Place Denfert-Rochereau; the Barrière du Trône, Place de la Nation; the Rotonde de la Villette, Place de Stalingrad; and the Rotonde de Monceau, Place de la République Dominicaine. The last shows Ledoux at his least adventurous, but the monumental building at the head of the Bassin de la Villette embodies his boldest aspirations. A giant arcaded drum is placed four-square on a solid, rectangular mass. At the core is a circular court. The silhouette is hard and sharp; and, though the detailing is strong, it is totally subservient to the geometry of the whole. Its air of primordial splendor is overwhelmingly impressive.

The extraordinary projects for which Ledoux is famous were not published as a group until 1804, two years before his death, when the first volume of *L'architecture considérée sous le rapport de l'art, des moeurs et de la législation* was issued. This contained his writings and one hundred and twenty-five plates illustrating the extant buildings and his project for an ideal city centered on the saltworks at Arc-et-Senans, on the edge of the forest of Chaux. Not until 1847 did his supposed son, Daniel Ramée, issue the second edition, containing two hundred and thirty extra plates, relating to Ledoux's realized work and unfulfilled commissions. Other isolated engravings exist—many of the plates included in the published volumes may have been distributed separately. The earliest dates from 1771, but this is unremarkable. Some of the designs for the buildings erected at Arc-et-Senans are dated 1776, just after the work there had begun; others are from 1780; but the first dated engraving for a design that is odd and altogether unconformable by contemporary standards is that of 1778 for an imagined hunting lodge for the Prince de Bauffremont. Later commissions—the Château de Maupertuis (c. 1780); the house for M. de Witt (1781); the Bishop's Palace at Sisteron (c. 1781); the Château d'Éguière, which must also be contemporary; and even that remarkable group of fifteen houses in the Rue St.-Georges, Paris, for M. Hosten (four were built from 1792 until 1795, just after Ledoux was released from prison)—are all unusual enough, but are not really so extraordinary. They are lacking in the brutal harshness of composition that makes so startling the prince's lodge, and, especially, the other famous designs for the Utopian city of Chaux—among them the Maison d'Éducation; the Cénobie (or commune) for sixteen families; the Panarethéon (or Temple of Virtue); the Oikema (or Temple of Love); and the cemetery. The last, not unlike Boullée's monument to Newton, may date from the late 1770s, though this seems unlikely; all were probably designed and engraved only after Catherine the Great's son, in the guise of the Comte du Nord, visited Paris in 1782 and accepted the dedication of the book (it was to be

Barriere de Bercy (*)

Barriere de Fontainebleau (*)

Barriere de la Rapée

Barriere de Gentilly.

Barriere d'Enfer (*)

Barriere St Jacques

Barriere du Mont Parnasse (*)

Barriere du Maine (*)

Barriere des Fourneaux (*)

Barriere de Vaugirard (*)

Barriere de l'Observation

Barriere de l'Ecole Militaire (*)

Barriere des Ministres (*)

Barriere du bord de l'eau

311. *Claude-Nicolas Ledoux, Barrière d'Enfer, Paris.*
312. *Claude-Nicolas Ledoux, Barrière d'Enfer, Paris, detail.*
313. *Claude-Nicolas Ledoux,* project for barrières, *Paris, 1785–89.*

Barriere de Passy (*)   Barriere des bons hommes.   Barriere de Longchamp

Barriere du Reservoir.   Barriere de Chaillot.   Barriere du Roule.   Barriere de Courcelle.

Barriere de la Croix blanche.   Barriere de Mouceau.   Barriere de Clichy.   Barriere de la rue Royale

314. *Claude-Nicolas Ledoux, Saline de Chaux, Arc-et-Senans, principal gate, 1775–79.*

315. *Claude-Nicolas Ledoux, ideal city of Chaux, Arc-et-Senans, aerial view.*

316. *Claude-Nicolas Ledoux, ideal city of Chaux, Arc-et-Senans, perspective view, from his* Architecture, *1804.*

317. *Claude-Nicolas Ledoux, house of the director of the Saline de Chaux, Arc-et-Senans, elevation.*

318. *Claude-Nicolas Ledoux, house of the director of the Saline de Chaux, Arc-et-Senans, section.*

319. *Claude-Nicolas Ledoux, project for a hunting lodge for the Prince de Bauffremont, 1778.*

320. *Claude-Nicolas Ledoux, project for the shepherd's house in the park at Maupertuis, 1780.*

321. *Claude-Nicolas Ledoux, Château d'Éguière, c. 1780.*

Elévation de la Maison du Directeur

Coupe du Batiment de la direction Prise sur la Largeur

322. *Claude-Nicolas Ledoux, the Cénobie, a multifamily dwelling in the ideal city of Chaux, Arc-et-Senans, from his* Architecture, *1804.*

323. *Claude-Nicolas Ledoux, Hosten Houses, four buildings in the Rue St.-Georges, Paris, elevation, 1792–95.*

324. *Claude-Nicolas Ledoux, Hosten Houses, Paris, elevation and section.*

325. *Claude-Nicolas Ledoux, cemetery for the ideal city of Chaux, Arc-et-Senans, section, from his* Architecture, *1804.*

326. *Claude-Nicolas Ledoux, project for a cooper's house in the ideal city of Chaux, Arc-et-Senans, from his* Architecture, *1804.*

dedicated, in the end, to his son, Alexander I). Ledoux was probably most active designing in the idle years that followed his release from prison in 1795. He built nothing then. From this period, also, must date the revisions to the works built early in his career, which make his engravings such telling evidence of his activity as an architect. The prospectus for his book did not come out until 1803.

For all the arbitrary nature of his refashioning, Ledoux's executed buildings from the late 1770s onward, and all his subsequent projects, reveal him as a designer of unparalleled power and vision, although his vision was less elevated than that of Boullée. He had a livelier imagination, clearly well-stimulated by knowledge of the odd and curious in architecture—and inspired also by the curious in literature, if we are to judge by a comparison of his account of a traveler to his ideal city with that of the hero in Tiphaigne de la Roche's *Giphantie* (1760), who discovers a new land where nature continues still to create new plant and animal species. Boullée, of course, responded also to the exotic, but he was careful always to distill such interests. Ledoux introduced minarets into the design of a country house without qualm. Like Boullée, he was intrigued by symbolism and mystery. He was, not surprisingly, a Freemason and seems to have been involved in an abortive initiation ceremony with William Beckford, possibly at Maupertuis. But whereas Boullée subordinated such rich and varied interests to a consistent and completely coherent vision of architecture, Ledoux was altogether erratic. He evolved no sustained or sustaining theory. His writings reveal him at his most wayward: He offered notions, not a philosophy. Some are acceptable, others incoherent and unintelligible. His style is rhapsodic and hortatory. Often, when his ideas can be connected to known facts or realities, he is revealed as commonplace enough, but his overblown language serves to distort and confuse. His text is a farrago. There is no clear organization, no argument, and much is already familiar. "Vous qui voulez devenir architecte," he wrote, "commencez par être peintre" (*L'architecture*, 1804, p. 113). His criteria throughout are not unlike those of Boullée: For example, his overwhelming responsiveness to nature, evident, in particular, in the natural and pleasant settings in which he placed his designs; his insistence on symmetry; his feeling for the qualities of solid geometry, light and shade, and poetry in architecture. "L'architecture," he wrote, "est à la maçonnerie ce que la poésie est aux belles-lettres: c'est l'enthousiasme dramatique du métier, ne peut en parler qu'avec exaltation" (ibid., pp. 15–16). He was fearful also of too much reason or knowledge: "L'érudition," he warned, "cette souveraine empesée, conduit rarement à l'heureux délire" (ibid.).

He aimed to be an inspired genius, and consciously thought of himself as the revolutionary prophet, both the architectural and moral kind. There is more social concern evident in his writings than in Boullée's. Indeed, he is often regarded as an early socialist, but most of his exhortations belong to the realm of post-Revolutionary cant. There is little evidence of sustained thinking. He dedicated his book to the czar of Russia, sent two hundred and thirty-seven of his drawings to the czar just before the Revolution, and was proud to recount his dealings with the king: "De tous temps," he wrote, "les souverains ont donné le ton" (ibid., p. 26). His hints as to the organization of the ideal city indicate that he envisaged an authoritarian regime, while his paean to the riches of nature as sufficient unto the needs of the poor, though it may recall Rousseau and Bernardin de Saint-Pierre, makes embarrassing reading. One may doubt at times that Ledoux was even a humanitarian. Yet he did design and build the saltworks at Arc-et-Senans as a noble architectural enterprise, which was unusual enough at the time, and in his visionary designs showed that canon forges could be conceived as elevating works of art; even the humblest dwellings, shepherds', coopers', and woodmen's houses, are of no less exalted an architecture than the house of the *Directeurs de la Loue*, or even the house of the *Directeur de la Saline* itself. This last had an altar in the center, dramatically lit, approached from a giant flight of steps. Everything was grist to Ledoux's creative mill and could be endowed with greatness and nobility. God, of course, was the supreme architect.

Ledoux, though, was infinitely less solemn than Boullée; he was livelier and less gloomy. "L'art sans éloquence," he wrote, "est comme l'amour sans virilité" (ibid., p. 16). Boullée produced endless projects for cenotaphs and cemeteries; indeed, most of his visionary designs have sepulchral overtones. All have a funerary ostentation and are set in desert landscapes. Ledoux concentrated rather on communal buildings and houses in attractive surroundings. His designs are undoubtedly more engaging than Boullée's, and all his works offered more possibilities for adaptation, but Ledoux was not often imitated. His architecture was thought to be undisciplined. Yet, much as Piranesi had set the tone and style that inspired Ledoux, so Ledoux suggested to architects how they might break from the classical norms to produce a new and radical architecture. Boullée provided the highest ideal; Ledoux offered a practical model. Together they were responsible for the profound change in architecture that is characterized as Revolutionary.

ENGLAND: *Dance and Soane*

In his *Description of the House and Museum on the North Side of Lincoln's Inn Fields*, of 1835–36, Sir John Soane wrote of the Breakfast Parlour

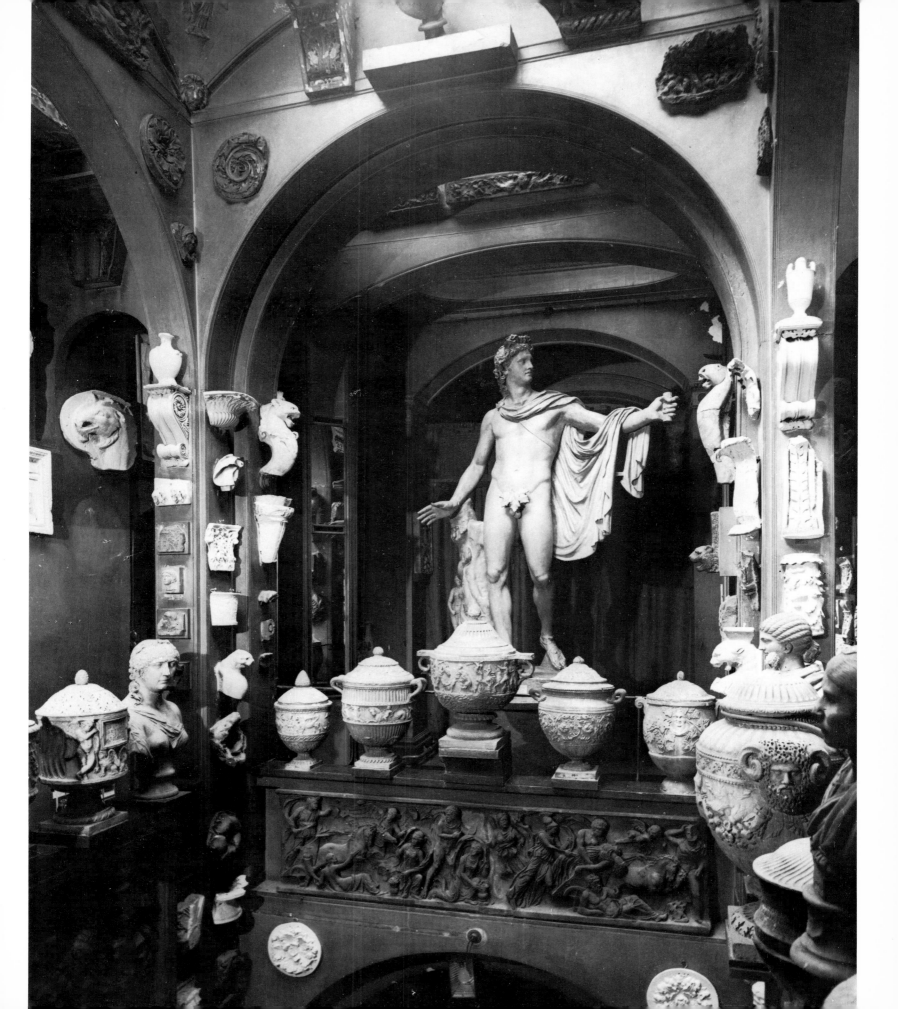

in his house: "The views from this room into the Monument Court and into the Museum, the mirrors in the ceiling, and the looking-glasses, combined with the variety of outline and general arrangement in the design and decoration of this limited space, present a succession of those fanciful effects which constitute the poetry of architecture."

The same sentiments and the same language occur, as we have seen, in Boullée's *Architecture, Essai sur l'art*, written in the 1780s and 1790s as part of his bizarre retreat from reality. In these years his long-suppressed ambition to be a painter finally surfaced in the form of demands for a poetic architecture of a vague ennobling symbolism, recalling the immutability of death, light, dark, and the stark geometry of the sphere, cube, and pyramid: "Nos édifices," he declared, "surtout les édifices publics, devroient être, en quelque façon, des poèmes. Les images, qu'ils offrent à nos sens, devroient exciter en nous des sentiments analogues à l'usage, auquel ces édifices sont consacrés" (see H. Rosenau, *Boullée and Visionary Architecture*, 1976, p. 118). But the buildings he most enjoyed designing were, ironically, the most functionless, as is the horrifying empty sphere of the celebrated Newton cenotaph. It is interesting to speculate to what extent Soane may have been aware of Boullée's obsession with "the poetry of architecture." Although Boullée's *Essai sur l'art* was not published until 1953, he was an energetic teacher of architecture, and through his pupils Soane may have learned of Boullée's ideas. In his Royal Academy lectures, first delivered in 1809, Soane observed: "The 'lumière mystérieuse,' so successfully practised by the French Artist, is a most powerful agent in the hands of a man of genius, and its power cannot be too fully understood, nor too highly appreciated. It is, however, little attended to in our Architecture, and for this obvious reason, that we do not sufficiently feel the importance of Character in our buildings, to which the mode of admitting light contributes in no small degree."

It is from Le Camus de Mézières's book *Le génie de l'architecture*, of 1780, that Boullée and Soane derived their belief in the creation of architectural character by means of the mysterious effect of light falling from hidden sources. Le Camus wrote of light that creates an architecture "mystérieux ou triste," and Boullée observed: "C'est la lumière qui produit les effets. Ceux-ci nous causent des sensations diverses et contraires, suivant qu'ils sont brillans ou sombres. . . . Si je peux éviter que la lumière arrive directement, et la faire pénétrer sans que le spectateur aperçoive d'où elle part, les effets résultans d'un jour mystérieux produiront des effets inconcevables, et en quelque façon, une espèce de magie vraiment enchanteresse" (see H. Rosenau, *Boullée and Visionary Architecture*, p. 126).

This could surely stand as an evocation of the effects aimed at

and achieved by Soane in such interiors as the Breakfast Parlour at Lincoln's Inn Fields, the Bank of England, and the Law Courts. Soane, indeed, was able, as Boullée was not, to forge within the classical tradition a personal style that was both poetic and practical. As Sir John Summerson has observed (*Sir John Soane*, 1952, p. 15): "In 1792, when [Soane's] style arrives suddenly at maturity, there was not, anywhere in Europe, an architecture as unconstrained by classical loyalties, as free in the handling of proportions and as adventurous in structure and lighting as that which Soane introduced at the Bank of England in that year." The sources of this style are to be found both in France and in England. Soane had been profoundly influenced by the Abbé Laugier's demand for a new architecture that would reconstitute the lightness and grace of Gothic structure in a purified and reformed version of the classical language. We know that Soane possessed eleven copies of Laugier's *Essai sur l'architecture*. What is less well known is that a manuscript survives of Soane's translation of the book from which many of Laugier's ideas were taken, Cordemoy's *Nouveau traité de toute l'architecture*. But Soane's sources were also English. He had worshiped at the shrine of his old master, George Dance, the younger (1741–1825), to whose work we now give our attention.

Adam, Chambers, and Mylne all arrived in Rome, the melting pot of early neoclassicism, in 1754–55, and the eighteen-year-old George Dance followed in 1759. He had been sent there by his architect father in order to join his brother Nathaniel, a painter, who had arrived four years earlier. Soon George Dance met Piranesi, and together they made the first accurate measured drawings of the Temple of Castor and Pollux in the Forum. In 1762 he entered the competition for a design for a public gallery for statues and pictures organized by the Accademia at Parma. The design with which he won the Gold Medal in 1763, characterized by stone domes and bleak rusticated walls, shows how much he had absorbed of the emergent neoclassicism of the French Grand Prix projects. This was the style of heroic grimness that M.-J. Peyre was to encapsulate in his *Oeuvres d'architecture*, of 1765, and that also inspired the dreams of the young Soane, Dance's junior by twelve years.

Dance returned to England late in 1764 and by the following spring was at work on his first commission, the church of All Hallows, London Wall, in the City of London. Inspired by the Roman Baths, and roofed with a barrel vault—not the coffered ellipse used by Inigo Jones and James Gibbs—the church has an internal Ionic order that lacks a full entablature and has instead a highly enriched frieze. This not very daring novelty, which was due to Dance's reading of Laugier's *Essai sur l'architecture*, we know shocked Soane when he first saw it. Dance's next building was Newgate Gaol (designed in 1768–

329. *George Dance, Newgate Gaol, London, 1768–80.*
330. *George Dance, Cranbury Park, Hampshire, detail of the ballroom ceiling, c. 1778.*

of which he wrote: "Whatever is fitted in any sort to excite the ideas of pain and anger . . . whatever is in any sort terrible . . . is a source of the sublime."

In the late 1770s Dance remodeled a country house, Cranbury Park, in Hampshire, for a family friend, providing a top-lit ballroom that contains the seeds of the mature Dance-Soane style. This vast room has semi-domes to east and west derived from the Roman Baths, but in the center is a beautiful, shallow cross vault in a starfish pattern that was adapted from a plate in Pietro Santi Bartoli's *Gli antichi sepolcri ovvero mausolei romani* (1697; new edition 1757). This important book, which was almost certainly known to Adam and was later owned by Soane, played a decisive role in disseminating knowledge of ancient Roman interior decoration. The groin vault in a starfish pattern, first imitated by Dance at Cranbury, became the hallmark of Soane's interiors, beginning with the study of his first house at Lincoln's Inn Fields, begun in 1792. The influence on Dance and Soane of this "sepulchral" architecture is particularly interesting in light of Boullée's obsession with the romantic effects of "buried architecture."

Dance developed the Cranbury theme in two interiors at the Guildhall in London, from 1777 to 1779. In the Common Council Chamber the dome and its pendentives are all parts of the same sphere, a device that may have been inspired by Jean-Baptiste de La Rue's *Traité de la coupe des pierres* (1728): Plate XXXIV shows the construction of a "cul-de-four en pendentifs sur un quarré." This is an attack on the Renaissance and Baroque conception of a domed space in which the dome is a separate handsome entity resting on clearly defined piers. At the Guildhall the dome is reduced to its essence. The whole room becomes a kind of dome, a basic tent or covering. This primitivist tent- or umbrella-like aspect is emphasized by the scalloped curves of decorative and nonstructural origin. The fluting applied to the dome is perhaps derived from the ruin of the Serapeum at Hadrian's Villa, which Dance may have seen and which was illustrated in the 1760s by Piranesi in *Vedute di Roma*. This type of fluting also became a feature of Grand Prix designs as, for example, in Sobre's Maison de Plaisance (1782). Another novelty of the Council Chamber was the space at the east and west ends that rose higher than that in the center, thus enabling the western end to be illuminated by two largely invisible windows casting light from a hidden source. This "lumière mystérieuse" was also a characteristic of the library that Dance designed within an uncompleted shell constructed by Adam at Lansdowne House, London, at the end of the 1780s. Dance remodeled Adam's vaults, creating semi-domes at each end of the long central space. The overall form of these domed spaces may derive from the Temple of Minerva Medica in Rome, but the sliced-off semi-domes,

69), which combines themes derived from Peyre with a Mannerist handling of rustication inspired by Giulio Romano. Elements from the powerful style of Vanbrugh also appear in the centrally placed Keeper's House, where they help reinforce the dramatic "narrative" content of the building, which was evidently intended to be expressive of its grim function. In the *Cours d'architecture*, which J.-F. Blondel began delivering to his students in 1743 (it was not published until 1771), the prison was upheld as the sole permanent building type for the style later described as "architecture parlante." This seems to relate not only to Newgate Gaol but also to Burke's category of the Sublime, with their concealed Diocletian windows, were inspired by a French Grand Prix precedent. We find them in Pierre-Nicolas Bernard's project for a *palais de justice*, of 1782, and in Sobre's *hôtel de ville*, of five years later.

A related obsession of Dance's was top-lit octagonal halls in a stripped Gothic style, such as those at St. Bartholomew-the-Less, London (1789); at St. Mary, Micheldever, Hampshire (1808); and at the house he built for the great patron and collector Sir George Beaumont at Coleorton, Leicestershire (1804). The combination of a kind of reductionist Gothic with Romantic toplighting echoes the ambitions of both Laugier and Boullée. In a very different interior at a London lunatic asylum, St. Luke's Hospital, Old Street (1781), Dance provided a nightmare-like, seemingly endless repetition of arches that anticipated the extreme shrill attenuation, both horizontal and vertical, of Bernard Poyet's Rue des Colonnes, Paris (1798), and Friedrich Weinbrenner's Kaiserstrasse, Karlsruhe (1808). Again we are reminded of Burke, who, in defining the delightful horrors of the Sublime, analyzed the effect of "infinity and things multiplied without end."

The abstraction and linearity that we also find in Dance's work make him an architectural counterpart to John Flaxman. Dance reduced both Gothic and classical styles to a strange disembodied synthesis that recalls Flaxman's depiction of the Greek world in his illustrations of Homer and Aeschylus, and of medieval Catholicism in his illustrations of Dante. But before we consign Dance to that chill vacuum let us recall what C. R. Cockerell said of him in his Royal Academy lectures in the 1840s: "Dance showed himself the most complete Poet Architect of his day—no one can doubt that Newgate is a prison, that St. Luke's is an asylum, prison or place of milder confinement for the unhappy and bewildered in mind, or that the front of the Guildhall, though anything but Gothic, is still the metropolitan and magnificent place of Government and civil authority."

What we have said of Dance is, in general, true of Soane, for never were two artists more mutually dependent on each other in the development of a common style. Dance, as the older man, often provided the motifs first, although the last design by him—of which we have a record—shows a definite dependence on Soane. This is his unexecuted project, dating from some time after 1815, for a house for Lord Bristol at No. 6 St. James's Square, London. It is basically a kind of warehouse, a three-storied glass box that was inspired by Soane's ruthlessly novel Loggia in the Waiting Room Courtyard at the Bank of England, of 1804–5. Soane was appointed Surveyor to the bank in 1788, succeeding Sir Robert Taylor. His extensive additions to and remodelings of Taylor's work occupied him on and off for the next

thirty-six years and undoubtedly represent the apotheosis of his unique architectural style. His first task was to rebuild completely Taylor's Stock Office immediately north of the Bartholomew Lane vestibule. Rain had seeped in through Taylor's lead roof and had decayed the principal roof timbers. Soane therefore concentrated his attention on a new roof set on stone piers with brick arches springing from them, replacing Taylor's interiors of lath and plaster and timber, which had been susceptible to both fire and water. Soane's vault was constructed of what he called cones—tapering hollow blocks of terra-cotta based on those used in the Byzantine buildings of Ravenna. He chose them

332. *Plate from Jean-Baptiste de La Rue's* Traité de la coupe des pierres, *1728.*

333. *George Dance, project for No. 6 St. James's Square, London, after 1815.*

334. *George Dance, design for the library, Lansdowne House, London, 1788–91.*

335.   *George Dance, St. Luke's Hospital, London, interior, 1781.*
336.   *Sir John Soane, Bank of England, London, 1788–1833. Ground-floor plan as in 1924.*
337.   *Sir John Soane, Bank of England, London, Lothbury Court, 1797.*

338. *Sir John Soane, Bank of England, London, Lothbury Court, detail of the colonnade.*

339. *Sir John Soane, Bank of England, London, entrance vestibule to the Waiting Room Courtyard, 1804–5.*

340. *Sir John Soane, Bank of England, London, Stock Office, 1792.*

341. *Sir John Soane, Bank of England, London, Old Colonial Office, 1818.*

342. *Sir John Soane, Pitzhanger Manor, Ealing, near London, Front Parlour, 1800–1802.*

343. *Sir John Soane, Privy Council Chamber, London, 1824.*▷

for their fireproof qualities as well as for their lightness. Soane's floating, disembodied space—marked by sharply incised lines, ribs, and grooves—owes something, as Summerson has shown, to the Baths of Diocletian, Dance's Common Council Chamber at the Guildhall, Taylor's Reduced Annuities Office (1782–88) at the Bank of England, Piranesi's engravings, and to Laugier's emphasis on considerations of structure and utility through analogy to the primitive hut. As an indication of the daring step Soane took at the Bank Stock Office we may compare it with a related interior of 1791–93, his Yellow Drawing Room at Wimpole Hall, Cambridgeshire. In this extraordinary, domed, T-shaped room Soane evidently went as far as he dared in adapting to domestic purposes the radical novelties pioneered by Dance at the Common Council Chamber, in 1777. At the bank he allowed himself more freedom. When he turned his attention, in 1794, to Taylor's Rotunda, also in need of repair, it emerged wondrously transformed. Where Taylor's space (see illustration 242) had been a pale echo of the Pantheon, Soane's is an imaginative re-creation of the spirit—not the letter—of an antique domed space. With Dance's help he provided an abstract synthesis in which the classical orders were reduced schematically to geometrical incised lines, the whole saved from totally chill austerity by the romantic lighting effects, the "lumière mystérieuse" of Le Camus de Mézières.

In the same style as the Bank Stock Office and Rotunda, Soane went on to turn Taylor's Transfer Office immediately north of the Rotunda into the Old Shutting Room. This dates from 1794–96, and was followed, in 1797–99, by the adjacent Consols Office, with its startling ring of caryatids, which, according to the original design, was to have been decorated even more richly. The development south of the Rotunda came much later, in 1812–23, but the stylistic consistency was remarkable. The caryatids of the Consols Office, greatly increased in height, turn up in the lantern of the Old Dividend or Four Percent Office, and are replaced by a noble Ionic colonnade in the Old Colonial or Five Percent Office, both completed in 1818. From 1804 to 1805 Soane provided a new western entrance to the bank in the newly realigned Prince's Street. The Picturesque vista from the barrel-vaulted Greek Doric entrance vestibule toward the dramatic open Loggia along the north side of the Waiting Room Courtyard is one of the most brilliant realizations of Soane's belief in the "poetry of architecture." Indeed, the whole bank could be seen as an embodiment of that belief. The way in which it grew slowly and haphazardly, with Soane obliged to combine and retain all manner of heterogeneous fragments of earlier buildings, and even to remodel his own, meant that the planning was empirical and not neoclassical.

None of the grand gateways really led anywhere; nothing was related to anything else in a way that an ancient Roman or a modern Frenchman would have understood. In its piecemeal, haphazard growth and plan it was thoroughly English and thoroughly Picturesque, yet in actual design no building in Europe was more neoclassical. Its poetry has never been better captured than by Sir Osbert Sitwell in his autobiographical volume *Great Morning* (1948), where he describes how in the evening "this one-storey building emptied altogether of life, and with its garden-courts and cloisters, resembled a monastery or a deserted temple rather than the most famous financial institution in the world. By one of the passionate paradoxes of its creator—surely the most original of all English architects—it seemed to offer a quiet, leafy, well-kept retreat from the world."

One type of interior not fully exploited at the Bank of England, but particularly associated with Soane's mature style, is that dominated by a kind of hanging ceiling or domed canopy. Its first tentative appearance is in the Front Parlour of Soane's own house, Pitzhanger Manor (1800–1802), at Ealing, near London. Of markedly funereal appearance, with sarcophagi in tomblike recesses and much other antique sculpture, this room must originally have been close in spirit to Thomas Hope's contemporary house-*cum*-museum in Duchess Street, London. The shadowy and funeral overtones of Soane's room were certainly not accidental and forcibly recall Boullée's ambition to create an "architecture ensevelie." Indeed, Boullée declared in his *Essai sur l'art* that the "Temple of Death" was the type of building that, more than any other, calls for the "poésie de l'architecture," so as to convey "l'image de l'architecture ensevelie, en n'employent que des proportions basses et affaissées et enfouies dans la terre, former enfin par les matières absorbant la lumière, le noir tableau de l'architecture des ombres dessiné par l'effet d'ombres encore plus noires. Ce genre d'architecture formé par des ombres," he proudly added, "est une découverte d'art qui m'appartient. C'est une carrière nouvelle que j'ai ouverte" (see H. Rosenau, *Boullée and Visionary Architecture*, pp. 124, 135). However, in such interiors as the Breakfast Parlour (1812) at Lincoln's Inn Fields, the National Debt Redemption Office, Old Jewry, City of London (1817), the Privy Council Chamber, Downing Street (1824), the Freemasons' Hall, Great Queen Street (1828), and the Law Courts at Westminster (1820s), Soane's obsession with toplighting and with high side lighting creates an eerie and mysteriously subterranean effect—occasionally inspired by Gothic vaulting and lighting arrangements—that represents the final and uniquely personal synthesis of the "lumière mystérieuse" of the visionary architecture of France and the Picturesque tradition of eighteenth-century England.

344. *Jean-François-Thérèse Chalgrin, Palais du Luxembourg, Paris, grand staircase, 1803–7.*

345. *Jean-François-Thérèse Chalgrin, Palais du Luxembourg, Paris, Salle du Sénat, 1803–7.*

FRANCE: *Percier and Fontaine to Garnier*

Building continued sporadically after the Revolution in France, but it was scarcely an auspicious time for architecture. There was little opportunity and a conspicuous lack of vigor in design. Arrangements and patterns evolved earlier in the eighteenth century were repeated to produce an array of neat, charming, and altogether well-planned and ornamented houses on the outskirts of Paris. But this was not the sort of activity to stimulate new talents. Architects turned to other occupations. Charles-Pierre-Joseph Normand (1765–1840) and Théodore Ollivier became engravers; others served as surveyors and military engineers in Napoleon's endless campaigns. Only Napoleon was able to act as a great patron, but not until after the coup d'état of 1799 that brought him finally to power. Most of the architects he employed on his larger projects had already made names for themselves before the Revolution. Rondelet restored once again the church of Ste.-Geneviève (now renamed the Panthéon). Chalgrin, who had started work on the Palais du Luxembourg in 1787, transformed its interior completely between 1803 and 1807 for the use of the Senate. The Salle du Sénat (disastrously redesigned in 1836 by Chalgrin's pupil Alphonse-Henri de Gisors) and the great extended stair with which Chalgrin replaced Rubens's gallery were unquestionably dramatic in a late eighteenth-century sort of way, but they were by then in the nature of established solutions. Chalgrin's Arc de Triomphe, the foundation stone of which was laid on August 18, 1806, was finer, though not as first conceived. He aimed, then, at the accepted grandeur of ancient Roman buildings, incorporating freestanding decorative columns, statues, and bas-relief panels. His projects of 1810, however, were more austere, and, as were all Chalgrin's works, faultless in proportion. Later Blouet was to complete the attic story of the Arc, destroying in the process the balance of Chalgrin's restrained classicism. Bélanger provided a design for an ambitious cast-iron dome for the court of the Halle aux Blés in 1805, two years after Legrand's and Molinos's timber dome burned down. He also began a very noble *abattoir* at Rochechouart in 1809, while Brongniart, as we have seen, started on the Bourse in the year before. Between 1806 and 1810 Gondoin, together with Jean-Baptiste Lepère (1761–1844), erected his most famous, if least enterprising, work, the Colonne Vendôme.

There were newcomers, though their architecture was even less precise and alive than that of the established practitioners. After much fuss and intrigue and no little competition, Ledoux's pupil Alexandre-Pierre Vignon (1763–1828) was commissioned in 1807 to build the Madeleine, incorporating some of the foundations of Contant d'Ivry's church. The result was a lifeless paraphrase of an antique Roman temple. The interior, in which the theme of the Roman Bath was

346. *Jacques Gondoin and Jean-Baptiste Lepère, column in the Place Vendôme, Paris, 1806–10.*

347. *Jean-François-Thérèse Chalgrin, Arc de Triomphe, Paris, begun 1806, completed 1836 by G.-A. Blouet.*

348. *Alexandre-Pierre Vignon, the Madeleine, Paris, 1807–45.*

349. *Jean-Jacques-Marie Huvé, the Madeleine, Paris, interior, 1825–45.▷*

Poyet—the architect admired by Durand—added a giant Corinthian portico to the old Palais-Bourbon (now the Chambre des Députés), in 1808. This, once again, was intended to commemorate the architecture of ancient Rome, but it is patently a facade, lacking in all solid dignity. Two years later Jacques-Charles Bonnard (1765–1818), who had worked for the Abbé de Saint-Non in Italy, began the vast Ministère des Affaires Étrangères (afterward called the Cour des Comptes but now demolished) on the banks of the Seine. This was an Italianate building with round-arched windows, applied columns, and a lot more besides, of a sort that had been attempted by a French architect only once before—in 1776, by P.-A. Pâris for the Prince Bishop of Basel's palace at Porrentruy (never completed). But to the younger generation Bonnard's building was a revelation. They rioted in 1826 when the secretary of the Académie disparaged Bonnard's work in an oration. The Italianate mode, however, was not the creation of Bonnard. He had merely applied it with a greater degree of richness. The architects responsible for the new manner of the early nineteenth century were Charles Percier (1764–1838) and Pierre-François-Léonard Fontaine (1762–1853), whom we have already encountered as an emulator of Boullée and also as the notorious runner-up for the Prix de Rome in 1785. Both were pupils of Antoine-François Peyre (1739–1823), younger brother of Marie-Joseph Peyre. Percier, in fact, did win the Grand Prix in 1786. By the following year Percier and Fontaine were both in Rome, where they met Bonnard and together explored the celebrated antiquities and the ancient aqueducts. But they examined also Renaissance palaces, not only in Rome but in Florence as well, and the villas and farms of Tuscany. These were to be their hostages for the future. When they returned to France they studied French Renaissance architecture, and even the Gothic style, for their tastes were eclectic. With wonderful finesse and tact, they were able to subordinate these strains from the past within the system of forms and measures that they had inherited from the eighteenth century, to produce a new style of some distinction and novelty, yet one that was perfectly decorous. Together they became modish designers of interiors. One of these was so admired by the Empress Josephine that she commissioned them, in 1799, to rebuild her newly acquired house at Malmaison. They proposed a scheme that was Palladian in inspiration, but so enlarged and extended beyond sensible measure that it aroused Napoleon's rage; instead, they redecorated the existing house with marvelous flair, taking up details from Bélanger's Bagatelle and Pâris's designs for the Menus-Plaisirs, and thus fashioning the style that was later to be identified as Empire, the epitome of neoclassical taste. Absolutely, it was not new; what they had done was to rely on a greater sense of interval, and a hard-

developed with dogged determination and success of a kind, was the work of Jean-Jacques-Marie Huvé (1783–1852), who took over in 1828 and completed most of the building twelve years later, though decoration continued until 1845.

On the same axis, on the opposite bank of the Seine, Bernard

352. *Charles Percier and Pierre-François-Léonard Fontaine, Château de Malmaison (Rueil-Malmaison), library.*

ness of outline and a crispness of detail, to effect the apparent change. Color was another aspect of their adaptation: They used more strong and acid tones than usual, chrome yellows, bottle greens, and azure blues, contrasting them with ebony or dark mahogany wood and bronze-gilt appliqués. Napoleon was much impressed. Before they

quarreled with Josephine as to the merits of a Picturesque garden, they had been made *Architectes des Palais du Premier et Deuxième Consuls.* Their official career began in January 1801.

For Napoleon they worked exhaustively. They were ultimately responsible for the administration of his extensive proposals for the

353. *Charles Percier and Pierre-François-Léonard Fontaine, Tuileries, Paris, Salle des Maréchaux and tribune, 1801 onward.*

354. *Charles Percier and Pierre-François-Léonard Fontaine, Palais Royal, Paris, staircase in the Montpensier wing, 1829.*

reorganization of Paris—the introduction of new roads, markets, and fountains, and the dispersal of the *abattoirs* and cemeteries to the periphery. They restored and decorated for him the old royal palaces at St.-Cloud, Compiègne, Fontainebleau and Le Raincy, Eu and Rambouillet, and throughout Europe prepared palaces for him and his nominees and family. Percier and Fontaine worked for the whole Bonaparte tribe. But their best efforts were expended on the Louvre and the Tuileries. They began in 1801 with the Tuileries, introducing a magnificent array of apartments, in style representing a continuation of the old Menus-Plaisirs, but wonderfully resourceful and distinctive. These were all destroyed in 1870 with the demolition of the Tuileries palace. In the same year they prepared designs for linking the Tuileries with the Louvre; the Rue de Rivoli and the related Rue des Pyramides are the results of these efforts. By 1808 they had started on the interiors of the Louvre itself, where their crisp and inventive but altogether static details may still be admired. Their greater ambitions were revealed in 1811 when they designed a gigantic palace, larger even than Versailles, on the heights of Chaillot for Napoleon's baby son, the Roi de Rome. This was started, as was an equally gargantuan scheme on the opposite bank of the Seine, in front of the École Militaire, for a series of four-square buildings serving as a center of learning—an archive, a university, and an École des Beaux-Arts. Here the dreams of Durand might have been realized. Percier and Fontaine were his worthy followers, both as practitioners and as teachers. They—or rather Percier—taught a whole generation of architects: Augustin-Nicolas Caristié (1783–1862), François Debret (1777–1850), A.-H. de Gisors (1796–1866), Huvé, Louis-Hippolyte Lebas (1782–1867), Achille-François-Rene Leclère (1785–1853), Jean-Baptiste-Ciceron Lesueur (1794–1883), and Louis-Tullius-Joachim Visconti (1791–1853) are only some of their better-known pupils. But their teaching, though altogether sensible and tolerant, as one might expect, was lax. Their followers had few firm convictions, and even fewer ideas. They relied for inspiration on those books that Percier and Fontaine published in successive years to enlarge the French classical repertoire so that it would accommodate a mixed Italianate style—the *Palais, maisons, et autres édifices modernes dessinés à Rome,* of 1798, and the *Choix des plus célèbres maisons de plaisance de Rome et de ses environs,* of 1809. Their own designs were illustrated in their *Recueil de décorations intérieures,* of 1801, and their *Résidences de Souverains . . . de France, d'Allemagne, de Suède, de Russie . . . ,* written in 1833.

It is scarcely to be wondered at that architects felt without strong guidance or convictions at the end of Napoleon's regime. Neither Louis XVIII nor Charles X was much interested in architecture, and

355. *Charles Percier and Pierre-François-Léonard Fontaine, Palais Royal, Paris, Galerie d'Orléans, 1829.*

356. *Charles Percier and Pierre-François-Léonard Fontaine, Rue de Rivoli and Place des Pyramides, Paris, begun 1803.*

357. *Charles Percier and Pierre-François-Léonard Fontaine, plan of Paris showing the Palais du Roi de Rome and the new university and administrative quarters, begun 1811.*

358. *Charles Percier and Pierre-François-Léonard Fontaine, project for the Palais du Roi de Rome, Paris.*

359. *Antoine-Chrysostome Quatremère de Quincy, pulpit in St.-Germain-des-Prés, Paris, 1829.*

they made no attempt to emulate Napoleon. "Il était un bon loca-taire," Louis XVIII remarked of Napoleon, and decided to alter nothing at the Tuileries. Leadership in architecture passed into the hands of the newly reestablished Académie des Beaux-Arts and the closely related Conseil Général des Bâtiments Civils. This, in effect, resulted in the dominance of one man, Antoine-Chrysostome Quatre-mère de Quincy, *Secrétaire Perpétuel de l'Académie des Beaux-Arts* from 1816 to 1839. Quatremère de Quincy was an unsuccessful sculp-tor who failed to win the Grand Prix but nonetheless traveled to Italy, where he became friendly with such men as Jacques-Louis David, Antonio Canova, and Sir William Hamilton. He was a great champion of Greek art, but this was a distant ideal, and in practical matters he preferred to rely on his knowledge of Roman antiquity. This was the model he upheld for French architects. He determined that only those architects who had traveled to Italy and inspected its antique remains for themselves should be employed on official commis-sions. Naturally, he was not altogether successful in this. But through the years he did impose his doctrinaire ideals with extraordinary strict-ness. Hundreds, probably thousands, of uninspired and rigid buildings —churches, *mairies, palais de justice,* barracks, prisons, and hospitals— attest to his limited tastes. The epitome of this taste, perhaps, is the Palais de Justice in Lyons, by Louis-Pierre Baltard (1764–1846), with a facade made up of an unbroken line of twenty-four giant Corinthian columns—the prototype of that official architecture so favored in Washington, D.C., even today. The Salle des Pas Perdus, consisting of a succession of neatly defined, low-domed spaces, has just that added variety and interest that Quatremère de Quincy was to admire later in life. His early aims are represented by the works of Étienne-Hippolyte Godde (1781–1869), who did not win the Grand Prix, but nonetheless showed in such churches as St.-Pierre-du-Gros-Caillou (1822–30), Notre-Dame-de-Bonne-Nouvelle (1823–30), and St.-Denys-du-St.-Sacrement (1826–35), all in Paris, that a routine and lackluster classical spirit could be cultivated in France even more successfully than in Rome. Quatremère de Quincy could not but applaud. These are the embodiments of the architecture hinted at in the backgrounds of David's paintings. The Imperial Roman opu-lence of Huvé's interiors at the Madeleine, initiated in 1828, was not to Quatremère de Quincy's liking. Even less so were the rich decora-tions introduced in the following year into the Chambre des Députés by another pupil of Percier and Fontaine, Jules-Jean-Baptiste de Joly (1788–1865). His adjoining vestibule and related Salon du Roi, built by 1833, and the richly decorated and gilded library (both, inciden-tally, incorporating paintings done by Delacroix from 1838 to 1847) seemed to Quatremère de Quincy utterly vulgar. But he was not

362. Louis-Hippolyte Lebas, Notre-Dame-de-Lorette, Paris, 1823–36.

363. Louis-Hippolyte Lebas, Notre-Dame-de-Lorette, Paris, interior.

364. Étienne-Hippolyte Godde, St.-Pierre-du-Gros-Caillou, Paris, interior, 1822–30.

365. Jacques-Ignace Hittorff and Jean-Baptiste Lepère, St.-Vincent-de-Paul, Paris, 1824, 1830–46.

366. *Jacques-Ignace Hittorff and Jules Jollivet, project for the decoration of the portico of St.-Vincent-de-Paul with enameled panels, one of which was painted in 1846, with six more to follow in 1852, all being taken down in 1861.*

367. *Jacques-Ignace Hittorff and Jean-Baptiste Lepère, St.-Vincent-de-Paul, Paris, interior.*

altogether opposed, as we have seen, to some liveliness of decoration or color in architecture. He always encouraged mural painting. His *Jupiter Olympien*, which was published in 1815, gave evidence of some ability to rethink conventions concerning the antique and would serve to stir the color controversy. Seven years later he organized a competition to provide a model for a new and marginally richer architecture than such men as Godde were able to offer. This was to be carefully controlled. The plan was to remain based on the established basilican pattern, but something of the old splendor of San Paolo fuori le Mure in Rome was introduced. The competition was won by a pupil of Percier and Fontaine, Louis-Hippolyte Lebas. Quatremère de Quincy was always distrustful of their students, and his misgivings in this instance were justified. Lebas built the church of Notre-Dame-de-Lorette during the next thirteen years, starting with a basilican plan, erecting on it a portico that was said to be proportioned on that of the Doric Temple of Hercules, at Cora in Italy, but that was endowed, nonetheless, with florid Corinthian columns. The interior was an extraordinary *pasticcio* of an Early Christian basilica, painted and gilded everywhere, that was both fastidious and coarse. He employed a great many sculptors and painters, and the church became at once a focus of artistic attention—an attention, when related to the ideas put forward in the *Jupiter Olympien*, that was to undermine, if not destroy, much that Quatremère de Quincy had stood for.

Hittorff, the exponent of a highly colored image of Greek antiquity, was the agent of change. In 1834, ten years after his return from Italy, and at the height of the quarrel concerning the application of color in Greek architecture, he designed two side altars for Notre-Dame-de-Lorette, gilded, pedimented affairs that incorporated panels of vividly colored enamel. The commission had been offered first to Jean-Auguste-Dominique Ingres, but he passed it on to Hittorff. Hittorff added brightly painted porticos to his Rotonde des Panoramas (1838–39) and, as we have seen, to the Cirque National—both on the Champs-Élysées—and elaborately decorated the Cirque d'Hiver, Boulevard des Filles-du-Calvaire. However, his real opportunity to demonstrate how the studied and serious classical style of the early nineteenth century might be transformed, but in conformity with antique precedents, came with the completion of St.-Vincent-de-Paul, overlooking the Place Lafayette, Paris. This church was sketched first, in 1824, by Hittorff's father-in-law, Lepère, who had worked with Gondoin on the Colonne Vendôme. But building was not begun in earnest until 1830, by which time Hittorff had revised the design completely. It is the largest basilican church of the period, with two tiers of columns inside supporting an open, timber-trussed roof. Exter-

368. *Jacques-Ignace Hittorff, Mairie du I*er*, Paris, 1855–61. The tower was built between 1858 and 1863 by Théodore Ballu.*
369. *Jacques-Ignace Hittorff, Gare du Nord, Paris, 1861–65.*
370. *Jacques-Ignace Hittorff, Gare du Nord, Paris, detail of the sheds.*

nally it is preceded by a large pedimented portico set against a flat masonry wall with a central projection, and is flanked by two square towers. The site and the setting lend some grandeur to the composition, but all feeling for mass is lacking and the detailing is disappointingly thin. Internally the same criticisms would apply were the interior not transformed into a riot of strong color: The columns are apricot; above, there are frescoes by a host of Ingres's pupils, including Jean-Hippolyte Flandrin; the roof trusses are brilliant blues and reds, all scattered with gold, in imitation of those at Monreale cathedral, which Hittorff saw as a latter-day expression of what he had imagined as the colorful architecture of Greek antiquity. Even today this interior is vibrant. For the outside Hittorff proposed something parallel. In 1846 he started to cover the wall of the portico with large, brightly colored enameled plaques, painted by Gros's pupil Jollivet. This panorama of biblical scenes was intended to extend over the entire surface. Seven of these were eventually put up, but the clergy was scandalized by the nudity of Adam and Eve—and everyone else by the blaze of color—and in 1861, at the clergy's behest, the plaques were taken down, though they still survive in a depot at Ivry-sur-Seine.

Hittorff built a great deal besides. Between 1836 and 1840 he flattened out Gabriel's Place Louis XV, by then renamed the Place de la Concorde, topped the pavilions with heavy statues, and added the obelisk, the fountains (of cast-iron), and the lamp standards. These were all originally gilt. He embellished the Champs-Élysées with an array of fountains, shelters, restaurants, and the circus and panorama already mentioned. Then in 1855 he designed the houses around the Place de l'Étoile and began what is now the Avenue Foch, leading to the Bois de Boulogne, where he began excavating the lakes. To the east of the Place de la Concorde he extended the Rue de Rivoli, designing the first of the large-scale *hôtels* in Paris on the American pattern, the Grand Hôtel des Chemins de Fer (now the Grands Magasins du Louvre). Opposite Perrault's Louvre facade he built the ungainly Mairie du I*er* between 1855 and 1861, as a pendant to St.-Germain-l'Auxerrois, which he was forced to paraphrase. He found no enjoyment in this task, for he loathed the Gothic style. But he was no favorite of Baron Haussmann, the all-powerful *Préfet de la Seine*, who was intent to embarrass him. They were involved soon enough in bitter litigation about the works in the Bois de Boulogne and the payment of fees. Hittorff won, but Haussmann had his revenge. By changing the alignments of the streets he saw to it that Hittorff's greatest work, the Gare du Nord, designed in 1859 and started two years later, did not act as a terminal feature to a main boulevard.

The Gare du Nord was a fitting conclusion to Hittorff's career. It reflected faithfully the disparities of his approach to architecture. The planning was excellent and sufficiently flexible to allow for the gradual transformation from a mixed goods and passenger terminal to one for people alone. The construction of the sheds was simple, economical, daring, and successful—A.-R. Polonceau's newly developed gable trusses were used, and all the ironwork was made in Glasgow. But the architecture of the facade was an assorted medley of classical motifs, all of unrelated scale, used neither correctly nor with sufficient panache to transcend the lack of convention. Hittorff was not a creative architect. Not one of his buildings is resolved. He applied decoration, usually of a meager kind, in an attempt to disguise his failure to compose convincingly, but even here he appeared to be fiddling. He was, however, wonderfully adventurous in other respects, especially as a technical innovator. In 1828 he introduced safety curtains of iron into the Théâtre de l'Ambigu Comique (demolished 1966). For the roof of his Rotonde des Panoramas he adapted the principle of the suspension bridge; for that of the Cirque National he employed an extremely elegant lattice timber truss, and repeated this with an even greater refinement at the Cirque d'Hiver. His prowess in this respect was always acclaimed and was slowly emulated. And his archaeological theories, too, though they had little enough to do with archaeology, opened the eyes of a whole generation of architects in France to the possibility of breaking from the established classical routine and developing a new architecture. The use of applied color in architecture after 1830 was a sign of rebellion.

The rebels of the 1830s are usually accounted as Guillaume-Abel Blouet, Émile-Jacques Gilbert, Félix-Jacques Duban, Henri Labrouste, Louis-Joseph Duc, and Léon Vaudoyer. But their contributions to architecture were very different and quite distinct.

Blouet (1795–1853) and Gilbert (1793–1874) emerged first. Blouet trained with Delespine, Gilbert with Durand at the École Polytechnique and then with Vignon at the École des Beaux-Arts. They both won the Grand Prix, Blouet in 1821, Gilbert in the year following; they worked together in Rome and again, after their return, when Blouet was appointed architect to the Arc de Triomphe in 1831, with Gilbert as his *Inspecteur*. Blouet, a protégé of Quatremère de Quincy, had been sent on an official mission to Greece in 1828; when his restoration studies of the Doric temple on Aegina were published in 1838, the temple was revealed in bright color, primarily blue and red. Gilbert made his attestation in the brilliantly colored interior of the chapel that forms the focus of his vast and very austere Asile d'Aliénés at Charenton, on the edge of Paris, built between 1838 and 1845. But Blouet's and Gilbert's idea of reform in architecture was based on nothing so superficial as the application of color.

They thought to enrich architecture by making moral and social aims determine its arrangement, as never before. Like many intellectuals of their generation, they were sustained by the humanitarian ideas of Saint-Simon and Charles Fourier. Saint-Simon was not at first much interested in architecture or even in art—"Il n'y a aujourd'hui d'hommes qui se vouent à la poésie que ceux qui ne peuvent pas réussir dans les travaux de l'intelligence," he wrote in 1813 in his *Mémoire sur la science de l'homme*. But by the year of his death, in 1825, when he wrote *Le nouveau christianisme*, he had reserved a place for architects among the leaders of society, alongside the engineers and the factory owners. He made no positive proposals himself, although his disciples, led by Émile Barrault, were to propound a doctrine at

373. *Victor Considerant, project for a phalanstère, 1834.*

374. *André Godin and E. André, familistère, Guise, begun 1859.*

375. *André Godin and E. André, familistère, Guise, interior court.*

376. *Louis-Hippolyte Lebas, house of detention for juvenile offenders,*
Place de la Roquette, Paris, plan, 1825.

both the Saint-Simonist expositions of 1828 and 1830, and, especially, in the pamphlet *Aux artistes: du passé et de l'avenir des beaux-arts*, issued in 1830, which held that the history of the arts followed a succession of "organic" and "critical" periods, the organic being identified as pre-Periclean Greek and that of the Middle Ages, expressive both of a unity of religious belief and social aspiration. The early Greek temple and the Gothic cathedral were thus seen as embodiments of integrated societies. Victor Hugo's architectural ideas, contained, in particular, in the second edition of his *Notre-Dame de Paris*, of 1832, were a direct response to such propaganda. But the Saint-Simonists themselves did not pursue these ideas to any consequence, nor were they to interpret them with any resounding success. Under the leadership of Barthélemy-Prosper Enfantin, a group of Saint-Simon's followers did set out in 1834 to build a city for the workers digging the Suez Canal. The plan of the city was in the shape of a human figure, the buildings corresponding to the functions of the body, administrative buildings and scientific institutes at the head, academies and temples at the heart, and so on. But the disciples did not get far with their plans. They were decimated by cholera. Fourier, however, suggested an architectural form for his ideas, at first reluctantly, but by 1829, when he published *Le nouveau monde industriel et sociétaire*, he included a sketch plan for one of his communes, which he called a *phalange*. This appeared as a bird's-eye perspective on the title page of *Le phalanstère* in June 1832, the year in which an attempt was made to found such a commune at Condé-sur-Vesgre, near Rambouillet. Victor Considerant was to depict his *phalanstère* as a palace of Versailles in 1834 in *Considérations sociales sur l'architecture*. But the opportunity for building such a community was to be rare. Only one was built in France, André Godin's *familistère* at Guise, begun in 1859, still standing and still working. No architect was involved. Godin employed a former art student, E. André, to prepare the drawings. The type was to become familiar in America—where Godin himself financed a phalanstery in Texas in 1853—but in France such experiments were so isolated and of so specific a nature that they had only an indirect influence on architecture. Later low-cost houses for workers, notably those built by Émile Müller for the Société Mulhousienne des Cités Ouvrières, beginning in 1853, and even his pupil Émile Cacheux's minimal houses, put up in Auteuil (Villa Émile Meyer and Villa Dietz Monnin) and elsewhere in Paris in the 1880s, all aimed to provide single dwellings with gardens, not collectives. The workers were to buy their houses and to become respectable members of the propertied classes.

Gilbert's and Blouet's model was provided by C. B. Beccaria in Italy and John Howard in England, who in the late eighteenth century had initiated a series of penal reforms that resulted in the gradual separation of criminals from the sick and the insane. Criminals, in turn, were categorized according to sex, age, and the nature of their crimes, so that by degrees the only means of ensuring that they did not adversely influence one another was to provide each with an individual cell—a self-contained unit, fully serviced, that might ensure total isolation and thus opportunity for moral redemption. Many prisoners went mad under these conditions and regrouping began once again. The architectural image that embodied these ideals was Jeremy Bentham's Panopticon. Though never realized, this was reflected in the arrangement of the ill-fated penitentiary erected at Millbank in London, between 1812 and 1821. The aim was the continuous surveillance of all prisoners from a single observation post; the obvious expression of this was the radial plan. This was introduced into France in 1825, when Lebas, architect of Notre-Dame-de-Lorette, won a competition for a model prison on the site of La Roquette in Paris. Though he had visited Millbank, it is evident that he had not grasped its rationale. He produced a plan of giant formality, a hexagon with six wings linked to the center. There, he placed a chapel. Prison reformers soon realized that the building was unlikely to prove satisfactory. In 1830 a magistrate, G. de Beaumont, was sent with Alexis de Tocqueville to study prisons in America, where remarkably efficient systems of organization were being evolved, especially in Philadelphia. De Tocqueville spent too much time collecting material for *La démocratie en Amérique* (1835, 1840). By 1836 another tour of American prisons was needed; on this occasion the magistrate F. A. Demetz was provided with Blouet as his companion. At the same time Gilbert was appointed to design La Nouvelle Force at Mazas, together with Jean-François-Joseph Lecointe (1783–1858), an early associate of Hittorff. Work there started in 1843. The great period of prison reform had begun, and an architecture embodying the new humanitarian ideals was initiated.

Gilbert continued always to use the patterns of organization and the stylistic details that he had inherited from Durand, and so the change was not so much in any alteration of form or details as in a careful consideration of their use in relation to the function they were to perform. Nothing in Gilbert's architecture was done for effect. Everything had a straightforward raison d'être. His prison, which was opened in 1850, consisted of an administrative block linked to a domed rotunda—an observation post on one floor, a chapel on the next—from which radiated six wings at a forty-five-degree angle to one another, containing three floors of individual cells. Each cell was fully serviced with hot and cold water, a WC, and a heating and ventilation system. The organization of life in the prison determined

377. Émile-Jacques Gilbert, Asile d'Aliénés, Charenton, chapel, 1838–45.

378. Émile-Jacques Gilbert, Asile d'Aliénés, Charenton, courtyard.

379. Émile-Jacques Gilbert and Arthur-Stanislas Diet, Hôtel-Dieu, Paris, 1864–76.

380. Émile-Jacques Gilbert and Arthur-Stanislas Diet, Hôtel-Dieu, Paris, courtyard.

381. Guillaume-Abel Blouet, penal reform farm colony, Mettray, near Tours, plan, designed 1839.

the architecture in every way, as it had in that even more strictly utilitarian structure from which Gilbert derived many ideas, the Pentonville prison, put up in London between 1840 and 1842 by Major Joshua Jebb. But the prison at Mazas was not looked upon simply as a solution to some readily defined problem. "Le prison de Mazas," Adolphe Lance wrote in the *Encyclopédie d'architecture* in December 1853, "n'est pas exclusivement une bâtisse bien entendu et un instrument administratif, c'est une oeuvre d'art" (pp. 175–82).

Gilbert's other buildings were all expressions of humanitarian reform in administrative guise, often of the most repressive if well-meaning kind. The new theories on the treatment of the insane led to his appointment in 1838 as architect of the Asile d'Aliénés, built during the next seven years on the hillside at Charenton, to the east of Paris, in a series of long, terraced pavilions, linked by colonnades, with a chapel, as we have seen, forming the focus. The different types of madmen were isolated here within the individual pavilions, men to one side, women to the other. Police reforms resulted in Gilbert's Préfecture de la Police on the Île de la Cité in Paris, of 1862 to 1876. Hospital reforms produced his Hôtel-Dieu nearby, put up between 1864 and 1876 with the aid of his son-in-law, Arthur-Stanislas Diet (1827–1890), who also completed Gilbert's asylum and prefecture. By the time the Hôtel-Dieu was completed, the simple geometrical ideals of Durand had proved inadequate to such a building. Even before it was finished part was dismantled and much redesigned. The doctors were never to be satisfied. But the sheer regularity of the architecture, the elegance even of the colonnaded courts, are undeniably impressive. Gilbert's only other building was the morgue erected on the Pont St.-Michel, Paris, opposite the east end of Notre-Dame, from 1861 to 1863. This has long since been demolished.

Blouet pursued his utilitarian aims largely through teaching. In 1846, when L.-P. Baltard died, a change in approach was at last possible in the training at the École des Beaux-Arts, and Blouet was appointed to succeed him as *Professeur de Théorie de l'Architecture*. The following year he began publication of his *Supplément à la traité théorique et pratique de l'art de bâtir de Jean Rondelet*, which, as we have remarked, was largely a catalogue of early nineteenth-century engineering achievements. He was responsible for only one noteworthy work of architecture—a church at Fontainebleau and the attic story of the Arc de Triomphe apart—a penal farm colony at Mettray, near Tours, designed in 1839, finished a few years later. The architecture here consists of no more than a series of dull utilitarian dormitory pavilions set formally on either side of a nondescript church, mildly medieval in inspiration, with the farm buildings behind. Yet Michel Foucault has recognized the system of reform that was enacted within as the ultimate limit of coercion on humanitarian grounds. Blouet became thereby the accepted authority on prison architecture.

The remaining members of the group of reform, Duban, Labrouste, Duc, and Vaudoyer, were less doctrinaire in their attitudes: They upheld the ideals of Durand, Rondelet, and the Saint-Simonists but did not allow them full play in their architecture; they were more concerned to infuse them into a renewed classical tradition. All were Grand Prix winners, starting with Duban in 1823 and continuing to 1826, when Vaudoyer was awarded the prize. In Rome, Duban and Labrouste met Hittorff and Blouet; all of them met Gilbert, who served as their mentor. They formed a close-knit group and continued through life to collaborate and support one another. But their architecture revealed them as very different. Félix-Jacques Duban (1797–1870), who had trained under Percier, had a passion for intricate and lively surface decoration, though it is fair to note that he integrated it far more successfully into his compositions than did Hittorff. In 1832 he took over the building of the École des Beaux-Arts from his brother-in-law François Debret. The foundations were already laid, but the great building facing the court on the Rue Bonaparte is his. It is a compression of all his Italian learning. The triumphal arches of Rome, the Colosseum, and the Cancellaria are all hinted at in the facade; inside, the frescoes of Pompeii no less than those of Raphael are recalled. The glass-covered courtyard with its cast-iron columns was conceived and designed by Duban but put up only between 1871 and 1874 by Ernest-Georges Coquart. The court in front and at the side was equally an assemblage, of fragments of medieval and Renaissance buildings rescued by Alexandre Lenoir for the Musée des Monuments Français. The whole was inordinately admired when it was completed, in particular the attic floor (for which Labrouste served as *Inspecteur*) and the treatment of the roof, which was regarded as something of a novelty. This was hipped with a prettily detailed iron ridgepiece. Duban's reputation was made. But he did not build much else of consequence, though his superb Italianate house at 7 Rue Tronchet, Paris, for the Swiss collector the Comte Pourtalès, is deserving of study. Duban was active largely as a restorer, starting with the Ste.-Chapelle in 1837, tackling then in turn the Château de Blois, that at Fontainebleau, and then the Louvre, where some richly modeled and gilded rooms survive to attest to his activity, together with some forlorn railings in the corners of the courtyard, for which he was ridiculed and therefore resigned. But in 1858 he did design a building of some nobility and largeness of scale, the extension to the École des Beaux-Arts on the Quai Malaquais. Curiously, critics who had spent years castigating him for the fussiness of his details thought this too bald and bold.

382. *Félix-Jacques Duban, Hôtel Pourtalès, Paris, 1836.*

383. *Félix-Jacques Duban, Hôtel Pourtalès, Paris, staircase.*

384. *Félix-Jacques Duban, École des Beaux-Arts, Paris, forecourt, 1832–40.*

385. *Félix-Jacques Duban and Ernest-Georges Coquart, École des Beaux-Arts, Paris, covered interior courtyard, designed 1863, built 1871–74.*

386. *Félix-Jacques Duban, École des Beaux-Arts, Paris, facade on the Quai Malaquais, 1858–62.*

387. *Félix-Jacques Duban, Galerie d'Apollon, the Louvre, Paris, 1848–52.*

388. *Pierre-François-Henri Labrouste, Collège Ste.-Barbe, Bibliothèque Ste.-Geneviève, and Keeper's house, Paris, plans, 1840–50.*

389. *Pierre-François-Henri Labrouste, Bibliothèque Ste.-Geneviève, Paris, cross section, 1842–50.*

390. *Pierre-François-Henri Labrouste, Bibliothèque Ste.-Geneviève, Paris, facade.*

391. *Pierre-François-Henri Labrouste, Bibliothèque Ste.-Geneviève, Paris, detail of the facade.*

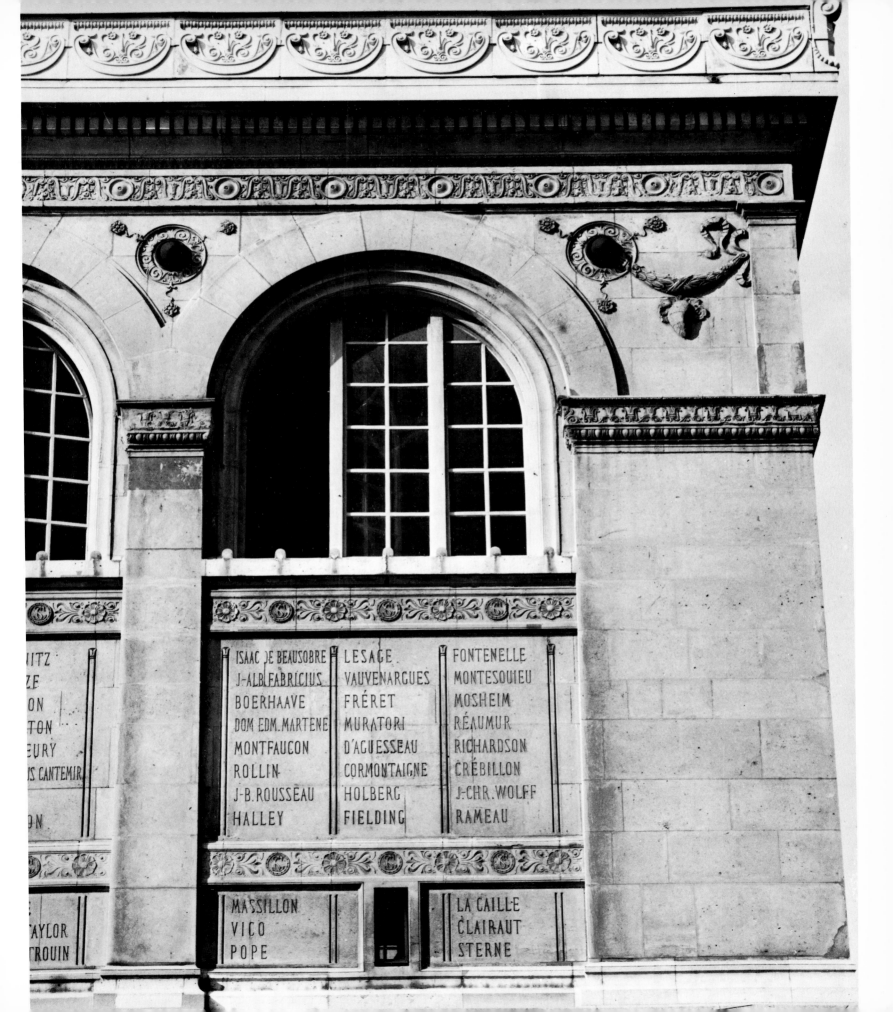

NITZ
ZE
ON
TON
EURY
S CANTEMIR

ON

ISAAC DE BEAUSOBRE   LESAGE   FONTENELLE
J.-ALB. FABRICIUS   VAUVENARGUES   MONTESQUIEU
BOERHAAVE   FRÉRET   MOSHEIM
DOM EDM. MARTENE   MURATORI   RÉAUMUR
MONTFAUCON   D'AGUESSEAU   RICHARDSON
ROLLIN   CORMONTAIGNE   CRÉBILLON
J.-B. ROUSSEAU   HOLBERG   J.-CHR. WOLFF
HALLEY   FIELDING   RAMEAU

TAYLOR
TROUIN

MASSILLON   LA CAILLE
VICO   CLAIRAUT
POPE   STERNE

Pierre-François-Henri Labrouste (1801–1875) was an architect of greater consistency and refinement, and of far greater stature. The beginning of his active career, however, was to be long delayed. He was a student of Lebas and A.-L.-T. Vaudoyer but was not prepared to accept their academic ideals without the most painstaking independent investigation. In 1824 he won the Grand Prix with a design for a *tribunal de cassation*. In 1828 he sent, as his fourth-year *envoi* from Rome, a restoration study of the three Doric temples of Paestum. His meticulous measurements proved that C. M. Delagardette's *Ruines de Paestum*, of 1799, was altogether untrustworthy. This was an affront to academic dignity. Labrouste went further: He developed a theory on the history of the people who had built the temples and showed how their social aspirations were reflected in their architecture. One of the buildings, he argued, was not a temple, but a civic structure. He illustrated this, hip-roofed—decked with large paintings, trophies, and inscriptions—as Jean Houel had done many years earlier, in 1787, in a restoration study of one of the Doric temples of Agrigento, illustrated in the fourth volume of his *Voyage pittoresque des îles de Sicile, de Malte, et de Lipari*. But Labrouste went further; he added graffiti. He wished to penetrate to the reality of the architecture, to present the buildings as they might really have existed. Naturally, he applied color. Many of his assumptions were wrong, but what roused the members of the Académie to fury was his deliberate dismissal of the ideal. And he compounded this rude rejection of established criteria in the following year, sending in as his fifth-year *envoi* a design for a frontier bridge between Italy and France that was modeled on a coarse Roman provincial work, the Flavian bridge at St.-Chamas, near Marseilles. For almost ten years the members of the Académie saw to it that he received no major commission. He became a student idol, and for twenty-six years from 1830 directed the most austerely intellectual *atelier* in Paris. Not one of his students won the Grand Prix. During this time he entered and won a number of competitions for utilitarian buildings, a Hospice d'Aliénés at Lausanne in 1837, a prison for Alessandria, Italy, in 1840, and an *abattoir* in Provins in 1841. None of these was built. His opportunity came in October 1838, when he was appointed architect to the new Bibliothèque Ste.-Geneviève, facing Soufflot's great church. There were difficulties over the acquisition of the site, but in January 1840 Labrouste's initial scheme was approved in principle, though the revisions were not settled for another two years and money not voted until 1843. A final plan was approved in July 1844 after work on the foundations had begun. The building, completed in December 1850, is very simple in arrangement. It is a long rectangle, entered on the ground floor, with stack rooms to the left, offices and rare books to the right. At the rear of the building is a separate stair hall leading up to the reading room, which occupies the whole of the upper level. This is a room of great dignity. The effect is achieved by means of a completely independent system of cast-iron columns and arches arranged to provide two long narrow naves, a spine down the center, hinting at the "civic" temple at Paestum and also at the medieval refectory at the former Abbaye de St.-Martin-des-Champs, Paris, which his pupil Lassus had recently measured and which his friend Léon Vaudoyer was about to turn into a library for the Conservatoire des Arts et Métiers—an echo, one must assume, of Saint-Simonist theory. There is, of course, nothing overtly Gothic about Labrouste's detailing. This, if anything, recalls his visits to Pompeii. The exterior is even more noble and purified. The arches inside are reflected in the arched openings of the upper floor—windows above, infilling panels below, each of which is, in turn, punctured by a small window to light the small workrooms arranged on the perimeter within. The ground floor is pierced by a row of round-headed windows and an equally reticent rounded doorway, decorated only with lamps of learning. The division between the two floors was at first marked by no more than a strong horizontal molding, but the members of the *Conseil Général des Bâtiments Civils* thought this too sharp. When the stack rooms were raised nineteen centimeters (seven and one-half inches) Labrouste introduced the frieze of garlands, which echoes that on the Panthéon opposite and, more important, provides just that degree of movement required to render the facade less static. The silhouette is strong and square. On either side Labrouste designed two buildings that show how he could vary his arrangements to relate to their functions and yet ensure a unified whole. To the east are the staff quarters (1847–48); to the west the Collège Ste.-Barbe (1845–47), his old school, of which one of his brothers was head. Another brother, Théodore Labrouste (1799–1885), collaborated with him here as architect.

The facade of the Bibliothèque Ste.-Geneviève is altogether Labrouste's own—though it should be remarked how closely it relates to that of the École de Dessin, nearby, at 8 Rue Racine, designed and built between 1841 and 1844 by Simon-Claude Constant-Dufeux (1801–1871), soon to be appointed *Professeur de Perspective* at the École des Beaux-Arts. Labrouste's facade, however, contains mnemonic references to many others that he had admired: Sir Christopher Wren's library at Cambridge; Leon Battista Alberti's Tempio Malatestiano in Rimini; Michelozzo's Banco Mediceo in Milan; and Jacopo Sansovino's Biblioteca Marciana in Venice. Even Egyptian temples are said to be embodied therein. This distillation of knowledge, which we have seen to lie also at the heart of Duban's work, was to be regarded as Labrouste's great contribution. From it, Neil Levine has suggested, was to spring that movement known somewhat inaccurately as the *néo-grec*. This flourished in France in the 1870s, though as late as 1911 the English architect A. E. Richardson was writing of it in the *Architectural Review* as the basis of renewal: "The true *néo-grec* style is the epitome of design, its interest a reflection of the tireless mind of the designer, who, having obtained a great many ideas on his subject, melts these very ideas in the crucible of his imagination, refining them again and again until the minted metal gleams refulgent. All material is the same to such a one. By these means and these alone, is original design possible" (July 1911, p. 28).

Labrouste did indeed succeed in restoring to nineteenth-century architecture some of the classic wholeness of that of the Greeks, but he aimed at a larger synthesis. He used his lifts, his heating and lighting systems, and his cast-iron columns not for utilitarian reasons alone, nor even to shock (though he did), but in order to relate his building organically to a nineteenth-century industrialized society, of which it

397. *Pierre-François-Henri Labrouste, Bibliothèque Nationale, Paris, main reading room, 1859–68.*

was to be a noble expression. He intended it to represent the moment of achievement in a third organic period of architecture (the Saint-Simonists, as we have seen, had recognized two others, the Doric Greek and the Gothic). Neil Levine has recently shown that to make quite explicit his aim he decided in August 1848—just after the riots of July that marked the end of the July Monarchy, and just after the publication of the *Discours sur l'ensemble du positivisme* by Auguste Comte, Saint-Simon's renegade disciple—to inscribe the names of the authors whose works were contained within the library on the panels of the facade, arranging them in chronological order from Moses to Berzelius (a Swedish chemist much admired at the time, to whom Michel Eugène Chevreul, for instance, had dedicated his book on color theory), illustrating the progress of humanity from monotheism to scientism. The name of Psellus is in the center just over the door, marking the meeting of east and west, the central stage in the history of metaphysics as outlined by Comte. The carving was completed in two months. The Bibliothèque Ste.-Geneviève thus became, demonstrably, a temple of all learning, a beginning of the new way. The letters were painted red.

Three years after completion, in 1853, Labrouste was appointed to succeed L.-T.-J. Visconti as architect at the Bibliothèque Nationale. He tidied up the existing conglomeration with skill and ruthlessness; then, in 1859, he began work on the main reading room, filling part of the court for which Boullée had prepared his designs. This was Labrouste's second masterpiece. But magnificent as it is, it represents no more than an extension of ideas already worked out to perfection at the Bibliothèque Ste.-Geneviève. Only his stack room, tiered galleries of cast iron, built between 1862 and 1867, shows him grappling to renewed effect with his initiatory themes. This, to early twentieth-century eyes, was his greatest creation. Even his contemporaries admired it, and for much the same reasons. "Tout," Louis-Auguste Boileau wrote in 1871 in *Le fer,* "jusqu'au moindre boulon et rivet, devient un objet d'art de nouvelle création."

Labrouste's other works need not detain us: a handful of tombs; a farm colony at Mesnil-St.-Fermin (1845–48); a large and dull seminary at Rennes (1854–72; now the Faculté des Lettres), whose construction he did not supervise; a house for the banker Louis Fould (1856–58; now gone), another for M. Vilgruy (1860–65; still standing at 9 Rue François 1er, Paris), and the Hôtel Rouvenat (1861; now gone) at Neuilly-sur-Seine, all three disappointing pastiches of the architecture of Louis XIII's reign; a small boxlike villa for a jeweler, M. Thouret (1860; still standing, though altered, at 68 Boulevard Bourdon, Neuilly-sur-Seine); and the Hôtel de l'Administration du Chemin de Fer PLM, Paris (1861–63; 44 Rue Neuves-des-Ma-

398. *Pierre-François-Henri Labrouste, Bibliothèque Nationale, Paris, detail of one of the cast-iron columns supporting the vault in the main reading room, 1859–68.*

399. *Pierre-François-Henri Labrouste, Hôtel Vilgruy, Paris, 1860–65.*
400. *Louis-Joseph Duc, Palais de Justice, Paris, facade on the Rue de Harlay, 1857–68.*

thurins), which he did not complete and which was torn down in part within a few years.

Louis-Joseph Duc (1802–1879) and Léon Vaudoyer (1803–1872) were, like Labrouste, to pour their energies into no more than one or two buildings. On his return from Rome in 1831, Duc became *Inspecteur* of the July Column, in the Place de la Bastille, under Jean-Antoine Alavoine (1778–1834). Soon he succeeded to the commission and at once started to apply decoration to Alavoine's sheer shaft. For the inauguration, in 1840, he designed some temporary pavilions, Greek in inspiration, brightly painted in yellow and red. In the same year he took over the work of completing the Palais de Justice in Paris. He did a great deal there, but the focus of all his effort was the Salle des Pas Perdus, referred to also as the Vestibule d'Assises, on the Rue de Harlay. This was started in 1857 and finished eleven years later, though much rebuilt and changed internally after damage suffered in 1870. Its hipped and heavily encrusted roof relates it at once to Duban's first building at the École des Beaux-Arts; its rhythmical bays, glazed above and filled in below with panels bearing inscriptions, link it to the Bibliothèque Ste.-Geneviève. But Duc wanted no fusion of structure, form, and expression. The structure—the arched vaulting within, the enclosing walls pierced with flattened arched openings—was to be seen and expressed as a humdrum working part of the architecture; the poetry, and all that mattered, were to arise from the artistic handling of an independent system of decoration, set in contradistinction to the rest. An array of columns derived from the Doric order, the highest form of expression in architecture, was thus set as a sculptural element in front of the wall. There was much more to Duc's composition—recollections of the Temple of Hathor in Egypt, details borrowed from the Temple of Athena Nike—but they need not be discussed. He aimed, clearly, to separate the practical and the expressive elements in architecture. And he was acclaimed. Viollet-le-Duc himself sat on the committee that awarded him the Prix de Cent Mille Francs in 1869 for the greatest work of art produced in France during the century.

Léon Vaudoyer made no such startling contribution to the development of architecture. He was closer to Labrouste, with whom he had been at school, and was said to be an intellectual, though we have little evidence of this. In 1838 he began work with his father, A.-L.-T. Vaudoyer, on the transformation of St.-Martin-des-Champs into the Conservatoire des Arts et Métiers. Work continued for years, right up to 1897, but it is of no great distinction or interest. The effects are contrived and awkward. But in 1845, the same year in which he took over from his father at St.-Martin-des-Champs, he prepared the first designs for his most important work, the cathedral at Marseilles.

Its horizontal banding appeared on his drawings only in 1852, a year after John Ruskin had published the *Stones of Venice*. Ruskin's influence here would be unlikely, though the cathedral is an extraordinarily eclectic work. Vaudoyer's range of sources here was wider, and also more overt in expression, than that employed by his friends. The plan is thirteenth-century Gothic; the forms and many of the details are Byzantine. But the most notable influence of all is that of the Florence

235

401. *Louis-Joseph Duc, Palais de Justice, Paris, Salle des Pas Perdus,*
1857–68.

402. *Léon Vaudoyer, cathedral, Marseilles, 1845, 1852–93.*
403. *Léon Vaudoyer, cathedral, Marseilles, interior.*

cathedral. Vaudoyer, less self-sure perhaps than Labrouste, aimed to provide an exemplar of a new architecture on the very threshold of an "organic period," at the end of an age of transition. He built on the basis of a Gothic plan because it was typically French. He selected Byzantine details because that style was a prelude to Gothic (he saw the pointed arch as a simple development of the arcade) and early Renaissance architecture because it marked the transition from an ecclesiastical authority to that of classical humanism. He had added, it seems, the Renaissance to the succession of "époques organiques" recognized by the Saint-Simonists. The result of all this thought and learning is not particularly impressive. Vaudoyer had insufficient feeling for the forms he was handling and assembled them without conviction. The building up of the docks alongside the cathedral has not enhanced its splendor, though in the interior something of the grand and thoughtfully—often brightly—colored architecture that he envisioned may still be experienced. The cathedral, finished only in 1893, was not much imitated in France, although echoes of it occur in the French colonies on the southern shores of the Mediterranean. And in Marseilles itself, Vaudoyer's pupil and assistant Henri-Jacques Espérandieu (1829–1874) took it as the point of departure for his first independent work of importance, the ungainly Notre-Dame-de-la-Garde (1853–64), which dominates the hill on the other side of the port. Vaudoyer's precepts, if we are to judge by Espérandieu's later buildings, all in Marseilles, were not of the stirring kind, nor were they sustaining. In 1858 Espérandieu started to design the Bibliothèque Municipale; four years later he began the flamboyant and highly ostentatious Palais de Longchamp, taking over ideas suggested a few years earlier by the sculptor Frédéric-Auguste Bartholdi. There was an ugly court case, but Espérandieu was exonerated. He went on, in 1862, to build the École des Beaux-Arts, which was a coarsened and undisciplined variant of Duban's; then followed the observatory and the *abattoir*. His works were florid and attractive only from afar; they give evidence of neither skill in design nor sustained intellectual effort.

Vaudoyer was no doubt aware of his inability to give convincing form to his ideas. He avoided building as long as he could—traveling at length in Germany, England, Spain, and Algeria, refusing many commissions—and was equally hesitant in expressing himself in writing. All his friends were agreed that he had thought long and hard about architecture, but he published no book on the subject, though he did contribute to such Romantic journals as the *Journal des artistes* and *Le magasin pittoresque* and, after its founding in 1840, to the *Revue générale de l'architecture et des travaux publics*. Indeed, his chief claim to fame is to have coined the term *architecture parlante* to describe the works of Ledoux, which he reviewed in *Le magasin pittoresque* in

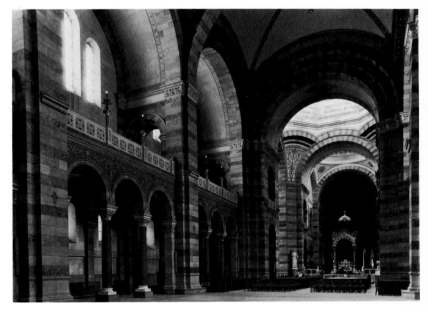

December 1852 (p. 388). He was intrigued, but did not approve. Ledoux's symbolism was to him too blatant by far.

The influence of the architects we have been considering was strongly felt in the second half of the century, in instigating both a more thoughtful eclecticism and a greater concern for precision in planning, engineering, and the design of details. Inevitably these

404. *Charles-Auguste Questel (attributed), Palais de Justice, Nîmes, begun 1838.*
405, 406. *Victor Baltard and Félix-Emmanuel Callet, Halles Centrales, Paris, exterior and interior, 1853–57.*

became richer and, in the hands of the less strictly trained architects, were debased and vulgarized. Espérandieu is a case in point. However, the career of Charles-Auguste Questel (1807–1888), a pupil of both Blouet and Duban, who himself worked on the largest scale at Nîmes (where he first noticed Espérandieu), at Grenoble, and at Paris, may be adduced to show a contrary process at work. On the whole, however, the extent and the pace of building during the Second Empire served to degenerate architecture; the rational tradition was disastrously weakened. But a few—very few—architects were able to turn this to their advantage. It became in their hands a liberating stimulus.

The greatest period of activity in the history of French architecture was initiated on June 22, 1853, when Baron Georges-Eugène Haussmann (1809–1891) succeeded Amédée Berger as *Préfet de la Seine*. On June 29, seven days after his appointment, Haussmann was called to St.-Cloud and shown a plan with the emperor's personal proposals for the remaking of Paris marked down in blue, red, yellow, and green, according to their relative urgency. It was this plan that Haussmann carried out in the years that followed. Paris was to be "la capitale des capitales." The city was virtually rebuilt. Streets and boulevards were opened up and lined with regular facades. The destruction was terrible. At intersections and focal points great public buildings and churches were erected; within the first ten years of Haussmann's administration more than fifteen large churches had been begun, and ten more were to follow. Almost all the old bridges over the Seine were rebuilt and five new ones begun. Markets were erected, including the great Halles Centrales. The latter were started afresh as an iron construction in 1853 by the architects Victor Baltard (1805–1874) and Félix-Emmanuel Callet (1792–1854). The Bois de Boulogne (1853–58), the Bois de Vincennes (1858–60), the Parc Monceau (1860–62), the Parc des Buttes-Chaumont (1864–67), the Parc de Montsouris (1867–68), and no fewer than thirty new squares were laid out and embellished with pavilions, railings, and appropriate street furniture. The streets were lighted by gas and the drainage system extended. Water in quantity was brought into the city. By the end of the Second Empire there were sixty public fountains in Paris. Paris itself was extended. On January 1, 1860, Passy, Auteuil, Les Batignolles-Monceau, Montmartre, La Chapelle, La Villette, Belleville, Charonne, Bercy, Vaugirard, and Grenelle were formally incorporated within the city. A few years later the building of *mairies* in these new *arrondissements* was begun. But from all this ferment only one or two names of interest emerge.

Haussmann, like his patron Louis-Napoleon, was a man of much common sense but less than common sensibility. Moreover, he mistrusted architects. He chose as his collaborators Eugène Belgrand

407. *Victor Baltard and Félix-Emmanuel Callet, Halles Centrales, Paris.*

(1810–1878), Maillebiau, and Jean-Charles-Adolphe Alphand (1817–1891), members all of the École des Ponts et Chaussées. Baullet-Deschamps, the only trusted architect, acted as surveyor of roads. Victor Baltard, who had won the Grand Prix in 1833, was appointed *Architecte en Chef de la Ville de Paris* and in that capacity redecorated and rebuilt a host of churches; but apart from the Halles Centrales and the church of St.-Augustin (1860–71), with cast-iron columns inside, he has little claim to architectural recognition. Hector-Martin

Lefuel (1810–1880), a pupil of Jean-Nicolas Huyot (1780–1840), was employed to reconstruct the Louvre and to link it finally to the Tuileries. He started in 1854, modestly enough, executing the plan that Visconti had left, but within a few years was piling sculpture and ornament onto the building with an exuberance that would have shocked Visconti. Lefuel's work was hurried and ill considered, but much appreciated in court circles. In 1853 he was commissioned to build the theater at Fontainebleau—which he designed in the eighteenth-century style that he had already introduced into the Salle des États in the Louvre.

Haussmann appointed Antoine-Nicolas-Louis Bailly (1810–1892), a pupil of Debret and Duban, to design the Tribunal de Commerce (1858–64), adapted at the emperor's request from the town hall at Brescia. Bailly's other important building of the period, the Mairie du IVe (1862–67), is no less pompous, if more prosaic. Théodore Ballu (1817–1885), a contractor's son and a disciple of Lebas, emerged also at this time. He completed Franz Christian Gau's Gothic pastiche Ste.-Clotilde, restored the Tour St.-Jacques, and, between Hittorff's Mairie du Ier and St.-Germain-l'Auxerrois, built that absurd tower that won for the ensemble the nickname of "porte-huilier." In 1861 he began work on La Trinité, a well-sited and richly adorned but not in the least impressive church. The Renaissance vaulting is all of *papier-mâché.* Ballu built several other churches. But of all the new architects employed by Haussmann only one produced anything of more than marginal worth, Gabriel-Jean-Antoine Davioud (1823–1881). His buildings are well considered and possessed always of some straightforward merit, though they are undeniably dull. He studied for three years at the École de Dessin, perhaps under Viollet-le-Duc, then in 1841 entered the *atelier* of Vaudoyer. His studies completed, he began work with Victor Baltard on the Halles Centrales, and on his recommendation was made *Inspecteur des Promenades* and put in charge of the Service des Fontaines. For Alphand he put up a host of pavilions and lodges in the Bois de Boulogne between 1855 and 1859, all intentionally Picturesque in an English sort of way, with an admixture of the Swiss-chalet style (one chalet was brought direct from Berne). Equally ambitiously, he worked at the Bois de Vincennes, the Parc des Buttes-Chaumont, and the Parc Monceau, where his showy grilles, inspired by those of Emmanuel Héré at Nancy, are particularly deserving of praise. For the Champs-Élysées, in 1857, he designed a new circus and panorama, still standing, a building of less structural quality than Hittorff's. Then, in the following year, he designed the first of his four great fountains, the Fontaine St.-Michel at the beginning of the Boulevard St.-Michel, a mass of metal and stone that was both praised and rudely dismissed. Charles Darcel remarked in the *Gazette des beaux-arts* in 1860, "C'est une oeuvre banale, sans signification et sans caractère" (p. 44), but César-Denis Daly (1811–1893), influential editor of the *Revue générale de l'architecture*, thought far too much of it. Later came the Fontaine de Château d'Eau (1867–74); the Fontaine de l'Observatoire (1870–75), with figures by Jean-Baptiste Carpeaux; and the Fontaine de la Place du Théâtre-Français (1872–74). In 1860 Davioud started on two mammoth theaters, the Théâtre du Châtelet and the Théâtre Lyrique (now Théâtre de la

Ville), both completed within two years. Darcel was as brutal in his comments as before; Daly published a magnificent monograph on the buildings. They are undeniably grand and were not uncomfortable, but as architecture they are altogether indigestible.

The Magasins Réunis, on the Place de la République, begun in April 1865 and completed in January 1867, are likewise adequate up to the point they reached and are distinguished by their planning and structural organization above much of the architecture of the time;

◁412. *Antoine-Nicolas-Louis Bailly, Tribunal de Commerce, Paris, staircase, 1858–64.*

413. *Antoine-Nicolas-Louis Bailly, Tribunal de Commerce, Paris.*

414. *Antoine-Nicolas-Louis Bailly, Mairie du IVe, Paris, 1862–67.*

415. *Gabriel-Jean-Antoine Davioud, Théâtre du Châtelet, Paris, 1860–62.*

416. *Gabriel-Jean-Antoine Davioud, Théâtre Lyrique (now Théâtre de la Ville), Paris, 1860–62.*

but that is all. As such later works as the Mairie du XIXe (1876–78) and the vast Palais du Trocadéro (1876–78) attest, Davioud was a thoughtful and extremely industrious architect who gave a great deal of attention to fine, finished detail. But he was incapable of communicating through architecture the feelings that had originally impelled him to take it up.

Many of Haussmann's architects were uninspired. Yet men such as Davioud were influential and widely imitated. And it would be a mistake to think that they achieved nothing in the field of architec-

ture and landscape design. The Parc des Buttes-Chaumont is a wonderfully rich amalgam of the traditional Picturesque and the railway age. The train tracks running alongside the park are integrated with perfect fluency into the landscape design, as is the vast panorama of the industrialized city. The new vistas and spaces that Haussmann gave to Paris, moreover, demanded a new breadth of scale and a grandness of public performance that one architect at least was able to perceive and respond to. This man was Jean-Louis-Charles Garnier (1825–1898). He expressed both the ostentation and the power of the

417. *Jean-Charles-Adolphe Alphand and Gabriel-Jean-Antoine Da-vioud, Parc des Buttes-Chaumont, Paris, 1864–67.*
418. *Jean-Charles-Adolphe Alphand and Gabriel-Jean-Antoine Davioud, Parc des Buttes-Chaumont, Paris, suspension bridge.*

and Louis Duc. Garnier was fifth. In the second stage of the competition Garnier was unanimously acclaimed. Garnaud died soon after, of grief, it was said. Ginain never forgave Garnier. The empress was furious. When he went to the Tuileries to show her his project, she exclaimed, "Qu'est cela, ce n'est pas un style; ce n'est ni du Louis XIV, ni du Louis XV, ni du Louis XVI." Garnier had his reply. "Madame," he said, "c'est du Napoléon III, et vous plaignez" (*Bulletin de la Société de l'Histoire de l'Art Français*, 1941–44, p. 83). Garnier thus gave a name to the style but, though the empress became reconciled, the building was not much admired by Louis-Napoleon, who visited it only once, in 1862, when he laid the foundation stone. The gala opening did not take place until January 5, 1875, more than four years after the battle of Sedan.

The most illuminating comments on the building were made by Garnier himself, first in *Le théâtre*, published in 1871, in which he outlined his aims, then in the texts to the two magnificently colored folios of *Le nouvel Opéra de Paris*, issued in 1878 and 1881, in which he judged of his success. He was clear and frank in all his explanations, sometimes facetious, never pretentious. He saw the Opéra as the embodiment of man's most primitive instincts: that of gathering together in ceremony around the campfire to share thoughts and dreams, to hear and to see and be seen. The spectacle was thus not to be enacted on the stage alone; theater involved all encounters, all actions. The spectators themselves were actors. And Garnier described in detail how he had fashioned his architecture with these ideas in mind. The Opéra was the entire society of the Second Empire. There were, of course, distinctions between different categories of people—those who paid more and those who paid less—and the part of each in the ritual was clearly assessed and defined. If one came by carriage or foot, there was a sequence prepared, and also a place for intermingling—even though this might be at a distance. Even the act of queuing for tickets was considered a part of the ceremony. Care was lavished on every detail. In the main foyer there were mirrors set into the columns so that women might glance at themselves and make last-minute adjustments to their dress or expressions before entering the great stair hall, a climax to the architecture. Here all excitement, all passion, was stirred. Here society disported itself in its splendor; people saw and were seen as they passed in procession up the stairs—which were copied, Garnier happily admitted, from Victor Louis's at Bordeaux. The lesser members of society watched from on high. The spectacle, the stuffs, the scents, and the diamonds were no less part of the architecture than the marbles, the draperies, and the chandeliers. "La lumière qui étincelera," he wrote in *Le théâtre*, "les toilettes qui resplendirent, les figures qui seront animées et souriantes,

Second Empire with such intensity and candid freshness when he built the Opéra that it is almost impossible not to be enthralled by it. Certainly he changed thereby the direction of French architecture.

For two years Charles Rohault de Fleury worked under the emperor's personal direction on the design of the new opera house; then, in 1860 he was suddenly dismissed, in order, it was widely thought, that the empress's favorite, Viollet-le-Duc, might be appointed architect. We may be thankful that Viollet-le-Duc proposed a competition instead. One hundred and eventy-one sentries were submitted, including one from the empress. Early in 1861 the winners in the first stage were announced. Paul-René-Léon Ginain was first; second came Botrel and Adolphe-Nicolas Crepinet, then Antoine-Martin Garnaud

419. *Jean-Louis-Charles Garnier, the Opéra, Paris, plan, 1862–75.*
420. *Jean-Louis-Charles Garnier, the Opéra, Paris, longitudinal section.*
421. *Jean-Louis-Charles Garnier, the Opéra, Paris.*

foyers, the stairs seem to provide the best of all possible ceremonial approaches to the auditorium, itself, sadly, one of the least remarkable features of this remarkable building. Garnier agreed, but, as always, he had his explanation. The auditorium, he said, would seem to be the natural climax for the architecture, yet when it was most in use attention was necessarily directed at the spectacle on the stage. The auditorium was then in semidarkness. Only for relatively short periods was it brilliantly lit and vibrant, but the audience was then static, and when the people moved they moved inevitably to the foyers and stairs, where they could enact their communal ceremonies with greater freedom. The lobbies and corridors were thus made larger than ever before, with areas for sitting, and with smoking rooms for the men (with fire and sun motifs) and ice cream parlors for the women (with lunar motifs). The decoration throughout was sumptuous. There was color everywhere, inside and out. Salviati the glassmakers' fortune was soon made. "Alors," Garnier wrote in *Le nouvel Opéra*, "vous ferez vos maisons moins blanches . . ." (vol. 1, p. 18).

Garnier rejoiced in his achievement. It expressed, he said, as all good architecture should, his entire personality: "J'ai beau chercher en parcourant le grand vestibule du nouvel Opéra, si je verrai quelques défauts à signaler; ma recherche est vaine, et je ne trouve vraiment rien à regretter dans cette partie du monument" (*Le nouvel Opéra*, vol. 1, p. 215). This, like other such pronouncements by the architect, is no more than a statement of fact. Garnier well knew how to satisfy practical requirements: He dismissed the heating and ventilating engineers who had worked on the Châtelet theaters because they thought of the Opéra only as a duct, and designed all this part himself, as well as the stage machinery and structure; and he searched France until he found marble blocks large enough for the columns in the stair hall. But he also understood how to achieve the maximum possibilities of architecture. He knew exactly when to be extravagant with space, with form, or with decoration. There is nothing coarse or vulgar about his building, as some of his contemporaries thought and as many people since have declared who believe themselves to have good taste. Le Corbusier detested it. Garnier could play with consummate mastery and gusto with most of those sacrosanct essentials of architecture—mass, rhythm, texture, and outline—and achieve a splendidly unified character. The silhouette of the Opéra when viewed from the Avenue de l'Opéra is superb. Even Haussmann admired it to the extent of eliminating the trees that were planned to line the avenue. The facade itself, massive and heavily decorated and gilded, is yet monumental in the best possible sense of the word; it possesses, as Garnier himself remarked, a considered dignity. "C'est l'art qui y séjourne," he wrote in *Le nouvel Opéra*, "et l'art ne doit pas être enta-

les rencontres qui se produiront, les saluts qui s'échangeront, tout aura un air de fête et de plaisir, et sans se rendre compte de la part qui doit revenir à l'architecture dans cet effet magique, tout le monde en jouira et tout le monde rendra ainsi, par son impression heureuse, hommage à ce grand art, si puissant dans ses manifestations, si élevé dans ses résultats".

The flights of Garnier's stairs soar with perfect fluency through the stair hall, they are at once easy and satisfying, yet they provide just that degree of surprise and excitement needed in all artistic success. There is a tension in every form. With their related corridors and

426. *Jean-Louis-Charles Garnier, Cercle de la Librairie, Paris, 1878–79.*
427. *Jean-Louis-Charles Garnier, Maison Hachette, Paris, plan of the second floor, 1882.*

428. *Jean-Louis-Charles Garnier, Maison Hachette, Paris.*
429. *Jean-Louis-Charles Garnier, Maison Hachette, Paris, elevation.*

ché de pruderie; il faut seulement que la richesse soit quelque peu digne, parce que si l'art peut danser la gavotte ou le menuet, il doit se garder du cancan" (vol. 1, p. 23). He did not even object to bad taste if there was in it passion and warmth.

All that Garnier did and admired was conditioned by his classical training. As a young man, a pupil of Lebas, he had won the Grand Prix with a design for a Conservatoire des Arts et Métiers, similar in style to the buildings Questel was later to build at Grenoble. He had developed these quattrocento and cinquecento tastes in Florence itself, where the Académie de France had moved from Rome under threat of attack from Garibaldi's army. But he undertook Roman studies as well—Trajan's Column and the Temple of Vesta—and later traveled to Sicily with the Duc de Luynes. In 1852, at the end of a three-year stay in Italy, when still a young man of twenty-eight, he traveled to Greece with Théophile Gautier and with Edmond About, who was later to write his account of the journey in *La Grèce contemporaine*. In Greece, Garnier felt, he perceived for the first time the true quality of classical architecture. He saw that there was emotion and human life latent in it, and a harmony and meaning not present in mere building: "Plaine de l'Attique, rocher de Minerve," he wrote in 1869 in *À travers les arts*, "c'est en vous voyant que j'ai compris la puissance magique de l'art et la majesté de l'architecture antique . . ." (p. 268). But his vision of Greek architecture was not that of Winckelmann. His restoration study of the Temple of Jupiter Panhellenius at Aegina was vibrantly colored, the columns in yellow, the walls of the cella and the architraves and friezes all bright red, with the metopes picked out in blue. There was, he admitted, no justification for this, other than that it pleased him. Between the columns were rich bronze grilles, once again no part of archaeological study.

Garnier always remained faithful to this Mediterranean inheritance; it was part of a world of smiling intelligence, unruffled by calculation and hardheaded need. In all his buildings he sought to stir this sense of buoyant ease and success. It is apparent in the Cercle de la Librairie (1878–79) at 117 Boulevard St.-Germain and, further along, in No. 195, the Maison Hachette (1882), a lavishly planned block of apartments; even more in those buildings he put up along the Riviera—a hotel, a school, a church, the Villa Bischoffsheim, and his own house at Bordighera; in the observatory at Nice; but most especially in the theater and casino at Monte Carlo, begun in 1878. This, before its gradual alteration, was another radiant masterpiece.

As a student, even before he entered the École des Beaux-Arts, Garnier had studied under Viollet-le-Duc at the École de Dessin (where he met Carpeaux, who was to design *Les Danseuses* for the Opéra). Later he worked as an assistant to Viollet-le-Duc, but he

251

432. *Jean-Louis-Charles Garnier, Casino, Monte Carlo, 1878–79. Extended by Schmit.*

433. *Paul-René-Léon Ginain, École de Medécine, Paris, facade on the Boulevard St.-Germain, 1878–1900.*

434. *Paul-Henri Nénot, Nouvelle Sorbonne, Paris, the great amphi-theater, 1885–91.*

came, as must be already evident, to reject all that Viollet-le-Duc stood for. He dismissed his architecture readily enough, together with that of all Viollet-le-Duc's followers: "On hésite dans l'appréciation de ses oeuvres plus personelles. Est-ce un souvenir du passé? Est-ce un essai de novation? Cela est difficile à dire" (À travers les arts, p. 48). And he went much further even in rejecting his theories: "Le raisonnement a priori est donc inutile, puis qu'il se produit inconsciemment. Il serait nuisible s'il voulait remplacer le sentiment et prendre la première place au detriment de la main qui opére et les yeux qui jugent. C'est pour cela que je repousse instinctivement et volontairement l'école utilitaire qui, voulant remplacer l'école de l'impression, part du raisonnement seul et, mal guidée dans son choix, repoussant le contrôle du sentiment, tombe à tout instant dans le faux et produit sous le spécieux prétexte de logique, des oeuvres bâtardes et incohérentes" (Le théâtre, p. 414). This was a theme he returned to again and again. He saw no future in an architecture based on rationalism, on science, on engineering, least of all on new materials: "Je le dis tout de suite, c'est là une erreur, et une grande erreur: le fer est un moyen, ce ne serais jamais une principe" (À travers les arts, p. 75). But if he was thus rejecting Viollet-le-Duc and his admirers, he was renouncing also that framework of reason, that particular thoughtfulness and concern, that had sustained the classical tradition in France. With Viollet-le-Duc were eliminated Durand, Rondelet, Gilbert, Blouet, and Labrouste. Certainly, Garnier did not expect that an artist should have moral or political convictions, or, if he had, that they should be allowed to inflect his work. One could not, he said, begin with fixed ideas, with any theory at all. The imagination must be allowed free play in works of creation. The rationale, if such was required, could be invented later.

If Garnier's works had not been so obviously successful, such statements would not have mattered. But the example of his easy mastery served, effectively, to destroy the thoughtful tradition of French architecture. His buildings were widely imitated, both inside and out. Opera houses all over the world commemorate his. An Italian, Squadrelli, conflated it with the Monte Carlo casino, throwing an admixture of Secessionist ironwork on top, to provide the local casino for San Pellegrino at the turn of the century. The result, as may be expected, was dreadful. Very few men possessed Garnier's talents. In France careful and serious architects did make a determined attempt to restore to the classical tradition its measured dignity and its system of belief: among them, E.-G. Coquart (1831–1902), Henri-Adolphe-Auguste Deglane (1855–1931), P.-R.-L. Ginain (1825–1898), Charles-Louis Girault (1851–1932), Julien-Azais Guadet (1834–1908), Victor-Alexandre-Frédéric Laloux (1850–1937), Paul-Henri Nénot

(1853–1934), and Jean-Louis Pascal (1837–1920). Guadet, Nénot, and Pascal, incidentally, trained at the Opéra. But they were no longer sustained by a faith, even of a specious sort. Architecture in France had for the moment lost its sap and its savor.

ENGLAND: *C. R. Cockerell to Barry*

It cannot be denied that in nineteenth-century England most of the finest minds and the most brilliant designers, with the exception of Cockerell, were drawn to the Gothic not the Classical Revival. There is simply no classical parallel to the astonishingly rich concatenation of Gothic Revivalists—A. W. N. Pugin, John Ruskin, William Morris, William Butterfield, George Edmund Street, and George Frederick Bodley. Harvey Lonsdale Elmes and George Basevi came close to matching them in achievement, but since they both died young, they appear as late Georgian rather than as Victorian architects. Sir James Pennethorne and Sir Charles Barry lacked imaginative greatness, while Alexander ("Greek") Thomson, though a brilliantly individual exponent of the classical tradition, somehow remains a figure of Scottish rather than of European importance.

With Charles Robert Cockerell English classicism achieved a new level of scholarship and imagination. During his remarkable *grand tour* of 1810–17 he became not only one of the leading archaeologists in Europe but also a greater expert on antique architecture than any English architect before or since. Excavating the late Archaic Temple of Jupiter Panhellenius on the island of Aegina with a group of English and German colleagues in 1811, Cockerell was involved in the discovery of the pedimental sculpture now housed in the Glyptothek in Munich. In the same year he was responsible for discovering the sculptured frieze of the fifth-century Temple of Apollo Epicurius at Bassae, and in 1813 he helped conduct the arrangements by which this sculpture was purchased by the British government. He incorporated casts of it in several of his buildings, notably the Ashmolean Museum, Oxford; the highly independent Ionic order of the temple also recurs with powerful effect in a number of his works. Indeed, his discoveries in Greece gave him a sense of the sculptural basis of Greek design, which influenced the development of his own architecture by enabling him to see the weaknesses of the current Greek Revival. We can trace this process in his diaries of the 1820s, where he criticizes not only the work of his contemporaries but also his own. Of his Literary and Philosophical Institution at Bristol (1821), he noted that the portico, based on the Temple of Vesta at Tivoli but with Corinthian capitals that imitate the one he had discovered at Bassae, was "inharmoniously attached" to the main-building. An even more revealing self-criticism is that of Lough Crew, a Greek Revival mansion that he built in Ireland from 1820 to 1825. In 1823 he already found it "very plain, too bald . . . its squareness left me an unpleasant impression . . . it would have been well to rusticate between the pilasters." Finding the Athenian Ionic capitals of the portico too minuscule to enliven a monumental building, he decided "never again [to] use Athenian order except in small scale."

One of the first buildings in which Cockerell began to realize his own stylistic ambitions was the Westminster Life and British Fire Office, in the Strand, London (1831; demolished 1908). Its Greek Doric order was not applied in the form of the usual attached portico but was deeply embedded in the facade. The depth and richness of articulation, the sense of layers within layers, are reminiscent of Italian Mannerism, particularly two buildings by Palladio: the Villa Barbaro at Maser (c. 1555–59) and the Loggia del Capitaniato at Vicenza (1571). Once formulated, this allusive style was soon used to create a series of highly independent yet highly classical masterpieces: Cambridge University Library (only partly executed), the Ashmolean Museum, Oxford, and the Royal Exchange, London (unexecuted), all of the late 1830s, and the branches of the Bank of England at Bristol, Manchester, and Liverpool, of 1844–45. Such a composition as his St. Giles's facade of the Ashmolean blends Greek, Roman, Renaissance, and Baroque vocabulary into a language "the study of which," as one critic observed of the Liverpool Bank of England, "is a liberal education" (H. H. Statham, *A Short Critical History of Architecture*, 1912, p. 527). What immediately strikes the visitor to any building by Cockerell, whether it be a major public building like the Cambridge University Library or the lodge to a country house, as at Wynnstay, Denbighshire (1827), is the sheer largeness of scale of the parts and of the whole. We feel at once that we are in the presence of a man possessed of a profound intelligence, who thinks architecturally with a persuasive conviction and authority. Exactly the same impression is given by the work of C.-N. Ledoux—both large buildings, such as the Rotonde de la Villette, Paris, and smaller ones, such as the *grenier à sel* at Compiègne. We know that Cockerell was an admirer of Ledoux, in particular of his Hôtel de Thélusson in Paris (see D. J. Watkin, *The Life and Work of C. R. Cockerell, R. A.*, 1974, p. 124).

In the early 1850s Cockerell designed the interiors of St. George's Hall, Liverpool, following the premature death of the architect of the building, Harvey Lonsdale Elmes (1814–1847). Cockerell's exquisite Concert Hall, in which the fine calligraphy of his rich classical ornament is demonstrated at its best, is an admirable foil to the harder sobriety of Elmes's exterior. St. George's Hall, of which the final designs were settled by Elmes in 1841, is in plan a brilliant imaginative re-creation of the *tepidarium* of the Baths of Caracalla, which Elmes

seems to have known from Blouet's *Restauration des thermes d'Antonin Caracalla à Rome* (1828). It is in no sense a mere archaeological restoration and ranks as one of the finest neoclassical public buildings in Europe.

The death of the gifted young Elmes in 1847 was a tragedy for the classical tradition in England. So, too, was that two years earlier of the fifty-one-year-old George Basevi. The latter was a favorite pupil of Soane, and his masterpiece was the Fitzwilliam Museum, Cambridge, a commission he was awarded after an open competition held in 1834–35. Like St. George's Hall, this massive building was inspired by the public architecture of the Roman Empire, in this case the Capitolium at Brescia, dating from the third quarter of the first century A.D. From this source comes the method by which Basevi's monumental Corinthian portico is extended on each side so as to form a colonnade and thus integrated powerfully into the body of the building in a way that one is tempted to call Baroque, although Basevi's stylistic sympathies are shown to be different by his architectural use of casts from the Bassae and Parthenon friezes in the interior.

For a variety of reasons, some of which seem to be accidental, the Gothic Revival was particularly associated with a religious, architectural, and intellectual tradition centered in Oxford, Cambridge, London, and the south of England generally. The classical tradition, by contrast, tended to flourish in Scotland and in the north of England. Thus, the "hyper-Corinthian luxury" (H. S. Goodhart-Rendel's apt characterization) of the Fitzwilliam Museum was echoed in the magnificent Town Hall, of 1845, at Leeds, Yorkshire, by Cuthbert Brodrick (1822–1905) and in William Hill's Town Hall at Bolton, Lancashire, of 1866. Liverpool also reflected a classical bias, from 1823, when John Foster designed St. Andrew's Church of Scotland, Rodney Street, manifestly inspired by Cockerell's Hanover Chapel, Regent Street, London (1821), to 1875, when Cornelius Sherlock (d. 1888) designed the Picton Reading Room, with its spectacular semicircle of Corinthian columns. In Edinburgh, the "Athens of the North," a more sternly Greek note was retained, as can be seen in Thomas Hamilton's Royal College of Physicians (1844–46) and in W. H. Playfair's National Gallery of Scotland (1850–57). In Glasgow a more masterly architect, Alexander Thomson (1817–1875), provided an astonishingly rich and powerful interpretation of the late international neoclassicism of Schinkel and Cockerell. His Caledonia Road Free Church of 1856 is a characteristic example of his work, which, confined to Glasgow, exercised little or no influence on his contemporaries elsewhere.

In London the one architect who seemed capable of perpetuating the intellectual classicism of Cockerell was Sir James Pennethorne

435. Charles Robert Cockerell, *Westminister Life and British Fire Office, London, 1831.*

436. Charles Robert Cockerell, *University Library, Cambridge, project for the west side of the courtyard, c. 1837.*

437. Charles Robert Cockerell, *Ashmolean Museum, Oxford, view from the southeast, 1839–41.*

438. Charles Robert Cockerell, *Bank of England, Bristol, 1844.*

439. *Harvey Lonsdale Elmes, St. George's Hall, Liverpool, plan, 1841.*
440. *Harvey Lonsdale Elmes, St. George's Hall, Liverpool, 1841–51.*
441. *Charles Robert Cockerell, Concert Hall, St. George's Hall, Liverpool, 1851–54.*

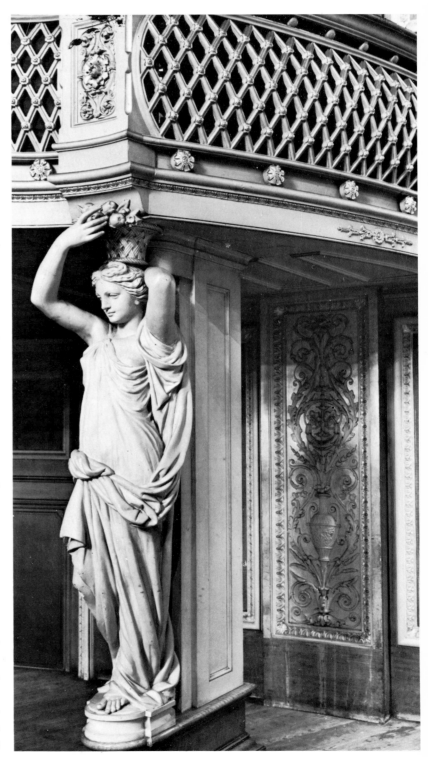

442. *Charles Robert Cockerell, Concert Hall, St. George's Hall, Liverpool, detail of a caryatid.*

(1801–1871). He was a pupil of John Nash, who told him, when Pennethorne was setting out on his *grand tour* of France and Italy in 1824, to seek the advice of Cockerell. Pennethorne later noted that "by Cockerell's urgent advice I paid more attention to the palaces and modern architecture of Italy than to the works of ancient art." The significance of this can hardly be overemphasized.

Perhaps Pennethorne's most important work was his Museum of Economic (or Practical) Geology, in Piccadilly, London, designed between 1844 and 1846, the first cultural monument of the Victorian age to be sponsored by the state. A building of great earnestness, sobriety, and authority, it showed what architects in the classical tradition were capable of when, assured of that tradition's refinement, logic, and dignity, they did not feel obliged to compete with the more immediately eye-catching effects of the fashionable Gothic and Italianate revivals. The museum's monumental but undemonstrative facades, in cream Colchester brick and Ancaster stone, concealed a dense and subtle plan that exploited interlocking volumes with a sophistication lacking in many later Gothic Revival buildings. Along the second story ran the great top-lit exhibition gallery, forty-seven meters (one hundred fifty-five feet) long, with a large rectangular opening in the floor that illuminated the Doric Hall below. The gallery, in which the horizontal and the vertical supports were of cast iron, was a space both formed and frankly defined by its construction. In this it differed from the two other great contemporary buildings in London that employed cast-iron construction: Robert Smirke's British Museum (1824–47), where the presence of cast iron is completely hidden, and J. B. Bunning's Coal Exchange (1847), where it is boldly exposed. Pennethorne adopted the perhaps more attractive solution of revealing that cast and wrought iron helped determine the shape of the room but then moderating the disclosure by covering the surface of the metal with plasterwork.

Pennethorne's geological museum was demolished in 1935, and his important interiors at Buckingham Palace (1852–58) were mutilated in 1902. His somewhat grim but constructionally interesting Public Record Office (1851–66) survives, as does his west wing (1856) at Sir William Chambers's Somerset House, where he brilliantly and modestly adapted Chambers's style. As architect to the Office of Works, Pennethorne enjoyed the kind of settled civil-service position that some other architects of the period, including Schinkel, occupied. He was thus preserved from the embarrassment of entering the scandalously conducted architectural competitions of the nineteenth century, which so impeded Cockerell's career. One of the fruits of Pennethorne's official position was the commission for buildings for the University of London in Burlington Gardens in 1866. However, he

443. *Charles Robert Cockerell and Edward Middleton Barry, Fitzwilliam Museum, Cambridge, detail of the cupola, 1845, 1870–75.*

444. George Basevi, Fitzwilliam Museum, Cambridge, 1834.
445. Cuthbert Brodrick, Town Hall, Leeds, 1853.

446. Cornelius Sherlock, Picton Reading Room, Liverpool, 1875.
447. Thomas Hamilton, Royal College of Physicians, Edinburgh, 1844–46.

became a pawn in the "Battle of the Styles," which was being played so absurdly between Liberal and Conservative politicians in the 1860s. He was thus obliged to present designs in both Gothic and Italianate modes in 1866–67, and the result is a dour piece of classicism with strongly French overtones. It is symptomatic of the failure of English architects to maintain the classical tradition in the face of competition from the Gothic and Italianate revivals.

The master of the Italianate Revival was Sir Charles Barry. Though comparatively of humble birth, he forged a career for himself that was one of the spectacular successes of the nineteenth century. His early work was varied, ranging stylistically from a Gothic manner reminiscent of Wyatt's Fonthill Abbey (St. Peter, Brighton, 1823–28), via the Schinkelesque trabeation of his Royal Institution, Manchester (1823), and Nos. 16–17 Pall Mall, London (1833–34; demolished 1913), to the early Italian Renaissance manner of Brunswick Chapel, Hove, Sussex, (1827) and two important buildings of 1829, the Attree Villa, Brighton, and the Travellers' Club in Pall Mall. He shot to fame in 1836 when he had the extraordinarily good fortune to be selected as architect of the New Palace of Westminster. The terms of the competition, in keeping with the sentimental and literary romanticism of an increasingly nationalist age, called for a "Gothic or Elizabethan" style in order to emphasize the supposed medieval roots of English government. Barry's complex masterpiece, with its essentially classical disposition (despite the elaborate Gothic detail provided by A. W. N. Pugin), was a curiosity that exercised no significant architectural influence but that has undoubtedly continued to color, up to the present day, the Englishman's notion of the political framework within which he expects his country to be governed.

Barry's choice of a Cinquecento Palazzo style for the Travellers' Club was fraught with consequences for the nineteenth century. It suggested that the Palladian Revival of early eighteenth-century England had returned, though the architects and styles that had come to be admired were not those that had appealed to Lord Burlington and his circle. Burlington had been interested in Palladio as an exemplar of order, harmony, and the antique, not as a representative of Italian culture; the Victorians were interested in the warmth and color of the Renaissance as an Italian phenomenon. The Travellers' Club was in some sense the culmination of Englishmen's obsession with the *grand tour*, an institution that had persisted without interruption from at least the time of the foundation of the Society of Dilettanti. The club members were anxious to build a noble mansion in which those who had made the *grand tour* could meet each other and return hospitality to the foreign gentlemen who had entertained them on their travels. It was not, therefore, inappropriate that its architecture should

Fig. 28. The Houses of Parliament, as finally completed: from A. Barry, *Life and Works of Sir Charles Barry* (1867).

be a tangible memorial of this *entente cordiale*. Barry chose as his model Raphael's Palazzo Pandolfini in Florence, though in execution he abandoned the elaborate rusticated surrounds to the ground-floor windows that had appeared in his first proposals for the Pall Mall facade. For the much larger Reform Club of 1837, farther along the same street, Barry chose as his model the grander Palazzo Farnese by Antonio da Sangallo and Michelangelo. But neither of Barry's clubs was in any sense a copy. The planning of both was extremely novel, particularly at the Reform Club, whose great central *cortile* became a recurrent theme in different Victorian building types. In tribute to the classical impetus that gave rise to these buildings, the Morning Room of the Reform Club was adorned with a cast of the Parthenon frieze, the Library of the Travellers' with a cast of the Bassae frieze (the latter doubtless on the recommendation of Cockerell, who was a founder-member).

Barry developed his Italianate style in a series of spectacular country houses: for example, Trentham, Staffordshire (1833 onward), Shrubland Park, Suffolk (1849–54), and Cliveden House, Buckinghamshire (1850). Others were quick to follow his lead. Thomas Cubitt provided mansions in this style during the 1840s for George Hudson, the railway king, at Albert Gate, London, and for Queen Victoria and Prince Albert at Osborne House on the Isle of Wight. Far more distinguished than anything by Cubitt and much by Barry was Dorchester House, Park Lane, London (1850–63), by Lewis Vulliamy (1791–1871). It was designed in close collaboration with its owner, R. S. Holford, the art collector and shipping magnate, who was evidently trying to rival Barry's Bridgewater House of 1846–51 for Lord Ellesmere. Based on Baldassare Peruzzi's Villa Farnesina, Rome (1509–11), Vulliamy's Dorchester House was one of the great buildings of the nineteenth century, and its destruction in 1929 was a major loss to British architecture. It expressed the culmination of those opulent, aristocratic Mediterranean sympathies that had developed in the 1830s and 1840s at the end of the long Georgian and Whig heyday. The sumptuously decorated interior reached a climax in the second-floor ballroom, or saloon, which, by a brilliant theatrical stroke, opened through three archways directly into the upper spaces of the stair hall. The whole house thus became alive with sound and movement on evenings when great balls and receptions were held. The dining room was designed by Alfred George Stevens (1817–1875), a pupil of Bertel Thorvaldsen and undoubtedly the finest of the Victorian sculptors. He was in deep sympathy with the cinquecento, particularly with Michelangelo, and was, of all nineteenth-century designers, the closest in temperament and talent to Cockerell. His Wellington Monument in St. Paul's cathedral (1856), a great triumphal arch of

454. *Sir Charles Barry, Shrubland Park, Suffolk, gardens, 1849–54.*

455. *Thomas Cubitt, Osborne House, Isle of Wight, aerial view, 1845–48.*

456. *Thomas Cubitt, Osborne House, Isle of Wight, drawing room.*

marble, is one of the noblest memorials to the nineteenth-century Italianate Revival. His magnificent chimneypiece in the dining room at Dorchester House took ten years to design and construct (1859–69). Its incredible cost of £1,778 shocked even the millionaire Holford.

To remind us of what we have lost at Dorchester House is a building in the same vein, though perhaps of even greater quality and originality: the Free Trade Hall, Manchester (1853), by Edward Walters (1808–1872), who had worked in the offices of both Cubitt and Vulliamy. William Bruce Gingell (1819–1900) was another talented architect in the Italianate manner. His West of England and South Wales District (now Lloyds) Bank at Bristol (1854) is a stylish variation on the theme of Pietro Sansovino's Libreria di S. Marco, Venice. Samuel Angell (1800–1866) had also made a special study of cinquecento architecture; he lectured on Giacomo da Vignola at the Royal Institute of British Architects in 1850, and in 1856 produced the sumptuous Clothworkers' Hall, Mincing Lane, London (destroyed 1940). An interesting offshoot of the taste for things Italian was the vogue in the 1840s for the "round-arch style" in church architecture, which included every kind of variant from Early Christian and Byzantine to Italian Romanesque and Norman. The most elaborate example of this taste is afforded by the church of St. Mary and St. Nicholas at Wilton, Wiltshire (1840–46), by Thomas Henry (1807–1880) and David Brandon. In a rich Italian Romanesque style, with a campanile over thirty meters (one hundred feet) high, it contains ancient Roman columns of black marble from the Temple of Venus at Porto Venere. A building of rare quality in the round-arch style is the museum of Trinity College, Dublin, of 1852–57, by Sir Thomas Newenham Deane (1828–1899) and Benjamin Woodward (1815–1861). Though organized around a central glazed courtyard, rather like Barry's Reform Club, the building has naturalistically carved capitals inspired by Ruskin and details in a Venetian early-Renaissance mode.

The Palazzo style was agreed upon as appropriate, for a variety of practical and associational reasons, for commercial premises and private clubs, but when it came to the style in which a great building of national and symbolic importance should be built, the latent battle between the exponents of the classical and the Gothic came with some violence to the surface. The particular victim of the strife was Sir George Gilbert Scott (1811–1878), who between 1856 and 1861 was forced more than once to remodel his Gothic design for the Foreign Office to suit the Renaissance tastes of the Prime Minister, Lord Palmerston. Ironically, the result was one of Scott's best buildings, though it must be said that he had much help from Matthew Digby Wyatt (1820–1877).

After the 1860s the classical tradition lost impetus and the best

457. *Lewis Vulliamy, Dorchester House, London, south (entrance) front, 1850–63.*

458. *Lewis Vulliamy, Dorchester House, London, stair hall and corridor on the second floor.*

459. *Lewis Vulliamy, Dorchester House, London, west facade, on Park Lane.*

460. *Lewis Vulliamy, Dorchester House, London, stair hall.*

463. *Sir Thomas Newenham Deane and Benjamin Woodward, Trinity College Museum, Dublin, stair hall, 1852–57.*

464. *Sir Thomas Newenham Deane and Benjamin Woodward, Trinity College Museum, Dublin.*

465. *Samuel Angell, Clothworkers' Hall, London, 1856.*

466. *Thomas Henry Wyatt and David Brandon, St. Mary and St. Nicholas, Wilton, Wiltshire, 1840–46.*

467. *Sir George Gilbert Scott and Sir Matthew Digby Wyatt, Foreign Office, London, 1856–73.*

architects worked in other veins. It was revived, together with an interest in Cockerell, between 1890 and 1910 with some surprisingly impressive results.

GERMANY

There were many similarities between the development of German and English architecture between 1790 and 1840; thus, a number of the major designs and buildings by Gilly, Schinkel, and Klenze have already been mentioned in the course of our discussion of the Greek

Revival and the Picturesque. Certainly the intensely eclectic work of the greatest German architect of these years, Karl Friedrich Schinkel, reminds us immediately not of France or Italy but of England. Schinkel also developed a "functional" interpretation of classicism, which was successfully revived in Germany between 1900 and 1940 as a reaction against both the Wilhelmine Baroque and Bauhaus bleakness. Schinkel particularly appealed to his countrymen during the first half of the twentieth century in part because of what they saw as his essential "Germanness." As head of the Public Works Department, Schinkel became identified with the creation of the new Germany

468. *Samuel Angell, Clothworkers' Hall, London, interior, 1856.*
469. *Sir George Gilbert Scott and Sir Matthew Digby Wyatt, Foreign Office, London, stair hall, 1862–73.*

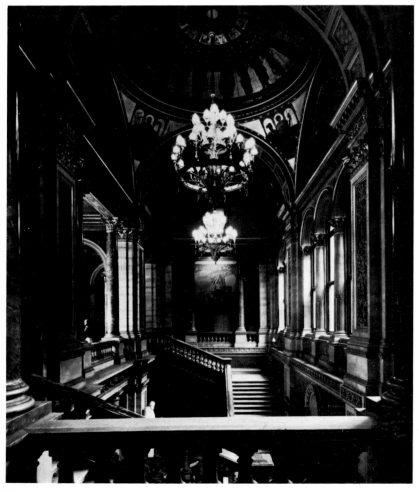

between the Napoleonic Wars and the foundation of the empire in 1871. Indeed, so much was he seen as part of its reforging that the royal family walked behind his coffin in his funeral procession.

He provided the center of Berlin with a number of striking monuments in different styles: Greek Revival for the Royal Guardhouse (1816–18), State Theater (1818–21), and Altes Museum (1822–28); Gothic for the grim brick Friedrich-Werdersche church (1821–30) and the cast-iron Kreuzberg War Memorial (1818); and a cross between Functional and North Italian quattrocento for the School of Architecture (1831–36). Despite the claims that have been made for his ability as a town planner (H. G. Pundt, *Schinkel's Berlin: A Study in Environmental Planning*, 1972), it must be confessed that, unlike John Nash in London, he was not able to make a coherent impact on the city of Berlin, which remained dominated by its Baroque and eighteenth-century planning and monuments.

One of the most prolific and eclectic architects of all time, Schinkel is difficult to sum up, to generalize about, to fit into a pattern. It is possible that his important study-tour of England in 1826 influenced the development of his "functional" style, with its prominent use of iron. He was both appalled and attracted by the architecture of the Industrial Revolution in England, and it seems that it was after observing the giant cotton mills that he conceived the idea of a fireproof architecture whose gridlike brick skin would wrap around an iron frame. The various explorations he made of this after his return from England include two unexecuted proposals—a bazaar for Unter den Linden (1827) and a State Library (1835–39) nearby—the Royal Customs Warehouses (1829), the School of Architecture, and the spectacular cast-iron staircases in two of the palaces in the Wilhelmstrasse that he remodeled for the king's sons, Prince Karl (1827) and Prince Albrecht (1829–33).

We have touched elsewhere on Schinkel's work in a Picturesque vein that, too, has English overtones: Schloss Glienicke, Schloss Charlottenhof, and Schloss Babelsberg. It culminated later in the 1830s in two unexecuted fantasies: a palace on the Acropolis for the king of Greece (Otto von Wittelsbach of Bavaria) and a palace at Orianda, in the Crimea, for the empress of Russia, who was a daughter of King Friedrich-Wilhelm III of Prussia. Both display a rich polychromy inspired by the researches of Hittorff, a great admirer of Schinkel; both are examples of Schinkel's special gift for distributing symmetrical Grecian forms in an asymmetrically landscaped composition; and both give the impression of sumptuous film sets. The palace on the Acropolis, which turned the Parthenon into a kind of glorified garden ornament, is the apotheosis of what some scholars have called Romantic classicism.

470. *Karl Friedrich Schinkel, Altes Museum, Berlin, 1822–23.*
471. *Karl Friedrich Schinkel, Altes Museum, Berlin, hall.*

Leo von Klenze (1784–1864), like Schinkel, was a North German who turned to architecture after meeting the visionary and influential young Friedrich Gilly. He studied in Paris in the opening years of the nineteenth century under Percier and Fontaine and also under J.-N.-L. Durand at the École Polytechnique. After working from 1808 to 1813 as court architect to Napoleon's youngest brother, Jérôme, who had been elevated to the throne of Westphalia, Klenze met Crown Prince Ludwig of Bavaria, in 1814. The young prince, who had purchased the Aegina Marbles in 1811, shared Klenze's passion for antiquity and in 1816 persuaded his father, Maximilian I, to appoint Klenze as supervisor of court buildings in Munich. This royal support in architectural endeavor finds a close parallel in the relationship between Schinkel and the crown prince in Berlin, between Percier and Fontaine and Napoleon in Paris, and between Nash and the Prince Regent in England. Klenze and the crown prince made the same kind of sweeping impact on Munich that Nash did on London, though the German architect and his patron worked in a style rather different from Nash's. Their principal contributions were the great Ludwigstrasse, running north from the royal Residenz, and the Königsplatz, which lay to the west of the Ludwigstrasse on the route into the city from the royal palace of Nymphenburg.

In 1816 Klenze designed two major buildings that reflect the influence of his French masters. The Glyptothek in the Königsplatz is notable as the first public sculpture gallery ever erected. It was commissioned by the crown prince, who wished to house the Aegina Marbles suitably. It contained Roman as well as Greek antiquities, and its Grecian portico is flanked by Roman aedicules. From the same year dates the very different Leuchtenberg Palace, off the Ludwigstrasse, designed for Napoleon's stepson, Eugène de Beauharnais, who had married the crown prince's sister. Perhaps the first major monument of the Renaissance Revival, it was inspired, like Barry's Reform Club of twenty-one years later, by the Palazzo Farnese. Klenze doubtless knew the engravings of Italian domestic architecture of the fifteenth and sixteenth centuries that Percier and Fontaine had published in their *Palais, maisons, et autres édifices modernes dessinés à Rome* (1798). The fifteenth-century Florentine style chosen by the crown prince for much of Klenze's street architecture in Munich may also owe something to the plates in *Architecture toscane*, published in 1815 by Auguste Grandjean de Montigny, Klenze's predecessor as architect to King Jérome. Klenze's Pinakothek, or Picture Gallery, in Munich (designed 1822–25; built 1826–36) antedates both Smirke's British Museum and Schinkel's Altes Museum and, unlike either of these, reflects a neo-Renaissance vocabulary. In 1823–24 Klenze visited Sicily and Paestum with the crown prince, and there he made detailed

472. *Karl Friedrich Schinkel, project for a palace on the Acropolis, Athens, 1834.*

473. *Karl Friedrich Schinkel, project for a palace, Orianda, Crimea, 1838.*

drawings of the Greek temples while the prince fell in love with the Palatine Chapel at Palermo. In 1824 he became director of the Building Authorities for Bavaria, and his position was further consolidated in the following year when the crown prince succeeded his father, as Ludwig I. Between 1826 and 1843 Klenze remodeled the Munich Residenz for Ludwig in a variety of styles ranging from that of the Königsbau (based on the Pitti Palace) to that of the Allerheiligen Hofkirche (based on the Palatine Chapel at Palermo).

Klenze's great monuments in the neo-antique, as opposed to the neo-Renaissance, tradition are the Walhalla (1830–42) near Regensburg, the Befreiungshalle (1842), near Kelheim, and, in Munich, the Ruhmeshalle (1843) and Propylaeon (1846–60; conceived in 1817). We have already described the Walhalla and the Propylaeon as the culmination of that neoclassical obsession with the Parthenon and the Athenian Propylaea, which, in nineteenth-century Germany, was colored by a growing nationalism. The Ruhmeshalle (Hall of Fame) is a bald Greek Doric stoa, whereas the Befreiungshalle (Hall of Liberation) is a vast, bizarre rotunda erected to commemorate the War of Liberation against Napoleon of 1813–15. Conceived by the architect Friedrich von Gärtner (1792–1847), the Befreiungshalle was completely remodeled after his death by Klenze, in whose hands it emerged as a stark, brutal, militaristic fortress.

The third member of the great trio of German nineteenth-century architects is Gottfried Semper (1803–1879), a generation younger than Schinkel and Klenze. Like them he was trained in both Germany and France: His masters were Gärtner, Gau, and Hittorff. From Hittorff he derived an interest in antique polychromy, which he studied in Italy and Greece from 1830 to 1833, and he published some of the results of his research in *Verläufige Bemerkungen über bemalte Architektur und Plastik bei den Alten* (1834). Unlike Hittorff and Klenze, he never worked in a neo-Greek mode but immediately opted for the Renaissance when he began to design major works in Dresden: the Opera House (1837–41), the Villa Rosa (1839), the Oppenheim Palace (1845), and the Königliche Gemäldegalerie (1845–48). Some of his best buildings in this vein were designed during his lengthy residence in Switzerland: the Town Hall at Winterthur (1863–67), the Fierz Commercial Building at Zurich (1864–65), and his project for the Zurich railroad station (1860). He later turned to the neo-Baroque, when, in the 1870s, he rebuilt the Dresden Opera House after a fire and designed major public museums in Vienna. However, it is not his buildings that principally concern us but his ideas on ornament and functionalism published in *Der Stil in den technischen und tektonischen Künsten* (2 vols., 1860–63; 2d ed., 1878–79), which we will discuss in a later chapter.

RUSSIA

From the time of its foundation by Peter the Great in 1703, St. Petersburg (Leningrad) was intended to be a port of entry for Western influence. The astonishing mélange of work done there by Italian, French, British, German, and Russian architects during the next century and a half realized as nowhere else Quatremère de Quincy's vision of a classical "communauté d'instruction et de connaissance, une certaine égalité du goût et du savoir . . . entre toutes les contrées de l'Europe." The fashion during the reign of the Empress Elizabeth (1741–62) was for rococo, and it was in that style that the palace of Tsarskoe Selo (1749–56), about fifteen miles from St. Petersburg, and the Winter Palace (1754–62), in the city itself, were executed, both by the Italian Count Bartolommeo Francesco Rastrelli (1700–1771). Catherine the Great (who reigned from 1762 to 1796) reacted against her aunt's tastes and adopted a neoclassical style that entered St. Petersburg in two buildings by the French architect Jean-Baptiste-Michel Vallin de la Mothe (1729–1800): the Old Hermitage (1764–67) and the Academy of Fine Arts (1765), which was based on a restrained design by his cousin, J.-F. Blondel. Ivan Yegorovich Starov, a Russian architect trained in Paris under de Wailly, continued to develop the new style in his church and belfry at Nikolskoe (1774–76; destroyed 1941) and in the Tauride Palace in St. Petersburg, whose impressive Catherine Hall is flanked on each side by eighteen pairs of Ionic columns. Giacomo Antonio Domenico Quarenghi (1744–1817), who traveled to Russia from Italy in 1779–80, introduced a monumental Palladianism at the English Palace in the English Park at Peterhof (1781–89) and at the Hermitage Theater (1782–87).

The most remarkable foreign importation was probably the mysterious Scottish architect Charles Cameron (c. 1743–1812), who was in Rome in the 1760s, published the *Description of the Baths of the Romans* in 1772, and was working for Catherine at Tsarskoe Selo in 1779. Her first choice had been Clérisseau, whom she invited in 1773 to design a house in the "antique" style to be built on the grounds of Tsarskoe Selo; however, she was annoyed by Clérisseau's proposals for a vast Roman palace combining elements from the Baths of Caracalla and Hadrian's Villa at Tivoli. Nevertheless, in 1780 she asked him for designs for a triumphal arch to be built in Russia by Cameron, and in the following year she bought more than a thousand of his drawings in Paris. Clérisseau's surviving model and drawings make it clear that the arch would have been of exceptional scale and originality, with the central round-headed opening flanked by square-headed openings with Doric columns. The commission for the additions to Tsarskoe Selo fell to Cameron, who, using some of Clérisseau's drawings, produced a breathtakingly lovely series of apartments in a glit-

273

477. Leo von Klenze, Glyptothek, Munich, portico, 1816–34.

477. Leo von Klenze, Glyptothek, Munich, portico, 1816–34.

478. Leo von Klenze, Allerheiligen Hofkirche, Residenz, Munich, 1826.
Engraving by Poppel.

479. Leo von Klenze, Königsbau, Residenz, Munich, 1826.

480. Leo von Klenze, Befreiungshalle, near Kelheim, 1842–63.

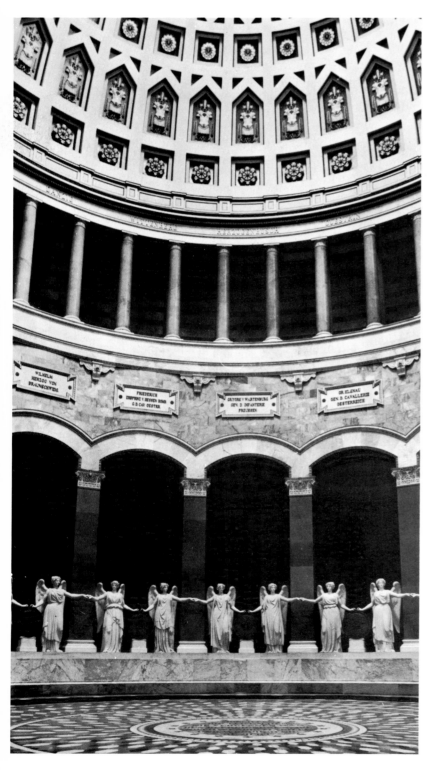

tering Adam style in 1779–84, and went on to add the Cameron Gallery and Agate Pavilion to Rastrelli's palace in 1782–85. The great open colonnades on the second floor of the Cameron Gallery are curiously similar to those on the south front of West Wycombe Park, Buckinghamshire (c. 1755), attributed to John Donowell. Because of the steeply sloping site, the gallery has at its south end a superb open staircase leading down to the lake in two widely curving arms that terminate in a single straight flight.

Cameron's other principal work was the palace at Pavlovsk, built for Grand Duke Paul between 1781 and 1785. Again, influence from Clérisseau and Adam is apparent, particularly in the magnificent Grecian Hall, inspired by Adam's great hall at Kedleston, Derbyshire (c. 1761 onward), and in the Italian Hall, the rotunda in the center of the palace, which is an echo of the saloon at Kedleston. In the park Cameron erected the circular Temple of Friendship in 1780 (demolished), the first building of the Greek Doric style in Russia.

Nineteenth-century classical architecture in Russia began spectacularly in 1804 with the St. Petersburg Exchange by the French architect Thomas de Thomon (1754–1813). This monumental templar building, combining elements taken from Boulleé and from the temples at Paestum (which de Thomon had visited), was part of the major redevelopment of the imperial capital carried out by Alexander I (reigned 1801–25) and his brother Nicholas I (reigned 1825–55) in emulation of the achievement of Catherine the Great and with the deliberate aim of making it a city unrivaled in the splendor of its public buildings. The Exchange was swiftly followed by perhaps the largest neoclassical building in the world, the Admiralty (1806–15), by Adrian Dimitrievich Zakharov (1761–1811), a Russian-born architect who had been trained under Chalgrin in Paris in 1782–86. The lateral facades of this brilliant and varied building provide reflections of Zakharov's stay in Paris, for they were inspired by Pierre Rousseau's archway at the Hôtel de Salm, under construction in 1782–85. Similarly, de Thomon's theater (destroyed 1813) was based on Peyre's and de Wailly's Théâtre-Français, in Paris. The French architect Auguste Ricard de Montferrand (1786–1858), a pupil of Percier, built St. Isaac's cathedral (1817–57) to a not very coherent design based on Soufflot's Ste.-Geneviève; nevertheless, it boasts an important iron-framed dome, whose exterior was inspired by Wren's dome at St. Paul's cathedral. The Academy of Mines at St. Petersburg (1806–11), by Andrei Nikiforovich Voronikhin (1760–1814), a pupil of de Wailly, has a giant twelve-columned Paestum-Doric portico, but the more important architect Karl Ivanovich Rossi (1775–1849) moved away from the néo-grec toward a style more Italianate and more festive. Italian-born but Russian-trained, he became the principal architect and

482. *Jean-Baptiste-Michel Vallin de la Mothe, Academy of Fine Arts, Leningrad, 1765.*
483. *Charles Cameron, Green Dining Room, Palace of Catherine the Great, Tsarskoe Selo (Pushkin), 1779–84.*
484. *Charles Cameron, bedroom, Palace of Catherine the Great, Tsarskoe Selo (Pushkin).*

town planner in St. Petersburg after 1816. Rossi's grand and rich style can be appreciated in the New Michael Palace (1819–23; now the Russian Museum), the General Staff Arch and flanking office buildings (1819–29) in front of the Winter Palace, the Alexandra Theater (1827–32), and the Senate and Synod (1829–34).

Though less striking than that of St. Petersburg, the transformation of Moscow into a city of great classical architecture during the late eighteenth and early nineteenth centuries bespeaks the vitality and adaptability both of Russian architects and of the classical style. The extent and quality of the work—which included public buildings, palaces, and mansions—are still little appreciated. Vasili Ivanovich Bazhenov, another pupil of de Wailly, conceived a remarkable scheme for rebuilding the Kremlin about 1772, but it was not executed. His highly ornamental Pashkov Palace (now the Lenin Library) of 1784–86 maintained links with the Baroque. The work of his assistant Matvei Feodorovich Kazakov (1733–1812), more than that of any other architect, gave the new Moscow its classical character. Kazakov's mighty triangular Senate Building in the Kremlin (now the Council of the Ministers of the USSR), of 1771–85, was a fulfillment of Bazhenov's Kremlin project. Its great Doric rotunda is flanked internally with impressive freestanding Corinthian columns, as is his Hall of the Noblemen's Assembly of 1784–86 (now the Hall of Columns, House of the Trade Unions). Kazakov, who had traveled in France and Italy, was an admirer of Palladio, as can be seen in both his public buildings (Golitsyn Hospital, 1796–1801) and his private palaces (Demidov House, 1789–91; and Batashev House, 1798–1802). He was also interested in reviving ancient Russian forms and mingling them with Gothic details, as he did with bizarre effect in the Petrovsky Palace (1775–82; altered 1840). Like Bazhenov's church of Our Lady of All Sorrows, Kazakov's Moscow churches of the 1780s and 1790s—SS. Cosmas and Damian, St. Philip the Metropolitan, Ascension, and St. Martin the Confessor—are asymmetrical in composition. The familiar Russian rotunda and tall campanile create a staccato effect oddly reminiscent of E.-M. Gauthey's church at Givry-sur-Saône (1770–91) and George Steuart's New St. Chad, Shrewsbury (1790).

A number of Moscow buildings of the turn of the century are associated with Quarenghi. He remodeled the Catherine (Golovin) Palace, incorporating a Tuscan colonnaded hall, and added a startling hemicycle of Tuscan columns to the facade by Yelezvoi Nazarov of the Sheremetev Pilgrims' Refuge. One of the grandest private palaces of the period was built at Ostankino in 1791–98 for Count Sheremetev by Quarenghi, Kazakov, and Ivan Petrovich Argunov. With its superbly ornamented theater and, on the grounds, the Italian and so-

485.   Charles Cameron, Cameron Gallery, Tsarskoe Selo (Pushkin), 1782–85.

486.   Charles Cameron, Palace of Grand Duke Paul, Pavlovsk, Grecian Hall, 1781–85.

487.   Charles Cameron, Palace of Grand Duke Paul, Pavlovsk, principal facade.

488.   Adrian Dimitrievich Zakharov, Admiralty, Leningrad, 1806–15.

489. *Adrian Dimitrievich Zakharov, Admiralty, Leningrad, detail.*
490. *Karl Ivanovich Rossi, Arch of the Winter Palace (now General Staff Arch), Leningrad, 1819–29.*
491. *Karl Ivanovich Rossi, Senate and Synod, Leningrad, 1829–34.*

called Egyptian pavilions, Ostankino has something of the quality of Cameron's work for Catherine the Great at Tsarskoe Selo.

In the early nineteenth century the principal Muscovite architects who followed Kazakov were the Italian-born Domenico Gilardi (1788–1845), Afanasy Grigoryev (1782–1868), and Osip Beauvais (1784–1834). By Grigoryev and Adam Menelaws is the Razumovsky House (1801–3). Its powerful facade is based on the motif by now familiar to us in the work of Kent, Adam, and Ledoux: an open screen of columns in front of a coffered apse. Gilardi's Khrushchev House (1814) and Lopukhin House (1817–22) are Palladian in theme, enlivened with crisp Empire decoration. Gilardi, however, did inject a more astringent note into Muscovite classicism, and his influence was, in some ways, comparable to the impact of Gilly in Germany. Strikingly reminiscent of Gilly are his adaptation of Kazakov's Music Pavilion of the Equerry on the Kuzminki estate (1819) and his completion in the late 1820s of Quarenghi's and Kazakov's Suburban Palace (begun 1788). Between 1809 and 1818, with his father, Giacomo, Gilardi built the Widows' House, and from 1823 to 1826 the Guardianship Council Building. The former is notable for a great octostyle portico of unfluted Greek Doric columns, the latter for a similar portico of Greek Ionic columns and a superb vaulted stair hall with two tiers of unfluted marble columns. His most impressive private house is the Lunin House (1818–23), on Nikitsky Boulevard, but his major work was the reconstruction, in 1817–19, of Kazakov's Moscow University of 1786–93. For Kazakov's elegant Ionic order on the entrance portico he substituted a powerful Greek Doric and also reworked the side pavilions in a harder, chunkier style. In a similar fashion, Menelaws remodeled the English Club (now the Museum of the Revolution of the USSR) with a Greek Doric portico. Greek Doric also are Osip Beauvais's squat, truncated columns set in a rusticated arch in the grotto of the Alexandrovsky Garden.

Beauvais's name is particularly associated with the planning in Moscow carried out after the disastrous fire of 1812, for he was director of the commission for rebuilding the city. In front of his Bolshoi Theater (1821–24) the Theater (now Sverdlov) Square merges with the Resurrection (now Revolution) Square. At the Tverskaya Zastava he built a splendid triumphal arch (1827–34), based on the Arch of Titus in Rome, to mark the spot where the victorious army had returned to Moscow from the Napoleonic Wars. It has now, unfortunately, been moved to the Mozhaiskoye Highway.

During the 1830s German influence penetrated where French and Italian had for so long held sway. In 1838, following the fire at the old Winter Palace in St. Petersburg in December 1837, Leo

492. *Matvei Feodorovich Kazakov, Senate Building, Kremlin, Moscow, 1771–85.*

493. *Giacomo Antonio Domenico Quarenghi, Matvei Feodorovich Kazakov, and Ivan Petrovich Argunov, Sheremetev Palace, Ostankino, near Moscow, 1791–98.*

494. *Giacomo Antonio Domenico Quarenghi, Matvei Feodorovich Kazakov, and Ivan Petrovich Argunov, Sheremetev Palace, Ostankino, near Moscow, view from the park.*

495, 496. *Giacomo Antonio Domenico Quarenghi, Matvei Feodorovich Kazakov, and Ivan Petrovich Argunov, Sheremetev Palace, Ostankino, near Moscow, views of the interior.*

von Klenze was called from Munich by Nicholas I to design the New Hermitage Museum. Klenze's vast building on the banks of the Neva next to the Hermitage Theater is an impressive amalgam of French, Russian, and German classicism: The monumental porch supported by giant *atlantes* carved by Alexander Ivanovitch Terebenev has a Russian grandiosity; the principal staircase echoes the one of 1803–7 by Chalgrin at the Palais du Luxembourg; the restrained Grecian trabeation of the facades was inspired by Schinkel, as was the careful layout of the galleries, with pictures hung on low side screens and with rooms allotted to the different schools of painting.

In Moscow the classical tradition came to an end in two great buildings by the German-born architect Konstantin Andreevich Ton (1794–1881): the Great Kremlin Palace (1838–49) and the huge church of the Redeemer (1839–83), whose odd, half-Byzantine, half-classical style points forward to the nationalistic Slav Revival of the later nineteenth century.

SCANDINAVIA

In the early nineteenth century the capital cities of Scandinavia—Copenhagen, Helsinki, and Christiania (Oslo)—produced a rich harvest of public buildings in the classical style that had been developed since the mid-eighteenth century in France, England, and Italy and that was to be so strikingly codified by Schinkel in Germany. Indeed, there is a strong German flavor to Scandinavian classicism in these years. However, the new style had been imported very early from France by two French architects, Nicolas-Henri Jardin (1720–1799), who lived in Denmark from 1755 to 1771, and Jean-Louis Desprez (1743–1804), who was employed by Gustavus III of Sweden beginning in 1784. Jardin's dining room of 1755–57 for Count A. G. Moltke in what is now the Amalienborg Palace in Copenhagen has been described as "the earliest surviving room decorated entirely in the Neo-Classical taste by a French architect" (S. Eriksen, *Early Neo-Classicism in France*, 1974, p. 57). Caspar Frederik Harsdorff (1735–1799), first a pupil of Jardin at the Royal Academy in Copenhagen, later studied under Blondel in Paris. His mortuary chapel for Frederik V in the cathedral at Roskilde, built in the 1770s, is a cool and beautiful blend of Blondel's and Adam's styles. Desprez, who was principally a stage designer, built the Botanicum at Uppsala in 1788 with a long, low portico of eight Greek Doric columns. This Greek enthusiasm had already been expressed in the designs of the Swedish-born Carl August Ehrensvärd (1745–1800), whose visit to Paestum in 1780–82 had resulted in his primitivist Doric project of 1785 for a dockyard gate at Karlskrona. The most important Scandinavian architect to emerge in these years was

Christian Frederik Hansen (1756–1845). In his architectural group composed of town hall, courthouse, and prison, with its attendant archways (1803–16), he brought to Copenhagen the Franco-Prussian style that Gilly had developed out of the work of Ledoux. Hansen's principal achievement is the cathedral at Copenhagen, the Vor Frue Kirke (designed 1808–10; built 1811–29), with its Doric colonnades supporting an immense coffered barrel vault reminiscent of Boullée's celebrated project for the new hall of the Bibliothèque Nationale. Hansen's pupil M. Gottlieb Bindesbøll (1800–1856) produced the memorable Thorvaldsen Museum in Copenhagen (1837–48), an idiosyncratic blend of styles borrowed from Egypt, Greece, and Schinkel. In his other works Bindesbøll tended toward the Rundbogenstil ("round-arch" style), as did his follower J. D. Herholdt (1818–1902), for example, in the Copenhagen University Library (1855–61).

The foundation of a new capital in Norway after that country's separation from Denmark in 1814 created great opportunities for the architect Christian Heinrich Grosch (1801–1865), a pupil of Hansen. At Christiania he built the Exchange (1826–52), using a baseless Tuscan order *in antis*, the Norwegian Bank (1828), and, most important, the University (1841–52), which has a markedly Schinkelesque trabeation. Here, a Greek Ionic portico leads into a fine Greek Doric hall.

Perhaps the most attractive project of the period in Scandinavia was the development of Helsinki after the city became a Russian grand duchy in 1809. The plan of the newly chosen capital of Finland is the work of the architect Johan Albrekt Ehrenström (1762–1847), but all the major public buildings and many private houses are by the German-born Johann Carl Ludwig Engel (1778–1840). He created the superb Senate Square, dominated by his cathedral (designed from 1818 onward; built 1830–51) at the top of a great flight of steps, and flanked by his University (1828–32) and Senate (1818–22). The University Library, with its magnificent colonnaded reading rooms, was designed in 1833 and later, and built from 1836 to 1845. Perhaps the most striking features of Engel's work are his Doric staircases: The massive, freestanding Paestum-Doric columns of the Senate staircase unexpectedly carry groin-vaulted ceilings, whereas two stories of fluted and unfluted columns create a complex web of trabeation in the staircase at the University Library.

ITALY

Italy was partially unified under the French from 1796 to the fall of Napoleon in 1814, but not until the late nineteenth century was it formally united under a single ruler, Victor Emmanuel II. For most

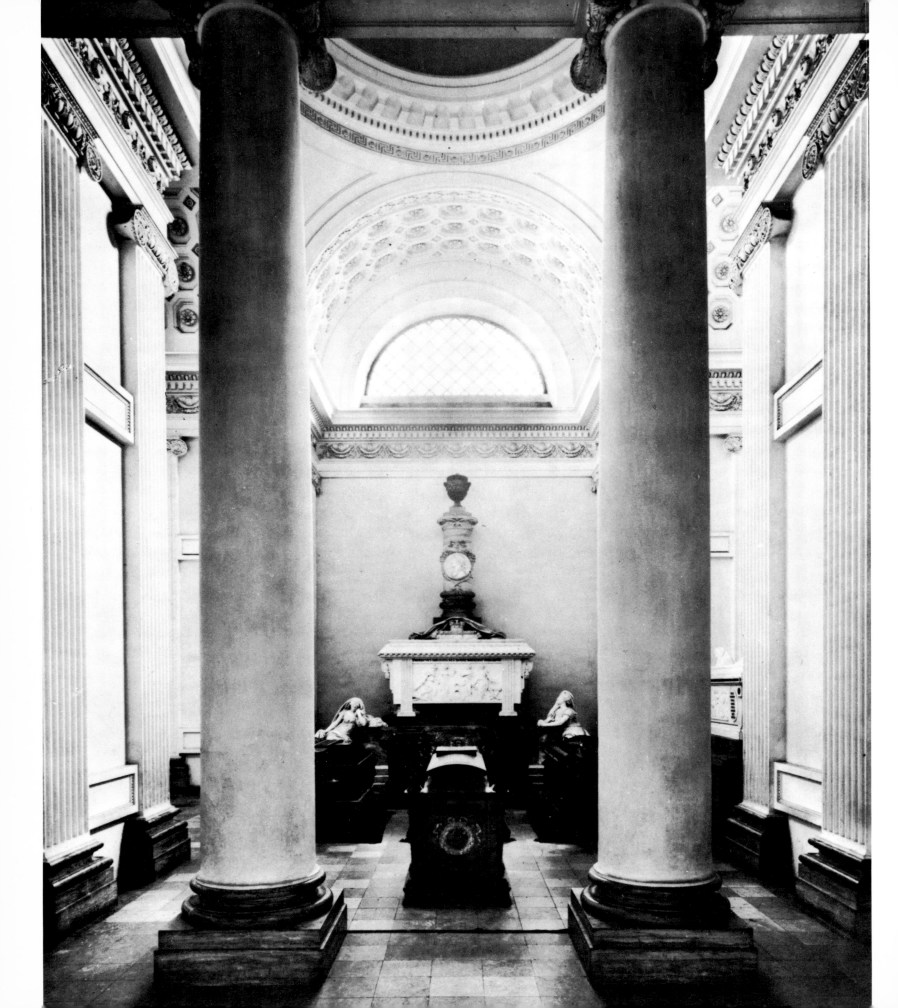

497. *Caspar Frederik Harsdorff, mortuary chapel for Frederik V, cathedral Roskilde, 1768–78. Completed 1821–25 by Christian Frederik Hansen.*

498. *Christian Frederik Hansen, courthouse and prison, Copenhagen, 1803–16.*

499. *Christian Frederik Hansen, Vor Frue Kirke, Copenhagen, 1811–29.*

of the period under consideration it was thus a conglomeration of odd and often opposing states, controlled for the most part by outside powers. Piedmont was completely oriented to France until the Treaty of Aix-la-Chapelle in 1748. Lombardy was a province of Austria until the arrival of Napoleon. Parma remained an outpost of French culture after 1748, when Louis XV's daughter married the Bourbon duke. Venice maintained a staunch independence until Napoleon dismissed the last doge. Trieste owed allegiance to Austria but became a free port in 1719, which inevitably changed things. And so one might continue. There was no common culture. From the middle years of the eighteenth century there was, in addition, very little money. Circumstances were not auspicious for architecture.

Early in the eighteenth century there was, indeed, a short but brilliant flowering of the late Baroque. In Piedmont Filippo Juvarra and Bernardo Antonio Vittone were busy; in Rome those monuments that still give pleasure without alloy—the Spanish Steps (1723–25), the Piazza S. Ignazio (1727–28), and the Fontana di Trevi (1732–62)—were being built. But in the middle years of the century this heady architectural splurge suddenly ceased. Activity continued in the south, where the Bourbons had taken over in 1738. Charles III summoned Ferdinando Fuga (1699–1782) and Luigi Vanvitelli (1700–1773) to Naples in 1751, and there they began some of the largest schemes ever devised for the Bourbons—Fuga's Albergo de' Poveri and the granary, Vanvitelli's royal palace at Caserta and the barracks. But inspiration was weak, and architecture in Italy entered the doldrums.

Even in Venice and on the nearby mainland, where building continued and the fiery Lodoli, as we have seen, was preaching his radical doctrines, little of interest was being done. Lodoli and his circle of intellectuals did not much influence the course of architecture, though Scipione Maffei's Museo Lapidario at Verona, completed about 1746 by Alessandro Pompei (1705–1772), must be regarded as a harbinger of neoclassicism, and Andrea Memmo's public-spirited works in Padua, the Prato della Valle and the hospital, both begun in 1775 by the local professor of architecture Domenico Cerato (1720–1792), were clearly intended to illustrate Lodoli's ideas. But architecture in the Veneto continued to be dominated by the influence of Palladio. Architects as diverse as the exuberant Giorgio Massari (1687–1766) and the over-fastidious Antonio Visentini (1688–1782), designer of the Palazzo Smith (now the Argentine Consulate), of 1751, and the Palazzo Coletti-Giusti, of 1766, both on the Grand Canal, used the elements and the compositional devices that Palladio had established. Ottavio Bertotti-Scamozzi, working in Vicenza on this same basis, was able to evolve an archi-

500. *Christian Frederik Hansen, Vor Frue Kirke, Copenhagen, interior, 1811–29.*

501. *M. Gottlieb Bindesbøll, Thorvaldsen Museum, Copenhagen, court-yard, 1837–48.*

502. *Johann Carl Ludwig Engel, cathedral, Helsinki, 1830–51.*

503. *Johann Carl Ludwig Engel, Senate, Helsinki, 1818–22.*

504. *Johann Carl Ludwig Engel, University Library, Helsinki, reading room, 1836–45.*

505. *Johann Carl Ludwig Engel, University Library, Helsinki, staircase.*
506. *Johann Carl Ludwig Engel, hospital, Helsinki, 1826.*

tecture of some power and conviction, but there was no fresh impulse. Yet a significant line of architectural descent can be traced in Venice, beginning with Massari's master, Andrea Tirali (1657–1737), and his nephew Giovanni Antonio Scalfarotto (1690–1764), designers, respectively, of the giant portico of S. Nicolò da Tolentino (1706–14) and of S. Simeone e Guida (1718–38), a high-domed, circular church, also fronted with a pedimented portico. Scalfarotto's nephew and disciple was Tommaso Temanza (1705–1789), architect of the small but robustly designed circular church S. Maria Maddalena (1760, 1763–78), but remembered chiefly as a stern teacher and propagandist, and especially as author of the *Vita dei più celebri architetti e scultori veneziani*, of 1778. Francesco Milizia was to derive much of his information from Temanza. Lodoli loathed him as an insufferable pedant. They were bitterly opposed, possibly in connection with the building of Temanza's first work, the Capella dei Sagredo, in S. Francesco della Vigna, also in Venice. But Temanza was to attain success through his pupil Giannantonio Selva (1754–1819), who traveled to Rome, Paris, London, and, later, Constantinople, before he settled down to design a number of well-proportioned and clear-cut buildings based on one or two themes and no more, but so competently handled that they are of more than provincial interest: the Teatro La Fenice, Venice, built rapidly between 1790 and 1792, and much reorganized by G. B. Meduna after a fire in 1836, but still today resplendent; the Palazzo Dotti-Vigodarzere, in the Via Rudena, Padua, of 1796; and the two Venetian churches S. Maurizio, begun in 1806, and S. Nome di Gesù, of nine years later, both completed by Selva's assistant Antonio Diedo (1772–1847). With Diedo, Selva also designed the dull facade of the duomo at Cologna Veneta (1810–17) and that most famous and even more boring work associated with his name, the great mausoleum for Antonio Canova at Possagno, of 1819 to 1833 (however, credit—or the reverse—for this conflation of the Parthenon and the Pantheon has not yet been fixed). Selva's most celebrated pupil was Giuseppe Jappelli (1783–1852), the first of these Venetian architects to win international recognition—largely, it must be admitted, for that hydra-headed work, the Caffè Pedrocchi and the Pedrocchino in Padua—part Egyptian, part classical, begun in 1826, part Picturesque Gothic, begun in 1838, all completed by 1842. But Jappelli was also responsible for other equally arresting works, including the stern Doric meat market (1819–24), now the Scuola Pietro Selvatico, and the Villa Treves de' Bonfili, with its *giardino inglese* (now a public park), both in Padua; outside Padua, at Saonara, the far better preserved villa and garden of the Conti Cittadella Vigodarzere (begun 1816); the Villa Gera on the Via F. Benini at Conegliano (1827); and the Villa Manzoni

507. *Alessandro Pompei, Museo Lapidario Maffeiano, Verona, elevation and plan, 1739 – c. 1746.*

at Patt di Sedico (1837), probably the largest in the province of Belluno. Altogether, Jappelli evolved a firm and competent style, one that impinges on international neoclassicism, even if it did not influence it.

When Napoleon reached Venice in 1807, he at once thought to make an impression by ordering large-scale works. Selva built the public gardens at Castello for him, now greatly altered, and also the cemetery, also modified; but most of the major commissions went to outsiders. Giuseppe Maria Soli (1747–1823), from Vignola (though he had trained in Bologna under Malvasia), began the west side of the Piazza S. Marco in 1810. Lorenzo Santi (1783–1839), from Siena, also a pupil of Selva, designed the great stair and the ballroom inside Soli's Ala Napoleonica in 1822. Then he undertook that lively yet

Doric-decked Caffè (1815–38), at the far end of the old Giardinetto Reale, now used as an air terminal, and finally the Palazzo Patriarcale tucked in at the side of the duomo (1837–50). There is nothing much to tell of architecture in Venice after this date.

In Rome, where the turmoil and intrigue occasioned by foreign visitors largely conditioned the form of international neoclassicism, there was even less sustained architectural activity. Piranesi, who arrived there from Venice in 1740, produced only the disappointing, if most intriguing, church of S. Maria del Priorato, high on the Aventine, begun in 1764. Quarenghi, who went in 1763 from Bergamo to Rome, where he met and studied with Selva, stayed long enough to rebuild the church of S. Scolastica at Subiaco (1771–77) before he was packed off to Russia in 1779 by Baron Friedrich Grimm. Carlo Francesco Giacomo Marchionni (1702–1786) was born in Rome but spent his early years in his family's native town of Montecelio, in the Marches. He was trained in Rome, under Filippo Barigioni, and in 1728 won first prize in the Concorso Clementino, at the Accademia di San Luca. By 1751 he had begun work on the Villa Albani, soon to become the mecca of Winckelmann and Mengs. This famous villa, heavily articulated both inside and out, with decorative details evidently influenced by Piranesi, was more or less complete by the end of 1762, though work in the interior continued until 1764, and on the terraces and garden buildings until 1767. It was a tour de force, but not one that had much influence. Nor indeed did Marchionni's other important work, the new sacristy of St. Peter's, erected between 1776 and 1784. This was viciously attacked by the only Italian critic of any acumen, Francesco Milizia (1725–1798), who had come from Otranto, via Naples, to Rome. He was hounded out of town for such effrontery. But his reputation had already been made with the publication in 1768 of the first edition of the *Vita degli architetti più celebri*, to be followed four years after by *Del teatro* and in 1781 by the *Principii di architettura civile*. These were all to be translated abroad.

Neoclassicism came to Rome only after the death of Winckelmann in 1768. He was succeeded as *Commissario dei Musei e Soprintendente alle Antichità* by the archaeologist Giovanni Battista Visconti, who at once initiated the transformation of Innocent VIII's casina in the Vatican as a museum. The alterations to the octagonal court were begun by Alessandro Dori, but in 1772 Michelangelo Simonetti (1724–1781) took up the work, which was to be continued with real enthusiasm only after the election of Pius VI in 1775, when Simonetti was joined by Pietro Camporese (1726–1781). The Sala delle Muse, the Sala a Croce Greca, and the new access stairs are all theirs, while the Braccio Nuovo, built between 1817 and 1822,

508. *Andrea Memmo and Domenico Cerato, Prato della Valle, Padua, 1775–90. Engraving by Piranesi.*

509. *Antonio Visentini, Palazzo Smith (now Argentine Consulate), Venice, 1751. Enlarged by Giannantonio Selva in 1784.*

510. *Tommaso Temanza, S. Maria Maddalena, Venice, 1760, 1763–78.*

511. *Giannantonio Selva, Teatro La Fenice, Venice, 1790–92.*
512. *Giannantonio Selva, S. Maurizio, Venice, begun 1806.*

513. *Giannantonio Selva and Antonio Diedo (attributed), mausoleum of Antonio Canova, Possagno, 1819–33.*
514. *Giuseppe Jappelli, Caffè Pedrocchi, Padua, 1826–31.*

is by Raffaello Stern (1774–1820); together, these rooms make up a sequence of varied spaces, each based on an antique precedent, with the details also of unusual archaeological correctness. The result is indeed neoclassical, and most impressive, but not readily applicable to smaller-scale works.

A confident, easily imitated neoclassical style appeared in Rome only with the arrival of the French. Giuseppe Valadier (1762–1839), who had worked long and hard in the Papal States, and in particular at Urbino, where he had rebuilt the duomo, presented an initial project for the planning and development of the Piazza del Popolo and the Pincio in 1793. This ambitious scheme, with its ramps and carriageways climbing the hill, was at once taken up by the French. Alexandre-Jean-Baptiste-Guy de Gisors (1762–1835) and Louis-Martin Berthault were sent from France to supervise both it and the superb Casina at the top. The final project was not approved, however, until April 1813, and when Pius VII assumed control in 1816 further modifications were made, so that the full splendor of the whole was not to be experienced before 1820. By then Valadier had done several other works of a neoclassical kind: restorations to the Arch of Titus (1819–20) and the Colosseum (1820), but mostly large and pretentious villas. The grandest to be built at this time, the Villa Torlonia, on the Via Nomentana, was begun early in the nineteenth century to the designs of Valadier, who was succeeded within a few years by Giovanni Battista Caretti (1803–1878). He laid out the gardens and the first pavilions, but the later ones and the ruins were built from 1840 to 1846 by Jappelli, Antonio Sarti, and others.

In Rome there was little succession to these works, though Valadier's pupil Lorenzo Nottolini (1785–1851) set up in Lucca, where he designed a noble stairway and sculpture gallery for the Palazzo Ducale in 1818 and, in 1826, proposed a grand layout for the Prato del Marchese not unrelated to Memmo's town-planning venture in Padua. During these years he built a succession of bridges and aqueducts, town houses, and, in particular, the Specola (Observatory) and Rotonda, at Marlia nearby, that conferred something of cosmopolitan sophistication on this provincial outpost.

Clearly, the development of architecture in Venice and Rome was, at first, sluggish, and when the pace quickened it was owing largely to outside influence. Selva was probably more indebted to the English example than to the French (though in his obituary Diedo described Selva's early work as in the "gusto francese'), but most architects took their cue from Paris. This is not, of course, to suggest that the Italians themselves had nothing to offer, but rather to indicate that the style of 1800 was one that the French had first fashioned and used—exploited, even—long before the Italians took it up and gave

517. *Michelangelo Simonetti and Pietro Camporese, Sala delle Muse, Vatican Museum, Rome, begun soon after 1775.*

518. *Michelangelo Simonetti and Pietro Camporese, Sala a Croce Greca, Vatican Museum, Rome, begun soon after 1775.*

519. *Raffaello Stern, Braccio Nuovo, Vatican Museum, Rome, 1817–22.*

it their own particular twist. The French provided not only the ideas and the examples but also the authority and power. They were invaders intent to make their presence felt and seen. They were great builders. The same, to a lesser extent, was true of the Austrians. Throughout Italy the impetus for change came from outside.

In Trieste, Germanic influences were strong, starting with Matteo Pertsch, who had trained under Giuseppe Piermarini in Milan and adapted his master's La Scala for his first works of importance, the Teatro Grande (now Verdi), in 1798–1806. His mature works, too, relate to Milanese classicism: the vast Palazzo Carciotti (1799–1806), conspicuously and rather ridiculously domed; nearby, also on the Riva 3 Novembre, the front of S. Nicolò dei Greci (1818–19); and—still within the new quarter of the town then being developed—the Rotonda dei Pancera (c. 1818). The second and far more able architect active in Trieste was Pietro Nobile (1774–1854), from the Ticino area of Switzerland, who trained from 1803 to 1805 in Rome. But he was soon established in Trieste, where he designed the Fontana House in 1813–16 (built only in 1827–30) and the Accademia di Commercio e Nautica (now the Biblioteca Civica Hortis), of 1817. His major work was S. Antonio Nuovo (1825–49), a noble church, beautifully sited at the head of the Canal Grande, and of more spatial interest than anything else of the period. His Costanzi House, of 1840, trim and unadorned, is in a style that was by then long out of fashion in the rest of Europe. In 1817 he was called to Vienna, where he was to build the Theseus Temple in the Volksgarten, of 1822, and the nearby Burgtor, of 1821 to 1824, in a heavy classical style still coherent and strong.

In Genoa the spark was kindled by de Wailly. Work on his salon for the Palazzo Spinola, commissioned in 1772, was supervised by Emanuele Andrea Tagliafichi (1729–1811), who traveled two years later to Paris, where he was made a corresponding member of the Académie. His original contribution came in the stair hall and salon of the Palazzo Durazzo-Pallavicini, in the Via Balbi, begun in 1780. But the only Genoan architect of consequence was Carlo Francesco Barabino (1768–1835), designer of the Teatro Carlo Felice and the related Palazzo dell' Accademia (1825–28; badly damaged in 1944) and of the first project for the cemetery of Staglieno (1835, 1844–51). He had trained in Rome with Giuseppe Barberi.

In Florence, activity was stirred by the work of redecorating the Palazzo Pitti, from 1796 onward, by Gaspare Maria Paoletti (1727–1813). He was responsible for the first design for the ballroom, while his pupils Giuseppe Cacialli (1778–1828) and Francesco Gurrieri Pasquale Poccianti (1774–1858) designed the highly articulated stairway in the garden wing. All were involved also in the rebuilding of the Villa del Poggio Imperiale, outside Florence, for Queen Marie Louise, whose kingdom of Etruria existed from 1801 to 1808. The powerful facade there was designed by Poccianti in 1806, but he left the work to Cacialli, to return to Florence, to the Pitti and to design the Sala d'Elci (1817–41) adjoining Michelangelo's Biblioteca Laurenziana. He also took up the system of aqueducts, filters, and cisterns in and around Livorno, which were to culminate in his Cisternone (1829–42), a not unworthy successor to Ledoux's gateway at Arc-et-Senans and certainly the most successful attempt in Italy, if not in all Europe, to realize the dreams of French visionaries. Giovanni Antonio Antolini, it seems, offered his advice, but Poccianti kept him at bay in Bologna by sending him his favorite salamis. The Cisternino, which came later, between 1837 and 1848, is powerful, too, but without dramatic impact.

Poccianti's facade for the Villa del Poggio Imperiale must have impressed deeply the young Antonio Niccolini (1772–1850), the stage designer, who worked there and also at Livorno. He reached Naples in 1808 (two years after the arrival of the French) and was commissioned one year later to design a new facade for G. A. Medrano's Teatro S. Carlo; the result was a tough Florentine (and French) leviathan, at odds with the sloppy Baroque architecture that the Bourbons had cultivated until then, *pace* the Vanvitellis. The facade was largely built in 1810. Six years later the old theater burned down and Niccolini was employed with Antonio de Simone to erect a new one behind it. For the Bourbons, who returned in 1815, he built extensively: On the Vomero he put up the Villa Floridiana (1817–19) and the adjoining Villa Lucia (1818) for Ferdinand I and his morganatic wife, Lucia Partanna; in the Piazza dei Martiri he refaced and decorated the Palazzo Partanna. Most of his energy was spent on designs for the reordering of the royal palace itself, but he saw none of this built. Outside Naples his chief works were in Bari: the Teatro Piccini (now part of the Palazzo Communale) and the church of S. Ferdinando, both projects supervised by his son Fausto.

The second altogether surprising and successful building begun at Naples under the French was the church of S. Francesco di Paola, enclosing the Piazza del Plebiscito with curved colonnades. The Foro Murat, as it was first called, was established by a decree of February 1808; demolition was begun at once but Leopoldo Laperuta's design was chosen only later in the year. The colonnades were built and the church started with the assistance of Antonio de Simone, but when the Bourbons returned they decided that it should become a dynastic chapel, dominating the square, now named the Foro Ferdinando. A competition for a new church was held. Eventually, after much intrigue and trickery, Pietro Bianchi (1787–1849), a pupil

521. *Matteo Pertsch, Palazzo Carciotti, Trieste (right). The Canal Grande and S. Antonio Nuovo are in the background.*
522. *Pietro di Nobile, S. Antonio Nuovo, Trieste, 1825–49.*
523. *Antonio Asprucci, Temple of Aesculapius, Villa Borghese, Rome, 1787.*

524. Francesco Gurrieri Pasquale Poccianti and Giuseppe Cacialli, Villa del Poggio Imperiale, Florence, begun 1806.
525. Francesco Gurrieri Pasquale Poccianti, Sala d'Elci, Biblioteca Laurenziana, Florence, 1816–41.

of Luigi Cagnola from the Ticino area, was commissioned to build it in 1817. It was completed by 1831, the most carefully detailed and richly finished of all new churches in Italy.

Related to, but distinct from, the activity in Naples was that in Sicily, in Palermo, where the break from the late Baroque was occasioned by the Frenchman Léon Dufourny. He spent six years there, and between 1789 and 1792 built the Villa Giulia, a botanical institute, stiff and four-square, clearly inspired by the Doric temples of the island. This was soon extended by two pavilions in an even more consciously primitive style by Giuseppe Venanzio Marvuglia (1729–1814). He had studied under Vanvitelli in Rome and had pursued an active if undistinguished career in Palermo until, inspired by Dufourny, he began La Favorita, or Palazzina Cinese, in 1799, a curious but captivating confection, part classical, part Chinese. In the garden he built the Fontana dell'Ercole, a monstrous Doric column supporting a tiny statue of Hercules. His other late work, the Villa Belmonte, of 1801, high on the slopes of Monte Pellegrino, was less engaging and far more restrained. In 1805 he was elected a corresponding member of the Institut National des Sciences et des Arts (later the Académie des Beaux-Arts) in Paris.

Architectural activity, though fervid during the Napoleonic interlude, was, on the whole, sporadic. Only in Lombardy was it sustained and consistent over a long period. The *locus classicus* for reform, however, was not in Milan but in Parma, where an academy was established in 1752, to which, on the Comte de Caylus's suggestion, Soufflot's pupil Ennemond-Alexandre Petitot was invited in the following year. He introduced and cultivated the French tradition both in his teaching and by his example. As court architect he built the new facade of S. Pietro (1761) and the Palazzo di Riserva (1764), both painted yellow; he drew up plans for La Pilotta (1766), an extended palace that was not to be built but that served nonetheless as a point of reference for his pupils; and he altered and enlarged the Palazzo Ducale (1767 onward), known also as the Palazzo del Giardino. Nearby, in Colorno, he built La Veneria (1753–55) and S. Liborio (1775–91), both of which were thought to be very French: La Veneria on account of its round-headed windows, the church because of the freestanding columns inside, which were more in evidence in the initial scheme than in the one executed. Petitot's style was scarcely advanced, despite the evidence of his student projects. However, he was able to handle the elements of A.-J. Gabriel's style with sufficient competence and confidence, and his academy became famous. When Catherine the Great decided to set up one of her own, she wrote to Petitot for advice. His pupils were legion: Agostino Gerli, Simone Cantoni, Carlo Felice Soave, Giocondo

Albertolli, Carlo Antonio Aspari, and Faustino Rodi (1751–1835) among them. Gerli, who worked also in Paris, perhaps with Honoré Guibert, is often thought to have marked the beginnings of late eighteenth-century classicism in Lombardy with his decorations for the main salons of the Villa Longhi at Vialba, begun in 1769. But there was more to the new style than decoration.

Power in Milan was long the Austrian prerogative, but after 1796 it passed several times into the hands of the French, causing upheavals and changes in personnel. Both administrations, however, were efficient and ambitious, and their aims were not dissimilar. The pattern of architectural development, if not the personalities involved, continued throughout almost uninterrupted.

When Caylus visited Milan in the first half of the century he found it a miserable city, but with the building of canals in the Lombardy plain and the consequent spectacular expansion of agriculture, landowners became richer and thought to build both town and country houses. The Austrians, moreover, were able to collect taxes with greater success than ever before. Milan was slowly rebuilt. Roads were constructed and new areas opened up on the sites of the monastic establishments that had been suppressed—twenty-six were closed down in 1782 alone. In 1790 the old gates were torn down and the city limits increased. The building of houses continued apace. Under Napoleon's administration even larger planning proposals were instigated and much was built. The nature of the city was not, however, to be greatly changed until the middle of the nineteenth century, when silk and cotton mills were opened up and industrialization began. This is part of a later history.

Under the Austrians architecture in Milan was dominated by Giuseppe Piermarini (1734–1808), who had worked for twelve years in Rome and Caserta with Vanvitelli and was brought by him to Milan in 1769, when he was invited to rebuild the Palazzo Ducale. Soon after, Piermarini took the project over and was made *Architetto di Stato*, a position he held until he fled from the French in 1796. For twenty-five years he controlled all building; nothing was erected of which he did not approve. He also ensured a continuance of his tastes by presiding over the Brera Academy, founded in 1776. His first independent work was the Accademia Virgiliana in Mantua, designed in 1770, built between 1773 and 1775. This is uninspiring, with an uneasy relationship between plan and elevation indicative of Piermarini's weakness as an architect. Not that this seems to have affected his career. He began in Milan with the vast Palazzo Belgioioso (1772–81) on the piazza of the same name, with a facade that is heavily articulated, though each element, even the individual rustications, retains a curious isolation. Other houses followed, the best

528. *Leopoldo Laperuta, Antonio de Simone, and Pietro Bianchi, S. Francesco di Paola, begun 1809, redesigned 1817, finished 1831.*
529. *Giuseppe Venanzio Marvuglia with Giuseppe Patricola, La Favorita (or Palazzina Cinese), Palermo, 1799–1802.*
530. *Ennemond-Alexandre Petitot, La Veneria, Colorno, 1753–55.*

of which are the Palazzo Greppi (1772–78); the Palazzo Moriggia (c. 1775), in the Via Borgonuovo; and the Casnedi House (c. 1776), with facades made up, as it were, of thin layers of rectangular panels. They are, for the rest, unadorned: "Ces indignes façades à la Piermarini," Stendhal wrote in his guide to Rome, Naples, and Florence. But the major work of this period was the Palazzo Ducale, which he took up in 1773 and continued until 1778. Here he introduced for the first time the most famous of the seven Albertollis, Giocondo (1742–1839), who had taught design at Parma for ten years, before moving in 1772 to Rome and then to Naples to work with Vanvitelli. By 1774 he was in Florence, cooperating with Paoletti on the Sala della Niobe in the Uffizi, and also at the Villa del Poggio Imperiale, to which he later returned. Late in 1774 Piermarini invited Albertolli to Milan, where he began on the interiors of the Palazzo Ducale—"il primo esempio," he said, "di buon gusto"—now sadly charred. He soon took over all the decorative work in Piermarini's buildings and began teaching also at the Brera Academy. He showed his students how to isolate forms and motifs and then assemble them in geometrical patterns. His pupils were numerous; it has even been suggested that Percier and Fontaine are to be numbered among them. Selva certainly was. Albertolli's publications, the *Ornamenti diversi inventati* (1782), *Alcune decorazioni di nobili sale ed altri ornamenti* (1787), and *Miscellania per i giovani studiosi del disegno* (1796), made his style even more readily available. This was of the heavy sort, not unlike that of Jean-Louis Prieur and of Neufforge. His only important independent building was the Villa Melzi (1805–15), at Bellagio, overlooking Lake Como. The facade, as in Piermarini's houses, is curiously flat.

Outside Milan, at Monza, Piermarini built the Villa Ducale (1776–80), once again decorated by Albertolli, though the chapel, still intact, was all to Piermarini's design. At Cassano d'Adda he erected a smaller variant in the extension to the Villa Borromeo (1780–85). Both these buildings are made up of cubic masses, the surfaces smooth and flattened, altogether without strength, as indeed was his last major work in Milan, the Teatro alla Scala (1776–78). The detail here is too lightweight. The interior has been many times altered. Yet within a year of laying the foundation stone Piermarini was busy on another theater in Milan, the Canobbiana (for those members of the aristocracy who had failed to get a box at La Scala), and was soon at work on others at Novarra (1777), Monza (c. 1778), Mantua (1782–83), Crema (1783–85), and Matelica (designed 1803; built 1805–12). Those for whom he did not build imitated him: at Trieste, as we have seen; at Piacenza; and even as far afield as Lisbon, where J. Costa y Silva built the new opera house

533. *Plate from Giocondo Albertolli's* Alcune decorazione di nobili sale ed altri ornamenti, *1787, showing interior decorations.*
534. *Giuseppe Piermarini, Villa Ducale, Monza, 1776–80.*

in 1792. Selva, who had been replaced as architect to the theater at Trieste by Piermarini's pupil Pertsch, disliked La Scala; it was, he noted, far too French. But there is really nothing particularly French about Piermarini's work. His contemporary Simone Cantoni (1739–1818), who had also worked for Vanvitelli but had trained between 1767 and 1768 in Parma and then with Tagliafichi in Genoa, was more French-inspired. Piermarini saw to it that he received no official commissions, but he built a great number of town and country houses and one public building, the Palazzo Ducale (1778–83) in Genoa. Milizia inspected the salon there and, even before its completion, conferred his approval. But the two works that reveal Cantoni at his most Gallic are the Palazzo Serbelloni (designed 1775; much revised and built 1779–94), 16 Corso Venezia, Milan, where Napoleon was received in 1796—though the grand salon was not complete until 1814—and the Palazzo Pertusati (1789–91), on the canal in Milan, now destroyed. The likes of these had not been seen in Italy. The first building has two attenuated Ionic columns set *in antis* within a central feature, topped by a steep pediment, screening a continuous bas-relief panel, a combination of motifs first used by Bélanger. The second was even more closely modeled on a Parisian *hôtel*, of the type of the Hôtel d'Argenson. But Cantoni was a wayward architect. For the Serbellonis he also built SS. Protasio e Gervasio at Gorgonzola (where in 1775 he had already designed the cemetery), a bold but broken composition consisting of a central portico linked by low arcades to two pavilions with great arched openings breaking into the pediments above. Behind the facade other features were piled up, topped by a lantern. The church, which shows Cantoni at his most idiosyncratic, was begun in 1802 and finished in 1842, when the campanile was completed by Giacomo Moraglia. Between these works came a long series of villas, starting with the Villa Olmo at Borgovico (1782–94), and including the Villa Giovio at Brescia (1790–95) and the Villa Gallarati-Scotti at Oreno (1790–93). Together they present an extraordinary medley of styles, some traditional, some more advanced, but having in common only Cantoni's consistent fondness for *atlantes* supported on attenuated pedestals in the attic story.

Piermarini's pupils Leopoldo Pollack (1751–1806) and Luigi Canonica (1764–1844) set the tone of a revised architecture more effectively. Pollack was trained in Vienna with his father, a builder, as was his younger brother Michael Johann, who was to become the most active architect in Budapest. In 1775 Pollack moved to Milan, where Piermarini at once set him to work on the Palazzo Ducale. Canonica, born in the Ticino, was trained by Piermarini at the Brera Academy and inherited thus his administrative skills. When the

French arrived in 1796 and Piermarini fled to his native Foligno, Canonica assumed the title of *Architetto di Stato*, for which he was not forgiven: "Capace," Piermarini said of him, "della più nera ingratitudine." Canonica was trusted by the French, though, who invited him to Paris in 1805, and also by the Austrians, for he retained his position until 1807, when it was thought more democratic to set up a commission of five (the Commissione d'Ornato) to control building activity in Milan. Canonica was judicious and competent always. He laid out much of Milan and erected many public and administrative buildings, in particular, the enlargement of the Collegio Elvetico for the senate. Tact was one of his great qualities. This is evident in his own works, which merge into the street pattern: the Palazzo Brentani-Greppi (1829–31), in the Via Manzoni, for example, with its recessed roundels above the windows of the *piano nobile*; on the same street, the Palazzo Anguissola-Traversi (1829–30), with fluted Corinthian pilasters and a rich frieze. Behind, in the Via Morone, is the Anguissola House (1775–78), by Carlo Felice Soave (1740–1803), another Ticenese taught at Parma; its detailing is very much more lively and well thought out, especially on the garden front and in the interiors. Together, these buildings reveal the extraordinary homogeneity of the style developed in Milan at this period. Canonica designed only one building that stands out—and it can hardly have done otherwise—the vast Arena in the park, laid out between 1805 and 1807 and completed in 1824, with a triumphal gateway of 1813. This is very simple, but of a size and scale that lend it grandeur. The inspiration was not Canonica's alone but derives in part from the perfervid activity in Milan of both Giuseppe Pistocchi (1744–1841), who came from Faenza, and Giovanni Antonio Antolini (1753–1841), who came also from Faenza after a long stay in Rome, in 1800. In Milan they indulged themselves in a series of public-spirited projects for the area around the Castello Sforzesco, which, in effect, meant mammoth projects, of which Canonica's Arena was the only built result.

Pollack was a less dutiful follower of Piermarini; he had a style of his own. This was evident from the first, when he took over from Piermarini the building of the University of Pavia: In 1785 came the anatomy theater (Aula Scarpa); in 1786 he began the third court; and by 1787 the physics theater (Aula Volta) was complete, all three in a fashionable French manner. The main stair, not greatly different, was built much later, in 1828, by Giuseppe Marchese. Petitot approved what he saw there: "Bon, bon," was his laconic comment. But Pollack's reputation was made, rather, by the Villa Belgioioso (later Reale), of 1790–96, in Milan. This hints, once again, at French sources, but has, in addition, that tight-packed quality of Piermarini's facades

at the Palazzo Belgioioso. The rich interiors provide an odd setting today for the Galleria d'Arte Moderna. The garden, to which Selva and Carlo Amati also contributed, is one of the earliest in the city in a full-fledged Picturesque style, preceding by almost a decade the publication in 1801 of Ercole Silva's pioneering study *Dell'arte dei giardini inglesi*, though not, of course, antedating Silva's own garden at the Villa Ghirlanda Silva in Cinisello Balsamo. Pollack's most distinguished works followed soon after, the Villa Casati at Muggio and the Villa Villani Rocca-Saporiti, known as La Rotonda, at Borgovico, in both of which the central oval salon plays a dominant part, though in neither instance is it an effective part of the planning arrangements. Pollack, like Piermarini and Canonica, was an indifferent planner. And, again like Canonica, his work is seen to best advantage in the context of contemporary architecture. This may still be done at Borgovico, on the western side of Lake Como, starting with the Villa Carminati (Resta Pallavicino), by Soave, arriving halfway along at La Rotonda, and ending at Cantoni's Villa Olmo and, down a side street, Soave's Villa Salazar. This architectural panorama is wonderfully varied, yet unified.

Only one architect of note succeeded these men, Luigi Cagnola (1762–1833). He represents the climax in the development from Piermarini, a development from a desiccated planar geometry applied to facades to a robust and very solid geometry of form. Cagnola had intended to be a diplomat and began his career in 1795 in Vienna. There he first dabbled actively in architecture, designing a gateway. His initial work in Italy was the Villa Zurla (Vimercati-Sanseverino) at Vaiano Cremasco, almost complete in 1802, when it was damaged by earth tremors. This low, colonnaded building was the outcome of a few years of study at the Academy in Venice and also of a particularly close inspection of the works of Palladio—not that Cagnola's borrowings were ever to be much in evidence. He was a rabid nationalist, which he thought the correct attitude for one of aristocratic descent at that time of unrest, and he turned thus to Italian sources for inspiration: to Palladio, to the Florentine Renaissance, and to ancient Rome. These sources conditioned even his earliest works. In Milan he built the Porta Ticinese (or Marengo), of 1801–14, a simple pedimented portico, and the Arco del Sempione (or della Pace), of 1806–38. Other gates built there in those years were the Porta Nuova (1810–13) by Giuseppe Zanoia (1752–1817); the Porta Comasina (now Porta Garibaldi), of 1826, by Giacomo Moraglia (1791–1860); and, best of all, the Porta Venezia (1827–33) by Rodolfo Vantini (1791–1856). Of these, Cagnola's Arco del Sempione was the one most deliberately based on ancient Roman precedents and executed with the richest of materials and sculptural details. The finest

535. *Giuseppe Piermarini, Teatro alla Scala, Milan, 1776–78.*

536. *Simone Cantoni, hall on the first floor, Palazzo Ducale, Genoa, decorated in 1783.*

537. *Simone Cantoni, project for the Palazzo Pertusati, on the Naviglio, Milan, 1789–91.*

538. *Giovanni Perego and Innocenzo Domenico Giusti, Palazzo Rocca-Saporiti, Milan, completed 1812.*

539. *Luigi Canonica, Arena, Milan, aerial view, 1805–24.*

540. *Giovanni Antonio Antolini, project for the Foro Buonaparte, Milan, 1801.*

541. Leopoldo Pollack, Villa Belgioioso (now Galleria d'Arte Moderna), Milan, plan of the gardens, 1790–96.
542. Luigi Cagnola, Porta Ticinese, Milan, 1801–14.

543. Leopoldo Pollack, Villa Belgioioso (now Galleria d'Arte Moderna), Milan, garden facade, 1790–96.
544. Luigi Cagnola, Arco del Sempione (or Arco della Pace), Milan, 1806–38.

panels were carved by Pompeo Marchesi. Cagnola was to prepare a design for Malmaison after the dismissal of Percier and Fontaine, but his next executed work was his own house. Begun a year or two before 1816, when he married his cousin Francesa del Marchesi d'Adda, it was continued for seventeen years after that date. This was his masterpiece. It is a great inflated piece of architecture set high on a hill overlooking Inverigo, all columns and pedimented porticos approached up giant stairways on one side, all rustications pierced with round-headed openings on the others. In the center is a flattened dome covering a circular hall. A small portico halfway up the hill has giant *atlantes* by Pompeo Marchesi. Formal geometry is the determining factor throughout. The internal planning and spatial organization are altogether inept. But having found his style, Cagnola stuck to it: at the Villa Cagnola at Verdello (c. 1820), which has surprisingly pretty floral frescoes in the rooms and romantic ruins in the garden; and at the colonnaded church of Concorezzo (1818–58) and that mammoth Pantheon-like one at Ghisalba (1822–33). For neither of these churches did he design the campanile, though he was responsible for the very stylish one at Urgnano (1824–29), near Ghisalba, and another at Chiari (1832), further to the southeast. He built very little in the last years of his life, but he was long held in awe, both by his students and by architects throughout Italy and even abroad. He designed a mausoleum for Metternich and an imperial palace for Vienna, neither of which was built. He was, in fact, a very limited architect, but he appeared to provide a focus in Italy for a style that was based on national precedents demonstrably large in scale, and strong. His appeal to all those architects who prepared vast designs in 1813 for the Monumento alla Riconoscenza al Moncenisio—Selva, Cantoni, and Pistocchi among them—must have been hard to resist. His ability is at once apparent when his work is compared with that of such a follower as Carlo Amati (1776–1852), architect of S. Carlo al Corso in Milan, built, despite well-founded alarms as to its structural stability, between 1839 and 1847. This overscaled church brings to a close the classical movement in Milan, if not in Italy. The rest is gutless niceties. The next phase, beyond the scope of this book, is represented by the Galleria Vittorio Emmanuele II, built by English entrepreneurs with English capital, between 1865 and 1877, to the designs of Giuseppe Mengoni (1829–1877). This is an aspect of the late nineteenth-century process of industrialization and large-scale replanning in Italy, the most disastrous result of which was the destruction of the heart of Florence in 1888.

In all this history there has not been much evidence offered of intellectual endeavor. Much of what there was came during the eighteenth century from France. Milizia's debt has already been men-

tioned; other authors could be adduced: Paolo Frisi, whose *Saggio sopra l'architettura gotica* was published in Livorno in 1766, or Ermenegildo Pini, author of *Dell'architettura dialogi*, of 1770. But these are of no great moment. They offered compilations of French thought.

During the nineteenth century the intrusion of new ideas was owing to the activities of the Gothic Revivalists—as it was throughout most of Europe. The Gothic Revival came late to Italy; it began in the early nineteenth century as a foreign import, largely from England, and largely connected with garden decoration. The first structure of any significance was La Margheria at Racconigi, near Turin, of 1834–39, designed by Pelagio Palagi (1775–1860). On the other side of Italy, in Padua, Giuseppe Jappelli had completed his Gothic wing at the Caffè Pedrocchi by 1842. But these were essentially lighthearted, frivolous structures. Gradually, with the growth of Italian nationalism, an interest was stimulated in Italy's own Gothic past; a serious revival was planned. The most influential exponents were Pietro Estense Selvatico (1803–1880) and Camillo Boito (1836–1914). Selvatico, from the Veneto, was no great revolutionary. He adopted ideas from Pugin, Ruskin, and Viollet-le-Duc, but added a few of his own. He did not build much of interest. However, he trained Boito. Boito, though born in Rome, was taught at the Brera Academy in Milan under Friedrich von Schmidt (1825–1891), who was there from 1857 to 1859 but resigned when Milan was finally lost to the Austrians. He devoted much of his later life to the completion of the cathedral at Cologne. It was from neither Selvatico nor Schmidt, however, that Boito borrowed his ideas; these came from the writings of Viollet-le-Duc, whom he may possibly have met when they acted as judges together at the competition for the facade of Florence cathedral. Boito taught in succession to Schmidt at the Brera Academy for no less than forty-eight years. He was thus of some influence in establishing a new and invigorated doctrine on the lines suggested by Viollet-le-Duc. Among his pupils were Giuseppe Brentano, Luca Beltrami, Gaetano Moretti, and Giuseppe Sommaruga. His own buildings, in a stripped, flattened, and very Italianate medieval style, are of more distinction than any others of this sort in Italy—though they are not in the least engaging. At Gallarate, north of Milan, are two of his early works, a cemetery built in 1865, when he was twenty-nine, and a hospital built six years later. These are comparatively restrained, but Boito's Gothic was already becoming more flamboyant and Venetian. At Padua, between 1872 and 1874, he built the Palazzo delle Debite and, five years later, the local museum. But the climax to his career was in Milan, the Casa Verdi, of 1899–1913, on the Piazza Buonarroti, complete

545. *Rodolfo Vantini, Porta Venezia, Milan, 1827–33.*
546. *Luigi Cagnola, S. Lorenzo (La Rotonda), Ghisalba, 1822–33.*
547. *Luigi Cagnola, Villa Cagnola (or La Rotonda), Inverigo, c. 1813–33.*

with Verdi's colorful tomb chamber. Verdi's librettist, the composer Arrigo Boito, was Camillo's brother.

There are a number of buildings of this sort in Italy, though few were so carefully detailed; for the most part they are funerary chapels. The real energies of the Gothic Revivalists went rather into the completion or rebuilding of the facades of medieval churches. Throughout Italy there were competitions, revisions, disputes, and finally long-drawn-out building programs to finish off the churches of the Middle Ages. There was also a handful of staggering Gothic houses built late in the century: Ernesto Pirovano's Villa Crespi at Capriate d'Adda, of 1890, and Gino Coppedè's Castello Mackenzie at Genoa, of a few years later; and there are many more, even in Sardinia. It was not these stylish extravaganzas, however, that were to be influential in the future but rather the writings and teachings of Boito. He encouraged architects to use a wide variety of materials chosen not for their visual interest alone but also for their appropriateness to the particular role they were to perform. Brick was very popular; sometimes it was plastered, though this was not considered to be "honest." Stone was chosen to trim window surrounds to give added strength to the openings. Only colored plaques and tiles were allowed a purely decorative role. Each element was to be made distinct and expressive. Though the buildings might be complex, the thinking behind them was direct and comparatively simple—simplistic, one might say. But Boito did provide the basis for the acceptance in Italy of Arts-and-Crafts ideas and, ultimately, of the Stile Florale—and thus of Futurism.

GREECE

Athens had shrunk to a settlement of less than ten thousand people by the end of the third decade of the nineteenth century. The revival of architecture, classical architecture in particular, was to start late; indeed, the movement was consolidated there only when it was already out of fashion in the rest of Europe. The style, paradoxical as it may seem, was a foreign import. It arrived in 1833 with the new monarch, Otto von Wittelsbach of Bavaria, likewise an import. The first plan for the renewed capital of Athens was drawn up by Stamatios Kleanthes—who had been trained by Schinkel in Berlin—together with Édouard Schaubert. But this plan was not accepted, nor was that drawn up in 1834 by no less a man than Leo von Klenze, who was sent to Greece to straighten things out by Otto's father, Ludwig I of Bavaria. Von Klenze proposed a vast palace in the Kerameikos district, not far from the Temple of Hephaestus. In the same year Schinkel, spurred by knowledge of this grand enterprise, proposed a royal palace on the Acropolis itself. It was a marvelous,

550. *Giuseppe Mengoni, Galleria Vittorio Emmanuele II, Milan, 1865–77.*

Picturesque cluster of classical forms, mingled with the ancient temples. The interiors were to be richly colored. But Schinkel did not visit Greece and could not press his claims. The new town plan and the royal palace were finally undertaken in 1836 to the designs of a less ambitious and more practical man, Friedrich von Gärtner. These German architects, though they built little (and, indeed, von Klenze's only building in Athens, the Roman Catholic church of Aghios Dionysios, built between 1858 and 1887, was in a Renaissance style), set the tone and the pattern for all major building to follow. Neoclassicism was adopted as the official style. This group of architects was succeeded, like the Bavarian dynasty, by Danes: Hans Christian Hansen (1803–1883) and his brother Theophilos Eduard Hansen (1813–1891). These men established neoclassicism in Greece, and set up an array of the most rigid, but also elegant and pristine, monuments to the style to be seen anywhere in the world today. Three of these are ranged together, the University (H. C. Hansen, 1839–49), the Academy (T. E. Hansen, 1859–87), and the National Library (T. E. Hansen, 1859, 1885, 1888–91). But they built a great deal more besides, and so did their pupil Ernst Ziller (1837–1923), who arrived in Athens in 1861, and their rivals and emulators, the Frenchmen François-Louis-Florimond Boulanger (1807–1875) and E. Troumpe and the Greek architects Panayotis Kalkos (1800–1870), Stamatios Kleanthes (1802–1862), and Lysandros Kaftanzoglu (1812–1885). Kaftanzoglu was trained in both Paris and Rome. These men were naturally active mainly in Athens, creating such extravaganzas as the circular court of the Zappeion (F.-L.-F. Boulanger began this in 1874, but it was taken over by T. E. Hansen) and Ilion Melathron, the house of no less a personality than Heinrich Schliemann (now the Supreme Court) by Ziller, of 1890. But major neoclassical buildings were put up also in Piraeus and scattered as far afield as Patras and the remoter islands. Their crisp, rigid forms and details were copied throughout Greece, transforming even the humblest of houses into models of classical rectitude. As late as 1920 the style survived, virtually unaltered and altogether intact. Now many of the lesser buildings are being destroyed. Others have been drastically altered, as was the Dimetrion House (1842–43) on Syntagma Square, by T. E. Hansen, which became the Hotel Grande Bretagne and survived as such until 1958, when it was demolished and rebuilt, only the ironwork being incorporated into the new hotel. Certainly this extraordinary postscript to the neoclassical movement has been much underestimated, by foreigners no less than by the Greeks themselves.

THE UNITED STATES OF AMERICA

The enthusiast for full-scale Greek Revival architecture will find no

551. *Pelagio Palagi, La Margheria, Racconigi, 1834–39.*
552. *Camillo Boito, Palazzo delle Debite, Padua, 1872–74.*
553. *Camillo Boito, Museo Civico, Padua, 1879.*

554. *Aerial view of Athens in 1932, showing the town as laid out in 1836 by Friedrich von Gärtner, with the principal neoclassical buildings: top right, the Royal Palace; grouped together on the left, the National Library, University, and Academy.*

555. *Hans Christian Hansen and Theophilos Eduard Hansen, National Library, University, and Academy, Athens, 1839–91.*

556. *François-Louis-Florimond Boulanger and Theophilos Eduard Hansen, Zappeion, Athens, circular court, begun 1874.*

country so satisfying as North America. Here in the first half of the nineteenth century flowered prolifically, if sometimes coarsely, the seed planted by James Stuart in his Doric temple at Hagley in 1758. Thomas Jefferson (1743–1826) and Benjamin Henry Latrobe (1764–1820) were the most interesting architects in late eighteenth-century America. Though many others were anxious to emulate their example during the Greek Revival of the nineteenth century, none possessed quite the quality of Latrobe. For another classical architect of comparable imagination, America had to wait for the emergence, in the 1870s, of Charles Follen McKim (1847–1909), trained in Paris.

The architect Charles Bulfinch (1763–1844) reflects the uncertain impact on America of the classicism of Chambers and Adam. His domed and colonnaded Massachusetts State House, Boston (1795–98), is a gross and inflated version of the work of Perrault, Chambers, and Adam, but it set the pattern for much official building in the nineteenth century. In the meantime, the more subtle Jefferson was working on the ever-changing designs for his own house, Monticello, at Charlottesville, Virginia. It was conceived in 1771 on a plan taken from Robert Morris's *Select Architecture* (1755) and adapted to a facade from Palladio's *Quattro libri*. The construction of this carefully thought-out, but not, by English standards, especially remarkable, building was carried out between 1771 and 1782. Work was resumed in 1793, and by 1809 the building had been completely transformed into a much more interesting and complex, though basically one-storied, house. With its varied and original planning, its Picturesque parkland setting, and its superb views of mountain scenery, Monticello realized Jefferson's dream of re-creating the Roman villas described by Pliny, admired by Lord Burlington and the English Palladians, and recorded in Robert Castell's *Villas of the Ancients Illustrated* (1728).

In 1785–89 Jefferson designed the Virginia State Capitol, at Richmond, with a vast and rather vapid Ionic portico supposedly inspired by the Corinthian-columned Maison Carrée at Nimes, which he had seen and admired a year or so earlier. In 1790 the site of the new federal city of Washington was selected and plans were drawn up by the Frenchman Pierre-Charles L'Enfant (1754–1825). On Jefferson's suggestion, competitions were held in 1792 for the president's house and the Capitol. The Irishman James Hoban (c. 1762–1831) won the competition for the former with an old-fashioned design copied from James Gibbs's *Book of Architecture* (1728). The competition for the Capitol was inconclusive, and the rather pedestrian pile executed between 1792 and 1828 was the outcome of an uneasy alliance between the Frenchman Stephen Hallet and three English-born architects, Dr. William Thornton (1758–1828), George

Hadfield (c. 1763–1826), and Benjamin Latrobe. The side wings and commanding dome with its cast-iron frame were added in 1851–65 by Thomas U. Walter (1804–1887).

It is a relief to turn from the Capitol to the novelty and charm of Jefferson's University of Virginia, at Charlottesville. The idea of an "academical village" consisting of small, linked buildings surrounded by grass and trees had been growing in Jefferson's mind between 1804 and 1810, but it was not until 1817 that the final plans were drawn up and the foundation stone laid. The captivating arrangement, with its two groups of five Palladian pavilions linked by colonnades and facing each other across a great lawn, seems to have been inspired (ironically, given the libertarian views of Jefferson) by the most remarkable monument of French absolutism, Louis XIV's Château de Marly, which Jefferson had visited with Maria Cosway when in Paris. In fact, Jefferson was anticipated by Soane, whose unexecuted designs of 1809 for the Royal Academical Institution in Belfast, Ireland, had also been inspired by the pavilion layout of Marly. With its low, detached buildings grouped around a huge lawn, William Wilkins's Downing College, Cambridge, England (designed 1804–6; executed 1807–20), was also a precedent for the University of Virginia. Each of Jefferson's ten pavilions, containing lecture rooms and living accommodations for ten professors, was differently designed than the others. Most contained references to such ancient Roman structures as the Ionic order of the Temple of Fortuna Virilis (Pavilion II) and the Doric order of the Baths of Diocletian (Pavilion I). Pavilion IX, with its central exedra, may have been inspired by Ledoux's Hôtel de Guimard (1770) or by Soane's project for Shotesham Park, Norfolk (1785). On Benjamin Latrobe's recommendation, Jefferson placed at the head of the whole composition a great Pantheon or Rotunda (executed 1823–27) containing a suite of three oval rooms and a superb circular library.

Latrobe arrived in Virginia in 1796, having been trained in England by the original if eccentric architect Samuel Pepys Cockerell. Latrobe's first important work in America was his State Penitentiary at Richmond, Virginia (1797–98), whose powerful arched entrance gate is in Soane's "primitivist" style. Latrobe was soon attracted northward to Philadelphia, the national capital from 1790 to 1800, and the largest city in America. In 1798 he received the commission for the Bank of Pennsylvania there. Latrobe's austere templar building, a simple rectangle with a Greek Ionic portico at each end, culminated in a central, circular domed space articulated with a logic and purity evidently derived from the doctrines of Laugier; the top-lit dome recalled Soane's Stock Office of 1792 at the Bank of

England. The demolition of Latrobe's building in the 1860s was a major loss for America. His next endeavor was the Philadelphia Waterworks (1798–1801; demolished 1827); here a rotunda rose from a rectangular base articulated with a radical Greek Doric order, and the whole seems to have echoed Ledoux's Rotonde de la Villette.

In 1803 Latrobe became Surveyor of the Public Buildings of the United States, a post that called for completing Thornton's Capitol Building in Washington, D.C. Latrobe's first House of Representatives was an oval colonnaded space with capitals derived from the Choragic Monument of Lysicrates in Athens. His Soane-like vestibule, with American maize-leaf capitals, built in the east basement in 1809, was rebuilt by him after the fire of 1814. Like Soane at the Bank of England and the Law Courts, Latrobe responded imaginatively to the task of working in cramped existing structures. After the fire he also rebuilt the Senate and House of Representatives on an improved plan incorporating a small rotunda with tobacco-leaf capitals of his own invention. Based on plans Latrobe had made as early as 1806–7, his Supreme Court Chamber, of 1815–17, beneath the Senate Chamber, is one of the most imaginative American classical spaces. Its trio of arches supported on stunted Greek Doric sandstone columns and its floating half-dome, strangely lobed, owe much to Ledoux and Soane.

Latrobe's best-known building is the Roman Catholic cathedral in Baltimore. With its low segmental dome and emphatically segmental arches, the interior recalls Soane's Bank of England, though the whole is unlike any church Soane ever designed. A masterpiece of sobriety and refinement, the building was designed in 1804–8 and executed in 1809–18; the onion-shaped tops to the belfry towers were added in 1832—but not to Latrobe's designs; his Ionic portico was not completed until 1863, and in 1890 the choir was tactfully lengthened.

Latrobe's pupils Robert Mills (1781–1855) and William Strickland (1788–1854) dominated the architectural scene until the 1840s. Mills worked in Latrobe's office from 1803 to 1808; his early works were centrally planned churches in Philadelphia and in Richmond, Virginia. In his octagonal Monumental Church in Richmond (1812), Mills interpreted the Greek Revival with a characteristically aggressive but thoughtful originality that established him as the heir of such architects as Bonomi and Gentz. In a similar vein was his County Records Office of 1822 at Charleston, South Carolina, designed in an unfluted Doric style and known, because of the manner of its construction, as the "Fireproof Building." His reputation was made with the Washington Monument at Baltimore (1814–29), a giant unfluted Doric column. After its completion, Mills moved to the

city of Washington. He quickly set his mark on the capital with such large public buildings as the Treasury, the Patent Office, and the Washington Monument—all designed in 1836—and the Post Office of 1839. Because of their giant porticos and colonnades and, in the case of the Washington Monument, huge height, they created a more powerful and effective national image than the comparable though slightly earlier buildings in England by Wilkins and Smirke.

William Strickland rose to prominence with his remarkable Second Bank of the United States (later Custom House; 1818–24) in Philadelphia, the first American public building to be based on the Parthenon. His United States Mint (1829–33), in Washington, is an unremarkable classical block, but in 1832–34 came his most imaginative contribution to the Greek Revival, the Philadelphia Merchants' Exchange. The circular Corinthian colonnade of the Exchange, crowned by a tall lantern based on the Lysicrates Monument, has an impressive drama lacking in his last major work, the Tennessee State Capitol, at Nashville (1845–49), where the Lysicratean lantern is less happily related to the building below.

At least as successful as Strickland were his pupils Thomas U. Walter and Alexander Jackson Davis (1803–1892), who formed a partnership in 1829 with Ithiel Town (1784–1844). Town's templar State Capitol for Connecticut, at Hartford (1827), was a worthy successor to Strickland's Second Bank in Philadelphia and led to commissions for similar capitol buildings. The Parthenon was also the model chosen by Davis and Town for their impressive United States Custom House, New York City (now the Sub-Treasury), of 1833–42, and then by Ammi B. Young (1800–1874) for his domed, colonnaded, granite-built Custom House in Boston, Massachusetts (1837–47). Ithiel Town's Bowers House, Northampton, Massachusetts (1825–26), with its giant Ionic portico, is characteristic of countless temple-like houses of the first half of the nineteenth century; James Coles Bruce's Berry Hill, Virginia (1835–40), in the Greek Doric style stands even closer to the paradigm: Wilkins's Grange Park of 1809. Yet another dramatically archaeological house worthy of comparison with Grange Park is Andalusia, north of Philadelphia, designed in 1835–36 by Thomas U. Walter. His patron was the influential Nicholas Biddle, who, unusual in his generation of Americans, had investigated Greek remains at first hand, in 1806. From Biddle also came the inspiration for Walter's singularly beautiful Girard College in Philadelphia (1833–47), whose centrally placed, Corinthian peripteral temple "contains an ingeniously planned three-story complex of groin-vaulted spaces, entirely of the latest (Millsian) fireproof construction" (W. H. Pierson, *American Buildings and Their Architects,* vol. 1, 1970, p. 437). The central temple is flanked on each side by a pair of templar dormitory buildings, the whole suggesting a highly colored version of the theme Wilkins had essayed at Downing College, Cambridge. For the giant portico of his Hibernian Hall in Charleston, South Carolina (1835), Thomas U. Walter adopted the Greek Ionic of the Erechtheum, but Henry Walter's Ohio State Capitol, Columbus (designed 1838 with the assistance of A. J. Davis; built from 1848 on by William Russell West and Nathan B. Kelly), is conceived on an altogether more heroic scale. Its vast octostyle Doric portico *in antis* builds up to a cylindrical cupola in a truly monumental composition. Uniting the styles of Ledoux and Schinkel, Walter here realized the fantastic unexecuted scheme of 1834 by Thomas Rickman and Edward Hussey for the Fitzwilliam Museum, in Cambridge, England.

This fecund classical tradition, gradually failing in quality if not in quantity, dominated American architecture until the 1860s. The return from Paris to Boston in 1865 of Henry Hobson Richardson (1838–1886) opened a new phase in the history of American architecture. Though he had been trained at the École des Beaux-Arts in Paris (1859–62) and had subsequently worked under Labrouste and Hittorff, Richardson did not import French classicism to America. His early works, including the Grace Episcopal Church, Medford, Massachusetts (1867–69), and the B. H. Crowninshield House, Marlborough Street, Boston (1868–69), owe something to contemporary Gothic Revival buildings in England. But in the 1870s, Richardson developed a rock-faced Romanesque—for example, the Brattle Square (now First Baptist) Church and Trinity Church in Boston, of 1870–72 and 1873–77—which owed more to France, and particularly to J.-A.-E. Vaudremer. Perhaps Richardson's finest works were such private houses of the 1870s and 1880s as the William Watts Sherman House, Newport, Rhode Island (1874–75), and Stoughton House, Cambridge, Massachusetts (1882–83), in a tile-hung Manorial style, with spreading plans recalling the work of Richard Norman Shaw.

Thus, Richardson has no real part in the present chapter. It was Charles Follen McKim, also a student at the École des Beaux-Arts (1867–70), and an assistant of Richardson, who instituted an academic classical revival in America. With his two partners, William Rutherford Mead and Stanford White, he produced a series of superlative classical masterpieces with a Roman rather than a French flavor. Despite the brilliance of their Boston Public Library (1887) and of their extensive work in New York City—the Villard houses (1882), Columbia University (1893), the University Club (1899), the Pierpont Morgan Library (1903), and the Pennsylvania Railroad Station (1904–10)—the determinist bias of recent architectural historians has prevented the firm of McKim, Mead & White from receiving the critical attention it deserves.

562. *William Strickland, Merchants' Exchange, Philadelphia, 1832–34.*

563. *William Strickland, Second Bank of the United States (later Custom House), Philadelphia, plan, 1818.*

564. *Thomas U. Walter, Andalusia (near Philadelphia) 1835–36.*

565. *Thomas U. Walter, Girard College, Philadelphia, main building, 1833–47.*

566. *Henry Walter, Ohio State Capitol, Columbus, designed 1838, built 1848 onward.*

567. *McKim, Mead & White, Low Library, Columbia University,*
New York City, 1893.

ENGLAND: *Walpole to Rickman*

By 1750 the Gothic Revival already had a long history in England. One of the most striking and earliest examples of the style is the library of St. John's College, Cambridge, of 1623–24 Justifying the elaborately Gothic design of its windows, a contemporary wrote to the master of the college: "Some men of judgement liked the best the old fashion of church window, holding it most meet for such a building." This justification of Gothic on grounds of environmental propriety was to be echoed for the next hundred years. Its most striking monuments are Sir Christopher Wren's Tom Tower at Christ Church, Oxford (1681), and Nicholas Hawksmoor's additions to All Souls' College, Oxford (1715–34), and his western towers at Westminster Abbey, London (1735–45). One of the first architects to imply that Gothic might have a romance and a quality in its own right was Sir John Vanbrugh, although he never employed the Gothic arch. However, his narrow, tall battlemented house at Greenwich, begun in 1717, is undoubtedly "emotionally Gothic" (J. Summerson, *Architecture in Britain, 1530–1830*, 5th ed., 1969, p. 237). He also argued keenly for the preservation of the "Holbein" Gate at Whitehall and, as we saw in Chapter 2, for the ruins of old Woodstock Manor in the park at Blenheim. If Vanbrugh provided a new emotional stimulus, William Kent created the new language of form that became known as "Georgian Gothic." Kent's innovatory role is thus of immense stylistic significance, but it is to be noted that the following list of his principal Gothic works contains not one that is anything more than an addition to an existing medieval or Tudor building: Esher Place, Surrey (1729–33); the gateway at Hampton Court, Middlesex (1732); the Courts of Chancery and of King's Bench, Westminster Hall (1739); and the pulpit at York Minster and choir-screen at Gloucester cathedral (both 1741). Kent's lighthearted, medievalizing style was basically an inaccurately Gothic treatment of the classical orders and, as such, proved easy to imitate. Batty Langley (1696–1751) developed Kent's hints and codified their details in his book confidently entitled *Gothic Architecture Improved by Rules and Proportions* (1747), though he evidently had some firsthand knowledge of medieval work.

The fruits of all this, in the later 1740s and 1750s, are particularly associated with the name of the Warwickshire squire and amateur architect Sanderson Miller (1717–1780). In addition to erecting sham castles at Edgehill, Warwickshire (1745–47), Hagley Park, Worcestershire (1747–48), and Wimpole Hall, Cambridgeshire (1750), Miller was one of a number of architects responsible for remodeling Arbury Hall, Warwickshire, from 1750 onward for Sir Roger Newdigate. Arbury was a Tudor house with pre-Reformation monastic

origins, so the choice of Gothic could be justified on associational grounds. Its dramatic and beautiful Gothicization, which extended throughout the second half of the eighteenth century, is largely the work of the architect Henry Keene (1726–1776), and, though it contains a number of references to medieval sources, the overall impression is entirely of the eighteenth century. At Lacock Abbey, Wiltshire, Sanderson Miller added a delightful Gothic gateway and great hall in 1754–55 intended to be in keeping with the existing monastic structures. But his most surprising Gothic building is one for which no claims to what we have called "environmental propriety" could possibly justify the choice of style. This is the astonishing Pomfret House built in Arlington Street, London, in 1760 for the widowed Countess of Pomfret. It was as though James Gibbs's Gothic temple at Stowe (1741) had been transferred from a rural to an urban setting.

The choice of Gothic as a style to be admired in its own right, not simply for associational reasons, had been anticipated by Horace Walpole at Strawberry Hill from 1749 to the 1790s. His selection of the Gothic style as a matter of taste is one of the three most important features of the house, the development of which has been so often told it scarcely need be repeated here. The two other points of importance are its asymmetrical growth, in which fortuitous development was emphasized, and the increasing archaeological knowledge that lies behind its stylistic details. With numerous borrowings from an astonishing variety of medieval sources, including tombs at Westminster Abbey and Canterbury, Salisbury, Ely, and Worcester cathedrals, as well as motifs taken from Old St. Paul's, Henry VII's Chapel at Westminster Abbey, and Rouen cathedral, Strawberry Hill was equally the product of collective endeavor as far as a "design team" was concerned. Between the 1750 and 1790s the learned amateurs Richard Bentley, John Chute, Thomas Pitt, and James Essex were assisted by a number of professional architects, including William Robinson, Robert Adam, James Wyatt, and the master mason at Westminster Abbey, Thomas Gayfere. Chute and Gayfere collaborated on the design of the Chapel in the Woods in 1772–74. With a facade based on Bishop Audley's chantry tomb at Salisbury cathedral, it was the most solid and convincing piece of Gothic at Strawberry Hill, for everywhere else the mood was one of rococo gaiety. Indeed, the house that Walpole had bought from the proprietress of a successful London toy shop always retained the aura of a plaything. Walpole's own attitude to it is captured both in a description of the staircase given to a friend in 1753—"[It is] so pretty and so small that I am inclined to wrap it up and send it to you in my letter"—and also in his comment, eight years later, "My build-

ings are paper, like my writings." Strawberry Hill, though visually so gay, was indeed a kind of paper architecture since many of its details were copied not directly from medieval buildings but from engravings of them in books in Walpole's library, notably Sir William Dugdale's *Warwickshire* (1656) and *St. Paul's* (1658) and John Dart's *Westminster* (1723) and *Canterbury* (1726). Paradoxically, the closest parallel to this Picturesque archaeology is the process by which the park at Shugborough, Staffordshire, was adorned by James Stuart during the 1760s with miniature versions of the Athenian buildings he was publishing with Revett in the *Antiquities of Athens*.

The product of a similar antiquarianism, of which Walpole highly approved, was the house of his friend Thomas Barrett, at Lee Priory, Kent (1783–90). Here James Wyatt, who had possibly been recommended by Walpole to Barrett, devised an extravaganza that was a little more archaeologically correct in some of its details than Strawberry Hill and yet, at the same time, almost more fanciful in its provision of an octagonal tower and spire. There were no medieval or monastic associations at Lee ("Priory" being a spurious addition by Barrett) so the choice of Gothic was purely aesthetic. Indeed, Wyatt prepared both classical and Gothic designs for Barrett to choose between. What particularly attracted Barrett and Walpole was Wyatt's ability to suggest growth and change in a building whose owner intended to create the impression of a small convent adapted for domestic use, presumably after the Reformation. In a letter of 1785 Walpole admired the make-believe that led one to "consider the whole as Gothic modernized in parts, not as what it is—the reverse." Its extreme irregularity of plan and outline also gave great pleasure to the eye nurtured on Picturesque principles. The domed octagonal library that forms the striking centerpiece of the whole composition may owe something to the fourteenth-century lantern over the crossing at Ely cathedral.

Ely, or possibly the plates in J. Bentham's *History and Antiquities of Ely* (1771), is also the source of the staggering central tower of Fonthill Abbey, Wiltshire, which Wyatt built for William Beckford between 1796 and 1807. But from Wyatt's imagination alone came the brilliant cruciform plan with its breathtaking vista, more than ninety meters (three hundred feet) long, from the oriel at the end of St. Michael's Gallery, through the central octagon, to the oratory at the north end of King Edward's Gallery. Beckford's original idea, analogous to Barrett's for Lee Priory, was to create a building resembling a convent, partly ruinous and partly converted to domestic use, which he could use for occasional picnics or supper parties. His obsession with the place grew until in 1805 he finally decided to live in it permanently. The grounds were landscaped and planted in such

an appropriately sublime and exotic manner that house and setting eventually became the high-water mark of Picturesque Gothic.

So far, we have seen the Gothic Revival as an aspect of the Picturesque theory that developed from Vanbrugh, through Strawberry Hill and Payne Knight's Downton Castle, to Fonthill Abbey and Nash's brilliant asymmetrical Irish castles Killymoon, near Cookstown (1803), Shanbally, County Tipperary (1812), and Lough Cutra, County Galway (c. 1817)—not forgetting, of course, Nash's own country seat, East Cowes Castle, Isle of Wight (c. 1798; now demolished). We must investigate two other traditions, associated respectively with castle and with church, which owe rather less to the Picturesque. At Clearwell Castle, Gloucestershire (1727), and Inveraray Castle, Argyllshire (begun 1745), Roger Morris (1695–1749) echoed the formal, symmetrical castles of the Middle Ages, which had already been revived in the Elizabethan and Jacobean periods at Mount Edgecumbe, Cornwall, Lulworth Castle, Dorset, and Ruperra Castle, Glamorganshire. From here it was but a step to James Wyatt's Kew Palace, Surrey (1802–11), and Ashridge Park, Hertfordshire (begun 1808); to Robert Smirke's Lowther Castle, Westmorland (1806); and to Eastnor Castle, Herefordshire (1812), and Taymouth Castle, Perthshire (1806–10), by Archibald and James Elliott (1760–1823; 1770–1810).

Church- far more than castle-building in the Gothic style seems almost to have had a momentum of its own. The numerous Gothic churches erected between the time, say, of the younger Wing's church at King's Norton, Leicestershire (1760–75), and of Charles Barry's St. Peter, Brighton (1823–28), do not reveal any substantial development in the understanding of medieval construction, although in his St. Luke, Chelsea (1819–25), James Savage introduced for the first time a masonry rather than a plaster vault. At the church of the Holy Trinity, Theale, Berkshire (1820–28), Edward Garbett and John Buckler (1770–1851) provided a strikingly complete and serious recreation of the lancet mode of Salisbury cathedral. Since Perpendicular was the mode usually adopted in eighteenth- and early nineteenth-century churches, Theale represents a significant attempt to enlarge historical understanding of medieval architecture. By basing the design of the tower on the demolished campanile of Salisbury cathedral, Garbett and Buckler delivered a sharp rebuke to eighteenth-century Gothicists, for the destruction carried out at Salisbury was attributed, not altogether fairly, to James Wyatt.

But the new and more serious phase of the Gothic Revival—of which the design of Holy Trinity, Theale, is a harbinger—was ushered in not so much by architects as by antiquarians and publishers in what J. M. Crook has called the "bibliographical revolution"

(C. L. Eastlake, *A History of the Gothic Revival*, 1872; rev. ed., 1970, ed. J. M. Crook). Between the 1790s and the 1830s John Carter (1748–1817) and John Britton (1771–1857) produced a series of influential books on medieval architecture, which combined scholarship with topography and, like Stuart's and Revett's *Antiquities of Athens*, provided architects with an authentic new vocabulary. Carter's publications included the books *Views of Ancient Buildings in England* (1786–93), *Ancient Architecture of England* (1795 and 1807), as well as numerous articles in the *Gentleman's Magazine* attacking the ill-treatment and ignorant restoration of medieval buildings. Britton's principal works were *The Architectural Antiquities of Great Britain* (1804–14) and, more important, the superbly illustrated, fourteen-volume *Cathedral Antiquities of Great Britain* (1814–35). Thomas Rickman's *An Attempt to Discriminate the Styles of English Architecture* (1817) provided a vocabulary of identification—"Early English," "Decorated," and "Perpendicular"—that was a reassuring parallel to the familiar "Doric," "Ionic," and "Corinthian" of classical architecture, and that had the similar advantage of being easily memorized and applied. Finally, Augustus Charles Pugin's *Specimens of Gothic Architecture* (1821–23) spelled out the language of Gothic detail in technical drawings for the benefit of craftsmen and draftsmen. The scene was now set for the arrival of the hero, and, at the risk of writing determinist or progressivist history, it cannot be denied that Pugin's celebrated son, Augustus Welby Northmore Pugin, seemed destined in every way to fulfill that very role.

ENGLAND: *Pugin and His Impact*

A. W. N. Pugin (1812–1852) has probably exercised as much influence over English architecture and architectural theory as any other architect of any period. In a series of compelling books, by turns amusing, polemical, and scholarly—*Contrasts* (1836), *The True Principles of Pointed or Christian Architecture* (1841), *The Present State of Ecclesiastical Architecture in England* (1843), and *An Apology for the Revival of Christian Architecture in England* (1843)—Pugin made a case for the adoption of Gothic, not as one of a number of styles chosen on grounds of beauty or association but as *the* style, indeed, as "truth." Gothic was the truthful expression of true construction and function, of true religion (i.e., Roman Catholicism), and of the true genius of the English people. Thus, Pugin could claim that what he was defending was "not a style but a principle" (*An Apology*, p. 44). In so doing, he laid the foundations of Victorian architecture and—by implying the special merit of a building that reveals its construction—of modern architecture as well. Whatever our feelings about his conclusions, it cannot be denied that Pugin was one of the few Englishmen

572. *Edward Hussey, Anthony Salvin, and William Sawrey Gilpin, view toward Scotney Old Castle, Kent, 1835–43.*
573. *Augustus Welby Northmore Pugin, St. Marie's Grange, Wiltshire, 1835. Watercolor by the architect.*
574. *Richard Norman Shaw, Adcote, Shropshire, designed 1875.*

who have theorized coherently about architecture; however, to say that he was English is not strictly true. A. C. Pugin was a French emigré, and it is to the intellectual tradition of French theorists from Perrault to Laugier and beyond that his son belonged. Pugin's first book, *Contrasts,* upheld the Gothic cause by an entertaining attack on the Reformation as the begetter of a false religion and a false (i.e., classical) architecture; however, five years later, guessing perhaps that an English Protestant audience might require a wider variety of argument, Pugin justified his passionate adherence to Gothic by echoing the language of eighteenth-century neoclassical rationalism. The equation of architectural beauty with structural honesty was familiar in France and Italy through the writings of such men as Cordemoy, Laugier, and Lodoli, but it had made little impact in England. The rational and academic analysis of Gothic structure as a basis for a modern architecture initiated by Cordemoy was brought to a climax by Pugin's contemporary Viollet-le-Duc. Pugin's contribution to this tradition was less influential than his sociological and ethical interpretation of architecture as the true index of the state of society. This was the vision that fired the Victorian Gothicists Butterfield, Street, Pearson, and Bodley: Christian architects creating a Christian society with Christian buildings, schools, colleges, parsonages, convents, and churches. One of Pugin's principal contributions to the language of form was his insistence that the elevation of a building should be subservient to its plan. Though this principle was derived from his belief in truthfulness, it led, ironically, to a type of self-consciously asymmetrical architecture that closely resembled the products of the Picturesque that Pugin was committed to despise.

In Chapter 2 we emphasized the importance of Salvin's Scotney Castle, Kent (1835–43), in the Picturesque tradition, particularly because of its relation through a landscaped garden to the ruins of the medieval Scotney Castle. Salvin's new building (see illustration 32) was itself equally revolutionary. The asymmetrical separation of part from part on the entrance front, the apparently functional placement of windows and chimneys contrasting eloquently with areas of blank wall, the vigorous diagonality of line—all this could be described as Puginesque, though, paradoxically, the twenty-three-year-old Pugin was not yet capable of work of this quality.

The kind of buildings Pugin was designing in 1835 we can see at his own house, St. Marie's Grange, Wiltshire. Here, though on a much smaller scale, is the same determined asymmetry that characterizes Scotney, and that is supposed to enable us to read the internal disposition of the building. The house was altered and enlarged, probably by Pugin himself, but its original appearance is recorded in a sketch by him of 1835 in which he is careful to show its relation

575. *Augustus Welby Northmore Pugin, Alton Castle, Staffordshire, 1847–51.*

576. *William Butterfield, vicarage, Coalpit Heath, Gloucestershire, 1844.*

577. *Augustus Welby Northmore Pugin, Scarisbrick Hall, Lancashire, 1837–45.*

to the distant view of Salisbury cathedral (and here, of course, is another parallel with Scotney). The cramped, narrow proportions of St. Marie's Grange, the aspiring verticality of its tall roofs and turrets, its steeply sloping site and drawbridge are all unexpected reminders of another pioneering house built by an architect for his own occupancy more than a century earlier, Vanbrugh Castle, Greenwich.

Though Salvin's later career was prolific and in many ways distinguished, he did not quite fulfill the particular promise of Scotney. It was Pugin who developed the language of domestic Gothic in a paradoxical combination of functional and Picturesque that was used to such brilliant effect by Richard Norman Shaw. Between St. Marie's Grange and Shaw's superb Adcote, Shropshire (designed 1875), lie Pugin's Scarisbrick Hall, Lancashire (1837–45), and especially Alton Castle, Staffordshire (1847–51), with its staccato separation of part from part, each functional element with its own appropriate and distinct shape and roof. A humbler line of dwellings also sprang from Pugin's early experiment at St. Marie's Grange. Between 1840 and 1843 he developed the theme of "Picturesque utility" (S. Muthesius, *The High Victorian Movement in Architecture, 1850–1870,* 1971, pp. 4–10) in a series of important and influential houses—Bishop's House, Birmingham (demolished), the Catholic school and teacher's house at Spetchley, Worcestershire, and his own house, The Grange, at Ramsgate, Kent. This earnest and supposedly "truthful" way of building caught on immediately with the Ecclesiological Society, which was busy popularizing in the Anglican church ideas Pugin had claimed were essentially Catholic. Butterfield's Coalpit Heath vicarage, Gloucestershire (1844), and the village of Baldersby, Yorkshire (1855–57); George Edmund Street's Colnbrook vicarage, Buckinghamshire (1853), and group of church, vicarage, and school at Boyne Hill, Maidenhead, Berkshire (1854); and William White's vicarages at Lurgashall, Sussex (1852), and Little Baddow, Essex (1857–58), are all unthinkable without the precedent of Pugin. Not least in importance is the building that stands at the end of this rather glum and cerebral development, Red House at Upton, near Bexleyheath, Kent, designed for William Morris (1834–1896) in 1859 by Philip Webb (1831–1915), which for so long, and so ironically, was hailed as a stepping-stone to the modern movement.

Pugin's church design had probably less influence on his contemporaries than his domestic design. Nonetheless, he has left us some singularly beautiful interiors, ranging from the early St. Chad's cathedral, Birmingham (1839), with its curiously attenuated proportions, to the solidly Early Victorian St. Giles, Cheadle, Staffordshire (1839–44)—elaborately stenciled in imitation of the treatment then being given to the Ste.-Chapelle in Paris—and finally to his late St. Augus-

580. *Augustus Welby Northmore Pugin, St. Giles, Cheadle, Stafford-shire, 1839–44.*

581. *Augustus Welby Northmore Pugin, St. Giles, Cheadle, Stafford-shire, interior.*

582. *Augustus Welby Northmore Pugin, St. Augustine, Ramsgate, Kent, choir, 1845–50.*

583. *John Loughborough Pearson, St. Mary, Dalton Holme, Yorkshire, 1858–61.*

584. *George Frederick Bodley, Holy Angels, Hoar Cross, Staffordshire, 1872–1900.*

585. *George Frederick Bodley, Holy Angels, Hoar Cross, Staffordshire, interior.*

586. Edward Buckton Lamb, Nunn Appleton Hall, Yorkshire, 1864.
587. William Butterfield, All Saints, Margaret Street, London, interior, 1849–59.

588. William Butterfield, All Saints, Margaret Street, London, plan.
589. William Butterfield, All Saints, Margaret Street, London, pulpit.

tine, Ramsgate, Kent (1845–50), possibly his finest church. At Ramsgate, which he paid for largely himself, Pugin was able to indulge his profound feeling for the powerful structure and profuse ornament of English early fourteenth-century Gothic. The result is a moving piece of living archaeology, which deeply influenced such followers of Pugin as Sir George Gilbert Scott, John Loughborough Pearson (1817–1897), and George Frederick Bodley (1827–1907). Pearson's opulent and sophisticated church of St. Mary at Dalton Holme, Yorkshire (1858–61), is a realization of the Puginesque dream as is the sumptuous, much later Holy Angels, Hoar Cross, Staffordshire (1872–1900), by Bodley, in whose career we can trace a Pugin revival. Bodley's All Saints, Cambridge (1861–70), came at the turning point when he rejected the exuberance of the 1850s for the calmer medievalism of Pugin.

ENGLAND: *High Victorian Architecture*

We have just spoken of exuberance as characteristic of the 1850s. It is generally accepted that between 1850 and 1870 the Gothic Revival passed rather unexpectedly through a violent period recognizably different from what preceded and succeeded it. It is by turns muscular and geometrical, naturalistic and polychromatic, often unaccommodating and even brutal. It is particularly associated with Butterfield, Lamb, Teulon, Burges, White, Brooks, and Street and Bodley in their early work. The elaborate secular buildings of Scott and Waterhouse must also be considered as High Victorian.

The oldest architect working in this new manner was Edward Buckton Lamb (1805–1869). His bizarre and assertive Gothic style had its origins in the Picturesque, pre-Puginesque world of John Claudius Loudon (1783–1843) and his circle. He found it early and did not develop it according to the doctrines of Pugin and Butterfield. He was consequently spurned by the Ecclesiological Society, yet the violence of his work in the 1850s and 1860s—for example, at Nunn Appleton Hall, Yorkshire (1864)—justifies his placement in the High Victorian movement. The harsh but roguish complexities of the tower of his Christ Church, West Hartlepool, County Durham (1854), reappeared with undiminished vigor at St. Martin, Vicars Road, Gospel Oak, London (1862–65). Of St. Martin's tower, Sir John Summerson brilliantly observed, "Most towers answer a question. This one asks" (*Victorian Architecture: Four Studies in Evaluation*, 1970, p. 73).

An architect with an equally individual and strident language was William Butterfield (1814–1900). With Pugin he was the most original and influential of the mid-century ecclesiastical architects. The Ecclesiologists were much more concerned than Pugin with the prob-

592. *George Edmund Street, St. James-the-Less, London, apse, 1859–61.*   593. *George Edmund Street, St. James-the-Less, London, interior.*

lems of urban church-building; they were more attracted by force and power in architectural form, and, though deeply influenced by his appeal for constructional honesty, tended to interpret this in terms of structural polychromy: Thus, the English country church of the fourteenth century, which had been Pugin's ideal, was temporarily forsaken in favor of an original amalgam that drew on the more massive forms of the thirteenth century and in which the polychromatic effects of the medieval architecture in Italy and Spain were daringly elaborated in brick. Butterfield's "model church" for the Ecclesiological Society—All Saints, Margaret Street, London (1849–59)—is a doctrinal statement of this new reformed Gothic. It is a forceful and compelling work in which it is hard not to discern a desire to shock. In his distinguished monograph *William Butterfield* (1971) Paul Thompson has tried to absolve Butterfield from the attachment to a kind of creative ugliness that has sometimes been seen in his work. Yet we should not overlook the fact that the Ecclesiological Society's own organ referred to a "deliberate preference of ugliness" in an article on the consecration of the church in 1859 (*The Ecclesiologist*, vol. 20, p. 185). In the early 1850s Butterfield dropped his structural polychromy but returned to it with passion in such churches as St. Alban, Holborn (1859–62), and in one of his most powerful and best-known masterpieces, Keble College, Oxford (1866–83).

As brilliant as Butterfield, and possibly more versatile, was George Edmund Street (1824–1881). His early vicarage and theological college at Cuddesdon, Oxfordshire (1852), and church at Boyne Hill, Maidenhead, contained the seeds of that massive and deceptively simple style that led Charles Eastlake to believe that Cuddesdon College and East Grinstead convent "have literally no architectural character beyond what may be secured by stout masonry, a steep roof, and a few dormer windows," though he claimed at the same time that "there is a genuine *cachet* on each design which it is impossible to mistake. They are the production of an artist hand" (*History of the Gothic Revival*, p. 323).

In 1855 Street published *Brick and Marble of the Middle Ages: Notes of a Tour in the North of Italy*, in which he defended the combination of motifs from different styles and countries. In the late 1850s and 1860s he went on to produce a group of vividly original churches in which he developed his firsthand knowledge of the color and constructional detail of Italian Gothic. From the year 1859 date three remarkable churches in very different parts of the country: St. John the Evangelist, Howsham, Yorkshire; St. Philip and St. James, Oxford; and St. James-the-Less, Westminster, London. The massive chunkiness of St. John the Evangelist, Howsham, with its somewhat

594. *Samuel Sanders Teulon, Bestwood Lodge, Nottinghamshire, 1862–64.*
595. *William White, St. Michael, Lyndhurst, Hampshire, 1858–59.*

Italianate western porch, reappears in the bigger and more sculptural church at Oxford, but it is St. James-the-Less that reveals Street at his most forceful and most brilliant. Of striped and diapered red and black brick it is an electrifying blend of Butterfield's style with early French and north Italian details, dominated by a massive Ruskinian campanile, forty-one meters (one hundred thirty-four feet) of unbuttressed brickwork. Its forceful exterior geometry is echoed internally in the insistent patterning of tile, marble, and mastic. For Charles Eastlake, the whole church was "evidence of a thirst for change which Mr. Street could satisfy without danger, but which betrayed many of his contemporaries into intemperance. Even here there is something to regret in the restless notching of edges, the dazzling distribution of stripes, the multiplicity of pattern forms, and exuberance of sculptural detail" (*History of Gothic Revival*, p. 321).

The "intemperance" Eastlake noted can surely be found in the work of William White (1825–1900) and Samuel Sanders Teulon (1812–1873). Notched, polychromatic, and willful is White's bizarre church of St. Michael at Lyndhurst, Hampshire (1858–59), which has many features in common with Street's St. James-the-Less but markedly lacks its overall balance. But even White's work pales into normality by the side of Teulon's Shadwell Park, Norfolk (1856–60), freakishly muscular, or Burges's additions to Gayhurst, Buckinghamshire (1859). Teulon's early work—for example, Tortworth Court, Gloucestershire (1849–53)—is rather in the busy manner of E. B. Lamb, but by the late 1850s he was producing work in a sculptural idiom similar to Street's but more assertive, exemplified by such buildings as St. Mark, Silvertown, Essex. But it was in country-house design that Teulon's idiosyncratic genius found its fullest expression. His Elvetham Hall, Hampshire (1859–62), for the fourth Lord Calthorpe, is a secular counterpart of Street's contemporary St. James-the-Less, as is also John Prichard's and John Pollard Seddon's Ettington Park, Warwickshire (1858–63). Perhaps the climax of this instantly recognizable and permanently unforgettable Teulon manner is Bestwood Lodge, Nottinghamshire (1862–64), a sensational building, which has inspired Mark Girouard to observe: "Anything striped, spiky, knobbly, notched, fungoid, or wiry fascinated him" (*The Victorian Country House*, 1971, p. 96). Bestwood was built for one of Teulon's characteristically aristocratic clients, the tenth duke of St. Albans, which forces us to question the popular modern notion that the High Victorian style was so vigorously self-assertive it must have been created for the new crude and self-educated captains of industry spawned by Victorian capitalism.

In 1857 John Loughborough Pearson, who had worked in Salvin's office, produced for a clergyman a High Victorian country

596. John Loughborough Pearson, St. Peter, Vauxhall, London, 1860–65.

597. James Brooks, St. Columba, Haggerston, London, 1867.

598. William Burges, Cardiff Castle, Glamorganshire, Banquet Hall, c. 1872–81.

599. William Burges, Cardiff Castle, Glamorganshire, Smoking Room ceiling, 1868–74.

600. *Deane and Woodward, University Museum, Oxford, 1854–60.*
601. *Deane and Woodward, University Museum, Oxford, interior.*

house, Quar Wood, Gloucestershire (mutilated 1954), in a manner similar to but more ordered than Teulon's. Pearson's quietly geometrical St. Peter, Vauxhall, London (1860), with its echoes of Street and Teulon, leads us stylistically to the work of James Brooks (1825–1901). Brooks became known for his powerful and moving churches in the slum areas of London: St. Michael, Shoreditch (1863); St. Saviour, Hoxton (1864); St. Columba (1867) and St. Chad (1868), both in Haggerston; and Christ Church, Clapton (1870).

One of the most attractive of this close-knit group of High Victorian designers was George Frederick Bodley. Poet, musician, and Christian gentleman, strongly disliking the business aspects of his work, he lived richly and well, surrounded by beautiful objects. Disapproving of architectural competitions as much as Butterfield did, he eventually turned to designing luxurious but fastidious churches for artistic dukes. But before this costly Puginesque sensitivity overtook him, he was essentially a part of the "vigour and go" of the High Victorian decades. Like Street and White, he was a pupil of Scott, and his early Normal School at Cheltenham, Gloucestershire (1854), derives, via Pugin, from Street's Cuddesdon of 1852. Bodley's St. Michael and All Angels, Brighton, Sussex (1858–62), is a brick urban church with early French plate-tracery and bands of Italianate structural polychromy. Far more engaging is his All Saints, Selsley, Gloucestershire (1858–62). In some sense Selsley might be regarded as the jewel of the whole High Victorian movement, combining with sobriety and originality on a small scale so many of the characteristics we have described in this chapter. The bold massing, the contrasts of voids and solids, the beautiful grouping on a sloping site—extraordinarily and eloquently emphasized by the external stone staircase leaping up to the two-storied sacristy—the French plate-tracery and the Germanic saddleback tower, effortlessly contained within a design that is still in many ways English, the beautiful Morris glass (possibly the firm's first ecclesiastical commission), with the Nativity in the apse and the Creation in the western rose window: All this adds up to an unforgettable reflection of the mid-Victorian Christian dream of Reformed Gothic and a reformed Anglican church.

In total contrast to Bodley was the architect William Burges (1827–1881), who produced some of the most exuberant and colorful buildings of the 1860s and 1870s. His extraordinarily imaginative remodelings of Cardiff Castle, Glamorganshire (1868 onward), and Castell Coch, Glamorganshire (c. 1875 onward), for his principal patron, Lord Bute, contain interiors which have to be seen to be believed.

It would be wrong to imply that the High Victorian aesthetic was expressed only in church and country-house design. The manner

602. *Sir George Gilbert Scott, competition project for the City Hall, Hamburg, Germany, 1854.*

603. *George Edmund Street, Law Courts, London, 1867 and later.*

604. *William Burges, competition project for the Law Courts, London, 1866.*

is also recognizable in certain public buildings, though the Second Empire style radiating from Paris to England and North America was generally found more convenient for such buildings, particularly those on a monumental scale. A seminal building was the Oxford University Museum, designed in 1854 by Benjamin Woodward, of the firm of Deane and Woodward. Displaying all the polychromy and abrupt angularity of detail and mass required by the "realist" High Victorians, the museum is nevertheless steadied by an impressive, symmetrical entrance facade dominated by a central tower. This memorable formula caught on immediately. It was employed, for example, by Sir George Gilbert Scott in his unexecuted schemes for the City Hall, Hamburg, Germany (1854), and for the Foreign Office, London (1856); by Edward William Godwin (1833–1886) in his impressive town halls at Northampton (1860–64) and Congleton, Cheshire (1864); and by Jeffery and Skiller at Winchester Guildhall (1870–73). More spectacular is Scott's St. Pancras Station Hotel, London (1867–74), with its pinnacled Gothic skyline and its dramatic staircase supported on exposed iron beams.

The competitions held for government offices in Whitehall in 1856 and for the Law Courts in the Strand ten years later produced a rich crop of paper architecture adhering with varying degrees of fantasy to High Victorian modes of thought. Apart from the design by Scott already mentioned, those by Street, by Deane and Woodward, and by Prichard and Seddon for the Foreign Office were the most memorable. A decade later the Law Courts entries were even more exuberant: Burges conducts us to a dream world of twelfth-century France as it never was; the proposals of John Pollard Seddon (1827–1906) seem equally other-worldly until we remember that he contrived to build something similar at Castle Hotel (subsequently University College), Aberystwyth, North Wales (1864); while the gusto of Alfred Waterhouse (1830–1905) shows him at a stage halfway between his early Scott- and Woodward-inspired Manchester Assize Courts (1859–64) and his Manchester Town Hall (1868–77), more freely Picturesque.

After 1870 the urgency of the demand for "truth" and "reform" could no longer be sustained. Something softer and more compromising seemed desirable. Richard Norman Shaw (1831–1912), in some ways the most brilliant architect of the century, is certainly the dominant figure in the story of Late Victorian architecture, yet much of the strength which prevented his architecture from going soft was derived from his High Victorian training in the office of G. E. Street. Such early works by Shaw as his unexecuted Exchange at Bradford, Yorkshire, and his now-demolished Holy Trinity, Bingley, Yorkshire, both designed in 1864, show his complete mastery of the

606. *Sir George Gilbert Scott, St. Pancras Station Hotel, London, stair hall, 1867–74.*

607. *Sir George Gilbert Scott, project for the Foreign Office, London, 1856.*

608. *Richard Norman Shaw, project for the Exchange, Bradford, Yorkshire, 1864.*

609. *Richard Norman Shaw, Leyswood, Groombridge, Sussex, 1866.*

610. *Charles-Auguste Questel, St.-Paul, Nimes, designed 1835, built 1838–50.*

611. *Charles-Auguste Questel, St.-Paul, Nimes, interior.*

style of Street, Butterfield, and Burges. His dazzling Leyswood, Groombridge, Sussex, designed in 1866 for a successful businessman, was a turning point. This theatrical and captivating building caught the "Old English" spirit in an impressionistic rather than a "truthful" way, and thus the step from High Victorian to Late Victorian was made.

FRANCE

During the seventeenth and eighteenth centuries, interest in Gothic in France was firmly subordinated to the tenets of the rational, classical tradition. The architecture of the Middle Ages was studied with the closest attention, even with enthusiasm, but the result of this careful inspection—and it was more painstaking than that conducted anywhere else, England included—was not that the outlines and details of Gothic architecture were imitated, rather that something of the structural finesse they thought to be discernible in Gothic was infused into classical buildings. Soufflot, as we have seen, in designing the greatest church of the eighteenth century, Ste.-Geneviève, sought to put up a building Gothic in its structural principles, classical in appearance. And this curious equation was attempted by a host of other architects in France. Toward the end of the eighteenth century, when they had learned to appreciate the solid, sculptural qualities of mass, French architects found the elegant refinements of Gothic of far less interest. Indeed, the study of Gothic virtually ceased at that time. This waning interest in what one might call the rational characteristics of the style coincided, however, with a new responsiveness to its visual effects. This was part of an English import: the cult of the Picturesque and the natural landscape-garden. In many respects no more than a frivolous fashion, this cult was yet a vital element in the development of the French architectural imagination. Architects felt free, for the first time since their rejection of the rococo style, to cultivate purely visual pleasures. The most earnest and serious practitioners delighted to build an array of exotic pavilions and kiosks —Chinese, Tartar, and Turkish, no less than Gothic—that were in no part addressed to their academic training and reason. They were awakening thus their visual responses. All too soon—as we have noted in the case of Boullée—this new-found pleasure in variety and richness of effect was subsumed into a theory of lighting and giant, geometrical formality, somewhat curiously described in the jargon of English Picturesque theory. But the fashion for Picturesque gardens, once initiated, persisted unchecked until the end of the second decade of the nineteenth century. Gothic garden pavilions continued to be built in considerable numbers. But their design demanded no great knowledge of Gothic architecture, and learning was scarcely enhanced by this activity.

Nor did the fashion impinge much on the mainstream of architecture. Throughout the period we have been considering, only one large building was erected in the Gothic style, the cathedral of Ste.-Croix at Orléans. This was begun in 1599, as a monument to Catholic continuity after its destruction by the Huguenots, and finished only in 1829, a monument to religious conservatism. Many of the greatest

612. *Pierre-Bernard Lefranc, chapel, Dreux, 1842.*

architects of the eighteenth century worked on the design of the west front—Gabriel, Trouard, E.-F. Legrand, and Pâris—and in this connection studied and measured a number of Gothic buildings; but they made no attempt to build anything else of the kind. Outside the field of garden follies nothing was built in France to constitute a Gothic Revival until well into the nineteenth century.

Though a frivolous, lighthearted Gothic Revival did not take hold in architecture, it penetrated the other arts. In the field of literature, for instance, the troubadour novel enjoyed an astonishing vogue in the closing years of the *ancien régime*, and the bland and rather lackluster tone of the genre was tainted with the sinister thrill of Gothic horror itself when, in 1764, F.-T.-M. de Baculard d'Arnaud's play *Le Comte de Comynges* was first produced. New sentiments, new emotions, were at once brought into play. The school of history painting was affected. Within ten years Horace Walpole's *Castle of Otranto* had been translated into French, and in the years immediately after the Revolution Mrs. Radcliffe's novels were to be read with particular pleasure. The *roman noir* became immensely popular. F.-G. Ducray Duminil's *Coelina; ou, l'enfant du mystère*, of 1799, is said to have sold more than a million copies.

Whatever these new and exaggerated sentiments may have owed to English inspiration—and its impact was to be reinforced in the years that followed, when the novels of Sir Walter Scott were translated—the French sought always to identify them with their own medieval past. National pride was strong. A.-L. Millin's *Antiquités nationales; ou, recueil de monumens pour servir à l'histoire générale et particulière de l'empire français*, published in six volumes between 1790 and 1796, is typical of this enhanced interest in medieval history. Such romantic tastes were to be even more effectively elaborated and satisfied in the Musée des Monuments Français that Alexandre Lenoir started to set up in 1795 in the Couvent des Petits Augustins, and that is now a part of the École des Beaux-Arts. Here Lenoir gathered together treasures and bric-a-brac, stained-glass windows, and bits of sculpture and architectural details from buildings ravaged during the Revolution and reassembled them with artifice and considerable inaccuracy to conjure up romantic sensations of the past. In the garden was a celebrated tomb, said to be that of Héloise and Abelard, made from fragments from the abbey church of St.-Denis and plaster figures modeled by Louis-Pierre Deseine. Within the museum the aura of myth and mystery was even more strongly evoked. Tombs and sculptural figures in the thirteenth-century rooms were dimly lit, and the low vaults of the old refectory of the Petits Augustins were painted in ultramarine and scattered with stars of gold. The fourteenth-century rooms were decorated in a more lively and buoyant manner. Lenoir moved thus through the centuries, producing a pageant of French history that profoundly inspired such men as Jules Michelet—"Que d'âmes," he wrote in the sixth volume of his *Histoire de la Révolution*, "ont pris dans ce musée l'étincelle historique, l'intérêt des grands souvenirs, le vague désir de remonter les âges! . . . C'est là, et nulle autre part que j'ai reçu d'abord la vive impression de l'histoire" (p. 117). Lenoir's museum was dismantled in 1816, but by then he had colored the imagination of more than one generation of Frenchmen.

François-Auguste-René de Chateaubriand himself was fascinated, inspired, and also enraged by what he called Lenoir's "Élysée." The opening lines of the short chapter on Gothic, in that chaotic work of genius *Le génie du christianisme* were an indictment of Lenoir's methods. "Chaque chose," Chateaubriand wrote, "doit être mise en son lieu, vérité triviale à force d'être répetée, mais sans laquelle, après tout, il ne peut y avoir rien de parfait" (vol. 3, bk. 1, chap. 3). The setting of a work of art, he said, was vital to it; to displace it was to destroy the *genius loci* and to dispel the veil of sanctity woven about it through the centuries. Age was a criterion of greater value than beauty. Chateaubriand sought thus to identify the spirit of ancient France with all vestiges and remains of Gothic architecture, however rude. He went even further: He offered Gothic architecture as a symbol of a renewed religious faith. Chateaubriand was not a devout Catholic when, in exile in England, he wrote *Le génie du christianisme* (he described his spiritual state then as "une nostalgie de dieu"), yet the publication of the work in 1802 was carefully timed to coincide with the signing of the Concordat and was at once looked upon as a Catholic creed.

Chateaubriand's Gothic metaphor was inevitably popularized; more people than ever before looked bemused at Gothic architecture. A welter of guidebooks was published. Writers, playwrights, and painters evoked Gothic images, but architects, as we have seen, remained largely aloof. On the occasion of Napoleon's coronation in 1804, Percier and Fontaine did put up a pretty, patterned portico in front of Notre-Dame, but the internal decorations were classical in spirit. What was needed to effect a serious Gothic Revival was archaeological knowledge. Such knowledge was but slowly accumulated.

The impetus came, once again, from England: from English scholars, active in Normandy, investigating the origins of the pointed arch. Andrew Coltee Ducarel's *Anglo-Norman Antiquities* was published in London in 1767, but more important were the studies of George Downing Whittington, who worked in Normandy during the very early years of the nineteenth century. He died before he could complete his investigations, but the results of his research were published by his friend the fourth earl of Aberdeen, in 1809, as *An Historical Survey of the Ecclesiastical Antiquities of France*. Whittington confirmed what the French had long believed, that Gothic was of French origin, and—in accord with the Benedictine historians of the eighteenth century—he upheld the excellence of the thirteenth-century style above all others'. Small wonder that the French responded to his ideas. Auguste Leprévost (1787–1859), a local scholar who had been inspired also by the Scots antiquary James Anderson, translated Whittington's book into French. In 1823 Leprévost, together with C.-A.-A.-D. de Gerville (1769–1853), another Norman scholar inspired by English antiquaries (he lived as a refugee in England from 1793 to 1801), founded the Société des Antiquaires de la Normandie. The third founding member was Arcisse de Caumont (1801–1873), the youngest, but even then the most learned. In the following year he read to the society his paper "Essai sur l'architecture religieuse du moyen-âge, particulièrement en Normandie" and was at once recognized as the soundest authority on Gothic architecture. His analysis and his method of dating buildings provided the basis for all future studies. He forged the science of Gothic archaeology. His greatest work, the *Cours d'antiquités monumentales*, was published between 1830 and 1841; his *Abécédaire* did not appear until 1851. In 1834 he founded the Société Française d'Archéologie, organizing congresses each year in different parts of France and publishing in the *Bulletin monumental* the papers that were read. The *Bulletin* was from the start, and has remained, a stern, authoritative journal. It demonstrated that the romantic ghost could be exorcised from medieval studies.

Not that an archaeological standard of taste was at once accepted by exponents of Gothic; such men were as much inspired by the rhetoric of Michelet's circle, and in particular by that of Victor Hugo, whose rallying cry was contained in the novel *Notre-Dame de Paris*, first published in 1831. He spurred two of the most active propagandists of the first phase of the Gothic Revival, Adolphe-Napoléon Didron (1806–1867) and Charles Forbes, Comte de Montalembert (1810–1870). Didron, then a young civil servant, wrote to Hugo enraptured when he had read *Notre-Dame de Paris*. Hugo advised him to travel to Normandy. During the following months he walked, rucksack on his back, from one medieval building to another, thus initiating those archaeological studies that he was to diffuse first as editor of the *Bulletin monumental*, then after 1844 in the pages of the *Annales archéologiques*. In 1845 he published the *Manuel d'iconographie chrétienne grecque et latine*. Montalembert's fascination with Hugo had been stirred earlier, in 1830, with the production of *Hernani*. He, too, was dispatched to Normandy, which he explored by carriage, moving thence to England and then to Ireland, before returning to take up the romantic Catholic revival preached by Félicité-Robert de Lamennais and J.-B.-Henri Lacordaire. Neither of these men had much liking for Gothic architecture. Lacordaire listened long to Montalembert's expositions on Gothic only to find that even Ste.-Croix at Orléans escaped his understanding; "Je crois avoir un peu compris," he wrote to Montalembert on September 1, 1831. Yet Montalembert managed to initiate in their paper, *L'avenir*, the policy of which he was to become the most consistent and effective exponent in France: of regarding Gothic architecture as the Catholic style par excellence. The papal suppression of *L'avenir* in 1832 diminished none of his

614. *Gustave Guérin and Charles-Victor Guérin, St.-Étienne, Tours, 1869–74.*

fervor; rather, it served to increase it. In Rome, where he traveled with Lamennais and Lacordaire, Montalembert met the German Nazarene painter Johann Friedrich Overbeck; in Florence he found a childhood acquaintance, Alexis François Rio (1797–1874), whom he inspired with his new-found passion. The result was *De la poésie chrétienne dans son principe, dans sa matière et dans ses formes*, the first volume of which Rio published in 1836. This won no immediate success: After five months no more than twelve copies had been sold. But in 1840 the English *Quarterly Review* devoted a long article to the book, and it later earned John Ruskin's respect, influencing much of the second part of his *Modern Painters*. The second part of Rio's book, *De l'art chrétien*, was published in 1855.

The only architect Montalembert inspired, Louis-Alexandre Piel (1808–1841), is likewise little known. His active career was extremely short. He was a pupil of François Debret but, spurred by Montalembert, he traveled to Germany (writing a series of articles in 1836, "Voyage en Allemagne," for *L'européen*) and returned to design a village church in the Franche-Comté and then, in 1837, St.-Nicolas at Nantes (which was to be taken over by J.-B.-A. Lassus). In 1840 he left for Rome, where he was received into Lacordaire's Dominican order. In 1841, at the age of thirty-three, he died. But his influence was not ineffectual. He had written two more articles for *L'européen*, "Le temple de la Madeleine" and "Déclamation contre l'art païen," which served to set fashionable opinion against the adaptation of classical forms for church architecture.

Montalembert's own collection of articles *Du vandalisme et du catholicisme dans l'art*, issued in 1839, was shallow and unsustained by vigorous thought. He relied largely on the ideas of Hugo, Overbeck, and Pugin; but although he described St. Marie's College at Oscott and employed the methods of the *Contrasts*, he made no mention of Pugin by name. Yet Montalembert's influence was felt strongly in France, and even in England. In 1844 the Camden Society made him an honorary member, an honor he hastened to reject, publishing a pamphlet in English in which he accused the members of the society of being guilty of mortal sin. Gothic in France was to be practiced as a Catholic religious discipline, and the first phase of the revival was thus confined—almost exclusively—to the design of churches.

For all practical purposes the Gothic Revival in France began about 1840. There were several earlier experiments: a Protestant chapel with Gothic trimmings, in the Rue d'Aguesseau, Paris, dating from 1835, and another in a thirteenth-century style, begun in the same year, for the Dames de la Congrégation Notre-Dame, 84 Rue de Sèvres, Paris (now demolished), by François-Marie Lemarié (1795–1854), a pupil of Debret. But the only noteworthy project of the Gothic Revival to date from before 1840 is that for St.-Paul at Nîmes, designed in competition with thirty other architects, in 1835, by Charles-Auguste Questel. This church is one of the great representative buildings of the Romanesque Revival in France and also, by a curious freak, the first. It is the work, moreover, of an architect who does not figure as an important influence in either the Romanesque or the Gothic revivals. However, it is fair to note that Questel's restoration of St.-Martin d'Ainay at Lyons and, in particular, the magnificent copper-gilt altar front and the furnishings he designed for that church were acclaimed and thoughtfully scrutinized by a great many visitors, French and foreign, when they were exhibited at the international exhibition in 1855, alongside Viollet-le-Duc's similar altar front and furnishings for the cathedral of Clermont-Ferrand. But Questel is remembered today for a dull, classical *palais de justice* at Nîmes or the livelier, if still academic, *préfecture* and library on the Place de Verdun at Grenoble.

St.-Paul was begun only in 1838, after the drawings had been considerably revised in accordance with the dictates of the Conseil Général des Bâtiments Civils, and was not completed until November 1850. It emerged then as an adequate if slightly gutless interpretation of southern Romanesque architecture, with ribbed vaults over the nave and aisles, an apse colorfully decorated with murals by Jean-Hippolyte Flandrin, and stained-glass windows by Maréchal Guyon of Metz, but all handled with greater confidence and maturity than one might be led to expect from a pupil of Duban, even a precocious one. Much was no doubt due to the help of the archaeologist Charles Lenormant, Questel's brother by adoption.

There were far more uncertainty and awkward lapses of knowledge in other early attempts to revive the medieval styles: in St.-Clément at Nantes, for instance, built between 1841 and 1847 by François-Léon Liberge (1800–1860); or in the large church that Alexandre-Charles Grigny (1815–1867) erected between 1842 and 1846 for the sisters of the Adoration Perpétuelle du Saint Sacrement at Arras. And even more laxity and indecisiveness are in that handful of maverick commissions awarded by Louis-Philippe: the chapel dedicated to Saint Louis at Carthage, designed by Charles-Joseph Jourdain and consecrated on April 25, 1841 (now gone); the fanciful Gothic *cloche* that was placed in 1842 by Pierre-Bernard Lefranc (1795–1856) over the family chapel at Dreux, built initially by Cramail in the form of a Doric temple between 1816 and 1822; and, most astonishing of all, the mausoleum for Ferdinand d'Orléans, the Chapelle St.-Ferdinand (now the Place de la Porte des Ternes), Paris, built between July 1842 and July 1843, in something of a Romanesque manner, by none other than P.-F.-L. Fontaine, with windows to the

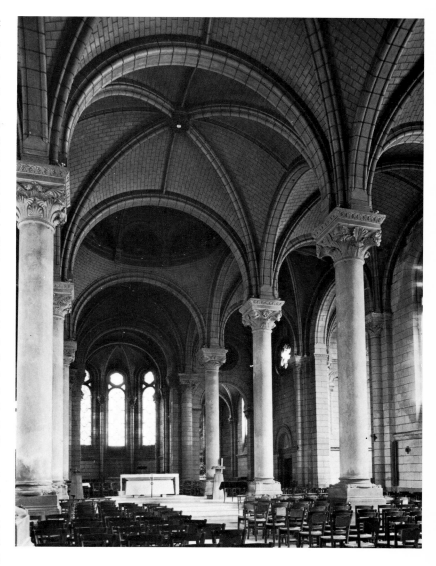

design of Ingres and surrounds drawn by Viollet-le-Duc. Other oddities and disasters could be listed, for, the liturgical enthusiasms of the clergy having once been aroused, there was much experimentation throughout France. But only a few of the early provincial exponents of Gothic need be considered before turning our attention to the focus of the revival, which was in Paris.

In Normandy, as was appropriate, two architects of more than usual distinction emerged, H.-C.-M. Grégoire (1791–1854) and Jacques-Eugène Barthélemy (1799–1882). Grégoire, who had studied under Percier, began his career in 1837 with a small chapel in brick

616. *Jean-Baptiste-Antoine Lassus and Eugène-Emmanuel Viollet-le-Duc, chapter house, Notre-Dame, Paris, 1846–50.*
617. *Jean-Baptiste-Antoine Lassus and Eugène-Emmanuel Viollet-le-Duc, chapter house, Notre-Dame, Paris, interior.*

"l'édifice hybride et disgracieux [*sic*]" (p. 188). Barthélemy, who later became diocesan architect to Rouen, was better informed. In 1840 he began Notre-Dame-de-Bon-Secours at Blosseville, just outside the town. By 1847 building was complete. The fittings and colorful decorations inside were added during the reign of Louis-Napoleon. The church, entirely of stone, was in the thirteenth-century style. The composition is careful rather than interesting, though Barthélemy showed himself singularly resourceful in adapting recondite elements and details. Altogether, it gives evidence of archaeological sensibility and stands thus as a landmark for the beginning of the Gothic Revival in France. It bears comparison, moreover, with many of Pugin's early works. In 1844 Barthélemy started on a chapel in the thirteenth-century style at the Château du Plessis, near Port Audemer; two years later he built a small church in the same manner at St.-Aubin, near Elbeuf. However, when in 1847 he was commissioned to design the church of Ventes-St.-Rémi, near Saint-Saëns, he chose a Romanesque style. All his works have pretensions to archaeological accuracy—pretensions that are not altogether unfounded.

Less well known though no less earnest than Barthélemy were the architects Hippolyte-Louis Durand (1809–1881), Victor Gay, and the brothers Charles-Victor and Gustave Guérin. Hippolyte Durand studied under Lebas and Vaudoyer at the École des Beaux-Arts. When he left the school he took to sending studies of Gothic buildings to the Salons and was soon rewarded with the commission to restore St.-Rémy at Rheims—a work that won Montalembert's praise. In 1845 Durand exhibited designs for a number of small churches in the thirteenth-century style and conceived the idea, together with Didron, of publishing a catalogue of them, "Parallèle de projets d'églises en style ogival du XIIIe siècle." The project was abandoned. But in the same year Durand began his first Gothic building, a thirteenth-century chapel for M. d'Orjault at Beaumont (Allier). In the following year he designed a church in the same style for Peyrehorade (Landes)—a church, as we shall see, that was to be the subject of some controversy at the Conseil Général des Bâtiments Civils. In 1849 Durand was made diocesan architect in the Basses-Pyrénées and in the years that followed built a number of churches in that area, all of them orthodox but dull. He was an architect of no great distinction.

Victor Gay, of whom much less is known, is perhaps more important. In 1846 he designed a large church—it was thirty-eight meters (one hundred twenty-five feet) long—for St.-Sulpice-les-Feuilles, near Arnac (Haute-Vienne). The church was conceived as a frame construction—the buttresses, the piers, and the ribs of the vaults of granite, the rest of the masonry of a light, less durable stone.

with trimmings of stone for the *hospice* at Yvetot (the similar chapel built there two years later for the seminary was by C.-L.-N. Robert). His major work was the fragile facade that he added to the late Gothic church of St.-Ouen at Rouen between 1845 and 1851. This was an architectural tour de force that displays neither originality nor real scholarship, yet evinces genuine powers of compositional skill. Not that Didron agreed: "Ce travail est inutile, nuisible, impossible," he wrote in the *Annales archéologiques* (p. 320) in 1845, when work was just begun; a year later he described the church as

The significance of the arrangement was at once apparent to all French theorists of Gothic construction, foremost among them Viollet-le-Duc, who was at that time publishing a series of articles on the subject in the *Annales archéologiques*. In the same year Gay designed a similarly organized chapel at Nanterre—it was exhibited at the Salon in 1846—but this seems to have aroused little interest in the architectural world. Indeed, almost nothing is known of Gay's activities after his early outburst. He designed some notable church furnishings, made by L. Bachelet, but, like Piel, may well have ended up in Rome, for the church of the Corpus Domini, on the Via Nomentana, is said to have been built by him.

It is Gustave Guérin who emerges as the first representative of the type that becomes so familiar with the advance of the Gothic Revival in France: the architect obsessed with Gothic as an exemplar of structural finesse. He was the son of Charles-Mathias Guérin, an architect of Tours. His first important commission was the restoration of the cathedral there. In 1844 he was asked to design the church of St.-Étienne at Tours, but he found, as many men must have found, that he was ill equipped to design and supervise the construction of a church in the Gothic style. Together with his brother Charles-Victor he began to inspect and to measure Gothic churches of the area. They planned a book on Gothic construction but published only one article, in 1847, in the *Revue générale de l'architecture*. The building of St.-Étienne was delayed until 1869, finished five years later, and it was not before April 1855, when Guérin started to restore his most famous church, Ste.-Anne, at Lariche Extra, Tours, that his ideas were to be given adequate expression. The rebuilt church is a complex structure, suggesting a deep understanding of Gothic construction, but little of the art of architecture.

Lassus and Viollet-le-Duc are the great representative figures of the Gothic Revival. The focus of their activity was in Paris, in particular on their works of restoration, where they trained the builders and craftsmen needed to sustain the revival. Jean-Baptiste-Antoine Lassus was a classically trained architect, a pupil of Henri Labrouste, but like other Labrouste disciples—Suréda, E. Boeswillwald, E.-L. Millet, J.-J.-G. Lisch, and J.-E.-A. de Baudot—he turned early to the study of thirteenth-century Gothic. In 1835 he was awarded a prize at the Salon for a restoration of the Ste.-Chapelle; two years later he submitted an analysis of the construction of the refectory of St.-Martin-des-Champs in Paris. Also in 1835, together with another of Labrouste's pupils, Adolphe-Gabriel Gréterin (1806–1852), he began the restoration of the late Gothic church of St.-Severin in Paris. Then, in 1838, he was made *Inspecteur* under Godde at St.-Germain-l'Auxerrois, and under Duban at the Ste.-Chapelle. Within another year he was in charge of the renovation of both these churches. He restored them to an almost unbelievable and highly colored medieval splendor. The painting on the porch at St.-Germain-l'Auxerrois, together with most of the internal furnishings, has now disappeared, though the window of the Passion, in the chapel behind the main altar, on which Didron, Louis-Adrien Lusson, and Louis-Charles-Auguste Steinheil collaborated, and which was made by Rebouleau, stands witness still to the beginnings of the stained-glass revival in France, heralded in 1837 by the publication of Ferdinand Charles Lasteyrie's *Histoire de la peinture sur verre*. At the Ste.-Chapelle, where

619. *Jean-Baptiste-Antoine Lassus, Sacré-Coeur, Moulins, 1849 onward.*

620. *Jean-Baptiste-Antoine Lassus, Sacré-Coeur, Moulins, interior.*

Lassus was joined in 1840 by Viollet-le-Duc and, soon after, by Suréda, the sumptuousness of the work is still evident and is daily admired by throngs of visitors. Pugin was one of the first. Didron took him to look at it in 1844. "I have seen the most glorious things," he wrote on May 28 to his patron, the earl of Shrewsbury, "far beyond my expectations; the restoration of the Ste.-Chapelle in Paris is worthy of the days of St. Louis. I never saw images so exquisitely painted." He returned, inspired, to design the colored wall paintings for St. Giles at Cheadle. Didron traveled, in turn, to England to witness the consecration of this church.

In April 1844 Lassus and Viollet-le-Duc were appointed architects for the restoration of Notre-Dame and the building of the new chapter house. Within a few years most of the craftsmen trained at St.-Germain-l'Auxerrois and the Ste.-Chapelle were working on the new site. The restoration proceeded steadily until 1864, when the spire of the crossing was finally finished, to the design of Viollet-le-Duc. The other altogether original feature of the building, the chapter house, was largely designed by Lassus. The fabric was complete by 1850, and the rich decorations were added in the years immediately following. The Maison du Personnel to the right of the west front, dating from 1866, is Viollet-le-Duc's alone.

Lassus's independent work is inevitably of interest, though of little appeal. In August 1843 he took over the design of St.-Nicolas at Nantes, begun by Piel. The church that he put up in the following years, however, was all his own. It was modeled in its parts on the cathedral at Chartres (restored by Lassus from 1848 onward) and was probably one of the most severe and rigorous interpretations of thirteenth-century work to be found in France at that period. It is a disappointment, though it is more coherent within than without. A few years later Lassus started on a chapel for the Château de Gezaincourt (Somme), consecrated in August 1848, but his most important building was the church of Sacré-Coeur, Place d'Allier, Moulins, where, in 1852, he was to begin a nave in the thirteenth-century style for the cathedral of Notre-Dame (taken over later by E.-L. Millet). A local architect, L.-D.-G. Esmonnot (1807–1880), who had originally been asked to prepare designs for the Sacré-Coeur, in 1844 proposed a building in the Romanesque style, but this was judged to be too expensive and in 1849 Lassus was called in to design the new church. As before, he took the cathedral of Chartres as his model, on this occasion providing twin towers for the facade. Esmonnot supervised building activities.

Four years later Lassus started on the smaller and simpler church of St.-Pierre at Dijon (July 1853–October 1858), an undertaking that was once again accompanied by related works of restoration, this

622. *Eugène-Emmanuel Viollet-le-Duc, De Courmont House, Paris,*
1846–49.

623. *Eugène-Emmanuel Viollet-le-Duc, Viollet-le-Duc House, Paris,*
1861–62.

time on the thirteenth-century church of Notre-Dame at Dijon. One
year later he began St.-Jean-Baptiste-de-Belleville, Paris (June 1854–
August 1859): "un monument ogival," his biographer Alfred Darcel
wrote in 1858, "vigoureux et solide, dont la nef est de proportions
excellentes, et la façade un vrai chef-d'oeuvre par l'ajustement des
flèches sur les tours qui l'accompagnent." Contemporary opinion
is more equivocal. The junction between the spires and the supporting
towers is gauche, and Lassus was at such great pains to subordinate his
artistic personality to the dictates of archaeological knowledge that
he must be judged to have blunted his sensibilities. His design is dull,

attenuated, and lacking in all vitality. But in this at least it gives an
impression of truthfulness to its period, and in particular to the stage
that the Gothic Revival had then reached in France. In the competition for the cathedral of Notre-Dame-de-la-Treille at Lille, of 1855,
for which Lassus submitted a similar design, he was awarded only
third prize, being easily overtaken by the Englishmen William
Burges—the winner, then quite unknown—and G. E. Street, who
came in second. *The Ecclesiologist* marked Lassus's work down as
"meager."

Lassus's other architectural works are of little interest. He added a porch to and designed the fittings for Lemarié's chapel in the Rue de Sèvres and carried out alterations and additions for other religious foundations. His domestic work is not exciting. He built a country house at Maisons Lafitte in a Louis XIII manner; a town house on the corner of the Rue Taitbout and the Rue de Provence, Paris, with thirteenth-century details; and in 1848 began a complex structure in the Avenue Montaigne, Paris, for Prince Soltykoff—at once a house and a museum for a mass of medieval and Renaissance *objets d'art*. The building, of brick and stone, was in the fifteenth-century style. The attracting feature, however, was a large rib-vaulted room copied from Mont Saint-Michel.

Lassus's literary contributions to the Gothic Revival were legion: articles on scale ("le module humain") in the *Annales archéologiques*; a great *Monographie de la cathédrale de Chartres* (1842–67), carried out with the help of Didron and the painter Eugène-Emmanuel Amaury-Duval; and the *Album de Villard de Honnecourt* (1858), completed after his death by Alfred Darcel. This work, dedicated to Henri Labrouste, contains an introduction in which the problems of the Gothic Revival are clearly outlined.

Viollet-le-Duc's contributions to the movement were even more solidly literary and intellectual. He was, in addition, the most active restorer in all France. But he was responsible also for a number of original works of architecture in which he tried, with failing conviction, to demonstrate how Gothic might be used as the basis for a nineteenth-century style. He began in 1846 with a house in the Rue de Berlin (now 28 Rue de Liège), Paris, for Henri de Courmont, a high-ranking official and a close friend of Prosper Mérimée. By 1849 the house was complete, the first of its kind (the gimcrack Maison des Goths, 116 Rue St.-Martin of 1826, apart) in which Gothic details were applied to a traditional Parisian street frontage. The stepped stringcourses, brackets, and moldings were not, of course, intended as mere decorative devices but rather as functioning elements. They are nonetheless deployed with remarkable firmness to produce an attractive pattern of horizontals and verticals. The facades on the court, of brick with stone trimmings, have a more grim, functional expression, with little overt Gothicism, the single pointed relieving arch in the brickwork carrying with it an air of appropriateness. In his later Parisian apartment buildings (15 Rue de Douai, of 1857–60, for instance, or his own house at 68 Rue Condorcet, of 1861–62) there are occasional hints of this fondness for Gothic, but Viollet-le-Duc seems to have rejected the style thereafter as unsuitable for city architecture. He used it, of course, for tombs (for Montalembert's family's in the Cimetière de Picpus, of 1850, and for Lassus's in the Cimetière Père-Lachaise, of 1857) and for a sequence of

projects for funerary chapels, none of great interest; but only for church-building did he adopt it with conviction, and later, on occasion, for country houses—but only for those built up on older, existing structures. These last were of little enough consequence and may be briefly listed: the Château de Montdardier, Le Vigan (Gard), for the Comte de Ginestou (1861–68; extended 1884–88); a project of 1861 for the Château de Chamousset, St.-Laurent-de-Chamousset (Rhône), for Comte Paul de Saint-Victor; the Château de Pupetières, Chabons (Isère), for the Marquis de Virieu (1861), executed by Denis Darcy (1823–1904); the Château de La Flachère (Rhône) for the

Comte de Chaponay (1863); and the Château d'Arragori, just outside Hendaye, for Antoinine d'Abbadia (1864–66), largely the work of a pupil, Edmond Duthoit. All these commissions arose from Viollet-le-Duc's close connection, through Prosper Mérimée, with the court of Louis-Napoleon. They were indiscriminate works for undiscriminating courtiers, parodies of that giant burlesque for Louis-Napoleon in which Viollet-le-Duc was indulging, the Château de Pierrefonds (Oise).

He had first proposed as a summer retreat for the court a restoration of a small château at Bonaguil (Lot-et-Garonne), but in April 1855 the emperor and empress traveled to England. They did not see Balmoral Castle, then barely complete, but they returned determined to emulate it. A month later Viollet-le-Duc prepared drawings for the conversion of the Château de Coucy (Aisne). Work was started at once and pursued for three years, but in 1858, on Viollet-le-Duc's persuasion, Coucy was rejected in favor of Pierrefonds. In February of the same year his designs were accepted. His presentation drawings of the following year show that the whole enterprise was considered as something of a medieval fantasia. Cavaliers and armored knights parade the court, kirtled ladies lean from the turrets, and buxom peasants are shown roasting oxen in the kitchen. Not that Viollet-le-Duc was constrained by such romantic images: He unflinchingly displayed girders of iron on his drawbridge and introduced trusses of iron and steel under his high-pitched roofs. His later sketches for the interiors, never to be completed, are intriguing also for indications of a new sense of style, sinuous and softly curving, especially in the design of the sofas and chairs. The emperor himself was enchanted: "J'ai là," he told Mérimée in 1866, "une chose *unique*." William Burges, long an admirer of Viollet-le-Duc and to a limited degree his emulator, was bitterly disappointed by his visit to Pierrefonds; he returned from France in 1873, horror-struck, to denounce the work: "I wish to point out to the younger members of the Institute," he said, "that antiquarianism and archaeology do *not* make an architect" (*The Architect*, 1873, p. 331).

Viollet-le-Duc's designs for churches, though far more seriously studied, serve only to confirm this opinion. He began in 1852 with a project for St.-Gimer outside Carcassonne, built with much difficulty and dispute as to costs, between 1853 and 1858. This brutal building—asymmetrical on account of foundation difficulties rather than compositional preferences—must be regarded essentially as a restoration study, related to the architect's rebuilding of the walled town close by. In 1855 he prepared drawings for a church at La Nouvelle (Aude) of an etiolated Gothic, happily not to be built; between 1859 and 1861 he put up a simple if colorfully decorated chapel for the Petit Sé-

627. *Émile Bœswillwald, church, Masny, sectional details.*

628. *Edmond–Armand–Marie Duthoit, Château de Roquetaillade (Gironde), Rose Bedroom, 1868–69.*

minaire, Rue de Vaugirard, Paris, which was moved in 1898 to Fontenay-aux-Roses, and enlarged; but not until 1860, when he designed St.-Denys-de-l'Estrée at Saint-Denis, outside Paris, and 1861, when he drew up the project for the church at Aillant-sur-Tholon (Yonne), did Viollet-le-Duc indicate the form that he might give to a considered revivalist work. The church at Aillant-sur-Tholon, built between 1863 and 1865 under the direction of the local architect,

Adolphe-Auguste Lefort, is strong and assertive and carefully composed with regard to the Picturesque balance of the townscape, but scarcely suitable as a model for other architects; St.-Denys-de-l'Estrée, erected between 1864 and 1866, was marginally more attractive, equally carefully related to the town, secular in its overtones, certainly more influential. This building showed Viollet-le-Duc at his most determined. The materials were chosen with the greatest

349

care; all the capitals and carvings were drawn out to full scale. Internally one is struck by the unusually wide and generous proportions of the bays, designed *ad quadratum*, the fullness of the moldings and profiles; but the suppression of the cross-ribs in the vaults—lightly decorated instead with painted arabesque motifs and scattered stars—seriously weakens the effect of the whole. The building is lacking in nobility and power; it is an ungainly and depressingly uninspired interpretation of a thirteenth-century structure. Modest as to his architectural abilities, Viollet-le-Duc might well have agreed. Yet Duban, reporting on the church in 1867, evidently regarded it with respect. In 1866 Viollet-le-Duc tried his hand at a far more ambitious variant, a design for St.-Pierre-de-Chaillot, intended for the site of the present Place des États-Unis, Paris; but though this was approved in 1868, it was to be rejected four years later. Viollet-le-Duc's only other excursion into ecclesiastical Gothic was the Protestant chapel on the Avenue de Rumine, Lausanne, built between 1876 and 1877, under the direction of the local architect Jules-Louis Verrey. This neat, domesticated building is perhaps the most successful, if unadventurous, of his Gothic essays. Clearly, he was inhibited in such endeavors. He was unable to give the lead expected, indeed demanded, of him.

Whatever Viollet-le-Duc's failings as an architect, he determined the course of the Gothic Revival virtually unaided, in particular through his power of patronage as architect to the Commission des Monuments Historiques and, perhaps even more effectively after 1853, as one of the three *Inspecteurs Générals* of the Service des Édifices Diocésains (of the other two inspectors, one was Henri Labrouste, said to be too old and infirm to mount the scaffolds, the other Paul Abadie, a pupil and unabashed admirer of Viollet-le-Duc). Indeed, all the serious acceptable architects who emerged in the 1850s and 1860s to support the Gothic Revival either had been trained by Lassus and Viollet-le-Duc or had worked for one of the two organizations dominated by the latter. It is fair to note, however, that they had, almost to a man, begun their careers under the aegis of Henri Labrouste. It was with no little perception that the critic Redon, writing in both *Le Figaro* and *La construction moderne* in 1900, should have remarked the final result of this influence, beginning with the works of the master himself: "L'architecture de Viollet-le-Duc est sèche, sectaire et sans âme; c'est une sorte de gothique *néo-grec*" (*La construction moderne*, p. 613).

At the Ste.-Chapelle Lassus and Viollet-le-Duc trained Suréda, who traveled to Spain in 1855 to set up a commission on historic monuments, and later became architect to the king; at Notre-Dame they indoctrinated Abadie, Boeswillwald, M.-A.-G. Ouradou, and Millet. Paul Abadie (1812–1884), the son of an architect of the same name from Angoulême, was a pupil of Achille Leclère, who was later to restore the cathedrals of both Angoulême and Périgueux. He started his independent career as diocesan architect with the churches of St.-Martial (1850–53) and St.-Ausone (1851–68), both at Angoulême. In 1854 he designed the church of Notre-Dame at Bergerac (first commissioned from Viollet-le-Duc), soon after, another at Valeyrac (Gironde), and then the Hôtel de Ville at Angoulême (1858–65) and the church of Ste.-Marie (1864–86) in the Bastide quarter at Bordeaux. His greatest work was the Sacré-Coeur at Montmartre, Paris, which he won in a competition with seventy-seven other architects in 1874. This was completed only in 1919. It confirmed him, even then, as the greatest exponent of the Romano-Byzantine style—a style sustained from the first by Félix de Verneilh's *Architecture byzantine en France, Saint Front de Périgueux et les églises à coupoles de l'Aquitaine*, published in 1851. Émile Boeswillwald (1815–1896), the son of a Strasbourg stonemason, had studied with Henri Labrouste before becoming *Inspecteur* at Notre-Dame in Paris in 1845. Within two years he had been appointed to restore the cathedral at Luçon and soon after began on Notre-Dame at Laon. In 1849 he became diocesan architect at Soissons, Orléans, and Bayonne. At Soissons he erected the dull, stripped Gothic church of St.-Waast; at Masny, near Douai (Nord), he built an equally ungainly but far more original church, designed in 1860 (the year in which the fourth volume of Viollet-le-Duc's *Dictionnaire raisonné de l'architecture française* appeared, with its challenging article on construction). This church incorporates columns of cast iron—once painted and stenciled in green, red, yellow, and black—with a brick superstructure, all exposed, and is equally harshly decorated inside and out with corbels and patterns and lintels of open brickwork set at forty-five-degree angles. This was clearly intended as more than a revivalist exercise; it was a determined attempt to give expression to Viollet-le-Duc's latest doctrines, and was acknowledged as such when it was finished, in 1864. The curé's house and the village hall, also by Boeswillwald, are in the same style, with an attempt at Picturesque grouping. But the architecture cannot be judged a success; nor was it of any great influence, though its decorative motifs were taken up later by Félix Narjoux for his schools in Paris. In the south of France, in the hills to the southeast of St.-Jean-Pied-de-Port, Boeswillwald built the small chapel of St.-Sauveur; at Biarritz, starting in 1863, and later at Beaumetz, he built other chapels, covered inside and out with geometrical designs in colored stone, brick, and tile. These were crude, self-conscious adaptations of Byzantine and other Eastern models to which the medieval architecture of the region was thought to relate. They owed something, no doubt, to A. L. Couchaud's *Choix d'églises byzantines de la Grèce*, of 1842, and even more, perhaps, to C. F. Texier's and R. P. Pullan's *Architecture byzantine*, of 1864. Boeswillwald's one ambitious domestic undertaking was the grotesque rebuilding of the Château de Montigny, near Masny (Nord), complete with octagonal towers of varying diameters and crow-stepped gables—all derived, it would seem, from an unexecuted project by Viollet-le-Duc, of May 1863, for the Château de Merinville. Boeswillwald was, through life, a close friend of Viollet-le-Duc and also of his mentor, Mérimée. In the autumn of 1854 he traveled with them to Germany; he owed the commission of the Biarritz chapel to Mérimée and in 1860 succeeded him as *Inspecteur Général des Monuments Historiques*, the first architect to be appointed to the post.

Maurice-Augustin-Gabriel Ouradou (1822–1884), a pupil of Lebas, the third of the early disciples of Viollet-le-Duc to be trained at Notre-Dame, became his son-in-law in 1857 and worked thereafter in close conjunction with him; indeed, such houses as that for Auguste Griois, at Ambrières-les-Vallées (Mayenne), designed in 1857 but begun only in 1865, and the Hôtel Duranti, 184 Boulevard Haussmann, Paris, both to be credited on completion to Ouradou, were commissioned from and first sketched by Viollet-le-Duc. One can well understand his reluctance to accept credit for these miserable works. Ouradou did little else to match even their small distinction—some minor restorations, church furnishings, and tombs. Eugène-Louis Millet (1819–1879), a pupil of Labrouste, entered the École des Beaux-Arts in 1837; three years later he was working for Viollet-le-Duc. He started in 1848 to restore the cathedrals of Châlons-sur-Marne and of Troyes, where he was to build the Chapel des Soeurs de la Providence, and in 1855 was commissioned to restore the Château de St.-Germain-en-Laye, near Maisons Lafitte, where in 1867 he began the new church in the Rue de la Muette. Three years after Lassus's death in 1857 Millet took over the work of the cathedral at Moulins and, similarly, succeeded to the restoration of the cathedral at Rheims in 1874, after Viollet-le-Duc's resignation as *Inspecteur Général des Édifices Diocésains*. Millet's special influence on the Gothic movement was exerted, however, not as an architect but as a teacher of craftsmen, in particular, the members of the Cercle des Ouvriers Maçons et Tailleurs de Pierres, for whom he built a small center in Paris, at 9 Rue des Chantiers.

To the list of architects already considered one might add the names of Jean-Charles Laisné (1819–1891), Victor-Marie-Charles Ruprich-Robert (1820–1887), Jean-Juste-Gustave Lisch (1828–1910), Joseph-Eugène-Anatole de Baudot (1834–1915), Édouard-Jules Cor-

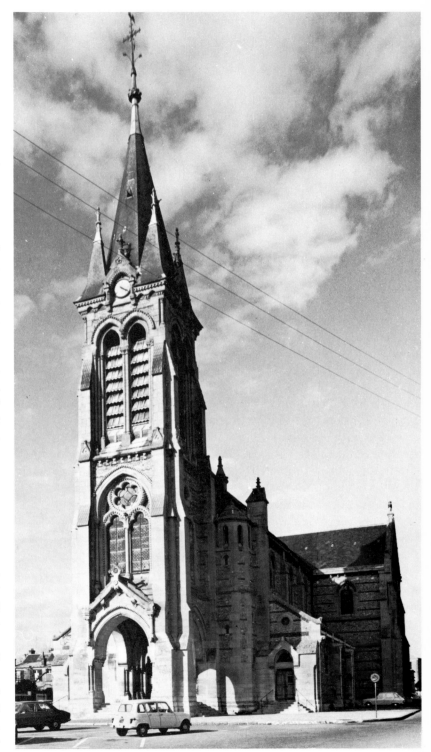

royer (1835–1904), Félix Narjoux (1836–1891), and Edmond-Armand-Marie Duthoit (1837–1889). All of these men worked long and with distinction both for the Commission des Monuments Historiques and for the Service des Édifices Diocésains and upheld, if in some cases only to a limited extent, the ideals of Viollet-le-Duc. But they were certainly not consistent Gothic Revivalists. Ruprich-Robert, a pupil of Constant-Dufeux, in 1840 became Viollet-le-Duc's assistant and later his successor at the École de Dessin. He began three churches in 1855, with the plates of the *Dictionnaire raisonné de l'architecture française* in mind: the church of Athis (Orne), St.-Jean-Baptiste at Flers (Orne; 1855–68), and the Chapelle du Petit Séminaire at Sées (Orne.). He built little else in this manner, but instead demonstrated his attachment to Viollet-le-Duc in theories of ornamental design, proposed first in 1866 in the *Flore ornamentale: essai sur la composition de l'ornement, éléments tirés de la nature et principes de leur application*, a work of considerable importance, completed in 1876. His great literary contribution, however, was *L'architecture normande aux XIᵉ et XIIᵉ siècles en Normandie et en Angleterre*, published posthumously.

Juste Lisch, a pupil of both Vaudoyer and Labrouste, likewise showed early Gothic sympathies, with his design for the bishop's palace at Luçon, though he turned soon after to classical sources for inspiration. His late works, the Gare de Le Havre and a host of buildings set up for the Paris exhibition of 1878—in particular, the Gare du Champ de Mars—and others for the Paris exhibition of 1889 (one of which survives as the Gare de Javel) were all designed with exposed frameworks of iron filled in with luridly colored panels of glazed bricks and tiles. They show undivided loyalties to the doctrines set down by Viollet-le-Duc in the second volume of the *Entretiens sur l'architecture*. Édouard-Jules Corroyer and Félix Narjoux, pupils of Constant-Dufeux, allied themselves always with Viollet-le-Duc and were active and sympathetic restorers of Gothic monuments. Corroyer began with the restoration of Mont Saint-Michel, a project later taken over by another of Viollet-le-Duc's disciples, his biographer, Paul-Émile-Antoine Gout (1852–1923). Narjoux started his career in 1857 with the restoration of the cathedral of Limoges. Both were early supporters of the Gothic Revival, Narjoux most notably in a house he built in his native Chalon-sur-Saône, closely modeled on the thirteenth-century houses of Cluny. Despite this interest in Viollet-le-Duc and Gothic architecture, both Corroyer and Narjoux spent most of their active careers developing a style that was far closer to the heart of Charles Garnier than that of Viollet-le-Duc. Only the three schools that Narjoux built in Paris (after 1872, when the Paris council voted to erect thirty-five such buildings) were to be organized and detailed in a manner responsive to the teachings of Viollet-le-Duc.

Anatole de Baudot and Edmond Duthoit alone of this group should be considered as determined and evolving exponents of the Gothic cause. Even so, their roles must be carefully defined. Duthoit was the son and the nephew of stone carvers at Amiens, trained and employed first by Viollet-le-Duc. But he spent much of his life outside France—in north Africa, where from 1872 onward he was actively engaged in restoration work, and in the Middle East, in Palestine and Syria in particular, where he traveled first in 1861, on the expeditions of the Comte de Vogüé and W. H. Waddington. There he measured and sketched a number of Early Christian and Byzantine churches, regularly sending drawings to the Salons and articles to the *Gazette des architectes et du bâtiment*. He was even tempted to try his hand at designing in the Eastern manner: He built two churches in Beirut. Yet his most adventurous work was done in France. For Viollet-le-Duc he supervised the reconstruction of the fifteenth-century Château d'Arragori, near Hendaye, on the Spanish border, designed for the explorer and astronomer Antoinine d'Abbadia. He greatly elaborated Viollet-le-Duc's designs, introducing an array of highly colored decorative motifs, partly Gothic in character but equally inspired by Eastern sources. "Mon arabe," he said, "sent le gothique, et mon gothique a un arrière gôut d'arabe ou de byzantin." His Château de Roquetaillade, southeast of Bordeaux, near Langon, once again begun on the basis of Viollet-le-Duc's designs in 1864, on this occasion for M. de Mauvesin, was even more spectacular. No detail, no piece of furniture, even, fails to show something of the exotic image Duthoit had evolved. The Rose Bedroom, the Green Bedroom, and the chapel are Duthoit's alone. It is the only building in France that may be compared—if unfavorably—to William Burges's contemporary work at Cardiff Castle (see illustrations 598, 599). Duthoit, unfortunately, produced little else: churches of a modest sort at Champeaux (Deux-Sèvres; c. 1878), Bryas (Pas-de-Calais; 1880–84), and Souverain-Moulin (Pas-de-Calais; c. 1883), and of a spectacular sort at Albert (Somme; 1883–97), where he erected the highly colored, almost exotic pilgrimage church of Notre-Dame-de-Brebières.

Anatole de Baudot was perhaps a more fitting heir to Viollet-le-Duc, his defender and constant support. He came to him first when Labrouste closed his *atelier* in 1856. By 1857 he had been set to work on the restoration of the cathedral at Puy-en-Velay (Haute-Loire) and was soon after appointed diocesan architect at Clermont-Ferrand. During the years that followed he restored no fewer than twenty-five churches. His original buildings are

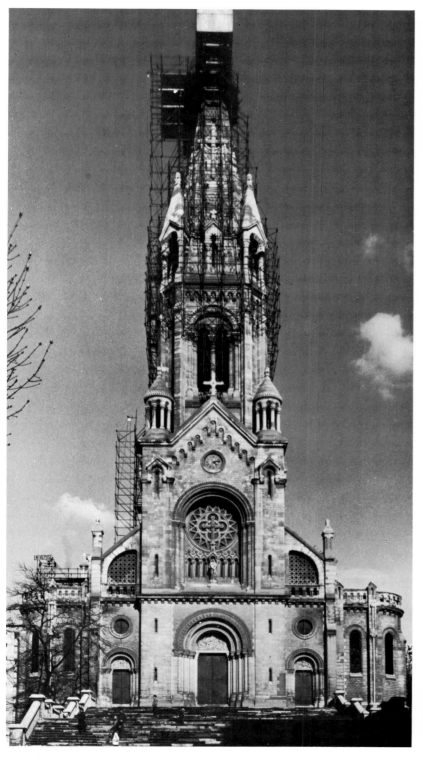

630. *Louis–Jean–Antoine Héret, Notre–Dame–de–la–Croix, Paris, 1863–80.*

631. *Louis–Jean–Antoine Héret, Notre–Dame–de–la–Croix, Paris, interior.*

much of its decoration in the form of outsized grotesques and gargoyles to his supervision. "Réussie ou non," de Baudot wrote in 1865 in the *Gazette des architectes et du bâtiment*, "cette façade a le mérite de l'originalité" (p. 83). At the same time he erected a more conventional building, with scarcely a hint of Gothic in its detailing, 21 Rue de Leningrad (originally Rue de Saint Petersbourg); then another at 34 Rue Saint-Lazare, finished in 1866, more boldly—one might say clumsily—detailed. This has something of the quality of Viollet-le-Duc's apartments for M. Milon, put up between 1857 and 1860, at 15 Rue de Douai. The Gothic features in the design, as one might expect at this period, are not obtrusive. De Baudot's slightly later church at La Roche Millay (Nièvre), of 1870, was likewise derived from a design by Viollet-le-Duc: the second for the tower and west front of St.-Martin at Ussel (Corrèze), dating from 1852 (the first was done in 1843), which was supervised by Millet and later credited to him. It is just possible that Viollet-le-Duc was indeed the designer of the La Roche Millay church also, for early sketches relating to it are still among his papers.

De Baudot's first important church, St.-Lubin at Rambouillet, designed in 1865 in competition with fifty-four other architects, relates rather to Viollet-le-Duc's more venturesome theories, taken up already, as we have seen, by Boeswillwald for the church at Masny. Along the nave are columns of iron, set two feet in front of piers of stone, serving together to support the walls and stone vaults above. The arrangement, taken perhaps from the lower chapel of the Ste.-Chapelle, or, more probably, from the fourteenth-century church of Tour (Calvados), restored later by de Baudot, avoids the use of flying buttresses while retaining an air of lightness internally. Though technically sound, the design was strongly attacked. Bourgeois de Lagny ridiculed it as a naive paraphrase of Gothic in the *Moniteur des architectes*, in 1866. César Daly followed up the attack in the *Revue générale de l'architecture* thirteen years later, when the church was finally completed. De Baudot determined not to use exposed ironwork in his later designs for churches, three of which—Levallois-Perret (1869), Sèvres (1870), and St.-Bruno at Grenoble (1870)—were won in competition and were at once castigated in the established architectural press, and then not built—though St.-Justin at Levallois-Perret was eventually erected, in a modified form, between 1892 and 1911. The project for the church at Privas (Ardèche), which de Baudot exhibited at the Salon in 1876, was, however, carried out. All were thoughtful if straightforward adaptations of simple thirteenth-century structures. They were related to Viollet-le-Duc's designs for the church at Aillant-sur-Tholon and, in particular, to St.-Denys-de-l'Estrée. What distinguishes all these churches, whether by Viollet-le-Duc or

almost as numerous, usually adventurous. However, it is difficult to assess his particular genius at this period, for his early works were designed under the watchful eye of Viollet-le-Duc, and only after his death did de Baudot learn to extend his abilities. Then he emerged as an innovator of great distinction. Not, of course, that he did not himself early inflect the works of his mentor. The house that Viollet-le-Duc built about 1863, for M. Sauvage, a building contractor, on a site bounded by Rue Le Peletier, Rue La Fayette, and Rue Chauchat in Paris, is largely the work of de Baudot, and undoubtedly owes

634. Joseph-Auguste-Émile Vaudremer, St.-Pierre-de-Montrouge, Paris.

635. Claude Naissant, Notre-Dame-de-la-Gare, Paris, 1855–64.

by his followers, is that they were modeled on the parish churches of France, not the cathedrals that Lassus and his contemporaries had sought to emulate, if only in miniature. The limited extent of the aspirations of both Viollet-le-Duc and de Baudot at this period is to be measured by the two lackluster volumes of their manual of instruction, *Églises de bourgs et villages*, published in 1867. Only long after Viollet-le-Duc's death did de Baudot demonstrate the truly startling quality of his imagination, beginning in 1882 with the building of the Lycée Lakanal at Sceaux, in which some of Boeswill-wald's innovations at Masny were to be exploited and developed, but especially after 1890, when he initiated his astonishing experiments in reinforced brickwork and concrete, including the Lycée Victor Hugo, 27 Rue de Sévigné (1894–96), and the church of St.-Jean-de-Montmartre (1894, 1897–1904), both in Paris. This development culminated in 1914 in his famous design for a giant exhibition hall, in all things a presage to the works of Pier Luigi Nervi. In de Baudot the intellectual promise of the Gothic Revival might be held to have been fulfilled.

There is a great deal more in the history of the Gothic Revival in France outside the orbit of Viollet-le-Duc urgently requiring investigation: the two early churches that Ferdinand Leroy is reported to have built at Châteauroux (Indre), by 1844, for example; or the ten that Paul Pechinet, an architect active at Langres, is said to have built in the Haute-Marne by 1846; or that extraordinary series on the outskirts of Paris, all by Claude Naissant (1801–1879), of a spare and taut geometry derived from Romanesque models. The critic of *The Ecclesiologist* had begun to remark upon some of the latter as early as 1855: St.-Lambert, Rue Bausset, Vaugirard (1848–56); Notre-Dame-de-la-Gare, Place Jeanne-d'Arc, Ivry (now Gobelins; 1855–64); St.-Charles-Borromée at Joinville-le-Pont (1856–66); St.-Pierre, Place de l'Église, Charenton-le-Pont (1857–59); Ste.-Geneviève, Rosny-sous-Bois (1857–66); and Notre-Dame-de-la-Médaille-Miraculeuse, 80 Avenue Pierre Larousse, Malakoff (1861). Also of interest is the imposing church of Notre-Dame-de-la-Croix, Rue Julien Lacroix, at Ménilmontant in Paris, by Louis-Jean-Antoine Héret (1821–1899), another of Lebas's pupils, built between 1863 and 1880, all in stone apart from the ribs of the vaults of the nave, which are of iron lattice construction. Even more demanding of comment is St.-Pierre-de-Montrouge, on the Place Victor Basch, Paris, built between 1864 and 1872 by Joseph-Auguste-Émile Vaudremer (1829–1914), the most outstanding of Blouet's and Gilbert's pupils. This church, though once again based on Romanesque models, was even more consciously indebted to a restoration study of Qal'at Saman, in Syria, that Duthoit had showed at the Salon and had

then published in the *Gazette des architectes et du bâtiment* in 1864, the year before the Comte de Vogüé's two great volumes *La Syrie centrale* started to appear. Vaudremer was attempting to produce a building of solid dignity—a quality noticeably lacking in the works of Viollet-le-Duc and his followers—that was clearly ecclesiastical in character, but in no way attested to the Gothic Revival. And he succeeded. St.-Pierre is perhaps the only church of the period of any architectural quality. He was less adept in his subsequent experiments—Notre-Dame-d'Auteuil, Place d'Auteuil, Paris, of 1876–80, which hints at a knowledge of Abadie's work; the gable-fronted Protestant Temple de Belleville, 97 Rue Julien Lacroix, Paris, put up between 1877 and 1880; the Greek Orthodox church in the Rue Georges Bizet, Paris, of 1890–95—though his last, St.-Antoine-des-Quinze-Vingts, 66 Avenue Ledru-Rollin, Paris, of 1901–3, reveals unusual and surprising powers of asymmetrical composition. Other classically trained architects sought similar evasive expedients along the lines suggested by the engineers François-Léonce Reynaud, in his *Traité d'architecture*, of 1850–58, and F. de Dartein in his *Étude sur l'architecture lombarde*, issued between 1865 and 1882. Lombard Gothic, it seemed, had the merit of being Italian, not French. Louis-Joseph Duc adopted it for the chapel of the Lycée Michelet, Paris, as did P.-R.-L. Ginain, to much less pleasing result at Notre-Dame-des-Champs, in the Boulevard du Montparnasse, Paris, of 1867–76. Such compromises, however, had little convincing effect. They made no impact on subsequent architecture.

Whether or not one notes and pursues the instances listed above, the pattern of the development of the Gothic Revival in France must already be clear. Support came in the first instance from the Commission des Monuments Historiques and later and more forcefully, after 1850, from the Service des Édifices Diocésains. Nearly all the architects we have considered had restored at least one Gothic building before they undertook to build anything new. They were thus amateur archaeologists and at once acknowledged an archaeological standard of taste. The focus for all their discussion, their source of information and ideas, was thus the *Annales archéologiques*, started by Didron in 1844. The tone of this review was from the first stridently militant. Didron delighted to provoke friends and enemies alike. The Gothic Revival was deliberately encouraged by scores of articles on medieval music, stained glass, and, above all, architecture. Félix de Verneilh established the national status of Gothic in a series of articles in 1845; Lassus preached the merits of the thirteenth-century style in the same year; while Viollet-le-Duc, as we have seen, beginning in 1844 and continuing until 1847, outlined in full those theories on Gothic that he was to elaborate later in life. These were the years of the highest hopes and excitement. Building in the Gothic style started just before 1840, though the first admired achievement, Barthélemy's Notre-Dame-de-Bon-Secours, was not completed until 1847. The Gothic movement during the 1840s was being firmly consolidated. In 1852 Didron estimated that two hundred churches of a mock-medieval kind had been built or were under construction in France. The chapter house of Notre-Dame in Paris was then complete, resplendent with murals and rich new furnishings, but the mature works of Lassus and Viollet-le-Duc were yet to come. At just this period, however, the sap and savor that had sustained the whole movement failed. Lassus remained a convinced revivalist, but Viollet-le-Duc, though he continued to design in a Gothic style, was no longer wholehearted in his support. He had given notice of this crisis of faith as early as 1844, concluding one of his articles in the *Annales archéologiques* with the words, "Ces secondes poussées n'ont jamais le vigueur, la sève des premières; elles sont souvent pâles et étiolées. Mais enfin ce sont encore les rejetons d'une bonne souche, et il faut bien se garder de les dédaigner" (p. 179). Already he was looking for an alternative form of architecture, Gothic in its principles but not in its appearance. He was determined to forge a new style. Although he remained friendly with Didron after 1848, he ceased to provide propaganda in the *Annales archéologiques.* Instead, he wrote after 1852 for the *Revue générale de l'architecture* and then for the *Encyclopédie d'architecture,* the review founded in 1851 by Adolphe Lance (1813–1874) and Victor Calliat (1801–1881). Viollet-le-Duc was not alone in his misgivings; many of the most active and serious-minded adherents of the Gothic movement sought a solution to the dilemmas of nineteenth-century architecture outside the restrictions of a revivalist doctrine. They built churches in the Gothic style—or in an interpretation of it—but little else. They were not sure of their cause. Apart from the limited creative ability of the architects involved, this lack of strong conviction must be held largely accountable for the rapid decline into eclecticism of the Gothic Revival in France. Very little of value in the way of building was to emerge.

The cause, the catalyst of this crisis of faith, was, paradoxically, the erection of Ste.-Clotilde, in Paris, the most conspicuous of the early monuments to the Gothic Revival, and one for which Didron and all his host had fought tenaciously. The history of this battle is little known. It begins, surprisingly, in 1834, when Prosper Mérimée, as *Inspecteur Général des Monuments Historiques,* suggested, wisely enough, that all plans for restoration work to be undertaken by the Commission des Monuments Historiques be submitted to the Conseil Général des Bâtiments Civils. This procedure was followed happily for five years and more, for Jean Vatout, president of the Commission, was at the same time president of the Conseil. But at the end of 1839 control of the Conseil was transferred from the Ministère de l'Intérieur to the Ministère des Travaux Publics. Vatout was obliged to resign his position on the Commission, which was thus deprived of its president and of the intimate cooperation of the staff of the Conseil. The Commission, now presided over by Ludovic Vitet, decided to assert its independence; in this it was successful, but at the expense of the Conseil's trust. Thereafter the two bodies were in all things opposed. And their antipathy became more marked with the quickening interest in Gothic, for, though the members of the Commission were by no means Gothic enthusiasts to a man, almost all the members of the Conseil opposed the Revival. They were, for the most part, members of the Académie.

The changes in administration had an irritating consequence for the Commission: the virtual loss of control over several important historic monuments, among them the church of St.-Denis, which François Debret had been restoring for a number of years. In 1839 he began work on the west front. More than an inch of stone was cut from the face of the building; niches and altogether unwarranted detail were also added to the north tower, which had been struck two years before by lightning. The Commission complained repeatedly. It demanded Debret's removal. Then, in 1844, the north tower was found to be collapsing under its own weight. All Gothic men were aghast. Didron attacked Debret and the Conseil viciously in the *Annales archéologiques*. The members of the Conseil lost no time in retaliating. Early in 1845 they arbitrarily refused to allow construction of three churches in the Gothic style strongly championed by Didron: St.-André, a diminutive version of St.-Nicaise, at Rheims; St.-Aubin at Toulouse, designed in competition the year before by Gaston Virebent; and St.-Étienne at Tours, by Gustave Guérin. The plans of St.-Étienne had already been passed and work was stopped only at the last moment by telegram. Didron was furious. He launched a new offensive. St.-André and St.-Aubin were not built, and St.-Étienne was begun only in 1869; but Didron's campaign resulted in the acceptance of the plans of the more conspicuous, and thus even more controversial, church of Ste.-Clotilde. The earliest plans for this, in the classical style, were by Jean-Nicolas Huyot (1780–1840). Two years before he died he was succeeded as architect by his friend Franz Christian Gau (1790–1854), a native of Cologne who had crossed the Rhine in 1809 to study under Lebas and Debret. The *Préfet de la Seine*, Claude-Philibert-Barthelot Rambuteau, a friend of Mérimée, demanded a church in the Gothic style. After some delay Gau produced a project in a fourteenth-century style. This was rejected by the Conseil in 1840 on the grounds that too many iron cramps and tie-rods were proposed in the construction. In the years that followed Gau modified his design no fewer than three times. On each occasion it was rejected. By 1845 Rambuteau had lost patience. He demanded acceptance of the design. The Conseil made no move. Then, early in 1846, the north tower of St.-Denis, collapsing slowly for two years, had to be hastily demolished. Debret was dismissed, but he was made a member of the Conseil. Rambuteau responded at once. Under the threat of a full-scale enquiry into the conduct of the work at St.-Denis, he forced the Conseil to approve the plans of Ste.-Clotilde. They were passed by one vote. Didron was triumphant. He disliked Gau and he disliked Gau's design, but he was overjoyed that a victory had been won for the Gothic cause in the teeth of the Conseil's—and thus the Académie's—opposition. The Académie was not yet prepared to concede the victory. A.-N. Caristie, a member of both the Conseil and the Commission, submitted a specially prepared questionnaire to the Académie. "Est-il convenable à nôtre époque," he asked, "de construire une église dans le style dit gothique?" This memoir and the discussion that followed were summarized by Désirée-Raoul Rochette and published at once as an academic encyclical. A copy was sent to the Ministère de l'Intérieur. Didron, Lassus, and Viollet-le-Duc all responded with vigor, and no fewer than six other pamphlets were written to support them. Viollet-le-Duc was appointed architect for the restoration of St.-Denis. In the same year, the Conseil attempted to prevent the erection of Hippolyte Durand's church at Peyrehorade, but was thwarted. By 1847 eighteen of the twenty plans for churches passed by the Conseil were in some medieval style or other.

Work was at once begun on Ste.-Clotilde. Responsibility, however, was placed in the hands of Théodore Ballu rather than of Gau, who had become deaf and unduly querulous. Ballu kept to Gau's designs as far as possible, being forced to reduce the height of the towers for reasons of economy. He retained the two spires, modifying their design. By December 1857 the church was complete. Didron disliked it with a rare intensity, as indeed did all committed revivalists. They thought it too florid in detail and were not proud of their victory.

The dispute forced many admirers of Gothic architecture to consider seriously the merits of a Gothic Revival; they had been unnerved by the feebleness of their own arguments, Viollet-le-Duc no less than anyone else, and there is ample evidence to suggest that they soon found the style insupportable. Churches like Gau's were not worth fighting for. The movement declined. It would not be unfair to say that it failed. The French had for only a very few years felt impelled to imitate Gothic.

638. *Plate from Christopher Dresser's* Principles of Decorative Design, *1873.*

Historians of modern architecture have looked to the nineteenth century, if at all, for prophets of the modern movement. Such theorists who have held rational, apparently utilitarian ideals—Horatio Greenough, A.W. N. Pugin, Edward Lacy Garbett, and Viollet-le-Duc—have been singled out and upheld as extraordinary visionaries who owed nothing or almost nothing either to their predecessors or to the societies in which they lived. Yet they evolved their ideas in relation to both, and if we hope ever to understand their intentions and meanings we must assess them in relation to the complex contexts from which they emerged. To abstract and isolate their ideas is to falsify them and to give them new meanings. This might, indeed, be stimulating. But to view history as a triumphant progress toward the present is to view it through a distorting glass.

The nineteenth-century radicals were not what they have seemed. Those moments in their careers when they have appeared to err or to falter have for the most part been ignored or set aside as embarrassments. Take Sir Joseph Paxton (1801–1865), the duke of Devonshire's head gardener at Chatsworth, who had already designed for the estate the Great Conservatory in 1836 and the *Victoria regia* greenhouse in 1850, before he put up the Crystal Palace, in London, in 1850–51. This marvel of prefabrication, of iron and glass—and also, it must be stressed, a great deal of timber construction—has a forceful clarity of expression that has rarely failed to satisfy. But it was not always thought of as "Architecture," which is how we have been taught to consider it. Paxton himself regarded the structure only as a specific solution to a particular dilemma. Iron and glass were not generally applicable to Victorian architectural needs, nor were the methods of building he had developed. When he launched into, among many other careers, that of architect after the Great Exhibition, he started to build Mentmore House in Buckinghamshire, a solid Elizabethan pastiche, for the Baron de Rothschild. He built much more of this sort. For the Rothschilds in France, with whom he had business dealings, he started a whole sequence of houses, beginning in 1853 with Ferrières, outside Paris, and ending, as we have seen, with the Château de Pregny, outside Geneva, where he was to be joined by Viollet-le-Duc. These great ungainly châteaux are all in a rich and florid style. They were clearly conceived as appropriate solutions to the problems Paxton considered as set; they were as fitted to their purposes as the Crystal Palace. And the lessons we have derived from this particular building—if lessons are wanted from history—we might as readily have read into the stones of Pregny.

Owen Jones (1809–1874), an architect of as clear and commonsensical a cast of mind as Paxton, was appointed Superintendent

of the Works at the Crystal Palace with the injunction to give it something of the effect of Architecture. He applied, as we might think proper, no ornamentation; instead, he invented a system of colored decoration designed to give body and depth to the framework of iron and timber. He painted the interior with stripes of red, yellow and blue, all separated by white, an arrangement based on Michel Eugène Chevreul's *De la loi du contraste simultané des couleurs,* of 1839—a law that Hittorff had tried to interpret so very differently at St.-Vincent-de-Paul—and also based on the color experiments of George Field. The theory was all science and calculation, but the effect was as of a fairy palace. "Looking up the nave with its endless rows of pillars," wrote the correspondent of the *Illustrated London News* on May 1, 1851, "the scene vanished from extreme brightness to the hazy indistinctness which Turner alone can paint." The outside was all blue and white. In 1856 Jones published his *Grammar of Ornament,* in which he made clear his belief that the generative forces of the nineteenth century—like religious or moral belief in the past— were science, industry, and commerce, and that it was the business of designers to express these. The artistry that was to give style to this utilitarian form—outlined in his thirty-seven propositions— consisted in proportional systems, geometrical arrangements of pattern and color, scientifically applied. At the end of his book were suggested decorative appliqués evolved from plant forms, a fashion that may have begun in England with Pugin's *Floriated Ornament,* of 1849. It was certainly taken up and marvelously expanded there by such men as James Kennaway Colling, John Lindley, Ralph Nicholson Wornum, Christopher Dresser, Frederick Edward Hulme, and Lewis Foreman Day. In France, as we have seen, Viollet-le-Duc and Ruprich-Robert pursued this path to somewhat different ends. The magical aura that Owen Jones had conjured up with his science at the Crystal Palace he successfully captured once again in his halls of arts and commerce—St. James's Hall, off Regent Street, London, of 1855 to 1858, the Crystal Palace Bazaar, between Great Portland and Oxford streets, London, of 1858, and Osler's shop, Oxford Street, of 1858 to 1860—all long since gone. Each had a roof of iron and glass and plaster painted in primary colors. They caused a sensation. But when it came to providing homes for the solid citizens who paid to hear music or shopped in these emporiums Owen Jones chose to design in a heavy Italianate style, as he did, for example, No. 8 Kensington Palace Gardens, London. He considered it appropriate to the station and needs of his clients.

When one turns to the career of that febrile French seer Hector Horeau (1801–1872), who in 1849, even before Paxton, submitted an iron and glass structure in the Crystal Palace competition, one finds the same candid acceptance of common propriety in the field of domestic and other architecture. A pupil of Eugène-Charles-Frédéric Nepveu (1777–1862) and then of François Debret, he failed to win the Grand Prix in 1826 but, like Owen Jones, traveled for three years throughout Europe and later, in 1837, to North Africa, before settling down to his chosen, constantly frustrating career. He published a spectacular and highly colored *Panorama de l'Égypte et de la Nubie* in 1841. But first he made a name for himself as a builder of iron and glass structures: In 1846 he designed a *jardin d'hiver* at Lyons (built in the following year) and the Château des Fleurs (a bandstand, in effect) for the corner of the Rue Vernet and the Rue Galilée, off the Champs-Élysées, in Paris, much praised in 1847 in the *Revue générale de l'architecture* (pp. 254, 410). He published a number of ambitious schemes for improving the drainage of the city, for *abattoirs*, markets, and exhibition buildings. His design for the Halles Centrales, the central market of Paris, a great iron and glass structure similar in appearance to Philibert de l'Orme's design for the Salles des Fêtes Royales, the forerunner of C.-L.-F. Dutert's Galerie des Machines, was first presented in 1844 and developed in the following years. When Victor Baltard and F.-E. Callet were appointed to build that market and began with a ponderous pavilion of stone, Horeau initiated a campaign that brought Baron Haussmann, in 1853, to order its demolition—thus leading to the erection of the iron and glass structures that Baltard and Callet eventually designed. Horeau was furious. He moved in 1855 to England, where he suggested a whole new range of street improvements and exhibited them all, four years later, in the Hanover Square Rooms, London. By then he had built a house in Surrey (untraced) and another at Primrose Hill, London (probably The Poplars, at 18 or 20 Avenue Road; demolished in 1934), illustrated in the review established by Viollet-le-Duc's son, the *Gazette des architectes et du bâtiment*, in 1868. The plan is imaginative, if symmetrical, with splayed wings, but the elevation is decorated with conventional Italian-inspired motifs. In the first volume of the elder Viollet-le-Duc's *Habitations modernes*, of 1875, another of Horeau's houses is illustrated, a farmstead at Ostend, in Belgium, with clumsy brick decoration around the door and window openings, and boldly projecting timber bargeboards and balconies with frets and rude arabesques. A Swiss chalet, it seems, has strayed. Later in life Horeau moved to Madrid, where in 1868 he designed an iron and glass market for the Plaza Cebada. A few years after—while serving a prison sentence in Paris for overenthusiastic support of the Commune—he sketched proposals for a new *hôtel de ville*, once again an ordinary enough, unpretentious sort of building, but with a great glass-roofed court in which all business was to be conducted.

Horeau was a hard thinker and a man of immense enterprise and no little adventure, but he, too, accepted, without qualm it seems, that for certain types of building, the conventional hybrid modes were the best.

In America James Bogardus (1800–1874), a manufacturer of machinery, was making four- and five-story fronts for buildings, all of iron and glass, from the late 1840s onward, but he chose to cast them in classically modeled molds, and with his increasing success made them ever more rich and intricate in decoration. The Renaissance style that he applied was to him an essential and fitting part of the whole conception. And, though he had an arrogant disregard of all conventional opinion and ranked the products of engineering extremely high, even James Fergusson (1808–1886), that bombastic philistine, one-time indigo merchant, and archaeologist, the architectural historian who was probably more widely read than any other during the nineteenth century, thought that such buildings as the Crystal Palace were lacking in a sense of solidity and mass, and could not, as he expressed it, "be elevated to the class of the Fine Arts." Fergusson, it is to be remarked, was general manager, from 1856 to 1858, of the Crystal Palace Company, at Sydenham, where Paxton and Jones had set up an even grander variant of the Hyde Park structure. His most entertaining and certainly most provocative book was *History of the Modern Styles of Architecture*, of 1862 (published together with his *Illustrated Handbook of Architecture*, of 1855, as part of the even more compendious *History of Architecture in All Countries, from the Earliest Times to the Present Day*, issued between 1865 and 1867). At the end of his *History of the Modern Styles of Architecture*, having rejected Greek and Gothic as moribund, and having ranted and raved at the shams of modern architecture, Fergusson yet felt compelled to recommend to his contemporaries that they take up a Renaissance style. "There is yet one other style within whose limits progress still seems possible," he wrote despairingly. "The Renaissance Italian is by no means worked out." Fergusson sought an architecture that was altogether sensibly designed and built, strong and durable, reflecting both in its forms and in its decoration—which he considered of the highest importance—the aspirations and the communal sense of the society that produced it: a banal aim, one might judge, but one that, together with so many other contemporaries, he thought best fulfilled in the Renaissance manner.

No less bathos attaches to those agonized theories offered in that now little-known but, in the nineteenth century, much-read *Rudimentary Treatise on the Principles of Design in Architecture*, first printed in 1850. The author was Edward Lacy Garbett, who was to appeal so much to Horatio Greenough and later American theorists. He staunchly upheld the importance of structural principles, recognizing two systems of structural purity, the Greek and the Gothic, but rejected them at length in favor of a third, as yet unresolved—that of the Italian Renaissance.

Other nineteenth-century prophets—those who most strongly affected nineteenth- and even twentieth-century sensibilities—came to somewhat different conclusions, though they inclined to agree with Fergusson as to the merits of the Crystal Palace. A. W. N. Pugin, that brilliant proselytizer of Gothic, described the building in casual asides in his letters as "the crystal humbug" and "a glass monster." This was not because he disapproved of iron construction or other modern devices and inventions, for he wrote in 1843 in *An Apology for the Revival of Christian Architecture in England*, "Any modern invention which conduces to comfort, cleanliness or durability should be adopted by the consistent architect." Moreover, he made clear in other of his works his approval of modern plumbing systems, gaslights, all manner of mechanical devices, and even the railways, provided that they were designed directly and simply with reference to their use. He liked best what he called "the substantial manner." He loathed the evident lack of mass of the Crystal Palace, and even more the evident indifference to Gothic that it reflected. The Medieval Court he set up in Paxton's building was, in its rich intensity, in sharp contrast to that pared-down structure. The principles that Pugin laid down in 1841 on the first page of *The True Principles of Pointed or Christian Architecture* have nothing overtly to do with Gothic. "The two great rules for design are these: 1st, that there should be no features about a building which are not necessary for convenience, construction, or propriety; 2nd, that all ornament should consist of enrichment of the essential construction of the building." However, it is evident throughout this book, and made quite plain in the second edition, that the only acceptable style is Gothic. Pugin countenanced no other. He fought throughout his short and active life for its revival, for it represented to him the last historical stage at which architecture had been a complete expression of communities imbued with a true spiritual faith. Pugin had been converted to Roman Catholicism in 1835. The Reformation, and all that was associated with it, was thus to him a second fall from grace. In his early years he adopted the late Gothic style, but as his belief grew that the Reformation was not the root cause of the fall, merely part of a more general decay in faith, he retreated to the styles of the early fourteenth and late thirteenth centuries; these became for him the only true architecture for the Revival.

Pugin's principles and much of his attitude toward Gothic—

even his identification of it as the true Catholic style—may be traced back, surprisingly, to so academic a source as Jacques-François Blondel's *Cours d'architecture*, to which Pugin was no doubt introduced by his father, an architectural illustrator from France. But Pugin's perfervid moralism is new to architectural theory. It was most forcefully expounded right from the start, in the most devastating of all his books, *Contrasts; or, A Parallel Between the Noble Edifices of the Fourteenth and Fifteenth Centuries, and Similar Buildings of the Present Day*, issued in 1836. The text is short, but the sixteen contrasted plates make his meaning clear: All the towns and buildings of the nineteenth century are degraded and mean; those of the Middle Ages are rewarding and full, burgeoning with ancient feelings and sentiments." 'Tis they alone that can restore pointed architecture to its former glorious state; without it all that is done will be a tame and heartless copy, true as far as the mechanism of the style goes, but utterly wanting in that sentiment and feeling that distinguishes ancient design" (2d ed., 1841, p. 43).

The moral note struck by Pugin was to be the real contribution of England to nineteenth-century architectural thought. John Ruskin (1819–1900) was the most eloquent spokesman of the ethical—though not the Catholic—attitude. His social convictions, however, were to be forcefully and dogmatically expressed only later in life. Yet already in his very first writings, "The Poetry of Architecture," published in 1837 and 1838, under the pseudonym Kata Phusin ("According to Nature"), in *Loudon's Architectural Magazine*, was his whole future understanding made evident. His editor John Claudius Loudon, it is worth remarking, was a man of a different stamp. All his activity was in sharp contrast to Ruskin's—his obsessive writing apart. Loudon was a caricature of the dour, industrious Scot; he got up at seven each morning, breakfasted, and then worked without a break until eight in the evening, writing in the course of his life over four million words, mostly on estate management and horticulture but on much else besides. He was forever producing practical proposals for such things as drainage systems and heating devices. He sought out the woman he was to marry because she had written what must rank as one of the first works of science-fiction, *The Mummy: A Tale of the Twenty-Second Century* (1827). He was building greenhouses years before Paxton and established the techniques of construction that Paxton was later to use at Chatsworth and the Crystal Palace. He was a very early protagonist of iron and glass architecture. But in his myriad publications he also offered all manner of architectural styles (he employed Charles Barry and those rogues E. B. Lamb and S. S. Teulon indiscriminately to make his designs), for, though he had explicit and very commonsensical ideas about

architecture, he cared not a jot what it should look like provided that it be usefully organized and soundly built. He cared for everything that Ruskin did not; yet he did care for Ruskin and was generous in his praise of his writings. Ruskin's "The Poetry of Architecture" dealt with qualities of landscape and the manner in which a chalet, a cottage, or a farmhouse might relate to it, in the tradition of Picturesque theory already widely applied in England. However, Ruskin's particular view of the way in which such inevitable, unassuming, and "natural" architecture is a reflection not only of the skills but of the whole way of life of the people who made it was new—though it may well have derived from Jean-Jacques Rousseau's enraptured description of the life and form of a mountain village near Neuchâtel, contained in his polemic of 1758 addressed to d'Alembert ". . .*Sur le projet d'établir un théâtre de comédie en [Genève]*." Goodness in architecture, for both men, arises from goodness in man. Later, in those two works most memorably concerned with architecture, *The Seven Lamps of Architecture*, of 1849, and *The Stones of Venice,* issued in three volumes in 1851 and 1853, Ruskin was to enlarge on this theme. In *The Queen of the Air*, of 1869, he was to turn it into an aphorism: "A foolish person builds foolishly, and a wise one sensibly; a virtuous one, beautifully; and a vicious one, basely."

The seven lamps—Sacrifice, Truth, Power, Beauty, Life, Memory, Obedience—have not much to do with architecture, certainly not in any conventional fashion. Ruskin was not greatly interested in the way a building might work, in its organization, or in its structure (though he was vehement in his denunciation of what he recognized as structural deceit). There are no more than one or two plans illustrated in his published works, and no sections; nor, if we are to judge by his drawings and descriptions, was he much taken with mass or volume in architecture. His skill as a draftsman and his passion in writing are directed to details: to doorheads and windows, to capitals and moldings. He focused always on discrete fragments. Architecture itself, he thought, resided in surface adornment, in moldings and sculpture. "Thus," he wrote in "The Lamp of Sacrifice," "I suppose no one would call the laws architectural which determine the height of a breastwork or the position of a bastion. But if to the stone facing of that bastion be added an unnecessary feature, as a cable moulding, *that* is Architecture." But what excited him above all else was surface pattern, the texture of things, whether in architecture or nature. His delight in drawing or describing such patterns was sensual, almost erotic. He saw in the surface, whether worked by man or weathered by time, the imprint of all nature, to be caressed by the hand and the eye. No matter if the surface was rough and ungainly, scarred and broken, provided it be a truthful expression. He abominated all restoration in architecture, battling furiously against it through life, and in 1874 refusing the Gold Medal of the Royal Institute of British Architects because the company included men who were defacing the ancient buildings he loved. The surface of structures had for him a sanctity that must not be disturbed (shades here of Chateaubriand). There was more to it than visual delight. The surface revealed the nature of the man who had worked it, giving expression to all his joys, passions, and beliefs; it thus also expressed the nature of the society of which that man was a part. For good architecture to arise, those responsible must have good lives and be happy.

Ruskin's ideal society was set somewhere in the Middle Ages, a notion he had derived first from Thomas Carlyle and later from Pugin. However, good Evangelical that he was and fearing lest he be tainted by Pugin's Catholicism, he sharply denied any such influence. He thus rejected all Renaissance architecture as a sham and upheld Gothic as an image of the good and the true. But just as there is not as much as one might expect of architecture in *The Seven Lamps*, so there is not much in it on Gothic—nor is there even in *The Stones of Venice*. Ruskin's crusade was not a national one. He disliked the damp and the gloom of the north and did not look long at the Gothic monuments of England, or even at those of France (though in time he learned to admire some of the latter). He preferred the south. Italian Gothic became for him the symbol of all he loved in architecture—Giotto's tower at Florence and, even more, the Doges' Palace, at Venice. Hastily written and added almost haphazardly to the second volume of *The Stones of Venice*, his chapter "The Nature of Gothic" served nonetheless as a catechism for the serious-minded architects of England. William Morris, of whom nothing need here be said, solemnly printed a separate edition at the Kelmscott Press in 1892. He described it then as "one of the very few necessary and inevitable utterances of the century." It was the spur to his career, and to that of Philip Webb, William Lethaby, and a great many others. "The Nature of Gothic" is, as might be expected, unspecific. Ruskin approaches his subject through broad categories: savageness, imperfection, changefulness, redundance, and rigidity. Yet one emerges from it inspired with a new reverence and feeling for the idea of Gothic. Absolutely, it was the most potent of all Ruskin's writings on architecture.

In time he turned his attention away from architecture: He thought rather on the nature of society and on what it might be. He became one of the most radical thinkers of his age. He aimed to make England a good, egalitarian society—with equal wages for all (he himself had been left £197,000 on his father's death). Architects, he saw, were impotent; only when the nature of society was changed would good architecture arise. In 1864 he was invited to lecture at the Mechanics Institute at Bradford, where a competition was being held for the design of a new exchange. He was expected to advise on the style, which no one doubted he would designate as Gothic. Instead, he told the assembled burghers and businessmen that *he* didn't care a damn what style they got, because *they* didn't. All that concerned them was the making of money. And he thundered on and on about the immorality of their lives and the consequent ugliness of their city. "The only absolutely and unapproachably heroic elements in the soldier's work," he told his audience, "seems to be—that he is paid little for it—and regularly: while you traffickers, and exchangers, and others occupied in presumably benevolent business, like to be paid much for it—and by chance. I never can make out how it is that a *knight*-errant does not expect to be paid for his trouble, but a *pedlar*-errant always does;—that people are willing to take hard knocks for nothing, but never to sell ribands cheap; that they are ready to go on fervent crusades, to recover the tomb of a buried God, but never on any travels to fulfil the orders of a living one;—that they will go anywhere barefoot to preach their faith, but must be well bribed to practise it, and are perfectly ready to give the Gospel gratis, but never the loaves and fishes.

"If you chose to take the matter up on any such soldierly principle; to do your commerce, and your feeding of nations, for fixed salaries; and to be as particular about giving people the best food, and the best cloth, as soldiers are about giving them the best gunpowder, I could carve something for you on your exchange worth looking at. But I can only at present suggest decorating its frieze with pendent purses" (*The Works of Ruskin*, ed. E. T. Cook and A. Wedderburne, vol. 18, p. 450).

The one building with which Ruskin was said to have been closely involved, the University Museum at Oxford, by Sir Thomas Deane and Benjamin Woodward, was not a successful expression of his ideals. He was less involved, though, than is usually thought. He was out of England for much of the building period and was writing hard for most of the rest of the time. The final design was made in 1854, and construction began in the following year, with workmen brought over from Ireland led by the rumbustious James O'Shea. He was to demonstrate in his work all Ruskin's cherished obsessions, though his insolent disregard for the dignitaries of Oxford led to his deportation in 1860, before the work of carving was complete. Woodward died in the following year, and funds were lacking, so little more was done. The bulk of the work was, however, by then largely executed, with a fantastical covered court all in iron and glass,

Gothic in style. Ruskin cannot have much approved of the use of iron, but he was never strongly critical about it. His concern for the joy of a man in his work and for the way he might make his mark on the finished surface had led him, inevitably, to reject the large-scale use of iron in architecture as well as all methods of prefabrication. The workman, he said, was thus degraded. Critics might see the effects of a painting by Turner (a painter he revered) in the nave of the Crystal Palace, but 1851, Ruskin retorted, was the very year in which Turner had died. In fact, Turner was keenly interested in the Crystal Palace. But for Ruskin there was nothing in it either of Turner or of Architecture. "The quantity of thought it expresses is, I suppose," he wrote in 1855 in a note to the second edition of *The Seven Lamps*—a note, incidentally, directed against Garbett—"a single and very admirable thought of Sir Joseph Paxton's, probably not a bit brighter than thousands of thoughts which pass through his active and intelligent brain every hour—that it might be possible to build a greenhouse larger than ever greenhouse was built before. This thought, and some very ordinary algebra, are as much as all that glass can represent of human intellect" (*Works*, vol. 9, p. 456). When he viewed the influence of his own works and writings in 1874 in the preface to the third edition of *The Stones of Venice*, "which has mottled our manufactory chimneys with black and red brick, dignified our banks and drapers' shops with Venetian tracery, and pinched our parish churches into dark and slippery arrangements for the advertisement of cheap coloured glass and pantiles," he felt bound to reject them, too, as pernicious.

On the Continent ethics and social morality were not permitted to dominate architectural theory: No one of any great influence took up architecture as a religious crusade, no one veered from architecture to political theory. Nonetheless, many—indeed, all the key figures—held strong, sometimes violent, political views. Gottfried Semper, the German spokesman, was forced to flee to Belgium and then to France when the antimonarchical revolution in which he was involved had failed. In France, Horeau, as we have seen, was imprisoned for his part in the Commune. Earlier, Gilbert, Blouet, Labrouste, and Duc had been passionately stirred by the ideas of Saint-Simon and Comte, while César Daly, editor of that most influential and sumptuous of journals, the *Revue générale de l'architecture*, was a Fourierist, and even designed a *phalanstère*, which he illustrated in outline in his *Revue*. But there was little else of this sort in it.

Viollet-le-Duc himself had fought on the barricades when young and, after the Franco–Prussian war, when the mood of the country was at a very low ebb, he thought to take up an active political stance.

He started to write regularly for *Le centre gauche, Le peuple*, and *Le bien public*. In 1873 he stood in the first municipal elections and was chosen as Republican candidate for Montmartre, a position he was to hold for no more than a year, for he decided then that the Republican government was without morality. He denounced it in *Le centre gauche* and resigned his seat and all government appointments, including that of *Inspecteur Général des Édifices Diocésains*. He was reelected to the city council, although under a different political banner, and sat on it until his death in 1879. These were honest and courageous steps to take, but there is no need to exaggerate their importance. Viollet-

le-Duc had for too long been a compliant courtier under the Second Empire; he had done nothing then to use his influence to improve the world.

The focus of all Viollet-le-Duc's interest in architecture was on construction. He was determined to show that the proper expression of structural principles would produce proper architecture. No one who has read Henry Adams's *Mont-Saint-Michel and Chartres*, packed with quotations from Viollet-le-Duc, can be in any doubt that he was also a man of sensitivity and feeling, acutely responsive to the poetry of Gothic architecture, and that he may be interpreted also in this light; but in his battle against the established architectural conventions, and in particular those established by the École des Beaux-Arts, he was forced to steel his arguments with the most ruthless logic and to interpret Gothic architecture—indeed, all good architecture, in which he included Greek and also Byzantine—as the readily explicable results of determined ends. The principles he adduced in his analyses were to be applied in the fashioning of an architecture for the nineteenth century and even after. He emerges thus as a harsh materialist, crude and overbearing. Yet even those structural principles he had so early explained in the pages of the *Annales archéologiques* were to be but tentatively applied to the exigencies of nineteenth-century architecture. From the first he accepted that new materials, especially iron, must serve as an essential part of nineteenth-century renewal. He was even prepared to use iron for restoration work: He ordered iron window frames for Ste.-Madeleine at Vézelay in 1845, just as Lassus had done for St.-Germain-l'Auxerrois. However, in a report to the Commission des Monuments Historiques of 1850 on the ridiculous cast-iron spire that J.-A. Alavoine had set on top of Rouen cathedral in 1824, Viollet-le-Duc firmly rejected—in much the same manner as had Pugin—the notion that iron might be used to reproduce forms or ornaments that had evolved under different circumstances. There was to be no cast-iron Gothic. He was vehement in his denunciation of all such experiments. On January 11, 1854, Louis-Auguste Boileau (1812–1896), the son of a joiner and himself the maker and carver of the organ loft at St.-Germain-l'Auxerrois, the architect also of a simple mock-Gothic church at Mattaincourt (Vosges) that included cast-iron pews, published a proposal in *La presse* for a church with columns of cast iron to be erected in the Chaussée-d'Antin. On February 18 this was again published, in *L'illustration*, with an enthusiastic commentary by Albert Lenoir. Within a short time a pupil of Percier and Fontaine, Louis-Adrien Lusson (1790–1864), had taken up the idea and proposed it to the archbishop of Paris for a site on the corner of the Rue Monthyon (now Rue Ste.-Cécile) and the Rue du Conservatoire. Work began in the month of March. Boileau, as might be expected, protested most strongly. He replaced Lusson as architect and by December 21, 1855, his new church of St.-Eugène had been consecrated. Externally it is an ordinary enough red-brick box, stuccoed here and there and broken by pointed windows, with three gables on the entrance facade. Internally it is a curious Gothic paraphrase similar to that designed (possibly in the same year) in England for the Ecclesiological Society, by William Slater, Richard Cromwell Carpenter's pupil and successor, but published in *Instrumenta ecclesiastica* only in 1856. All the columns and ribs and even the

651. *Eugène-Emmanuel Viollet-le-Duc, section of a Gothic church showing how iron and wood might be substituted for stone structural elements, from his* Dictionnaire raisonné de l'architecture française, *1859.*

traceries of Boileau's church are of iron. The vaults are covered with sheets of metal. The building caused much excitement and comment. César Daly condemned it early, in February 1855, long before its completion, in the *Revue générale de l'architecture*, as a conception of the utmost naivety. Two years later he was to reject it as too much the railway shed: "Dans lesquelles toutefois la colonne en fonte réussit très-bien, parce que là l'effet d'art résulte uniquement de l'aménagement, non pas le plus monumental, dans le sens propre du mot, mais le plus commode, d'un grand espace qu'on doit disposer, autant que possible, de façon à en utiliser toutes les parties et à y laisser largement pénétrer le jour; dans une église, au contraire, la colonne, il nous semble, est tout à la fois faite pour soutenir et pour meubler" (p. 100). But Michel Chevalier published a highly appreciative account of Boileau's paraphrase in the *Journal des débats* on June 1, 1855, and at once proposed that the system be adopted for the cathedrals of Moulins and Marseilles and also for the new churches at Montpellier and Lille. Chevalier's tribute drew forth a rude reply from Viollet-le-Duc. In the *Encyclopédie d'architecture*, in the same month, he wrote, "Un système dont toute la solidité réside dans l'extrême précision des assemblages se rapproche plus de l'art du mécanicien que de l'art de l'architecture. . . . M. Boileau, le directeur de la construction de Saint-Eugène, quelque ingénieux qu'il soit, n'était pas architecte, c'était un fort habile menuisier, et quoi qu'on fasse, la première éducation pratique ne se remplace pas." It was, he added, a puerile pastiche in bad taste. Boileau replied in the following month with more restraint than might be expected. He was doing no more, he said, than Viollet-le-Duc himself had suggested in his writings. Approving of the principles of Gothic construction, he had tried to interpret them in the way in which thirteenth-century masons themselves might have done had they had present-day resources. Viollet-le-Duc's distaste, he suggested, was aroused because the forms and arrangements of Gothic had not been slavishly copied. Viollet-le-Duc was enraged. He responded in the same issue of the *Encyclopédie d'architecture*, raising a host of technical issues and also that question pertinent to the whole problem: "Pourquoi des arcs, quand on peut avoir des poutres de fonte ou de tôle d'une énorme portée? Pourquoi ne pas se servir de ces matières comme les ingénieurs anglais et français sont arrivés à le faire, c'est-à-dire en simplifiant de jour en jour les formes, en rompant franchement avec les vieilles traditions imposées par la routine?" But there is small cause to think that Viollet-le-Duc would have liked St.-Eugène any better had it resembled more closely a railway shed. Along with César Daly and most of his fellow critics in France, he had not admired the Crystal Palace. Henri Sirodot had dismissed it in the *Revue générale de l'ar-*

652. *Eugène-Emmanuel Viollet-le-Duc, project for a concert hall with a ceiling vaulted in iron and brick, from his twelfth* Entretien sur l'architecture, *c. 1866.*

653. *Eugène-Emmanuel Viollet-le-Duc, diagram showing that the equilateral triangle must be the basic principle of all architecture, from his* Dictionnaire raisonné de l'architecture française, *1866.*

chitecture in 1851 as no more than a giant greenhouse, without pretensions to architecture (p. 154).

Boileau was unabashed. Already in a small brochure issued in September 1854 he had published his first, and even more startling, project for a church of iron as *La nouvelle forme architecturale.* He showed tenuous columns of iron supporting a system of segmental arches and ribs of iron, carrying in turn an array of ribbed vaults, built up one against another to form a pyramidal composition. The curved vaults are exhibited both inside and out. The columns of iron, boldly expressed inside, are sheathed on the outside perimeter with stone. But the window areas between remain unusually large. The traceries with which they are filled are yet more unusual. They are made up of intersecting arcs to form a pattern of lines that relates to the segmental arches of the vaults. Two towers of a similar idiosyncratic composition stand at the west end of the church. Altogether, the design is freakish, inspired not only by Gothic examples but also, there is little doubt, by Moorish architecture (extracts from Owen Jones's lavish book on the Alhambra were published in the *Revue générale de l'architecture* in 1844, and one plate in particular seems to have provided the prototype for Boileau). He was later to produce many and far more ambitious variations on this design, to illustrate them, and to issue them together with the most persuasive of literary propaganda: In 1881 he published *Les principes et exemples d'architecture ferronière,* five years later the *Histoire critique de l'invention en architecture,* and in 1889 *Les préludes de l'architecture du XXᵉ siècle et l'exposition du centenaire,* a work of prophetic intention. But, apart from the great Magasins du Bon Marché, a department store begun, together with his son Louis-Charles, in 1869, his executed works showed little advance on St.-Eugène, if indeed they attained its standard of consistency. He added an iron-ribbed dome to his early reinforced-concrete church of Le Vésinet (Yvelines) in 1863, in the same year began St.-Paul, Place J. Dormoy, at Montluçon (Allier), and then in 1869 started work on St.-Étienne at Juilly (Seine-et-Marne)—where Lamennais and his disciples had installed themselves in 1830—a church not unlike St.-Eugène. In 1868 he built Notre-Dame-de-France in Leicester Place, London, a curious, iron-framed structure (demolished in 1957) set within the circular shell of Robert Barker's old panorama.

Viollet-le-Duc ignored this activity. His disciple J.-E.-A. de Baudot, however, attacked Boileau's designs for the church at Le Vésinet in 1863 in the *Gazette des architectes et du bâtiment* and three years later castigated the project Boileau had submitted in the Rambouillet competition (won, it may be remembered, by de Baudot himself, with a design incorporating columns of iron). "Le parti

654. *Eugène-Emmanuel Viollet-le-Duc, tomb of the Duc de Morny, Père-Lachaise cemetery, Paris, 1865–66.*

how iron, and timber, too, might be substituted for the structural members of a Gothic church, suggesting in this way how iron might be used in the nineteenth century. He himself used it thus unenterprisingly (as Butterfield and other such Gothic enthusiasts had done earlier in England) for the trusses of the sacristy of the cathedral at Rheims, designed in July 1862, but not built until 1870, and also for the more adeptly designed trusses for the roofs of the Château de Pierrefonds (1862). The Maison du Personnel at Notre-Dame in Paris, also with simple trusses of iron, was built in 1866. The use of iron was a particularly sensitive issue for Viollet-le-Duc at this period (hence de Baudot's shamefaced attack on Boileau's Rambouillet design) because Alfred Darcel, reviewing architecture at the Salon of 1864 in the *Gazette des beaux-arts* and, more important, César Daly in the editorial and in an assessment of a confessional designed twenty years earlier by Lassus for St.-Germain-l'Auxerrois included in the *Revue générale* in 1866, and also Bourgeois de Lagny in his review of the Salon of the same year in the newly founded *Moniteur des architectes,* had all vigorously attacked those tendencies that they associated then with Viollet-le-Duc. The Rambouillet church designs were a particular pretext for scorn. "L'école rationaliste," wrote Daly (thus categorizing Viollet-le-Duc and his disciples), "qui tend en ce moment à transformer l'*art architectural* en *architecture industrielle,* proclam[e] ainsi devant tous son scepticisme en matière d'art, son respect exclusif pour la science et l'utile" (p. 5). Bourgeois de Lagny, like Darcel earlier, even associated Viollet-le-Duc and his disciples with Boileau—an association they dreaded. Everyone regarded Boileau as a crank. But Bourgeois de Lagny was perhaps even more damaging when he linked them with the Realists, then being so widely discussed. "Le réalisme architectural (ou la construction avec l'absence d'art)," he concluded, "n'a qu'un rôle très-secondaire à remplir dans le développement de l'art monumental" (p. 81). Viollet-le-Duc had long been a friend of Champfleury and, in the *Journal des débats,* on August 7, 1863, had reviewed his collected essays, *Réalisme,* with what best tact he could. However, when he commented on other products of the Realist school, the novels of Flaubert, in letters to Mérimée, he was unequivocal in his contempt. Mérimée shared his opinions: "J'ai lu le roman de Flaubert," he wrote on December 29, 1869, of *L'éducation sentimentale.* "Hélas! C'est un mathématicien qui se trompe," a remark that both Daly and Bourgeois de Lagny would willingly have applied at that time to Viollet-le-Duc.

Viollet-le-Duc's answer to this onslaught was the astounding designs contained in the twelfth *Entretien,* dating from 1866 or just after. There, in illustrations for a *hôtel de ville* supported by V-poles

général adopté par l'architecte," he wrote, "n'est pas un système, mais simplement l'application de métal à des formes qui ne résultent pas des propriétés des matériaux employés" (p. 97). De Baudot sought thus firmly to disassociate his design from Boileau's. Later he was to find that Boileau was, after all, a liberating stimulus; when he came to design a church at Montmartre he took up a great deal from him. But the dispute with Boileau forced Viollet-le-Duc at once to consider more seriously the role of iron in architecture. In the article on construction in the fourth volume of the *Dictionnaire raisonné de l'architecture française,* issued in 1860, he showed very simply

655. *Jules Saulnier, Menier chocolate factory, Noisiel-sur-Marne, 1869, 1871–72.*

656. *Eugène Train, Collège Chaptal, Paris, 1863–75, a celebrated example of mixed brick, terra-cotta, colored ceramic, and exposed iron construction that started a fashion even before its completion.*

657. *Louis-Ernest Lheureux, Bibliothèque de l'École de Droit, Paris, facade, 1876–78.*

and for other large halls combining struts and frameworks of iron supporting masonry vaults—but especially in his hall for three thousand people—he showed how an architecture for the future might be forged (see illustration 27). Modest in his estimation of his creative abilities, he no doubt saw that his designs were ungainly and lacking in style, but they were yet an attempt of a determined and desperate sort to achieve style. The polyhedral hall is indeed a naive illustration of style as defined in that very same year, 1866, not in the *Entretiens*, as one might expect, but in the eighth volume of the *Dictionnaire raisonné de l'architecture française*. "Le style," Viollet-le-Duc wrote (no longer part, if it ever had been for him, of period styles), "*est la manifestation d'un idéal établi sur un principe*" (p. 475). To him, this great guiding principle was, ultimately, that of the world, of the universe itself. The secret of all its structure, of all its stability, was the equilateral triangle, upon which all the structure of all matter, all fine form, was based. The earth's crust had style. There is a lot more to his argument, and more subtlety than is here indicated, but even this short exposition is enough to demonstrate how he had moved from Gothic Revivalism to the most inclusive of guiding principles and how he hoped that they might be interpreted.

658. *Louis-Ernest Lheureux, Bibliothèque de l'École de Droit, Paris, interior, 1876–78.*

659. *Louis-Ernest Lheureux, Bibliothèque de l'École de Droit, Paris, second reading room, 1880, 1893–98.*

No one would say that he succeeded, but the breadth of his outlook was without equal.

Not many of his contemporaries were better equipped than Viollet-le-Duc to take up his challenge or to provide an example of his intentions. Those that did make the attempt were not trained by him. A pupil of Horeau, Jules-Désiré Bourdais (1835–1915), about 1868 built a small chapel at Négreplisse (Tarn-et-Garonne) with a roof supported by four conspicuous timber struts, composed in a manner reminiscent of the illustrations offered in the *Entretiens.*

Jules Saulnier completed a series of great brick structures for the Menier chemical factory at Saint-Denis in 1865; then, four years after, began the design of that celebrated iron-framed building across the Marne at Noisiel, for the Menier chocolate works. Building did not start for another two years but was sufficiently advanced for Viollet-le-Duc to draw it to the attention of his readers in the eighteenth *Entretien,* written in 1871 or early in 1872. It was illustrated in full in the *Encyclopédie d'architecture* in 1874 and in the years that followed, together with Saulnier's subsidiary buildings and remarkable workers' housing. The splendid building over the river gleaming with richly colored and patterned glazed bricks is thought to be the first complete iron-framed structure ever erected. This may indeed be the case. But the diagonal metal framework that is so boldly exposed on the facade commemorates a timber-framed structure erected on the same site between 1840 and 1855 by Saulnier's master, Bonneau, which in turn was based on a surviving medieval construction. Viollet-le-Duc may, nonetheless, have acted as a stimulus to Saulnier. Less doubtful is his influence on the architect of the library of the École de Droit, Rue Cujas, Paris, built between May 1876 and June 1878 by Louis-Ernest Lheureux (1827–1898), a pupil of Henri Labrouste. Lheureux had worked with Labrouste on the Collège Ste.-Barbe, just across the street, where he also built the Salle de Dessin. All these buildings—the facade of the Collège apart—are now gone, as is the second hall that Lheureux added to the first, beginning in 1880. In both, arrangements of cast-iron brackets and ceiling beams, with infilling panels of brick-work, were striking interpretations of Viollet-le-Duc's ideas but they were even more notable as examples of the reserve and monumental splendor that one associates with the name of Labrouste. The stone facade of the first hall, admirably articulated with three tall arches and a panel of lettering, was among the finest examples of French nineteenth-century architecture. Lheureux did little else of this quality, though his designs for the Entrepôt, the wine warehouses, at Bercy, Paris, approved in 1877 by Viollet-le-Duc himself—in his role as committee member for the city council—were not unworthy successors: iron-framed buildings, with infilling panels of glazed brick-work. The first phase of building was complete by 1886, but this has now disappeared. There is not much else dating from this period to bear witness to the theories of Viollet-le-Duc.

"Nous faisons de l'architecture de sentiment," Viollet-le-Duc wrote angrily in 1871 in the seventeenth *Entretien*, "comme nous avons fait de la politique de sentiment, la guerre de sentiment. . . . Il faudrait songer à faire intervenir en tout ceci la froide raison, le bon sens pratique, l'étude des nécessités du temps, des perfectionnements fournis par l'industrie, des moyens économiques, des questions d'hygiène et de salubrité" (p. 296). This was the note he struck again in the conclusion to the *Entretiens*, an emphasis upon practical wisdom and analytical investigation, which he believed was best expressed in the work of engineers: in particular, that engineer of the École des Ponts et Chaussées Auguste Choisy (1841–1909).

Choisy, in his studies of the art of construction in history, even more perhaps in his devastating *Histoire de l'architecture*, of 1903, fittingly resolved all these issues, over which Viollet-le-Duc had pondered and puzzled, in a most ruthless conclusion. Choisy's brilliant

illustrations reduced the complexities of all architecture to a few simple lines. Choisy provides the natural ending to the period we have studied, for he condensed not only Viollet-le-Duc's but all architectural theory into the simplest of aphorisms and diagrams. His very last work was an edition of Vitruvius, published in 1909, the final occasion on which that old Roman was edited for architects—and how very different it was from Perrault's, though one can see the connection. But there is yet one more architect who demands consideration before our conclusion is reached: That man is Gottfried

662. *Gottfried Semper, Town Hall, Winterthur, staircase, 1863–69.*

663, 664. *Gottfried Semper, Eidgenössische Technische Hochschule, Zurich, north facade and* aula magna, *1858–64.*

Semper, a pupil of Gärtner, an architect of a distinctly lackluster kind.

Semper, like Viollet-le-Duc, was ultimately concerned with the problem of style. His preoccupation with this question antedated even Viollet-le-Duc's. His first attempt to explain it was in *Die vier Elemente der Baukunst*, published in Brunswick late in 1851, but based on lectures he had prepared in London, where he was established from 1851 to 1855. While in London, he was in close contact with Owen Jones and Henry Cole, for whom he acted as an investigator of Meyer's enameling process at Sèvres and Minton's tileworks at Trent. Semper was also responsible for the arrangement of some of the exhibits at the Crystal Palace. He could not, however, approve of this building since he believed that iron, when thus logically used, was unable to produce monumental form. One of his pupils, whom we know only by his initials, L. H., writing in 1900 in *La construction moderne*, summed up his beliefs: "Il y a deux catégories de constructions: 1ᵉ celles dont chaque élément est en lui-même stable (comme le temple de Paestum). C'est ce qui caractérise la construction monumentale; 2ᵉ celles dont les éléments ne doivent leur stabilité qu'à leur assemblage; c'est ce qui caractérise la construction des meubles, des chaises, par example. Entre ces deux extrêmes il y a toute une série de degrés qui donnent des structures plus ou moins monumentales suivant qu'elles se rapprochent de l'un des systèmes ou de l'autre. La cathédrale gothique serait donc moins monumental que le temple de Paestum, et le Palais de cristal ne serait pas du tout monumental" (p. 525). But it was there, at the Crystal Palace, overwhelmed by the sheer number and variety of artifacts, that he determined to evolve some system whereby the meaning of all such creative endeavor might be grasped and explained. He had earlier marveled in Paris at the ordering devices adopted at the Jardin des Plantes by that great biologist Georges Cuvier, who had first put forward a classificatory system based not on the resemblance of creatures and their parts but rather on the functioning of their organs and other vital processes. The key to the theory that Semper was to propose for the works of man was a small exhibit at the Crystal Palace, a model of a Carib hut, from the village of Arima, near Port of Spain, Trinidad. This was the work of Manuel Sorzano and was filled with utensils and other objects, mostly of Spanish or modern West Indian origin. It was not a primitive hut, but it made manifest the four processes that Semper was to uphold as the prime generators of everything made by man. He made no differentiation between the arts and the crafts. His developed theory is contained in *Der Stil*, published in Munich in two volumes, in 1860 and 1863. The third volume, which was to treat of architecture, was never completed. But this scarcely matters. The tenor of the theory is clear. Semper conceived four essential processes of making: weaving, molding, building in timber, and building in stone, sometimes reduced to heaping (to which he reluctantly appended metalworking). Each of these involved particular materials: textiles, ceramics, wood, and stone. Each in turn resulted in a particular element of architecture: the enclosing wall and all decorative pattern; the base and the hearth; the system of support; and the masonry wall, which might eventually serve to replace any of the former. Everything in art and architecture and all the crafts he held to be reducible to these processes and the materials associated with them. The highest form of expression was architecture, as it contains them all. But it was not, as must already be evident, the first of the arts to emerge; indeed, it derived from the four crafts, and thus suggests that Semper upheld a theory of the practical and useful origin of all art and architecture. His "materialist" stance has often been derided. But this is to misinterpret him willfully, for he believed that the crafts were originally developed for symbolical purposes. Long before man made a house, before he molded a hearth or a pot, he had started to weave and to plait, to make a wreath. The wreath is offered at the beginning of *Der Stil* as the first of the fully fashioned, expressive products of man.

According to Semper's theory, most patterns spring from the art (or the craft, if we prefer to call it that) of weaving. Patterns thus precede the development of structural form, so that ornament may be seen as more basic than structure. The developed theory also includes the way in which religious, social, and political institutions condition the processes of making to give fit and poetic expression to forms. But Semper himself was never to succeed in giving adequate shape to his ideas—not even to the extent that Viollet-le-Duc did. He built hugely—in Dresden, where he put up two successive opera houses (begun in 1837 and 1871); in Zurich, where he became professor in 1855 at the Eidgenössiche Technische Hochschule and began to build the new school in 1859; and in Vienna, where he started construction on the Kunst und Naturhistorisches Museums and Hofburgtheater in 1872. There was a lot more besides, but his architecture is all undistinguished. In the prolegomena to *Der Stil* he was able to hold up no more challenging a style for future development than that of the cinquecento, it "not being complete in itself." "Die Gefahr für die Erhaltung jener Baukunst der Wiedergeburt die, zugleich mit der Malerei und der Bildnerei des Cinquecento, und in gleichem Grade, unübertroffen dasteht, ohne, wie das Gothische, in sich fertig zu sein, keine Seite zu weiterer Entwicklung zu bieten, liegt in der Thatsache, dass sie nur durch wahrhaft künstlerische Hand ausführbar ist, aber durch Pfuscherei, die heutzutage verlangt wird, sofort in trivialste Formengemeinheit ausartet" (vol. 1, p. xvii). Semper despised Gothic, in particular after 1844 when he was overtaken by Sir George Gilbert Scott in the Nikolaikirche competition at Hamburg. The ideas of the three great European theorists—Ruskin, Viollet-le-Duc, and Semper—were not readily absorbed. They were not to be taken up outside their own countries until late in the century. Semper's stay in England from 1851 to 1855 no doubt ensured an early interest in his work, in particular in the orbit of the South Kensington Schools of Design, but none of his works was translated. His ideas on the design of urns or vases were adopted in 1862 by Christopher Dresser (1834–1904) for *The Art of Decorative Design*, and later, without acknowledgment, for *Principles of Decorative Design* (1873). Yet as late as 1884, when Lawrence Harvey read "Semper's Theory of Evolution in Architectural Ornament" to the Royal Institute of British Architects, he began with the words, "Perhaps many of my British colleagues have never heard of Semper" (*Transactions*, 1885, vol. 1, p. 29).

One might think that Semper's earlier sojourns in France, in 1826 and 1827, in 1829 and 1830, and from 1849 to 1851, also ensured a heightened interest in his works when they appeared, but there is no hint of any. Viollet-le-Duc owned a copy of *Der Stil*, but was not equipped to read it. His analysis of urns or water vessels in the sixth *Entretien*, which might be taken as a rebuke to or even as a parody of Semper's, was written in 1859, before the publication of Semper's book. Semper, however, had read the four *Entretiens* issued in 1858, for he was quick to reject Viollet-le-Duc's notions on the design of Doric columns; he mocked him in *Der Stil* as a materialist.

Ruskin, so widely read in England, was but slowly acknowledged in France. Mérimée intended to write an article on him as early as 1856, a few years after Mérimée's return from England with Viollet-le-Duc, but nothing came of it. Viollet-le-Duc made no mention of Ruskin. The first article to appear in France on Ruskin, signed "J. C," in the *Revue britannique* of 1856, was hostile. The first important studies were J.-A. Milsand's two articles in the *Revue des deux mondes* of July 1860 and August 1861, issued together as a book in 1864. But it was not for his architectural criticism that Ruskin was admired. Robert de La Sizeranne's celebrated *Ruskin et la religion de la beauté* produced the same reaction in France in 1897 that had been provoked exactly twenty years before in England, when Walter Pater's blasphemous essay "The School of Giorgione" was published in the *Fortnightly Review*. "Art, then," Pater wrote (and he thought this of architecture too), "is . . . always striving to be independent of the mere intelligence, to become a matter of pure perception, to get rid of its responsibilities to its subject or material" (p. 530). Ruskin's message was seen in France in this light; the moral and intellectual elements in art that he so staunchly upheld were largely overlooked—though it is fair to note that Charles Lucas, writing his obituary in *La construction moderne*, in January 1900, described Ruskin as a moralist. Marcel Proust became his greatest admirer; to him Ruskin and Pater represented all that Viollet-le-Duc was not. By 1904 Proust had published his translation of *The Bible of Amiens*. Four years earlier *The Seven Lamps of Architecture* had appeared in French. By then Ruskin had died, like Pugin, mad.

Ruskin himself, surprisingly, looked upon the works of Viollet-le-Duc with a measured respect. He saw to it that the great *Dictionnaire raisonné de l'architecture française* was purchased for his students at Oxford, though he mentioned it only with passing scorn in his lectures of 1873; but he returned to the subject eleven years later as Slade Professor:

> And here I must advise you that in all points of history relating to the period between 800 and 1200, you will find M. Viollet-le-Duc, incidentally throughout his *Dictionary of Architecture*, the best-informed, most intelligent, and most thoughtful of guides. His knowledge of architecture, carried down into the most minutely practical details—(which are often the most significant,) and embracing, over the entire surface of France, the buildings even of the most secluded villages; his artistic enthusiasm, balanced by the acutest sagacity, and his patriotism, by the frankest candour, render his analysis of history during that active and constructive period the most valuable known to me, and certainly, in its field, exhaustive. Of the latter nationality his account is imperfect, owing to his professional interest in the mere *science* of architecture, and comparative insensibility to the power of sculpture (*Works*, vol. 33, p. 465).

This passage, long, eloquent, and rambling, is typical of the late Ruskin, but its general tone is unexpected in its sympathy. For, though fully conscious of what he regarded as Viollet-le-Duc's failings in sensibility, and horrified by them, Ruskin was yet willing to recognize the achievement represented by the *Dictionnaire raisonné de l'architecture française*: "Were you not glad when that book came out?" Sir Sidney Cockerell asked him in 1888. "No, I was very jealous," he replied, "I ought to have written it myself." Certainly he read it again and again, and recommended it often. He was fascinated by it, and also by Viollet-le-Duc. On October 18, 1882, he recorded this poignant note in his diary: "Disturbed sleep, dreaming I had introduced myself to M. Viol[let]-le-Duc and that he wouldn't have anything to say to me."

But perhaps more revealing of Ruskin's relation to Viollet-le-Duc is his response to another of his books, *Le massif du Mont Blanc*, of 1876. Almost exact contemporaries, strongly opposed in sentiment and outlook, Ruskin and Viollet-le-Duc yet shared interests to an uncanny degree. Both were passionate geologists, both traveled on all possible occasions to view the Swiss Alps. After the disappointments of 1863, when he was hounded out of the École des Beaux-Arts by the students he had thought to indoctrinate, Viollet-le-Duc first sought solitude, strength, and reassurance in the healing springs of alpine scenery. Thereafter he went back each year, for eight weeks in the summer. In 1872 he built himself a chalet at Chamonix, two years later a house at Lausanne, La Vedette (demolished in 1976), where he died and was buried. Viollet-le-Duc was not a climber, but his relentless urge to activity drove him up the mountains. He started to survey Mont Blanc, often climbing steadily for eight hours to reach a vantage point, only to find the mountains obscured by clouds. Undeterred, he would return the next day to take his readings. He was tireless in his task. By 1876 he was able to issue both a most detailed map of Mont Blanc and a study of that mountain. Cutting the leaves of that book in this same year, as he set out on his journey to Switzerland, Ruskin contemplated, he wrote, "the splendid dash of its first sentence into space—'La croûte terrestre, refroidie au moment du plissement qui a formé le massif du Mont Blanc,'—with something of the amazement, and some manner of the praise, which our French allies are reported to have rendered to our charge at Balaclava: 'c'est magnifique: mais ce n'est pas—la géologie.'" From the Simplon inn, he wrote on September 2 to Dr. John Brown, "At last my enemy *has* written a book." There were more fallacies on physical laws, he noted, than one could count.

When Ruskin wrote of the Alps he remarked on the masses and forms, the patterns and textures and hues of the rocks, digressed on their formation, and read therein lessons of nature. He derived lessons also on human fortitude and dignity when he observed the manner in which people had adapted their ways of living and building to that world of violent contrasts. This was a note he had struck first, in his earliest writings, "The Poetry of Architecture." Viollet-le-Duc made no acknowledgment of the people; he liked best the high, desolate regions of rock and everlasting ice. And, though his work might have seemed and been intended to seem a straightforward technical account of the formation of Mont Blanc, there was another, not darker but certainly more wayward, purpose. His last chapters reveal his aim. He wished to present to the mind's eye the spectacle of the mountain as it once existed, hard and neat and new. What Viollet-le-Duc offers is nothing less than a gigantic restoration study. There is no more than a sketch of his proposal in the book, but on the wall of his studio in Paris he hung a large, carefully colored vision of the mountain as it might be: "Fin de l'époque glacière: étude de restitution." He left this on his death to his mistress, Mme. Sureda. Restoration, of course, was anathema to Ruskin.

Le massif de Mont Blanc was among the first of Viollet-le-Duc's books to be translated and issued in England in its entirety. Charles Wethered translated an extract from the *Dictionnaire raisonné de l'architecture française—On Restoration*—in 1875. During the same period Benjamin Bucknall (1833–1895), who was to translate both *Le massif de Mont Blanc* in 1877 and the *Entretiens* (as *Lectures on Architecture*), in 1877 and 1881, issued three English versions of the popular studies that Viollet-le-Duc had contrived for the young, *How to Build a House, Annals of a Fortress*, and *The Habitations of Man in All Ages* (Viollet-le-Duc fondly envisaged these as equivalents of Jules Verne's stories). But Viollet-le-Duc had long since won fame in England: As early as 1855 Matthew Digby Wyatt had written to ask permission to translate the *Dictionnaire raisonné de l'architecture française* and had worked seriously at the task until he became convinced that no English publisher would support the scheme. Five years later another prospective translator appeared in Martin Macdermott, and once again nothing resulted. But Viollet-le-Duc's achievements were sufficiently esteemed by 1864 for the Royal Institute of British Architects to award him their Gold Medal (on the advice of Daly). He did not travel to England to receive this honor. Even before then a succession of admirers from Sir George Gilbert Scott to William Burges and Alfred Waterhouse had plundered the pages of both *Dictionnaires* in search of gables, finials, crockets, and gargoyles, and all manner of medieval details. When Scott came to design the main stair of St. Pancras Station Hotel, it was clear that he had learned to respond—and swiftly—to the designs in the twelfth *Entretien*. Waterhouse used exposed iron girders and struts in the ways suggested by Viollet-le-Duc in many of his later works. Slowly Viollet-le-Duc won renown as a prophet of an independent architecture, based, indeed, on the principles abstracted from a study of the buildings of the Middle Ages, but owing nothing to them in appearance.

In America, as might be imagined, the reception of the three great theorists was not dissimilar from their reception in Europe. Ruskin's works were read and absorbed almost as soon as they were published in England, following, as early as 1839, Loudon's praise of "The Poetry of Architecture," reprinted in the *Journal of the Franklin Institute*. American editions of volumes one and two of *Modern Painters* were published in 1847 and 1848; the following year *The Seven Lamps of Architecture* appeared; and in 1851 the first volume of *The Stones of Venice* was issued—without plates. Critics found Ruskin both admirable and absurd, inspiring and confusing. He was accused of cant and inconsistency, but to judge from the many editions of his works that were printed, he was steadfastly read. Henry van Brunt (1832–1903), a young architect trained at Harvard University, no doubt reflected informed opinion when, in his paper "Cast Iron in Decorative Architecture," read to the Institute of Architects in December 1858, he judged Ruskin to be altogether sound in his observations on the art of the Middle Ages, but of little relevance to architects in the nineteenth century. These, van Brunt claimed, operated in an age of machines, not of handicrafts. "Labor," he concluded, "now is the means and not the end of life." Van Brunt had also read Owen Jones and, probably, Viollet-le-Duc, whose *Entretiens* he was to translate two years before Bucknall as *Discourses on Architecture*, in 1875, the second volume appearing in 1885. This was not the first of Viollet-le-Duc's works to be printed in America. *Histoire d'une maison*, translated by G. M. Towle, had already appeared as *The Story of a House* in 1874. These were followed, in 1876, by Bucknall's translation of *Histoire de l'habitation humaine* (*The Habitations of Man in All Ages*) and, in 1881, by *Learning To Draw*, a translation of *L'histoire d'un dessinateur; comment on apprend à dessiner*, by Virginia Champlin (a pseudonym). The American equivalent of Scott's interpretation of the drawings in the *Entretiens* was the stupendous covered court of The Rookery, La Salle Street, Chicago, designed in 1885 by John Wellborn Root (1850–1891), of the firm of Burnham and Root. Root was also the man who first published translations from Semper's *Der Stil* in America—in the *Inland Architect and New Record*, in 1889–90—though Semper's works were certainly read in Chicago long before that. Indeed, it has even been suggested that the term "curtain walling," which is so strongly associated with the late nineteenth-century architecture of Chicago, commemorates Semper. In 1891, Bernard Maybeck (1862–1957), far away from Chicago, in California, started to translate *Der Stil*, but did not get very far.

After the turn of the century, Frank Lloyd Wright redecorated the covered court at The Rookery with surprisingly little tact—surprisingly, because of the many members of the Chicago School who responded to the writings of Viollet-le-Duc, Wright absorbed them to the most splendid and rewarding effect, regarding them always as the spur to his greatness. He even made his son read the *Dictionnaires*. Other architects, very different in their ways, gave to their interpretations of these teachings a wholeness of vision never achieved in Viollet-le-Duc's lifetime. One thinks of Antonio Gaudí in Spain, of Victor Horta in Belgium, of Hendrikus Petrus Berlage in Holland—all of whom based their thinking on his—and also, perhaps, of the whole school of Russian Constructivists.

BIOGRAPHIES

General sources of reference used in compiling the biographies include the following: Architectural Publication Society, *The Dictionary of Architecture,* London, 1848–92. J. Balteau, M. Barraux, and M. Provost, eds., *Dictionnaire de biographie française,* Paris, 1933–. C. Bauchal, *Nouveau dictionnaire biographique et critique des architectes français,* Paris, 1887. E. Bellier de la Chavignerie and L. Auvray, *Dictionnaire général des artistes de l'école français,* Paris, 1868, 1886. H. M. Colvin, *A Biographical Dictionary of English Architects, 1660–1840,* London, 1954; rev. ed., 1978. P. Portoghesi, *Dizionario enciclopedico di architetture e urbanistica,* Rome, 1968–69. L. Stephen and S. Lee, eds., *Dictionary of National Biography,* London, 1885–1909. U. Thieme and F. Becker, eds., *Allgemeines Lexikon der bildenden Künstler,* Leipzig, 1907–47.

ABADIE, Paul (Angoulême, 1812–Châtou, 1884)

Son of an architect of the same name active in Angoulême, he was a pupil in Paris of A.-F.-R. Leclère. He turned early to the Gothic style, beginning work under J.-B.-A. Lassus and E.-E. Viollet-le-Duc on the restoration of Notre-Dame in Paris and then joining the Service des Édifices Diocésains. Most of his work was done in this capacity, in the southwest of France, but the building for which he is most famous, the Sacré-Coeur, is in Paris. This commission was won in competition in 1872.

Principal executed works, excluding restorations:
Notre-Dame, Bergerac, 1855–56.
Hôtel de Ville, Angoulême, 1858–65.
Hôtel de Ville, Jarnac.
St.-Ferdinand, Rue de la Croix de Seguey, Bordeaux, ?–1869.
Ste.-Marie, Avenue Thiers (Bastide quarter), Bordeaux, 1864–86.
St.-Bernard, Mussidan (Dordogne).
St.-Barthélemy, Faux (near Florac).
Sacré-Coeur, Montmartre, Paris, 1874–1919. The work was taken over on Abadie's death by P.-G.-H. Daumet, then by C.-J. Laisné and H.-P.-M. Rauline, in 1891 by Rauline alone, and in 1904 by Lucien Magne, who designed the tower.

ADAM, Robert (Kirkcaldy, Fife, 1728–London, 1792)

He was one of the four sons of the Scottish architect of country houses William Adam (1689–1748). In 1754 he became a friend of C.-L. Clérisseau in Paris, and, shortly after, of Giambattista Piranesi in Rome. In 1757 he and Clérisseau traveled to Split (Spalato), in Dalmatia, to explore and measure the ruins of Diocletian's palace. The results of their rapid research were published as *Ruins of the Palace of the Emperor Diocletian at Spalatro* (1764). On his return to England, Adam embarked on a brilliant career in which he was to transform the Palladianism established by the third earl of Burlington into a new, instantly recognizable classical style inspired by the visions of Piranesi and based on antique and Renaissance sources. He further popularized this style in the books he published with his brother, *The Works in Architecture of Robert and James Adam, Esquires* (1773, 1779, 1822).

Principal executed works:
Harewood House, Yorkshire, alterations, 1759–71.
Admiralty, Whitehall, London, screen-wall, 1759.
Kedleston Hall, Derbyshire, 1760–70.
Osterley Park, Middlesex, remodeling, 1761–80.
Lansdowne House, Berkeley Square, London, 1762–68. Demolished 1936.
Syon House, Middlesex, 1762–69.
Nostell Priory, Yorkshire, remodeling, 1765–75, 1776–85.
Kenwood House, Hampstead, London, remodeling, 1767–69.
Newby Hall, Yorkshire, additions, 1767–85.
Adelphi Buildings, Strand, London, 1768–72. Demolished 1936.
No. 20 St. James's Square, London, 1771–74.

Derby House, No. 23 Grosvenor Square, London, 1773–74. Demolished 1862.
Home House, Portman Square, London, 1773–76.
Register House, Edinburgh, 1774–92.
Culzean Castle, Ayrshire, 1777–90.
University, Edinburgh, 1789–93.
Charlotte Square, Edinburgh, 1791.

Literature: A. T. Bolton, *The Architecture of Robert and James Adam,* 2 vols., London, 1922. A. T. Bolton, "The Classical and Romantic Compositions of Robert Adam," *Architectural Review* (London) 57 (Jan.–May 1925). J. Lees-Milne, *The Age of Adam,* London, 1947. D. Stillman, *The Decorative Work of Robert Adam,* 1966. M. Whinney, *Home House,* 1969. All of Adam's major country houses are the subject of articles in *Country Life* magazine.

ALAVOINE, Jean-Antoine (Paris, 1778–Paris, 1834)

He studied architecture under C.-E. Dumas and J.-T. Thibault but traveled to Italy on military service before returning to complete his studies at the École des Beaux-Arts, Paris. He then went to Spain, returning in 1807 to Paris, where he worked first for Jacques Cellerier at the Théâtre des Variétés, then on the Fontaine de l'Éléphant at the Place de la Bastille. He replaced Cellerier as director of the latter project in 1812, laying the foundations and putting up the plaster model of the elephant. Between 1815 and 1823 he restored the church of St.-Denis outside Paris, then in 1823 began work at Rouen cathedral, for which he built an amazing filigree Gothic spire of cast iron that was to be completed against much opposition only in 1884. This was his one noteworthy achievement. In 1830 he returned to the Place de la Bastille to erect a commemorative column rather than the projected elephant; work on this July Column was taken over in 1834 by L.-J. Duc.

Literature: P. Chirol, *Jean-Antoine Alavoine,* Rouen, 1920. J.-P. Desportes, "Alavoine et la flèche de la cathédrale de Rouen," *Revue de l'art,* no. 13, 1971, pp. 48–62.

ALBERTOLLI, Giocondo (Bedano, 1742–Milan, 1839)

For ten years he studied sculpture and architecture at the Academy in Parma, but his career was to be that of a decorator. In 1770 he was in Florence, working under G. M. Paoletti on the decorations of the Villa del Poggio Imperiale at nearby Caiano; soon after, Paoletti took him to work on the Sala della Niobe in the Uffizi and the apartments of the Meridiana at the Palazzo Pitti. By 1772 he was in Rome and then in Naples, working for Luigi Vanvitelli, but he was back home in Bedano by 1774, for Giuseppe Piermarini found him there and took him to work on the Palazzo Ducale in Milan. There he worked brilliantly for two years, before beginning the decorations of the Villa Ducale at Monza. He worked subsequently in many other palaces in Milan—Belgioioso, Arconato, Greppi, Casnedi, Melzi, etc.—setting a style modeled on that of J.-L. Prieur for the whole of Lombardy. From 1776 to 1812 he directed

the school of decorative design at the Accademia di Brera, publishing several works to establish his models: *Ornamenti diversi inventati* (1782); *Alcune decorazioni di nobili sale ed altri ornamenti* (1787); and *Miscellanea per i giovani studiosi del disegno* (1796). He designed only one building of importance, the Villa Melzi at Bellagio, overlooking Lake Como (1808–15). This is large and bland. His own house at Lugano (now the Banco Nazionale) is of more interest.

Literature: A. Kauffmann, *Giocondo Albertolli, Ornamentiker des italienischen Klassizismus,* Strasbourg, 1911. G. Mezzanotte, *Architettura neoclassica in Lombardia,* Naples, 1966.

ALPHAND, Jean-Charles-Adolphe (Grenoble, 1817–Paris, 1891)

His schooling was completed in Paris at the Lycée Charlemagne. In 1835 he entered the École Polytechnique and the year after the École des Ponts et Chaussées, where he spent two years. In 1838 he took up an engineering post at Bordeaux, where he established himself and was noticed by the local *préfet,* G.-E. Haussmann. When Haussmann was appointed *Préfet de la Seine,* he took Alphand with him to Paris and charged him with the layout and development of the Bois de Boulogne. By 1857, however, he had risen to become *Ingénieur en Chef* to the Service des Promenades et Embellissements de Paris. By 1861 he had become *Directeur Administratif des Promenades* and six years later was named *Directeur de la Voie Publique et des Promenades.* In all his activities he was closely allied to Haussmann, as one might expect, for his projects were extensive and wide-ranging. He was responsible for the planting of trees and flowers throughout Paris; he laid out most of the new squares and all the major parks. Later he was also to take on the task of laying out the new roadways and sewers and during the Commune assumed the additional task of making ammunition. He refused to accept the post of *Préfet* after the downfall of Haussmann but was nonetheless made *Directeur des Travaux de Paris* in 1871. From 1869 on he was also *Inspecteur Général des Ponts et Chaussées.* He wrote numerous official reports; the most notable records of his achievements, however, are contained in the *Atlas des travaux de Paris* and in his *Promenades de Paris,* 1867–73.

Literature: P. Strauss, "M. Alphand et les travaux de Paris," *Revue bleue* 48 (1891), pp. 761–65. Ville de Paris, *Discours prononcé à l'occasion des funérailles de J. C. A. Alphand,* Paris, 1892. G. Lafenestre, *Notice sur la vie et les oeuvres de M. Alphand,* Paris, 1899. A. de Cilleuls, *L'administration parisienne sous la IIIᵉ République,* Paris, 1910, pp. 34–40, 148–58, 317–18, 344–45, 352.

AMATI, Carlo (Monza, 1776–Milan, 1852)

He studied first in Monza, then in Milan, probably under G. P. Parini. In 1796 he became an assistant to Leopoldo Pollack, later he worked for Giocondo Albertolli, and finally was engaged by Giuseppe Zanoia.

In 1817 he succeeded Zanoia as professor of architecture at the Accademia di Brera; four years later he was appointed to the Commissione d'Ornato. He was a dull, uneven designer, with little technical skill, and one may be thankful that he put up only one building of prominence, S. Carlo al Corso in Milan. He also saw to it that C. F. Soave's design for the Milan cathedral was more or less completed by 1813.

Principal executed works:
Villa Sormani, Coronate, 1802.
Villa Durini, Monza, c. 1815.
S. Carlo al Corso, Milan, first project 1832, built 1839–47.

Literature: G. Mezzanotte, *Architettura neoclassica in Lombardia,* Naples, 1966.

ANGELL, Samuel (1800–1866)

He was an attractive but minor architect whose work reflects the shift of emphasis during his career from Greek archaeology to Renaissance practice. With William Harris he made important discoveries of Greek sculpture at Selinunte in 1823. These were eagerly inspected by J.-I. Hittorff for traces of color shortly before they were dispatched from Palermo to London. Harris died of malaria at Palermo, and Angell published the results of their work, with Thomas Evans, as *Sculptured Metopes . . . of the Temples of the Ancient City of Selinus in Sicily, Discovered by William Harris and S–A–* (1826). Angell's principal building, Clothworkers' Hall, London (1856; destroyed 1940), is not Greek but Italian Renaissance in style.

ANTOINE, Jacques-Denis (Paris, 1733–Paris, 1801)

He was the son of a cabinetmaker, Jean-Baptiste Antoine, and appears to have had no formal architectural training. He began as a builder. But in the competition of 1762 for the design of the Hôtel des Monnaies in Paris, his project was chosen above those of E.-L. Boullée and P.-L. Moreau-Desproux. This was to be his greatest work: a noble and dignified building overlooking the Seine, with a series of grand interiors that are infinitely to be preferred to the rather dull exterior. He soon established himself as a sound and trustworthy architect. He became a member of the Académie Royale d'Architecture in 1776 and in 1789 was charged with the completion of C.-N. Ledoux's tollgates around Paris, much embittering Ledoux.

Principal executed works:
Hôtel des Monnaies, Quai de Conti, Paris, 1767–75. (M. Mosser, *L'information d'histoire de l'art,* no. 2, 1971, pp. 94–101.)
Hôtel Brochet de Saint-Prest, 28 Rue des Sts.-Pères, Paris, 1768–73. Now part of the École des Ponts et Chaussées.
Château de Mussy-l'Évêque (near Langres), before 1777.
Château de Herces, Brechères-sur-Vesgre (near Houdan).
Palacio Alba y Berwick, Madrid, grand staircase, 1778.

The house was begun by Guilbert.
Château de Buisson (Eure), 1782.
Hôtel de Jaucourt, 45 Rue de Varennes, Paris.
Hôtel de Mirabeau, Rue de Sèvres, Paris.
Palais de Justice, Paris, staircase, writing hall, and record office, 1782–85.
Hôtel de Ville, Cambrai, facade, in association with N.-H. Jardin, completed by 1786.
Église des Filles-Sainte-Marie, Nancy. Now a boys' school.

Literature: M. Gallet, *Paris Domestic Architecture of the 18th Century,* London, 1972.

ANTOLINI, Giovanni Antonio (Castelbolognese, 1753–Bologna, 1841)

He was an important figure in the movement for architectural reform in north Italy in the years around 1800 and gave freely of his advice to several patrons and other architects, but he built very little indeed, winning his reputation largely on the basis of the grandiose designs he prepared in 1800 and 1801 for the Foro Buonaparte in Milan, published in the following year as *Disegni del foro Buonaparte in 24 gran tavole.* He studied first in Imola with the engineer Francesco Baruzzi, then moved to Bologna, where he studied architecture at the university. By 1775 he was in Rome, where he stayed for about twenty years in the employ of Cosimo Morelli. In the late 1780s he was active in Umbria. By 1797 he was in Faenza, in competition with Giuseppe Pistocchi, three years later in Milan, once again in competition with Pistocchi, but in 1804 he was made professor of architecture at the Accademia di Belle Arti at Bologna, from where he plagued F. G. P. Pocciantti in Livorno and G. M. Soli in Venice, the latter having taken over his design for the Ala Napoleonica on the Piazza S. Marco.

Literature: G. Mezzanotte, *Architettura neoclassica in Lombardia,* Naples, 1966. A. Emiliani et al., *L'età neoclassica a Faenza 1780–1820,* exhib. cat., Faenza, 1979.

BAILLY, Antoine-Nicolas-Louis (Paris, 1810–Paris, 1892)

A pupil of François Debret and then, in 1829, of F.-J. Duban, he was later draftsman to P.-M. Letarouilly. He was chosen by Baron Haussmann to design the Tribunal de Commerce in Paris, built between 1858 and 1864, a muddle of Renaissance forms and motifs modeled, at the emperor's request, on the town hall at Brescia. Bailly's other notable building of the period, the Mairie du IVe, of 1862–67, is more prosaic but no less pompous. He was also responsible for the Lycée St.-Louis, on the Place Sorbonne, Paris.

Principal executed works:
Hôtel Schneider, Paris.
Hôtel Montmorency-Luxembourg, Paris.
Hôtel Ganay, Paris.
Château Lagoutte, Choisy-le-Roi.
Château de Theuville (Seine-Maritime).
Château de Cany (Seine-Maritime).

Crédit Foncier, Paris.
Tribunal de Commerce, Paris, 1858–64.
Lycée St.-Louis, Paris, extension, 1860–65.
Mairie du IVe, Paris, 1862–67.

Literature: A. Ancelet, *Notice sur M. A. N. Bailly,* 1892. H. Delaborde, P. Dubois, Bonnat, *Funérailles de M. Bailly,* 1892.

BALLU, Théodore (Paris, 1817–Paris, 1885)

A pupil of L.-H. Lebas at the École des Beaux-Arts, Paris, beginning in 1835, he won the Grand Prix in 1840 and traveled to Rome and then to Greece. Five years after his return to Paris, in 1850, he was appointed *Inspecteur* at Ste.-Clotilde, which he was to take over on F. C. Gau's death, in 1854, completing the spires to a modified design of his own in 1857. The following year he began another Gothic pastiche, the tower next to St.-Germain-l'Auxerrois, completed in 1863. In 1860 he was appointed architect to the fourth section of the Travaux de la Ville de Paris, the one concerned with church building, and in this capacity built a number of equally unlovely but even more richly decorated buildings in a Renaissance mode. In 1871 he was appointed *Inspecteur Général des Travaux de la Ville de Paris,* a position he held until 1876. He won the competition in 1873 for the restoration of the Hôtel de Ville in Paris, which had been destroyed by the Commune.

Principal executed works:
Tour St.-Jacques, Paris, restoration, 1856.
St.-Germain-l'Auxerrois, Paris, tower, 1858–63.
La Trinité, Square de la Trinité, Paris, 1861–67. (T. Ballu, *Monographie de l'église de la Ste. Trinité,* 1868.)
Temple du St.-Esprit, Rue d'Astorg and Rue Roquépine, Paris, 1862–65. Now replaced.
St.-Ambroise, 71 bis Boulevard Voltaire, Paris, 1863, 1865–69. (T. Ballu, *Monographie de l'église Saint-Ambroise,* 1874.)
St.-Denis, Rue Henri Barbusse, Argenteuil, Paris, 1866.
St.-Joseph, 161 and 163 Rue St.-Maur, Paris, 1867–74.

Literature: P. Sédille, *Théodore Ballu, architecte,* 1886. H. Daumet, *Notice sur M. Th. Ballu,* Paris, 1886. H. Delaborde, *Notice sur la vie et les ouvrages de M. Théodore Ballu,* Paris, 1887.

BALTARD, Louis-Pierre (Paris, 1764–Lyons, 1846)

A pupil of A.-F. Peyre, he worked with Richard Mique and also, it seems, with C.-N. Ledoux on the construction of the Paris tollgates. He spent the years 1788 to 1791 in Rome. In 1796 he was appointed to a teaching post at the École Polytechnique, Paris, and a few years later he became official architect to the department of prisons. In this capacity he built the noblest, if staidest, of his buildings, the Palais de Justice at Lyons, begun in 1835. He is remembered as a staunch upholder of the academic tradition, publishing the *Grands prix d'architecture,* together with A.-L.-T. Vaudoyer, from 1818 to 1834 and teaching at the École des Beaux-Arts, Paris, from 1818 until his death.

Literature: T. de Puylaroque, "Pierre Baltard, peintre et dessinateur (1764–1846)," in *Bulletin de la Société de l'Histoire de l'Art Français*, Année 1976 (1978), pp. 331–39.

BALTARD, Victor (Paris, 1805–Paris, 1874)

Son of Louis-Pierre Baltard, he studied under his father at the École des Beaux-Arts, Paris, winning the Grand Prix in 1833. He replaced E.-H. Godde in 1849 as architect to the city of Paris chiefly responsible for churches. He restored a number of these from 1851 to 1863, painting their interiors brightly and inaccurately. To his own designs he built St.-Augustin, with columns and ribs of exposed ironwork; however, his earlier, more utilitarian use of iron at the Halles Centrales is regarded as more memorable and became more famous. Baltard and his partner, F.-E. Callet, began to construct the market with solid stone pavilions, but, under the influence of Hector Horeau, Baron Haussmann ordered these to be demolished and a new iron structure set up. The building was commemorated in Baltard's and Callet's magnificent *Monographie des Halles Centrales de Paris*, of 1863, with a revised second edition of 1873.

Principal executed works:
Halles Centrales, Paris, 1844 (first sketches), 1853–57, designed in partnership with F.-E. Callet. Demolished 1972–73.
St.-Augustin, Place St.-Augustin, Paris, 1860–71.

Literature: M. Deurbergue, *Victor Baltard: projets inédits pour les Halles Centrales*, Bibliothèque Historique de la Ville de Paris, Paris, 1978 (with a bibliography).

BARABINO, Carlo Francesco (Genoa, 1768–1835)

He studied first in Genoa at the Accademia Lingustica, then from 1788 to 1793 in Rome at the Accademia della Pace under Giuseppe Barberi. Thereafter, he was active chiefly in Genoa as a town planner, in particular after 1818, when he was appointed architect to the Commune by the Corpo Decurionale. Between 1825 and 1828 he opened up the Via Carlo Felice, established the Piazza S. Domenico (now de Ferrari) with the Teatro Carlo Felice and the Palazzo dell' Accademia, and planned a succession of new residential quarters.

Principal executed works:
Palazzo Negrone de Cavi, Piazza Fontane Marose, Genoa, internal redecoration.
Chiesa del Rimedio, Via Giulia, Genoa, altar and decorations, 1796. The church was reconstructed in 1904 in the Piazza Alimonda, with the original altar.
Casa Massucone, Piazza Nuova, Genoa.
Lavatorio, Vai Madre di Dio, Genoa, 1797.
S. Siro, Genoa, facade, 1819–21.
Oratorio del Rosario, Salita S. Francesco di Paola, Genoa, 1824–26.
Teatro Carlo Felice and Palazzo dell'Accademia, Piazza de Ferrari, Genoa, 1825–28. Damaged 1944, largely demolished 1976.
Chiesa dell'Annunziata, Genoa, 1834, 1843–.

Staglieno cemetery, Genoa, 1835, 1844–51, built under the guidance of G. B. Resasco.

Literature: M. Labò, "Un architetto neoclassico: C. Barabino," *Emporium* 54 (Oct. 1921), pp. 207–23. Achille Neri, "Il Barabino e la cultura urbanistica di Genova nell' Ottocento," *Casabella Continuatà*, no. 228, 1959, pp. 40–53. C. Maltese, "Appunti per una storia del neoclassicismo a Genova," in *Neoclassicismo. Londra 1971. Atti del convegno internazionale promesso del Comité International d'Histoire de l'Art*, Genoa, 1973. E. de Negri, *Ottocento rinnovamento urbano. Carlo Barabino*, Genoa, 1977.

BARBIER, François

He was a pupil at the school of the Académie Royale d'Architecture, in Paris, between 1764 and 1765, but his career is otherwise little documented. His chief activity was in the field of garden design, most notably at the Désert de Retz, near Chambourcy, where he seems to have been responsible for the famous house and garden of Racine de Monville, and at the Hôtel de Thélusson, Paris, where he laid out the gardens in accord with C.-N. Ledoux's designs.

Literature: M. Gallet, *Paris Domestic Architecture of the 18th Century*, London, 1972.

BARRY, Sir Charles (London, 1795–London, 1860)

One of the most successful of all nineteenth-century architects, he trained not as an architect but as a surveyor (from 1810 to 1816). He made a *grand tour* to Italy, Greece, Egypt, and Syria in 1817–20 and on his return found that the quickest way of establishing an architectural practice was to design churches in the Gothic style, then popular with the Commissioners for Church Building. His study and love of Italian Renaissance architecture was put to good use in the design of clubs and institutional buildings, beginning with the Travellers' Club in 1829. As an alternative to the Greek Revival his rich Italianate style proved popular, particularly with the aristocracy, who commissioned him to transform their Georgian country houses into sumptuous *palazzi*. In 1836 he won the biggest British architectural prize of the nineteenth century, the commission to design the new Houses of Parliament. His superbly planned structure, with its rich Perpendicular Gothic detail and its unforgettable silhouette, is one of the great buildings of the world.

Principal executed works:
St. Peter, Brighton, Sussex, 1823–28.
Royal Institution of Fine Arts (now City Art Gallery), Manchester, 1823–35.
Travellers' Club, Pall Mall, London, 1829–31. (*Country Life* 140 [1966], p. 1270; *Journal of the Royal Institute of British Architects* 59 [1952], p. 417; London County Council, *Survey of London* 29–30 [1960].)
King Edward VI's Grammar School, Birmingham, 1833–37. Demolished 1936.
Trentham Hall, Staffordshire, rebuilding, 1833–42.

Demolished 1910. (*Country Life*, Jan. 25–Feb. 8, 1968.)
Kingston Lacy, Dorsetshire, remodeling, 1835–39.
Highclere House, Hampshire, 1837–c. 1850. (*Country Life* 126, p. 18.)
Reform Club, Pall Mall, London, 1837–41. (*Country Life* 108 [1950], p. 1498; J. M. Crook, *The Reform Club*, 1973; London County Council, *Survey of London* 29–30 [1960].)
Trafalgar Square, London, layout and fountains, 1840.
Palace of Westminster and Houses of Parliament, London, 1836–. (M. H. Port., ed., *The Houses of Parliament*, New Haven, Conn., 1976.)
Harewood House, Yorkshire, alterations, 1843–50. (*Country Life*, Oct. 5, 1901, July 4, 1914, Feb. 25, 1922; M. Mauchline, *Harewood House*, 1974.)
Bridgewater House, Green Park, London, 1846–51. (London County Council, *Survey of London* 29–30 [1960]; *Country Life*, May 13, 1949.)
Shrubland Park, Suffolk, alterations and additions, 1849–54. (*Country Life* 114, pp. 1654, 1734.)
Cliveden House, Buckinghamshire, rebuilding, 1850–51. (*Country Life* 32, pp. 808, 854.)
Clumber House, Nottinghamshire, alterations, 1857. Demolished 1938. (*Country Life*, Sept. 12–19, 1908.)
Halifax Town Hall, Yorkshire, 1859–62, with his son, E. M. Barry.

Literature: W. H. Leeds, *The Travellers' Club House . . . and the Revival of the Italian Style, by Charles Barry*, London, 1839. A. Barry, *The Life and Works of Sir C. Barry*, London, 1867. M. Binney, "The Making of an Architect," *Country Life* 146 (1969), pp. 494, 550, 622.

BARTHÉLEMY, Jacques-Eugène (Rouen, 1799–Rouen, 1882)

He came from a family of architects in Rouen, where, as architect to the Service des Édifices Diocésains, he was to be responsible for the general repair and restoration of many churches. In 1840 he began construction of one of the most important churches of the Gothic Revival, Notre-Dame-de-Bon-Secours, at Blosseville, on the outskirts of Rouen. This was largely completed by 1847, though the decorative murals and furnishings were added in the following years.

Literature: *Église de Notre-Dame-de-Bon-Secours, près Rouen*, Rouen, 1848. J. Loth and Sauvage, *Notre-Dame de Bon Secours*, Rouen, 1851. M. Simon, "Notice," *Précis des travaux de l'académie de Rouen*, 1881–82, pp. 591–94.

BASEVI, George (London, 1794–Ely, 1845)

He was born into a prosperous Jewish family that had arrived in England from Verona in 1762. Described by the author of his obituary in *The Builder* as "cold and somewhat haughty," he undoubtedly felt that his race made him an outsider in English society (though his first cousin Benjamin Disraeli became prime minister). He was a favorite pupil of Sir John Soane and spent the years 1816–19 in Greece and Italy. Though not an archaeologist, he was deeply impressed by the discovery of traces of color on antique architecture, and in his principal building, the Fitzwilliam Museum, he imparted a new sculptural richness to the Greek Revival.

Principal executed works:
St. Thomas, Stockport, Cheshire, 1822–25.
Gatcombe Park, Gloucestershire, additions and alterations, c. 1822.
Belgrave Square, London, 1826–28.
Painswick House, Gloucestershire, alterations and additions, 1828–30. (*Country Life* 42 [1917], p. 204.)
Beechwood, Highgate, London, 1834. (*Country Life*, Mar. 7, 1952.)
Fitzwilliam Museum, Cambridge, 1834–44. Completed by C. R. Cockerell, 1845–48, and E. M. Barry, 1870–75. (*Country Life* 132 [1962], pp. 1278–81, 1340–43.)
Conservative Club, St. James's Street, London, 1843–45, with S. Smirke. Largely gutted 1951. (London County Council, *Survey of London* 29–30 [1960].)

BAUDOT, Joseph-Eugène-Anatole de (Sarrebourg, 1834–Paris, 1915)

He was a pupil at the École des Beaux-Arts, Paris, where he had enrolled in the studio of P.-F.-H. Labrouste. When this closed down in 1856 he and a number of other students asked E.-E. Viollet-le-Duc to open an *atelier*. This venture did not long survive, but de Baudot worked from that time on for Viollet-le-Duc. He supervised the building of Notre-Dame and in time assumed an important role in the Service des Édifices Diocésains. In 1872 he was made secretary to the committee and within seven years he was *Inspecteur Général*. In the same year he became a member of the Commission des Monuments Historiques and remained one until 1892. De Baudot built little of importance while Viollet-le-Duc was alive but soon after his death, beginning in 1882 with the Lycée Lakanal at Sceaux, showed that he could be a designer of originality and power. Ten years later, in his own house at 1 Rue de Pomereu, Paris, he began his experiments with reinforced concrete and brickwork that culminated in the church of St.-Jean-de-Montmartre. He later prepared a number of projects for houses and exhibition buildings of reinforced concrete that are of the highest interest. Throughout life he wrote articles for architectural journals, in particular the *Gazette des architectes et du bâtiment*, the *Encyclopédie d'architecture*, and the *Journal de serrurerie*, on all of which he served for a time as editor. His most important published works are *L'architecture et le beton armé*, of 1905, and *L'architecture, le passé, le présent*, of 1916. The latter was a result of his teaching at the Trocadéro, where he was appointed *Professeur d'Architecture Française* in 1887.

Principal executed works:
Apartment house, 21 Rue de Leningrad, Paris, 1863.
Apartment house, 34 Rue Saint-Lazare, Paris, 1865–66.
St.-Lubin, Rambouillet, 1865–69.
St.-Justin, Place d'Estienne d'Orves, Levallois-Perret, Paris, 1870, 1882, 1892–1911.
Church, La Roche Millay (Nièvre), 1870.
Church, Privas (Ardèche), designed 1876.

Château, Beaumont, Belgium, partly a restoration.
Maison de Campagne, Lourcieux (Loire), 1881.
Lycée Lakanal, Rue du Lycée Lakanal, Sceaux, 1882–88.
Lycée, Tulle (Corrèze), 1889.
Hôtel de Baudot, 1 Rue de Pomereu, Paris, 1892–93.
Three workers' houses, Rue Gabriel-Peri, Antony, 1893.
Lycée Victor Hugo, 27 Rue de Sévigné, Paris, 1894–96. The earliest structure, the gymnasium in the court at the rear, was demolished in 1960.
St.-Jean-de-Montmartre, 19 Rue des Abbesses, Paris, 1894, 1897–99, 1902–4 (using Paul Cottancin's system).
Théâtre Municipal, Tulle (Corrèze), 1896, 1889–99, with the town architect Auberty.

Principal unexecuted projects:
Pavilions for the Exposition Universelle, Paris, 1878.
Pavilions for the Exposition Universelle, Paris, 1900.
Concours pour la Fondation Rothschild, 1905.
Grande salle des fêtes et d'exposition, 1910.
Salle d'exposition, 1914.

Literature: F. Berce, "Anatole de Baudot," *Les monuments historiques de la France*, no. 3, 1965. F. Boudon, "Recherche sur la pensée et l'oeuvre d'Anatole de Baudot, 1834–1915," *Architecture, mouvement, continuité*, no. 28, Mar. 1973.

BÉLANGER, François-Joseph (Paris, 1744–Paris, 1818)

An active and prolific architect, Bélanger was important in particular for his decorative works, usually executed by Lhuilier, which set the style for the Empire period. He was a pupil of J.-D. Le Roy and Pierre Contant d'Ivry. He did not travel to Rome but rather to England, probably in 1766. In the following year he was appointed *Dessinateur aux Menus-Plaisirs*, three years later *Dessinateur du Comte de Provence*. By 1777 he had been promoted to *Inspecteur des Menus-Plaisirs* and *Premier Architecte du Comte d'Artois*. His commissions came, for the most part, through his intimate relations with the actresses Sophie Arnould and, later, Mlle. Dervieux.

Principal executed works:
Pavillon Lauraguais, garden of the Hôtel de Brancas (Hôtel de Lassay), 1 Rue Taitbout, Paris, 1769.
Pavillon de Bagatelle, Bois de Boulogne, Paris, Sept. 21–Nov. 26, 1777. The Picturesque garden was completed by 1780. (B. Scott, "Bagatelle—Folie of the Comte d'Artois," *Apollo*, June 1972, pp. 478–85.)
Stables for the Comte d'Artois, Rue du Faubourg St.-Honoré and Rue Neuve de Berry, Paris, 1778–88.
Hôtel Bélanger, Rue des Bois, Paris.
Folie Saint-James, 34 Avenue de Madrid, Neuilly-sur-Seine, 1778–84. (E. de Ganay, "Les jardins de Saint James," *Revue de l'art ancien et moderne*, Jan.-June 1922, pp. 392–98; R. Wahl, *La folie Saint-James*, Neuilly-sur-Seine, 1955.)
Château, Méréville, alterations and extensive gardens for the banker J.-J. de Laborde, later taken over by Hubert Robert, 1784–. (E. de Ganay, "L'art des jardins dans les jardins de Jeurre," *Revue de l'art ancien et moderne*, June–Dec. 1926, pp. 310–16; J. de Cayeux, "Hubert Robert dessinateur des jardins

et sa collaboration au parc de Méréville," *Bulletin de la Société de l'Histoire de l'Art Français*, 1968, pp. 127–33; O. Choppin de Janvry, "Méréville," *L'oeil*, Dec. 1969, pp. 30–41, 83, 96; S. de Lassus, "Quelques détails inédits sur Méréville," *Bulletin de la Société de l'Histoire de l'Art Français*, Année 1976 [1978], pp. 273–87.)
Hôtel, 20 Rue Neuve des Capucins, Paris.
Hôtel de Puysegur, Rue de la Chaussée-d'Antin and Rue Neuve des Capucins, Paris.
Hôtel de Mirepoix, Rue de Provence (now Pigalle), Paris, 1788.
Hôtel de Weymerange, Rue des Mathurins and Rue de la Ferme, Paris.
Water pumps at Chaillot (1781) and Le Gros Caillou (1786), Paris.
Halle aux Blés, Paris, dome, designed 1805, built 1808–13. (*L'architecture*, 1933, p. 249; *Art Bulletin* 55 [1973], pp. 262–79.)

Principal unexecuted projects:
Gallery for Lord Shelburne, Lansdowne House, London, 1778.
Opera house on the Place du Carrousel, Paris, 1781.
Hôtel d'Artois and a new residential quarter, "La nouvelle Londres," on the site of the nursery gardens at Roule, Paris, 1783.
Abattoir de Rochechouart, Paris, designed 1808.

Literature: J. Stern, *À l'ombre de Sophie Arnould: François-Joseph Bélanger, architecte des Menus-Plaisirs, premier architecte du Comte d'Artois*, 2 vols., Paris, 1930.

BELLICARD, Jérôme-Charles (Paris, 1726–Paris, 1786)

He was an architect who turned archaeologist and, for a time, engraver. A pupil of Denis Jossenay, he won the Grand Prix in 1747, reaching Rome early in 1749. There he did a design for the Festa della Chinea, worked with Giambattista Piranesi, and met the Marquis de Vandières (de Marigny), C.-N. Cochin, and J.-G. Soufflot, who were responsible for his small future success. He was made a member of the Académie Royale d'Architecture and *Contrôleur* at the châteaux of Compiègne and Fontainebleau, where he remained until 1777. For Cochin he engraved the plates of *Observations sur les antiquités de la ville d'Herculaneum* (1754), for Soufflot those of the first project for Ste.-Geneviève. He built nothing of any significance and died ruined by gambling.

Principal executed work:
Hôtel for the Marquise de Matharel, Rue Notre-Dame-des-Champs, Paris, 1758–59.

Literature: S. Eriksen, *Early Neo-Classicism in France*, London, 1974, pp. 154–55.

BIANCHI, Pietro (Lugano, 1787–Lugano, 1849)

He studied in Milan at the Accademia di Brera, under Luigi Cagnola, by whom he was sent to Naples to take up the building of S. Francesco di Paola in 1817. The church was completed by 1831. Bianchi was a member of the academies of Rome, Vienna, and Brussels.

Literature: A. Venditti, *Architettura neoclassica a Napoli,* Naples, 1961.

BINDESBØLL, Michael Gottlieb Birkner (Ledøje, 1800–Copenhagen, 1856)

He entered the Academy of Fine Arts, Copenhagen, in 1817 and traveled in Germany, Italy, France, Greece, and Turkey. He was appointed Royal Inspector of Buildings for Holstein in 1839, for Jutland in 1850, and for Copenhagen in 1851. He was deeply influenced by the discovery in the 1820s and 1830s by J.-I. Hittorff and others of traces of color on antique architecture. His principal building, the Thorvaldsen Museum in Copenhagen (1837–48), owes much to this discovery.

Literature: H. Bramsen, *Gottlieb Bindesbøll—Liv og Arbejder,* Copenhagen, 1959.

BLONDEL, Jacques-François (Rouen, 1705–Paris, 1774)

He was possibly the nephew of Jean-François Blondel, but little is known of his early life or activities. He arrived in Paris about 1729; on May 6, 1743, he opened a school of architecture in the Rue de la Harpe, which was merged with the school of the Académie Royale d'Architecture when he was appointed professor there in 1762. He taught virtually without a break until his death and was without doubt the most important and most influential teacher of architecture in Europe. Many foreigners attended his classes. His ideas were also disseminated through his publications: *De la distribution des maisons de plaisance,* of 1737–38; *Recueil de l'architecture française,* of 1752–56; *Cours d'architecture,* of 1771–73 (the last two volumes, by Pierre Patte, were published in 1777); and *L'homme du monde éclairé par les arts,* of 1774.

Principal executed works:
Hôtel Petit de Marivat, Place Dauphine, Besançon.
Aubette, Strasbourg.
Place d'Armes, Metz, 1764–65. He also designed the doorway for the cathedral, now much altered. (J. Lejeaux, *La Place d'Armes de Metz,* Strasbourg, 1927.)

Literature: A. Prost, *Jacques-François Blondel et son oeuvre,* Metz, 1860. J. Lejeaux, "Jacques-François Blondel (1705–1774)," *L'architecture,* Jan. 15, 1927, pp. 23–27. J. Lejeaux, "Un architecte français, Jacques-François Blondel," *Revue de l'art ancien et moderne,* 1927, vol. 2, pp. 223–34, 271–85. R. Middleton, "Jacques-François Blondel and the *Cours d'Architecture,*" *Journal of the Society of Architectural Historians* (U.S.A.), Dec. 1959, pp. 140–48. M. Gallet, *Paris Domestic Architecture of the 18th Century,* London, 1972.

BLOUET, Guillaume-Abel (Passy, 1795–Paris, 1853)

His interest in architecture was first awakened by Macquet, a student at the École des Beaux-Arts, Paris, where he enrolled and studied under P.-J.-N. Delespine. He won the Grand Prix in 1821. In Rome he proved himself a model student and was allowed to

stay on longer than usual. He was much influenced in these years by E.-J. Gilbert. Then in 1828 he was sent on an official mission to survey the buildings of southern Greece, the results of which were published as *L'expédition scientifique de Morée* in three volumes in 1831, 1833, and 1838. On his return he took over the work on the Arc de Triomphe, which, with Gilbert as his *Inspecteur,* he finally completed in 1836. A year later he was sent on a tour of inspection of American prisons. He also found time to draw Niagara Falls and to publish a book on the subject. Prisons proved to be his great interest, and he served for years as *Inspecteur Général des Prisons.* His other abiding interest was the art of construction, which he taught at the École des Beaux-Arts from 1846 on as *Professeur de Théorie de l'Architecture,* and which he publicized in a two-volume supplement to J.-B. Rondelet's *Traité théorique et pratique de l'art de bâtir* in 1847–48.

Principal executed works:
Arc de Triomphe, Paris, completion and attic story, 1832–36.
Penal farm colony, Mettray, designed 1839. (*Colonie agricole et pénitentiaire de Mettray,* c. 1853.)
Church, Fontainebleau, 1852.

Literature: D.-R. Rochette, *Funérailles de M. Blouet,* Paris, 1853. A. Lance, *Abel Blouet: sa vie et ses travaux,* Paris, 1854 (also published in the *Encyclopédie d'architecture,* June 1854, p. 81 ff., July 1854, p. 97 ff.). A. Hermant, *Abel Blouet,* Paris, 1857.

BODLEY, George Frederick (Hull, 1827–Water Eaton, Oxfordshire, 1907)

He was one of the most prolific of all church architects of the nineteenth century, and is often regarded as the "climax of the Gothic Revival." The first pupil of Sir George Gilbert Scott, he reacted against his master's work in his early buildings, choosing instead a vigorous mode of High Victorian composition based on thirteenth-century French models. The turning point in his career, when he reverted to the English models admired by A. W. N. Pugin, came in the early 1860s with All Saints, Cambridge, and St. Salvador, Dundee. There followed a seemingly endless number of exquisite churches of ever-increasing refinement, from the richly stenciled St. John the Baptist, Tue Brook, Liverpool, to the light and graceful Holy Trinity, Kensington. From 1869 to 1897 he was in partnership with Thomas Garner, with whom he and G. G. Scott, Jr., had founded the firm of Watts & Co. to produce church and domestic furnishings to their own designs.

Principal executed works:
St. John the Baptist, France Lynch, Gloucestershire, 1854–57.
St. Michael and All Angels, Brighton, Sussex, 1858–62.
All Saints, Selsley, Gloucestershire, 1858–62.
All Saints, Cambridge, 1861–70.
St. Salvador, Dundee, 1865–70.
All Saints, Scarborough, Yorkshire, 1868.
St. John the Baptist, Tue Brook, Liverpool, 1868–71.
Cathedral, Hobart, Tasmania, 1868–94, 1903.
Houses, Malvern Link, Worcestershire, 1869.

St. Augustine, Pendlebury, Lancashire, 1870–74.
Holy Angels, Hoar Cross, Staffordshire, 1872–1900.
St. Michael and All Angels, Folkestone, Kent, 1873–83.
St. Michael, Camden Town, London, 1876–81.
St. Mary of Eton, Hackney, Wick, London, 1880.
St. German, Roath, Cardiff, 1883–84.
St. Mary, Clumber, Nottinghamshire, 1886–89.
Queens' College Chapel, Cambridge, 1890–91.
St. John the Evangelist, Cowley, Oxford, 1894–1902.
St. Mary, Eccleston, Cheshire, 1899.
Holy Trinity, Prince Consort Road, Kensington, London, 1902–6.
St. Chad, Burton-on-Trent, Staffordshire, 1903–10. Completed by Cecil Hare.
SS. Peter and Paul cathedral, Washington, D.C., 1906, with Vaughan and Hare.
Cathedral, San Francisco, California, 1906–15. Completed by Cecil Hare.

Literature: E. Warren, "The Life and Work of G. F. Bodley," *Journal of the Royal Institute of British Architects* 17 (1910), pp. 305–40. D. Verey, "Two Early Churches by Bodley," *Country Life,* May 20, 1971, p. 1246. D. Verey, "George Frederick Bodley: Climax of the Gothic Revival," in J. Fawcett, ed., *Seven Victorian Architects,* London, 1976, pp. 84–101.

BOESWILLWALD, Émile (Strasbourg, 1815–Paris, 1896)

The son of a stonemason at Strasbourg, Boeswillwald was educated in Munich and in Paris, where he attended the École des Beaux-Arts, a student in the *atelier* of P.-F.-H. Labrouste. Later, in 1845, he became *Inspecteur* to the restoration of Notre-Dame, under J.-B.-A. Lassus and E.-E. Viollet-le-Duc, with whom he was to be associated through life. In 1849 he became diocesan architect to Soissons, Orléans, and Bayonne, and was thus responsible for restoring and repairing a number of churches in those areas. His greatest restoration was the cathedral at Laon. He put up several buildings on his own account, notably two polychromed chapels, at Biarritz and at Baumetz, and the church of St.-Waast at Soissons and that at Masny (Nord) with columns of iron. In 1860 he succeeded Prosper Mérimée as *Inspecteur Général des Monuments Historiques,* thus becoming the first architect to hold the post.

BOGARDUS, James (Catskill, New York, 1800–New York City, 1874)

He was primarily an inventor, who produced a machine for engraving postage stamps that was adopted in England, but he is chiefly famous as the manufacturer, sometimes designer, of a series of cast-iron buildings, begun in 1848, most of which are in New York City.

Principal executed works:
Laing Stores, Washington and Murray streets, New York City, 1848. Now dismantled.
Bogardus Factory, Centre and Duane streets, New York City, 1849. Demolished 1859.
Baltimore Sun Building, Baltimore, 1851, with the architect Hatfield.

Harper's Book Building, Franklin Square, New York City, 1854, with J. B. Corlies. Demolished 1920.

Ahrenfeldt China Store, Murray Street, New York City, 1857. Taken down 1956.

P. J. Munro Building, 254–60 Canal Street, New York City, 1857.

Warehouse, 85 Leonard Street, New York City, 1860.

Literature: C. W. Condit, *American Building Art: The Nineteenth Century*, New York, 1960. W. Sturgis Knight, ed., *The Origins of Cast-Iron and Architecture in America*, New York, 1970. W. R. Weisman, "Mid-Nineteenth-Century Commercial Building by James Bogardus," *Monumentum* 9 (1973), pp. 63–76.

BOILEAU, Louis-Auguste (Paris, 1812–Paris, 1896)

Son of a watchmaker, he was trained as a joiner and woodcarver, and began his career by making the pulpit of St.-Antoine at Compiègne. Shortly afterward he made the more spectacular organ loft for St.-Germain-l'Auxerrois in Paris. This was completed by 1839, one of the first full-scale examples of the Gothic Revival in church furnishings. He moved at this period to the Vosges, where, between 1840 and 1842, he made the furniture and, in particular, the rood-screen for St.-Pierre at Aire-sur-la-Lys (Nord) and in 1843 opened a workshop and school for craftsmen at Mirecourt. He also put up his first building, the church at Mattaincourt. This was in no way a remarkable structure, though the surviving cast-iron Gothic pews are certainly odd. Soon after, he moved to Paris and started to experiment with such new structural materials as iron and, later, reinforced concrete, in an attempt to produce a new architecture. In 1850 he made a design for a chapel at St.-Denis with a structural framework of iron. This was to serve as the basis of all his later projects—from those illustrated in *La nouvelle forme architecturale*, of 1853, to those in his *Histoire critique de l'invention en architecture*, of 1886. He was a close friend of L.-A. Piel from 1838 until the latter architect's departure to Rome in 1840 and through him had come in contact with Philippe Buchez and those theories contained in the *Introduction à la science de l'histoire ou science du développement de l'humanité*, published in 1833. Boileau thus believed in successive periods of architectural synthesis, and to illustrate this concept he designed and exhibited his famous model of a "cathédrale synthétique" in 1850, at his home at 11 Rue de Sèvres. His architecture found little favor; only Théophile Gautier emerged as an admirer, in an article published in *La presse* on October 1, 1850. But in 1854, taking over from L.-A. Lusson, who had plagiarized his designs, Boileau was able to give convincing form to his concept of a new architecture of iron in the church of St.-Eugène in Paris. He built more churches of this kind all over France. But though he exhibited much and wrote even more he was to be strongly opposed by most established critics and architects, from César Daly to E.-E. Viollet-le-Duc. His ideas found their best expression in the Magasins du Bon Marché, Paris, built between 1869 and 1879, largely to the designs of his son, Louis-Charles Boileau (1837–1896), who had worked also with Théodore Ballu. His grandson was

an architect, too, Louis Boileau, designer of the Palais de Chaillot.

Principal executed works:
Church, Mattaincourt (Vosges), 1843–49.
Church, Hymont (Vosges), begun c. 1850, not yet completed 1862.
Church, Valleroy-aux-Saules (Vosges), begun c. 1850, not yet completed 1862.
St.-Eugène, Rue Ste.-Cécile and Rue du Conservatoire, Paris, March 6, 1854–Dec. 21, 1855. (C. Beuther, "Saint-Eugène et la Bibliothèque Nationale: Zwei Eisenkonstruktionen und ihr Ideengehalt," *Miscellanea pro arte Hermann Schnitzler*, Düsseldorf, 1966, pp. 315–26.)
St.-Germain-de-Marencennes (Charente-Maritime).
Notre-Dame, Rochefort-sur-Mer (Charente-Maritime), c. 1862–65.
Church, Le Vésinet (Yvelines), Paris, 1863–65.
St.-Paul, Place J. Dormoy, Montluçon (Allier), 1863–66.
Church, L'Abergement-Clémenciat (Ain), 1866–68.
Magasins du Bon Marché, Rue de Sèvres, Paris, 1869–79, with Louis-Charles Boileau.
Notre-Dame-de-France, Leicester Place, London, 1868. (N. Pevsner, *Architectural Review* [London] 101, no. 603, p. III.)
Church, Gua (near Aubin [Aveyron]), 1868.
St.-Étienne, Juilly (Seine-et-Marne), 1868–69. Stained glass and painting, 1900–1902.
Chapel, Hôpital Civil, Clermont (Oise), c. 1870.

Literature: B. Foucart, "La 'cathédrale synthétique' de Louis-Auguste Boileau," *Revue de l'art*, no. 3, 1969, pp. 49–66.

BOITO, Camillo (Rome, 1836–Milan, 1914)

He studied first at the Accademia, Venice, then at the Facoltà di Matematica in Padua. In 1855 he returned to the Accademia, to take over P. E. Selvatico's chair, but he did not stay long. In 1856 he moved to Tuscany, then in 1859 to Milan, where he was to succeed Friedrich von Schmidt in the following year as professor of architecture at the Accademia di Brera. He clearly aimed to be a teacher and published a number of books and articles, the most significant of which was *Architettura del medioevo in Italia*, of 1880. Taking up the idea and the ideals of E.-E. Viollet-le-Duc, he here proposed a reform in architecture based on a study of the buildings of the Middle Ages. His teachings seemed nothing less than revolutionary in Italy, though they contained nothing that was new. His buildings—and he was no less active as an architect than as a teacher—are in a medieval style of the ungainly kind.

Principal executed works:
Cemetery, Gallarate, 1865.
Ponti tomb, Gallarate, 1865.
Hospital, Gallarate, 1871.
Palazzo delle Debite, Padua, 1872–74.
School, Via Galvani, Milan, 1888.
Casa di Riposa dei Musicisti, and tomb of Giuseppe Verdi (Casa Verdi), Piazza Buonarroti, Milan, 1899 and 1913.

Literature: L. Grassi, *Camillo Boito*, Milan, 1959.

BONNARD, Jacques-Charles (Paris, 1765–Bordeaux, 1818)

A pupil of Renard and C.-H. Watelet, he won the Grand Prix in 1788 but fled soon after to England and later to Italy. Returning to France, he succeeded Renard as architect to the Ministère des Affaires Étrangères and in 1810 won a competition for the new ministry on the Quai d'Orsay, in Paris. He was engaged with this for four years, when work was stopped, to be taken up again, after Bonnard's death, by his pupil Jacques Lacornée.

Literature: Quatremère de Quincy, *Notices historiques*, Paris, 1834, pp. 335–45. J.-M. Léri, "Le palais du Quai d'Orsay (1810–1871)," *Bulletin de la Société de l'Histoire de l'Art Français*, Année 1976 (1978), pp. 387–93.

BONOMI, Joseph (Rome, 1739–London, 1808)

He was trained in Rome by C.-L. Clérisseau and by the Marchese Teodoli, a nobleman-architect. He was called to England in 1767 by the Adam brothers, but he also worked for Thomas Leverton. His principal achievement is the church at Packington, Warwickshire, in the Revolutionary style of C.-N. Ledoux and Friedrich Gilly.

Principal executed works:
Packington Hall, Warwickshire, Long Gallery, 1782–88. (D. FitzGerald, "A Gallery after the Antique," *Connoisseur* 181 [1972], pp. 2–13; *Country Life* 148 [1970], pp. 102, 162, 226.)
St. James, Great Packington, Warwickshire, 1789–90. (*Country Life* 150 [1971], p. 110.)
Longford Hall, Shropshire, 1789 (*Country Life* 132, p. 354.)
Portman House, Portman Square, London, ballroom, c. 1790. Demolished 1940.
Eastwell Park, Kent, 1793–1800. Demolished 1926.
Blickling Park, Norfolk, mausoleum, 1794.
Laverstoke, Hampshire, 1796–99.
Roseneath, Dunbartonshire, 1803–6. Demolished 1961.

BOULANGER, François-Louis-Florimond (Douai, 1807–Paris, 1875)

Joint winner, with Clerget, of the Grand-Prix in 1836, he traveled to Rome and returned to Paris, exhibiting at the Salons between 1840 and 1855, but he spent most of his active life in Athens.

Principal executed works:
Palea Vouli (old House of Parliament), off Stadiou Street, Athens, 1871–.
Zappeion, Athens, 1874–. Taken over by T. E. Hansen.

BOULLÉE, Étienne-Louis (Paris, 1728–Paris, 1799)

He appears to have been related, through his mother, to François Boucher and, indeed, wanted to be a painter.

He was always a visionary. He began his studies under J.-B. Pierre but was subsequently sent to the architects Jacques-François Blondel and J.-L. Legeay. He himself taught from the age of nineteen at the École des Ponts et Chaussées, Paris. Boullée did not travel to Italy. He began his active career in 1752, together with Pierre and E.-M. Falconet, with a design for the Chapelle Calvaire at St.-Roch, Paris, and followed it with a succession of town and country houses, but he gave up this practice within a few years. In 1775 he became *Intendant des Bâtiments* to the Comte d'Artois but resigned this position within two years. However, in 1780 he prepared drawings for d'Artois for a *grand hôtel* on the site of the nursery gardens at Roule (as did F.-J. Bélanger). This was one of the first of the vast, overscaled designs for which he was to become famous. In October 1778 he became *Contrôleur* at the Hôtel Royal des Invalides and two years later at the École Militaire but resigned both positions in 1782. He continued to execute official commissions in Paris, transforming the Hôtel de Force into a prison (1780–82), the Hôtel Tubeuf into a Bourse (1784), and the Hôtel Langlée into the Loterie Royale (1788), but devoted his attention, rather, to the design of stupendous, overbearing buildings, many of which were intended as illustrations to his short *Essai sur l'art*, published only in the twentieth century. Boullée was an assiduous member of the Académie Royale d'Architecture from his election in 1762 to its suppression in 1793.

Principal executed works:
Hôtel Alexandre, 16 Rue de la Ville-l'Évêque, Paris, 1763–66.
Hôtels de Monville, Rue de la Ville-l'Évêque, Paris, 1764. Both demolished.
Château, Chaville (Seine-et-Oise), 1764–66. Demolished.
Hôtel de Pernon, Rue de la Chaussée-d'Antin, Paris, 1768–71. Demolished.
Hôtel de Thun, Rue de la Chaussée-d'Antin, Paris, 1769–71. Demolished.
Hôtel de Brunoy, Rue du Faubourg St.-Honoré, Paris, 1775–79. Demolished.

Principal unexecuted projects:
Conversion of Giovanni Girardini's Palais-Bourbon, Paris, for the Prince de Condé, 1764.
Métropole, 1777–81.
Hôtel d'Artois, Pépinières du Roule, Paris, 1780.
Grand projet for the palace at Versailles, 1780.
Theater, Place du Carrousel, Paris, 1781.
Museum, 1783.
Library, 1784.
Cenotaph for Isaac Newton, 1784.

Literature: J. M. Pérouse de Montclos, ed., *E. L. Boullée: Architecture, essai sur l'art,* Paris, 1968. J. M. Pérouse de Montclos, *Étienne-Louis Boullée: de l'architecture classique à l'architecture révolutionnaire,* Paris, 1969. H. Rosenau, *Boullée and Visionary Architecture,* London and New York, 1976.

BOURDAIS, Jules-Désiré (Brest, 1835–1915)

He worked first under Hector Horeau and in 1860 took up an administrative post in Brest; a few years later he became architect to the Tarn-et-Garonne department but by 1874 was in Paris, working with G.-J.-A. Davioud on the Palais du Trocadéro. With Davioud he was able to enter and win the competition for the theater at Cannes in 1875 and later to design and build the Mairie du XIXᵉ in Paris.

BRODRICK, Cuthbert (Hull, 1822–Hull, 1905)

The son of a shipowner, he was a pupil of Henry Lockwood. He became the leading architect in Yorkshire, working in a powerful style based on Italian Renaissance and Baroque precedents. The Town Hall, Leeds, is his masterpiece.

Principal executed works (all in Yorkshire):
Royal Institution, Hull, 1852–54.
Town Hall, Leeds, 1853–58.
Corn Exchange, Leeds, 1860–63.
Grand Hotel, Scarborough 1863–67. (*Architectural Review* [London] 145 [Mar. 1969].)
Congregational Church Headingley Lane, Leeds, 1864–66.
Institute of Science, Art and Literature, Leeds, 1865–68.
Oriental Baths, Leeds, 1866. Demolished 1969.

Principal unexecuted projects:
Cathedral, Lille, 1856.
Government Offices, London, 1857.
Assize Courts, Manchester, 1859.
Town Hall, Bolton, Lancashire, 1865.
National Gallery, London, 1866.
Town Hall, Manchester, 1866.

Literature: T. B. Wilson, *Two Leeds Architects: Cuthbert Brodrick and George Corson,* Leeds, 1937. D. Linstrum, *Historic Architecture of Leeds,* 1969. D. Linstrum, "Cuthbert Brodrick," *Journal of the Royal Society of Arts,* Jan. 1971.

BRONGNIART, Alexandre-Théodore (Paris, 1739–Paris, 1813)

An altogether competent, if not greatly original architect, he was responsible for a number of private houses in Paris, many of which survive, if only in part. He was a pupil of Jacques-François Blondel and of E.-L. Boullée, and also a student at the Académie Royale d'Architecture, Paris, under Hubert Pluyette. He became a member of the Académie in 1781. The largest and dullest of his buildings was the Bourse, in Paris.

Principal executed works:
Theater, Caen, 1765.
Hôtel de Montesson, Rue de la Chaussée-d'Antin, Paris, 1770–71. Demolished. (*Gazette des beaux-arts* 64 [1964], pp. 161–76.)
Hôtel de Sainte-Foix, Rue Basse-du-Rempart, Paris, 1775. Demolished.
Hôtel de Monaco, 57 Rue St.-Dominique, Paris, 1775–77. Much altered and extended, in part by F.-J. Duban.
Couvent des Capucins de la Chaussée-d'Antin, Paris,

1780–83. Survives as St.-Louis-d'Antin and the Lycée Condorcet, 63 Rue Caumartin.
Hôtel de Mlle. de Bourbon-Condé, 12 Rue Monsieur, Paris, 1780–81.
Hôtel Brongniart, 49 Boulevard des Invalides, Paris, 1781. A story has been added.
Hôtel de Montesquiou, 20 Rue Monsieur, Paris, 1781. Only the shell survives.
St.-Germain-l'Auxerrois, Romainville, Paris, 1785–87.
Hôtel Masserano, 11 Rue Masseran, Paris, 1787.
Hôtel Chamblin, 3–5 Rue Masseran, Paris, c. 1789.
Père Lachaise cemetery, Paris, 1804.
Bourse, Paris, 1807, 1808–15. Court covered over with glass in 1823 by E.-E. de Labarre, who completed the work in 1827; wings added in 1903 by E.-G. Coquart.

Literature: J. Silvestre de Sacy, *Alexandre-Théodore Brongniart, 1739–1813: sa vie, son oeuvre,* Paris, 1940.

BROOKS, James (Hatford, Berkshire, 1825–Stoke Newington, London, 1901)

He was moved by J. L. Pearson's St. Peter, Vauxhall (1860–65), to develop the type of high, brick-built church in the style of the early thirteenth century, with lancet windows and an apse, with which he is particularly associated. He had a highly developed sense of form, and his austere churches, often in poor areas, are undeniably impressive.

Principal executed works:
St. Michael, Shoreditch, London, 1863.
St. Saviour, Hoxton, London, 1864. Demolished.
St. Columba, Haggerston, London, 1867.
St. Chad, Haggerston, London, 1868.
Annunciation Church, Chislehurst, Kent, 1868–70.
St. Andrew, Plaistow, Essex, 1870.
Christ Church, Clapton, London, 1870.
Ascension Church, Lavender Hill, Battersea, London, 1873.
Transfiguration Church, Lewisham, London, 1880.
St. Peter, Hastings, Sussex, 1885.
All Saints, Southend, Essex, 1889.
All Hallows, Gospel Oak, London, 1889.

BROWN, Lancelot ("Capability") (Kirkharle, Northumberland, 1716–London, 1783)

He was the principal designer of landscaped parks in eighteenth-century England. Developing ideas taken from William Kent, with whom he had worked at Stowe in the 1730s, he formulated the "natural" style of gardening in which formal vistas and axial planning were replaced by the studied asymmetry of serpentine lakes, smooth hills, and clumps of trees. His finest surviving parks include those at Warwick Castle, Croome Court, Bowood, Blenheim Palace, and Dodington Park. He was appointed Surveyor to His Majesty's Gardens and Waters at Hampton Court in 1764. He was also an architect of country houses and collaborated with Henry Holland, his future son-in-law, for a few years after about 1771.

Principal executed buildings:

Croome Court, Worcestershire, 1751–52. (*Country Life* 37, p. 482; *Country Life* 87, p. 14.)

Corsham Court, Wiltshire, alterations. 1761–64. (*Country Life* 82, pp. 516, 548.)

Claremont House, Surrey, 1770–72, with Henry Holland. (*Country Life*, July 7, 1950.)

Benham Place, Berkshire, 1772–75, with Henry Holland.

Literature: D. Stroud, *Capability Brown*, 1950 (3d ed., 1975).

BUCKNALL, Benjamin (Rodborough, Gloucestershire, 1833–Algiers, 1895)

He is significant as the only serious follower of E.-E. Viollet-le-Duc in nineteenth-century England. He went to France to meet him in 1861, corresponded with him from 1862 to 1875, and translated his *Histoire d'une maison* in 1874, *Histoire d'une forteresse* in 1875, *Histoire de l'habitation humaine* in 1876, and *Entretiens sur l'architecture* in 1877 and 1881. Bucknall's most important building is Woodchester Park. His point of departure was a plan made in 1846 by A.W. N. Pugin for a house on the site. But Bucknall achieved what Pugin never attempted, a buildling all of stone: with stone vaults, stone staircases, stone drainpipes, and even a stone bath. Though uncompleted, it is one of the most impressive buildings of its date anywhere in Europe. He settled in Algiers about 1875.

Principal executed works, dating from before his move to Algiers:

Woodchester Park, Gloucestershire, c. 1854–68. (*Country Life*, Feb. 6, 1969; D. Verey, "Woodchester Park," in H. Colvin and J. Harris, eds., *The Country Seat*, 1970, pp. 237–43.)

Our Lady and St. Michael, Abergavenny, 1857–60.

Tocknells House, Painswick, Gloucestershire, c. 1860.

St. Stephens (a stone cottage), Nympesfield, Gloucestershire, c. 1860.

St. Wulstan, Little Malvern, Worcestershire, 1862.

West Grange, Stroud, Gloucestershire, 1866.

Dominican Convent of St. Rose of Lima, Stroud, Gloucestershire, 1867; and chapel, 1888–95.

Holy Trinity, Slad, Gloucestershire, reconstruction, c. 1869.

BULFINCH, Charles (Boston, Massachusetts, 1763–1844)

He was educated at Harvard University and traveled in Europe from 1785 to 1787. Much of the layout of Boston is attributable to him, and from 1817 to 1830 he was in charge of work on the Capitol in Washington, D.C. He was influenced by the style of English seventeenth- and eighteenth-century architecture.

Principal executed works:

Beacon Monument, Boston, Massachusetts, 1789.

Connecticut State House, Hartford, 1792–96.

Massachusetts State House, Boston, 1795–98.

Holy Cross Church, Boston, Massachusetts, 1805.

Courthouse, Boston, Massachusetts, 1810.

New South Church, Boston, Massachusetts, 1814.

Literature: C. A. Place, *Charles Bulfinch: Architect and Citizen*, Boston and New York, 1925 (repr. New York, 1968). H. Kirker, *The Architecture of Charles Bulfinch*, Cambridge, Mass., 1969.

BURGES, William (London, 1827–London, 1881)

The son of a successful engineer, trained by Edward Blore and M. D. Wyatt, he was an architect in whose work hard constructional reality mingled with wild fantasy. Despising perspectives, he produced architectural drawings that were severe, unshaded, linear patterns. Inspired by the stern style of French architecture in 1200, fashionable in the 1850s and 1860s, his buildings echo to some degree the work and ideas of E.-E. Viollet-le-Duc. But Burges's artistic imagination was infinitely richer than the French architect's, and he was encouraged to develop it by his exotic patron from 1868 to 1881, the millionaire Lord Bute, for whom he created his most colorful and extravagant interiors, at Cardiff Castle and Castell Coch. Burges's enthusiasm for the Middle Ages, unlike that of many of his fellow architects, was romantic and visual rather than religious; he thus felt free to introduce motifs from other cultures into his work. That he did not take up the Domestic Revival of W. E. Nesfield and R. N. Shaw but preserved the sometimes overpowering bulk and weight of the architecture of the 1860s to the end of his career also set him apart from his contemporaries. He was a creative designer of jewelry, ceramics, metalwork, and furniture and published *Art as Applied to Industry* in 1865.

Principal executed works:

Waltham Abbey, Essex, restoration and east end, 1859.

Gayhurst, Buckinghamshire, alterations and additions, 1859–60.

St. Finbar's cathedral, Cork, 1862–76. (C. Handley-Read, "St. Fin Barre's Cathedral, Cork," *Architectural Review* [London] 141 [1967], pp. 422–30.)

St. Michael, Lowfield Heath, Surrey, 1867.

Cardiff Castle, Glamorganshire, 1868–81. (*Country Life*, Apr. 6–20, 1961.)

Knightshayes, Devonshire, 1869–71. (J. M. Crook, *National Trust Year Book 1975–76*, pp. 44–55.)

Christ the Consoler Church, Skelton, Yorkshire, 1871–72.

St. Mary, Studley Royal, Yorkshire, 1871–78.

Speech Room, Harrow School (near London), 1872.

All Saints, Murston, Kent, 1873–74.

Trinity College, Hartford, Connecticut, 1873–80.

No. 9 Melbury Road, Kensington, London, 1875–80. (*Country Life* 139 [1966], pp. 600–604; London County Council, *Survey of London* 37 [1973], pp. 114–18.)

Castell Coch, Glamorganshire, 1875–81. (*Architectural Review* [London] 109 [1951], pp. 39–46; *Country Life*, May 10–17, 1962.)

Principal unexecuted projects:

Cathedral, Lille, 1855, with Henry Clutton.

Crimean Memorial Church, Constantinople (Istanbul), 1856–57 and 1858.

Cathedral, Brisbane, 1859.

School of Art, Bombay, 1865.

Law Courts, London, 1866.

Literature: R. P. Pullan, *The Architectural Designs of William Burges*, 2 vols., 1883–87. R. P. Pullan, *The Designs of William Burges*, 1885. R. P. Pullan, *The House of William Burges*, 1885. C. Handley-Read, "William Burges," in P. Ferriday, ed., *Victorian Architecture*, London, 1963, pp. 187–220. C. Handley-Read, "William Burges' Painted Furniture," *Burlington Magazine* 105 (1963), pp. 496–509.

BURLINGTON, third earl of (Richard Boyle) (London, 1695–Chiswick, 1753)

This patron, collector, and architect did more to determine the pattern of eighteenth-century British taste than any other individual. He studied Andrea Palladio's architecture in Vicenza on a visit to Italy in 1719 and subsequently bought a large collection of Palladio's drawings, which he published as *Fabbriche antiche disegnate da Andrea Palladio Vicentino* (1730). This combined interest in Palladio and in the antique was brilliantly expressed in his Assembly Rooms at York, based on Palladio's interpretation of Vitruvius's Egyptian Hall.

Principal executed works:

Tottenham Park, Wiltshire, 1721. Largely demolished.

Westminster School, London, dormitory, 1722–30.

House for General George Wade, No. 29 Great (now Old) Burlington Street, London, 1723. Demolished 1935.

Chiswick House, Middlesex, c. 1723–29.

Assembly Rooms, York, 1730. ("Lord Burlington's Work at York," in R. Wittkower, *Palladio and English Palladianism*, 1974.)

Literature: London County Council, *Survey of London* 31–32 (1963). "Lord Burlington and William Kent," "Lord Burlington's Work at York," and "Lord Burlington at Northwick Park," in R. Wittkower, *Palladio and English Palladianism*, 1974.

BUTTERFIELD, William (London, 1814–1900)

He was the leading Gothic Revivalist in the High Church Anglican party that was making the same analogies as A. W. N. Pugin among the Roman Catholics between architecture and religion. Butterfield was less directly inspired by medieval precedent than Pugin and developed a bizarre method of building and decoration that relied for its effect on geometrical patterns in polychrome brickwork. Characteristic examples can be seen at Keble College and Rugby School. In a quieter key, some of his domestic buildings played an important part in the vernacular revival later associated with the name of Philip Webb.

Principal executed works:

St. Saviour, church and vicarage, Coalpit Heath, Gloucestershire, 1844–45.

St. Augustine College, Canterbury, Kent, 1844–48.

Cathedral, Perth, 1847–90.
Cathedral, Adelaide, 1847–78.
St. Matthias, Stoke Newington, London, 1849–58.
All Saints, Margaret Street, London, 1849–59. (*Country Life*, Jan. 14, 1965.)
Milton Ernest Hall, Bedfordshire, 1854–64. (*Country Life* 146 [1969], p. 1042.)
Baldersby village, Yorkshire, church, school, and cottages, 1855–57.
St. Alban, Holborn, London, 1859–62.
Rugby School, Warwickshire, 1860–86.
Winchester Hospital, Hampshire, 1863.
All Saints, Babbacombe, Devonshire, 1865–74.
Keble College, Oxford, 1866–83.
Cathedral, Melbourne, 1877–86.
Chanter's House, Ottery St. Mary, Somersetshire, 1880.

Literature: J. Summerson, "William Butterfield," *Architectural Review* (London) 64 (1945), pp. 166–75 (repr. in J. Summerson, *Heavenly Mansions, and Other Essays on Architecture,* London, 1949, pp. 159–76). P. Thompson, *William Butterfield,* 1971. J. Summerson, "Pugin and Butterfield," *Architectural Review* (London) 152 (1972), pp. 97–99.

CACIALLI, Giuseppe (Florence, 1778–1828).

He studied in Florence and was a pupil of G. M. Paoletti, with whom he was associated in the rebuilding and decoration of the Villa del Poggio Imperiale and the Palazzo Pitti. He taught for many years at the academy in Florence.

CAGNOLA, Luigi (Milan, 1762–Inverigo, 1833)

He was born to a family of aristocratic pretension that had made money supplying the occupying Austrian army. He was sent first to Rome to study literature, then to Pavia to study law, then, in 1795, to Vienna to study diplomacy. He returned after a few months to Milan, where he started to practice law, but he had fallen already among painters and architects and when the French army arrived and he was forced to flee to the Veneto and Venice he took advantage of the occasion to study architecture there. He was much taken by the works of Andrea Palladio and when he returned to Milan he determined to initiate a reform in architecture that was Palladian in spirit, and thus Italian. He did not at first endorse French taste. When he was elected to the Commissione d'Ornato, in 1807, he saw to it that nothing in the French manner was approved for building. He was a man of strong personality, eccentric and rude on occasion, and was very influential. He did not build much, but his arid, though grand, architecture was held in awe throughout Italy.

Principal executed works:
Villa Zurla, Vaiano Cremasco, 1801–2.
Porta Ticinese (or Porta Marengo), Milan, 1801–14.
Arco del Sempione (or Arco della Pace), Milan, 1806–38. Some of the reliefs are by Pompeo Marchesi.
Villa Cagnola (or La Rotonda), Inverigo, c. 1813–33.

The carved figures of *atlantes* are by Marchesi. The furnishings, all designed by Cagnola, were sold off in 1950.
Burgtor, Vienna, designed 1818. Built between 1821 and 1824 by Pietro Nobile.
Church, Concorezzo, 1818–58. The campanile was designed in 1842 by A. Pizzala.
Villa Cagnola, Via Roma and Via Cavour, Verdello, c. 1820.
S. Lorenzo (or La Rotonda), Ghisalba, 1822–33. The campanile was added later.
Campanile, Urgnano, 1824–29.
Campanile, Chiari, 1832.

Principal unexecuted projects:
Project undertaken for the Empress Josephine for the completion of Malmaison, c. 1812. (G. Hubert, "Cagnola, architecte de l'Impératrice Josephine?" *Gazette des beaux-arts* 88 [1976], pp. 137–44.)
Monumento alla Riconoscenza, Moncenisio, 1813.
Extensions to the Imperial Palace, Vienna, 1819–24.
Mausoleum for Metternich, Vienna, c. 1820.

Literature: G. Mezzanotte, *Architettura neoclassica in Lombardia,* Naples, 1966.

CALLET, Félix-Emmanuel (Paris, 1792–Paris, 1854)

A pupil of P.-J.-N. Delespine, he won the Grand Prix in 1819. He was an architect of no distinction, although he built much in Paris and in the French provinces. He is distinguished only as having been the collaborator of Victor Baltard at the Halles Centrales, Paris.

Principal executed works:
Gare d'Orléans, Paris, 1835. He was replaced by F.-L. Reynaud.
Halles Centrales, Paris, 1851–54, with Victor Baltard. Demolished 1972–73.
Hôtel des Commissaires-Priseurs (later Chambre de Commerce), Place de la Bourse, Paris.
Hôtel Casimir et Lecomte, Place St.-Georges, Paris.
Villa Barthelony, Secheron (near Geneva).
Villa Dufour, Bellevue.
Château de Saulsure (near Vernon).

CAMERON, Charles (c. 1743–St. Petersburg [Leningrad], 1812)

Little is known about his early life and training except that he was in Rome in 1768, presumably collecting material for his important publication of 1772, the *Description of the Baths of the Romans.* About 1778 Catherine the Great summoned him to St. Petersburg; his buildings for her are characterized by sumptuous decoration inspired by C.-L. Clérisseau, Robert Adam, and the Roman Baths of Titus.

Principal executed works:
Palace of Catherine the Great, Tsarskoe Selo (Pushkin), interiors, 1779–84; Cameron Gallery and Agate Pavilion, 1782–85.
Temple of Friendship, Pavlovsk, 1780.
Palace of Grand Duke Paul, Pavlovsk, 1781–85.

Rasumovski Palace, Baturin, Ukraine, 1799–1802.
Naval hospital and barracks, Kronstadt (Kotlin Island), c. 1805.

Literature: G. K. Loukomski, *Charles Cameron,* 1943. T. Talbot Rice and A. A. Tait, eds., *Charles Cameron,* exhib. cat., London, 1967–68. I. Rae, *Charles Cameron, Architect to the Court of Russia,* 1971.

CAMPBELL, Colen (1676–London, 1729)

He was chief promoter of the revived Palladian Villa style, which was to be so popular in Britain and then in Europe. In 1718 Lord Burlington employed him to take over the remodeling of Burlington House from James Gibbs, who was then remodeling it in a Baroque style. Campbell commemorated British Palladian architecture in the three volumes of his *Vitruvius Britannicus* (1715, 1717, and 1725).

Principal executed works:
Shawfield Mansion, Glasgow, 1712. Demolished 1792. (G. L. M. Goodfellow, "Colen Campbell's Shawfield Mansion in Glasgow," *Journal of the Society of Architectural Historians* [U.S.A.], Oct. 1964.)
Wanstead House, Essex, 1715. Demolished 1824. (*Country Life* 108 [1950], p. 607.)
Burlington House, Piccadilly, London, rebuilding, 1718–19. (London County Council, *Survey of London* 32 [1963], pp. 390–429.)
Newby (now Baldersby) Park, Yorkshire, 1720–21.
Houghton Hall, Norfolk, 1721. (*Country Life* 49 [1921], pp. 14, 40, 64, 98.)
Stourhead, Wiltshire, c. 1720–24. (*Country Life* 83 [1938], pp. 608, 638; *Country Life* 109 [1951], p. 38.)
Mereworth Castle, Kent, c. 1722. (*Country Life* 47 [1920], pp. 808, 876, 912; *Country Life Annual,* Jan. 1966, p. 28.)

Literature: H. Stutchbury, *The Architecture of Colen Campbell,* Manchester, 1967.

CAMPORESE, Pietro (Rome, 1726–1781)

He became a member of the Accademia di San Luca in 1775 and was active in Rome and the surrounding area. He began the duomo at Subiaco and the rooms of the new Vatican museum. The former was to be completed by his two sons, Giulio (1754–1840) and Giuseppe (1763–1822), the latter by Giuseppe alone, who worked on the atrium, the Sala della Biga, the vestibule to the Galleria dei Candelabri e degli Animali, and the Sala Rotonda. Giulio's son, named, like his grandfather, Pietro (1792–1873), rebuilt the basilica of S. Paolo fuori le mura, together with P. Bosio and P. Belli.

Literature: J. Arnaud, *L'Académie de Saint-Luc,* Paris, 1886, p. 202.

CANONICA, Luigi (Reveredo di Tesserete, Lugano, 1764–Milan, 1844)

He was a pupil and perhaps the chief disciple of Giuseppe Piermarini, whom he succeeded as *Architetto di Stato* in Milan when the French replaced the Austrians in Lombardy, thus earning Piermarini's most bitter resentment. Canonica prospered under the French and took over the work of building the Foro Bonaparte, substituting for Giuseppe Pistocchi's and G. A. Antolini's visionary designs more practical, though no less vast, proposals. In 1805 he visited Paris to inspect the work of Percier and Fontaine; later in the same year he began his Arena in Milan and prepared initial designs for the new gateways of the city. He was an altogether competent and active architect, chiefly of the administrative sort, building throughout Lombardy right up to the year of his death, but he left little of special interest or note.

Principal executed works:
Teatro Carcano, Milan, 1802–3. Demolished.
Foro Bonaparte, Milan 1803–. Very little of this was built.
Arena, Milan, 1805–13, completed 1824.
Teatro della Concordia, Cremona, 1808.
Teatro Sociale, Sondrio, 1820–24.
Teatro Sociale, Mantua, 1820–25.
Palazzo Anguissola-Traversi, 10 Via Manzoni, Milan, 1829–30.
Palazzo Brentani-Greppi, 6 Via Manzoni, Milan, 1829–30.

Literature: G. Mezzanotte, *Architettura neoclassica in Lombardia*, Naples, 1966.

CANTONI, Simone (Muggio di Mendrisio, 1739–Milan, 1818)

He began working with his father, a builder, but was soon in the employ of Luigi Vanvitelli and then, from 1767 to 1768, a student under E.-A. Petitot at Parma. He built extensively in Lombardy and in related provinces, scarcely at all in Milan, where Giuseppe Piermarini held sway, but his most influential building, the Palazzo Serbelloni, was in Milan, and it served to set a new standard of taste there. This palace was demonstrably a neoclassical work, but much of Cantoni's output is more heterogeneous—indeed, messy.

Principal executed works:
Cemetery, Gorgonzola, 1775–76.
Palazzo Serbelloni, 16 Corso Venezia, Milan, designed 1775, built 1779–94; salon, 1814.
Palazzo Ducale, Genoa, rebuilding of facade and salon, 1778–83.
Villa Olmo, Borgovico, Como, 1782–94.
Palazzo Vailetti-Medolago, Bergamo, 1783–91.
Palazzo Pertusati, Milan, 1789–91.
Villa Gallarati-Scotti, Oreno, 1790–93.
Villa Giovio, Brescia, Como, 1790–95.
SS. Protasio e Gervasio, Gorgonzola, 1802–6. Work was taken up again in 1818 by Giacomo Moraglia. The building was consecrated in 1820, and the campanile was erected in 1842 by Moraglia to Cantoni's design.
S. Ambrogio, Morazzone, 1814.

Literature: G. Mezzanotte, *Architettura neoclassica in Lombardia*, Naples, 1966.

CARISTIE, Augustin-Nicolas (Avallon, 1783–Paris, 1862)

The son and grandson of architects, a pupil of Charles Percier and of A.-L.-T. Vaudoyer, he won the Grand Prix in 1813. Yet his small distinction was to have been recognized as a violent opponent of the Gothic Revival. His chief activity was the restoration of the Roman arch at Orange, in 1821–29, though he was also responsible for several monuments of his own and a handful of public buildings at Rheims.

Principal executed works:
Napoleonic Monument, Orange, 1823–30.
Monument, Quiberon (Morbihan), 1825.
Palais de Justice, Rheims, 1841–45.

CARMONTELLE, Louis Carrogis de (Paris, 1717–Paris, 1806)

He was born Louis Carrogis, the son of a *maître cordonnier*, but he learned the techniques of the surveyor and was able to join the Orléans dragoons in Westphalia. He changed his name. He was noticed by one of his officers, M. de Pont-Saint-Maurice, who was tutor to the Duc de Chartres, and who obtained for Carmontelle the position of reader to the young duke. In this society he came into his own. He became the all-round entertainer, writing charades, presenting them, and recording them. His *Proverbes dramatiques* were published in six volumes between 1774 and 1776. His drawings of the celebrated company entertained by the Duc de Chartres found their way into collections throughout Europe. The Duc d'Aumale had more than five hundred of Carmontelle's portraits in his collection at Chantilly. But it was another aspect of his delight in entertainment that was to win Carmontelle more lasting fame: He laid out the gardens of the Duc de Chartres's *folie* at Monceau as a series of conversation pieces, based—though he denied this strongly—on the fashionable *jardin anglais*. His settings, his ruins, and his tableaux are recorded in the *Jardin de Monceau*, of 1779. He was later to lay out other gardens.

Literature: M. C. de Mery, ed., *Proverbes dramatiques de Carmontelle, précédés de la vie de Carmontelle*, rev. ed., Paris, 1822. F. A. Gruyer, *Chantilly: les portraits de Carmontelle*, Paris, 1902. *Paris au XVIIIe siècle: Restif de la Bretonne. Le Paris populaire. Carmontelle. Le Paris mondain*, exhib. cat., Musée Carnavalet, Paris, 1934–35.

CARR, John (Horbury, Yorkshire, 1723–Askham Richard, Yorkshire, 1807.)

He was a competent architect, working in an elegant, late Palladian style enlivened by Robert Adam's influence, who built up a large circle of patrons who commissioned country houses and public buildings in Yorkshire and Nottinghamshire.

Principal executed works:
Kirby Hall, Yorkshire, c. 1750. Built by Carr from designs by Lord Burlington and Roger Morris. Demolished 1920.
Arncliffe Hall, Yorkshire, c. 1750–54. (*Country Life*, Dec. 25, 1920.)
Heath Hall (near Wakefield), Yorkshire, 1754. (*Country Life* 144, pp. 692, 756, 816.)
Grandstand, Knavesmire racecourse, York, 1755–56. Largely demolished.
Harewood House, Yorkshire, 1759–71, with Robert Adam. (*Country Life*, Oct. 5, 1901; *Country Life*, July 4, 1914; *Country Life*, Feb. 25, 1922; M. Mauchline, *Harewood House*, 1974.)
Wentworth Woodhouse, Yorkshire, additions, 1760–1804. (*Journal of the Royal Institute of British Architects* 41 [1933].)
Tabley House, Cheshire, 1761–67. (*Country Life*, July 1923, pp. 84, 114.)
Welbeck Abbey, Nottinghamshire, additions, 1763–77.
Kirkleatham Hall, Yorkshire, 1764–67. Demolished 1954–56.
Thoresby Park, Nottinghamshire, 1768. Demolished 1868.
Town Hall and Assembly Rooms, Newark, Nottinghamshire, 1773–76.
County Assize Courts, York Castle, 1773–77.
Basildon Park, Berkshire, 1776.
Denton Park, Yorkshire, 1778. (*Country Life*, Nov. 4, 1939.)
Thornes House (near Wakefield), Yorkshire, 1779–81. Demolished 1951.
The Crescent, Buxton, Derbyshire, 1779–84.
Clifton Hall, Nottinghamshire, rebuilding, 1778–97. (*Country Life*, Aug. 25, 1923.)
Grimston Garth (near Aldborough), Yorkshire, 1781–86. (*Country Life*, Oct. 17, 1952.)
Farnley Hall (near Otley), Yorkshire, additions, c. 1786. (*Country Life* 115, pp. 1618, 1714, 1808, 2098.)
Town Hall, Chesterfield, Derbyshire, 1787. Demolished.

Assembly Rooms, Nottingham, alterations, 1790.

CELLERIER, Jacques (Dijon, 1742–1814)

A pupil of Jacques-François Blondel and of J.-D. Le Roy, he traveled to Rome and returned to Paris to establish himself as an architect of theaters. About 1785 he rebuilt the Théâtre de l'Ambigu Comique on the Boulevard du Temple, Paris, and in 1808 the Théâtre des Variétés, Boulevard Montmartre. Later, in 1810, he began the theater at Dijon, finished only in 1825. Cellerier is also remembered as the designer, in 1810, of the fountain in the form of an elephant for the Place de la Bastille, Paris, begun and set up in plaster by J.-A. Alavoine.

Principal executed works:
Hôtel de Verrière, Rue Verte St.-Honoré, Paris, 1774.
Hôtel, 21 Rue de la Chaussée-d'Antin, Paris, 1775–79.
Hôtel de Mme. d'Epinay, 5 Rue de la Chaussée-d'Antin, Paris, 1776–77.
Maison du Duc de Laval, Boulevard Montparnasse, Paris, 1777–89. Demolished 1867.
Hôtel de Montigny, Rue de Provence, Paris, 1778–82.
Hôtel de la Maréchale de Nicolai, Rue Louis-le-Grand, Boulevard de la Chaussée-d'Antin, Paris, 1779.

Veterinary school, Alfort, before 1786.

Hôtel du Prince de Soubise, Rue de l'Arcade, Paris, 1787–88.

Triumphal arch, Champ de Mars, Paris, 1790.

Hearse for transporting Voltaire's ashes to the Panthéon, Paris.

Theater, Dijon, 1810–25.

Literature: M. Gallet, *Paris Domestic Architecture of the 18th Century*, London, 1972.

CERATO, Domenico (1720–Padua, 1792)

He was active first in Vicenza as *Professore di Architettura Civile*, then, from 1772 onward, in Padua, as *Pubblico Professore di Architettura Pratica* and as *Pubblico Architetto*. He built much in Padua, starting in 1761 with the construction of the university observatory within and atop the Castello, and other such works as the installation of the Scuola di Veterinaria in the Convento delle Maddalene, in 1776, and the erection of the Pubblica Casa d'Agricoltura in the Borgo Santa Croce. He was a sound practitioner rather than a man of inspiration. But under the guidance of Andrea Memmo he was responsible for two works that were of more than local importance, the Prato della Valle and the Ospedale Civile.

Principal executed works:

Specola (observatory), Castello Vecchio, Padua, 1761–67.

Prato della Valle, Padua, 1775–90, conceived by Andrea Memmo. (N. Gallimberti, "Il Prato della Valle, Andrea Memmo e il Cerato," *Padova e la sua provincia* 13 [1967], pp. 20–26.)

Ospedale Civile, Padua, 1776, 1778–98, conceived by Andrea Memmo.

Literature: G. Passadore, "Domenico Cerato architetto a Padova," *Bolletino del Centro Internazionale di Studi di Architettura Andrea Palladio* 5 (1963), pp. 318–29.

CHALGRIN, Jean-François-Thérèse (Paris, 1739–Paris, 1811)

Trained by L.-A. Loriot, E.-L. Boullée, and G. N. Servandoni, Chalgrin won the Grand Prix in 1758 and from November 1759 to May 1763 lived in Rome, from where he corresponded with J.-G. Soufflot. On his return to Paris he became *Inspecteur des Travaux de la Ville de Paris*, under P.-L. Moreau-Desproux, and in this capacity, between 1765 and 1767, supervised the building of the Hôtel de Saint-Florentin, 2 Rue Saint-Florentin, to the designs of A.-J. Gabriel. He himself designed the entrance to the court and the main doorway. In 1770 he was elected to the Académie Royale d'Architecture and established himself as a fashionable designer with a temporary ballroom erected for the Austrian ambassador's celebrations of the dauphin's marriage. The building for which he is best remembered, however, is the church of St.-Philippe-du-Roule, designed soon after his return from Rome but not begun until 1772. He served as *Premier Architecte* to the

Comte de Provence from 1775 on, and as *Intendant des Bâtiments* to the Comte d'Artois beginning in 1779.

Principal executed works:

St.-Philippe-du-Roule, Place Chassaigne-Goyon, Paris, c. 1764, 1768–84. The choir and Chapelle de la Vierge were added behind the columns of the apse in 1846 by E.-H. Godde. The Chapelle des Catéchismes was added in 1853 by Victor Baltard.

Chapelle du St.-Esprit, 30 Rue Lhomond, Paris, 1768.

St.-Sulpice, Place St.-Sulpice, Paris, main doorway and organ loft, 1776; north tower, 1777; baptistery, 1780–88.

Collège de France, Place Marcelin Berthelot, Paris, 1780–84. Extended in 1831–42 by P.-M. Letarouilly.

Hôtel de Langéac, Rue de Berry, Paris. (H. C. Rice, *L'hotel de Langéac*, 1947.)

Pavillon de la Comtesse de Provence, Avenue de Paris, Versailles, 1781–84.

Hôtel des Écuries d'Artois, Versailles.

Palais du Luxembourg, Rue de Vaugirard, Paris, grand staircase, 1803–7.

Arc de Triomphe, Place de l'Étoile, Paris, 1806–36. After Chalgrin's death work was taken over by L. Goust, then by J.-N. Huyot, and finally by G.-A. Blouet, who added the attic to his own design.

Literature: C.-F. Viel, *Notice nécrologique sur J. F. T. Chalgrin*, Paris, 1814. A.-C. Quatremère de Quincy, *Notice sur Chalgrin*, Paris, 1816. M. Gallet, *Paris Domestic Architecture of the 18th Century*, London, 1972.

CHAMBERS, Sir William (Göteborg, 1723–London, 1796)

He was born in Sweden of Scottish parents. In the service of the Swedish East India Company from 1739 to 1749, he visited China and Bengal. He was a pupil of J.-F. Blondel in Paris from 1749 to 1750, after which he spent five years studying architecture in Italy. He gradually rose to the top of the architectural profession in England and was appointed Surveyor-General and Comptroller of the Works in 1782. He helped found the Royal Academy in 1768 and published *Designs of Chinese Buildings* (1757). *Treatise on Civil Architecture* (1759), and *Plans . . . of the Gardens and Buildings at Kew in Surrey* (1763).

Principal executed works:

Kew Palace, Surrey, gardens and garden buildings, 1757–62. (*Apollo*, Aug. 1963).

Casina, Marino (near Dublin), 1758–76.

Pembroke House, Whitehall, London, alterations, 1760, 1773–74. Demolished 1913.

Duddingstone (near Edinburgh), 1762–67.

Gower (Carrington) House, Whitehall, London, 1765–74. Demolished 1886.

Milton Abbey, Dorsetshire, 1769–75. (*Country Life* 139 [1966], pp. 1586, 1650, 1718; *Country Life* 140 [1966], pp. 152, 208.)

Somerset House, London, 1776–96. (*Country Life* 142, pp. 1248, 1340.)

Principal unexecuted projects:

Mausoleum for Frederick, Prince of Wales, 1751–52.

Harewood House, Yorkshire, 1756.

Literature: J. Harris, *Sir William Chambers*, 1970.

CLÉRISSEAU, Charles-Louis (Paris, 1722–Auteuil, 1820)

A pupil of Jacques-François Blondel and of G. Boffrand, Clérisseau won the Grand Prix in 1746 but reached Rome only toward the end of 1749. He remained there until 1754, when he turned north to Florence. There he encountered Robert Adam, for whom, and for whose brother James, he was later to serve as *cicerone*. He stayed in Italy for another eight years, measuring the ruins of Diocletian's palace at Split (Spalato), Dalmatia, on Robert Adam's account, and returned to France in 1767. Two years later he was made a member of the Académie Royale de Peinture et de Sculpture, the only architect in France, except for Charles de Wailly, who was to be thus honored. But though he produced thousands of drawings, for the most part of ruins, and did several notable designs—in particular, that for Father le Sueur's cell, painted to represent a ruined room, at S. Trinità dei Monti, Rome; those for the garden ruins of the Villa Farsetti, Sala, of 1767; and the salons in both the Parisian *hôtels* of Grimod de la Reynière—Clérisseau left little work of any real distinction, certainly not enough to sustain the reputation he enjoyed in his lifetime. He was admired by a great many connoisseurs in Italy and France. He was induced by the Adam brothers to travel in 1771 to England, where he worked for them until 1773. He was invited to Russia by Catherine the Great, who in 1781 purchased quantities of his drawings, and he was later consulted with considerable reverence by Thomas Jefferson, who had been much struck by the Maison Carrée at Nimes, illustrated in the only volume of Clérisseau's *Antiquités de la France* to appear, in 1778.

Principal executed works:

Ruin Room, S. Trinità dei Monti, Rome, designed c. 1765. (*Connoisseur* 149 [Apr. 1962], pp. 239–43.)

Hôtel Grimod de la Reynière, Rue Boissy-d'Anglas, Paris, salon, 1774 or 1775. Now in the Victoria and Albert Museum, London. (*Apollo*, Nov. 1963, pp. 377–83.)

Palais du Gouverneur (now Palais de Justice), Metz, 1776–89.

Literature: T. J. McCormick, "Virginia's Gallic Godfather," *Arts in Virginia* 4, no. 2 (1964), pp. 2–13. T. J. McCormick, "Charles-Louis Clérisseau and the Roman Revival," Ph.D. diss., Princeton University, 1971. T. J. McCormick, "Piranesi and Clérisseau's Vision of Classical Antiquity," in G. Brunel, ed., *Piranèse et les français*, Rome, 1978, pp. 303–14.

COCKERELL, Charles Robert (London, 1788–1863)

He was one of the most distinguished upholders of the classical tradition in nineteenth-century European architecture. He was a pupil of his father, S. P. Cockerell, and of Robert Smirke. He spent the years 1810–17 on an extended *grand tour*, during which he made important archaeological discoveries that he later published in *The Temples of Jupiter Panhellenius at Aegina, and of Apollo Epicurius at Bassae* (1860). In his architecture he early showed dissatisfaction with the Greek Revival and developed instead a richer but highly fastidious style in which Roman and Mannerist elements were grafted onto a Greek stem. He succeeded his father as surveyor to St. Paul's cathedral in 1819 and Sir John Soane as architect to the Bank of England in 1833. He did not train pupils in his office but educated a whole generation of architects through the brilliant lectures he delivered from 1841 to 1856 as professor at the Royal Academy, London.

Principal executed works:
Oakly Park, Shropshire, 1819–36. (*Country Life* 119 [1956], pp. 380–83, 486–89.)
Lough Crew, County Meath, 1820–25. Demolished 1960.
Hanover Chapel, Regent Street, London, 1821. Demolished 1896.
Holy Trinity, Hotwells, Bristol, 1828. Interior gutted 1940–41.
Cambridge University Library, 1837. Only the north wing was executed.
London and Westminster Bank, Lothbury, London, 1837. Demolished 1924.
Ashmolean Museum, Oxford, 1839–41. (*Country Life* 155 [1974], pp. 242–45.)
Sun Fire Office, Threadneedle Street, London, 1839–41. Demolished 1971.
Bank of England, Manchester, 1844.
Bank of England, Liverpool, 1844.
St. George's Hall, Liverpool, interiors, 1851–54.
Liverpool and London Insurance Company, Liverpool, 1855.

Principal unexecuted projects:
Palace for the Duke of Wellington, 1816.
University College, London, 1825.
National Gallery, London, 1833.
New Palace of Westminster, London, 1835.
Reform Club, Pall Mall, London, 1837.
Royal Exchange, London, 1839.
Carlton Club, Pall Mall, London, 1844.

Literature: S. P. Cockerell, ed., *Travels in Southern Europe and the Levant, 1810–1817: The Journal of C. R. Cockerell, R. A.,* 1903. J. Harris, "C. R. Cockerell's 'Iconographica Domestica,'" *Journal of the Society of Architectural Historians of Great Britain* 14 (1971), pp. 5–29. D. J. Watkin, *The Life and Work of C. R. Cockerell, R. A.,* 1974.

COCKERELL, Samuel Pepys (1753–London, 1827)

A pupil of Sir Robert Taylor, he became surveyor to the Admiralty, to the Foundling and Greenwich hospitals, to the Grafton and Pulteney estates, to the sees of Canterbury and London, to the East India Company, and to St. Paul's cathedral. He also found time to design some unusual country houses and churches and to train some well-known pupils, including Benjamin Latrobe, William Porden, and his son, C. R. Cockerell.

Principal executed works:
House for the First Lord of the Admiralty, Whitehall, London, 1786–91. (Viscount Cilcennin, *Admiralty House, Whitehall,* 1960.)
Daylesford House, Gloucestershire, 1788–93. (P. F. Norton, "Daylesford: S. P. Cockerell's Residence for Warren Hastings," *Journal of the Society of Architectural Historians* [U.S.A.], Oct. 1963.)
Church, Banbury, Oxfordshire, 1792–97.
Middleton Hall, Carmarthenshire, 1793–95. Demolished.
Nutwell Court, Devonshire, 1802.
St. Ann's, Soho, London, tower, 1802–6. (London County Council, *Survey of London* 33 [1966], pp. 262–64.)
Sezincote House, Gloucestershire, c. 1805. (*Country Life,* May 13–20, 1939.)

CONSTANT-DUFEUX, Simon-Claude (Paris, 1801–Paris, 1871)

He studied at the École des Beaux-Arts, Paris, under François Debret and also with L.-T.-J. Visconti, winning the Grand Prix in 1829. His most important building was his first and, indeed, his smallest, the École de Dessin, begun in 1842. This was to influence P.-F.-H. Labrouste when he came to design the Bibliothèque Ste.-Geneviève. Constant-Dufeux built little else; he won fame rather as a teacher, a *chef d'atelier,* beginning in 1836, and as *Professeur de Perspective* at the École des Beaux-Arts from 1845 onward. He propagated ideas on the symbolical role of architecture, to which he first gave expression in the tomb of Admiral Dumont d'Urville.

Principal executed works:
École de Dessin, 8 Rue Racine, Paris, 1841–44. Only the facade survives.
Tomb of Admiral Dumont d'Urville, Montparnasse cemetery, Paris, 1842–44.
Alcée-Billaud family tomb, Montmartre cemetery, Paris.
Hôtel, Rue de Vendôme, Paris.
Monument to Admiral de Brueys, Uzès, 1861.
St.-Laurent, Paris, west front, 1863–66.

Literature: P. Feraud, *Notice sur M. Constant-Dufeux,* Paris, n.d.

CONTANT D'IVRY, Pierre (Ivry-sur-Seine, 1698–Paris, 1777)

A pupil of Nicolas Dulin, he became a member of the Académie Royale d'Architecture in 1728. He was an important architect, vitally interested in problems of construction, but essentially representative of that period of transition between rococo and neoclassicism proper. He was architect to the Duc d'Orléans from 1752 to 1777.

Principal executed works:
Château de Bissy (near Vernon, Eure), stables, 1741–42.
Abbaye Royale de Penthémont, 106 Rue de Grenelle, Paris, 1747–56.
Abbaye St.-Vaast, Arras, 1750, 1754–. Completed in

the nineteenth century and rebuilt after World War II, the church is today the cathedral.
Saint-Vasnon, Condé-sur-l'Escaut, 1751.
Palais Royal, Paris, interiors and, in particular, the surviving grand staircase, 1756–70.
Madeleine, Paris, designed 1761. Work was begun in 1764 but halted at the time of the Revolution, and the building was altered by A.-P. Vignon into its present form.

Literature: M. Gallet, "Un modèle pour la Madeleine, d'après le projet de Contant d'Ivry," *Bulletin du Musée Carnavalet,* June 1965, pp. 14–19. M. Gallet, *Paris Domestic Architecture of the 18th Century,* London, 1972.

COOLEY, Thomas (1740–1784)

Originally apprenticed to a London carpenter, he was working by the 1760s as an assistant to Robert Mylne on the building of Blackfriars Bridge. From Mylne he acquired an up-to-date classicism in the tradition of Sir William Chambers, which he put to good use in his winning design for the Royal Exchange in Dublin. He subsequently set up practice in Dublin, where he helped give that city its new grandly classical aspect.

Principal executed works:
Royal Exchange (now City Hall), Dublin, 1769–79.
Hibernian Marine School, Dublin, 1770–73.
Newgate Prison, Dublin, 1773. Demolished.
Public Offices, Inns Quay, Dublin, 1779. Completed by James Gandon as the Four Courts.
Caledon Castle, County Tyrone, 1779. (*Country Life* 80, p. 324; *Country Life* 81, pp. 224–50.)
Cathedral, Armagh, tower.

Literature: M. Craig, *Dublin, 1660–1860,* 1952.

COQUART, Ernest-Georges (Paris, 1831–Paris, 1902)

A pupil of L.-H. Lebas at the École des Beaux-Arts, Paris, he won the Grand Prix in 1858. Thirty years later he consolidated his academic career by becoming a member of the Institut de France. He was a *chef d'atelier,* thus a careful and cautious architect expending much of his energy on refinements of detail. He worked for years under L.-J Duc at the Palais de Justice. He particularly enjoyed designing tombs and monuments, of which he did many: the tombs of Général Lecomte and Général Clément Thomas at the Père-Lachaise cemetery, Paris (1875); the Rougevin and Henri Regnault monuments at the École des Beaux-Arts, Paris (the latter in collaboration with J.-L. Pascal); the monument to the Battle of Coulmiers, at Coulmiers (1877); and the Crespel-Dellisse tomb in the cemetery at Arras.

Principal executed works:
Palais de Justice, Paris, Chambre Civile de la Cour de Cassation, 1880–90.
École des Beaux-Arts, Paris, Musée des Antiques et de la Renaissance, in the court of F.-J. Duban's first building, 1871–74.

Literature: E. Saint-Lanne, *Dictionnaire illustré des contem-*

porains, Paris, 1891. C. E. Curinier, *Dictionnaire national des contemporains*, Paris, 1899–1905. G. Larroumet and P. Dubois, *Funérailles de M. Coquart*, Paris, 1902.

CORROYER, Édouard-Jules (Amiens, 1835–Paris, 1904)

A pupil of E.-E. Viollet-le-Duc and of C.-A. Questel, he was early employed by both the Commission des Monuments Historiques and the Service des Édifices Diocésains. His most notable restorations were of the cathedral at Soissons and of the abbey of Mont Saint-Michel (1873–88), about which he was to publish no fewer than three books.

Principal executed works:
Casino, Vichy, 1862.
Château, Ain, 1868–69.
Hôtel de Ville, Roanne (Loire).
Church, Vouzy (Marne).
Church, Villers.
Church, St.-Cyr-les-Vignes (Marne).

Literature: C. E. Curinier, *Dictionnaire national des contemporains*, Paris, 1899–1905. A. Soubiès, *E. J. Corroyer, 1835–1904*, Paris, 1904.

DALY, César-Denis (Verdun, 1811–Paris, 1893)

He was the son of an English officer and spent his early years in England. Later a pupil of F.-J. Duban, he considered building a *phalanstère* along the lines suggested by F.-M.-C. Fourier and was proposed in 1843 by Flora Tristan as architect of a grand Palais de l'Union Ouvrière, but he was to build nothing of this kind. He restored the cathedral of Albi beginning in 1848, adding a balustrade of his own design. He was active above all as editor of the most influential of the French architectural periodicals, the *Revue générale de l'architecture*, begun in 1840, closed down in 1890, and a number of other sumptuous and somewhat vulgar architectural publications (*L'architecture privée au XIXᵉ siècle*, 8 vols., 1860–77; *Motifs historiques d'architecture et de sculpture d'ornement*, 4 vols., 1869–80; and *Architecture funéraire contemporaine*, 1871). In 1892 he was awarded the Gold Medal of the Royal Institute of British Architects.

Literature: *Journal of Proceedings of the Royal Institute of British Architects* 8 (1892), pp. 357–65. *Transactions of the Royal Institute of British Architects* 8 (1892), pp. 27–31. H. Lipstadt, "César Daly et l'habitation," *Architecture, mouvement, continuité*, no. 42, June 1977, pp. 37–40. H. Lipstadt, "Housing the Bourgeoisie," *Oppositions* 8 (1977), pp. 34–47. A. Lorenz Van Zanten, "Form and Society," *Oppositions* 8 (1977), pp. 136–45. H. Lipstadt, "César Daly: Revolutionary Architect?" *Architectural Design* 11–12 (1978), pp. 18–29.

DANCE, George, the younger (London, 1741–1825)

He was one of the most original, if eccentric, eighteenth-century architects. He was trained in Rome, Naples, Florence, and Parma from 1759 to 1764, and, on his return, he succeeded his father in 1768 as Clerk of the City Works, a position that put him in charge of official building in the City of London. A thoughtful, inward-looking designer, he was influenced by the theories of the Abbé Laugier and of the Picturesque, and also by the Greek and Gothic revivals, but his work was never merely eclectic since he was determined to reduce architecture to its elemental principles. This move toward a disembodied, reductionist style profoundly influenced his devoted pupil Sir John Soane. To C. R. Cockerell, Dance was "the most complete Poet Architect of his day."

Principal executed works:
All Hallows, London Wall, London, 1765–67.
Pitzhanger Manor, Ealing, 1768. Rebuilt 1800–1802 by J. Soane.
Newgate Gaol, London, 1768–80. Demolished 1902. (H. D. Kalmann, "Newgate Prison," *Journal of the Society of Architectural Historians of Great Britain* 12 [1969], pp. 5–61; J. Summerson, "Catalogue of Drawings of Newgate Gaol in Sir John Soane's Museum," *Journal of the Society of Architectural Historians of Great Britain* 2 [1959], pp. 41–49.)
Cranbury Park, Hampshire, additions and alterations, c. 1776. (*Country Life* 120, pp. 944, 1058, 1116.)
Guildhall, London, alterations and additions, 1777–79, 1787–89. Partly demolished.
Finsbury Square and Circus, London, 1779. Demolished.
Lansdowne House, Berkeley Square, London, library, 1788–91. Rebuilt. (*Country Life* 77 [1935], pp. 490–95; D. Stillman, "The Gallery of Lansdowne House," *Art Bulletin* 52 [1970], pp. 74–80.)
Stratton Park, Hampshire, rebuilding, 1803–6. Demolished 1961, except for the portico.
Coleorton House, Leicestershire, 1804–8.
Royal College of Surgeons, Lincoln's Inn Fields, London, 1804–13. Rebuilt 1835–37. (*Country Life*, July 10, 1961.)
Laxton Hall, Northamptonshire, remodeling, 1812.
Ashburnham Place, Sussex, 1813–17. Demolished 1959. (*Country Life* 113, pp. 1158, 1246, 1334.)

Principal unexecuted projects:
Camden Estate, St. Pancras, London, 1780s.
Crescent, St. George's Fields, Southwark, London, 1786.
Port of London, 1796–1800.
No. 6 St. James's Square, after 1815.

Literature: D. Stroud, *George Dance, Architect (1741–1825)*, 1971.

DAUMET, Pierre-Gérôme-Honoré (Paris, 1826–Paris, 1911)

A pupil of Saint-Père, Trouillet, G.-A. Blouet, and E.-J. Gilbert, he won the Grand Prix in 1855. From Rome he traveled to Greece with J.-A.-E. Vaudremer in 1858 and again in 1862 with Léon Heuzey, returning to Paris in the same year to become a *chef d'atelier*. He continued to teach until 1894. He worked notably with L.-J. Duc at the Palais de Justice, Paris, from 1867 on; later, in succession to F.-J. Duban, at the Château de Chantilly; and later still as successor to Paul Abadie

at the Sacré-Coeur, Paris. He also restored the Château de St.-Germain-en-Laye. An altogether competent and able designer—as his interiors at Chantilly so eloquently demonstrate—he was nonetheless an architect of no great originality. He worked late in his life for Leopold II of Belgium at the Palais Royal, Brussels, at the Château de Laeken, and on Leopold's estate in the south of France.

Principal executed works:
Ecce Homo sanctuary, Jerusalem.
Faculté du Droit, des Sciences, et des Lettres, Grenoble.
Château, Chantilly, 1875–82.
Palais de Justice, Paris, with L.-J. Duc. Daumet's chief contribution was the Cour d'Appel, begun 1879.
Palais de Justice, Grenoble, 1890–97 (chiefly a work of restoration).
Chapelle du Pensionnat des Dames de Sion, Paris.
Château de Perreuse, Jouarre (Seine-et-Marne).

Literature: M. d'Espouy, "Daumet," *L'architecture*, 1912, p. 17. C. Girault, *Notes sur la vie et les oeuvres de Honoré Daumet*, Paris, 1919.

DAVIOUD, Gabriel-Jean-Antoine (Paris, 1823–Paris, 1881)

He studied first at the École de Dessin, Paris, with A.-M.-F. Jay, then with Léon Vaudoyer at the École des Beaux-Arts He did not win the Grand Prix but began working for Victor Baltard and was soon to have an extremely active and prestigious career, working largely for the Haussmann administration in the Service des Promenades et Plantations de Paris, to which he was appointed chief architect in 1857. He laid out innumerable squares and parks. By 1872 he had become *Inspecteur Général des Travaux de la Ville de Paris*.

Principal executed works:
Bois de Boulogne, Paris, lodges and minor buildings, 1855–59. (T. Vacquet and A. Alphand, *Le Bois de Boulogne architectural*, Paris, 1860.)
Panorama, Champs-Élysées, Paris, 1857.
Fontaine St.-Michel, Paris, 1858–60.
Parc Monceau, Paris, 1860–62. His most notable contributions were the richly decorated gateways.
Théâtre du Châtelet and Théâtre Lyrique (now Théâtre de la Ville), Place du Châtelet, Paris, 1860–62. (C. Daly and J. Davioud, *Les théâtres du Place du Châtelet*, 1874.)
Magasins-Réunis, Place de la République, Paris, 1865–67.
Parc des Buttes-Chaumont, Paris, lodges, garden buildings, and restaurants, 1864–67.
Parc Montsouris, Paris, lodges and decorative buildings, 1867–68.
Fontaine de l'Observatoire, Paris, 1870–75.
Fontaine, Place du Théâtre-Français, Paris, 1872–74.
Palais du Trocadéro, Paris, 1876–78, with J.-D. Bourdais. Demolished.
Mairie du XIXᵉ, Paris, 1876–78, with J.-D. Bourdais.

Literature: Destors, "Notice sur la vie et les oeuvres de G. Davioud," in *Bulletin de la Société Centrale des Architectes*, Paris, 1881. J. Bourdais, "Gabriel Davioud," *Encyclopédie d'architecture* 10 (1881), p. 35ff.

DEANE AND WOODWARD

Woodward was the most important figure in this partnership, the history of which is as follows: Sir Thomas Deane (1792–1871), of Cork, set up a partnership with Benjamin Woodward (1815–1861) and also, about 1850, with his son, Sir Thomas Newenham Deane (1828–1899). The younger Deane, in turn, formed a partnership with his son, Thomas Manly Deane, in 1878; their work was mainly done in Ireland. The most important building associated with the firm of Deane and Woodward is the Oxford Museum, muscular Gothic outside, amazing iron and glass within. The profuse sculptural oramentation is the result of Woodward's enthusiasm for John Ruskin.

Principal executed works:
Museum, Trinity College, Dublin, 1852–57. By Deane and Woodward. (*Country Life,* May 6 and 20, 1976.)
University Museum, Oxford, 1854–60. By Sir T. Deane, Son, and Woodward. (P. Ferriday, "The Oxford Museum," *Architectural Review* [London] 132 [1962], pp. 408–16.)
Crown Life Office, New Bridge Street, Blackfriars, London, 1855. By Deane and Woodward. Demolished.
Llys Dulas, Anglesey, 1856. By Woodward.
Union Buildings, St. Michael's Street, Oxford, 1857. By Woodward.
Kildare Street Club, Dublin, 1858.
Middleton Hall, St. Giles's Street. Oxford, north range, c. 1858. By Woodward.
Picture Gallery, Kilkenny Castle, Ireland, 1859–62. By Deane and Woodward.
St. Hilda's College, Oxford, north range, 1862. By Deane and Woodward.
Meadow Building, Christ Church, Oxford, 1862–64. By T. N. Deane.
Crown Life Office, Fleet Street, London, 1866. By T. Deane. Demolished.
Pitt Rivers Museum, Oxford, 1885–86. By T. N. and T. M. Deane.

DEBRET, François (Paris, 1777–St.-Cloud, 1850)

A pupil of Charles Percier, he succeeded Jacques Cellerier in 1813 as architect to the restoration of St.-Denis, a task he pursued during the following years with neither tact nor skill, so that in 1846 the north tower had to be taken down. His post there was taken over by E.-E. Viollet-le-Duc. Debret preferred the Italianate mode, which he developed with surprising exuberance during the 1820s in his theater facades and with more restraint at the École des Beaux-Arts, Paris. He began the École in 1822, completing the Bâtiment des Loges in 1828, before he was succeeded, in 1832, by his brother-in-law, F.-J. Duban.

Principal executed works:
Théâtre Louvois, Paris. Demolished.
Théâtre des Nouveautés, Place de la Bourse, Paris. Demolished.
Opéra, Rue Grange Batelière (now Drouot), Paris, 1820–21. Demolished.
École des Beaux-Arts, Rue Bonaparte, Paris, Bâtiment des Loges, 1822–28.

DEGLANE, Henri-Adolphe-Auguste (Paris, 1855–1931)

A pupil of Jules André, he won the Grand Prix in 1881 and served, very properly, as an administrative architect and a *chef d'atelier* beginning in 1890. His most notable work was the architectural shell of the Grand Palais, Paris, for the Exposition Universelle of 1900. The grand internal halls and flamboyant stairs of the building behind were designed by Louis-Albert Louvet.

DELESPINE, Pierre-Jules-Nicolas (Paris, 1756–Paris, 1825)

The son and grandson of architects, he built little of interest or importance. He was responsible for the markets of the Blancs-Manteaux, 1813, and of St.-Gervais, 1822–23, the latter begun by E.-E. de Labarre. In 1824 he was appointed professor at the École des Beaux-Arts, Paris.

DEVEY, George (London, 1820–Hastings, 1886)

He enjoyed one of the busiest practices in country houses of the nineteenth century. Unlike his principal rival, R. N. Shaw, he did not publicize his buildings, and his patrons were chiefly aristocrats and bankers. He was a pupil of the watercolorists J. D. Harding and J. S. Cotman, who developed his appreciation of vernacular architecture and the English rural scene. His (very large) country houses are in the Old English, or Manorial, style, which, with W. E. Nesfield and Shaw, he pioneered.

Principal executed works:
Betteshanger, Kent, 1856–82.
Coombe Warren, Surrey, c. 1865–70.
Brantingham Thorpe, Yorkshire, 1868–72.
Broomford Manor, Devonshire, c. 1870–71.
Denne Hill, Kent, 1871–75.
Hall Place, Kent, 1871–76.
Goldings, Hertfordshire, 1871–77.
St. Alban's Court, Kent, 1874–78.
Ascott, Buckinghamshire, 1874–88. (*Country Life* 108 [1950], p. 826.)
Durdans, Surrey, c. 1875.
Killarney House, County Kerry, 1877–80. Demolished.
Knowle Park, Surrey, 1882–83.
41 Grosvenor Square, London, 1884–85.
Melbury House, Dorsetshire, 1885–86.

Literature: W. H. Godfrey, "The Work of George Devey," *Architectural Review* (London) 21 (1907), pp. 23, 83, 293. W. H. Godfrey, "George Devey, F. R. I. B. A.," *Journal of the Royal Institute of British Architects* 13 (1906), p. 501. M. Girouard, "George Devey in Kent," *Country Life,* Apr. 1–8, 1971.

DIEDO, Antonio (Venice, 1772–1847)

He was a pupil, assistant, and successor to G. Selva—and his most faithful follower. He collaborated with Cicognara and Zanotto on the *Descrizione della fabbriche più cospicue di Venezia.*

Principal executed works:
Palazzo Giustiniani-Recanati, Venice, facade.
S. Maurizio, Venice, in succession to G. Selva.
S. Nome di Gesù, Venice, in succession to G. Selva.
Church, Schio, 1805–20.
Duomo, Cologna Veneta, 1810–17, in succession to G. Selva; it is likely, however, that he was in part responsible for the design.
Church, Cenda, Polsine.

Literature: E. Bassi, *Giannantonio Selva, architetto veneziano,* Florence, 1935. E. Bassi, *Architettura del sei e settecento a Venezia,* Naples, 1962.

DIET, Arthur-Stanislas (Amboise, 1827–Paris, 1890)

He studied first under Hérard, then, for two years, with Alphonse Durand. In 1846 he entered the École des Beaux-Arts, Paris, studying in the *atelier* of F.-J. Duban and later, when he began work on the Louvre, with G.-A. Blouet, winning the Grand Prix in 1853 with a design for a museum. He stayed no more than a few months in Rome, returning to marry the daughter of E.-J. Gilbert. He began his career by completing the museum at Amiens (the staircase, however, is his alone) and continued in much the same fashion with the lunatic asylum at Charenton and the Hôtel-Dieu (after 1867) and the Préfecture de la Police (after 1869) in Paris, all designed and begun by his father-in-law. As a result of this exacting and dull activity, he rose to the position of *Architecte en Chef de la Ville de Paris.* In 1879 he became *Inspecteur Général* of the Conseil des Bâtiments Civils. At Sèvres he built a small house for himself and his family.

Literature: A. Normand, *Notice sur la vie et les travaux de Diet,* Paris, 1892.

DOBSON, John (Chirton, Northumberland, 1787–Newcastle upon Tyne, 1865)

He was a pupil of the Newcastle architect David Stephenson and of the London watercolorist John Varley. He quickly became the leading architect of Durham and Northumberland, at home in both Greek and Gothic styles. He was also interested in engineering, as is borne out by his Newcastle Central Railway Station. His practice was enormous, and he executed churches, town-planning projects, and public buildings as well as the austerely classical country houses for which he is probably best known.

Principal executed works:
Eldon Square, Newcastle, 1824–26.
Longhirst, Northumberland, 1824–28.
Nunnykirk, Northumberland, 1825.
St. Thomas, Newcastle, 1825.
Lilburn Tower, Northumberland, 1828–43. (*Country Life,* Nov. 8, 1973.)
Meldon Park, Northumberland, 1832.
Grey Street, Newcastle, 1835–39.
Beaufront Castle, Northumberland, 1836–42. (*Country Life,* Feb. 5 and 12, 1976.)
Railway station, Newcastle, 1846–50.

Literature: L. Wilkes and G. Dodds, *Tyneside Classical:*

The Newcastle of Grainger, Dobson and Clayton, 1964. M. Girouard, "Longhirst, Meldon and Nunnykirk," *Country Life*, Feb. 17 and 24, 1966.

DONTHORN, William John (Swaffham, Norfolk, 1799–Hastings, 1859)

A pupil of Sir Jeffry Wyatville from 1817 to 1820, Donthorn is a little-known architect who worked in an exceptionally chaste and spare style derived from George Dance, the younger, and Sir John Soane, which offers a parallel to the outline techniques of the artists A. J. Carstens and John Flaxman. His principal surviving work in this vein is probably High House, West Acre, Norfolk, but his Highcliffe Castle, Hampshire, shows that he had learnt from Wyatville how to handle Gothic Picturesquely, on an asymmetrical plan.

Principal executed works:
Hillington Hall, Norfolk, 1823–31. Demolished c. 1946.
High House, West Acre, Norfolk, 1829.
Elmham Hall, Norfolk, c. 1830. Demolished 1924.
Highcliffe Castle, Hampshire, 1830–34. (*Country Life* 91, pp. 806, 854, 902.)
Bure Homage, Hampshire, c. 1835. Demolished 1956.
Heronden Hall, Kent, 1846.

Literature: Royal Institute of British Architects, *Drawings Catalogue (C–F)*, London, 1972.

DRESSER, Christopher (Glasgow, 1834–Mulhouse, 1904)

He studied at the Government, School of Design in Somerset House, London, but was for many years active and famous as a botanist rather than as a designer. In 1860 he was awarded an honorary doctoral degree by the University of Jena, "in consideration of the services he has rendered to botanical science." But in 1856 he prepared a plate illustrating a geometrical arrangement of flowers for Owen Jones's *Grammar of Ornament* and in the following year began a series of articles for the *Art Journal* on the adaptation of natural forms for ornamental design. In 1859 he published both *The Rudiments of Botany* and *Unity in Design. The Art of Decorative Design* followed three years later. Soon he was busy not only writing articles and books—the most sumptuous was *Studies in Design*, of 1874—but also producing designs of all kinds for manufacturers and traders. He was probably the highest-paid designer in Britain. In 1877 he spent four months in Japan, where he bought quantities of "objects for ordinary domestic use," and two years later started a business with Charles Holme to import such articles into England. His account of his visit, *Japan: Its Architecture, Art and Art Manufacturers*, was issued in 1882.

Literature: N. Pevsner, "Christopher Dresser, Industrial Designer," *Architectural Review* (London), Apr. 1937, pp. 183–86. S. Durant, *Christopher Dresser, 1834–1904*, exhib. cat., Fine Art Society, Ltd., London, 1972. C. Dresser, *The Principles of Decorative Design*, ed. S. Durant, London, 1973.

DUBAN, Félix-Jacques (Paris, 1797–Bordeaux, 1870)

He intended to become a writer, but his sister had married François Debret, for whom he began to work. He then enrolled at the École des Beaux-Arts, Paris, where he studied under Charles Percier and won the Grand Prix in 1823. He was of the progressive generation of P.-F.-H. Labrouste, L.-J. Duc, and Léon Vaudoyer, and on his return to France he attempted to initiate a reform in architecture. But he delighted in rich and intricate decoration and surface pattern, and his contribution lay rather in his skill in combining and coordinating the classical and Italianate heritages than in any new approach to design. His greatest building was the École des Beaux-Arts, off the Rue Bonaparte, Paris, which he took over from Debret in 1832. He was responsible for much else besides, chiefly of a decorative nature, but late in life, in the Bâtiment de la Salle Melpomène, at the École des Beaux-Arts, he showed that he could design in a grand, monumental manner. He directed the restoration of the Ste.-Chapelle, the Louvre, and the châteaux of Blois and Fontainebleau.

Principal executed works:
Palais des Études, École des Beaux-Arts, Rue Bonaparte, Paris, 1832–58. Duban laid out the forecourt with, fragments remaining from Alexandre Lenoir's Musée des Monuments Français. The internal court was roofed over in 1871–74 by E.-G. Coquart in accordance with a design made by Duban in 1863.
Hôtel Pourtalès, 7 Rue Tronchet, Paris, 1836. The interiors were much enriched between 1865 and 1873 by Hippolyte Destailleur.
Château, Chantilly, interiors, 1840–48. Taken over later by P.-G.-H. Daumet.
Hôtel Galliéra, Paris.
Château de Dampierre (near Rambouillet), decoration of interiors, in particular the Salle de la Minerve, the setting for J.-D. Ingres's painting *L'Age d'Or*, 1840–.
Louvre, Paris, Galerie d'Apollon, Salon Carré, Salle des Sept-Cheminées, and facade along the Seine, 1848–52.
Bâtiment de la Salle Melpomène, École des Beaux-Arts, Quai Malaquais, Paris, 1860–62.
Château de Chalay (Loire-et-Cher).
Château de Sandat (Lot-et-Garonne).

Literature: L. Vaudoyer, *Discours à l'enterrement de Duban*, Paris, 1870. C. Daly, "Funérailles de Félix Duban," *Revue générale de l'architecture* 28, p. 199 ff. C.-A. Questel, "Notice sur M. Duban," Paris, 1872. Beulé, *Éloge de Duban*, Paris, 1872. *Catalogue de l'exposition des dessins de Félix-Jacques Duban*, Paris, 1872.

DUC, Louis-Joseph (Paris, 1802–Paris, 1879)

At the age of nineteen he enrolled at the École des Beaux-Arts, Paris, where he worked under Charles Percier and A. M. Châtillon. In 1825 he won the Grand Prix. Upon his return from Rome, where he was in close contact with P.-F.-H. Labrouste and Léon Vaudoyer, he began work on J.-A. Alavoine's July Column, on the Place de la Bastille, Paris, but his greatest work was the Palais de Justice, Paris, which occupied him for years, and on which he was to be associated with a number of architects, though the Salle des Pas Perdus, or Vestibule des Assises, on the Rue de Harlay, is his alone and won for him the most extravagant praise from his contemporaries, including E.-E. Viollet-le-Duc.

Principal executed works:
July Column, Place de la Bastille, Paris, 1831–40. J. A. Alavoine, who had begun this, died in 1834, after which the design was greatly altered.
Palais de Justice, Paris, 1840–70. Many architects were involved in this project. The Salle des Pas Perdus, on the Rue de Harlay, is Duc's special contribution. Begun in 1857, it was more or less completed by 1868 but was damaged by the Commune and rebuilt and altered internally thereafter.
Lycée Michelet, Rue Julien, Vanves, Paris, 1862–.
Château, Biarritz, 1870–71, with L.-F. Roux.

Literature: H. Delaborde, *La vie et les ouvrages de M. Duc*, Paris, 1879. P. Sédille, "J.-L. Duc," *Encyclopédie d'architecture*, 1879, p. 65 ff. J.-L. Pascal, "Duc," *Gazette des beaux-arts*, 1879, p. 430 ff. Cernesson, "Louis Duc," *Revue générale de l'architecture* 37 (1880), pp. 75 ff., 150 ff.

DUFOURNY, Léon (Paris, 1754–Paris, 1818)

A pupil of J.-D. Le Roy and of Peyre, he traveled in 1782 to Italy, where he was to stay for more than ten years, chiefly in Palermo. There, between 1789 and 1792, he built the Villa Giulia in the botanical gardens, and it served to establish the neoclassical style in Sicily. In 1803 he became professor in succession to Le Roy at the École Imperiale d'Architecture, Paris, and in 1805 he was made a corresponding member of the Institut de France.

Literature: A.-C. Quatremère de Quincy, "Notice historique sur la vie et les ouvrages de M. Dufourny," *Recueil des notices historiques lues dans les séances publiques de l'Académie Royale des Beaux-Arts*, Paris, 1834, p. 201.

DUMONT, Gabriel-Pierre-Martin (Paris, 1720–Paris, 1791)

He won the Grand Prix in 1737 but did not travel to Rome until 1742. There he was to spend many years, accompanying J.-G. Soufflot on his journey to Paestum in 1750 and publishing their observations in 1764 as *Suite de plans . . . de trois temples . . . de Paestum*. This was soon plagiarized in England and in Holland. Dumont published much else besides: *Détails des plus intéressantes parties d'architecture de la basilique de St. Pierre de Rome*, of 1763; *Recueil de plusieurs parties de l'architecture sacrée et profane de différents maîtres*, of 1764–67, which contained plates by J.-L. Legeay and others with whom Dumont was associated in Rome; and *Parallèles des plans des plus belles salles de spectacles d'Italie et de France*, which was first issued in 1764 or 1765, but ran into three subsequent revised editions.

Literature: M. Gallet, *Paris Domestic Architecture of the 18th Century*, London, 1972.

DURAND, Hippolyte-Louis (Paris, 1809–1881)

A pupil of L.-H. Lebas and of Vaudoyer at the École des Beaux-Arts, Paris, Durand turned early to the study of Gothic architecture, submitting designs in this style at the Salons beginning in 1845. In 1849 he became architect to the Service des Édifices Diocésains in the departments of Basses-Pyrénées and Gers, and it was there that he was chiefly active, designing and altering a number of churches, among them St.-Jacques at Tartas, begun in 1849; St.-André at Bayonne, begun in 1856, in collaboration with Hippolyte Guichenne of that city; and Notre-Dame at Lourdes, completed in 1872. The most noteworthy, however, was his first church, that of St.-Martin at Peyrehorade (Landes), the subject of much discussion at the Conseil Général des Bâtiments Civils. It was sketched first in 1846 but begun only six years later and completed in December 1857. With Guichenne he also built the Hôtel de Ville at Peyrehorade (1865, 1868–, enlarged 1890–92).

DURAND, Jean-Nicolas-Louis (Paris, 1760–Thiais [Seine-et-Marne], 1834)

He studied first with Pierre Panseron and then, at the age of sixteen, he entered E.-L. Boullée's office, a step that enabled him to attend the Académie Royale d'Architecture, where he was awarded the second Grand Prix in 1779 and in 1780. His first independent work, the Hôtel Lathuile, dates from those years. But he was to build little else. During the post-Revolutionary period he entered eleven competitions with J.-T. Thibault for grand, monumental buildings proposed by the Convention and won four of these, but saw none of them built. In 1795 he was made professor at the École Centrale des Travaux Publics, which soon after became the École Polytechnique, and there he taught until 1830. His famous books, the *Recueil et parallèle des édifices de tout genre anciens et modernes* (1800), the *Précis des leçons d'architecture données à l'École royale polytechnique* (1802–5), and the *Partie graphique des cours d'architecture faits à l'École royale polytechnique* (1821), were the outcome of his teaching and served to disseminate his rigid and most restricted doctrines throughout France; indeed, throughout Europe—in Germany in particular.

Principal executed works:
Hôtel Lathuile, Rue du Faubourg Poissonnière, Paris, 1779–80.
Lermina House, Chézy (near Lagny).
Laplace House, Thiais.
House, 39 Rue Maurepas, Thiais.

Literature: J. M. Pérouse de Montclos, *Étienne-Louis Boullée: de l'architecture classique à l'architecture révolutionnaire*, Paris, 1969, pp. 214–16. M. Gallet, *Paris Domestic Architecture of the 18th Century*, London, 1972. W. Szambien, "Das Landhaus des Jean-Nicolas-Louis Durand (1760–1834) in Thiais," *Architectura* 8 (1978), pp. 73–87.

DUTHOIT, Edmond-Armand-Marie (Amiens, 1837–1889)

Descended from a long line of masons and stone carvers originally from Lille but settled from 1796 onward in Amiens, he was trained as a mason. In this capacity he was early employed by E.-E. Viollet-le-Duc, who was commissioned in 1849 to restore the cathedral at Amiens. In 1857 Duthoit moved to Paris to study in Viollet-le-Duc's *atelier* and then to work in his office, but his first independent commission came from his father and uncle, Aimé and Louis Duthoit, who were restoring the church and abbey of St.-Riquier (Somme). For the Chapelle du Petit Séminaire Duthoit designed a magnificent altar and ciborium in 1860. In the following year he went, on Viollet-le-Duc's recommendation, to Cyprus and Syria with William Henry Waddington and the Comte de Vogüé and produced most of the measured drawings and views in the Comte de Vogüé's publications *Le temple de Jerusalem* (1864–65) and *Syrie centrale: architecture civile et religieuse du Ier au VIIe siècle* (1865–77). While on the expedition he designed two churches in Beirut. Late in 1862 Duthoit returned to Paris and took up work once again with Viollet-le-Duc, supervising the restoration, enlargement, and decoration of three of his most notable châteaux, Roquetaillade, d'Arragori (d'Abbadia), and Chamousset, each of which he in time took over from Viollet-le-Duc as designer. In 1865 Duthoit traveled once again to Cyprus and Asia Minor. In 1866 he was appointed *Inspecteur* by the Commission des Monuments Historiques for the Somme and Oise departments, restoring the cathedral at Senlis (1866, 1885), the churches at Bertaucourt-les-Dames (1875) and Mogueville (1875), and St.-Étienne at Beauvais (1885). He returned in 1870 to Amiens and there established a modest practice, consisting largely of designing tombstones but also including several commissions for churches, the most spectacular of which was the pilgrimage church at Albert, in which he demonstrated to an extraordinary and colorful degree that a love of Gothic could be combined with a taste for Early Christian, Byzantine, and Arab architecture, all of which he saw as interrelated. In 1872 he was chosen by the Commission des Monuments Historiques to prepare a report on the antiquities of Algeria, and from then until his death he spent three to six months of each year excavating and restoring the Roman and Arab remains in Algeria and Tunisia for the Commission.

Principal executed works:
Church for the Orphelinat Français, Beirut, 1862–65. Altered in execution.
Church of the Capuchins, Beirut, 1862–65.
Château de Roquetaillade (Gironde), 1864–70, 1875–77. Begun by E.-E. Viollet-le-Duc, who was responsible for the exterior, the stair hall, and dining room. Duthoit's bedrooms, complete with furnishings, date from 1868–69, his chapel from 1875–77. (*Connaissance des Arts*, May 1971.)
Château d'Arragori (d'Abbadia), Bidassoa, near Hendaye (Basses-Pyrénées), 1864–79, begun with Viollet-le-Duc. Duthoit's furnishings date from 1869–79, his chapel from 1876–79.
Fountain, Neuilly-Saint-Front (Aisne), c. 1867.
Church, Champeaux (Deux-Sèvres), c. 1878.
Church, Bryas (Pas-de-Calais), 1880–84.
Church, Souverain-Moulin (Pas-de-Calais), c. 1883.

Notre-Dame-de-Brebières, Albert (Somme), 1883, 1884–97. Completed by Henri Bernard and Louis Duthoit. Rebuilt to the original design after World War I.

Literature: Edmond Duthoit architecte, 1837–1889, Amiens, 1890. P. Foucart, *L'hôtel Bouctot-Vaguiez et son architecte Louis Duthoit*, Amiens, 1978. B. Bergdoll, "The Architecture of E. A. M. Duthoit," B.A. diss., University of Cambridge, 1979.

EHRENSVÄRD, Carl August (1745–Örebro, 1800)

He was taught drawing from 1763 to 1765 but adopted a naval career and became, like his father, an admiral. He was in Italy between 1780 and 1782, and there he was much impressed by the masculinity of the Doric architecture of Paestum. He imitated this in his unexecuted projects for a monument in the Gustav Adolf Square, Stockholm (1782), and for a dockyard gate at Karlskrona (1785). In 1795 he built a copy of the Athenian Temple of Hephaestus at Mälby.

Literature: F. Josephson, *Carl August Ehrensvärd*, Stockholm, 1963. H. Frykenstedt, *Carl August Ehrensvärd (1745–1800): An Original Swedish Aesthetician and an Early Functionalist*, Uppsala, 1965. H. Frykenstedt, *Studier in Carl August Ehrensvärds författarskap*, Uppsala, 1965.

ELMES, Harvey Lonsdale (Oving, Sussex, 1814–Jamaica, B.W.I., 1847)

He was trained by his father, James Elmes (1782–1862), a minor London architect. In 1841 he unexpectedly produced plans for what was to be one of the finest public buildings of nineteenth-century Europe, St. George's Hall, Liverpool. In 1839–40 Elmes had won two competitions for a concert hall and assize courts at Liverpool. His final design for St. George's Hall was prepared as a consequence of the City Corporation's decision to unite the two functions in a single building. Though he had never visited Greece or Italy he "was able to conceive a building . . . combining the refinement of Greek detail with the scale of Imperial Rome" (Colvin, *Biographical Dictionary*). St. George's Hall was his only work of consequence. After his premature death, it was completed by Rawlinson and C. R. Cockerell.

Literature: R. P. Jones, "The Life and Work of Harvey Lonsdale Elmes," *Architectural Review* (London) 15 (1904), p. 231.

ENGEL, Johann Carl Ludwig (Berlin, 1778–1840)

He studied at the school of architecture in his native city. In 1816 he moved to Helsinki and became the most important town planner and architect in Finland. In Helsinki he laid out the Senate Square (begun 1818), with its Senate (1818–22), University (1828–32), cathedral (1830–51), and University Library (1833–45).

Literature: C. Meissner, *Carl Ludwig Engel*, 1937. N. E.

Wickberg, *Engel*, exhib. cat., Berlin, 1970.

ERDMANNSDORFF, Friedrich Wilhelm, Freiherr von (Dresden, 1736–Dessau, 1800)

He introduced into Germany, following his first visit to England, in 1763, fashionable mid-eighteenth-century English architecture, decoration, and garden design. In 1765–66 he traveled in Italy with his principal patron, Herzog Franz von Anhalt-Dessau. There he met Giambattista Piranesi, C.-L. Clérisseau, J. J. Winckelmann, and Sir William Hamilton. The outcome of these experiences was Schloss Wörlitz (1769–73), designed for Anhalt-Dessau. Inspired by Sir William Chambers, by Robert Adam, and by Robert Wood's *Ruins of Palmyra*, it also contained English furniture and chimneypieces after designs by Piranesi. The Picturesque landscaped park was dotted with garden buildings by Erdmannsdorff, including a copy of the island-tomb of J.-J. Rousseau at Ermenonville. In 1794 a Greek Doric Temple of Venus, a pantheon, and the Stein Pavilion, with remarkable interior decoration in a revived Etruscan mode, were added. Erdmannsdorff's elegant style was soon superseded in Germany by the Franco-Prussian style of Friedrich Gilly. His later buildings at Dessau and the interiors he remodeled in the Berliner Schloss have all been destroyed.

Principal executed works (all in East Germany):
Schloss, Dessau, remodeling of interiors, 1767–68.
Schloss Wörlitz (near Dessau), 1769–73; garden buildings, 1775–96.
Schloss Luisium (near Dessau), 1774. Demolished.
Schlosstheater, Dessau, 1777. Demolished.
Schloss Georgium (near Dessau), 1780. Demolished.
Berliner Schloss, remodeling of interiors for Friedrich Wilhelm II, 1787. Demolished.
Stables and riding school, Dessau, 1790. Demolished.

Literature: E. P. Riesenfeld, *Erdmannsdorff*, Berlin, 1913.

ESPÉRANDIEU, Henri-Jacques (Nîmes, 1829–Marseilles, 1874)

He worked first for C.-A. Questel at Nîmes, entered the École des Beaux-Arts in 1847 as a pupil of Léon Vaudoyer, and then, from 1855 on, worked for Vaudoyer at Marseilles, where he was in charge of the cathedral works. All Espérandieu's major and most conspicuous buildings are in Marseilles. Though a Protestant, he was commissioned to design Notre-Dame-de-la-Garde.

Principal executed works:
Notre-Dame-de-la-Garde, Marseilles, 1853–64.
École des Beaux-Arts and Bibliothèque Municipale, Rue de la Bibliothèque, Marseilles, 1862–69.
Palais de Longchamp, Jardin Zoologique, Marseilles, 1862–69. This was based on a design by the sculptor Frédéric-Auguste Bartholdi. (H.-J. Espérandieu, *Palais de Longchamp*, 1869.)
Château de Pharo, 1867–.

Literature: E. Reinaud, *H. Espérandieu et le palais de Longchamp*, 1905.

FONTAINE, Pierre-François-Léonard (Pontoise, 1762–Paris, 1853)

The son of an architect, he was sent to work at L'Isle-Adam under André but soon after went to Paris to study at the *atelier* of A.-F. Peyre. There he met Charles Percier, who was to be his lifelong partner. At the Académie Royale d'Architecture, they had different masters: Percier was the pupil of J.-D. Le Roy, Fontaine of François Heurtier. Fontaine won the second Grand Prix in 1785, the main prize being withheld from him because it was thought that his superb drawing might encourage those who followed him to concentrate on presentation alone. He determined nonetheless to go to Rome and was awarded a pension at the Académie in 1786. Percier won the Grand Prix in that year. Fontaine returned to Paris, on foot, in 1790, Percier in the following year. They set up in business together and within ten years had established a fashionable practice. In 1801 they published their influential *Recueil de décorations intérieures*. The fruit of their Italian studies, the *Palais, maisons, et autres édifices modernes dessinés à Rome* and *Choix des plus célèbres maisons de plaisance de Rome et de ses environs*, appeared in 1798 and 1809, respectively. In 1800 they began to work at the Château de Malmaison for Josephine, and though they were to quarrel with the empress as to the nature of the garden layout, the success of their interiors there won Napoleon's attention. In 1801 they were appointed his official architects. They refurbished and redecorated the Tuileries and the Louvre, they built the Rue de Rivoli and the Arc du Carrousel. Throughout Europe they were responsible for preparing residences for him and his representatives. On the Colline de Chaillot they planned a vast palace for his son, the Roi de Rome, and on the opposite bank of the Seine they laid out an even grander quarter with a university and other official buildings, some of which were begun. They were the most powerful and influential architects in France in the early years of the nineteenth century. Many of the Grand Prix winners of that period were taught by them—or rather, by Percier, for he was chiefly responsible for the conduct of the *atelier* they opened in 1791. Fontaine lived long enough to build for the Orléans dynasty, but the work for which the two men became famous was all done for Napoleon. Percier and Fontaine were buried, together with Bernier, a friend of their Roman years, in the same tomb in the Père-Lachaise cemetery. Not one of them had married—in accord with a pact they had made in Rome.

Principal executed works:
Hôtel Chauvelin, Rue Chantereine, Paris, 1799.
Château de Malmaison (Rueil-Malmaison), interiors, 1800–1802.
Tuileries, Paris, interiors, 1801–. Destroyed 1870.
Rue de Rivoli, Paris, 1801–.
Arc du Carrousel, Paris, 1806.
Louvre, Paris, interiors, 1808–.
Palais du Roi de Rome, Colline de Chaillot, Paris, 1811–. Never completed.
Palais des Archives, Palais de l'Université, École des Beaux-Arts, etc., Quai d'Orsay, Paris, 1812–. Never completed.

Literature: M. L. Biver, *Pierre Fontaine, premier architecte de l'Empéreur*, Paris, 1964.

FRÉZIER, Amédée-François (Chambéry, 1682–Brest, 1773)

He moved early from Savoie to Paris, where he studied first theology and then mathematics under La Hire and Varignon at the Collège de France. He traveled during this period to Italy and in 1705 published his *Traité des feux d'artifice pour le spectacle* (revised in 1747). In 1707 he enrolled in the Corps de Génie and remained in that employ until he retired in 1764. He was sent in 1711 on a mission to South America to appraise the strength of the Spanish fortifications there, visiting Brazil, Chile, Bolivia, and Peru (in particular, the antiquities of Cuzco). He disembarked at Marseilles in 1714. In 1719 he was sent to Santo Domingo, where he stayed for nine years, laying out the town and building up the fortifications. On his return to France he was posted for a short time to Phalsbourg, then to Landau, where he remained for ten years. There he put up one significant building, the military hospital, in 1732–37, and there he wrote his great works on construction and architectural theory, the *Théorie et pratique de la coupe des pierres . . .; ou, traité de stéréotomie à l'usage de l'architecture*, of 1738–39, and the *Dissertation sur les ordres d'architecture*, of 1738. In 1740 he became *Directeur des Fortifications* in Britanny. He worked in Brest, drawing up many projects, mostly not to be built, but he was responsible for the completion of the church of St.-Louis to Garangeau's designs, and he himself designed the baldachino for the high altar, using four antique columns shipped from Leptis Magna (1742–58). This was all destroyed in World War II. For Jacques-François Blondel's school in Paris he wrote a simplified and shortened version of his famous treatise, *Éléments de stéréotomie*, published in 1760. But he impinged on the world of architectural theorists even more strongly through his attacks in the *Mémoires de Trévoux* and the *Mercure de France* on the writings of J.-L. de Cordemoy and the Abbé Laugier.

Literature: P. du Colombier, "Amédée-François Frézier," in *Festschrift für Karl Lohmeyer*, ed. K. Schwingel, Saarbrücken, 1954, pp. 159–66.

GABRIEL, Ange-Jacques (Paris, 1698–Paris, 1782)

He was the son of Jacques Gabriel V, *Premier Architecte du Roi*, by whom he was trained and to whose post he succeeded in 1742. He became at the same time *Directeur de l'Académie d'Architecture*. He worked for the king and the court alone, expending a great deal of his energy on administrative work, minor and even major alterations to the royal palaces, *grands projets* for Versailles and Compiègne, etc., but he also found time to build a number of beautifully detailed and proportioned works, some among the finest of the century.

Principal executed works:
Salle de l'Opéra, Versailles, 1748–70. (*Revue de l'art*, no. 13, 1971, pp. 87–97.)

Ermitage de Mme. de Pompadour, Château de Fontainebleau, 1749.
Gros-Pavillon, Château de Fontainebleau, 1751.
Château de Compiègne, 1751–64.
École Militaire, Paris, 1751–88. (R. Laulan, *L'École Militaire de Paris*, 1950.)
St.-Hubert (a hunting lodge near Versailles), 1755–57.
Place Louis XV (now Place de la Concorde), Paris, 1755–75. (S. Granet, *La place de la Concorde*, 1963.)
Petit Trianon, Versailles, 1761, 1762, 1764–68.
Suite (Petits Appartements) for Mme. du Barry, Versailles, 1770.
Cour de Marbre, Versailles, reconstruction, 1772–73. (C. Tadgell, "Gabriel's Grands Projets," *Architectural Review* [London], 1974, pp. 155–64.)

Literature: Comte de Fels, *Ange-Jacques Gabriel, premier architecte du roi*, Paris, 1924. Y. Bottineau, *L'art d'Ange-Jacques Gabriel à Fontainebleau (1735–1774)*, Paris, 1962. M. Gallet, *Paris Domestic Architecture of the 18th Century*, London, 1972. C. Tadgell, *Ange-Jacques Gabriel*, London, 1978.

GANDON, James (London, 1743–Lucan [near Dublin], 1823)

A pupil of Sir William Chambers, he settled in 1781 in Dublin, where he became the leading architect and worked in a style of French-inspired classicism. In stamping Dublin with the mark of classical magnificence, he completed the work begun by Thomas Cooley.

Principal executed works:
County Hall and prison, Nottingham, 1770–72.
Custom House, Dublin, 1781–91. Gutted 1921.
Parliament House (now Bank of Ireland), Dublin, additions, 1785–89.
Four Courts, Dublin, 1786–1802. Gutted 1922.
Emo Park, County Laoighis, c. 1790–1800. (*Country Life*, May 23 and 30, 1974.)

Literature: J. Gandon, Jr., and T. J. Mulvany, *The Life of James Gandon*, Dublin, 1846 (repr. London, 1969, ed. M. Craig). M. Craig, *Dublin, 1660–1860*, 1952.

GANDY, Joseph Michael (London, 1771–London, 1843)

He was Sir John Soane's draftsman and is best known for the watercolors depicting Piranesian architectural fantasies that he exhibited at the Royal Academy from 1789 to 1838. In 1805 he published two volumes of designs for vernacular architecture, *The Rural Architect and Designs for Cottages . . .*, in a stark and totally different vein. His most interesting buildings are Storrs Hall, Westmorland (1808), and Doric House, Sion Hill, Bath (c. 1810), both in the Greek Doric style.

Literature: "The Vision of J. M. Gandy," in J. Summerson, *Heavenly Mansions, and Other Essays on Architecture*, London, 1949, pp. 111–34.

GARNIER, Jean-Louis-Charles (Paris, 1825–Paris, 1898)

He had the humblest of beginnings but moved from the office of Demoyencourt to the *atelier* of Leveil and then to that of L.-H. Lebas, and thus to the École des Beaux-Arts, where he won the Grand Prix in 1848. He traveled to Rome and to Athens and then to Constantinople. In 1862 he won the competition for the design of the new Opéra in Paris, his most splendid and successful work, which was to occupy him until 1875 and even later. This building, more than any other, may be said to have set the style of the Second Empire, though it was not much to the liking of Napoleon III, and was visited by him only in 1862, when he laid the foundation stone. But the Opéra, together with Garnier's other great work of celebration, the Casino at Monte Carlo, was taken to represent all that was most fashionable in France in the late nineteenth century and was imitated throughout the world. Garnier commemorated his achievement in the superbly illustrated volumes of *Le nouvel Opéra de Paris*, 1878–81.

Principal executed works:
Opéra, Place de l'Opéra, Paris, 1862–75.
Magasin de Décors de l'Opéra, Boulevard Berthier, Paris.
Villa Garnier, Bordighera, 1872.
Casino, Monte Carlo, 1878–79. Extended to the east in 1898 by Schmit.
Cercle de la Librairie, 117 Boulevard St.-Germain, Paris, 1878–79.
Maison Hachette, 195 Boulevard St.-Germain, Paris, 1882.
Casino, Vittel, 1882. Demolished.
Panorama de Balaklava, Champs-Élysées, Paris, 1883. Transformed in 1894 into the Théâtre Marigny.
Panorama Français, 251 Rue St.-Honoré, Paris. Reconstructed in 1884 as the Nouveau Cirque. Demolished.
Church, La Capelle-en-Thiérache (Aisne).
Observatory, Nice.
Villa Sarcey, Rosendaele (Nord).
Villa Bishchoffsheim, Bordighera. (*L'oeil*, Jan.–Feb. 1977.)
Church and school, Bordighera.

Literature: G. Larroumet, *Notice historique sur la vie et les travaux de M. Charles Garnier*, Paris, 1899 (also in *L'architecture* 12 [1899], pp. 421, 429). J.-L. Pascal, *Charles Garnier*, Paris, 1899 (also in *L'architecture* 12 [1899], pp. 245, 257). F. Jourdain, "Charles Garnier," *Musica*, Oct. 1904. A. Laprade, *Charles Garnier et l'Opéra*, exhib. cat., Paris, 1961. M. Steinhauser, *Der Architektur der Pariser Oper*, Munich, 1969.

GAU, Franz Christian (Cologne, 1790–Paris, 1854)

A pupil of François Debret and of L.-H. Lebas, he attended the École des Beaux-Arts, Paris, but did not win the Grand Prix. However, in 1815 he traveled to Italy, where he measured the Vatican and soon published the result of these studies. He then went to Egypt, publishing afterward, in 1823, *Antiquités de la Nubie; ou, monuments inédits des bords du Nil*. Back in Italy, he took up the completion of François Mazois's work on the ruins of Pompeii. He returned to France to enroll in the architecture department of the city of Paris, beginning work in 1827 with the design of the presbytery of St.-Séverin, then taking on the restoration of St.-Julien-le-Pauvre and the completion of the church of St.-Sacrement. Between 1831 and 1844 he also served as architect to the prison and hospital administrations of Paris, erecting new buildings for the Bicêtre between 1831 and 1835. His most famous and controversial building was the mock-Gothic church of Ste.-Clotilde in Paris, completed by Théodore Ballu.

Principal executed works:
Mairie du IIe, 8 Rue de la Banque, Paris, 1846–49. Completed by Victor Baltard.
Ste.-Clotilde, Square Ste.-Clotilde, Paris, 1846–57. Completed by Théodore Ballu.

Literature: J.-I. Hittorff, *Discours sur la tombe de Gau*, 1854.

GAUTHEY, Émiliand-Marie (Chalon-sur-Saône, 1732–Paris, 1808)

After completing his schooling he went to Versailles to study mathematics with his uncle and then to Paris to study architecture with G.-P.-M. Dumont. He began teaching at the École des Ponts et Chaussées, at the same time attending J.-R. Perronet's courses. In 1758 he became *Sous-Ingénieur* to Burgundy and was charged with preparing a design for a system of canals. At first he built roads but soon he was building the canal linking the Saône and the Loire and working on other equally ambitious canal projects, in particular, the Canal du Centre. In 1782 he became *Ingénieur en Chef* to Burgundy. In 1792 he moved to Paris as *Inspecteur Général des Ponts et Chaussées*. His close connection with the building of Ste.-Geneviève in Paris began in 1770, when he took up J.-G. Soufflot's defense, writing memoirs to refute Pierre Patte's attacks and building a machine to measure the resistance of stones. The small church he built at Givry-sur-Saône, begun in 1770, was designed as a test model for Ste.-Geneviève. At this period he built the gateway that served as a town hall at Givry-sur-Saône. His best-known building is the town hall at Tournus.

Principal executed works:
Church, Givry-sur-Saône, 1770–91.
Hôtel de Ville, Givry-sur-Saône, 1770–.
Hotel de Ville, Tournus, 1774–77.
Palais des États, Dijon, north wing, 1776–80.
Theater, Chalon-sur-Saône, 1778–84. An earlier project was drawn up in 1769.
Château, Chagny, 1780.
Immeuble des Mines de Blanzy, Chalon-sur-Saône.

Principal unexecuted projects:
Church, Chagny.
Church, Louhans, 1785.
Reconstruction of the Abbaye de Cluny.

Literature: M. Navier, ed., *Oeuvres de M. Gauthey*, Paris, 1809–16. F. de Dartein, "La vie et les travaux de Émiliand Gauthey," *Études sur les ponts en pierre . . .*, vol. 4, 1909, pp. 1–89.

GAY, Victor

Virtually nothing is known of him, though he is recorded as architect of St.-Sulpice-les-Feuilles, near Arnac (Haute-Vienne), designed in 1846 and later, a church in the Gothic style conceived as a frame construction. During 1846 he exhibited at the Salon a sketch for a chapel at Nanterre. Later he designed church furnishings that were considered to be of some quality.

GENTZ, Heinrich (Breslau, 1766–Berlin, 1811)

He was taught by the artist A. J. Carstens and later, in the 1780s, by the architect Karl von Gontard at the Berlin Academy. He visited the Greek buildings of Italy and Sicily and, on his return to Berlin in 1795, was made Inspector of Royal Buildings. In 1798 he became professor at the Berlin School of Architecture. He pioneered in the introduction of Greek Doric architecture into Germany, and his style is close to that of his partner and brother-in-law, Friedrich Gilly.

Principal executed works:
Mint, Berlin, 1798–1800. Demolished 1886.
Schloss Ziebingen, c. 1800.
Schloss Weimar, interiors, 1801–4.

Literature: A. Doebber, *Heinrich Gentz*, Berlin, 1916.

GILBERT, Émile-Jacques (Paris, 1793–Paris. 1874)

He was one of the very few architects of importance trained by J.-N.-L. Durand at the École Polytechnique, Paris. He entered that school in 1811 but transferred two years later to the École des Beaux-Arts. where he worked under Vignon. In 1822 he won the Grand Prix. His stern rationalism strongly influenced such men of his generation as G.-A. Blouet, P.-F.-H. Labrouste, L.-J. Duc, and Léon Vaudoyer. He sought to restore to architecture those life-giving qualities which he felt the fashionable practice of Percier and Fontaine and their host of disciples and imitators had drained from it; he wished it to have a moral and social purpose. His whole career was devoted to the design of buildings in which the human condition was most degraded: hospitals, prisons, and asylums. His soberness of outlook survived even into the late nineteenth century in the works of such men as J.-A.-E. Vaudremer, the most gifted of his pupils.

Principal executed works:
La Nouvelle Force (prison), Mazas, Paris, 1836, 1843–50, designed with J.-F.-J. Lecointe.
Asile d'Aliénés (lunatic asylum), Charenton (near Paris), 1838–45. Completed by his son-in-law, A.-S. Diet.
Morgue, Pont St.-Michel, Île de la Cité, Paris, 1861–63. Demolished.
Préfecture de la Police, Paris, 1862–76. Completed by his son-in-law, A.-S. Diet.
Hôtel-Dieu, Place du Parvis Notre-Dame, Paris, 1864–76. Completed and altered by his son-in-law, A.-S. Diet.

Literature: P. Abadie, *Notice sur Gilbert*, Paris, 1874. L. Cernesson, *Émile Gilbert, sa vie et ses oeuvres*, Paris, 1875.

GILLY, Friedrich (Stettin, 1772–Karlsbad, Czechoslovakia, 1800)

He was a pupil of his father, David Gilly, and of C. G. Langhans, Friedrich Becherer, and F. W. von Erdmannsdorff at the Berlin Academy. His visionary schemes, particularly his monument to Frederick the Great, of 1797, inspired a whole generation of German architects, icluding K. F. Schinkel and Leo von Klenze. The Francophile tendencies already evident in his Frederick the Great Monument were heightened by his visit in 1797–98 to Paris, where he particularly admired F.-J. Bélanger's Pavillon de Bagatelle and J.-G. Legrand's Théâtre Feydeau. He was partner and brother-in-law of the architect Heinrich Gentz.

Principal projects, both unexecuted:
Monument to Frederick the Great, Berlin, 1797.
Prussian National Theater, Berlin, 1798.

Literature: A. Oncken, *Friedrich Gilly*, Berlin, 1935. A. Rietdorf, *Gilly*, Berlin, 1943. "Description de Bagatelle," *L'oeil*, June 1965.

GINAIN, Paul-René-Léon (Paris, 1825–Paris, 1898)

A pupil of L.-H. Lebas, he won the Grand Prix in 1852. In Italy he did a restoration study of the Greek theater at Taormina and pursued the academic path through life, becoming a *chef d'atelier* at the École des Beaux-Arts, Paris, and, in 1881, a member of the Institut de France. The building for which he is, and always was, most admired, the École de Médecine in the Boulevard St.-Germain, is a perfect example of the refined *néo-grec* style favored in Paris at the end of the nineteenth century.

Principal executed works:
Notre-Dame-des-Champs, 91 Boulevard du Montparnasse, Paris, 1867–76.
Clinique d'Accouchement, 89 Rue d'Assas, Paris, 1877–80.
Musée Galliéra, 10 Avenue Pierre I de Serbie, Paris, 1878–88.
École de Médecine, Boulevard St.-Germain, Paris, 1878–1900.
Hospice Ferrari-Galliéra, Clamart (Seine), 1886.

Literature: G. Larroumet, *Funérailles de M. L. Ginain*, 1898.

GINGELL, William Bruce (1819–1900)

He was articled to a firm of Bath architects and set up practice in Bristol with T. Royse Lysaght. He became architect to the West of England and South Wales District (later Lloyd's) Bank. He also developed an industrial side to his practice, designing breweries, factories, and warehouses in a powerful, arcuated manner halfway between K. F. Schinkel's Rundbogenstil and H. H. Richardson's Romanesque. His obituary in *The Builder* (June 2, 1900, p. 548) lists the following industrial premises, all in Bristol: Messrs. E. S. & A. Robinson's Redcliff Street works; Bristol United Breweries; Messrs. W. J. Rogers, Ltd., brewery; Messrs. Champion & Co.'s works; Messrs. J. Robinson &

Co.'s mill, Bathurst Wharf. Professor H. R. Hitchcock has attributed the following buildings in Bristol to him: the warehouse at 12 Temple Street (c. 1855); Messrs. Simonds's brewery, between Old Market Street and Jacob Street (c. 1865).

Principal executed works (all in Bristol):
Bristol General Hospital, Cumberland Road, 1853–57.
West of England and South Wales District (now Lloyd's) Bank, Corn Street, 1854–58.
National Provincial Bank, Corn Street, 1864.

GISORS, Alexandre-Jean-Baptiste-Guy de (Paris, 1762–Paris, 1835)

He studied at the school of the Académie Royale d'Architecture, Paris, where he was a pupil of J.-F.-T. Chalgrin. He did not win the Grand Prix. He began his career as an *Inspecteur* at the Palais Bourbon, where Jacques-Pierre de Gisors, probably his cousin, was commissioned by the Directory to design the Salle des Cinq-Cents, a commission he himself was to take over. The Conseil des Cinq-Cents was replaced and there was much changing of responsibilities, but A.-J.-B.-G. de Gisors eventually took over the work of refurbishing and redecorating (he was later replaced by Bernard Poyet). Gisors went on to pursue a successful official career, becoming *Inspecteur Général des Bâtiments Civils*. His one important building, which he hoped would serve as a model, was the basilican church of St.-Vincent at Mâcon, designed in 1807, built between 1808 and 1816 (cf. A. Morgand, *Ann. Acad. Mâcon*, p. 36, 1942–43, pp. 145–52).

Literature: E. Joyant, "Les Gisors architectes," *Bulletin de la Société de l'Histoire de l'Art Français*, 1937, pp. 270–93. B. Foucart and V. Noël-Bouton, "Les projets d'église pour Napoléonville (1802–1809) de Guy de Chabrol à Guy de Gisors," *Bulletin de la Société de l'Histoire de l'Art Français*, Année 1971, pp. 235–58.

GISORS, Alphonse-Henri de (Paris, 1796–Paris, 1866)

The nephew of A.-J.-B.-G. de Gisors, he was a pupil of Charles Percier at the École Royale d'Architecture, Paris, from 1814 until he entered the employ, in 1817, of the Conseil Général des Bâtiments Civils. By 1824 he had been promoted to architect and soon began work on the École de Médecine and carried out similar projects of maintenance and extension. In 1834, however, he was appointed to design the Chambre des Pairs in the Palais du Luxembourg, where he at once set up a temporary assembly hall, the scene of the anarchist Fieschi's attack. In 1836 he began a new assembly room, totally eclipsing the Salle du Sénat installed by Chalgrin in 1804. This was completed by the beginning of 1841. He also refashioned Chalgrin's grand staircase and rebuilt much of the garden front of the palace. He commemorated his achievement in a slight monograph, *Le palais du Luxembourg*, of 1847.

Literature: E. Joyant, "Les Gisors architectes," *Bulletin de la Société de l'Histoire de l'Art Français*, 1937, pp. 270–96.

GISORS, Jacques-Pierre de (1755–Paris, 1818)

He studied first with Guillaumot, then with E.-L. Boullée, and won the Grand Prix in 1779. He stayed in Rome for no more than a few months in 1780. He settled in Paris, where he evidently built a number of houses and prepared several projects of the large-scale kind then fashionable. In 1793 he designed the assembly room for the Convention in the Tuileries, assisted by E.-C. Leconte. Charles Percier was also working for him during this period. Between 1795 and 1797 he built the hall for the Conseil des Cinq-Cents in the Palais-Bourbon. A.-J.-B.-G. de Gisors served as his *Inspecteur* here (under Napoleon he was to supersede Jacques-Pierre as architect at the Palais-Bourbon). Little is known of his later career, though beginning in 1811 he worked for the Conseil Général des Bâtiments Civils and was responsible for the design and layout of several *abattoirs* around Paris.

Literature: E. Joyant, "Les Gisors architectes," *Bulletin de la Société de l'Histoire de l'Art Français*, 1937, pp. 270–93.

GODDE, Étienne-Hippolyte (Breteuil-sur-Oise, 1781–Paris, 1869)

A pupil of C.-M. Delagardette, he worked with Jacques Molinos in the architecture department of the city of Paris, gradually rising through the administrative hierarchy, until he was in charge of the erection, restoration, and extension of all churches within the city. His ministrations to the Gothic churches were later judged to have been disastrous. His own designs were rigid, and formal in the manner of St.-Philippe-du-Roule, which, incidentally, he also enlarged with slight understanding.

Principal executed works:
Séminaire de St.-Sulpice (now Contributions Indirectes), Place St.-Sulpice, Paris, 1820–38.
St.-Pierre-du-Gros-Caillou, 92 Rue St.-Dominique, Paris, 1822–30.
Notre-Dame-de-Bonne-Nouvelle, 25 bis Rue de la Lune, Paris, 1823–30.
St.-Denys-du-St.-Sacrement, 68 bis Rue de Turenne, Paris, 1826–29, formally consecrated 1835.
Chapel, Père-Lachaise cemetery, Paris, 1834.

GONDOIN, Jacques (St.-Omer, 1737–Paris, 1818)

His father was a royal gardener. He studied with Jacques-François Blondel and, though in 1758 he was awarded only the second Grand Prix, he was sent by the king to Italy, where he was a *pensionnaire* from 1761 to 1763. In 1766 he traveled to Holland and England. He worked at the Garde-Meubles de la Couronne beginning in 1767 and in 1769 became *Dessinateur du Mobilier de la Couronne*. This was to be his chief occupation. But he also designed one building of supreme importance in the history of French architecture of the late eighteenth century, the École de Chirurgie, commemorated in his *Description des Écoles de Chirurgie*, of 1780. He later returned to Italy and while there attempted to buy the site of Hadrian's Villa.

Principal executed works:
École de Chirurgie (now École de Médecine), Rue de l'École de Médecine, Paris, 1769–75. (*L'architecture*, May 15, 1934.)
Villa des Eaux-Vives, near Melun, on the banks of the Seine, completed c. 1795.
Colonne Vendôme, Place Vendôme, Paris, 1806–10, with L.-B. Lepère.

Literature: A.-C. Quatremère de Quincy, "*Notice historique sur M. Gondoin,*" Académie des Beaux-Arts, Paris, 1821. M. Gallet, *Paris Domestic Architecture of the 18th Century*, London, 1972. S. Eriksen, *Early Neo-Classicism in France*, London, 1974, p. 186.

GOUT, Paul-Émile-Antoine (Paris, 1852–1923)

He studied at the École des Beaux-Arts, Paris, under J.-C. Laisné, then with J.-E.-A. de Baudot, and was drawn thus into the Commission des Monuments Historiques and the Service des Édifices Diocésains, for which he was to do much restoration work. He was early connected with E.-E. Viollet-le-Duc and his son, becoming an editor of the *Encyclopédie d'architecture* and later, in 1914, writing Viollet-le-Duc's biography. He built much on his own account; especially notable are his schools in Paris, and in particular the magnificent Lycée Racine, 20 Rue du Rocher, of 1891 (extended in 1906).

GUADET, Julien-Azais (Bordeaux, 1834–Paris, 1908)

A pupil of P.-F.-H. Labrouste and of Jules André, Guadet was the ringleader of the opposition to the reforms instigated at the École des Beaux-Arts in 1863 by E.-E. Viollet-le-Duc. He had been excluded as a candidate for the Grand Prix by the imposition of a new age limit. In the following year Viollet-le-Duc and his friends changed this regulation and awarded Guadet the Grand Prix, but they were never to win his friendship or his respect. He worked later for Charles Garnier on the Opéra. He practiced as an architect, and his Hôtel des Postes was held in some esteem, but he won fame as a teacher, as a *chef d'atelier*, and as *Professeur de Théorie de l'Architecture* at the École des Beaux-Arts. His theories are contained in *Éléments et théorie de l'architecture*, of 1901–4.

Principal executed works:
Hôtel des Postes, 52 Rue du Louvre, Paris, 1880.
Théâtre-Français, Palais-Royal, Paris, reconstruction.
Apartment house, 240 bis Boulevard St.-Germain, Paris.

Literature: J.-L. Pascal, *Notice sur la vie et les ouvrages de J. Guadet*, Paris, 1910 (repr. from his *Éléments et théorie de l'architecture*, 4th ed., Paris, 1909, and *L'architecture* 21 [1908], p. 253). J. Guadet, "Souvenirs de 1863," in *Recueil publié à l'occasion de la millième adhésion à la Société des Architectes Diplomés par le Gouvernement*, Paris, 1911. S. Kuthy, "Julien Guadet et l'enseignement d'architecture," in *Architecture, mouvement, continuité*, no. 16 (Société des Architectes Diplomés par le Gouvernement, no. 176), Feb. 1970, pp. 26–32.

GUÉRIN, Gustave

The son of an architect at Tours, Charles-Mathias Guérin. He worked first on the restoration of the cathedral in that town. He won his small renown in 1844, when he was commissioned to design the church of St.-Étienne there. The difficulties this involved and the research he undertook, together with his brother Charles Victor, into the niceties of Gothic construction formed the subject of several articles in the *Révue générale de l'architecture* and comments in the *Annales archéologiques*. Building was not begun until 1869. By then Guérin had built his only other work of importance, Ste.-Anne, at Lariche Extra, Tours (1855–).

HAMILTON, Thomas (Glasgow, 1784–Edinburgh, 1858)

He was a pupil of his father, an Edinburgh carpenter and builder. He became the leading architect in his native city, and his many Greek Revival buildings transformed it into the "Athens of the North."

Principal executed works:
Royal High School, Edinburgh, 1825–29.
George IV Bridge and Johnson Terrace, Edinburgh, 1827.
Arthur Lodge, Edinburgh, 1827–30 (attributed).
Assembly Rooms, Ayr, 1827–30.
Burns Monument, Edinburgh, 1830.
Dean Orphanage, Edinburgh, 1833–36.
Royal College of Physicians, Edinburgh, 1844–46.

Principal unexecuted project:
National Gallery, Edinburgh, 1848–50.

Literature: A. J. Youngson, *The Making of Classical Edinburgh, 1750–1840*, Edinburgh, 1966. A. Rowan, "Georgian Edinburgh," *Country Life* 142 (1967), pp. 956, 1052.

HANSEN, Christian Frederik (Copenhagen, 1756–1845)

The principal neoclassical architect of Denmark, he studied at the Academy of Fine Arts in Copenhagen from 1766 to 1769 and in Italy from 1782 to 1784. He was appointed Royal Inspector of Buildings for Holstein in 1783 and Chief Inspector of Buildings in 1808. He built up a large domestic practice in Altona from 1783 to 1808. In 1803 he began to rebuild the town hall, courthouse, and prison in Copenhagen and later the Christansborg Palace. His principal building was the Vor Frue Kirke (Cathedral Church of Our Lady), Copenhagen (designed 1808–10, built 1811–29).

Literature: W. Jakstein, *Landesbaumeister Christian Friederich Hansen der nordische Klassizist*, Neumünster, 1937. *Christian Hansen*, exhib. cat., Altona, 1968.

HANSEN, Theophilos Eduard (Copenhagen, 1813–Vienna, 1891)

Like his elder brother Hans Christian (1803–1883), he studied at the Academy of Fine Arts, Copenhagen, under Gustav F. Hetsch, winning a bursary in 1838 that enabled him to travel through Germany and north Italy and on to Greece, where his brother was already active building the new University of Athens, which T. E. Hansen was to take over. In Athens, thanks to the support of Édouard Schaubert, he was awarded the commission for the new observatory, and he also built a house for Antonio Dimitrios, which later became the Hôtel Grande Bretagne. Even more important for his future career was an encounter with the editor of the *Allgemeine Bauzeitung*, Ludwig Förster, whose daughter Sophie he was to marry in 1850. Förster invited him to Vienna, where they worked together and where Hansen's reputation was made. He arrived in 1846, entered several competitions, and put up an array of small buildings. The first of note was the war museum, begun in 1856, of brick with an admixture of terra-cotta and glazed ceramics, all compounded together in something of a Byzantine style—one that he was to take up again and again, most notably for the Greek church in Vienna. But he became known for his great buildings in the classical taste, ranging from a heavy-handed Italianate to the more refined "griechischen Renaissance" of his grandest and most opulent work, the Reichsrathsgebäude, in Vienna. During the last years of his life he was eagerly consulted—for such buildings as the town hall of Copenhagen and Hamburg, the royal palace at Corfu, and, in Berlin, the Reichstag (1882) and the Museuminsel (1884–86).

Principal executed works:
University, Athens, 1837, 1839–49, begun by H. C. Hansen.
Observatory, Athens, 1839–49.
A. Dimetrion House, Syntagma Square, Athens, 1842–43. Demolished.
Villa Pandchoulitseff, Traunkirchen-am-Traunsee, 1852.
Chapel, Protestant cemetery, Vienna, 1856–58.
Waffensmuseum (a war museum), Artillerie-Arsenal, Vienna, 1856–60.
Greek church, Fleischmarkt, Vienna, 1858.
Academy, Athens, 1859, 1861–87.
National Library, Athens, 1859, 1885, 1888–91.
Palast Sina, Hohen Markt, Vienna, 1859–60.
Villa Genthon, Vevay.
Villa Kratzer, Oberdöbling, Vienna.
Todesco House, Vienna, with L. Förster.
Haus der Gesellschaft der Musikfreunde, Karlsplatz, Vienna, 1864–69.
Palast des Deutschordensmeisters, Parkring, Vienna, 1868.
Palast Epstein, Burgring, Vienna, 1870–73.
Palast Ephrussi, Schottengasse, Vienna, 1872–73.
Akademie der Bildenden Künste, Vienna, 1872–76.
Borse, Schottenring, Vienna, 1873–77.
Reichsrathsgebäude, Vienna, 1873–83.

Literature: G. Niemann and F. V. Feldegg, *Theophilos Hansen und seine Werke*, Vienna, 1893.

HARRISON, Thomas (Richmond, Surrey, 1744–Chester, 1829)

He had no formal architectural training but from 1769 to 1776 was in Rome, where he produced designs for improving the Piazza del Popolo that show he had absorbed the vocabulary of international neoclassicism. On his return he worked chiefly in northwest England. His Greek Revival buildings with their beautifully handled masonry prompted C. R. Cockerell to say of him, "He has a spark divine."

Principal executed works:
Chester Castle, 1785–1822.
Lancaster Castle, Lancashire, remodeling, 1786–99.
Broomhall, Fife, 1796. (*Country Life*, Jan. 29, 1970.)
Lyceum, Liverpool, 1800–1803.
Portico Library, Manchester, 1802–6.
Watergate House, Chester, 1820.
Grosvenor Bridge, Chester, 1827–32.

Principal unexecuted projects:
Cortile del Belvedere, Vatican, Rome, remodeling as a museum, 1770.
Piazza del Popolo, Rome, alterations, 1773.
New sacristy, St. Peter's, Rome, 1774.

Literature: J. M. Crook, "The Architecture of Thomas Harrison," *Country Life* 149 (1971), pp. 876–79, 944–47, 1088–91, 1539.

HARSDORFF, Caspar Frederik (Copenhagen, 1735–1799)

He was taught at the Academy of Fine Arts in Copenhagen by N.-H. Jardin. He traveled in France and Italy for six years, from 1756 to 1762, during which time he was taught by Jacques-François Blondel in Paris. He was appointed Inspector of Buildings in Copenhagen in 1764, professor at the academy in 1766, and Royal Inspector of Buildings in 1770. His elegant French style can be admired in his Frederikskirke, Copenhagen, in the royal mortuary chapels in Roskilde cathedral, and in his town houses in Copenhagen.

Literature: F. Weilbach, *Architekten C. F. Harsdorff*, Copenhagen, 1928.

HÉRET, Louis-Jean-Antoine (Paris, 1821–Paris, 1899)

He trained under Denise and then, beginning in 1844, with L.-H. Lebas at the École des Beaux-Arts, Paris, and pursued an active career building chiefly schools and asylums. His only work of significance is the church of Notre-Dame-de-la-Croix, Ménilmontant, Paris, designed in a thirteenth-century Gothic manner (1863–80).

Literature: *L'architecture* 12 (1899), p. 89.

HITTORFF, Jacques-Ignace (Cologne, 1792–Paris, 1867)

He crossed the Rhine to study in Paris under Charles Percier at the École des Beaux-Arts and then with F.-J.

Bélanger, who at that time was working on the Abattoir de Rochechouart and in charge of court fêtes and spectacles. Hittorff succeeded him in the latter activity in 1818. But in 1822 he traveled to Italy, where he met Thomas Leverton Donaldson, who first stirred his interest in the new notion that ancient Greek architecture may have been colored. Hittorff then journeyed to Sicily, where he found traces of color on a temple at Selinunte. He at once initiated a campaign, culminating in his *Restitution du temple d'Empédocle à Selinonte; ou, l'architecture polychrome chez les grecs* (1846–51), to propagate the notion that Greek temples had been colored overall with yellow paint and the moldings and sculptural details picked out in brilliant reds, blues, greens, and gold. A celebrated controversy ensued. This was Hittorff's only real claim to fame, but he built extensively, too, chiefly in Paris, where he clashed with Baron Haussmann and the church authorities alike when he tried to implement his notions of an updated polychromy at the church of St.-Vincent-de-Paul, begun by his fatherin-law, J.-B. Lepère. Hittorff's grandest work was his last, the Gare du Nord, which bears witness to the curious duality in all his architecture: an intense and adventurous interest in structural and technical innovation coupled with a slack and diffuse application of ornamental motifs.

Principal executed works:
Théâtre de l'Ambigu Comique, Boulevard St.-Martin and Rue René Boulanger, Paris, 1827–28, designed with J.-F.-J. Lecointe. Demolished 1966.
St.-Vincent-de-Paul, Place Lafayette (now Place Franz Liszt), Paris, begun 1824 by J.-B. Lepère, taken over and revised by Hittorff 1830–46. (H. Doisy, *La paroisse et l'église Saint Vincent de Paul*, Paris, 1942.)
Place de la Concorde, Paris, rebuilding, 1836–40. A.-J. Gabriel's layout was almost effaced: The moats were filled and the obelisk, fountains, and lamp standards introduced.
Champs-Élysées, Paris, embellishments, 1836–40. Hittorff's major contribution, the street furniture and the five fountains apart, was the reconstruction of the Ambassadeurs and Ledoyen restaurants, the Alcazar d'Été, the Pavillon Guillamin Laurent, the Rotonde des Panoramas (1838–39), and the Cirque National (1840; demolished 1899).
Caserne des Sapeurs-Pompiers, between Rue de Pontoise and Rue de Poissy, Paris, 1845.
Cirque Napoléon (Cirque d'Hiver), Boulevard des Filles-du-Calvaire, Paris, 1852.
Fondation Eugénie-Napoléon, Rue de Picpus, Paris, 1853–57.
Extension of the Rue de Rivoli, Paris, from the Rue de l'Échelle to the Rue de Rohan, including the erection of the Grand Hôtel des Chemins de Fer (now Grands Magasins du Louvre), 1854–55, with C. Rohault de Fleury, Alfred Armand, and A.-J. Pellechet.
Mairie du Ve, Place du Panthéon, Paris, 1855. It is a rough copy of J.-G. Soufflot's École de Droit, opposite.
Houses around the Place de l'Étoile, Paris, 1855, with C. Rohault de Fleury, Alfred Armand, and A.-J. Pellechet.
Gare du Nord, Place de Roubaix, Paris, 1861–65. (R. Clozier, *La gare du Nord*, Paris, 1940.)

Literature: A. E. Richardson, "Jacques-Ignace Hittorff," Architectural Review (London) 36 (1914), p. 106. O. Lancaster, "Jacques Ignace Hittorff," Architectural Review (London), Aug. 1937, p. 69. K. Hammer, Jakob Ignaz Hittorff: Ein Pariser Baumeister, 1792–1867, Stuttgart, 1968. D. D. Schneider, "The Works and Doctrine of Jacques Ignace Hittorff," Ph.D. diss., Princeton University, 1971.

HOLLAND, Henry (London, 1745–1806)

He was trained by his father, a London master builder. He became a partner of Capability Brown in 1771, soon taking over the architectural side of his practice and marrying his daughter, in 1773. His Brooks's Club, designed in 1776, brought him to the attention of the fashionable Whig circle, from which later came most of his clients. He was not interested in archaeology and did not travel in the Mediterranean but evolved for himself a singularly sophisticated neoclassical manner with marked overtones of the Louis XVI style. He was interested in the technical side of building and made use of fireproof plating, cone vaulting, and mathematical tiles.

Principal executed works:
Claremont, Esher, Surrey, 1771–74, with Capability Brown. (Country Life, July 7, 1950.)
Hans Town, Chelsea, London, c. 1771–. Largely demolished.
Brooks's Club, St. James's Street, London, 1776–78. (Country Life 111, p. 290.)
Berrington Hall, Herefordshire, 1778. (Country Life 116 [1952], pp. 2102, 2182.)
Carlton House, Pall Mall, London, alterations and additions for George, Prince of Wales, 1783–89, 1794. Demolished 1827. (J. M. Crook and M. H. Port, The History of the King's Works, vol. 6 [1782–1851], 1972.)
Pavilion, Brighton, for George, Prince of Wales, 1786–87. Later rebuilt.
Dover House, Whitehall, London, alterations and additions, 1787. (London County Council, Survey of London 14 [1931].)
Althorp, Northamptonshire, reconstruction, 1787–89. (Country Life, June 18–25, 1921; Country Life, May 22, 1960.)
Woburn Abbey, Bedfordshire, alterations and additions, 1787–1801. (Country Life 117 [1955], pp. 854–58, 987; Country Life 118 [1955], 434–37, 488–91; Country Life 138 [1965], pp. 98–102, 158–61.)
Broadlands, Hampshire, additions and alterations, 1788. (Country Life, Mar. 31–Apr. 7, 1923.)
Drury Lane Theatre, London, 1791–94. Burned 1809. (London County Council, Survey of London 35 [1970].)
Southill House, Bedfordshire, 1795. (A. E. Richardson et al., Southill: A Regency House, 1951.)
Wimbledon Park House, Surrey, 1801. Demolished 1949.

Literature: D. Stroud, Henry Holland, 1966.

HOPE, Thomas (Haarlem, 1769–London, 1831)

He was born into a rich Dutch banking family of Scottish descent. He undertook an extensive grand tour from 1787 to 1795, after which he settled in England. As collector, patron, author, architect, and designer, he exercised the same kind of sway over fashionable taste in England that Lord Burlington had done at the beginning of the eighteenth century. His pamphlet of 1804 entitled Observations on the Plans . . . by James Wyatt, Architect, for Downing College dealt the death-blow to Wyatt's Roman classicism and ushered in the Greek Revival. In the same year he opened to the public his magnificent London house, the contents of which he later illustrated in a book called Household Furniture and Interior Decoration (1807). This was influential in popularizing an English version of the Empire style associated with Percier and Fontaine. With the help of the architect William Atkinson, he designed for himself a bizarre but Picturesque country house, The Deepdene, the diagonality of which was probably inspired by Jeffry Wyatville.

Principal executed works:
No. 1 Mansfield Street, London, remodeling and extension, 1799–1804, 1818. Demolished 1851.
The Deepdene, Surrey, remodeling and extension, 1818–23, with William Atkinson. Demolished 1836, 1969.

Literature: D. J. Watkin, Thomas Hope (1769–1831) and the Neo-Classical Idea, 1968.

HOREAU, Hector (Versailles, 1801–Paris, 1872)

A student at the École des Beaux-Arts, Paris, first in the atelier of E.-C.-F. Nepveu, then with François Debret, he failed to win the Grand Prix in 1826 but started out soon afterward on a grand tour through Italy, to Greece, and to Egypt. The outcome of this was his Panorama de l'Égypte et de la Nubie, of 1841. On his return to France he made a name for himself as a builder of iron-and-glass structures. In 1846 he designed a jardin d'hiver at Lyons and the Château des Fleurs (a bandstand, in effect) off the Champs-Élysées in Paris (not to be confused with Rigolet's slightly later Jardin d'Hiver). During these years he exhibited and published schemes for improving the sewers, for laying out new roads and squares, and for building prisons, abattoirs, markets, and exhibition halls. The most influential of his designs was that for a new Halles Centrales for Paris, presented late in 1844. His concept of an iron-and-glass structure was later taken up by Baron Haussmann and imposed on the architects Victor Baltard and F.-E. Callet, who had begun the Halles Centrales, in stone, in 1851. Angered at not winning this commission, Horeau turned his attention to England—where in 1849 he failed to win the competition for the 1851 world exhibition pavilion with an iron-and-glass structure—and settled there in 1855. In London he exhibited his design for street improvements and other structures. About 1868 he built a house at Primrose Hill, London. Soon after, he was in Madrid, where he designed a market, and then in Paris, where he was imprisoned for the part he played in the Commune. He designed a hôtel de ville during his stay in prison.

Literature: E. Bosc, "Hector Horeau," Le moniteur des architectes, Sept. 30, Oct. 31, 1872, pp. 225–27, 241–47. J. Doin, "Hector Horeau," Gazette des beaux-arts, 1914, pp. 11–30. F. Boudon, F. Loyer, P. Dufournet, Hector Horeau, 1801–1872, exhib. cat., Paris, 1979.

HUVÉ, Jean-Jacques-Marie (Versailles, 1783–Paris, 1852)

Son of the architect Jean-Jacques Huvé, and a pupil of Charles Percier, he pursued an official career, succeeding C.-F. Viel as architect to the Paris hospital administration, and in 1827 becoming architect to the Administration des Postes. He was in charge of the works at the châteaux of Compiègne and St.-Ouen, but his distinction rests in his work at the Madeleine, in Paris, which he took over from A.-P. Vignon, completely designing the interior.

Principal executed works:
Château, St.-Ouen, 1819–20.
Madeleine, Place de la Madeleine, Paris. The present building was begun in 1807 by A.-P. Vignon, with Huvé as Conducteur des Travaux. Later he rose to the post of Inspecteur en Chef and, on Vignon's death in 1828, took over as architect. His interior dates from 1825 to 1845.

HUYOT, Jean-Nicolas (Paris, 1780–1840)

He began his studies at the École de Dessin, Paris, then entered the studio of David and, soon after, that of A.-F. Peyre. In 1807 he won the Grand Prix. After five years in Italy he returned to France to take up an official position, but in 1817 he left on an archaeological mission, under M. de Forbin, in Greece and the Middle East. He did not return to Paris until 1822, when he took up the chair of architectural history at the École des Beaux-Arts. He was much admired by A.-C. Quatremère de Quincy, who saw to it that he was nominated, in 1823, as architect to the completion of the Arc de Triomphe, in association with L. Goust. There was some dispute as to the design to be adopted and as to the architect who should control the works. Building was not pursued very actively. G.-A. Blouet finally replaced all the contenders in 1832. Huyot was no more successful in his other major undertakings: The site at Bellechasse for which he designed a classical church was taken over and used for F. C. Gau's Ste.-Clotilde, and the vast pilgrim church he began on Mont Valerien was destroyed in 1840, eventually replaced by a fortress.

INWOOD, Henry William (London, 1794–1843)

He was trained in the office of his father, William Inwood, a London surveyor and architect, with whom he subsequently cooperated in the design of several London churches. He visited Athens in 1819 and published the results of his researches there as The Erechtheion (1827). He also published The Resources of Design in the Architecture of Greece (1834). He was drowned at sea on a voyage to Spain in 1843.

Principal executed works (with his father):
St. Pancras, Euston Road, London, 1819–22.
All Saints, Camden Town, London, 1822–24.
St. Peter, Regent Square, Holborn, London, 1822–25. Demolished 1967.
St. Mary, Somers Town, St. Pancras, London, 1824–27.

JAPPELLI, Giuseppe (Venice, 1783–1852)

He studied first at the Accademia Clementina at Bologna but moved in 1803 to Venice, where he became Giannantonio Selva's assistant. He was to be active chiefly in the Veneto, building much in Padua in a more adept and well-mannered neoclassical style than almost any other architect of that period in Italy. He won fame, though, for that odd work the Caffè Pedrocchi and the Pedrocchino, part classically inspired, part Gothic, on the Piazza Cavour, Padua, of 1826–42. He was no doubt influenced in its design by his journey to France and England in 1836–37.

Principal executed works:
Villa dei Conti Cittadella Vigodarzere, Saonara, 1816–.
Meat market (now Scuola Pietro Selvatico), Via Leonardo Loredan, Padua, 1819–24.
Caffè Pedrocchi and the Pedrocchino, Piazza Cavour and Via 8 Febbraio, Padua, 1826–31, 1838–42.
Villa Gera, Via F. Benini, Conegliano, 1827. (*L'architettura*, 1967, pp. 682–89.)
Villa Treves de' Bonfili, Padua. The *giardine inglese* are now a public park.
Villa Manzoni, Patt di Sedico, c. 1836.
Villa Torlonia, Via Nomentana, Rome, garden pavilions, 1838–40, supervised later by Antonio Sarti and others.

Literature: N. Gallimberti, *Giuseppe Jappelli*, Padua, 1963.

JARDIN, Nicolas-Henri (St.-Germain-des-Noyers, 1720–Paris, 1799)

A pupil of A. A. Mollet, he won the Grand Prix in 1741 and stayed in Rome as a *pensionnaire* from December 1744 to November 1748. On his return to Paris he worked under Tannevot but in 1754 was invited to Denmark to work for Frederik V. He stayed in Denmark from 1755 to 1771, journeying to Paris in 1762, and to England, Holland, and Belgium in 1768–69. He was responsible for the introduction into Denmark of the neoclassical taste, notably through the dining room he designed for Count A. G. Moltke, but his major work was the royal church in Copenhagen, much modified and completed long after he had left the country.

Principal executed works:
Dining room for Count A. G. Moltke (now part of the Amalienborg Palace), Copenhagen, 1755–57.
Royal church, Copenhagen, 1757.
Marienlyst (near Elsinore), 1759–62.
Military barracks, Copenhagen, 1765–69.
Hospital, Lagny, 1772–86.

Mme. de Vieillard House, Ivry-sur-Seine.
Hôtel de Ville, Cambrai, facade, finished by 1786, designed with J.-D. Antoine.

Literature: C. Elling, *Jardin i Rom*, Copenhagen, 1943. *Piranèse et les français, 1740–1790*, exhib. cat., Académie de France à Rome, Rome, 1976, pp. 155–59. C. Elling, "Le séjour romain de Nicolas-Henri Jardin," in G. Brunel, ed., *Piranèse et les français*, Rome, 1978, pp. 181–98.

JEFFERSON, Thomas (Albemarle County, Virginia, 1743–Monticello, Virginia, 1826)

President of the United States from 1801 to 1809, he was in Paris as Minister to France from 1785 to 1789. There he formed his architectural tastes. His architectural designs lack the quality of those of Benjamin Latrobe, and it is as an influence on others that he is most important.

Principal executed works:
Monticello, Virginia, 1771–82, 1793–1809.
Virginia State Capitol, Richmond, 1785–89.
University of Virginia, Charlottesville, 1817–27.

Literature: F. Kimball, *Thomas Jefferson, Architect*, Boston, 1917. W. B. O'Neal, *Jefferson's Buildings at the University of Virginia: The Rotunda*, Charlottesville, 1960. F. Doveton Nichols, ed., *Thomas Jefferson's Architectural Drawings*, Boston and Charlottesville, 1961. J. A. Baer, Jr., *Jefferson at Monticello*, Charlottesville, 1967. H. C. Rice, Jr., *Thomas Jefferson's Paris*, Princeton, N. J., 1976.

JOLY, Jules-Jean-Baptiste de (Montpellier, 1788–Paris, 1865)

A pupil first of C.-M. Delagardette, then of P.-J.-N. Delespine, he did not win the Grand Prix, but seems nevertheless to have traveled to Italy. In 1821 he succeeded Bernard Poyet as architect to the Chambre des Députés, Paris. For this he was to design his richest and liveliest interiors, complete with paintings by Eugène Delacroix.

Principal executed works:
Chambre des Députés, Quai d'Orsay, Paris, Salle de Séances, 1829–33; three salons, lobbies, and library, 1828–33. The paintings by Delacroix were done later, between 1838 and 1847.

JONES, Owen (London, 1809–London, 1874)

At sixteen he entered the office of Lewis Vulliamy and remained there for six years. In 1831 he set out on a *grand tour*, traveling to France, Italy, Sicily, and Greece, where he encountered a French architectural student, Jules Goury. Together they sailed to Egypt and then to Spain, where they arrived in 1834, and began to draw and measure the Alhambra, intending to publish the results of their survey. Goury died there and Jones returned to England in 1836. But the following year he set out for Granada again and spent another year

at work at the Alhambra. Back in London, he continued work on the publication, teaching himself to prepare color plates. The result was *Plans, Elevations, Sections and Details of the Alhambra*, published between 1842 and 1845, the first and also one of the most sumptuous books printed in color. Jones was to follow this up with many others. He then began to work for Messrs. Longman and De la Rue, designing stamps, playing cards, and other such things. In all his designs he used strong colors and avoided the imitation of relief. "I always *design* in color," he claimed. In 1842 he issued *Designs for Mosaics and Tessellated Pavements*. He designed shops along Regent Street, London, for Houbigant's and Jay's, and a house in Kensington Palace Gardens. His great opportunity came, however, in 1851 when, as Superintendent of the Works at the Crystal Palace, he devised the entire scheme of color decoration. He became Director of Decoration also to the Crystal Palace Co. at Sydenham. The theories he evolved in working on the Crystal Palace he recorded in the *Grammar of Ornament*, of 1856, the most important of his books. In 1857 he was awarded the Gold Medal of the Royal Institute of British Architects. During the remainder of his career he designed several shops, many interiors in conjunction with Messrs. Jackson and Graham, and prepared designs for exhibition buildings in Paris and elsewhere. Throughout he remained a propagandist for color.

Principal executed works:
No. 8 Kensington Palace Gardens, London, c. 1850. Demolished.
Crystal Place, Hyde Park, London, painted decorations, 1851.
Crystal Palace, Sydenham, London, architectural courts and painted decorations, 1854, with Sir. M. D. Wyatt and other architects.
St. James's Hall, Regent Street Quadrant, London, 1855–58. Demolished.
Iron kiosk for Bombay, 1856, set up temporarily in the gardens of the Royal Horticultural Society, South Kensington, London. It was made by Messrs. Trollope and cast by Handyside of Derby.
Crystal Palace Bazaar, Oxford Street, London, 1858. Demolished.
Osler's shop, Oxford Street, London, 1858–60. Demolished.
Fonthill House, Wiltshire, interior decorations for the display of Alfred Morrison's collection of Chinese porcelain. Demolished.
Fishmonger's Co., London, interior decorations.
Alfred Morrison House, Carlton House Terrace, London, interiors.
Preston Hall, interior decoration of the hall, dining and drawing rooms for Henry Brassey. Jones also decorated Brassey's London house.
Douglas Castle, Lanarkshire, decoration of the drawing room for Lord Home.
Beech Grove, Newcastle upon Tyne, interior decorations.
Overstone Hall, Northampton, interior decorations.
Eynsham Hall, Oxfordshire, interior decorations.

Principal unexecuted projects:
Palace for the People, Muswell Hill, London, 1858.

Palais de Cristal de St.-Cloud, Paris, 1861.
St. Pancras Station Hotel, London.

Literature: The Architect, Apr. 25, 1874, pp. 235–36.
The Builder 32 (May 9, 1874), pp. 383–85. M. Darby
and D. Van Zanten, "Owen Jones' Iron Buildings of
the 1850s," *Architectura* (Munich) 1 (1974), pp. 53–75.

KENT, William (Bridlington, Yorkshire, 1685–London, 1748)

He was one of the most versatile and influential designers in eighteenth-century England, and his architecture, furniture, and garden design anticipated later
Gothic Revival, neoclassical, and Picturesque developments. He was working as a painter in Rome when Lord
Burlington brought him back to England to act as his
associate in promoting the Palladian Revival. A number
of his designs were published by J. Vardy in *Some Designs of Mr. Inigo Jones and Mr. William Kent* (1744) and
others by I. Ware in *Designs of Inigo Jones and Others*
(c. 1735).

Principal executed works:
Houghton Hall, Norfolk, interiors, c. 1726–31. (*Country
  Life* 49, pp. 14, 40, 64, 98.)
Chiswick House, Middlesex, interiors, c. 1727. (*Country
  Life* 43, pp. 130, 160; *Country Life* 104, pp. 470, 728.)
Esher Place, Surrey, additions, 1729–33. Partly de-
  molished.
Treasury buildings, Whitehall, London, 1734–36.
  (*Country Life* 122, pp. 978, 1034.)
Holkham Hall, Norfolk, c. 1734. (*Country Life* 23, pp.
  822, 870.)
Stowe, Buckinghamshire, garden buildings, 1730s.
  (*Country Life* 102, pp. 526, 578, 626; *Country Life*
  145, p. 78.)
Rousham, Oxfordshire, addition of wings and garden
  buildings, 1730s. (*Country Life* 99, pp. 900, 946,
  1084, 1130.)
No. 44 Berkeley Square, London, 1742–44. (*Country
  Life* 86, p. 12; *Country Life* 132, p. 1648.)
Wakefield Lodge, Northamptonshire, c. 1745. (*Country
  Life*, Aug. 2, 1973.)

Literature: F. Kimball, "William Kent's Designs for
the Houses of Parliament," *Journal of the Royal Institute
of British Architects*, Aug. 6 and Sept. 10, 1932. M.
Jourdain, *The Work of William Kent*, 1948. "Lord
Burlington and William Kent," in R. Wittkower,
Palladio and English Palladianism, 1974.

KLENZE, Leo von (Halberstadt, 1784–Munich, 1864)

He turned from the study of law to architecture after
meeting Friedrich Gilly in 1800. Like all German architects of this period he looked to Paris for inspiration
and was, in fact, trained there by J.-N.-L. Durand and
by Percier and Fontaine. He was court architect to King
Jérome at Kassel from 1808 to 1813. In 1816 he was
appointed Supervisor of Court Buildings to Ludwig
I of Bavaria and in 1824 became Director of the Building
Authorities for Bavaria. With Ludwig he transformed
Munich into the Florence of the nineteenth century

with such buildings as the Königsbau of the Residenz,
based on the Palazzo Pitti. Klenze was an archaeologist
of distinction, publishing many books on antique
architecture, and his own inclinations were toward
Greek rather than quattrocento sources. His most important Greek Revival buildings were the Glyptothek
and Propylaeon in Munich and the Walhalla near
Regensburg. However, his adoption of a neo-Renaissance vocabulary makes him comparable to Sir Charles
Barry in England.

Principal executed works:
Leuchtenberg Palace, Munich, 1816.
Glyptothek, Munich, 1816–34. Gutted.
Pinakothek, Munich, 1822–25, 1826–36. Gutted.
Residenz, Munich, additions and alterations, 1826–43.
Walhalla (near Regensburg), 1830–42.
New Hermitage Museum, Leningrad, 1839.
Befreiungshalle, Kelheim, 1842–63, with Friedrich von
  Gärtner.
Ruhmeshalle, Munich, 1843.
Propylaeon, Königsplatz, Munich, first projected in
  1817, executed in 1846–60.

Principal unexecuted projects:
Royal Palace, Athens, 1834.
Pantechneion, Athens, 1836.

Literature: L. von Klenze, *Sammlung architektonischer
Entwürfe*, 10 pts., Munich, 1830–50. O. Hederer, *Leo
von Klenze*, Munich, 1964.

KNIGHT, Richard Payne (Wormesley, Herefordshire, 1750–London, 1824)

He was a Herefordshire squire who built Downton
Castle for himself in 1772–78. Designed in an asymmetrical, castellated style partly derived from the background buildings in Claude Lorrain's paintings, it was
to have considerable influence on British architecture
and particularly on John Nash. Knight later developed
his theories on the Picturesque in two influential books,
The Landscape, a Didactic Poem (1794) and *An Analytical
Inquiry into the Principles of Taste* (1805). He also published *An Account of the Worship of the Remains of Priapus*
(1786) and *An Inquiry into the Symbolical Language of
Ancient Art and Mythology* (1818). Unfortunately for
his reputation, however, he failed to recognize the
quality of the Elgin Marbles, claiming in 1806 that they
were not Grecian but Hadrianic.

Principal executed work:
Downton Castle, Herefordshire, 1772–78. (*Country
  Life* 42, p. 36; A. Rowan, "Downton Castle, Here-
  fordshire," in H. Colvin and J. Harris, eds., *The
  Country Seat*, London, 1970, pp. 170–73.)

Literature: J.-J. Mayoux, *Richard Payne Knight et le
pittoresque*, Paris, 1932. N. Pevsner, "Richard Payne
Knight," *Art Bulletin* 31 (1949), pp. 293–320 (repr. in N.
Pevsner, *Studies in Art, Architecture and Design*, vol. 1,
1968, pp. 109–25). S. Lang, "R. Payne Knight and the
Idea of Modernity," in J. Summerson, ed., *Concerning
Architecture*, 1968, pp. 85–97. F. J. Messman, *Richard
Payne Knight*, The Hague, 1974.

LABROUSTE, Pierre-François-Henri (Paris, 1801–
Fontainebleau, 1875)

He planned to become a painter but in 1818 enrolled
at the École des Beaux-Arts, Paris, where he won the
Grand Prix in 1824. In Rome he worked with G.-A.
Blouet, E.-J. Gilbert, and F.-J. Duban, and later with
L.-J. Duc and Léon Vaudoyer. He allied himself with
their aims of reform. For his fourth-year *envoi* he sent
back a restoration study of the temples of Paestum that
was taken as an affront to professional thinking by the
members of the Académie, and became the cause of
some scandal. Labrouste was for years given no great
commissions by the established authorities. He was at
once looked upon, though, by the young, as an idol.
In 1830 he opened an *atelier* from which many of the
Gothic Revivalists were to emerge. When he closed his
atelier in 1856, half his pupils went to E.-E. Viollet-le-
Duc. His real opportunity to build came in 1838, when
he was commissioned as architect of the new Bibliothèque Ste.-Geneviève. He erected one of the noblest
buildings of the century and followed this success
with the reordering of the buildings of the Bibliothèque
Nationale and the design of the new reading room and
stacks there. His reputation was, and has always remained, high.

Principal executed works:
Bibliothèque Ste.-Geneviève, Place du Panthéon, Paris,
  1838, 1842–50; Keeper's house and administrative
  offices, Place du Panthéon and Rue Valette, Paris,
  designed 1845–47, built 1847–48.
Collège Ste.-Barbe (now Faculté de Droit), 2 Rue
  Cujas, Paris, 1845–47. Only Labrouste's facade re-
  mains, built in conjunction with his brother Théo-
  dore.
Colonie Agricole (farm colony), Mesnil-St.-Firmin,
  1845–49.
Bibliothèque Nationale, Paris, 1853–69; main reading
  room and stacks, 1859–68.
Grand Séminaire (now Faculté des Lettres), Rennes,
  1854–72. Supervised by Charles Langlois.
Hôtel Fould, 27 Rue de Berry, Paris, 1856–58. De-
  molished.
Thouret House, 68 Boulevard Bourdon, Neuilly-sur-
  Seine, 1860. Altered.
Hôtel Vilgruy, 9 Rue François Ier, Paris, 1860–65.
Hôtel Rouvenat, Neuilly-sur-Seine, 1861.

*Literature: Souvenirs d'Henri Labrouste. Notes recueillies
et classées par ses enfants*, Paris, 1928. *Catalogue de
l'exposition des oeuvres de Henri Labrouste à la Bibliothèque
Nationale*, Paris, 1953. R. Plouin, "Henry Labrouste, sa
vie, son oeuvre," dissertation, Université de Paris, 1965,
in the Bibliothèque d'Art et d'Archéologie, Paris. "H.
Labrouste," *Les monuments historiques de la France* 6 (1975).
Neil Levine, "The Romantic Idea of Architectural
Legibility: Henri Labrouste and the Néo-Grec," in A.
Drexler, ed., *The Architecture of the École des Beaux-
Arts*, New York, 1977. P. Saddy, *Henri Labrouste
architecte, 1801–1875*, Paris, 1977.

LABROUSTE, Théodore (Paris, 1799–1885)

The elder brother of P.-F.-H. Labrouste, he studied under A.-L.-T. Vaudoyer and L.-H. Lebas at the École des Beaux-Arts, Paris, winning the Grand Prix in 1827. He returned from Rome to work under his brother at the Collège Ste.-Barbe, both in Paris and in the rural institution at Fontenay-aux-Roses. In 1841 he was appointed architect to the Bibliothèque de l'Arsenal, a position he held until 1880. In 1845 he succeeded F. C. Gau as architect of the hospitals of Paris. This was to be his main occupation.

Principal executed works:
Maison Municipal de Santé, Rue du Faubourg Saint-
    Denis, Paris, 1856–58.
Headquarters of the Assistance Publique, Paris, 1857–59.
Bibliothèque de l'Arsenal, Paris, 1859–60.
Hospice des Incurables, Ivry-sur-Seine, 1864–72.
Hospice des Ménages, Paris.
Hospice de Villas, Issy-les-Moulineaux, Paris.

LAISNÉ, Jean-Charles (Fontenay-aux-Roses, 1819–1891)

He was a pupil at the school of M. Morin at Fontenay-aux-Roses, which later became Ste.-Barbe-des-Champs, and there he first encountered E.-E. Viollet-le-Duc and Émile Trélat, with whom he was to be associated through life. He studied at the École des Beaux-Arts, Paris, first in 1835 in the *atelier* of J.-J.-M. Huvé, later in that of Huvé's nephew, Charles Lenormant, who introduced him to his adopted brother, C.-A. Questel, for whom Laisné was to work at Nîmes and, later, at Versailles. In 1848 he entered the service of the Commission des Monuments Historiques, for which he restored the Pont du Gard, Notre-Dame, Dijon (1866–) and a great deal more. In 1856 he began working for the Service des Édifices Diocésains, for which he also restored a number of buildings. He succeeded P.-G.-H. Daumet as architect to the works of the Sacré-Coeur in Montmartre, Paris. He was also architect to the Banque de France. In connection with Viollet-le-Duc's attempt to reform the École des Beaux-Arts, in 1863 Laisné was appointed to open an official *atelier*, which, despite all opposition, he maintained until 1879, when he was succeeded by P.-R.-L. Ginain.

Principal executed works:
Lycée, Cognac, 1864–70.
Lycée, Guéret, 1864–70.
École Normale Supérieure, Cluny, 1865.
École de Pharmacie, Avenue de l'Observatoire, Paris,
    1876–85. Extended 1938.
Lycée Janson de Sailly, Passy, Paris, 1880.

Literature: Exposition des oeuvres de Laisné, Millet et Ruprich-Robert, Union Syndicale des Architects Français, Paris, 1891.

LAMB, Edward Buckton (1805–London, 1869)

He was one of the most bizarre and original interpreters of the Gothic Revival in England during the first half of the nineteenth century. As a Broad Churchman, he was not committed to perpetuate the long chancels of medieval churches but was free to experiment in the Gothic style with the sort of centrally planned church established by Sir Christopher Wren in the seventeenth century. He was the pupil of L. N. Cottingham, a Gothic specialist and restorer of medieval churches, and he contributed most of the designs for Gothic and Elizabethan furniture and all the designs for villa interiors to J. C. Loudon's influential *Encyclopaedia of Cottage, Farm and Villa Architecture* (1832). Lamb also produced many of the individual designs in *Loudon's Architectural Magazine* (1834–38) and propounded his particular view of Picturesque architecture in his own *Studies of Ancient Domestic Architecture* (1846). His violently assertive Gothic is characterized by the contrast of large and small features and by an extreme complexity of window tracery, wooden roofs, and skyline.

Principal executed works:
Elkington Hall, Lincolnshire, 1841.
Allenheads, Northumberland, 1846.
St. Stephen, Aldwark, Yorkshire, 1846–53.
Holy Trinity, Prestwood, Buckinghamshire, 1849.
Rectory, Aston Clinton, Buckinghamshire, 1850.
All Saints, Thirkleby, Yorkshire, 1850.
St. Margaret, Leiston, Suffolk, 1853.
Christ Church, West Hartlepool, County Durham,
    1854.
St. Mary, Braiseworth, Suffolk, 1857.
Newton Hall, Essex, 1858.
SS. Simon and Jude, Englefield Green, Surrey, 1859.
Hughenden Manor, Buckinghamshire, 1862. (*Country
    Life* 113, pp. 1604, 1698.)
Aldwark Manor, Yorkshire, 1862.
St. Mary, Bagby, Yorkshire, 1862.
St. Martin, Vicars Road, Gospel Oak, London, 1862–65.
Nunn Appleton Hall, Yorkshire, addition, 1864. De-
    molished. (*The Builder* 22 [1864], pp. 188–90.)
St. Mary Magdalene, Canning Road, Addiscombe,
    Surrey, 1868–70.

LANGHANS, Carl Gotthard (Landeshut, 1732–Grüneiche, 1808)

He is best known for his Brandenburg Gate, the most important neoclassical building in Berlin dating before those by K. F. Schinkel. In 1775 he became Architectural Adviser for Public Buildings in Silesia, and in 1788 he went to Berlin as Director of the Royal Office of Public Buildings.

Principal executed works:
Palais Hatzfeld, Breslau, 1766–86.
Theater, Breslau, c. 1780.
Theater, Schloss Charlottenburg, Berlin, 1788–91.
Marble Palace, Potsdam, 1789.
Brandenburg Gate, Berlin, 1789–91.
Royal Palace, Breslau, extensions, 1794–95.
Theater, Berlin, 1800–1802. Demolished 1817.
Theater, Potsdam, 1795.
Theater, Danzig, 1798–1801.

Principal unexecuted project:
Monument to Frederick the Great, Berlin, 1797.

Literature: W. T. Hinrichs, *Carl Gotthard Langhans,* Strasbourg, 1909.

LANGLEY, Batty (Twickenham, 1696–London, 1751)

The son of a gardener, he produced numerous pattern books of early Georgian classical architecture for country builders and craftsmen: *The Builder's Chest Book; or, a Compleat Key to the Five Orders of Columns in Architecture* (1727), *New Principles of Gardening* (1728), etc. But he is best remembered for his eccentric attempt to reduce William Kent's Gothic style to a system of orders in his *Ancient Architecture Restored and Improved* (1741; reissued 1747).

Literature: A. Rowan, "Batty Langley's Gothic," in G. Robertson and G. Henderson, eds., *Studies in Memory of D. Talbot Rice,* Edinburgh, 1975. E. Harris, "Batty Langley, a Tutor to Freemasons, 1696–1751," *Burlington Magazine,* May 1977, pp. 327–35.

LAPERUTA, Leopoldo

He was the first architect of the church of S. Francesco di Paola, Naples, begun in 1810. His design was superseded in 1817 by that of Pietro Bianchi.

Literature: A. Venditti, *Architettura neoclassica a Napoli,* Naples, 1961.

LASSUS, Jean-Baptiste-Antoine (Paris, 1807–Vichy, 1857)

A pupil of P.-F.-H. Labrouste, a student at the École des Beaux-Arts, Paris, Lassus turned early to Gothic architecture, submitting a study of the Ste.-Chapelle to the Salon of 1835 and, two years after, a study of the refectory of the former Abbaye de St.-Martin-des-Champs, Paris. In 1838 he started work under E.-H. Godde on the restoration of St.-Germain-l'Auxerrois and in the same year was called in to assist F.-J. Duban with the restoration of the Ste.-Chapelle. Within a few years he was in charge of both these undertakings. In 1844 he was appointed, together with E.-E. Viollet-le-Duc, to restore Notre-Dame in Paris and to build its new chapter house. He restored much else besides, including the cathedral of Chartres, on which he wrote a monograph. He was the staunchest of all the French Gothic Revivalists, building much in that style and publishing a great deal of literary propaganda, in particular a theory on "le module humain" as it applied to Gothic architecture. His *Album de Villard de Honnecourt* was published posthumously in 1858.

Principal executed works:
St.-Nicolas, Nantes, 1843–52. (B. Foucart and V. Noël-
    Bouton, "Saint-Nicolas de Nantes," in *Congrès
    Archéologique de France, Haute Bretagne,* 126ᵉ session,
    Paris, 1968, pp. 136–81.)
Chapter house, Notre-Dame, Paris, 1846–50, with E.-E.
    Viollet-le-Duc.
Petit Séminaire, Rue Notre-Dame-des-Champs, Paris.
Couvent de la Visitation, Montauban.
Hôtel Soltykoff, Avenue Montaigne, Paris, begun
    1848. Demolished.
Sacré-Coeur, Moulins (Allier), 1849–81. Begun 1844
    by L.-D.-G. Esmonnot.
Notre-Dame, Moulins (Allier), west end, 1852–.

St.-Pierre, Dijon, 1853–58.
St.-Jean-Baptiste-de-Belleville, Paris, 1854–59.
Apartment house, 41 Rue Taitbout, Paris.
House, Rue Albine, Maisons-Lafitte.
St.-Saturnin, Cusset (Allier), 1857–63.

Literature: E. Viollet-le-Duc, "Nécrologie J. B. A. Lassus," *Encyclopédie d architecture,* Aug. 1857. A Darcel, "Notice sur Lassus," in J.-B.-A. Lassus, *Album de Villard de Honnecourt,* Paris, 1858. J.-M. Leniaud, "Recherches sur Jean-Baptiste Lassus (1807–1857)," *Position des thèses de l'École de Chartres,* Paris, 1976, pp. 77–88.

LATROBE, Benjamin Henry (Fulneck, Yorkshire, 1764–New Orleans, Louisiana, 1820)

He was the most original and influential architect to work in North America before the return to Boston from Paris of H. H. Richardson in 1865. Born in England and educated in Germany, he became a pupil in 1786 of S. P. Cockerell. He also studied engineering under John Smeaton, the builder of the Eddystone Lighthouse. In 1796 he emigrated to America, where he became, in 1803, Surveyor of the Public Buildings to the federal government. By his work in an independent Greek Revival manner in Richmond, Philadelphia, Baltimore, and Washington, D.C., he turned American classicism into a tradition of international rather than purely national significance.

Principal executed works:
Hammerwood Lodge, Sussex, c. 1790.
Ashdown House, Sussex, c. 1790.
State Penitentiary, Richmond, Virginia, 1797–98. Demolished 1927.
Bank of Pennsylvania, Philadelphia, 1798–1800.
Sedgeley, Philadelphia, Pennsylvania, 1799.
Capitol, Washington, D.C., alterations and additions, 1803–11. Rebuilt 1814.
Cathedral, Baltimore, Maryland, 1804–18.
Exchange, Baltimore, Maryland, 1816–20. Demolished 1904.

Principal unexecuted project:
Second Bank of the United States, Philadelphia, Pennsylvania, 1818.

Literature: T. Hamlin, *Greek Revival Architecture in America,* New York, 1944. T. Hamlin, *B. H. Latrobe,* Oxford and New York, 1955.

LEBAS, Louis-Hippolyte (Paris, 1782–1867)

He studied first with A.-L.-T. Vaudoyer, then under Charles Percier. On completing his studies, he traveled to Italy, to which country he was to return in 1806, as part of Murat's army, and yet again on his own account in 1811. His first important work was the church of Notre-Dame-de-Lorette in Paris, a commission won in competition in 1823. Three years later he began the new house of detention for juvenile offenders on the Place de la Roquette, Paris. Both these buildings were intended to set new standards for architecture. The first did, indeed, inspire J.-I. Hittorff when he

came to build St.-Vincent-de-Paul, but the second showed only how inept was Lebas at utilitarian, rational planning. He was soon outpaced as a reformer of prison architecture by E.-J. Gilbert.

Principal executed works:
Notre-Dame-de-Lorette, 1 Rue Fléchier, Paris, 1823–36.
House of detention for juvenile offenders, Place de la Roquette, Paris, 1826–36. Demolished 1974.
Palais de l'Institut, Quai de Conti, Paris, Salle de Séances and library, 1831–36.
Tomb of Joseph Halévy, Père-Lachaise cemetery, Paris.

LE CAMUS, Louis-Denis

Little is known of his career. He won the second Grand Prix in 1742 and was *Contrôleur Général des Bâtiments à l'Hôtel Royale des Invalides* until 1778. Earlier he had become architect to the Duc de Choiseul, for whom he designed the Quartier Choiseul in Paris and at whose instigation he built the giant vauxhall, the Colisée in Paris, between 1769 and 1771, which was recorded by his pupil G. L. Le Rouge in the small *Description du Colisée élevé aux Champs-Élysées* in 1771. This pleasure dome was demolished in 1785. For the Duc de Choiseul Le Camus also designed the pagoda and other pavilions in the gardens at Chantelou, on the Loire.

Literature: M. Gallet, *Paris Domestic Architecture of the 18th Century,* London, 1972. A. C. Gruber, "Les 'vauxhalls' parisiens au XVIIIe siècle," *Bulletin de la Société de l'Histoire de l'Art Français,* Année 1971 (1972), pp. 134–35.

LE CAMUS DE MÉZIÈRES, Nicolas (Paris, 1721–1789)

Little is known of him, and he is often confused with Louis-Denis Le Camus, about whom even less is known, but he did design and build (1763–67) the Halle aux Blés in Paris (later to have a dome added by J.-G. Legrand and Jacques Molinos) and he was the author of the influential treatise *Le génie de l'architecture; ou, l'analogie de cet art avec nos sensations,* of 1780, and a manual of building construction, *Le guide de ceux qui veulent bâtir,* of 1781. He also wrote a bucolic novel *Aabba; ou, le triomphe de l'innocence,* published in 1784. The record of his major work he left incomplete, though the plates were all engraved: "Plan coupes et élévations des halles couvertes et incombustibles pratiquées pour les grains, farines et grenailles, en l'emplacement de l'ancien Hôtel de Soissons, quartier de St. Eustache."

Literature: M. Gallet, *Paris Domestic Architecture of the 18th Century,* London, 1972. A. C. Gruber, "Les 'vauxhalls' parisiens au XVIIIe siècle," *Bulletin de la Société de l'Histoire de l'Art Français,* Année 1971 (1972), pp. 134–35.

LECLÈRE, Achille-François-René (Paris, 1785–Paris, 1853)

A pupil first of J.-N.-L. Durand, then of Charles Per-

cier, he won the Grand Prix in 1808 and traveled for six years in Italy and the south of France, carefully measuring the Roman and Renaissance monuments, which he later published. He built nothing of importance or even of interest. He restored many châteaux in the provinces but was active, above all, as a teacher, beginning in 1815, and as an administrative architect.

Principal executed works:
Tomb of Casimir Périer, Père-Lachaise cemetery, Paris, 1833.
Château de Mme. de Mortefontaine, Verneuil.
Château de Montesquiou, Villebois.
Monument to C.-M.-A. de Bonchamp, St.-Florent.

LEDOUX, Claude-Nicolas (Dormans [Marne], 1736–Paris, 1806)

He was the pupil first of Jacques-François Blondel, then of L.-F. Trouard. His first work, the decorations for the Café Godeau (or Café Militaire), Rue St.-Honoré, Paris, dates from 1762. He was active in the years immediately following, not in Paris but in Burgundy, Champagne, and the Franche-Comté, where he built small churches, bridges, and other utilitarian structures for the Service des Eaux et Forêts. His real debut in Paris dates from 1766, when he prepared designs for the Hôtel d'Hallwyl and the Hôtel d'Uzès. Within a few more years he was building a succession of varied and highly imaginative houses in Paris. In 1771 he began the Pavillon de Mme. du Barry at Louveciennes. The two commissions that served to establish his reputation, and which still provoke the highest interest, were the saltworks at Arc-et-Senans (Doubs), designed in 1774, and the *barrières* (tollgates) of Paris, started in 1785 but taken over after the Revolution by J.-D. Antoine. Ledoux began a series of engravings of his works about 1780 that showed them in a more up-to-date style than that originally envisaged. By 1786 the first sheaf of these was ready for publication as a book, *L'architecture considérée sous le rapport de l'art, des moeurs et de la législation,* but this was to be delayed until long after the Revolution, in 1804, just before his death. By then an extraordinary text had been compiled to accompany the illustrations. The second edition was not issued until 1847, by Ledoux's supposed son, Daniel Ramée: *L'architecture de Claude-Nicolas Ledoux.*

Principal executed works:
Café Godeau, Rue St.-Honoré, Paris, *boiserie,* 1762. (M. Gallet, *Bulletin du Musée Carnavalet,* June 1972, pp. 12–17.)
Hôtel d'Hallwyl, 28 Rue Michel-le-Comte, Paris, 1766–67.
Hôtel d'Uzès (on the site of the Rue d'Uzès), Paris, 1767–69. Demolished c. 1870. (M. Gallet, *Bulletin du Musée Carnavalet,* no. 2, 1969, pp. 2–23.)
Hôtel de Montmorency, Boulevard de Montmorency and Rue de la Chaussée-d'Antin, Paris, 1770–.
Hôtel de Guimard, Rue de la Chaussée-d'Antin, Paris, 1770, 1773–76.
Château de Bénouville (Calvados), 1770–77.

Pavillon de Mme. du Barry, Louveciennes, 1770–.
Hôtel Tabary, Rue du Faubourg Poissonnière, Paris, 1771–73.
Stables for Mme. du Barry, 5 Avenue de Paris, Versailles, 1773.
Ledoux House, Rue de l'Université, Paris, 1773–.
Saline de Chaux, Arc-et-Senans (Doubs), 1774, 1775–79. (B. Stoloff, "C. N. Ledoux et la saline d'Arc-et-Senans, genèse d'une oeuvre achevée," *Gazette des beaux-arts* 89 [1977], pp. 65–72.)
Theater, Besançon, 1775, 1778–84. (E. de Ganay, *Revue de l'art ancien et moderne* 52 [1927], pp. 4, 17.)
Hôtel de Thélusson, Rue de Provence, Paris, 1778–83.
Château de Maupertuis (near Coulommiers), c. 1780.
Grenier à sel, Rue de l'Étoile, Compiègne, 1783.
Barrières (tollgates), Paris, 1785–89. Not completed until c. 1798. Only four survive. (E. Frémy, *Bulletin de la Société de l'Histoire de Paris* 118 [1912]; *Bulletin de la Société de l'Histoire de l'Art Français* 69 [1929].)
Palais de Justice and prison, Aix-en-Provence, 1786. Demolished.
Hosten Houses, Rue St.-Georges, Paris, 1792–95.
There are many other works by Ledoux worthy of note and a vast range of unexecuted projects, most of them illustrated in his book.

Literature: G. Levallet-Haug, *Claude-Nicolas Ledoux,* Paris and Strasbourg, 1934. J. Langner, "Claude-Nicolas Ledoux, die erste Schaffenzeit (1762–1774)," Ph.D. diss., University of Freiburg im Breisgau, 1959. W. Herrmann, "The Problem of Chronology in Ledoux's Engraved Works," *Art Bulletin* 42 (1960), pp. 191–210. M. Gallet, "La jeunesse de Ledoux," *Gazette des beaux-arts,* Feb. 1970, pp. 65–92. M. Gallet, "Ledoux et sa clientèle parisienne," *Bulletin de la Société de l'Histoire de Paris et de l'Île de France,* Année 1974–75 (1976), pp. 131–73. B. Stoloff, *L'affaire Claude-Nicolas Ledoux, autopsie d'un mythe,* Brussels, 1977. M. Gallet, *Ledoux et Paris, Cahiers de la rotonde* 3, Paris, 1979.

LEFUEL, Hector-Martin (Versailles, 1810–1880)

He began working with his father, a building contractor, studied also at the École des Beaux-Arts, Paris, and in the *atelier* of J.-N. Huyot. After a break in his studies he won the Grand Prix in 1839 and, having spent five years in Rome, returned to Paris to act as an *Inspecteur* at the Chambre des Députés. In 1853 he began work at the Château de Fontainebleau, where he built the theater, and on the strength of this was appointed in 1854 to take over the mammoth task begun by L.-T.-J. Visconti of linking the Louvre and the Tuileries. This was his major occupation throughout life. He greatly enriched and elaborated Visconti's project, setting a fashion for lively and playfully decorated roofs.

Principal executed works:
Theater, Château de Fontainebleau, 1853–.
Louvre and Tuileries, Paris, restoration and extension, 1854–.
Hôtel Fould, Paris.
Hôtel de Nieuwerkerke, Paris.

Literature: J.-L. Pascal, "Notice sur Lefuel," *Revue générale de l'architecture,* 1881, p. 259 ff.

LEGEAY, Jean-Laurent (Paris, c. 1710–after 1788)

An important catalyst in the activities of the French *pensionnaires* in Rome in the 1740s, he was an architect who never fulfilled his promise. He won the Grand Prix in 1732 but left for Rome only at the end of 1737, staying there until January 1742. He collaborated with Giambattista Piranesi and other engravers on the plates of G. D. Campiglia's *Il quinto libro del nuovo teatro delle fabbriche et edifici in prospettiva in Roma* and Fausto Amidei's *Varie vedute di Roma antica e moderna* (1745), giving evidence then of small facility as an engraver. Skill came later, however, when he published his four known suites of etchings—*Fontane* (1767), *Rovine* (1768), *Vasi,* and *Tombeaux*—all issued together with six extra plates in Paris in 1770. After his return to Paris he designed a new Catholic church for Berlin, completed only in 1773 under the supervision of J. G. Büring. In October 1748 Legeay went to Schwerin as *Baumeister* to the Herzog of Mecklenburg and continued on in the employ of his son, preparing designs after 1756 for Ludwigslust that were to be taken over and much altered by J. J. Busch. In 1756 Legeay moved to Berlin to become *Baumeister* to Frederick II, for whom he designed the new palace, the Grands Communs, facing Sans Souci. This was erected, once again to altered designs, by Karl von Gontard after Legeay's departure in 1763. It is probable that he then went to England, where he was in contact with Sir William Chambers and may have had a hand in the design of the Casino at Marino, outside Dublin. By 1770 Legeay was back in Paris but moved soon after to the Toulouse region, where he taught drawing in a Benedictine establishment. There is a record of him in Bordeaux in 1785 and another in Narbonne in the following year. He aimed then to go to Rome, where he is known to have been in 1788.

Literature: J. Harris, "Le Geay, Piranesi and International Neoclassicism in Rome (1740–1750)," in *Essays in the History of Architecture Presented to Rudolf Wittkower,* London, 1967, pp. 189–96. J. M. Pérouse de Montclos, *Étienne-Louis Boullée: de l'architecture classique à l'architecture révolutionnaire,* Paris, 1969, pp. 39–46. G. Erouart, "Jean-Laurent Legeay—recherches," in G. Brunel, ed., *Piranèse et les français,* Rome, 1978, pp. 199–212.

LEGRAND, Étienne-François

The son of the architect Étienne Legrand, he is often confused with Jacques-Guillaume Legrand. He worked on the completion of the cathedral at Orléans and designed the Hôtel Gallifet, 75 Rue de Grenelle, of 1780–87, and the Hôtel Jarnac, 8 Rue Monsieur, of 1788, both in Paris. The controversial church of St.-Louis in Port Marly (Yvelines), of 1778, has recently been attributed to him also.

Literature: M. Gallet, *Paris Domestic Architecture of the 18th Century,* London, 1972. M. Gallet, "Louis-François Trouard et l'architecture religieuse dans la région de Versailles au temps de Louis XVI," *Gazette des beaux-arts* 88 (Dec. 1976), pp. 201–18.

LEGRAND, Jacques-Guillaume (Paris, 1743–Saint-Denis, 1808)

A pupil of both J.-R. Perronet and Jacques-François Blondel, he is best remembered for the dome that he and Jacques Molinos designed in 1782 for the Halle aux Blés in Paris. He was also the son-in-law of C.-L. Clérisseau, the text of whose *Antiquités de la France* he wrote, and the first biographer of Giambattista Piranesi, though this work was not published until the twentieth century.

Principal executed works:
Halle aux Blés, Paris, dome, 1782–83, with Jacques Molinos. Destroyed 1802. (*L'architecture,* 1933, p. 249; *Art Bulletin* 55 [1973], pp. 262–79.)
"Lantern of Diogenes," park of St.-Cloud.
Hôtel, 6 Rue St.-Florentin, Paris, 1789.
Théâtre Feydeau, Paris, 1789. Destroyed.

Literature: M. Gallet, *Paris Domestic Architecture of the 18th Century,* London, 1972.

LE LORRAIN, Louis-Joseph (Paris, 1715–St. Petersburg [Leningrad], 1759)

He was not an architect, but his architectural extravaganzas had so considerable an influence on architecture that he must be listed here. He was a pupil of the painter Dumont le Romain; he won the Grand Prix in 1739 and traveled at the end of the following year to Rome, where he remained for eight years. There he took up engraving, cooperating with Giambattista Piranesi on the *Opere varie,* and designed and engraved a series of *macchine* for the Festa della Chinea, in particular those of 1745, 1746, and 1747, that served to set a new style for architecture in Paris in the following decade. After returning to Paris, he was taken up by the Comte de Caylus, for whom he engraved two plates after descriptions of antique paintings, and by whom he was persuaded to help J.-D. Le Roy tidy up the drawings for that architect's influential book *Les ruines des plus beaux monuments de la Grèce.* Between 1756 and 1758 he designed for Ange-Laurent La Live de Jully the suite of furniture, now at Chantilly, that started the fashion for things "à la grecque," though it can scarcely be thought of as Greek. In the spring of 1758 he set off for Russia to direct the Académie des Arts, but fell ill and died in the following year.

Literature: S. Eriksen, *Early Neo-Classicism in France,* London, 1974. *Piranèse et les français, 1740–1790,* exhib. cat., Academie de France a Rome, Rome, 1976. P. Rosenberg, "Louis-Joseph Le Lorrain (1715–1759)," *Revue de l'art,* nos. 40–41, 1978, pp. 173–202.

LEPÈRE, Jean-Baptiste (Paris, 1761–1844)

He was first instructed in the free schools of Paris. In 1787 he left for Santo Domingo, where he stayed for two years and is said to have built several houses. Soon after his return to Paris, where he worked on the details of the Théâtre-Français, he left in 1796 for Constantinople, intending to help establish a canon foundry. He was back in France within two years but left again in 1798 on Napoleon's famous expedition to Egypt. After again returning to France, he was appointed to succeed Charles Percier and P.-F.-L. Fontaine at the Château de Malmaison in 1802 and, three years later, to assist Jacques Gondoin in the detailed design of the column in the Place Vendôme. He was responsible for the maintenance and restoration of a number of the royal châteaux but is associated with only one design of interest, that of the church of St.-Vincent-de-Paul, which he sketched first and began in 1824. He was succeeded in this project by his son-in-law J.-I. Hittorff, who took up the work, after a period of inactivity, in 1830. The church is usually credited to Hittorff, who completed the building in 1846, but the exterior may be based largely on Lepère's design.

Literature: "Notice biographique sur M. J. B. Lepère," *Revue général de l'architecture* 5 (1844), pp. 367–72.

LE ROY, Julien-David (Paris, 1724–Paris, 1803)

He won the Grand Prix in 1750 and traveled to Rome, but his fame was to spring from his journey to Greece, whither he set out in 1754, prompted by the prospectus of James Stuart and Nicholas Revett. He managed to measure the principal buildings in Athens, Corinth, and other places and to publish them as *Les ruines des plus beaux monuments de la Grèce* in 1758, several years before Stuart and Revett. They were to be scathing about his standards of accuracy. But he had his reply in the second edition of his work published in 1770. This work won for him the post of Professor of Architectural History at the Académie Royale d'Architecture. He was active chiefly as a teacher, but he also published *Histoire de la disposition et des formes différentes que les chrétiens ont données à leurs temples*, in 1764, *Les observations sur les édifices des anciens peuples*, in 1767, and a handful of pamphlets on the sailing boats of antiquity. Giambattista Piranesi was to attack him violently for setting the Greeks above the Romans, but this outburst was prompted by national pride and personal involvement in the selling of plates of Roman antiquities rather than by any serious scholarly dispute.

Literature: *Piranèse et les français, 1740–1790*, exhib. cat., Académie de France à Rome, Rome, 1976.

LESUEUR, Jean-Baptiste-Cicéron (Clairefontaine, 1794–Paris, 1883)

A pupil of Charles Percier and of Auguste Famin, he shared the Grand Prix in 1819 with F.-E. Callet and used his time in Italy to study carefully the architecture of the late Renaissance, which was to inspire all his works. In the 1830s he built several large apartment buildings in Paris that caused some stir, but his most important work was the extension and decoration of Domenico da Cortona's sixteenth-century Hôtel de Ville in Paris, an undertaking he began in 1835 with E.-H. Godde. By 1846 the exterior was completed. Work on the interiors continued until 1854 (Victor Baltard assumed responsibility for some, after 1852). Long before its completion this building had exerted its influence. The detailing was bad, but in its sheer picturesqueness the composition had more breadth and assurance and a firmer emphasis than any other attempt at a revival of late French Renaissance forms. The treatment of the mansard roofs set a fashion, inspiring L.-T.-J. Visconti's Bibliothèque Nationale design and later Visconti's and H.-M. Lefuel's Louvre projects. And the fashion was soon to be even more widespread. In 1861 Lesueur was awarded the Gold Medal of the Royal Institute of British Architects.

Principal executed works:
Church, Vincennes, 1826–30.
Notre-Dame, 33 Rue de Paris, Vincennes, 1830–32.
Apartment house, 7 Boulevard des Capucines, Paris, 1834.
Apartment house, 5 Boulevard des Capucines, Paris, 1835.
Hôtel de Ville, Paris, extension and decoration of Domenico da Cortona's building, 1835–54.
Conservatoire de Musique, Geneva.

LHEUREUX, Louis–Ernest (Fontainebleau, 1827–Passy, Paris, 1898)

A pupil of P.-F.-H. Labrouste, he worked with his teacher on the Collège Ste.-Barbe in Paris and later built a major extension to it on the Rue Vallette. His most important work, however, was the Bibliothèque de l'École de Droit, in the Rue Cujas—directly opposite Labrouste's entrance to the Collège Ste.-Barbe—built between May 1876 and June 1878. From 1880 to 1898 he added another reading room to this, with a facade in a richer vein on the Rue St.-Jacques. He worked in the Service des Travaux d'Architecture de la Ville de Paris, beginning in 1856, erecting buildings for the most part in the fourth, fifth, and twelfth *arrondissements*. His chief work in this capacity was the completion of the Entrepôt de Bercy, begun by L. Cernesson. Lheureux's plans for this were approved in 1876.

Principal executed works:
Church, Bray (Seine-et-Oise). Partly a work of restoration.
Collège Ste.-Barbe, Rue Vallette, Paris. Demolished.
Lheureux House, Rue Largillière, Passy, Paris. Demolished.
Ateliers et Magasins d'Orfèvrerie, 6 Rue d'Antin, Paris. Demolished.
Bibliothèque de l'École de Droit, Rue Cujas, Paris, 1876–78; extension in the Rue St.-Jacques, begun 1880, built 1893–98. Both demolished 1973.
Entrepôt de Bercy, Paris, completion, 1876–. Demolished.
École, Rue St.-Louis-en-l'Île, Paris.

Literature: G. Vapereau, *Dictionnaire universel des contemporains*, Paris, 1893. C. Lucas, "M. Louis-Ernest Lheureux," *La construction moderne* 14 (1898–99), p. 155. L. Capitaine, "L.-E. Lheureux," *L'architecture* 11 (1898), pp. 473–74.

LISCH, Jean-Juste-Gustave (Alençon [Orne], 1828–Paris, 1910)

He was a pupil of A.-L.-T. Vaudoyer and of P.-F.-H. Labrouste at the École des Beaux-Arts, Paris, where he enrolled in 1847. He was to be associated with the Service des Édifices Diocésains and the Commission des Monuments Historiques; to the latter he was appointed *Inspecteur Général*. He designed in a number of established styles but also built some remarkable exposed-iron-frame buildings with infilling panels of tile for the railway companies and for the expositions in Paris of 1878 and 1889.

Principal executed works:
Bishop's palace, Luçon.
École Commerciale, Avenue Trudaine, Paris.
École des Jeunes Filles, Rue de la Santé, Paris.
Couvent des Dames des Oiseaux, Issy-les-Moulineaux.
Couvent des Dames Augustines, Fontainebleau.
Chapel, Couvent des Dames Auxiliatrices du Purgatoire, 16 Rue St.-Jean-Baptiste-de-la-Salle, Paris, 1873–76. Interior redecorated 1956.
Palais de Justice, Agen (Lot-et-Garonne).
Séminaire, Dijon.
Railroad station, Le Havre.
St.-Géraud, Aurillac.
École Normale, Aurillac.
Gare St.-Lazare extension and Terminus Hotel, Paris.
Château d'Athis (Orne).
Gâre des Invalides and stations of the Moulineaux line, Bois de Boulogne and Porte-Maillot.
Apartment house, Rue St.-Lazare, Colombes (Seine).

Literature: C. E. Curinier, *Dictionnaire national des contemporains*, Paris, 1899–1905.

LODOLI, Carlo (Venice, 1690–Padua, 1761)

Lodoli was not an architect, though in 1742 he made some alterations to the pilgrim hostel attached to S. Francesco della Vigna in Venice that reveal something of his ideas as a theoretician. He inclined the wall of the access gallery outward so that two men carrying luggage on their shoulders could pass one another. He curved the underside of the stones of the windowsills and of the thresholds of the doors to give them greater resistance. This arrangement was illustrated in G. Ziborghi's *L'architettura di Jacopo Barozzi da Vignola*, printed in Venice in 1748. Lodoli's radical attempt to relate the forms of architecture to use and to the proper expression of the function of building materials did not have immediate effect in Venice, where he was active, though it was certainly not without influence later. He taught architecture, among other things, to the sons of Venetian noblemen from about 1720 to 1730 and, intermittently, from about 1734 to the time of his death. His theories were never properly recorded. Francesco Algarotti offered a version in his *Saggio sopra l'architettura*, of 1757, which Lodoli considered unsatisfactory. Another disciple, Andrea Memmo, set down a more extensive account in 1784. It was reworked by Angelo Comolli in 1786 and published in part as the *Elementi dell' architettura Lodoliana; ossia, l'arte del fabbricare con solidità scientifica e con eleganza non capricciosa.* This was slightly revised and issued with the second volume only in 1833–34.

Literature: F. Haskell, *Patrons and Painters: A Study in the Relations Between Italian Art and Society in the Age of the Baroque*, London, 1963. A. C. Murat, "Indagini sulla teori veneta dell'età neoclassica," *Bollettino del Centro Internazionale di Studi di Architettura Andrea Palladio* 5 (1963), pp. 99–114. J. Rykwert, "Lodoli on Function and Representation," *Architectural Review* (London), July 1976, pp. 21–26.

LOUDON, John Claudius (Cambuslang, Lanarkshire, 1783–London, 1843)

His father was a farmer, and his first and most sustained interests were in estate management and horticulture. He set out for London in 1803 and soon established himself as a landscape gardener. He returned to Scotland the following year to alter the palace gardens at Scone and at that time published the first in a long series of books on horticulture: *Observations on the Formation and Management of Useful and Ornamental Plantations.* The year after, still in Scotland, he published *A Short Treatise on Some Improvements Lately Made in Hothouses.* This focused on another of his interests, building in iron and glass. He perfected the methods of construction to be taken up by Sir Joseph Paxton at Chatsworth and later at the Crystal Palace. His publications and practical inventions are too numerous even to list here. He was indefatigable. He traveled throughout western Europe and on to Russia. In 1826 he established *The Gardener's Magazine*, six years later, *An Encyclopaedia of Cottage, Farm and Villa Architecture*, which proved an instant success and had a considerable influence on the design of small buildings in England. In 1834 he started *Loudon's Architectural Magazine*; it lasted only four years, but John Ruskin was to be first published in its pages, and it was to serve as the forerunner of the greatest of all architectural periodicals, *The Builder*. In view of his adventurous and enterprising attitude to all things, his own house, 3–5 Porchester Terrace, London, must be judged something of a disappointment. He didn't care a fig for style or styles; to him they were all equal.

Literature: J. Gloag, *Mr. Loudon's England*, London, 1970.

LOUIS, Louis-Nicolas-Victoire, known as Victor Louis (Paris, 1731–Paris, c. 1807)

In 1746 he enrolled at the Académie Royale d'Architecture, Paris, where he became the pupil of L.-A. Loriot and in 1755 was awarded a Gold Medal and the equivalent of the Grand Prix, though his drawings did not conform to the stipulated program. He arrived in Rome in September 1756 and stayed there three years. By the time he returned to Paris he had changed his name to Victor Louis. He designed a remarkable chapel in 1763 for Ste.-Marguerite-de-Charonne, painted in *trompe l'oeil* by P. A. Brunetti. Late in 1764, on the recommendation of Mme. Geoffrin, he started work for the king of Poland and became his official architect. He was in Warsaw in 1765, designing the new palace. But nothing much was to come of this activity. It was rather through the Duc de Richelieu, whose house in the Rue Neuve-St.-Augustin he had redecorated, that Louis

obtained his great opportunity. In 1772 he was commissioned to build the new theater at Bordeaux. He built much else besides in that town and in its environs, conferring upon the region a cosmopolitanism unrivaled by any other provincial center in France. Later he worked in Paris at the Palais-Royal, on the same large scale that had by then become a feature of his style.

Principal executed works:
Chapel, Notre-Dame-de-Bon-Secours, Rue de Charonne, Paris, 1760.
Chapelle des Âmes du Purgatoire, Ste.-Marguerite-de-Charonne, Rue de Charonne, Paris, 1763–65. Decorations painted by P. A. Brunetti.
St.-Vincent, Place St.-Vincent, Metz.
St.-Clement, off the Rue du Pontiffroy, Metz, facade.
Temporary ballroom for the Spanish ambassador's celebration of the dauphin's marriage to Marie Antoinette, Vauxhall de Torré, Paris, 1770.
Vauxhall, Bois de Boulogne, Paris, 1770.
Hôtel de Richelieu, Rue Neuve-St.-Augustin, Paris, 1772–73.
Hôtel de l'Intendance (now Préfecture), Rue Charles-Nodier, Besançon, 1772–76. Built by N. Nicole.
Grand Théâtre, Bordeaux, 1773–80. (V. Louis, *Salle de spectacle de Bordeaux*, 1782.)
Hôtel Fontfrède, 1 Cours du Chapeau-Rouge, Bordeaux, 1774–76.
Hôtel Legrix (now Préfecture), 22 Rue Esprit-des-Lois, Bordeaux.
Hôtel Saige (now Préfecture), 23 Cours du Chapeau-Rouge, Bordeaux, 1774–80.
Hôtel de la Molère, 4 Rue Esprit-des-Lois, Bordeaux.
Hôtel de Rolly, Place de la Comédie, Bordeaux. Demolished.
Hôtel de Nairac, 17 Cours de Verdun, Bordeaux, begun 1775. Altered internally.
Château de Virasel (near Marmande).
Palais-Royal, Paris, galleries and theater (now Théâtre-Français), 1781. Rebuilt 1902 by Julien and Paul Guadet.
Château de Bouilh, St.-André-de-Cubzac (Gironde), begun 1786. Never completed. (*Country Life*, Jan. 13, 1977, pp. 70–73.)

Literature: C. Marionneau, *Victor Louis, sa vie, ses travaux et sa correspondance, 1731–1800,* Bordeaux, 1881. F. G. Pariset and S. Lorenz, *Victor Louis et Varsovie*, exhib. cat., Bordeaux and Paris, 1958. F. G. Pariset, *Histoire de Bordeaux, 1714–1814*, vol. 5, Bordeaux, 1968. J. Foucart-Borville, "Les projets de Charles de Wailly pour la gloire de la cathédrale d'Amiens et de Victor Louis pour le maître autel de la cathédrale de Noyon," *Bulletin de la Société de l'Histoire de l'Art Français*, Année 1974 (1975), pp. 131–44. *Piranèse et les français, 1740–1790*, exhib. cat., Académie de France à Rome, Rome, 1976.

LOYER, Toussaint-Noël (Rouen, 1724–Lyons, 1807)

He studied in Paris, where he was taken up by J.-G. Soufflot, who about 1747 sent him to Lyons to supervise the building of the convent of St.-Augustin (Génovéfains), of the dome of the Hôtel-Dieu, and later of the

new theater. In 1758 he designed the Hôtel de Varey, 2 Rue Auguste-Comte, Lyons, overlooking the Place Bellecour, Lyons, simple enough externally, but with paneling in the rooms on three of the floors that marks the beginning of the new interior style of the late eighteenth century. The designs, though innovatory, are clumsy— very close to those illustrated in the same years in J.-F. de Neufforge's *Recueil*. In 1803 Loyer became *Architecte de la Ville de Lyons.* J.-B. Rondelet was his pupil.

Principal executed works:
Hôtel de Varey, 2 Rue Auguste-Comte, Lyons, 1758–c. 1760.
St.-Polycarpe, Lyons, facade, 1760.
Hôtel Dervieux-du-Villars, Lyons.

Literature: E.-L.-G. Charvet, *Lyon artistique: architectes, notices biographiques et bibliographiques,* Lyons, 1899, p. 226. S. Eriksen, *Early Neo-Classicism in France*, London, 1974.

LUSSON, Louis-Adrien (La Flèche, 1790–Rome, 1864)

He studied first with Lahure and then at the École des Beaux-Arts, Paris, under Charles Percier and P.-F.-L. Fontaine. He began his career in 1820, at Le Mans, where he built the market, but he then moved to Paris, where he worked for the administration. In 1829 he was appointed architect to the Place Louis XV (Place de la Concorde) and in the following year won a competition for the erection of iron fountains there. J.-I. Hittorff, who later took over as architect, was to adopt this idea. But Lusson himself adopted the idea of columns of iron for the church of St.-Eugène in Paris from L.-A. Boileau, by whom he was soon succeeded as architect. Lusson was an active propagandist for the use of iron in architecture. He published much on this and other subjects but built nothing of interest. His most arresting work was the customs house in the Rue Chauchat, Paris, built in 1827, transformed in part into a church in 1843 by F. C. Gau.

McKIM, Charles Follen (Chester County, Pennsylvania, 1847–St. James, Pennsylvania, 1909)

He studied engineering at Harvard University and then architecture at the École des Beaux-Arts, in Paris, from 1867 to 1870. He worked in H. H. Richardson's office on his return, before setting up a partnership with W. R. Mead and, a little later, with Stanford White. His grandiose classical style, looking to Rome and the Renaissance rather than to Greece for inspiration, is of such brilliance that he must be considered one of the two or three greatest architects America has produced. His masterpieces were the Boston Public Library and the Pennsylvania Railroad Station, New York City.

Principal executed works:
H. Victor Newcomb House, Elberon, New Jersey, 1880–81.
Isaac Bell, Jr., House, Newport, Rhode Island, 1881–82.
Villard Houses, Madison Avenue, New York City, 1882.
Charles A. Tiffany House, New York City, 1882–83.

W. G. Low House, Bristol, Rhode Island, 1887.
Boston Public Library, Boston, Massachusetts, 1887.
Germantown Cricket Club, Philadelphia, 1891.
Madison Square Garden, New York City, 1891. Demolished.
Washington Triumphal Arch, New York City, 1892.
Columbia University, New York City, 1893.
University Club, New York City, 1899.
Morgan Library, New York City, 1903.
Pennsylvania Railroad Station, New York City, 1904–10. Demolished.
Madison Square Presbyterian Church, New York City, 1906.

Literature: A Monograph of the Work of McKim, Mead and White, 4 vols., New York, 1915–25. C. H. Reilly, *McKim, Mead and White*, 1924. C. Moore, *The Life and Times of Charles Follen McKim*, Boston and New York, 1929 (repr. 1970).

MARCHIONNI, Carlo Francesco Giacomo (Rome, 1702–Rome, 1786)

He studied first under Filippo Barigioni, a pupil of Carlo Fontana. In 1728 he won the Concorso Clementino at the Accademia di San Luca, thus establishing a reputation for himself. His first works, both in Rome, were at the Castel Sant' Angelo, where he was associated with the sculptor Pietro Bracci, and at S. Croce in Gerusalemme, where he was responsible for the tomb of Benedict XIV. His great work was the Villa Albani, which has been variously dated: His connection with Cardinal Alessandro Albani dates from 1738, at least, but the first designs for the villa are of 1746, and Marchionni's work began on the garden in 1751. G. B. Nolli collaborated on the garden layout and ornamentation and, after 1757, J. J. Winckelmann no doubt advised on the design, in particular on that of the two temple porticos composed of antique fragments. The building was ready for occupation at the beginning of 1763. Marchionni's other important commission, the new sacristy of St. Peter's, was no doubt granted because of his connection with Cardinal Albani, but he had been called in as early as 1752 to act as assistant architect to the fabric by his old master Barigioni and was to work there also under Luigi Vanvitelli. He designed the doorway for the Museo Profano. The sacristy was begun in 1776, the year after Marchionni had been elected director of the Accademia di San Luca.

Principal executed works:
Villa Albani (now Villa Torlonia), Via Salaria, Rome, 1751–67.
S. Domenico, Ancona, facade and related buildings, 1763–86. (R. Elia, "La chiesa di San Domenico in Ancona," *Studia piceno* 23 [1955], pp. 53–86.)
S. Maddalena de Cassinesi, Messina, 1763–.
New sacristy, St. Peter's, Rome, 1776–84.

Literature: J. Gaus, *Carlo Marchionni: Ein Beitrag zur römischen Architektur des Settecento*, Cologne, 1967.

MARVUGLIA, Giuseppe Venanzio (Palermo, 1729–1814)

He studied under Luigi Vanvitelli in Rome but was chiefly active in Sicily, where he was to be strongly influenced later in life by the French architect Léon Dufourny.

Principal executed works:
Oratorio di S. Filippo Neri, Palermo, 1769.
Villa Giulia, Palermo, extension to Léon Dufourny's building.
La Favorita (or Palazzina Cinese), Palermo, 1799–1802. (*Country Life*, 1947, pp. 724–25).
Villa Belmonte (near Palermo), 1801.

Literature: S. Caronia Roberti, *Venanzio Marvuglia*, Palermo, 1934.

MEMMO, Andrea (Venice, 1729–Venice, 1793)

He was not an architect but, taught by Carlo Lodoli, he determined to sponsor a more radical and public-spirited form of architecture. When serving as *Provveditore* (governor) of Padua from March 1775 to 1776, he initiated plans for both the new hospital and the famous Prato della Valle, built under the direction of the local architect Domenico Cerato. The latter was completed only in the nineteenth century. In 1779, when serving as *Bailo* (ambassador) to Constantinople, Memmo prepared a design for a new embassy that incorporated windows with curved undersides to the sills, similar to those Lodoli had built into the pilgrim hostel at S. Francesco della Vigna in Venice. The embassy was not built. Memmo recorded what he recalled of Lodoli's theories in 1784 and published them with the help of Angelo Comolli in 1786 as *Elementi dell' architettura Lodoliana; ossia, l'arte del fabbricare con solidità scientifica e con eleganza non capricciosa.* The second volume was published only in 1833–34.

Literature: G. F. Torcellan, *Una figura della Venezia settecentesca, Andrea Memmo*, Venice and Rome, 1963.

MILLER, Sanderson (Edgehill, Warwickshire, 1717–1780)

A country gentleman and amateur architect, he was one of the principal pioneers of the Gothic Revival. His best-known work is perhaps the pseudo-Gothic castle at Edgehill, admired by Horace Walpole; his most unexpected work is another Gothic "castle" in Arlington Street in the heart of London.

Principal executed works:
Radway Grange, Warwickshire, remodeling, 1744–46. (*Country Life*, Sept. 6, 1946.)
Castle, Edgehill, Warwickshire, 1745–47. (*Country Life*, Sept. 13, 1946.)
Castle, Hagley Park, Worcestershire, 1747–48. (*Country Life*, Sept. 19, 1957.)
Castle, Wimpole Hall, Cambridgeshire, 1750. (*Country Life*, May 21, 1927.)
Arbury Hall, Warwickshire, 1750–. Here Miller assisted in the remodeling. (*Country Life*, Oct. 8, 15, 29, 1953.)
Lacock Abbey, Wiltshire, remodeling, 1754–55. (*Country Life* 53, pp. 280, 314, 352.)

Hagley Hall, Worcestershire, 1754–60. (*Country Life*, Sept. 19–26, 1957.)
Pomfret House, Arlington Street, London, 1758–60. Demolished 1920. (J. Cornforth, "A Countess's London Castle," *Country Life Annual*, 1970, pp. 138–39.)

MILLET, Eugène-Louis (Paris, 1819–Cannes, 1879)

He entered the École des Beaux-Arts, Paris, in 1837 as a pupil of P.-F.-H. Labrouste but was to be associated rather with E.-E. Viollet-le-Duc and the Commission des Monuments Historiques, whose service he entered in 1849. He was active largely as a restorer, working on the cathedrals of Troyes (1848–), Moulins (1860–), and Rheims (1874–), and also on the Château de St.-Germain-en-Laye (1855–). When Viollet-le-Duc attempted to reform the École des Beaux-Arts in 1863, Millet took over the course on construction and taught at that school for two years before resigning to teach instead the members of the Cercle des Ouvriers Maçons et Tailleurs de Pierres, for whom he built a small center at 9 Rue des Chantiers, Paris. He built little of interest. His most important works were the Greffulhe Hospice, Levallois-Perret, of 1869 (demolished in 1969), and the parish church at Maisons-Lafitte (designed in 1867). His tomb, in the cemetery at St.-Germain-en-Laye, was the last of Viollet-le-Duc's designs.

Literature: Eugène Millet, sa vie, ses oeuvres, son tombeau, Paris, 1881.

MILLS, Robert (Charleston, South Carolina, 1781–1855)

A pupil of Benjamin Latrobe from 1803 to 1808, he is best known for his big, bland, late classical public buildings in Washington, D.C.

Principal executed works:
Pennsylvania State House, Harrisburg, 1810.
Monumental Church, Richmond, Virginia, 1812.
Washington Monument, Baltimore, Maryland, 1814–29.
County Records Office, Charleston, South Carolina, 1822.
Patent Office Building, Washington, D.C., 1836–40.
Treasury Department Building, Washington, D. C., 1836–42.
Washington Monument, Washington, D.C., designed 1836, built 1848–84.
Post Office Building, Washington, D.C., 1839.

Literature: H. Gallagher, *Robert Mills*, New York, 1935.

MIQUE, Richard (Nancy, 1728–Paris, 1794)

Son of a local architect, he was sent first to Strasbourg to study with an engineer and then to Paris, where he became a pupil of Jacques-François Blondel. He established himself first in Nancy, as architect to King Stanislas, serving as chief engineer in the Ponts et Chaussées de Lorraine et Barrois and then, on Emmanuel Héré's death in 1763, as *Directeur Général des Bâti-*

ments du Roi de Pologne. In 1766 he was induced by Marie Antoinette to become her architect, chiefly at the Petit Trianon, so he moved to Versailles. On A.-J. Gabriel's death in 1782 he became *Architecte du Roi* and *Directeur de l'Académie Royale d'Architecture.* He was guillotined for trying to help Marie Antoinette to escape.

Principal executed works:
Theater and garden buildings, Petit Trianon, Versailles. (P. de Nolhac, *Le Trianon de Marie Antoinette,* Paris, 1914.)
Couvent des Augustines (now Lycée Hoche), Versailles, 1767–72. (A. Hachette, *Le couvent de la reine à Versailles,* 1922.)
Église des Carmelites (now "Petite Paroisse"), Saint-Denis, 1775.
Chapel, Hospice de St.-Cloud, St.-Cloud, 1788.

Literature: P. Lavedan, "Richard Mique, architecte de Marie Antoinette," *Bulletin de la Société de l'Histoire de l'Art Français,* 1941/44, p. 25. M. Gallet, *Paris Domestic Architecture of the 18th Century,* London, 1972.

MOLINOS, Jacques (Lyons, 1743–1831)

He worked with J.-G. Legrand from 1782 to 1783 on the design and construction of the great timber dome of the Halle aux Blés in Paris. Two years later, they traveled together to Italy. Molinos appears to have built nothing more of much interest, though he held a succession of important administrative posts and continued to be active until 1829, when he was made a member of the Institut.

Principal executed works:
Jacquin House, Les Près-St.-Gervais, 1775.
Château de Puisieux (near Villers-Cotterêts), 1780–85.
Halle aux Blés, Paris, dome, 1782–83, with J.-G. Legrand. Destroyed 1802. (*Art Bulletin* 55, no. 2, pp. 262–79.)

Literature: M. Gallet, *Paris Domestic Architecture of the 18th Century,* London, 1972.

MORAGLIA, Giacomo (Milan, 1791–1860)

He was an architect of no great distinction who pursued the classical path already explored by others. Much of his work involved the completion of buildings begun by such architects as Simone Cantoni, Luigi Cagnola, and Luigi Canonica.

Principal executed works:
SS. Protasio e Gervasio, Gorgonzola, continuation of Simone Cantoni's work and campanile, 1818–20, 1842.
Palazzo Civico, Lugano, 1839–44.
SS. Crocifisso, Stresa, 1842–47.

Literature: G. Mezzanotte, *Architettura neoclassica in Lombardia,* Naples, 1966.

MOREAU-DESPROUX, Pierre-Louis (1727–1793)

He came from an architectural dynasty that held the post of *Maître des Bâtiments de la Ville de Paris.* In 1752 Charles de Wailly, who had won the Grand Prix, offered to share the prize with Moreau-Desproux (who had won the second prize in 1750, 1751, and 1752), and the two men stayed in Rome from October 1754 to December 1756. On his return Moreau was commissioned to design the Hôtel de Chavannes, which had been completed by May of 1758. This won acclaim as an early example of a new, more consciously classical style and was praised by the Abbé Laugier in his *Observations.* But Moreau-Desproux was not an innovator. He was scarcely even adequate to the role he inherited as *Maître des Bâtiments de la Ville de Paris,* a post he held from 1763 to 1787.

Principal executed works:
Hôtel de Chavannes, Boulevard du Temple, Paris, 1756–58.
Théâtre de l'Opéra, Palais-Royal, Paris, 1763–70.
Fontaine des Haudriettes, Rue des Haudriettes and Rue des Archives, Paris, 1764.
Pavillon Carré de Beaudouin, 121 Rue de Ménilmontant, Paris, 1770.
Hôtel de Gontaut, Rue Louis-le-Grand, Paris, 1772.
Hôtel Saint-Julien, Rue d'Artois, Paris.

Literature: M. Gallet, "Dessins de Pierre-Louis Moreau-Desproux pour les édifices parisiens," *Bulletin du Musée Carnavalet,* Nov. 1961, pp. 6–15.

MORRIS, William (Walthamstow, Essex, 1834–Hammersmith, London, 1896)

He was not an architect, though he worked for a time in the office of G. E. Street, and he had no direct architectural influence. His Red House at Upton (1859), reflecting the parsonage style of William Butterfield, Street, and William White and designed for him by Philip Webb, was already old-fashioned when it was built. His campaigns against the restoration of medieval buildings did not meet with much success, nor did his proposals for abolishing the ugliness in towns caused by the Industrial Revolution. It is as a decorative designer of superlative quality that Morris is important. For the firm of Morris, Marshall & Faulkner, which he founded in 1861, he produced an endless stream of lovely designs, based on medieval and Renaissance sources, for stained glass, wallpaper, tiles, printed textiles, carpets, and tapestries. The various aspects of his achievement as a designer can best be appreciated in the works listed below.

Principal executed interiors (extant):
Red House, Upton (near Bexleyheath), Kent, 1859. (*Country Life* 127 [1960], p. 1382.)
Green Dining Room, Victoria and Albert Museum, London, 1866.
Tapestry Room and Armory, St. James's Palace, London, 1866–67.
Chapel, Jesus College, Cambridge University, Cambridge, 1867–74.
Hall and Combination Room, Peterhouse, Cambridge University, Cambridge, 1868–74.
Hall, Queens' College, Cambridge University, Cambridge, 1875.
Standen, Sussex, 1891–94. (*Country Life* 147, pp. 494, 554.)

Wightwick Manor, Staffordshire. (*Country Life* 133, pp. 1242, 1316.)

Literature: W. Morris, *The Unpublished Lectures of William Morris,* ed. E. D. Lemire, Detroit, 1969. W. Morris, "The Revival of Architecture," *Fortnightly Review,* May 1888 (repr. in N. Pevsner, *Some Architectural Writers of the 19th Century,* Oxford, 1972, pp. 315–24). N. Pevsner, "William Morris and Architecture," *Journal of the Royal Institute of British Architects* 64 (1957), pp. 172–77 (repr. in N. Pevsner, *Studies in Art, Architecture and Design,* vol. 2, 1968, pp. 108–17). P. Henderson, *William Morris: His Life, Work and Friends,* 1968. P. Thompson, *The Work of William Morris,* 1968. A. C. Sewter, *The Stained Glass of William Morris and His Circle,* 2 vols., New Haven, Conn., 1974–76.

NAISSANT, Claude (1801–1879)

He was official architect to the town of Sceaux from 1843 to 1866 and in this capacity built a number of churches in the area. These might be described as Romanesque Revival of an unusual kind, perhaps influenced by the works of the German architect C. von Lassaulx, who was early publicized in France in the pages of the *Annales archéologiques.*

Principal executed works:
St.-Lambert, Rue Bausset, Vaugirard, Paris, 1848–56.
Notre-Dame-de-la-Gare, Place Jeanne d'Arc, Ivry (now Gobelins, Paris), 1855–64.
Sous-Préfecture, Sceaux, 1855–66.
St.-Charles-Borromée, Joinville-le-Pont, 1856–66.
St.-Pierre, Place de l'Église, Charenton-le-Pont, 1857–59.
Ste.-Geneviève, Place Carnot, Rosny-sous-Bois, 1857–66.
Notre-Dame-de-la-Médaille-Miraculeuse, 80 Avenue Pierre Larousse, Malakoff, 1861.
Mairie, Issy-sur-Seine, 1863.

NARJOUX, Félix (Chalon-sur-Saône [Saône-et-Loire], 1836–Sèvres, 1891)

He studied first with his father, a local architect, then under S.-C. Constant-Dufeux in Paris, where he enrolled in 1854 in the École des Beaux-Arts. He soon became associated with E.-E. Viollet-le-Duc and in 1857 was appointed architect to the restoration of Limoges cathedral. In 1860 he became *Architecte de la Ville de Nice* and ten years later *Architecte de la Ville de Paris.* In the latter capacity he was responsible for several new schools, among them the Groupe Scolaire, Rue Curial (now 41 Rue de Tanger), of 1875–76, and the École Voltaire, 12–14 Rue Titon, of 1881–82. He wrote several small books on the schools of various countries: *Écoles primaires* (1879), *Écoles publiques en France et en Angleterre* (1876), *Écoles publiques en Belgique et en Hollande* (1878), and *Écoles publiques en Suisse* (1879). But his important compilations were those of the buildings of the capital: *Paris: monuments élevés par la ville, 1850–1880* (1880–83) and *Architecture communale* (1870–80). He also wrote a somewhat embarrassing novel on the life of an Oxford don, *L'aventure de William Knobbs* (1882).

Literature: J. Lermina, *Dictionnaire universel . . . de la France contemporaine*, Paris, 1884. G. Vapereau, *Dictionnaire universel des contemporains*, Paris, 1893.

NASH, John (London, 1752–Isle of Wight, 1835)

A pupil of Sir Robert Taylor, he was established as an architect and speculative builder in London by 1777, but in 1783 he went bankrupt. He then set up an architectural practice in Wales but returned to London in 1796, when he formed a partnership with the landscape gardener Humphry Repton. This connection with Repton emphasized Nash's role as the leading Picturesque architect, composing scenery in which house and setting blended into a unity. Nash's unique contribution to English architecture was to bring this particular skill to London in the development of Regent's Park and Regent Street. The Prince Regent was an active patron of Nash and commissioned him to remodel Carlton House, Brighton Pavilion, and Buckingham Palace.

Principal executed works:
East Cowes Castle, Isle of Wight, begun c. 1798. Demolished 1950.
Luscombe Castle, Devonshire, 1799–1804. (*Country Life* 119 [1956], pp. 248, 292, 336.)
Cronkhill, Shropshire, c. 1802.
Dairy, c. 1805, and Blaise Hamlet, 1811, Blaise Castle, near Bristol.
Ravensworth Castle, County Durham, 1808. Demolished.
Caerhays Castle, Cornwall, 1808.
Attingham Park, Shropshire, picture gallery, c. 1810. (*Country Life* 49 [1921], pp. 158, 186.)
Caledon, County Tyrone, additions, 1812. (*Country Life*, Feb. 27–Mar. 6, 1937.)
Brighton, Royal Pavilion, remodeling, 1815–21. (H. D. Roberts, *History of the Royal Pavilion*, Brighton, 1939; C. Musgrave, *Royal Pavilion: An Episode in the Romantic*, 1959.)
Regent Street quadrant, London, 1818–20. Demolished 1906–.
Regent's Park, London, terraces, 1821–30.
Buckingham Palace, London, remodeling and extension, 1825–30. (H. Clifford Smith, *Buckingham Palace*, 1931; J. Harris et al., *Buckingham Palace*, 1968.)
United Service Club, London, 1827. (*Country Life* 131, p. 832.)
St. James's Park, London, planting and layout, 1827.
Carlton House Terrace, London, 1827–33.

Literature: J. Summerson, *John Nash*, 1935, 2d ed., 1949. T. Davis, *The Architecture of John Nash*, 1960. T. Davis, *John Nash: The Prince Regent's Architect*, 1966.

NÉNOT, Paul-Henri (Paris, 1853–1934)

A pupil of P.-E. Lequeux, of C.-A. Questel, and of J.-L. Pascal, he worked also with J.-L.-C. Garnier. He won the Grand Prix in 1877, and in 1882 received first prize in the competition for the Victor Emmanuel II monument in Rome. This he was not to build. But in 1884, in Paris, he won another competition and put up a building almost as large and of the same inflated scale: the Nouvelle Sorbonne. He published a mono-

graph on this with Liard, *La nouvelle Sorbonne*, in 1895.

Principal executed works:
Nouvelle Sorbonne, Paris, 1885–1901.
Institut Océanographique, 195 Rue St.-Jacques, Paris, 1910.
Banque Dreyfus, Rue de la Banque, Paris.
Bureaux de la Compagnie Générale Transatlantique, Paris.
Administration de la Compagnie d'Assurance, La Nationale, Paris.
Administration de la Compagnie Internationale des Wagons-Lits, Paris.
Apartment house, Rue du Luxembourg, Paris.

Literature: C. E. Curinier, *Dictionnaire national des contemporains*, Paris, 1899–1905. E. Joseph, *Dictionnaire biographique des artistes contemporains*, Paris, 1934. "Henri-Paul Nénot," *Architectural Review* (London), July 1917, pp. 5–10.

NEUFFORGE, Jean-François de (Comblain-au-Pont [near Liège], 1714–Paris, 1791)

He is said to have studied under Jacques-François Blondel and with the engraver P. E. Babel. His fame was based on the plates of his *Recueil élémentaire d'architecture*, issued in nine volumes from 1757 to 1772. The nine hundred illustrations served to promote a somewhat heavy-handed revival of the Louis XIV style, which, however, impinged often enough on the neoclassicism of the late eighteenth century. Though he does not appear to have been a designer of originality, Neufforge was quick to take up ideas and to publicize them. He also engraved eighteen of the plates for J.-D. Le Roy's *Ruines des plus beaux monuments de la Grèce*, of 1758.

Literature: S. Eriksen, *Early Neo-Classicism in France*, London, 1974.

NICCOLINI, Antonio (San Miniato al Monte, 1772–Naples, 1850)

He trained first in Florence and worked initially at the Villa del Poggio Imperiale under F. G. P. Poccianti. Then he went to Livorno, where Poccianti was restoring the Teatro Avvalorati. He was invited in 1806 to Naples as a set designer but took up the offer only two years later, when Murat became king. He worked at the Fondo and the S. Carlo theaters. A new facade for the latter—built by G. A. Medrano in 1737—was required at the time, and Niccolini was shown the design submitted by the French architect Lecomte. He dismissed this and proposed a competition, which he won. His massive, large-scale facade, hinting at an intimate knowledge of Poccianti's designs for the Villa del Poggio Imperiale, was begun late in 1809 and finished within a year, establishing his reputation and introducing a new, sterner manner into Neapolitan architecture. The theater behind burned down in 1816 and he was commissioned at once, together with Antonio de Simone, to rebuild it in the new style. He became, and remained, the court architect, spending years elaborating plans for the extension of the royal palace, by the side

of his theater. Nothing came of these giant schemes, but he did build a number of villas for the royal favorites and others. In 1816 he was made director of the Scuola di Scenografia and four years later *Professore di Prospettive* at the Istituto di Belle Arti, for which he designed a dull building in 1822.

Principal executed works:
Teatro S. Carlo, Naples, facade, 1810–11; auditorium, 1816–17, with Antonio de Simone.
Villa Floridiana, Vomero, Naples, 1817–19. Now a museum.
Villa Lucia, Vomero, Naples, 1818.
Palazzo Partanna, Piazza dei Martiri, Naples, refacing and redecoration.
Palazzo Pignatelli-Strongoli, Riviera di Chiaja, Naples, 1820.
Tondo di Capodimonte, Naples, 1836.
Teatro Piccini, Bari, 1854, carried out by Niccolini's son Fausto after his death. Now part of the Palazzo Communale.

Literature: A. Venditti, *Architettura neoclassica a Napoli*, Naples, 1961.

NICOLE, Nicolas (Besançon, 1702–Besançon, 1784)

He was trained first as a wood carver and then worked with Jacques-François Blondel in Paris. By 1739 he had returned to Besançon to design the Chapelle du Refuge and to begin his career. He put up a number of buildings in the Franche-Comté in the following years, the most important of which was La Madeleine in Besançon. In 1771 he undertook to supervise the construction of the Hôtel de l'Intendance (now the Préfecture) to the designs of Victor Louis, then in Bordeaux. This was completed by 1776.

Principal executed works:
Chapelle du Refuge (Chapelle de l'Hôpital), Besançon, 1739–45.
La Madeleine, Place Claude de Jouffroy, Besançon, 1746–66.
St.-Pierre, Jussey (Haute-Saône), nave and west front, 1750–60. The choir dates from the sixteenth century.
Church, Voray-sur-l'Ognon (Haute-Saône), 1770.

Literature: R. Tournier, "L'architecte Nicolas Nicole, 1702–1784," *Académie des Sciences, Belles-Lettres et Arts de Besançon*, 1938, pp. 112–26. R. Tournier, *L'architecte Nicolas Nicole, 1702–1784*, Besançon, 1942.

NOBILE, Pietro (Campestro [Ticino], 1774–Vienna, 1854)

In 1785 he arrived in Trieste, where he grew up and studied, but he was also for a time in Vienna and, between 1803 and 1805, in Rome, where he encountered the sculptor Antonio Canova. By 1807 he was back in Trieste, where for ten years he was in charge of all official works and director of the Accademia di Belle Arti. He was responsible for several notable buildings in Trieste, of a purer and more restrained style than had hitherto been seen in that town. His most important and certainly most successful building was the church of S. Antonio Nuovo. During his later life, from 1817 on, he was active in Vienna and also in Graz.

Principal executed works:
Accademia di Commercio e Nautica (now Biblioteca Civica Hortis), Piazza A. Hortis, Trieste, 1817. The upper floor was added in 1856.
Burgtor, Vienna, 1821–24, based in part on Luigi Cagnola's design of 1818.
Theseus Temple, Volksgarten, Vienna, 1822.
S. Antonio Nuovo (or S. Antonio Taumaturgo), Piazza S. Antonio, Trieste, 1825–49 (the first sketches date from 1808).
Fontana House, 4 Via del Pesce, Trieste, 1827–30 (the initial projects date from 1813–16).
Lanterna Vecchia, Trieste, 1833.
Costanzi House, Piazza Piccola, and Via della Muda Vecchia, Trieste, 1840.

Literature: L'architettura 1 (1955), pp. 49–52, 378–84. M. Walcher Casotti, *L'architettura a Trieste della fine del settecento agli inizio del novecento,* Udine, 1967. L. T. Zucca, *Architettura neoclassica a Trieste,* Trieste, 1974.

NOTTOLINI, Lorenzo (Segromigno [near Lucca], 1787–Lucca, 1851)

He studied first under Giovanni Lazzarini in Lucca but in October 1811 went to Florence under the patronage of the grand duchess to enroll at the Accademia delle Belle Arti under Paoletti and Vannini. In 1812 he transferred, for three months, to the Accademia Clementina at Bologna, to work with G. A. Antolini and then, in November of the same year, traveled to Rome to study at the Accademia delle Belle Arti and the Accademia di San Luca. He stayed in Rome until 1817, working, it seems, for Giuseppe Valadier. Back in Lucca, he was appointed architect to the court in 1818 and soon after was placed in charge of all the public works of the town and the surrounding areas. He reorganized the walls, laid out new streets, greatly enlarged the Palazzo Ducale, and finished off these urban improvements with a series of fountains. But his major works were in the countryside, where he built a magnificent aqueduct and bridges and designed a vast royal residence, though of this project only a hunting lodge and an observatory were built. Many drawings survive to attest to his activity in the region of Lucca. Many of his projects, all but one in the classical style, are on the grandest of scales, and it is scarcely to be wondered at that they were not built. His sole vagary was a design made in 1835 for a Gothic church for Stiava, though the classical design he prepared in 1817 in Rome for a church in Limerick for the Irish congregation of St. Clement may be accounted another extraordinary commission.

Principal executed works:
Palazzo Ducale, Lucca, vaulted entranceway, grand stairway, Galleria delle Statue, 1818; Palazzina on the north courtyard, 1834.
Reggia, Viareggio, 1820–25. Only a small part of the original project was built, incorporating the Villa Cittadella.
Aqueduct and related structures outside Lucca, 1820–34.
Capella Orsetti, Camposanto, Lucca, 1822.

Villa Reale and Specola (observatory), Marlia, 1822–25.
Timber grandstand, Lucca, 1826.
Monastero dell' Angelo, Monti di Brancoli, Vinchiana (near Lucca), rebuilding and new church, 1827–34.
Piazza Antelminelli, Lucca, 1832–35.
Fountains, Piazza S. Salvatore, Via del Fosso, and Via del Gonfalone, Lucca.
Casina di Caccia di Carlo Lodovico (a hunting lodge), pass of Pieve Santo Stefano (near Lucca), rebuilding, 1837–43.
Suspension bridge, Fornoli, 1839.

Literature: M. D. Bardeschi et al., *Lorenzo Nottolini architetto a Lucca,* Lucca, 1970.

OURADOU, Maurice-Augustin-Gabriel (Paris, 1822–1884)

A pupil of L.-H. Lebas, he worked later for E.-E. Viollet-le-Duc and became his son-in-law. He supervised the construction of several minor buildings designed by Viollet-le-Duc, and these were later to be credited to Ouradou. On Viollet-le-Duc's behalf, he traveled to Russia in March 1877, to check observations made in the text of his father-in-law's *Art russe* (1877).

PAINE, James (Andover, Hampshire, 1717–France, 1789)

A prolific architect of country houses, he developed the neo-Palladian tradition with great refinement. He published much of his work in two volumes in 1767 and 1783 as *Plans . . . of . . . Houses . . . Executed in the Counties of Derby, Durham, Middlesex, Northumberland, Nottingham and York.*

Principal executed works:
Nostell Priory, Yorkshire, c. 1735–50. (*Country Life* 111, pp. 1248, 1492, 1572, 1652; *Country Life* 112, p. 1028.)
Mansion House, Doncaster, Yorkshire, 1745–48.
Kedleston Hall, Derbyshire, 1757–61. Completed by Robert Adam. (*Country Life* 34, pp. 892, 928.)
Stockeld Park, Yorkshire, 1758–63. (*Country Life* 145, p. 466.)
Gibside, County Durham, chapel and mausoleum, 1760. (*Country Life,* Feb. 8–15, 1952.)
Brocket Hall, Hertfordshire, 1760s–. (*Country Life,* July 4–18, 1925.)
Wardour Castle, Wiltshire, 1770–76. (*Country Life,* Nov. 22–29, 1930.)

PALAGI, Pelagio (Bologna, 1775–Turin, 1860)

He studied painting first in Rome. From 1815 until 1832, when he moved to Turin, he was active in Milan, working in part under Giocondo Albertolli. His work in Milan is of minor importance, but already he was designing in the gimcrack Gothic style on which his future distinction was to rest.

Principal executed works:
Palazzo Aresi, Milan, c. 1830.

Villa Traversi, Desio, tower in the Gothic style.
La Margheria, Racconigi, 1834–39.
Palazzo Reale, Turin, main ballroom, 1835–42.

Literature: A. Boidi, "Pelagio Palagi e il neogotico in Piemonte," *Bolletino della Società Piemontese di Architettura e Belle Arti* 19 (1965), pp. 49–67.

PAOLETTI, Gaspare Maria (Modena, 1727–1813)

He established the Accademia delle Belle Arti in Florence in 1766 and was for years associated with all the major architectural projects instituted there by the grand duke, in particular the works at the Villa del Poggio Imperiale at nearby Caiano, from 1770 to 1781, and at the Uffizi, where he designed the Sala della Niobe in 1779. He was responsible also for the Bagni della Valdinievole at Montecatini, of 1773.

PÂRIS, Pierre-Adrien (Besançon, 1745–Besançon, 1819)

His father was *Intendant des Bâtiments du Prince-Évêque de Bâle.* He studied in Paris under L.-F. Trouard, failed to win the Grand Prix, but was sent nonetheless to Rome in 1770. There he taught Giambattista Piranesi's son Francesco and became acquainted with the Abbé de Saint-Non, for whose *Voyage pittoresque* he drew a number of plates. He returned in 1774 to Paris, where he worked for the Duc d'Aumont. Through him, Pâris was appointed to succeed M.-A. Challe at the Menus-Plaisirs in 1778 and then, after a second journey to Italy with Trouard in 1783, was named *Architecte des Menus-Plaisirs.* Later he traveled to Rome again and settled there for a time, serving briefly as director of the Académie de France. He returned in 1817 to Besançon, where his marvelous collection of drawings is now installed in the museum and his own collected designs in the local library. He built very little of note, though much that was attractive.

Principal executed works:
Hôtel (now Hôtel de Crillon), Place de la Concorde, Paris, interiors for the Duc d'Aumont. Now in the Hôtel de la Tour d'Auvergne, 2 Avenue de La Motte-Picquet, Paris, and the Metropolitan Museum of Art, New York.
Hôtel de Chastenoye, 120 Rue du Faubourg St.-Honoré, Paris.
Hôtel Boulogne de Malanville, Rue d'Angoulême-St.-Honoré, Paris.
Hôtel de Richebourg, Rue de Courcelles, Paris.
Hôtel de Ville, Neuchâtel. Built to a modified design, 1784–90.
Hospital, Bourg-en-Bresse. (A. C. Gruber, *Monuments historiques de la France,* vol. 6, 1975, pp. 70–72.)
Salle des Notables and Salle des États-Généraux, Hôtel des Menus-Plaisirs, Versailles, 1787.

Literature: C. Weiss, *Catalogue de la bibliothèque de M. Pâris, suivi de la description de son cabinet,* Besançon, 1821. M. L. Cornillot, *Collection Pierre-Adrien Pâris, Besançon,* Paris, 1957. M. Gallet, *Paris Domestic Architecture of the 18th Century,* London, 1972. A. C. Gruber,

"L'oeuvre de P. A. Pâris à la cour de France, 1779–1791," *Bulletin de la Société de l'Histoire de l'Art Français*, 1974, pp. 213–27. A. C. Gruber, "La Villa Albani vue par un artiste du XVIIIe siècle," in G. Brunel, ed., *Piranèse et les français*, Rome, 1978, pp. 281–92.

PASCAL, Jean-Louis (Paris, 1837–Paris, 1920)

A pupil of E.-J. Gilbert and of C.-A. Questel, he worked also for J.-L.-C. Garnier and won the Grand Prix in 1866. He became, in 1872, a *chef d'atelier* and, in 1890, a member of the Institut de France. He was, like P.-R.-L. Ginain, an architect of the impeccable classical kind who maintained the high standards of the French academic tradition, though he did not advance them. He was awarded the Gold Medal of the Royal Institute of British Architects in 1914.

Principal executed works:
Bibliothèque Nationale, Paris, continuation of the work of P.-F.-H. Labrouste and design of the Salle Ovale, with his pupil Recoura.
Faculté de Médecine et de Pharmacie, Bordeaux, 1880–88.
Hôtel, 12 Rue de Prony, Paris, 1883.
Château du Doux, Altillac (Corrèze). (*L'architecte* 3 [1908], p. 9.)
Villa Renouard, Pau.
Château de Maubuisson, Clairefontaine.
Apartment house, 197 Boulevard St.-Germain, Paris.
Apartment house, 105 Rue Notre-Dame-des-Champs, Paris.

Literature: G. Vapereau, *Dictionnaire universel des contemporains*, Paris, 1893. C. E. Curinier, *Dictionnaire national des contemporains*, Paris, 1899–1905. R. Blomfield, "The Royal Gold Medal 1914," *Journal of the Royal Institute of British Architects* 21 (1915), pp. 533–43. C. M. Widor, *Pascal, Séance de l'Académie des Beaux-Arts*, Nov. 4, 1920.

PATTE, Pierre (Paris, 1723–Mantes, 1814)

He was the pupil and biographer of Germain Boffrand but started his career as an engraver, selling copies of Giambattista Piranesi's etchings, working for Jacques-François Blondel, but chiefly active on behalf of the publishers of the *Encyclopédie*. In 1759 he quarreled with them and began working for the publishers of the *Description des arts et métiers*. His finest engravings were done for his own magnificent work *Monumens érigés en France à la gloire de Louis XV*, of 1765. The text reveals that he had developed a keen interest in problems of construction, an interest that was to be further publicized in a series of articles and memoirs and, in particular, in his celebrated *Mémoire sur la construction du dôme projeté pour couronner l'église de Sainte-Geneviève*, published in 1770. Patte was J.-G. Soufflot's most damaging opponent in the arguments that raged during the late eighteenth century concerning the structural stability of Soufflot's great church. The attack was continued even in the last two volumes of J.-F. Blondel's *Cours d'architecture*, published in 1777, written

for the most part by Patte. Though he was vitally interested in structure, he built little, and nothing of importance.

Principal executed works:
Hôtel de Charost, Place St.-Sulpice, Paris, c. 1764. Replaced by the Mairie du VIe.
Church, Bolbec, 1776–84.

Literature: M. Matthieu, *Pierre Patte, sa vie, son oeuvre*, Paris, 1940.

PAXTON, Sir Joseph (Milton Bryan, Bedfordshire, 1801–Sydenham, 1865)

He was a gardener, architect, and planner of great genius. In 1826 he was appointed Superintendent to the Gardens at Chatsworth, Derbyshire, and later became confidential adviser to the sixth duke of Devonshire as House Steward and Manager of the Devonshire estates in Derbyshire. His ingenious idea of applying constructional principles long familiar in conservatories to the design of the Great Exhibition building in 1850 has justly earned him a place in history books. But he was not obsessed by this notion, as some of his more recent apologists have been, and was content to design country houses in the rich styles of earlier periods, as was then expected, although they contained advanced technology in the form of artificial ventilation and hot-water heating. His layout of Birkenhead Park, with picturesque villas and terraced housing, is an attractive development of John Nash's Regent's Park.

Principal executed works:
Great Conservatory, Chatsworth, Derbyshire, 1836–40, with D. Burton. Demolished 1920.
Model village of Edensor, Derbyshire, 1838–42.
Barbrook House, Edensor, Derbyshire, 1842–47, 1851–52.
Birkenhead Park, Wirral, Cheshire, layout, 1843–47.
The Park, Buxton, Derbyshire, layout, c. 1845.
Burton Closes, Bakewell, Derbyshire, 1846–47, with A. W. N. Pugin.
Crystal Palace, London, 1850–51. Reconstructed 1854. Destroyed 1936.
Mentmore, Buckinghamshire, 1850–55, with G. H. Stokes.
Lismore Castle, County Waterford, 1850–58, with A. W. N. Pugin and G. H. Stokes. (*Country Life*, Aug. 13, 1964.)
Ferrières (near Paris), 1853–59, with G. H. Stokes.
People's Park, Hopwood Lane, Halifax, Yorkshire, layout, 1856.
Château de Pregny, Geneva, 1860–64, with G. H. Stokes. The mansard roofs were added later by Francis Gindroz. E.-E. Viollet-le-Duc and Félix Narjoux designed a gallery for the château in 1875. (G. Fatio, *Pregny: Commune genevoise et coteau des altesses*, Pregny, 1947.)
Battlesden House, Bedfordshire, 1860–64, with G. H. Stokes. Demolished 1885.

Literature: V. Markham, *Paxton and the Bachelor Duke*, 1935. G. F. Chadwick, *The Works of Sir Joseph Paxton*, 1961.

PEARSON, John Loughborough (Brussels, 1817–London, 1897)

An impressive if rather unlovable Gothic Revival architect, he is especially associated with working out a form for the nineteenth-century urban church, often incorporating stone vaults. Some of his earlier churches, for example, those at Daylesford and Appleton-le-Moors, have a strident sculptural vigor in a "primitivist" Anglo-French style, whereas his later work is quieter, but always strong. He was a pupil of I. Bonomi, of Philip Hardwick, and of Anthony Salvin.

Principal executed works:
Church, house, and school, Treberfydd, Brecknockshire, 1848–50.
Holy Trinity, Bessborough Gardens, London, 1848–50. Destroyed c. 1940.
Roundwick House, Sussex, 1856.
Quar Wood, Gloucestershire, 1857. Altered 1954.
St. Leonard, Scarborough, Yorkshire, 1857–59.
St. Mary, Dalton Holme, Yorkshire, 1858–61.
St. Peter, Daylesford, Gloucestershire, 1859–61.
St. Peter, Vauxhall, London, 1860–65.
Christ Church, Appleton-le-Moors, Yorkshire, 1863–66.
Vicarage, Freeland, Oxfordshire, 1868–73.
St. Augustine, Kilburn, London, 1870–c. 1877.
Lechlade Manor (now St. Clotilde's convent), Gloucestershire, 1872–73.
St. John, Red Lion Square, London, 1874–78. Destroyed c. 1940.
St. John, Norwood, London, 1875–87.
St. Michael, Croydon, Surrey, 1876–85.
St. Alban, Birmingham, 1879–81.
Westminster Abbey and Hall, London, major restoration, 1879.
Cathedral, Truro, Cornwall, 1880–1910.
Westwood, Sydenham Hill, London, 1881.
St. Stephen, Bournemouth, Hampshire, 1881–98.
St. Agnes, Sefton Park, Liverpool, 1882–85.
All Saints, Hove, Sussex, 1889–91.
Sidney Sussex College, Cambridge University, Cambridge, north range, 1890.

Literature: D. Lloyd, "John Loughborough Pearson: Noble Seriousness," in J. Fawcett, ed., *Seven Victorian Architects*, 1976, pp. 66–83. A. Quiney, *John Loughborough Pearson*, New Haven, Conn., and London, 1979.

PENNETHORNE, Sir James (Worcester, 1801–Worcester Park, Surrey, 1871)

He became a pupil of John Nash in 1820, an architect to the Commissioners of Woods and Forests in 1838, and Surveyor to the Land Revenue Department in 1840. Admired by C. R. Cockerell, he was potentially an architect of distinction in the classical manner, but, partly because of his heavy duties as a civil servant and partly because of competition from the Gothic Revivalists, he failed to fulfill his early promise.

Principal executed works:
No. 10 St. James's Street, London, 1832.
Swithland Hall, Leicestershire, 1834.

Dillington House, Somersetshire, alterations, late 1830s.
Christ Church, Albany Street, St. Pancras, London, 1838.
Kennington Park, Lambeth, London, 1841–51.
Victoria Park, Hackney, London, 1842–45.
Kensington Palace Gardens, London, layout, 1843.
Museum of Economic (or Practical) Geology, Jermyn Street, London, 1844–46. Demolished 1935. (London County Council, *Survey of London* 29–30 [1960].)
Eastward extension of Oxford Street, London, 1845–47.
Public Record Office, Chancery Lane, London, 1851–66.
Buckingham Palace, London, ballroom wing, 1853–55.
Somerset House, London, west wing, 1856.
Battersea Park, London, 1858.
London University, Burlington Gardens, London, 1866–67. (London County Council, *Survey of London* 31–32 [1963].)

PERCIER, Charles (Paris, 1764–Paris, 1838)

He worked first for J.-F.-T. Chalgrin, then for P.-A. Pâris, and then entered the *atelier* of A.-F. Peyre, where he met his future partner, P.-F.-L. Fontaine (see that entry for information about their joint careers).

Literature: M. Fouché, *Percier and Fontaine*, Paris, 1907. J. Duportal, *Charles Percier: reproductions de dessins conservés à la bibliothèque de l'Institut*, Paris. 1931.

PERRAULT, Claude (Paris, 1613–Paris, 1688)

The brother of Charles Perrault, who was personal secretary to Jean Baptiste Colbert and, later, author of *Contes du temps passé de ma mère l'oye*, Claude Perrault trained first as a doctor and was active as a scientist long before he turned his attention to architecture. His first surviving drawing dates from 1666. The following year, when he was already fifty-four, he was appointed, along with Louis Le Vau, *Premier Architecte du Roi*, and Charles Le Brun, *Premier Peintre du Roi*, to sit on a small committee set up by Colbert to design the east front of the Louvre, for which Gianlorenzo Bernini had earlier executed plans. To what extent the notable facade that was built between 1667 and 1674 was Perrault's design unaided one cannot be sure. Le Vau has been proposed as the architect and so has his chief assistant, François d'Orbay, but those who saw the original drawings before they were destroyed in flames at the Hôtel de Ville in Paris in 1870 have usually upheld Perrault's authorship. He designed a few other buildings, interesting enough in themselves but in no way as influential as the Louvre facade. He made his mark also, however, as a theorist. At Colbert's prompting, he undertook a new translation into French of Vitruvius's ten books on architecture. This was published first in 1673 but appeared in a more fully annotated and infinitely more useful edition in 1684. The year before, he issued the complementary *Ordonnance des cinq espèces de colonnes selon la méthode des anciens*. He became one of the protagonists in the famous quarrel between the Ancients and the Moderns, though it was his brother, Charles, who battled with Nicolas Boileau to uphold the concept of progress.

Principal executed works:
Grotte de Thetis, Versailles, decorative details, c. 1667. (L. Lange, *Art de France*, vol. 1, 1961, p. 133 ff.)
Observatoire, Paris, 1667–72. (M. Pezet, *Zeitschrift für Kunstgeschichte*, vol. 30, 1967, p. 1 ff.)
Louvre, Paris, east facade, 1667–74, with Louis Le Vau and Charles Le Brun. (M. Whiteley and A. Braham, "Louis Le Vau's Project for the Louvre and the Colonnade," *Gazette des beaux-arts*, Nov., 1964 pp. 285–96, Dec., 1964, pp. 347–62; "Les soubassements de l'aile orientale du Louvre," *Revue de l'art*, no. 4, 1969, pp. 30–43.)
Porte Saint-Antoine, Paris, triumphal arch, 1668–. Never completed. Demolished 1716.

Literature: H. Kortum, *Charles Perrault und Nicolas Boileau*, Berlin, 1967. W. Kambartel, *Symmetrie und Schönheit*, Munich, 1972. M. Sorriano, *Le dossier Perrault*, Paris, 1972. W. Herrmann, *The Theory of Claude Perrault*, London, 1973.

PERRONET, Jean-Rodolphe (Suresnes, 1708–Paris, 1794)

The son of a Swiss officer, he was sent to study in Paris under the architect Debeausire. In 1735 he entered the Corps des Ponts et Chaussées, then by no means an engineering body alone, and was sent to work at Alençon, where he rose rapidly to become chief engineer of the Généralité. He was occupied mainly with the building of roads but he also started to draw up maps of the road network, and it was on this account that he was called to Paris in February 1747 to organize the training of whole teams of surveyors and draftsmen to map France. This was the beginning of the École des Ponts et Chaussées, of which he was to be director for forty-seven years, building up an engineering school without equal in the world. Jacques-François Blondel was called in to teach architecture there. But Perronet's real achievement was to revolutionize the building of bridges, to make that procedure a carefully calculated science rather than a matter of cautious precedent. He was *Premier Ingénieur* of France by 1763. He built eleven major bridges; the best-known and the most important were those at Neuilly-sur-Seine (1766, 1768–74, with Chézy and Demoustier; and 1771–86, with Dausse and Demoustier) and, at Paris, the Pont de la Concorde (1771, 1787–91). These were magnificently recorded in 1783 in the *Description des projets et de la construction des ponts de Neuilly, de Mantes, d'Orléans*, known as the *Oeuvres de Perronet*, issued again in a greatly enlarged edition containing seventy-five plates in 1788. Perronet also designed and built the Canal de Bourgogne (1775–1832) and the Canal de l'Yvette (1769–). He also acted as architect on occasion, beginning in 1745, when he built a new tower over the crossing of Notre-Dame at Alençon. But his real contribution came as adviser to J.-G. Soufflot in the building of Ste.-Geneviève in Paris. He was Soufflot's chief defender against the attacks of Pierre Patte. He may also have come into close contact with C.-N. Ledoux as *Inspecteur Général des Salines*, a post he held from 1757 to 1786.

Literature: S. de Prony, *Notice historique sur Jean-Rodolphe*

Perronet, 1829. "La vie et les travaux de Jean-Rodolphe Perronet," in F. de Dartein, *Études sur les ponts en pierre*, vol. 2, Paris, 1907.

PERTSCH, Matteo (Mätthaus) (Trieste, c. 1774–Trieste, 1836)

He was trained at the Accademia di Brera, in Milan, probably under Giuseppe Piermarini, whose style, particularly as expressed at the Teatro alla Scala, he imposed on his own theater in Trieste, the Teatro Grande (now Verdi), for whose erection he was responsible in 1806. (The competition for the design was won in 1798 by Giannantonio Selva, who was much embittered by Pertsch's takeover). All Pertsch's major works are in Trieste.

Principal executed works:
Palazzo Carciotti, 13 Riva 3 Novembre, Trieste, 1799–1806.
S. Nicolò dei Greci, Riva 3 Novembre, Trieste, facade, 1818–19.
Rotonda dei Pancera, Via S. Michele and Via della Rotonda, Trieste, c. 1818.
Steiner House, 4 Corso Italia, Trieste, 1824.
Pertsch House, 12 Via Barriera, Trieste. Demolished 1935.

Literature: M. Walcher Casotti, *L'architettura a Trieste della fine del settecento agli inizio del novecento*, Udine, 1967. L. T. Zucca, *Architettura neoclassica a Trieste*, Trieste, 1974.

PETITOT, Ennemond-Alexandre (Lyons, 1727–Parma, 1801)

The son of an architect, he worked first for J.-G. Soufflot at Lyons, then enrolled in the school of the Académie Royale d'Architecture, in Paris, where he was taught by Denis Jossenay. In 1745 he won the Grand Prix and traveled to Rome, where he was commissioned to design one of the architectural extravaganzas of the Festa della Chinea in 1749 and did other remarkable large-scale projects. In 1750 he returned to Paris, where he was taken up by the Comte de Caylus, for whom he engraved plates for the latter's *Recueil d'antiquités* and on whose recommendation, in 1753, he was appointed *Architetto delle Fabbriche Ducali* at Parma. There he remained for the rest of his extremely active life, building a great deal and establishing, in 1757, an architectural academy that set the pattern and the standards for the future development of architecture in Lombardy. He published *Raisonnements sur la perspective*, in 1758, *Suite de vases*, in 1764, *Descrizione delle feste celebrate in Parma . . . l'anno 1769*, and a satire on the fashion for things Greek, *Mascarade à la greque*, in 1771.

Principal executed works:
La Veneria, Colorno, 1753–55.
S. Pietro, Parma, facade, 1761.
Palazzo di Riserva (now Museo Glauco Lombardi), Parma, 1764.
Casino, garden of the Palazzo Ducale, Parma, 1767.

Palazzo Ducale (or Palazzo del Giardino), Parma, alterations and redecoration, 1767–.
S. Liborio, Colorno, 1775, 1777–91.

Literature: M. Pellegri, *E. A. Petitot, 1727–1801*, Parma, 1965. G. Mezzanotte, *Architettura neoclassica in Lombardia*, Naples, 1966.

PEYRE, Antoine-François (Paris, 1739–Paris, 1823)

The brother of Marie-Joseph Peyre, he studied under him, winning the Grand Prix in 1762. In Rome he pursued his interest in painting rather than architecture, and back in Paris he took up an official and none too active career. But in 1779 he began to work for the Elector of Trèves, at Coblenz, where he built a palace that was not much admired in France. He returned before the Revolution and was appointed architect to the Château de Fontainebleau, where he himself was to be imprisoned after the Revolution. He was a notable teacher. He published his works in *Oeuvres d'architecture*, in 1819–20.

Literature: A.-C. Quatremère de Quincy, *Notice historique sur la vie et les ouvrages de M. Peyre*, 1823.

PEYRE, Marie-Joseph (Paris, 1730–Choisy-le-Roi, 1785)

He was the brother of Antoine-François Peyre. A pupil of J.-L. Legeay, of Jacques-François Blondel, of Denis Jossenay, and of L.-A. Loriot, he won the Grand Prix in 1751, studying in Rome from May 1753 to the beginning of 1756. He prepared large-scale designs during this period, one of which was awarded a prize at the Accademia di San Luca. On his return to Paris, he built the extremely simple, Palladio-inspired *folie*, the Hôtel Leprêtre de Neubourg, completed in 1762. Soon after, he designed a vast palace for the Prince de Condé on a site opposite the Palais du Luxembourg on which he was later to build the Théâtre-Français (now Théâtre de France), together with Charles de Wailly. He published all his early designs in 1765 in *Oeuvres d'architecture*, a book of fundamental importance in the history of late eighteenth-century architecture. It had a further impact in 1795, when the second edition was issued, for it contained his collected articles on the use of columns and the planning of houses in antiquity and other such subjects. He built little, serving as architect to the châteaux of Fontainebleau and Choisy.

Principal executed works:
Hôtel Leprêtre de Neubourg, Clos Payen (near Paris), 1762. Demolished.
Hôtel de Nivernais, 10 Rue de Tournon, Paris. Now a barracks.
Théâtre-Français (later Théâtre de l'Odéon, now Théâtre de France), Place de l'Odéon, Paris, 1767–70, 1779–82, designed with Charles de Wailly. Restored by J.-F.-T. Chalgrin after a fire in 1799, rebuilt after another fire in 1818, and modified internally several times since. (D. Rabreau and M. Steinhauser, "Le théâtre de l'Odéon de Charles de Wailly et Marie-Joseph Peyre, 1767–1782," *Revue de l'art,* no. 19,

1973, pp. 8–49; M. Rambaud, "Un projet de M. J. Peyre pour l'Opéra de Paris," *Bulletin de la Société de l'Histoire de l'Art Français,* Année 1976 (1978), pp. 241–53.
Hôtel de Luzy, 6 Rue Ferou, Paris (attributed).

Literature: A.-M. Peyre, "Notice sur la vie de l'auteur," in M.-J. Peyre, *Oeuvres d'architecture*, 2d ed., 1795.

PIEL, Louis-Alexandre (Lisieux, 1808–Bosco [Piemonte], 1841)

A pupil of François Debret, he was taken up early by the Comte de Montalembert and persuaded to uphold the cause of the Catholic Gothic Revival. He designed a small church in the Franche-Comté and prepared the first set of drawings for St.-Nicolas at Nantes (later to be taken over by J.-B.-A. Lassus), before departing for Rome in 1840 to enter J.-B.-H. Lacordaire's Dominican order. He died the following year, of consumption.

Literature: A. Teyssier, *Notice biographique sur L.-A. Piel*, Paris, 1843. A. de Calonne, "Louis-Alexis Piel," *Revue générale de l'architecture*, 1844, pp. 273–76 (review of A. Teyssier's *Notice biographique*). B. Foucart and V. Noël-Bouton, "Saint-Nicolas de Nantes," *Congrès Archéologique de France, Haute Bretagne,* 126e session, Paris, 1968, pp. 136–81.

PIERMARINI, Giuseppe (Foligno, 1734–Foligno, 1808)

He was the most dominant and, indeed, dominating architect in Milan, and thus in all Lombardy, in the late eighteenth century. But his work is as dull as his planning abilities were slight, and one must assume that his stature and power were owing to his strength of personality and administrative skills rather than his architectural sensibilities. He studied first with Paolo Posi and then with Carlo Murena. Between 1756 and 1764 he worked for Luigi Vanvitelli in Rome and then from 1765 to 1768 at Caserta. Vanvitelli brought him to Milan in 1769, when he was asked to advise on the new Palazzo Ducale. Piermarini at once established himself in Milan, where he became *Architetto di Stato*, responsible for a number of public buildings and much new planning, controlling the design of all new structures within the city through the Commissione d'Ornato and reorganizing the teaching at the Accademia di Brera so that it reflected his point of view. He worked closely with the Austrian authorities but fled to Foligno in 1796, when the French arrived; however, he returned later.

Principal executed works:
Accademia Virgiliana, Mantua, 1770, 1773–75.
Palazzo Greppi, Via S. Antonio, Milan, 1772–78. Demolished.
Palazzo Belgioioso, Piazza Belgioioso, Milan, 1772–81.
Palazzo Ducale, Milan, 1773–78. Largely destroyed. The interior plasterwork was by Giocondo Albertolli.
Teatro alla Scala, Milan, 1776–78. Extended 1830 by A. Sanguirico.
Villa Ducale, Monza, 1776–80.

Teatro della Canobbiana, Milan, 1777–79. Parts survive in the Teatro Lirico.
Villa Borromeo, Cassano d'Adda, extension, c. 1780–85.

Literature: E. Filippini, *Giuseppe Piermarini nella vita e nelle opere*, Foligno, 1936. A. Caleca, *Disegni di G. Piermarini nella Biblioteca Communale di Foglino*, Pisa, 1962. G. Mezzanotte, *Architettura neoclassica in Lombardia*, Naples, 1966.

PIÈTRE, Henri (c. 1725–after 1785)

He was a pupil of J.-S. Cartaud, with whom he later worked, and also of Pierre Contant d'Ivry, whom he succeeded in 1777 as *Premier Architecte* to the Duc d'Orléans. His interiors at the Palais-Royal and, in particular, those in the Hôtel Mélusine, of 1766, suggest that he was a designer of some enterprise and power. His work at the Pavillon d'Orléans, Rue de Provence, of 1774–85, and at the adjoining Hôtel de Montesson in the Rue de la Chaussée-d'Antin, Paris, sometimes attributed to A.-T. Brongniart alone, was more spectacular, however, and confirmed him as an architect of the highest fashion.

Literature: M. Gallet, "Les dessins de l'architecte Henri Piètre pour la décoration du Palais-Royal," *Bulletin du Musée Carnavalet*, June 1960, pp. 8–15. M. Hébert, "Les hôtels du Duc d'Orléans et de Mme. de Montesson à la Chaussée d'Antin," *Gazette des beaux-arts*, Sept. 1964, pp. 161–76. M. Gallet, *Paris Domestic Architecture of the 18th Century*, London, 1972.

PIRANESI, Giambattista (Mogliano [Veneto], 1720–Rome, 1778)

He studied first with his uncle, Matteo Lucchese, an engineer, then with Giovanni Scalfarotto, and then with Carlo Zucchi, etcher of views. But in 1740, at the age of nineteen, he went on an embassy to Rome, where he worked once again briefly and in rapid succession for the Valeriani brothers, the stage designers, and then for another etcher of views, Giuseppe Vasi. In July 1743 he published his first suite of etchings, *Prima parte di architetture e prospettive*. He then moved to Naples, but by May 1744 was back in Venice, where he worked for a short time with G. B. Tiepolo. By 1745 he had returned to Rome for good. He began as a print seller but was soon preparing and selling his own magisterial series of etchings of imaginary prisons, ancient and modern views of Rome, and fantastical inventions of his own inspiration. He colored the imagination of all visitors to Rome, and thousands took back copies of his works. His influence on the language of vision in the eighteenth century can scarcely be overestimated. His celebrated quarrels with Lord Charlemont, with P.-J. Mariette, and with J.-D. Le Roy ensured him even greater fame (or notoriety). But though he stubbornly insisted on calling himself an architect he built almost nothing, apart from the church of S. Maria del Priorato (begun in 1764) and the piazza outside, high on the Aventine, in Rome.

Literature: H. Focillon, *Giovanni-Battista Piranesi*, Paris, 1918. A. M. Hind, *Giovanni Battista Piranesi: A Critical Study*, London, 1922. A. Hyatt Mayor, *Giovanni Battista Piranesi*, New York, 1952. J. Scott, *Piranesi*, London, 1975. *Piranèse et les français, 1740–1790*, exhib. cat., Académie de France à Rome, Rome, 1976. J. G. Legrand, "Notice historique sur la vie et sur les ouvrages de J. B. Piranesi," in *GRAFICA grafica II:2*, Calcografia Nazionale, Rome, 1976. G. Brunel, ed., *Piranèse et les français*, Rome, 1978. J. Wilton-Ely, *The Mind and Art of Giovanni Battista Piranesi*, London, 1978.

PISTOCCHI, Giuseppe (Faenza, 1744–Faenza, 1814)

An architect who worked and traveled widely in Italy, he achieved fame for a design for the Foro Buonaparte, which he did not build, in Milan, a city in which he built nothing of interest. He trained first with Giuseppe Boschi in Faenza, then in Rome, where he began in 1760 to work under Murena. In 1766 he moved to Pesaro and continued to work in that town, though he was chiefly active during this period in his native Faenza, where he put up several *palazzi* in a restrained classical style. In 1801 he was invited to Milan to supervise the building of the new military quarters, and at that time he drew up his large-scale project for the Foro Buonaparte. By 1802 he was back in Faenza. In 1804 he was made a member of the Accademia di Belle Arti at Bologna. In 1812 he was in Mantua, as architect to the Palazzo Ducale; two years later he was appointed professor at the University of Pavia.

Principal executed works:
S. Matteo, Faenza, 1772. Destroyed.
Palazzo Bandini-Spada, 97 Corso Mazzini, Faenza, 1775–80.
Theater, Piazza della Molinella, Faenza, 1780–87.
Palazzo Gessi, 54 Corso Mazzini, Faenza, 1786.
Pistocchi House, 21 Corso Mazzini, Faenza, 1787–88.
Caldesi House, 9 Corso Garibaldi, Faenza, c. 1800.

Principal unexecuted projects:
Teatro Fenice, Venice, 1789.
Foro Buonaparte, Milan, 1800–1801.

Literature: E. Golfieri, "Architetture neoclassiche di G. Pistocchi faentino, 1744–1814," in *Atti dei convegni nazionale di storia dell'architettura*, vol. 9, Milan, 1939, pp. 309–20. E. Godoli, *Giuseppe Pistocchi (1744–1814), architetto giacobino*, exhib. cat., Faenza, 1974.

PLAYFAIR, William Henry (London, 1789–Edinburgh, 1857)

He was the son of the distinguished and original neo-classical architect James Playfair. He was trained in Edinburgh by William Stark and rose to prominence by winning the competition to complete Robert Adam's Edinburgh University building.

Principal executed works:
University, Edinburgh, completion, 1817–24.
Dollar Academy, Clackmannanshire, 1818.
New Observatory, Calton Hill, Edinburgh, 1818.
Royal Scottish Academy, Edinburgh, 1822–26, 1832–35.
National Monument, Calton Hill, Edinburgh, 1824–29, with C. R. Cockerell.
St. Stephen, Edinburgh, 1826.
Surgeons' Hall, Edinburgh, 1829.
Donaldson's Hospital, Edinburgh, 1842–51.
New College, Edinburgh, 1846–50.
National Gallery of Scotland, Edinburgh, 1850–57.

Literature: A. J. Youngson, *The Making of Classical Edinburgh*, Edinburgh, 1966.

POCCIANTI, Francesco Gurrieri Pasquale (Bibbiena, 1774–Florence, 1858)

He was taught in Florence by G. M. Paoletti and established himself there as an architect to successive administrations, contributing notably to the works undertaken at the Palazzo Pitti. It was in Livorno and in the surrounding countryside, however, that his grandest buildings were erected, all related to the waterworks there.

Principal executed works:
Palazzo Pitti, Florence. The first proposals were accepted in 1796, but the major works were undertaken later: wings overlooking the piazza, 1818–40; Meridiana, 1819–41; first-floor rooms, including ballroom, 1819–40; new secondary stair, 1820–47; new corridor linking the palace to the observatory, 1820–31; new vestibule, 1823–36.
Villa del Poggio Imperiale, Caiano, project for rebuilding, 1806 (design soon taken over by Giuseppe Cacialli and much revised); conservatory, 1824–32.
Sala d'Elci, Biblioteca Laurenziana, Florence, 1816–41.
Scuola di Anatomia, hospital of S. Maria Nuova, Florence, 1818–26. Demolished.
Purgatorio, Pian di Rota, Livorno, 1827–45.
Cisternino, Livorno, project approved 1827, built 1837–48.
Cisternone, Livorno, 1829–42.

Principal unexecuted project:
S. Lorenzo, Florence, completion of facade, 1836–.

Literature: *Pasquale Poccianti architetto, 1774–1858*, exhib. cat., Bibbiena, 1974. F. Borsi, G. Morelli, and L. Zangheri, *Firenze e Livorno e l'opera di Pasquale Poccianti*, Rome, 1974.

POLLACK, Leopoldo (Vienna, 1751–Milan, 1806)

The son of a builder employed by the Italian chancery in Vienna, he trained first under P. U. Triendl and then at the academy under Vincenz Fischer but moved in 1775 to Milan, where he studied for a year under Giuseppe Piermarini and then began to work for him at the Palazzo Ducale. He was Piermarini's favorite pupil but managed to develop a varied style of his own that was more robust than his teacher's. He built widely in Lombardy, largely in Milan, but was also active in Vienna (indeed, he was thrown into prison in 1798 by the French authorities occupying Milan when they found that he was building a theater in Vienna). He taught at Milan's Accademia di Brera from 1796 on. His brother Michael Johann (1773–1855) joined him in Milan in 1794 and worked with him for four years before moving to Budapest, where he established himself as a leading architect.

Principal executed works:
University, Pavia, rebuilding and redecoration under Giuseppe Piermarini; anatomy theater (Aula Scarpa), 1785; third court, 1786; physics theater (Aula Volta), 1787 (vaulting inserted 1828).
Villa Villani Rocca-Saporiti (known as La Rotonda), Borgovico, Como, 1790–93.
Villa Belgioioso (later Villa Reale, now Galleria d'Arte Moderna), Milan, 1790–96.
S. Vittore, Varese, facade, 1791–95.
Villa Mezzabarba, Casatisma, Pavia, 1791–96.
Church, Rho, facade, 1795.
Palazzo Agosti-Grumelli, Via S. Salvatore, Bergamo, 1796–97.
Teatro dei Filidrammatici, Milan, facade, 1798. The auditorium appears to have been designed by Giuseppe Piermarini and Luigi Canonica.
Villa Pesenti-Agliardi, Sombreno (Bergamo), 1798–1801.
Villa Casati (now town library and clinic), Muggio, c. 1800.
Teatro Sociale, Bergamo, 1803–5.

Literature: G. Mezzanotte, *Architettura neoclassica in Lombardia*, Naples, 1966. Italia Nostra, *Leopoldo Pollack, architetto, 1751–1806*, exhib. cat., Bergamo, 1978.

POMPEI, Alessandro (Verona, 1705–Garda, 1772)

He was opposed to the Baroque and sought to establish a sterner classicism, largely under the inspiration of Scipione Maffei, but his active architectural career was extremely short, as he was compelled to take on the running of the family estates after the death of his brother in 1746. His ideas were expressed with particular force and clarity in his *Cinque ordini dell'architettura civile di Michele Sanmicheli*, of 1735.

Principal executed works:
Villa di Illasi (near Verona), 1731–37.
Museo Lapidario Maffeiano, Verona, 1739–c. 1746. (V. Vercelloni, "Verona: Palazzo della Dogana e Museo Lapidario," *Bollettino di Italia nostra*, no. 15, pp. 23–24; L. Magagnato, "Letteratura critica e tradizione sanmicheliana nel periodo neoclassico a Verona," *Bolletino del Centro Internazionale di Studi di Architettura Andrea Palladio* 13 [1971], pp. 169–78.)
Palazzo Pindemonte, Vo, 1742.

Literature: C. Semenzato, "Un architetto illuminista," in *Arte Veneta*, 1963, pp. 192–200.

POTAIN, Nicolas-Marie (1713–1796)

He won the Grand Prix in 1738 and traveled to Rome. He was later associated with the Marquis de Marigny and prepared a study on theater designs at the marquis's instigation. He built little. He worked under A.-J. Gabriel at the Place Louis XV (now Place de la Concorde) from 1755 to 1770 and succeeded J. G. Soufflot as architect of the cathedral at Rennes, completed only in the nineteenth century. He was the author of the *Traité des ordres d'architecture*, of 1767.

Principal executed work:
St.-Louis, St.-Germain-en-Laye, 1764–66, 1787–89, 1823–24. Completed to their own design by A.-J. Malpièce and A.-J. Moutier.

POYET, Bernard (Dijon 1742–1824)

He studied under Charles de Wailly. Though he won only a second Grand Prix, in 1768, he obtained permission nonetheless to travel to Italy. He is notable for his projects rather than his executed buildings, in particular, for the Hôpital Ste.-Anne, in Paris, a giant radial structure designed in 1785 and much admired by J.-N.-L. Durand. Begun in 1788, it was thought impractical and outrageously expensive, and work on it was soon stopped.

Principal executed works:
St.-Sauveur, Paris, 1780–96. Demolished.
Chambre des Députés, Quai d'Orsay, Paris, portico, 1804–7.

PRICE, Sir Uvedale (Foxley, Herefordshire, 1747 Foxley, 1829)

He was a Herefordshire squire, and his three-volume *Essay on the Picturesque*, of 1794, defined the Picturesque for the first time as an aesthetic category distinct from the Sublime and the Beautiful as defined by Edmund Burke. He brought out an expanded version of his influential book in 1810.

Literature: N. Pevsner, "Uvedale Price," *Architectural Review* (London) 95 (1944; repr. in N. Pevsner, *Studies in Art, Architecture and Design*, vol. 1, 1968, pp. 126–37). M. Allentuck, "Sir Uvedale Price and the Picturesque Garden: The Evidence of the Coleorton Papers," in *The Picturesque Garden and Its Influence Outside the British Isles*, Dumbarton Oaks, 1974.

PUGIN, Augustus Welby Northmore (London, 1812– Ramsgate, Kent, 1852)

The most influential architect in nineteenth-century England, he was trained by his French father, A. C. Pugin (1762–1832), who arrived in England in 1792 and played an important role in John Nash's office, specializing in Gothic detail. A. W. N. Pugin was converted to the Catholic church in 1835 and in a series of widely read publications—among them, *Contrasts* (1836) and *The True Principles of Pointed or Christian Architecture in England* (1841)—elaborated a confusion between the principles of religion and those of architectural design that was to color all subsequent thought on architecture in the nineteenth century. The poverty of the Catholics in England in Pugin's lifetime meant that few of his many churches could be as well con-

structed or as richly adorned as he would have liked. Perhaps his finest achievements are the Catholic churches at Cheadle (paid for by Lord Shrewsbury) and Ramsgate (paid for by himself) and the decoration of the Houses of Parliament.

Principal executed works:
St. Marie's Grange, Alderbury, Wiltshire, 1835. (*Architectural Review* [London], 98 [Mar. 1945], pp. 90–96.)
Alton Castle, Staffordshire, remodeling, 1837–. (*Country Life*, June 9, 1960.)
St. Mary, Derby, 1837–39.
Scarisbrick Hall, Lancashire, 1837–45. (*Country Life* 123, pp. 506, 580.)
St. John's Hospital, Alton, Staffordshire, 1839. (*Country Life* 128, p. 1226.)
St. Chad's cathedral, Birmingham, 1839.
St. George's cathedral, Southwark, London, 1839–40. Largely destroyed.
St. Giles, Cheadle, Staffordshire, 1839–44.
Bishop's house, Birmingham, 1840–41. Demolished.
St. Barnabas's cathedral and bishop's house, Nottingham, 1841.
St. Mary, Brewood, Staffordshire, 1842.
Alton Castle, Staffordshire, 1847–51. (*Country Life* 128, p. 1226.)
The Grange, Ramsgate, Kent, 1843. (*Architectural Review* [London], Apr. 1948, pp. 163–66.)
Houses of Parliament, London, decoration, 1844–52. (M. H. Port, ed., *The Houses of Parliament*, New Haven, Conn., 1976; *Country Life*, Nov. 11, 1976.)
St. Augustine, Ramsgate, Kent, 1845–50. (*Architectural Review* [London], Apr. 1948, pp. 163–66.)
St. Edmund's College, Ware, Hertfordshire, 1846–52.
The Rolle Mortuary Chapel, Bicton Grange, Devonshire, 1850.

Principal unexecuted projects:
Downside Abbey, Somersetshire, 1839.
Balliol College, Oxford University, Oxford, 1843.
Woodchester Park, Gloucestershire, 1845–46.
Milton Abbey, Dorsetshire, remodeling and redecoration, 1847–48.

Literature: B. Ferrey, *Recollections of A. N. Welby Pugin*, 1861. M. Trappes-Lomax, *Pugin: A Mediaeval Victorian*, 1932. D. R. Gwynn, *Lord Shrewsbury, Pugin and the Catholic Revival*, 1946. P. B. Stanton, *Pugin*, 1971.

QUARENGHI, Giacomo Antonio Domenico (Capiatone de Rota Fuori nella Valle Imagna, 1744–St. Petersburg [Leningrad], 1817).

He began to study painting at Bergamo and moved in 1763 to Rome to continue under A. R. Mengs and Stefano Pozzi. In Rome, however, he met the young Roman architect Vincenzo Brenna, whom he was later to encounter in Russia. Brenna persuaded him to take up architecture. He worked next under Paolo Posi, the French architect A. Dervizet, and N. Giansimoni. He traveled later through Italy, to France, and on to England. In 1779 he was invited to Russia to work for Catherine the Great. There he established himself and built extensively and enormously. His works are il-

lustrated best in the *Fabbriche e disegni di Giacomo Quarenghi* (2d ed., Mantua, 1845).

Principal executed works:
S. Scolastica, Subiaco, rebuilding of interior, 1771–77. (P. Arizzoli-Clementel, "Giacomo Quarenghi à Subiaco: lettres inédites," *Revue de l'art*, no. 19, 1973, pp. 97–108.)
Merchants' Arcade, Moscow, 1780.
Bezborodko Palace and garden pavilion, Leningrad, 1780–90.
Church of the Annunciation, Kuzmin, Tsarskoe Selo (now Pushkin), 1780–90.
Church, Tsarskoe Selo, 1780–90.
Church, Pulkovo (near Tsarskoe Selo), 1780–90.
Church and hospital, Pavlovsk, 1781.
Tsarskoe Selo, courtroom, designed 1782, built 1784–88; two iron bridges, 1782–86; ruin in the park, 1785–86; Alexander Palace, 1792–96.
College of Foreign Affairs, Leningrad, 1782–83.
Hermitage Theater, Leningrad, 1782–87.
Academy of Science, Leningrad, 1783–89.
State Bank, Leningrad, 1783–90.
Saltykov House, Leningrad, 1784–88.
Winter Palace, Leningrad, St. George's Hall, 1786–95; Nevskaja Rooms, 1792–94.
Vintingov Palace, Leningrad, 1788.
Slobodskoi Palace, Moscow, 1788–89.
Yusupov Palace, Leningrad, 1790–1800.
Old Merchants' Yard, Moscow, 1790–1805.
Sheremetev Palace, Ostankino (near Moscow), 1791–98, with M. F. Kazakov and I. P. Argunov.
Zavadovskij Palace, Ljaliči (near Brjansk), 1794–95.
Sheremetev Pilgrims' Refuge, Moscow, additions, 1794–1807.
Church of the Knights of Malta, Vorontsov Palace, Leningrad, 1798–1800.
Orthodox church, Vorontsov Palace, Leningrad, 1798–1800.
Catherine Palace, Lefortovo (near Moscow).
Mary Hospital (now Kujbiscesvskaja), Leningrad, 1803–5.
Catherine Institute (now Saltykov–Ščedrin Library), Leningrad, 1804–7.
Little Hermitage, Leningrad, east wing, 1804–7.
Cavalry barracks, Leningrad, 1804–7.
Smolny Institute, Leningrad, 1806–8.
English church, Leningrad, 1810.
Triumphal arch (near Narva Gate), Leningrad, 1814. Timber construction.

Literature: L. Hautecoeur, *L'architecture classique à St. Pétersbourg à la fin du XVIIIe siècle*, Paris, 1912. M. Iljin, "Giacomo Quarenghi," *Bolletino del Centro Internazionale di Studi di Architettura Andrea Palladio* 5 (1963). *Disegni di Giacomo Quarenghi*, exhib. cat., Vicenza, 1967.

QUESTEL, Charles-Auguste (Paris, 1807–Paris, 1888)

An orphan, he was adopted early by the Lenormant family and thus had the scholar and archaeologist Charles Lenormant for his brother. The latter was no doubt influential in preparing the design for Questel's first and perhaps most significant work, the church of St.-Paul at Nîmes, in the Romanesque style. But Questel was also trained by Vincent, by A.-F. Peyre, and by G.-A. Blouet (1826–28), and worked as *Sous-Inspecteur* for L.-H. Lebas at the Collège de France, Paris, in 1830–31. He spent two years, 1831–32, in Italy and returned to work for F.-J. Duban at the École des Beaux-Arts, Paris, thus learning to pursue the classical path with greater determination. He took over E.-J. Gilbert's and Blouet's *atelier* in 1856. He built a number of large and carefully considered buildings and has long been an admired architect, though one of no great qualities.

Principal executed works:
St.-Paul, Boulevard Victor Hugo, Nîmes, 1835, 1838–50.
Place de la Libération, Nîmes, 1844, 1846–48. The fountains were designed with Pradier, 1846–51.
Monument to Saint Louis, Aigues-Mortes, 1848.
Hospital, Gisors (Eure), 1859–61.
Préfecture, Place de Verdun, Grenoble, 1860–67, supervised by F. F. Riondel.
Asile Ste.-Anne, Rue Cabanis, Paris, 1861–76.
Bibliothèque-musée, Place de Verdun, Grenoble, 1863, 1865–70. (B. Foucart, "Questel et la bibliothèque-musée de Grenoble [1862–1872]," *Bulletin de la Société de l'Histoire de l'Art Français*, Année 1975 [1976], pp. 281–301.)
Banque de France, Paris, Galerie Dorée, 1868.

Literature: A.-N.-L. Bailly, *Discours sur Questel*, Paris, Feb. 1888. G. Raulin, *Charles-Auguste Questel, sa vie, ses oeuvres 1807–1888*, Paris, 1888 (repr. in *L'architecture* 2 [1889], pp. 52–56). H. Delaborde, *Notice sur la vie les ouvrages de M. Questel*, Paris, 1890.

REPTON, Humphry (Bury St. Edmunds, 1752–Hare Street, Essex, 1818)

He succeeded Capability Brown as chief British landscape gardener in the new "natural" style. The subordination of nature and architecture to an essentially pictorial conception, so much a part of the English Picturesque movement, is a characteristic feature of Repton's *Red Books*. In these manuscript volumes he used his skill as a watercolorist to present a series of theatrical views with movable flaps showing the house and grounds of a prospective client before and after his proposed remodeling. Though not primarily an architect (he relied on the services of John Nash and of his sons John Adey Repton and George Repton), he prepared elaborate designs for remodeling Brighton Pavilion in the Hindu style and Magdalen College, Oxford University, in the Gothic Style. Characteristic parks by Repton survive at Woburn, Welbeck, Uppark, Harewood, Holkham, and Sheringham. He was author of *Sketches and Hints on Landscape Gardening* (of 1795), which, with publications of a similar though less practical nature by Sir Uvedale Price and by Richard Payne Knight, served as a handbook of Picturesque ideas.

Literature: D. Stroud, *Humphry Repton*, 1962. E. Malins, *The Red Books of Humphry Repton*, 1976.

REVETT, Nicholas (Brandeston, Suffolk, 1720–1804)

He was trained in Rome as a painter. He was in Athens from 1751 to 1753 with James Stuart, with whom he collaborated on the most important archaeological book of the eighteenth century, *Antiquities of Athens*, published in four volumes between 1762 and 1816. His visit to Asia Minor in 1764–66 with Richard Chandler and William Pars resulted in a two-volume study, *Antiquities of Ionia*, published in 1769 and 1797.

Principal executed works:
Standlynch (now Trafalgar) House, Wiltshire, alterations and additions, c. 1766. (*Country Life* 98, pp. 68, 112.)
West Wycombe Park, Buckinghamshire, alterations and additions, 1770–80. (*Country Life* 73, pp. 466, 494.)
Church, Ayot St. Lawrence, Hertfordshire, 1778.

Literature: L. Lawrence [Lewis], "Stuart and Revett: Their Literary and Architectural Careers," *Journal of the Warburg Institute* 2 (1938–39), pp. 128–46.

REYNAUD, François-Léonce (Lyons, 1803–Trouville, 1880)

In 1818 he went to Paris to complete his education, enrolling three years later at the École Polytechnique, where he had J.-N.-L. Durand for his master. Within a few months, however, he was expelled from the school on suspicion of belonging to a cell of the *carbonari*. He was so incensed by the accusation that a year later he did join that radical group. He also entered J.-N. Huyot's *atelier*. A few years later, in 1828, he traveled to Italy to erect outbuildings on an estate near Florence. His client died within a few days of his arrival, but he managed to stay on to study Tuscan architecture and to travel to Rome and Naples before returning to Paris. There he gave lessons in mathematics to support himself. During this period he began to associate with the Saint-Simonists. He knew B.-P. Enfantin well, though he broke with him in time, as he did not approve of the mystical turn he had given to Saint-Simon's doctrines. His brother Ernest Reynaud was even more closely associated with the Saint-Simonists. He changed his name to Jean, entered the community in the Rue Monsigny, Paris, and traveled throughout the Midi with Pierre Leroux to preach the new social religion. F.-L. Reynaud was gradually reconciled to this branch of the Saint-Simonists, becoming close to Leroux, to Édouard Charton, who founded the *Magasin pittoresque*, to C.-A. Sainte-Beuve, and to Hippolyte Fourtoul, future *Ministre de l'Instruction Publique*. All contributed to the magazine that Pierre Leroux and Ernest (Jean) Reynaud founded, the *Encyclopédie nouvelle*. After the July Revolution Léonce was permitted to enter the École des Ponts et Chaussées. At the end of 1834 he began his career with an appointment as engineer to the lighthouse of Héaux de Bréhat, off Brittany. This was the first, perhaps the most significant, in a series of no less than sixty-one lighthouses, together with one hundred and eighty-seven beacons, that he and his associates built along the coast of France.

He became *Directeur des Phares* in 1846 and retained that position until 1878. His skill and intellectual grasp were at once recognized. In November 1837 he was appointed professor at the École Polytechnique, where he continued to teach for thirty years. He also taught the history of architecture at the École des Ponts et Chaussées from 1842 to 1869, when he became director of the school. He served in this capacity until 1873. His teachings were published in a two-volume *Traité d'architecture* (1850–58), which ran to no less than four editions. He offered a rationalist interpretation of architectural history and of architecture, firmly opposed to E.-E. Viollet-le-Duc's and thus strongly approved by the Académie. In 1869 he was elected to the Conseil Supérieur de l'École des Beaux-Arts. Despite the stern rationalism of his ideas, however, he admired greatly J.-L.-C. Garnier's new Opéra. What he came to dislike was Gothic. In an article, "Architecture," published in 1839 in the *Encyclopédie nouvelle*, he had shown himself a tolerant interpreter of the style and even in 1853, when he was appointed as one of the three *Inspecteurs Générals* of the Service des Édifices Diocésains, he had been sympathetic in his reports on the restoration of Gothic buildings. However, in the *Traité* he revealed himself as a violent opponent of all forms of Gothic Revivalism. His firm stand served to distinguish him even among other detractors. Reynaud sat on numerous commissions and juries and was active in most spheres of French architecture. Apart from his lighthouses he did not build much: the first Gare du Nord (1842–46) and the Dépôt Central des Phares (1865–68). His major publications, in addition to the *Traité*, were *Les travaux publics de la France* (1878–80) and *Atlas des ports maritimes de la France*.

Literature: F. de Dartein, *M. Léonce Reynaud, sa vie et ses oeuvres*, Paris, 1885.

RICHARDSON, Henry Hobson (St. James, Louisiana, 1838–Boston, Massachusetts, 1886)

He was educated at Harvard University and from 1859 to 1862 at the École des Beaux-Arts, in Paris. He subsequently worked under P.-F.-H. Labrouste and J.-I. Hittorff, but the style he brought back to America was not theirs but a Romanesque one inspired by J.-A.-E. Vaudremer. He also worked in a Picturesque domestic vein, which owed something to the work of R. N. Shaw and W. E. Nesfield in England.

Principal executed works:
Grace Episcopal Church, Medford, Massachusetts, 1867–69.
Brattle Square (now First Baptist) Church, Boston, Massachusetts, 1870–72.
Trinity Church, Boston, Massachusetts, 1873–77.
William Watts Sherman House, Newport, Rhode Island, 1874–75.
Cheyney Block (now Brown-Thompson Department Store), Hartford, Connecticut, 1875–76.
Sever Hall, Harvard University, Cambridge, Massachusetts, 1878–80.
Crane Memorial Library, Quincy, Massachusetts, 1880–83.

Austin Hall, Harvard University, Cambridge, Massachusetts, 1881–83.

Stoughton House, Cambridge, Massachusetts, 1882–83.

Allegheny County Jail, Pittsburgh, Pennsylvania, 1884–88.

Glessner House, Chicago, 1885–87.

Marshall Field Wholesale Building, Chicago, 1885–87. Demolished.

Ames Building, Harrison Avenue, Boston, Massachusetts, 1886–87.

Literature: M. G. Van Rensselaer, *Henry Hobson Richardson and His Works*, Boston and New York, 1888 (repr. 1969). H. R. Hitchcock, *The Architecture of H. H. Richardson and His Times*, 3d ed., Cambridge, Mass., 1966.

RODI, Faustino (Cremona, 1751–Cremona, 1835)

He studied under E.-A. Petitot at the Accademia di Parma from 1770 to 1776 and then moved to Genoa, but within a few years had returned to Cremona, where he established both himself and the new classical style. He taught at the local school, where his chief pupils were Luigi Voghera and Domenico Moglia.

Principal executed works:
Hospital, Cremona, a full conversion of the old convent of S. Francesco, 1780–.
Palazzo Silva, Cremona, c. 1784.
Palazzo Stanga, S. Vincenzo (Cremona).
Palazzo Vescovile, Cremona, 1793–1817.
Palazzo Pallavicino, Cremona. Completed after his death by Luigi Voghera.

Literature: G. Mezzanotte, *Architettura neoclassica in Lombardia,* Naples, 1966.

RONDELET, Jean-Baptiste (Lyons, 1734–Paris, 1829)

He worked first for his father, a building contractor at Lyons, then for T.-N. Loyer. He went in 1763 to Paris to enroll in Jacques-François Blondel's school and then in 1770 to work for J.-G. Soufflot at Ste.-Geneviève. He became Soufflot's closest collaborator, completing that church after his death, and was responsible also for the later alterations to ensure its stability and to purify its style. In 1783 he went to Italy for two years to study the building techniques of the Romans. He advised Gaspard Monge in 1795 on the establishment of the École Centrale des Travaux Publics, later the École Polytechnique, in Paris, where J.-N.-L. Durand was that year appointed professor of architecture. He himself preferred to teach at the École des Beaux-Arts, Paris, where he went in 1799 and remained throughout his life. In 1802–3 he published his accumulated technical knowledge in *Traité théorique et pratique de l'art de bâtir*, which had run to five editions by 1830.

Literature: E. L. G. Charvet, *Lyon artistique: architectes, notices biographiques et bibliographiques,* Lyons, 1899, pp. 340–44.

ROOT, John Wellborn (Lumpkin, Georgia, 1850–Chicago, 1891)

In 1864 he fled from the threat of conscription into the Confederate army to Liverpool, where he studied for a year at the Clare Mount School, in Wallasey. Returned to America in 1866, he enrolled at New York University and studied science and civil engineering. In 1869 he began work in New York City with the architects James Renwick and Joseph Sands. A year later he moved to the office of J. B. Snook, then to that of P. B. Wright, a staunch upholder of the theories of E.-E. Viollet-le-Duc. This firm soon moved to Chicago, to join that of Asher Carter and W. H. Drake. There Root met Daniel Hudson Burnham (1846–1912). The two architects set up a partnership in 1873. Their first important building was the John B. Sherman House, erected in a Gothic style, in 1874. They built a dozen or more houses of this sort during the next few years, but their fame was to spring from their great commercial buildings of the 1880s, beginning with the Grannis Block, of 1880–81. Twenty-six more buildings were to follow in Chicago alone; others were commissioned for Kansas City, Missouri, Cleveland, Ohio, and San Francisco. The practice was extensive and the range of buildings involved considerable, but the best-known—then and today—are those early Chicago landmarks The Rookery, the Monadnock Block, and the Reliance Building.

Principal executed works:
John B. Sherman House, Twenty-first and Prairie, Chicago, 1874. Destroyed.
Grannis Block, 21–29 North Dearborn, Chicago, 1880–81. Destroyed.
Montauk Block, 64–70 West Monroe, Chicago, 1881–82. Destroyed.
Calumet Clubhouse, Twentieth and Michigan, Chicago, 1881–83. Destroyed.
Burlington and Quincy General Office Building, Franklin and Adams, Chicago, 1882–83. Destroyed.
Sidney Kent House, 2944 South Michigan, Chicago, 1882–83.
Calumet Building, 111–17 South La Salle, Chicago, 1882–84. Destroyed.
Santa Fe Building, Ninth and Jackson, Topeka, Kansas, 1883–84. Destroyed.
Counselman Building, La Salle and Jackson, Chicago, 1883–84. Destroyed.
Rialto Building, 132–48 West Van Buren, Chicago, 1883–86. Destroyed.
Insurance Exchange Building, La Salle and Adams, Chicago, 1884–85. Destroyed.
Traders' Building, 305–15 South La Salle, Chicago, 1884–85. Destroyed.
McCormick Harvesting Machine Building, Wacker and Jackson, Chicago, 1884–86. Destroyed.
E. E. Ayer House, State and Banks, Chicago, 1885–86. Destroyed.
Art Institute, Michigan and Van Buren, Chicago, 1885–87. Destroyed.
Phenix Building, 111 West Jackson, Chicago, 1885–87. Destroyed.
The Rookery, La Salle and Adams, Chicago, 1885–88.
St. Gabriel's, 4501 South Lowe, Chicago, 1886–87.

Midland Hotel, Seventh and Walnut, Kansas City, Missouri, 1886–88. Destroyed.
Board of Trade Building, 210 West Eighth, Kansas City, Missouri, 1886–88.
Rand-McNally Building, 165 West Adams, Chicago, 1888–90. Destroyed.
Chicago (Great Northern) Hotel, Dearborn and Jackson, Chicago, 1889–91. Destroyed.
Reliance Building, State and Washington, Chicago, 1889–91, 1894–95.
Monadnock Block, Dearborn and Jackson, Chicago, 1889–92.
Masonic Temple, State and Randolph, Chicago, 1890–92. Destroyed.
Mills Building, Montgomery and Bush, San Francisco, 1890–92.

Literature: D. Hoffmann, *The Architecture of John Wellborn Root,* Baltimore and London, 1973.

ROUSSEAU, Pierre (Nantes, 1751–Paris, 1810)

A pupil of N.-M. Potain, he won only the second Grand Prix in 1773 but was nonetheless allowed to go to Rome as a *pensionnaire*. In 1791 he succeeded Potain, by then his father-in-law, as architect to the church at St.-Germain-en-Laye, not to be completed until 1827. His best-known building is the Hôtel de Salm (now Palais de la Légion d'Honneur) in Paris.

Principal executed works:
Hôtel des Gardes de la Porte du Roi, Fontainebleau.
Hôtel de Dreuneue, Rue de Provence, Paris.
Hôtel de Salm (now Palais de la Légion d'Honneur), 64 Rue de Lille, Paris, 1782–85. Redecorated 1812 by A.-F. Peyre; restored 1871–78, after a fire, by Mortier.
Hôtel, 26 Rue de la Rochefoucauld, Paris, 1788.
Chinese pavilion and muniment room, Hôtel de Montmorency, Boulevard Montmartre, Paris.

Literature: M. Gallet, *Paris Domestic Architecture of the 18th Century*, London, 1972.

RUPRICH-ROBERT, Victor-Marie-Charles (Paris, 1820–Cannes, 1887)

He entered S.-C. Constant-Dufeux's *atelier* in 1836. Two years later he enrolled at the École des Beaux-Arts, Paris. He worked thereafter in Paris as *Inspecteur* at the Chambre des Députés (1843–48) and at the École de Dessin, under E.-E. Viollet-le-Duc, who induced him, in 1849, to join the Commission des Monuments Historiques and the Service des Édifices Diocésains. He restored the cathedrals of Sées (Orne), Bayeux, Nevers, and later, in succession to E.-L. Millet, Rheims. He was responsible for a number of minor works, St.-Jean-Baptiste at Flers (Orne; 1855–68); the church at Athis (Orne); the Chapelle du Petit Séminaire at Sées; his own house, 10 Rue Assas, Paris; and the tomb of Constant-Dufeux, in the Montparnasse cemetery. He won renown for his decorative designs—the sacred crown presented by Napoleon III to the Abbey of Einsiedeln, the Chinese museum at Fontainebleau, the furnishings of the pope's apartment there and those for Anne of Austria's room at the Val-de-Grâce—and, above all, for his book on decorative motifs drawn from nature, the *Flore ornamentale* (1866–76). His greatest work, however, was historical: *L'architecture normande aux XIe et XIIe siècles en Normandie et en Angleterre* [1884–89].

Literature: L. Dassy, "Ruprich-Robert," *Forum Artistique,* July 1887. *L'architecture* 1 (1888), p. 280. *Exposition des oeuvres de Laisné, Millet et Ruprich-Robert,* exhib. cat., Union Syndicale des Architectes Français, Paris, 1891.

SALVIN, Anthony (Worthing, Sussex, 1799–Hawksfold, Surrey, 1881)

A pupil of John Nash, he subsequently specialized in the restoration and improvement of medieval castles. He also designed several large, brilliant houses in Tudor and Jacobean styles from the 1820s to the 1860s.

Principal executed works:
Mamhead, Devonshire, 1828. (*Country Life* 117, pp. 1366, 1428.)
Harlaxton Manor, Lincolnshire, 1831–53. (*Country Life* 121, pp. 704, 764.)
Scotney Castle, Kent, 1835–43. (*Country Life* 120, pp. 420, 526.)
Peckforton Castle, Cheshire, 1844–50. (*Country Life,* July 29–Aug. 5, 1965.)
Keele Hall, Staffordshire, 1855–61. (*Country Life,* Feb. 29, 1908.)
Thoresby, Nottinghamshire, 1864–75. (*Country Life* 133, p. 1312.)

SANTI, Lorenzo (Siena, 1783–Venice, 1839)

He moved to Venice while young. There he studied at the school of the Accademia under Giannantonio Selva and later taught there himself. His chief works in Venice are the Corpo di Guardia, later converted into the post office, of 1822, in G. M. Soli's Ala Napoleonica, on the Piazza S. Marco; and the Palazzo Patriarcale, adjoining S. Marco, of 1837–50. In 1838 he also designed, in lighthearted mood, the Caffè at the end of the Giardinetto Reale, now used as an air terminal.

SAULNIER, Jules

His master was Bonneau, architect of the first factory for the Menier chocolate company built on the Marne, at Noisiel, from 1840 to 1855. This building was itself an imitation of a medieval timber-framed mill that had earlier stood on the site. Saulnier's famous iron-framed building with infilling panels of glazed brickwork was started in 1869 and completed three years later. He was responsible for many other buildings for the company; particularly notable is his workers' housing, of 1871 to 1872.

Principal executed works:
Menier chemical works, Saint-Denis, 1860–65.

Chocolat Menier, Noisiel-sur-Marne, 1860–72.
House, Mureaux (Seine-et-Oise), 1878.

SCHINKEL, Karl Friedrich (Neuruppin, 1781–Berlin, 1841)

The greatest architect of nineteenth-century Germany, he was a pupil of Friedrich Gilly in Berlin from 1798 to 1800. His long official career as an architectural civil servant began with his appointment in 1810 to the Prussian Oberbaudeputation (Public Works Department), which regulated state and royal building; in 1830 he was appointed head of this department. The colossal scale of his building operations in Berlin and throughout Prussia identified him with that move to establish Prussia as the leading state in a newly united Germany which culminated in the foundation of the empire in 1871. His beautifully lucid architecture has a strongly intellectual quality and a stylistic astringency regardless of the "style" he was working in: Greek, Gothic, *Rundbogenstil,* or Functional. At the same time, he had a strong feeling for the Picturesque relationship of buildings to their surroundings. He had acquired this during the years he spent before 1815 as a panorama painter and stage designer, at a time when building activity in Prussia had virtually ceased. He was deeply interested in the theoretical principles and the practical aspects of architecture, and from 1820 to 1830 he worked on the text and illustrations of an unpublished book entitled "Architektonisches Lehrbuch." He also produced, with P. C. Beuth, a series of designs for mass-produced articles called *Vorbilder für Fabrikanten und Handwerker* (3 vols., Berlin, 1821–37). He gave wide publicity to his own architectural designs in the following books: *Sammlung architektonischer Entwürfe* (28 portfolios, 1819–40) and *Werke der höheren Baukunst für die Ausführung erfunden* (2 vols., Athens and Orianda, 1842–48).

Principal executed works:
Royal Guardhouse (Neue Wache), Unter den Linden, Berlin, 1816–18. Interior gutted.
State Theater, Platz der Akademie, Berlin, 1818–21. Interior gutted.
Schloss Tegel, Berlin, 1820–24.
Friedrich-Werdersche Church, Berlin, 1821–30. Interior gutted.
Altes Museum, Lustgarten, Berlin, 1822–28. Interior largely gutted.
Schloss Glienicke, Klein-Glienicke, Berlin, 1824–26.
Palace for Prince Albrecht, Wilhelmstrasse, Berlin, remodeling and additions, 1829–33. Demolished 1946.
Schloss Charlottenhof, Potsdam, 1826–27; garden buildings, 1829–36, with Ludwig Persius.
School of Architecture, Berlin, 1831–36. Demolished 1961.
Schloss Babelsberg, Potsdam, 1833–44.
Jagdschloss Granitz, Rügen, 1838.
Schloss Kamenz, Silesia, 1838–40.

Principal unexecuted projects:
Gothic mausoleum for Queen Luise, 1810.
National Memorial Church, Berlin, 1814.
Town Hall, Berlin, 1817.

Master plan for remodeling central Berlin, 1817.
Bazaar, Unter den Linden, Berlin, 1827.
Palace for Prince Wilhelm, Pariser Platz, Berlin, 1829.
Palace for King Otto I, Acropolis, Athens, 1834.
State Library, Berlin, 1835–39.
Palace for the empress of Russia, Orianda (near Yalta), Crimea, 1838.

Literature: A. F. von Wolzogen, *Aus Schinkels Nachlass,* 4 vols., Berlin, 1862–64. A. Grisebach, *Schinkel,* Leipzig, 1924. P. O. Rave, ed., *Karl Friedrich Schinkel: Lebenswerk,* Berlin, 1941–. L. Ettinger, "A German Architect's Visit to England," *Architectural Review* (London) 97 (May 1945), pp. 131–34. "Schinkel," in N. Pevsner, *Studies in Art, Architecture and Design,* 1968, vol. 1, pp. 174–95. H. G. Pundt, *Schinkel's Berlin: A Study in Environmental Planning,* Cambridge, Mass., 1972. D. J. Watkin, "Schinkel: Royal Patronage and the Picturesque," *Architectural Design* 49 (1979), pp. 56–71.

SCOTT, Sir George Gilbert (Gawcott, Buckinghamshire, 1811–London, 1878)

He was a phenomenally successful architect with a practice that brought him more than seven hundred fifty commissions. The mood of evangelical self-satisfaction that dominates his *Personal and Professional Recollections* (1879) has not endeared him to modern readers, who have sometimes seen in him the unacceptable face of Victorian England. But despite much dull work and much harsh restoration of medieval churches, several of his buildings have commanding merit, in particular St. Pancras Station Hotel and the Foreign Office, in London. As a self-made man in search of a popular *via media,* he forged for himself a prosperous career, and his productive energy is especially characteristic of nineteenth-century Britain. He began humbly as an assistant to Sampson Kempthorne, an architect of workhouses, and was knighted in 1872.

Principal executed works:
Cambridge House Hospital, Flax Bourton, Somersetshire, 1837–38.
St. Mary, Henwell, Middlesex, 1841.
Martyrs' Memorial, Oxford, 1841.
Reading Gaol, Berkshire, 1842–44.
Royal Wanstead School, Essex, 1843.
Christ Church, Turnham Green, Chiswick, 1843.
St. Giles, Camberwell, London, 1843.
Parish church, Doncaster, Yorkshire, 1854.
Broad Sanctuary, Westminster, London, 1854.
Kelham Hall, Nottinghamshire, 1858–62. (*Country Life* 141, pp. 1230, 1302.)
Home and Foreign Offices, Whitehall, London, designed 1856–61, built 1862–73, with M. D. Wyatt. (*Country Life,* Feb. 6, 1964.)
Chapel and master's lodge, St. John's College, Cambridge University, Cambridge, 1863–69.
Albert Memorial, Kensington, London, 1863–72. (P. Ferriday, "Syllabus in Stone," *Architectural Review* [London] 135 [1964], pp. 422–28.)
Chapel and library, Exeter College, Oxford University, Oxford, 1866–69.
St. Pancras Station Hotel, London, 1867–74. (*Country*

Life, Nov. 18, 1965, pp. 1314–17.)
Parish church, Kensington, London, 1869–72.
St. Mary's Episcopal cathedral, Glasgow, 1871–74.

SEDDON, John Pollard (London, 1827–1906)

An intriguing architect, the son of a prominent Regency furniture maker, he was articled to the late-classical architect T. L. Donaldson. This was odd training for an architect who was to produce one of the most audacious examples in the country of constructional polychromy: Ettington Park. It was designed in collaboration with John Prichard, a pupil of A. W. N. Pugin. Seddon was in practice with Prichard at Llandaff from 1852 to 1862, and during these years they collaborated on the rebuilding of Llandaff cathedral. In 1852 Seddon published *Progress in Art and Architecture* and in 1862 moved to London, where he was in partnership with J. C. Carter from 1885 to 1904. Perhaps his most unexpected building is St. Catherine, Hoarwithy, designed in a rich Italian Romanesque style.

Principal executed works:
Southerndown Hotel, Bridgend, Glamorganshire, 1852–53.
Ettington Park, Warwickshire, 1858–63, with John Prichard.
Castle Hotel (now University College), Aberystwyth, Cardiganshire, 1864–66.
Powell Almshouses, Fulham, London, 1869.
St. James, Great Yarmouth, Norfolk, 1870–78.
Abermad (near Aberystwyth), Cardiganshire, c. 1872.
St. Mary, Ullenhall, Warwickshire, 1875.
St. Catherine, Hoarwithy, Herefordshire, 1880–85.

Principal unexecuted projects:
Law Courts, London, 1866.
Monumental Halls, Westminster, London, 1890.

SELVA, Giannantonio (Venice, 1754–1819)

He was a pupil of Tommaso Temanza, who advised him to travel to Rome and the south, where he spent three years. Two more years were spent journeying through France, Holland, and England, and Constantinople. He returned to Venice only at the end of 1781. There he settled, winning fame as the designer of the Teatro La Fenice, establishing the style of neoclassicism in that city of rich and rococo decorative fantasies. He was a close friend of the sculptor Antonio Canova, whose memorial at Possagno he most probably designed in 1818. It was built between 1819 and 1833 by Selva's pupil Antonio Diedo.

Principal executed works:
Villa Manfrin (later Villa Margherita), S. Artemio, Treviso, 1782–83.
Teatro La Fenice, Piazza S. Fantino, Venice, 1790–92. Rebuilt 1836 by G. B. Meduna.
Palazzo Dotti-Vigodarzere, Via Rudena, Padua, 1796.
S. Maurizio, Venice, facade, begun 1806, completed by Antonio Diedo. The interior is by Pietro Zaguri, with furnishings by Selva.

Giardino Pubblico Castello, Venice, 1808–10. Much altered.
S. Nome di Gesù, S. Chiara, Venice, 1815–34, completed by Antonio Diedo.

Principal unexecuted projects:
Studio for Antonio Canova, Zattere, Venice, 1809.
Monumento alla Riconoscenza al Moncenisio, 1813.

Literature: E. Bassi, *Giannantonio Selva: architetto Veneziano*, Florence, 1935.

SELVATICO, Pietro Estense (Padua, 1803–Padua, 1880)

At the age of nineteen he took up the study of law at the University of Padua, but at the same time studied painting under Giovanni Demin and architecture under Giuseppe Jappelli. He later undertook several minor architectural commissions, but his fame was to spring from his activity as a critic, historian, and teacher. He began his academic career as *Professore di Estetica* at the Accademia di Belle Arti in Venice. He introduced into Italy a new, widespread knowledge of the writings of such men as F.-A. Rio and the Comte de Montalembert, A. W. N. Pugin, John Ruskin, and E.-E. Viollet-le-Duc, and he cultivated the German Nazarenes and other such primitive painters. In 1867 he opened his school for craftsmen and artists in Padua; two years later he was in Rome advising on the whole pattern of artistic education in Italy. His successor in all this activity was Camillo Boito. Together they may be said to have prepared the way for the neo-Liberty movements, and also for Futurism.

Principal executed works:
S. Pietro, Trento, facade.
Monument to Francis I of Austria, Padua.
High altar, S. Giovanni Battista, Mezzolombardo.

Literature: N. Gallimberti, "P. Selvatico architetto," *Bolletino del Museo Civico di Padova*, 1933. L. Gaudenzio, *La regia Scuola d'Arte "P. Selvatico" di Padova*, Padua, 1943. F. Bernabei, *Pietro Selvatico nella critica e nella storia delle arti figurative dell' ottocento*, Vicenza, 1974.

SEMPER, Gottfried (Hamburg, 1803–Rome, 1879)

He studied mathematics and law at Göttingen University, attending courses on classical archaeology at the same time. He then turned to architecture, becoming a pupil of Friedrich Gärtner in Munich. In 1826 and 1827 he was in France, and in 1829 he went to Paris, where he remained for almost a year, working for F. C. Gau and coming into constant contact with J.-I. Hittorff and the painter J.-A.-D. Ingres. In August 1830 he set off for Italy, Sicily, and Greece, returning to Hamburg in December 1833. The following year he took up a teaching post at the Dresden Academy, where he remained until 1849, when he was forced to flee after having taken part in an abortive revolution. He went to Belgium and France, then to England, where he arrived in 1851 and stayed until 1855. He was at once made use of by Henry Cole, who appointed him to help

with the displays in the Crystal Palace and then to teach the technology of metals at the newly formed Department of Practical Art at Marlborough House. During this period he wrote and published his first attempts to establish a systematic framework for ordering the arts: *Die vier Elemente der Baukunst* (1851) and *Wissenschaft, Industrie und Kunst* (1852). In 1855 he moved to Zurich, where he was made professor at the Eidgenössische Technische Hochschule. He built much at that time and also wrote the most important of his books, *Der Stil in den technischen und tektonischen Künsten*, published in two volumes in 1860 and 1863. The third volume, dealing with architecture, was never written. In 1871 he went to Vienna, where he became *Baurat* to the emperor and built the new museum and opera house. He was not a successful architect, but as a theorist he was more searching, certainly more wide-ranging in his scope, than anyone else of the period.

Principal executed works:
Opera house, Dresden, 1837–41.
Oppenheim Palace, Bürgerwiese, Dresden, 1845–48.
Königliche Gemäldegalerie, Dresden, 1845–48.
Polytechnikum, Zurich, 1858–64.
Railroad station, Zurich, 1860.
Sternwarte der ETH (an observatory), Zurich, 1861–64.
Town Hall, Winterthur, 1863–69.
Fierz Commercial Building, 8 Zurichbergstrasse, Zurich, 1865–66.
New opera house, Dresden, 1871–78.
Hofburgtheater, Vienna, 1871–78.
Kunst und Naturhistorisches Museum, Vienna, 1872–82.

Literature: C. Lipsius, *Gottfried Semper in seiner Bedeutung als Architekt*, 1880. H. Semper, *Gottfried Semper*, 1880. M. Fröhlich, *Gottfried Semper*, Basel and Stuttgart, 1974. A. M. Vögt, C. Reble, M. Fröhlich, eds., *Gottfried Semper und die Mitte des 19. Jahrhunderts*, Basel and Stuttgart, 1976.

SERVANDONI, Giovanni Niccolò (Florence, 1695–Paris, 1766)

He studied under the painter G. P. Panini and the architect G. I. Rossi in Rome. He moved in 1724 to Paris, where he became *Premier Peintre Decorateur* to the Académie Royale de Musique in 1728. Though he held this position for eighteen years and lived in Paris, he traveled widely throughout Europe, doing designs for the theater and for fêtes and fireworks displays. In 1755 he went to Dresden as *Premier Architecte* to King Augustus. His greatest work was the west front of St.-Sulpice in Paris, the commission for which he won in competition in 1732, and which was slowly built and modified during the years of construction. It was completed only in 1777 by J.-F.-T. Chalgrin.

Principal executed works:
St.-Sulpice, Place St.-Sulpice, Paris, west front, 1732–77. (C. Hamel, *Histoire de l'église Saint-Sulpice*, 2d ed., Paris, 1909; G. Lemesle, *L'église Saint-Sulpice*, Paris, 1931; E. Malbois, "Projets de la place devant Saint Sulpice par Servandoni," *Gazette des beaux-arts*, 1933, pp. 34–46.)

Church, Coulanges-la-Vineuse (Yonne).
High altar, Sens cathedral, 1742.
High altar, St.-Bruno, Lyons, 1745. The executed design was altered by J.-G. Soufflot.
Chapel, Hôtel de La Live de Jully, Rue Cambon, Paris.
Temple in the park, Gennevilliers.
Servandoni House, 6 Place St.-Sulpice, Paris, 1752, 1754–57. This is the only part of his project for the new square that was built. (*Gazette des beaux-arts*, 1922, pp. 283–92.)

Literature: E. L. G. Charvet, *Lyon artistique: architectes, notices biographiques et bibliographiques*, Lyons, 1899, pp. 362–65.

SHAW, Richard Norman (Edinburgh, 1831–Hampstead, London, 1912)

He was trained by William Burn and worked in the office of Anthony Salvin and of G. E. Street before setting up an architectural office with W. E. Nesfield in 1863. In 1862–64 he and Nesfield devised the Old English Manorial style, which was to revolutionize English and North American domestic architecture. The key building in the new manner was Leyswood (1866–69), a dramatic fantasy, and the architect soon followed it up with Cragside, an essay in Burke's Sublime. However, his training under Street is reflected in the Ruskinian High Victorian Gothic of his contemporary Holy Trinity, Bingley. He produced a magnificent chain of town houses in London, culminating in No. 185 Queen's Gate. He came to feel that his Old English style was a fake and turned to classicism for reality, as he did, for example, in his house, Chesters, and in his designs for Regent Street. His avowed aim now became to unite in his work "the contradictory geniuses of Cockerell and Pugin." In many of his major buildings (of whatever style), he relied extensively on iron or steel girders to ease spatial planning and to create new forms and dispositions. Indeed, his last building, Portland House, was one of the first major English office blocks of reinforced concrete; its facade is in a subdued Cockerell-inspired classicism.

Principal executed works:
Holy Trinity, Bingley, Yorkshire, 1864–69. Demolished 1974. (*Country Life*, Dec. 27, 1973.)
Glen Andred, Groombridge, Sussex, 1866–68. (*Country Life,* Sept. 6, 1973.)
Leyswood, Groombridge, Sussex, 1866–69. Largely demolished 1955. (*Country Life*, Sept. 6, 1973.)
Farnham Bank, Castle Street, Farnham, Surrey, 1866–69. Demolished 1933.
Cragside, Rothbury, Northumberland, 1869–. (*Country Life*, Dec. 18–25, 1969.)
Grims Dyke, Harrow Weald, London, 1870–72.
New Zealand Chambers, Leadenhall Street, London, 1871–73. Destroyed 1941.
Lowther Lodge, Kensington Gore, London, 1872–75. (London County Council, *Survey of London* 38 [1975], pp. 327–31.)
No. 196 Queen's Gate, London, 1874–76. (London County Council, *Survey of London* 38 [1975], pp. 331–33.)

No. 6 Ellerdale Road, Hampstead, London, 1874–.
No. 8 Melbury Road, London, 1875–76. Gutted. (London County Council, *Survey of London* 37 [1973], pp. 143–44; *Country Life*, Nov. 16, 1972.)
Cheyne House, Chelsea Embankment, London, 1875–77.
Swan House, Chelsea Embankment, London, 1875–77. Gutted.
No. 31 Melbury Road, London, 1875–77. (London County Council, *Survey of London* 37 [1973], pp. 148–49; *Country Life*, Nov. 16, 1972.)
St. Margaret, Ilkley, Yorkshire, 1875–79.
Adcote, Shropshire, 1875–81. (*Country Life*, Dec. 25, 1909; *Country Life*, Oct. 22, 1970.)
Albert Hall Mansions, Kensington Gore, London, 1876, 1882, 1884. (London County Council, *Survey of London* 38 [1975], pp. 342–45.)
Flete, Devonshire, 1877–. (*Country Life*, Nov. 20, 1915.)
Church, houses, inn, club, Bedford Park, Turnham Green, London, 1877–80. (*Country Life*, Dec. 7–14, 1967.)
Clock House Chelsea Embankment, London, 1878–80.
Alliance Assurance Offices, 1–2 St. James's Street, London, 1881–83.
Dawpool, Thurstaston, Cheshire, 1882–86, 1892. Demolished 1927, except for stables. (*Country Life*, Feb. 18, 1911.)
No. 180 Queen's Gate, London, 1883–85. Demolished 1971. (*Country Life*, Aug. 30, 1956; London County Council, *Survey of London* 38 [1975], pp. 333–34.)
New Scotland Yard, London, 1886, 1897. (S. Beattie, *Architectural History*, vol. 15, 1972, pp. 68–81.)
No. 170 Queen's Gate, London, 1888–90. (London County Council, *Survey of London* 38 [1975], pp. 334–38.)
No. 185 Queen's Gate, London, 1889–91. Destroyed 1940. (London County Council, *Survey of London* 38 [1975], pp. 338–40.)
All Saints, Richards Castle, Shropshire, 1889–93.
Bryanston, Dorsetshire, 1889–94.
Chesters, Northumberland, 1890–94. (*Country Life*, Feb. 17, 1912.)
Haggerston Castle, Northumberland, 1892–97. Demolished 1931.
White Star Offices, James Street, Liverpool, 1895–98.
Parr's Bank, Castle Street, Liverpool, 1898–1901. (*Architectural Review* [London] 10 [1901], pp. 146–55.)
Gaiety Theater and Restaurant, Aldwych, London, 1901–3. Largely demolished.
Alliance Assurance Offices, 88 St. James's Street, London, 1901, 1904–5. (London County Council, *Survey of London* 30 [1960], pp. 485–86.)
Town Hall, Bradford, Yorkshire, extension, 1902, 1905–9.
Regent Street quadrant, Piccadilly and Piccadilly Circus, London, rebuilding scheme, 1904–11. Partly executed. (London County Council, *Survey of London* 31 [1963], pp. 87–95.)
Portland House, Lloyds Avenue, London, 1907–8. Gutted 1971–72. (*Concrete* 6 [1972], pp. 30–34.)

Literature: R. Blomfield, *Richard Norman Shaw, R. A.,* 1940. M. Girouard, "Early Norman Shaw Commissions," *Country Life*, Aug. 30–Sept. 6, 1973. N.

Halbritter, "Norman Shaw's London Houses," *Architectural Association Quarterly* 7, no. 1 (1975), pp. 3–19. A. Saint, "Norman Shaw's Letters: A Selection," *Journal of the Society of Architectural Historians of Great Britain* 18 (1975), pp. 60–85. A. Saint, *Richard Norman Shaw*, New Haven, Conn., 1976.

SIMONE, Antonio de

He was partner or assistant to Leopoldo Laperuta, architect of S. Francesco di Paola at Naples, begun in 1810 but taken over and altogether redesigned in 1817 by Pietro Bianchi.

Literature: A. Venditti, *Architettura neoclassica a Napoli*, Naples, 1961.

SIMONETTI, Michelangelo (Rome, 1724–1781)

He was a papal architect, chiefly occupied with the reorganization and rebuilding of the Vatican museums under the direction of the *Soprintendente alle Antichità*, G. B. Visconti, beginning in 1772. Before that date he is recorded only as a member, in 1769, of the Virtuosi del Pantheon. In 1772 he took over the work begun by Alessandro Dori on the Casina of Innocent VIII. He destroyed the chapel decorated by Andrea Mantegna, slowly forming the related rooms of the new museum. The octagonal courtyard reflects in part his design, of 1773, but it was only under Pius VI that work on the Museo Chiaramonti began in earnest. Simonetti was then joined by Pietro Camporese, the elder, and together they built the Galleria dei Candelabri e degli Animali, the Sala delle Muse, the Sala a Croce Greca, and the Sala Rotonda. Simonetti's staid, archaeological tastes served to effect something of a revolution in Roman classicism.

SOANE, Sir John (Goring-on-Thames, 1753–London, 1837)

Perhaps the most original architect at work in Europe in 1800, he combined Continental neoclassicism with a romanticism derived from English Picturesque theory. The son of a bricklayer, he became a pupil of George Dance, the younger, in 1768 and an assistant of Henry Holland in 1772. After designing a number of country houses, he was appointed Surveyor to the Bank of England, in 1788; Clerk of the Works at Whitehall, Westminster, and St. James, in 1790; and one of the three architects attached to the Board of Works, in 1814. His remarkable house-*cum*-museum in Lincoln's Inn Fields, London, he left to the British nation by act of Parliament in 1833. He published several volumes of his own designs and also, in 1835–36, *Description of the House and Museum on the North Side of Lincoln's Inn Fields*.

Principal executed works:
Shotesham Park (near Norwich), 1785–88. (*Country Life*, Aug. 10, 1967.)
Chillington Hall, Staffordshire, remodeling, 1786–89.

(*Country Life* 103, pp. 326, 378, 426; *Country Life* 114, p. 785.)
Bank of England, London, remodeling, 1788–1833. Largely demolished 1930.

Nos. 12–14 Lincoln's Inn Fields, London, remodeling as Sir John Soane's Museum, 1792–1824. (*Country Life*, May 25, 1972.)

Tyringham Hall, Buckinghamshire, also lodge and bridge, 1793–1800. (*Country Life* 42, p. 628; *Country Life* 114, p. 784.)

Pitzhanger Manor, Ealing, 1800–1802.

Dulwich College, Camberwell, London, picture gallery and mausoleum, 1812.

House of Lords, House of Commons, and Law Courts, Westminster, London, additions, 1820–26. Demolished.

Pelwall House, Staffordshire, 1822–28.

Literature: A. T. Bolton, *The Works of Sir John Soane, R. A.,* 1924. A. T. Bolton, *The Portrait of Sir John Soane, R. A.,* 1927. J. Summerson, *Sir John Soane,* 1952. D. Stroud, *The Architecture of Sir John Soane,* 1961.

SOAVE, Carlo Felice (Lugano, 1740–Milan, 1803)

He built little, and only a handful of these works were in Milan, where he settled, for Giuseppe Piermarini, who controlled most of the building done in that city, did not altogether approve of his style, which was at first strongly influenced by that of E.-A. Petitot, under whom Soave studied at Parma in 1772. But his few buildings mark him as an infinitely more interesting architect than Piermarini, in particular his Anguissola House, in Milan. He was architect to the Milan cathedral from 1795 to his death and designed a facade for the building in 1791 that was built eventually by Carlo Amati.

Principal executed works:
Anguissola House, Via Morone, Milan, 1775–78.
Hospital, Codogno, 1781.
S. Margherita, Pandino (Cremona), 1783–91.
Palazzo Bovara, Milan, 1787.
Villa Salazar, Borgovico, Como.
Villa Carminati (Resta Pallavicino), Borgovico, Como.
Villa Crivelli-Serbelloni, Luino, c. 1795.

Literature: G. Mezzanotte, *Architettura neoclassica in Lombardia,* Naples, 1966.

SOLI, Giuseppe Maria (Vignola, 1747–Modena, 1823)

He studied first at the Accademia Clementina, Bologna, under Malvasia, then, from 1770 to 1783, in Rome. In 1784 he took charge of the teaching of architecture at the Accademia in Modena, and became court architect there. But his best-known work is in Venice.

Principal executed works:
Ala Napoleonica, Piazza S. Marco, Venice, 1810. Designed by G. A. Antolini.
Accademia di Scienze, Lettere e Arti, Modena, extension and new facade, 1814–24.
Palazzo Bellucci, Vignola.

Literature: M. Valdrighi, *Giuseppe Soli,* n. d.

SOUFFLOT, Jacques-Germain (Irancy [Auxerre], 1713–Paris, 1780)

He seems to have had little formal architectural training. He was sent to Paris to study law but abandoned it and set off for Rome, where he arrived in 1731. Three years later he was admitted to the Académie de France à Rome, where he remained until 1738. He then returned to Lyons, where he built a number of important buildings and became *Architecte de la Ville.* In 1749 he was chosen by Mme. de Pompadour as companion, together with C.-N. Cochin and the Abbé Leblanc, for her brother, Abel Poisson (soon to be made Marquis de Vandières, later Marquis de Marigny). Poisson was being sent to Italy in preparation for his receipt of the post of *Directeur Général des Bâtiments.* The party set forth in December 1749; Poisson returned in the following year, but Soufflot stayed on to inspect the temples of Paestum, which he published, together with G.-P.-M. Dumont, in 1764. By February 1751 Soufflot was back in Lyons, and in the following year he moved to Paris, where he became *Contrôleur des Bâtiments du Roi au Département de Paris* in 1755 and was commissioned to build the new church of Ste.-Geneviève, now known as the Panthéon. This was his greatest work, one that embodied all the most advanced theories on structure and on design. Its construction was followed with the keenest interest by architects throughout Europe. In Paris it was the subject of considerable controversy. The structure was not altogether sound, and much reinforcement had to be effected later by Soufflot's pupil J.-B. Rondelet. The design itself was much changed by alterations conducted at the behest of A.-C. Quatremère de Quincy in the early nineteenth century. But the church has always been considered a masterpiece of eighteenth-century architecture.

Principal executed works:
Hôtel-Dieu, Quai Jules Courmont, Lyons, facade and central feature, 1741–48.
Loge du Change (now Église Réformée), Place du Change, Lyons, 1747–49.
Grand Théâtre, Lyons, 1754–56. Demolished 1828.
Notre-Dame, Paris, sacristy, 1756. Demolished.
Ste.-Geneviève (now the Panthéon), Place du Panthéon, Paris, 1756–90. (A. Braham, *Burlington Magazine,* Oct. 1971.)
Nymphaeum, 2 Avenue du Château, Chatou (near Paris), after 1762.
Château de Ménars (Loire), nymphaeum and orangery, 1764. (M. Mosser, *Bulletin de la Société de l'Histoire de l'Art Française,* Année 1972, pp. 269–93.)
Hôtel de Marigny, Rue St.-Thomas-du-Louvre, Paris, c. 1767. Demolished.
Hôtel de Marigny, Faubourg du Roule, Paris, 1769. Demolished.
École de Droit, Place du Panthéon, Paris, 1771–83.

Literature: E. L. G. Charvet, *Lyon artistique: architectes, notices biographiques et bibliographiques,* Lyons, 1899, p. 366. J. M. Monval, *Soufflot, sa vie, son oeuvre, son esthétique,* Paris, 1918. M. Mathieu, *Pierre Patte, sa vie,* son oeuvre, Paris, 1940. M. Petzet, *Soufflots Sainte-Geneviève und der französische Kirchenbau des 18. Jahrhunderts,* Berlin, 1961. P. Chevalier and D. Rabreau, *Le Panthéon,* Paris, 1977.

STERN, Raffaello (Rome, 1774–Rome, 1820)

He was the son of the architect Giovanni Stern. His archaeological interests were given full play in his one important and, in neoclassical terms, altogether successful work, the Braccio Nuovo of the Museo Chiaramonti in the Vatican, of 1817–22. He built little else, though he was in part responsible for the decoration of the apse of S. Pudenziana and the Cappella Paolina in the Palazzo del Quirinale, Rome. He began the restoration of the Colosseum and the Arch of Titus, both of which were continued by Giuseppe Valadier.

STEVENS, Alfred George (Blandford Forum, 1817–Haverstock Hill, 1875)

The greatest sculptor of nineteenth-century England was trained, in a somewhat haphazard way, in Naples, Rome, Florence, Milan, and Venice between 1832 and 1842. He was deeply influenced by Michelangelo and was also interested in architectural design. From 1845 to 1847 he taught architectural drawing, perspective, and modeling at the Government School of Design, Somerset House, London. He had a special aptitude for design in metalwork and designed the railings in front of the British Museum as well as many grates and stoves for the firm of iron founders H. E. Hoole. His greatest work was the Wellington Monument, a commission he owed largely to the efforts of C. R. Cockerell, who was stylistically in deep sympathy with him.

Principal executed works:
Deysbrook, West Derby, Liverpool, decoration in Pompeian style of drawing room and dining room, 1847. Demolished (some panels in Walker Art Gallery, Liverpool).
Wellington Monument, St. Paul's cathedral, London, 1856. (J. Physick, *The Wellington Monument,* Victoria and Albert Museum Publication, 1970.)
Dorchester House, Park Lane, London, dining room, 1859–69. Demolished 1929 (chimneypiece in Victoria and Albert Museum, London). (*Journal of the Royal Institute of British Architects* 35 [1928], pp. 623, 667; *Country Life* 63, pp. 646, 684.)
Dome mosaics, St. Paul's cathedral, London, c. 1860–64.

Principal unexecuted projects:
Royal Reception Room, Paddington Station, London, decoration, c. 1852.
Reading room, British Museum, London, decoration, c. 1853.

Literature: W. M. Conway, "The Work of Alfred Stevens in Liverpool," *The Builder* 54 (1888), pp. 223–24. H. Stannus, *Alfred Stevens and His Work,* 1891. K. R. Towndrow, *Alfred Stevens,* 1939. S. McMorran, "Alfred Stevens," *Journal of the Royal Institute of British Architects* 71 (1964). S. Beattie, *Alfred Stevens, 1817–75,* Victoria and Albert Museum Publication, 1975.

STREET, George Edmund (Woodford, 1824–London, 1881)

He was a High Churchman, and his buildings have all the aggressive vigor of the High Victorian decades. Like William Butterfield, he was interested in constructional polychromy and published *Brick and Marble of the Middle Ages: Notes of a Tour in the North of Italy* (1855). He was a pupil of G. G. Scott and set up a practice in Oxford in 1852; Philip Webb and William Morris were among his first assistants. In 1855 he moved his practice to London, where he designed one of his most striking churches, St. James-the-Less, Westminster. His greatest secular commission, the Law Courts, has been described as the swan song of the Gothic Revival.

Principal executed works:
St. Mary, Par, Cornwall, 1847.
Cuddesdon College and vicarage, Cuddesdon (near Oxford), 1852.
St. Peter, Bournemouth, 1853.
Vicarage, Colnbrook, Buckinghamshire, 1853.
All Saints, Boyne Hill, Maidenhead, Berkshire, with vicarage and school, 1854–60.
St. George, Oakengates, Shropshire, 1855.
St. John the Evangelist, Howsham, Yorkshire, 1859.
St. Philip and St. James, Oxford, 1859.
St. James-the-Less, Westminster, London, 1859–61.
All Saints, Denstone, Staffordshire, 1860–62.
St. John, Torquay, Devonshire, 1861–71.
All Saints, Clifton, Bristol, 1863–68.
Law Courts (Royal Courts of Justice), Strand, London, 1866–82.
St. Mary Magdalen, Paddington, London, 1868–78.
St. John the Divine, Kensington, London, 1870–74.
St. Mary, Holmbury St. Mary, Surrey, 1879.

Principal unexecuted projects:
Oxford University Museum, Oxford, 1853.
Cathedral, Lille, 1855.
Foreign Office, London, 1856.
Crimean Memorial Church, Istanbul, 1856–57.
St. Dionis Backchurch, London, 1857.
National Gallery, London, 1866.

Literature: A. E. Street, *Memoir of G. E. Street,* 1888. H. R. Hitchcock, "G. E. Street in the 1850's," *Journal of the Society of Architectural Historians* (U.S.A.) 19 (1960), pp. 145–71. B. Clarke and J. Piper, "Street's Yorkshire Churches and Contemporary Criticism," in J. Summerson, ed., *Concerning Architecture,* 1968, pp. 209–25.

STRICKLAND, William (Philadelphia, 1788–Nashville, Tennessee, 1854)

He was a pupil of Benjamin Latrobe. Like his fellow student Robert Mills, he worked extensively in a more than competent classical manner but lacked Latrobe's genius. His principal building is the temple-like Second Bank of the United States, Philadelphia, a commission he took over from Latrobe. He was also an engineer, much involved in the construction of canals and railways.

Principal executed works:
Masonic temple, Philadelphia, 1810. Rebuilt after a fire, 1819–20.
Second Bank of the United States (later Custom House), Philadelphia, 1818–24.
United States Naval Asylum, Washington, D.C., 1827.
United States Mint, Washington, D.C., 1829–33.
Merchants' Exchange, Philadelphia, 1832–34.
Tennessee State Capitol, Nashville, 1845–49.

Literature: A. A. Gilchrist, *William Strickland: Architect and Engineer, 1788–1854,* Philadelphia, 1950.

STUART, James (London, 1713–London, 1788)

He was not trained as an architect but opened the eyes of Europe to Grecian architecture by the accurate measured drawings he published with Nicholas Revett in *The Antiquities of Athens* (4 vols., 1762–1816). On his return to England from Greece in 1755, Stuart was much in demand among the members of the Society of Dilettanti and their friends (who had financed his studies in Athens from 1751 to 1753) as the designer of buildings in the new Greek manner. A certain natural indolence made Stuart much less of a threat to the success of Robert Adam than must have appeared probable in the 1760s. Stuart was, however, an important and successful furniture designer.

Principal executed works:
Hagley Park, Worcestershire, Greek Doric temple, 1758. (*Country Life,* Sept. 19, 1957.)
Spencer House, Green Park, London, interiors, 1759–66. (*Country Life,* Oct. 30–Nov. 6, 1926; London County Council, *Survey of London* 30 [1960].)
Church, Nuneham Park, Oxfordshire, 1764. *Country Life,* Oct. 7–14, 1941.)
Shugborough, Staffordshire, garden buildings, 1764–70. (*Country Life* 115, pp. 1126, 1220.)
Montagu (later Portman) House, Portman Square, London, c. 1775–82. Demolished.
Royal Hospital, Greenwich, remodeling of chapel, 1779–88. (L. Lawrence [Lewis], "Greece and Rome at Greenwich," *Architectural Review* [London], Jan. 1951; "The Architects of the Chapel of Greenwich Hospital," *Art Bulletin* 29 [1947], p. 260.)

Literature: L. Lawrence [Lewis], "Stuart and Revett: Their Literary and Architectural Careers," *Journal of the Warburg Institute* 2 (1938–39), pp. 128–46. N. Goodison, "Mr. Stuart's Tripod," *Burlington Magazine,* Oct. 1972, pp. 695–705; *Burlington Magazine,* Dec. 1972, p. 874.

TAGLIAFICHI, Emanuele Andrea (Genoa, 1729–1811)

An architect active in Genoa, he studied in Rome but returned to his native city to establish himself. In 1772–73 he supervised the redecoration of the salon and adjoining terrace of the Palazzo Spinola (now Palazzo Campanella, 12 Via Garibaldi), designed by Charles de Wailly. In 1774 he traveled to Paris and in 1778

was made a corresponding member of the Académie Royale d'Architecture.

Principal executed works:
Palazzo Durazzo-Pallavicini, Via Balbi, Genoa, courtyard and main salon, begun 1780.
Villa Rosazza (or Villa della Scoglietto), interior redecoration and garden pavilions, 1787.

Literature: C. Maltese, "Appunti per una storia del neoclassicismo a Genova," in *Neoclassicismo. Londra 1971. Atti del convegno internazionale promesso del Comité International d'Histoire de l'Art,* Genoa, 1973.

TARDIEU, Jean-Jacques (Paris, 1762–Paris, 1833)

A pupil of J.-D. Le Roy, he won the second Grand Prix in 1788 and went the following year to Rome as a *pensionnaire.* Many of his monumental designs were illustrated in the *Annales du musée* and other such publications, but not much is known of his other activities.

TAYLOR, Sir Robert (Woodford, 1714–London, 1788)

The son of a successful mason-contractor, he was trained as a sculptor by Henry Cheere. He turned to architecture after 1750 and specialized in the design of London offices and country villas for city merchants. Stylistically his work was transitional between Palladianism and neoclassicism. The plans of his villas are particularly attractive. Like S. P. Cockerell, the most successful of his pupils, he acquired a fortune through his activities as a surveyor (to the Admiralty, Bank of England, Customs, Greenwich and Foundling hospitals, Lincoln's Inn, and Grafton and Pulteney estates, among other clients).

Principal executed works:
Harleyford Manor, Buckinghamshire, 1755.
Asgill House, Richmond, Surrey, 1758–67.
Bank Buildings, Threadneedle Street, London, 1764–66. Demolished 1844.
Bank of England, London, alterations and additions, 1765–83. Largely demolished c. 1930. (H. R. Steele and F. R. Yerbury, *The Old Bank of England,* 1930; M. Binney, "Sir Robert Taylor's Bank of England," *Country Life* 146 [1969], pp. 1244–48, 1326–30.)
Purbrook, Hampshire, c. 1770. Demolished 1829.
Ely House, Dover Street, London, c. 1772. (C. Hussey, *The Story of Ely House,* 1953.)
Stone Buildings, Lincoln's Inn, London, 1774–80.
Gorhambury, Hertfordshire, 1777–90. (*Country Life* 74, p. 556; *Country Life* 120, p. 430.)
Heveningham Hall, Suffolk, 1778–c. 1780. (*Country Life,* Sept. 19–26, 1925.)

Literature: M. Binney, "The Villas of Sir Robert Taylor," *Country Life* 142 (1967), pp. 17–21, 78–82; *Country Life* 145 (1969), pp. 52–55, 1014–17.

TEMANZA, Tommaso (Venice, 1705–1789)

He trained in Venice with his uncle Giovanni Scalfarotto and was associated with him as engineer to the city's sea defenses. He worked also as an architect, building a handful of small churches and pavilions that reflect his conservative classical tastes. But his distinction rests above all in his activity as a teacher—he was the master of Giannantonio Selva, Antonio Diedo, and Leopoldo Cicognara—and as a scholar. He excavated and measured a number of ancient Roman buildings at Rimini, though he actually went to Rome itself only in 1762. His great work was *Vita dei più celebri architetti e scultori veneziani*, published in Venice in 1778, a work that was widely read and much used by such later compilers as Francesco Milizia and A.-C. Quatremère de Quincy.

Principal executed works:
Capella dei Sagredo, S. Francesco della Vigna, Venice.
S. Margherita, Via S. Francesco, Padua, facade, 1748.
Oratorio, Villa Contarini, Piazzola sul Brenta.
Garden pavilion, Ca' Zenobio, 2593 Fondamenta Foscarini, Venice. Now part of the Armenian boys' school.
S. Maria Maddalena, Campo della Maddalena, Venice, 1760, 1763–78.

Literature: E. Bassi, *Architettura del sei e settecento a Venezia,* Naples, 1962. N. Ivanoff, "Tommaso Temanza," *Bolletino del Centro Internazionale di Studi di Architettura Andrea Palladio* 5 (1963), pp. 202–11.

TEULON, Samuel Sanders (Greenwich, 1812–1873)

He was perhaps the most aggressively assertive of all the High Victorian Gothic architects. There seems to be a deliberate will to shock in his buildings that must be of aesthetic rather than sociological origin since there is no reason to suppose that his patrons were men of exceptional violence. Trained in the office of an obscure London architect, he specialized in country residences for aristocratic clients. His most startling houses are Shadwell Park, for Sir. R. J. Buxton, Bart., and Bestwood Lodge, for the duke of St. Albans.

Principal executed works:
St. Stephen, Manciple Street, Southwark, London, 1849–50. Demolished.
Tortworth Court, Gloucestershire, 1849–53.
Christ Church, Croydon, Surrey, 1851–52.
Holy Trinity, Hastings, Sussex, 1851–59.
St. James, Edgbaston, Birmingham, 1852.
Enbrook, Kent, 1853.
St. Andrew, Lambeth, London, 1854. Demolished.
St. John the Divine, Burringham, Lincolnshire, 1856.
St. Thomas, Wells, Somersetshire, 1856.
Shadwell Park, Norfolk, 1856–60. (*Country Life* 136, pp. 18, 98.)
Gisborough Hall, Yorkshire, 1857.
St. Mark, Silvertown, Essex, 1859.
Elvetham Hall, Hampshire, 1859–62.
Hawkleyhurst, Hampshire, 1860–61.
Bestwood Lodge, Nottinghamshire, 1862–64.
Church, vicarage, school, village, Hunstanworth, County Durham, 1863.
SS. Peter and Paul, Hawkley, Hampshire, 1865.
St. Stephen, Rosslyn Hill, Hampstead, London, 1869–76.
Woodlands Vale, Isle of Wight, 1870–71.

Literature: M. Girouard, "Acrobatic Gothic: S. S. Teulon," *Country Life*, Dec. 31, 1970, pp. 1282–86.

THIBAULT, Jean-Thomas (Montier-en-Der [Haute-Marne], 1757–Paris, 1826)

He trained first at the École des Beaux-Arts, Paris, then began work in 1778 at L'Isle-Adam on the estate of the Prince de Conti. He submitted a drawing in 1780 to one of the *concours* of the Académie Royale d'Architecture and was noticed by E.-L. Boullée, whose office he then entered. He stayed there until 1788, when he set off for Italy. Returning to Paris in 1792, he earned his living by making designs for the theater and, together with J.-N.-L. Durand, entered a number of competitions, several of which they won, though they were to see nothing built. He worked later at the Palais de l'Élysée, Paris, and the Château de Neuilly for Caroline Murat and at the Château de Malmaison for the Empress Josephine. In 1810 he went to Holland to work for Louis Bonaparte. He was appointed *Professeur de Perspective* at the École des Beaux-Arts in 1819.

Literature: N. Chapuis, "Notice sur J.-T. Thibault," in J.-T. Thibault, *Application de la perspective linéaire aux arts du dessin*, Paris, 1827. J. M. Pérouse de Montclos, *Étienne-Louis Boullée: de l'architecture classique à l'architecture révolutionnaire,* Paris, 1969, pp. 213–14.

THOMON, Thomas de (Nancy, 1754–St. Petersburg [Leningrad], 1813)

He trained in Paris and visited Italy, where he saw the Greek temples of Paestum. After spending some time in Vienna he went in 1790 to St. Petersburg, where Alexander I later commissioned him to build a theater and what was to be his masterpiece, the Exchange (1804). He also built warehouses on the Salni Embankment (1804–5) and the memorial chapel to Paul I at Pavlovsk. In 1806 he published *Recueil des principaux monuments construits à Saint-Pétersbourg.*

Literature: G. Loukomski, "Thomas de Thomon," *Apollo* 42 (1945), p. 297 ff.

THOMSON, Alexander (Balfron, Stirlingshire, 1817–Glasgow, 1875)

He was trained in Glasgow, where nearly all his important buildings are to be found. Because of his powerful classical work in Glasgow (mainly town planning and churches), he became known as "Greek" Thomson. He worked in an impressive and original style that reflected and developed the manner of K. F. Schinkel in Germany.

Principal executed works (all in Glasgow):
Nos. 3–4, Dunlop Street, 1849.
Free church, Caledonia Road, 1856.
Holmwood House, Cathcart, 1856–58.
Walmer Crescent and Queen's Park Terrace, 1857.

Church, Vincent Street, 1859.
Grecian Building, Sauchiehall Street, 1865.
Northpark Terrace, 1866.
Great Western Terrace, 1867.
Church, Queen's Park, 1867.
Egyptian Halls, Union Street, 1871.

Principal unexecuted project:
Natural History Museum, South Kensington, London, 1864.

Literature: G. Law, " 'Greek' Thomson," *Architectural Review* [London], May 1954, pp. 307–16. A. Gomme and D. Walker, *Architecture of Glasgow*, 1968.

TOWN, Ithiel (Thompson, Connecticut, 1784–New Haven, Connecticut, 1844)

He was a prolific and versatile architect whose numerous public buildings and state capitols transformed the American architectural scene. His Greek Revival country houses are also striking. From 1829 to 1843 he worked in partnership with M. E. Thompson and A. J. Davis.

Principal executed works:
Bowers House, Northampton, Massachusetts, 1825–26.
Connecticut State Capitol, Hartford, 1827.
Center Church, New Haven, Connecticut.
Trinity Episcopal church, New Haven, Connecticut.
Indiana State Capitol, Indianapolis, 1831.
North Carolina State Capitol, Raleigh, 1831.
United States Custom House, New York City, 1833–42.
Illinois State Capitol, Springfield, 1837.
Ohio State Capitol, Columbus, 1839.

Literature: R. Hale Newton, *Town and Davis, Architects,* New York, 1942.

TROUARD, Louis-François (Paris, 1729–1794)

A pupil of L.-A. Loriot, he won the Grand Prix in 1753 and left the following year for Rome. On his return he was attached to the King's Works at Versailles and was to be chiefly active there. He indulged in the fashion for the *goût grec* in one or two houses, including his own, in Paris.

Principal executed works:
Trouard House, 9 Rue du Faubourg Poissonnière, Paris, 1758. This was his own house.
Trouard House, 1 Rue du Faubourg Poissonnière, Paris, 1762. Demolished.
Château de Carlepont (near Noyon), 1762.
Barracks of the Gardes-françaises, Place d'Armes, Versailles.
St.-Symphorien de Montreuil, Versailles, 1764–70.
Chapelle des Catéchismes, St.-Louis, Versailles, 1764–70.
Cathedral, Orléans, continuation of the west front, following Jacques (V) Gabriel's design, 1766–73.
Trouard House, Rue de Provence, Paris, 1778.

Literature: M. Gallet, *Paris Domestic Architecture of the 18th Century,* London, 1972. M. Gallet, "Palladio et l'architecture française dans la seconde moitié du XVIIIe siècle," in *Les monuments historiques de la France,* vol. 2, 1975, pp. 51–54. M. Gallet, "Louis-François Trouard et l'architecture religieuse dans la région de Versailles au temps de Louis XVI," *Gazette des beaux-arts* 88 (Dec. 1976), pp. 201–18.

VALADIER, Giuseppe (Rome, 1762–1839)

He was the most important architect active in Rome in the early nineteenth century. In 1786 he was appointed *Architetto Camerale* and by 1810 had risen to the position of *Direttore dei Lavori Pubblici di Beneficenza,* together with Giuseppe Camporese and C. Fea. With them he projected designs for the restoration of the major monuments of Rome, planned new roads and public works, and thought to make the Tiber navigable up to Perugia. He built much and published much, but he is remembered best for the Piazza del Popolo in Rome, where he was to be associated with a succession of French architects.

Principal executed works:
Cathedral, Urbino, interior restoration and decoration, 1789–. The facade is now attributed to Camillo Morigia.
Piazza del Popolo, Rome. Initial project, 1793; second and much altered design made 1813, further modified, extended, and approved 1815. Garden and Casina, 1816–17; reorganization of Agostiniani, 1818–21; Caserma dei "Cherubinieri," 1822; realignment of entry to Via del Babuino and Via di Ripetta, 1821–22. (G. Matthiae, *Piazza del Popolo,* Rome, 1946; P. Hoffmann, *Il monte pincio e la casina Valadier,* Rome, 1967.)
S. Salvatore hospital, Mont' Olmo, 1794.
College, Monsampietrangeli, designed 1798, built 1823–69.
Cathedral, Rieti.
Villa Poniatowski (now Villa Vagnuzzi), Rome, 1800–10.
S. Pantaleo, Rome, facade, 1806.
S. Cristina, Cesana, 1814–22.
Castellani House, at S. Lorenzo in Lucina, Rome.
Palazzo Lezzani, Corso, Rome.
S. Rocco a Ripetta, Rome, facade, 1831.

Literature: E. Schultze-Battmann, *G. Valadier, ein klassizist Architekt Roms,* Dresden, 1939. F. Stoppani, "Un francese a Roma, l'architetto G. Valadier," *Capitolium* 6 (1959). P. Marconi, *Giuseppe Valadier,* Rome, 1964.

VALLIN DE LA MOTHE, Jean-Baptiste-Michel (Angoulême, 1729–1800)

Cousin and pupil of Jacques-François Blondel, he was summoned to St. Petersburg [Leningrad] by Count Ivan Shuvalov in 1759 to undertake the construction of the Academy of Fine Arts with Alexander Kokorinov (1765). Vallin de la Mothe designed the first Hermitage (built 1764–67) and the markets on the Nevski Prospect in St. Petersburg.

Literature: L. Réau, "Vallin de la Mothe, documents inédits," *L'architecture* 35 (1922), pp. 173–80.

VANBRUGH, Sir John (London, 1664–Greenwich, 1726)

He was a soldier, playwright, and architect. The Picturesque "movement" of his buildings influenced such neoclassical architects as Robert Adam and Sir John Soane.

Literature: L. Whistler, *The Imagination of Vanbrugh and His Fellow Artists,* 1954. K. Downes, *Vanbrugh,* 1977.

VANVITELLI, Luigi (Naples, 1700–Caserta, 1773)

Son of the Dutch landscape painter Gaspar van Wittel, who settled early in Rome, he began as a painter but came under the influence of Filippo Juvarra, who directed his attention toward architecture. In 1726 he began working as architect to St. Peter's and soon after established something of a reputation with designs for the facade of S. Giovanni in Laterano and for the Trevi fountain. Clement XII then sent him to the Marche, where he built much. He was recalled in 1746 to Rome, where he worked for four years, mainly on restorations. He was invited in 1751 by the Bourbon king, Charles III, to Naples, where he began work on the enormous and magnificent new Palazzo Reale at Caserta. For the Bourbons he built extensively in the following years, not only in Naples and the surrounding region, but also in Sicily. He was probably the most famous architect in Italy in the second half of the eighteenth century, and his advice was eagerly sought.

Principal executed works:
Palazzo Reale, Caserta, designed 1751, begun 1752, completed 1774 by his son Carlo Vanvitelli (1739–1821). (G. Chierici, *La reggia di Caserta,* Rome, 1937; F. Defelippis, *Il palazzo reale di Caserta e i Borbone di Napoli,* Naples, 1968.)
Palazzo del Principe d'Angri, Naples, c. 1755. Supervised by Carlo Vanvitelli.
Palazzo Calabritto, Naples, redecoration and new stairway, c. 1755.
Cavalry barracks, Ponte della Maddalena, Naples, 1757–; elliptical chapel, 1764.
Palazzo Correo, Madrid, c. 1760. Supervised by his sons and his pupil Sabatini.
SS. Annunziata, Naples, 1760–82. Completed by Carlo Vanvitelli.
Villa Campolieto, Resina, refacing, redecoration, and extension, 1766–.
Palazzo Teora, Naples, redecoration of the ballroom, 1768.
Chiesa della Trinità, Naples, 1770–. Completed by Carlo Vanvitelli.
Palazzo Perelli, Naples, restoration and redecoration, new ballroom and theater, 1772.

Literature: L. Vanvitelli, *Vita dell' architetto L. Vanvitelli,* Naples, 1823. F. Fichera, *L. Vanvitelli,* Rome, 1937. R. De Fusco et al., *Luigi Vanvitelli,* Naples, 1973.

VAUDOYER, Antoine-Laurent-Thomas (Paris, 1756–Paris, 1846)

His father refused to allow him to become an architect; only after his death was he able to enter the École Royale d'Architecture, Paris, and the *atelier* of A.-F. Peyre. He won the Grand Prix in 1783 and traveled to Italy, where he stayed for five years. In 1793, when the official schools of architecture were closed, he opened a small one in the Louvre. In 1804 he was appointed to prepare the Collège des Quatre Nations for the installation of the Institut de France, and the Couvent des Petits Augustins nearby to receive the Musée des Monuments Français. Five years later he opened his *atelier* again, and it was as a doctrinaire teacher that he won fame. With L.-P. Baltard he published the *Grands prix d'architecture,* from 1818 to 1834.

Principal executed works:
Salle des Séances, Institut de France, Paris, 1806.
Marché des Carmes, Paris, 1812–18.
Collège de France, Paris, extension.

VAUDOYER, Léon (Paris, 1803–Paris, 1872)

The son of A.-L.-T. Vaudoyer, he was taught by him and his cousin L.-H. Lebas at the École des Beaux-Arts, Paris. In 1826 he won the Grand Prix and in Rome encountered P.-F.-H. Labrouste and L.-J. Duc. Thereafter he traveled to Germany, England, Spain, and North Africa, and, though he was appointed architect to the Conservatoire des Arts et Métiers in Paris in 1838 (together with his father), he showed little inclination to settle down. Not until 1845, just before his father's death, did work begin in earnest on the site. In the same year he designed the most notable of his works, the cathedral at Marseilles, a great church inspired by the cathedral of Florence, but with a French Gothic plan. This has never been greatly admired. It was Vaudoyer who first used the term "architecture parlante" to describe the works of C.-N. Ledoux.

Principal executed works:
Tomb of General Foy, Père-Lachaise cemetery, Paris, 1825–32. Restored 1891 by Hippolyte Destailleur.
Conservatoire des Arts et Métiers, 292 Rue St.-Martin, Paris, 1845–97.
Ste.-Marie-Majeure, Place de la Cathédrale, Marseilles, 1845, 1852–93. The towers were built after Vaudoyer's death by his pupil H.-J. Espérandieu; the decorations are largely the work of H. Révoil.

Literature: V. Baltard, *Funérailles de M. Vaudoyer,* Paris, 1872. E. Beulé, *Funérailles de M. Vaudoyer,* Paris, 1872. G. Davioud, *Funérailles de M. Léon Vaudoyer,* Paris, 1872. L. Duc, *Funérailles de M. Vaudoyer,* Paris, 1872. *Catalogue de l'exposition des dessins de L. Vaudoyer à l'École des Beaux-Arts,* Paris, 1873.

VAUDREMER, Joseph-Auguste-Émile (Paris, 1829–Antibes, 1914)

The pupil of Adhémar, G.-A. Blouet, and E.-J. Gilbert, he won the second Grand Prix in 1854, traveling through Italy and, in 1858, to Greece with P.-G.-H.

Daumet. He upheld throughout his life the purified classical ideals of his masters and of the École des Beaux-Arts. There is a nobility and a fine restraint in all his works, whether of the monumental or the utilitarian sort, but there is, in addition, evidence of an unusual ability to take up other styles—Byzantine and Romanesque—and subordinate them to his own stern aesthetic ideals. He was an architect of the exceptional kind.

Principal executed works:
Prison and reformatory, Rue de la Santé, Paris, 1862–85.
St.-Pierre-de-Montrouge, Place Victor Basch, Paris, 1864–72.
Notre-Dame-d'Auteuil, 2 Place d'Auteuil, Paris, 1876–80.
Villa, Aulnay (Seine).
Bishop's palace, Beauvais.
Hôtel, 13 Rue du Pont Neuf, Paris.
Temple de Belleville, 97 Rue Julien Lacroix, Paris, 1877–80.
Groupe Scolaire, Rue d'Alésia, Paris.
Lycée, Montauban, 1884–87.
Lycée, Grenoble, 1885–86.
Lycée Molière, 71 Rue du Ranelagh, Paris, 1885–88.
Lycée Buffon, Boulevard Pasteur and Rue de Vaugirard, Paris, 1885–90, 1895–99.
Hôtel, 65 Avenue d'Antin, Paris.
Greek Orthodox church, 5 Rue Georges Bizet, Paris, 1890–95.
Apartment house, 27 Avenue Georges Mandel, Paris.
Hôtel, Rue Chardin, Paris, 1895–96.
St.-Antoine-des-Quinze-Vingts, 66 Avenue Ledru-Rollin, Paris, 1901–3, with Lucien Roy.

Literature: C. E. Curinier, *Dictionnaire national des contemporains*, Paris, 1899–1905. J. Hermant, *L'architecture*, 1914, p. 65.

VIEL, Charles-François (Paris, 1745–Paris, 1819)

He studied first with J.-F.-T. Chalgrin and until 1780 supervised that architect's works at St.-Sulpice and the Collège de France, in Paris. In 1781 he was appointed architect to the Hôpital Général, and the remainder of his career was taken up with the maintenance, extension, and building of new hospitals in Paris. His works, both architectural and theoretical, are well documented, as he published them together in 1805 in five volumes: *Principes de l'ordonnance et de la construction des bâtimens*. He revealed himself there as a reactionary, somewhat eccentric theorist, certainly the most provocative of the period.

Principal executed works:
Mont-de-Piété, Rue des Blancs-Manteaux, Paris, begun 1777; extensions on the old Rue de Paradis (now Crédit Municipal, 61 Rue des Francs-Bourgeois), 1784–89. The annex, installed in two *hôtels* in the Rue des Petits-Augustins, was built between 1809 and 1811 on the site of the Académie de Médecine, Rue Bonaparte.
Hôpital St.-Jacques–St.-Philippe (now Hôpital Cochin), Rue du Faubourg St.-Jacques, Paris, 1780–82. This

was built at the end of the site of the Hôpital des Vénériens, by J.-B.-E. Saint-Far, the gateway of which, 111 Boulevard de Port-Royal, survives.

Literature: J. M. Pérouse de Montclos, "Charles-François Viel," *Bulletin de la Société de l'Histoire de l'Art Français*, Année 1966 (1967), pp. 257–69.

VIEL DE SAINT-MAUX, Jean-Louis

The details of his life are as yet unknown, but he was probably the brother of Charles-François Viel, with whom he is sometimes confused. He trained first as a painter and was active chiefly in Marseilles, where he worked as a naval architect. He was the author of *Lettres sur l'architecture des anciens et des modernes, dans lesquelles se trouve développé le génie symbolique que préside aux monuments de l'antiquité* (Paris, 1787).

Literature: J. M. Pérouse de Montclos, "Charles-François Viel," *Bulletin de la Société de l'Histoire de l'Art Français*, Année 1966 (1967), pp. 257–69.

VIGNON, Alexandre-Pierre (Lagny, 1763–Paris, 1828)

He is often confused with Barthélemy Vignon (1762–1846), who worked for the Empress Josephine at the Château de Malmaison and for Caroline Murat at the Château de Neuilly and elsewhere. A pupil of C.-N. Ledoux (who was to leave him half his wealth and goods), then of J.-D. Le Roy at the school of the Académie Royale d'Architecture, he began his career by building barracks and armories in Paris. In 1790 he was appointed architect to the Arsenal. During the following years he prepared several projects for buildings incorporating the foundations, walls, and portico surviving from the Madeleine in Paris begun by Pierre Contant d'Ivry and continued after his death by G.-M. Couture. His great opportunity came in 1807, when, in competition with eighty-one other architects, he was appointed to turn the unfinished church into a Temple de la Gloire. Building began in the following year. By the time of Vignon's death the new masonry structure had virtually been completed. J.-J.-M. Huvé took over in that year. The chaneling of the columns began in 1833, the iron roof truss was put in place above the vaults in the following year, and the building, by then redesignated as a church, was consecrated in 1842.

Literature: E. L. G. Charvet, *Lyon artistique: architectes, notices biographiques et bibliographiques,* Lyons, 1899, p. 392. G. Vauthier, "Pierre Vignon et l'église de la Madeleine," *Bulletin de la Société de l'Histoire de l'Art Français,* 1910, pp. 380–422.

VIOLLET-LE-DUC, Eugène-Emmanuel (Paris, 1814–Lausanne, 1879)

As a young man he worked briefly for J.-J.-M. Huvé and then in the *atelier* of A.-F.-R. Leclère. He refused, however, to enroll at the École des Beaux-Arts; instead, he traveled to Italy on his own account. Only on his return, after a visit of eighteen months, was he drawn into the orbit of the medievalists, by no less a

man than Prosper Mérimée, then *Inspecteur Général des Monuments Historiques*. In 1840 he was commissioned to restore Ste.-Madeleine at Vézelay. Within the same year he began work under J.-B.-A. Lassus and F.-J. Duban at the Ste.-Chapelle, and within four more years had started the restoration of Notre-Dame in Paris, once again with Lassus. Viollet-le-Duc at once identified himself with the Gothic Revivalists, outlining his theories on Gothic architecture in A.-N. Didron's *Annales archéologiques*. Throughout his life he was to set himself in opposition to the École des Beaux-Arts, the Académie, and all they represented, upholding the excellence of Gothic architecture, but he realized early enough that if he were to make any real impact on the course of architecture in France he would have to put forward a theory of architecture wider in scope than one based on Gothic alone. Taking up the rationalist tradition of the seventeenth and eighteenth centuries, he sought to show that not only Gothic but Greek and Byzantine—indeed, all good architecture—was founded on a rational system of structure and organization, and that if the principles that he had thus adduced from his study of the historical styles were to be interpreted within the social context of the nineteenth century and with the new materials available, a new architecture capable of style might arise. His most widely read books were the *Dictionnaire raisonné de l'architecture française du XIe au XVIe siècle* (ten vols., 1854–68) and *Dictionnaire raisonné du mobilier français de l'époque carlovingienne à la renaissance* (six vols., 1858–75), but his most intriguing and, in the long run, most influential work was the *Entretiens sur l'architecture*, published between 1858 and 1872, containing some ungainly but novel suggestions as to the form the new architecture might take. Viollet-le-Duc's notions were taken up by architects as different as Antonio Gaudí, Frank Lloyd Wright, Auguste Perret, and Ludwig Mies van der Rohe. He himself was responsible for almost eighty buildings, restorations apart, but never once succeeded in giving anything like convincing form to his ideas.

Principal executed works, excluding restorations:
Henri de Courmont House, 6 Rue de Berlin (now 28 Rue de Liège), Paris, 1846–49.
St.-Gimer, Carcassonne, 1852–58.
Château de M. Dollfus (now Maison de Repos du Geisbuhl), Dornach, 1854–56. Later extended.
Milon House, 15 Rue de Douai, Paris, 1857–60.
Griois House (now Château du Tertre), Ambrières-les-Vallées (Mayenne), designed 1857, begun 1865 under the supervision of M. Gudin. Published in E.-E. Viollet-le-Duc, *Habitations modernes*, vol. 2, 1875, as the work of M.-A.-G. Ouradou.
École Polonaise (now École des Garçons), 80 Boulevard du Montparnasse, Paris, 1858–60.
Chapelle du Petit Séminaire, Rue de Vaugirard, Paris, 1859–61. Now at Fontenay-aux-Roses.
Sabatier House (now École Secondaire d'Agriculture), Pierrefonds (Oise), 1860–63.
St.-Denys-de l'Estrée, Saint-Denis, 1860–66.
Viollet-le-Duc House, 68 Rue Condorcet, Paris, 1861–62.
Sauvage House, Rue Lafayette, Rue Le Peletier, and Rue Chauchat, Paris, 1863–64.

Church, Aillant-sur-Tholon, 1863–65.
Château d'Arragori (near Hendaye), 1864–66.
Tomb of the Duc de Morny, Père-Lachaise cemetery, Paris, 1865–66.
Château Jacquesson (now La Slavia administrative building), Châlons-sur-Marne, 1865–67.
La Vedette, 29 Avenue du Leman, Lausanne, 1874–78, supervised by Jules-Louis Verrey. Demolished 1975.
Protestant chapel, Avenue du Rumine, Lausanne, 1876–77, supervised by Jules-Louis Verrey.

Literature: Paul Gout, *Viollet-le-Duc, sa vie, son oeuvre, son doctrine,* Paris, 1914. "Viollet-le-Duc and the Rational Point of View," in J. Summerson, *Heavenly Mansions, and Other Essays on Architecture,* London, 1949, pp. 135–58. P. M. Auzas et al., *Eugene Viollet-le-Duc, 1814–1879,* exhib. cat., Paris, 1965. M. Bailleux, *Viollet-le-Duc au château d'Eu (1847–1879),* exhib. cat., Eu, 1979.

VISCONTI, Louis-Tullius-Joachim Rome, 1791–Paris, 1853)

Son of the famous keeper of antiquities at the Vatican Ennius Quirinus Visconti, who fled in 1798 to France, he studied architecture at the École des Beaux-Arts, Paris, under Charles Percier. He began work in 1822 as *Inspecteur* at the Ministère des Finances, under Hippolyte Destailleur. His first independent work was the Fontaine Gaillon, of 1824, the first in a series of splendid fountains he built in Paris. But his most important work was done at the Bibliothèque Nationale, where he took over from Lannoy in 1825, and at the Louvre, the design for which he did in 1851, and where he was succeeded soon after by H.-M. Lefuel.

Principal executed works:
Fontaine Gaillon, Carrefour Gaillon, Paris, 1824–28.
Mlle. Mars House, Rue Tour-des-Dames and Rue de la Rochefoucauld, Paris, 1825.
Nos. 1, 3, 7, and 9 Rue Tour-des-Dames, Paris.
Fontaine Louvois, Square Louvois, Paris, 1835–39.
Fontaine Molière, Rue Molière and Rue Richelieu, Paris, 1841–43.
Tomb of Napoleon, Église du Dôme, Paris, 1842.
Fountain, Place St.-Sulpice, Paris, 1843–49.
Hôtel de Pontalba, Rue du Faubourg St.-Honoré, Paris.
Hôtel de Lauriston, Avenue des Champs-Élysées, Paris, 1845.
Hôtel Collot, Quai d'Orsay, Paris.

VISENTINI, Antonio (Venice, 1688–1782)

He began as a painter, studying with Antonio Pellegrini, and is remembered best as an engraver, but he turned also to architecture, helping to establish the Accademia in Venice in 1755. There he taught perspective drawing until 1778. He produced two notable but dull works for Consul Smith, with whom he was closely associated, and made several attempts, both published and unpublished, to arrive at a revised Palladian architectural theory. His most significant observations, based on the works of another man, for whom he acted as editor, Teofilo Gallaccini, were published as *Osservazioni al trattato di Teofilo Gallaccini sopra gli errori degli architetti,* in 1771.

Principal executed works:
Palazzo Smith (later Palazzo Mangili-Valmarana, now the Argentine Consulate), Grand Canal, Venice, 1751. Enlarged by one floor and decorated inside by Giannantonio Selva, 1784.
Villa Smith, Mogliano, Veneto. Destroyed.
Palazzo Coletti-Giusti, Grand Canal, Venice, 1766.

Literature: E. Bassi, *Architettura del sei e settecento a Venezia,* Naples, 1962. A. C. Murat, "Il neoclassicismo nel Veneto," *Bolletino del Centro Internazionale di Studi di Architettura Andrea Palladio* 5 (1963), pp. 99–257.

VULLIAMY, Lewis (London, 1791–London, 1871)

A pupil of Robert Smirke, he built up a very large practice, mainly of fairly minor commissions. Like Thomas Hopper, he was successful partly because of his versatility: He commanded the Greek, Gothic, Tudor, Romanesque, and Renaissance styles. His masterpieces, both for his rich patron R. S. Holford, were the Italianate Dorchester House and the Jacobean Westonbirt House. He published *Examples of Ornamental Sculpture in Architecture from Greece, Asia Minor, and Italy,* in 1823.

Principal executed works:
Syston Hall, Lincolnshire, alterations, 1824. Demolished 1934.
Boothby Pagnell Hall, Lincolnshire, 1825.
St. Barnabas, Addison Road, Kensington, London, 1827–29.
Law Institution, Chancery Lane, London, 1828–32.
Christ Church, Woburn Square, London, 1831–33.
Royal Institution, Albemarle Street, London, remodeling, 1838. (*Country Life,* Sept. 2, 1965.)
Dorchester House, Park Lane, London, 1850–63. Demolished 1929. (C. Hussey, "Dorchester House," *Journal of the Royal Institute of British Architects* 35 [1928], pp. 623, 667; *Country Life* 63, pp. 646, 684.)
Westonbirt House, Gloucestershire, 1863–70. (*Country Life,* May 18–25, 1972.)

WAILLY, Charles de (Paris, 1730–Paris, 1798)

He studied briefly with J.-L. Legeay, then worked with Jacques-François Blondel and G. N. Servandoni. At the school of the Académie Royale d'Architecture, Paris, his master was the mathematician C.-E.-L. Camus. He won the Grand Prix in 1752 and generously offered to share it with P.-L. Moreau-Desproux. They spent just over two years together in Rome. There de Wailly recorded an extraordinary range of buildings, paintings, and sculpture, including the ceiling of Il Gesù and Bernini's *Throne of Saint Peter.* This diversity, or rather eclecticism, marked all his future work. His rich, profusely decorated interiors for the Palazzo Spinola in Genoa and the Chapelle de la Vierge at St.-Sulpice in Paris mark one aspect of his style; the Château de Montmusard near Dijon and the Théâtre-Français (now Théâtre de France) in Paris, built in conjunction with M.-J. Peyre, represent an altogether different approach to design. But his range was evidently greatly appreciated, for he built much in Paris and prepared designs for the empress of Russia and other rulers in Kassel and Brussels. He was *Contrôleur* at Versailles and at Choisy.

Principal executed works:
Château de Montmusard (now part of the École St.-Dominique), Rue Claude Bouchu, Dijon, 1764–72. Never completed.
Théâtre-Français (later Théâtre de l'Odéon, now Théâtre de France), Place de l'Odéon, Paris, 1767–70, 1779–82, designed with M.-J. Peyre. Rebuilt twice after fires, once by J.-F.-T. Chalgrin, and modified several times since internally. (D. Rabreau and M. Steinhauser, "Le théâtre de l'Odéon de Charles de Wailly et Marie-Joseph Peyre, 1767–1782," *Revue de l'Art,* no. 19, 1973, pp. 8–49.)
Chapelle du Reposoir, Rue Hoche, Versailles, 1769.
Palazzo Spinola (now Palazzo Campanella), 12 Via Garibaldi, Genoa, 1772–73, supervised by A. Tagliafichi. (C. Maltese, "Appunti per una storia del neoclassicismo a Genova," in *Neoclassicismo. Londra 1971. Atti del convegno internazionale promesso del Comité International d'Histoire de l'Art,* Genoa, 1973.)
St.-Leu-St.-Gilles, Paris, crypt, 1773–80.
Hôtel de Wailly and Hôtel Pajou, Rue de la Pépinière, Paris, 1776–79.
Chapelle de la Vierge (1777–78) and pulpit (1789), St.-Sulpice, Place St.-Sulpice, Paris.
Château de Rocquencourt, 1781–86.

Literature: A. Braham, "Charles de Wailly and Early Neo-Classicism," *Burlington Magazine,* Oct. 1972, pp. 670–85. J. Foucart-Borville, "Les projets de Charles de Wailly pour la gloire de la cathédrale d'Amiens," *Bulletin de la Société de l'Histoire de l'Art Français,* Année 1974 (1975), pp. 131–44. *Piranèse et les français, 1740–1790,* exhib. cat., Académie de France à Rome, Rome, 1976.

WALPOLE, Horace (4th earl of Orford) (London, 1717–1797)

He was a wealthy connoisseur, collector, and author. His celebrated house, Strawberry Hill, Middlesex, shaped the Gothic Revival in eighteenth-century England. Strawberry Hill, elaborated asymmetrically for Walpole by a number of architects between the 1750s and the 1790s, was important both as an example of architecture used for associational and literary purposes and as the expression of a belief that medieval work could be imitated in exactly the same way that contemporary neoclassicists imitated antique architecture. There is an extensive modern literature on Walpole, but the most up-to-date summary of current knowledge about Strawberry Hill is by J. M. Crook (*Country Life,* June 7–21, 1973).

WALTER, Thomas Ustick (Philadelphia, 1804–Philadelphia, 1887)

He was a pupil of William Strickland, whose style he maintained until the mid-nineteenth century.

Principal executed works:
Girard College, Philadelphia, 1833–47.
Hibernian Hall, Charleston, South Carolina, designed 1835.
Andalusia (near Philadelphia), designed 1835–36.
Capitol, Washington, D.C., addition of dome and wings, 1851–.

WALTERS, Edward (London, 1808–Brighton, 1872)

He was a pupil of his father, John Walters, who was Surveyor to the London Hospital. Having worked for Thomas Cubitt, Lewis Vulliamy, and Sir John Rennie, he set up practice in 1839 in Manchester, where he specialized in the design of banks, commercial buildings, and warehouses in an impressive neo-Renaissance style. His masterpiece is the Free Trade Hall, Manchester.

Principal executed works:
Warehouse, 15 Mosley Street, Manchester, 1839.
Queen's Hotel, Portland Street, Manchester, 1845.
District Bank, Sankey Street, Warrington, Lancashire, 1847.
Congregational church, Cavendish Street, Manchester, 1847–48.
Warehouse, 9 Portland Street, Manchester, 1851.
Free Trade Hall, Peter Street, Manchester, 1853–56.
Nos. 10, 12, and 34 Charlotte Street, Manchester, 1857, 1860, 1855.
William Deacon's Bank, Mosley Street, Manchester, 1860.

WATERHOUSE, Alfred (Liverpool, 1830–Yattendon, Berkshire, 1905)

He was a prolific architect of impressive, intelligently planned, but charmless buildings in imperishable terracotta and harsh red brick. That he was a Quaker set him apart from his fellow architects, and his religious convictions are, perhaps, reflected in the intellectual austerity and individuality of his work. The structural basis of his great public and commercial Gothic Revival buildings is not the Gothic arch but, rather, iron. The rolled iron beam that he employed extensively is expressed in the insistent vertical paneling of his facades. Perhaps his finest and most characteristic

building, after his Gothic Town Hall in Manchester, is the Romanesque Natural History Museum, London, a ruthlessly symmetrical pile of terra-cotta, steel, and glass, humanized by its delightful naturalistic sculpture. Waterhouse was president of the Royal Institute of British Architects from 1888 to 1891 and was much in demand as an adjudicator in architectural competitions.

Principal executed works:
Hinderton, Hooton, Cheshire, 1856.
Assize Courts, Manchester, 1859–64. Demolished.
Hutton Hall, Guisborough, Yorkshire, 1864–68.
Easneye, Hertfordshire, 1867–69.
Allerton Priory, Liverpool, 1867–70.
Gonville and Caius College, Cambridge University, Cambridge, Tree Court, 1868.
Town Hall, Manchester, 1868–77.

Blackmoor House, Hampshire, 1869–73, 1882.
Eaton Hall, Cheshire, 1870–82. Largely demolished. (*Country Life*, May 29, 1920.)
Girton College, Cambridge, 1872.
Natural History Museum, London, 1873–81. (London County Council, *Survey of London* 38 [1975], 206–14.)
Pembroke College, Cambridge University, Cambridge, hall (since altered) and library, 1874.
Iwerne Minster, Dorsetshire, 1877–78.
Prudential Assurance Buildings, Holborn Bars, London, 1877–79, 1899–1906.
Yattendon Court, Berkshire, 1878–81. Demolished.
Town Hall, Hove, Sussex, 1879.
St. Paul's School, Hammersmith, London, 1881. Demolished.
City and Guilds of London Central Technical Institution, Kensington, London, 1881–84. Demolished.
Grinkle Park, Easington, Yorkshire, 1882.
Lyndhurst Road Congregational church, Hampstead, London, 1883.
National Liberal Club, London, 1884–87.
King's Weigh House chapel, Duke Street, Mayfair, London, 1889–91.
University College Hospital, London, 1896.

Literature: S. A. Smith, "Alfred Waterhouse: Civic Grandeur," in J. Fawcett, ed., *Seven Victorian Architects*, 1976, pp. 102–21.

WEBB, Philip (Oxford, 1831–Worth, Sussex, 1915)

A ruthless and austere domestic architect with a firm belief in the importance of construction and the integrity of materials, he exercised a profound influence on the Domestic Revival and the Arts-and-Crafts movement despite his attempts to avoid both publicity and hiring architectural assistants. By blending medieval and eighteenth-century details, he tried to create a styleless vernacular language—but in so doing, of course, created his own individual style, which is always recognizable. He owed much to his master, G. E. Street, in whose office he met William Morris. He joined Morris's firm, and much of his work was done in association with him.

Principal executed works:
Red House, Upton (near Bexleyheath), Kent, 1859. (*Country Life* 127 [1960], p. 1382.)
Arisaig, Inverness, 1863. Partly demolished.
Washington Hall, Durham, c. 1864.
1 Palace Green, Kensington, London, 1867 (London County Council, *Survey of London* 37 [1973], pp. 185–87.)
19 Lincoln's Inn Fields, London, 1868–69.
Joldwynds, Dorking, Surrey, 1873. Demolished. (*Country Life* 76, p. 276; *Country Life* 101, p. 47.)
Rounton Grange, Yorkshire, 1873–76. Demolished. (*Country Life* 37 [1915], p. 906.)
St. Martin and two houses, Brampton, Cumberland, 1874–78.
Smeaton Manor, Yorkshire, 1877–79. (J. Brandon-Jones, "Notes on the Building of Smeaton Manor," *Journal of the Society of Architectural Historians of*

Great Britain 1 [1958], pp. 31–59.)
Clouds, Wiltshire, 1879–91. Partly demolished. (*Country Life* 16 [1904], p. 738.)
Tangley Manor, Surrey, 1883. (*Country Life*, Jan. 21, 1905.)
Bell Brothers Offices, Zetland Road, Middlesbrough, Yorkshire, 1883.
Coneyhurst, Ewhurst, Surrey, 1885.
Forthampton Court, Gloucestershire, 1891.
Standen, East Grinstead, Sussex, 1891–94. (*Country Life* 27 [1910], p. 666; *Country Life* 147, pp. 494, 554.)
Exning House, Newmarket, Cambridgeshire, 1896.

Literature: G. Jack, "An Appreciation of Philip Webb," *Architectural Review* [London] 38 (July 1915), pp. 1–6. W. R. Lethaby, *Philip Webb and His Work*, Oxford, 1935. J. Brandon-Jones, "The Work of Philip Webb and Norman Shaw," *Architectural Association Journal* 71 (June–July 1955). J. Brandon-Jones, "Philip Webb," in P. Ferriday, ed., *Victorian Architecture*, 1963, pp. 149–65.

WHITE, William (1825–1900)

He was an architect of considerable quality and originality but is little known, partly because he built no public buildings or prominent churches. From 1845 to 1847 he worked in G. G. Scott's office, where fellow assistants included G. F. Bodley and G. E. Street, whose work he influenced. He thought deeply about architectural matters and published several important papers on modern design (in *The Ecclesiologist* and elsewhere) in which he advocated a kind of picturesque utility.

Principal executed works:
Rectory, Ruan Lanihorne, Cornwall, c. 1850.
All Saints, Notting Hill, London, 1852–55.
St. Lawrence's vicarage, Lurgashall, Sussex, 1852.
St. Hilary, St. Hilary, Cornwall, 1854.
St. Michael's retreat house, Wantage, Berkshire, 1855.
Bank House, St. Columb Major, Cornwall, 1857.
Little Baddow vicarage, Essex, 1857–58.
St. Michael, Lyndhurst, Hampshire, 1858–59.
Bishop's Court, Clyst Honiton, Devon, 1860–64.
SS. Philip and James, Merifield, Cornwall, 1863–71.
Winscott (near St. Giles-in-the-Wood), Devonshire, 1864. Demolished.
St. Saviour, Aberdeen Park, Islington, London, 1865.
Humewood Castle, County Wicklow, 1867–70. (*Country Life* 143, pp. 1212, 1282.)
Quy Hall, Cambridgeshire, 1868.

Literature: *British Architect*, Sept. 16, 1881, p. 465. *The Architect* 23 (1880), p. 363. *The Builder* 63 (1900), p. 91. *Journal of the Royal Institute of British Architects* 7 (1900), p. 145. P. Thompson, "The Writings of William White," in J. Summerson, ed., *Concerning Architecture*, 1968, pp. 226–37.

WILKINS, William (Norwich, 1778–Cambridge, 1839)

With Robert Smirke, he became one of the leaders of the Greek Revival in early nineteenth-century England.

He spent four years, beginning in 1801, studying antique architecture in Greece, Asia Minor, and Italy and published the results of his research as *Antiquities of Magna Graecia* (1807), *Atheniensa; or, Remarks on the Topography and Buildings of Athens* (1816), *The Civil Architecture of Vitruvius* (1812), and *Prolusiones Architectonicae* (1837). He lacked imagination as a classical architect and quickly switched to the Gothic style following a change in public taste.

Principal executed works:
Haileybury College, Herefordshire, 1806–9. (J. M. Crook, *Haileybury and the Greek Revival: The Architecture of William Wilkins*, Hoddesdon, 1964.)
Downing College, Cambridge University, Cambridge, 1807–20.
Grange Park, Hampshire, 1809. (J. M. Crook, "Grange Park Transformed," *The Country Seat*, ed. J. Harris and H. M. Colvin, 1970; *Country Life*, May 8–15, 1975.)
Dalmeny House, West Lothian, 1814–17.
Tregothnan, Cornwall, 1816–18. (*Country Life* 119 [1956], pp. 1051, 1112.)
Trinity College, Cambridge University, Cambridge, new court, 1821.
United University Club, Pall Mall East, London, 1822–26. Demolished 1902.
Corpus Christi College, Cambridge University, Cambridge, new court, 1823–27.
King's College, Cambridge University, Cambridge, new court and screen, 1824–28.
University College, Gower Street, London, 1827.
St. George's Hospital, Hyde Park Corner, London, 1828. (*Country Life*, Nov. 11, 1976.)
National Gallery, London, 1834. (*Burlington Magazine*, June 1971, pp. 218–29.)

WOOD, Robert (1716–1771)

A member of the Society of Dilettanti beginning in 1763, he left Rome for Syria in 1750 with James Dawkins and the Italian draftsman Giovanni Battista Borra ("Il Torquilino"). He published the impressive results of his research as *The Ruins of Palmyra* (1753) and *The Ruins of Balbec* (1757). In 1769 he published *An Essay on the Original Genius of Homer*. Though not an architect, he was well known in architectural circles: Robert Adam wrote in 1755, "We are at a vast loss for the want of Mr. Wood whose character is one of the most perfect among the Human Race. He is of universal learning."

Literature: C. A. Hutton, "The Travels of 'Palmyra' Wood in 1750–51," *Journal of Hellenic Studies* 47 (1927), pp. 102–28.

WYATT, James (Weeford, Staffordshire, 1746–near Marlborough, 1813)

One of the most prolific and best-known of late eighteenth-century British architects, he was the son of the Staffordshire architect Benjamin Wyatt (1709–1772). He spent six years in Italy, beginning in 1762, where he was a pupil in Venice of Antonio Visentini.

His Pantheon in Oxford Street, London (1769–72), brought him sudden fame, and he soon acquired an extensive and fashionable practice as a country-house architect. He elegantly plagiarized the Adam manner, but also made a speciality of the increasingly popular Gothic style inspired by Strawberry Hill. He restored many medieval cathedrals and received numerous official appointments, culminating in the post of Surveyor General and Comptroller of the Works in 1796.

Principal executed works:
Pantheon, Oxford Street, London, 1769–72. Demolished 1937. (London County Council, *Survey of London* 31–32 [1963].)
Heaton Hall, Lancashire, 1772. (*Country Life*, Aug. 29–Sept. 5, 1925.)
Radcliffe Observatory, Oxford, 1776–94. (*Country Life*, May 10, 1930.)
Bryanston House, Dorsetshire, 1778. Demolished 1890.
Heveningham Hall, Suffolk, c. 1780–84. (*Country Life*, Sept. 19–26, 1925.)
Lee Priory, Kent, 1783–90. Demolished 1955.
Brocklesby Park, Lincolnshire, mausoleum, 1787–94. (*Country Life*, Mar. 3, 1934.)
Castle Coole, County Fermanagh, 1790–97. (*Country Life*, Dec. 19–26, 1936.)
Goodwood House, Sussex, 1790–1806. (*Country Life*, July 9–16, 1932.)
Fonthill Abbey, Wiltshire, 1796–1807. Demolished. (J. Wilton-Ely, "A Model for Fonthill Abbey," in *The Country Seat*, ed. H. Colvin and J. Harris, 1970.)
Stoke Poges Park, Buckinghamshire, 1798–99. (*Country Life* 14, p. 168.)
Dodington Park, Gloucestershire, 1798–1813. (*Country Life* 120, pp. 1176, 1230.)
Norris Castle, Isle of Wight, 1799.
Belvoir Castle, Leicestershire, additions and alterations, 1801–13. (*Country Life* 120, pp. 1284, 1402, 1456, 1500.)
Kew Palace, Surrey, 1802–11. Demolished 1827.
Ashridge Park, Hertfordshire, 1808–13. (*Country Life* 50, pp. 160, 192.)

Literature: A. Dale, *James Wyatt*, Oxford, 1936 (2d ed., 1956). R. Turner, *James Wyatt*, 1950.

WYATT, Lewis William (c. 1777–Isle of Wight, 1853)

A nephew of James Wyatt, probably trained by his uncle Samuel Wyatt, he was a minor classicist but produced one work of great quality, Willey Park.

Principal executed works:
Tatton Park, Cheshire, completion, 1807–12. (*Country Life* 136, pp. 162, 232, 292.)
Hackwood, Hampshire, remodeling, 1807–13. (*Country Life*, May 14–21, 1913.)
Willey Park, Shropshire, 1812–15. (*Country Life*, Feb. 19, 1921.)
Cuerden Hall, Lancashire, additions, 1815.

Principal unexecuted project:
Downing College, Cambridge University, Cambridge, 1805. (D. J. Watkin, *The Triumph of the Classical: Cambridge Architecture 1804–34*, Cambridge, 1977.)

WYATT, Sir Matthew Digby (Rowde, Wiltshire, 1820–Dimlands Castle, S. Wales, 1877)

He was a pupil of his brother, T. H. Wyatt, and traveled on the Continent from 1844 to 1846, completing the drawings for his book *Specimens of Geometrical Mosaics of the Middle Ages* (1848). He subsequently published many books and articles on polychromatic decoration, metalwork, textiles, and the applied arts. He was at the center of the circle including Henry Cole and Owen Jones, who believed both in reform through ornament and in harnessing the new powers released by the Industrial Revolution. In 1851 Wyatt was appointed Secretary to the Executive Committee of the Great Exhibition, and when Sir Joseph Paxton's Crystal Palace was moved to Sydenham in 1854, he designed its interior courts in Pompeian, Byzantine, Gothic, and Renaissance styles. His faith in the spirit of the modern world and in technology set him apart from most Victorian architects. Thus, he generally avoided Gothic and worked in a Renaissance or arcuated mode, which was thought to be more fitting in the nineteenth century. Unfortunately, he was a poor architect, so his experiment lost much of its force.

Principal executed works:
Aldingham Hall, Lancashire, 1846–50.
Crystal Palace, Sydenham, London, interior courts, 1854. Destroyed 1936.
Paddington Station, London, 1854–55, with I. K. Brunel as engineer.
Garrison Church, Woolwich, London, 1862, with T. H. Wyatt.
Addenbrooke's Hospital, Cambridge, 1864–65. Additions made later.
Rothschild mausoleum, West Ham Jewish cemetery, London, c. 1867.
India Office, London, courtyard, 1867. (*Country Life*, Feb. 6, 1964.)
Possingworth Manor, Sussex, 1868.
Oldlands Hall, Sussex, 1869.
Alford House, Kensington, London, 1872. Demolished.

Principal unexecuted projects:
Albert Memorial, London, 1863.
National Gallery, London, 1866.

Literature: N. Pevsner, *Matthew Digby Wyatt*, Cambridge, 1950 (repr. in N. Pevsner, *Studies in Art, Architecture and Design*, vol. 2, 1968, pp. 96–107; 266–68).

WYATT, Samuel (Weeford, Staffordshire, 1737–Chelsea, London, 1807)

He was the son of Benjamin Wyatt (1709–1772), a Staffordshire farmer, timber merchant, builder, and architect. He settled in London, where he established an important country-house practice and worked in a style more than rivaling in elegance the classical manner of his brother, James Wyatt.

Principal executed works:
Baron Hill, Anglesey, 1776–79. Ruinous.
Hurstmonceux Place, Sussex, c. 1777.

Doddington Hall, Cheshire, 1777–98. (*Country Life* 113, pp. 344, 414.)
Hooton Hall, Cheshire, 1778. Demolished c. 1935.
Albion Mills, Blackfriars, London, 1784–86. Destroyed by fire 1791.
Tatton Park, Cheshire, 1785–91. (*Country Life* 136, pp. 162, 232, 292.)
Soho House, Handsworth, Birmingham, 1789. (*Country Life*, Nov. 6, 1915.)
Kinmel Park, Denbighshire, 1790–1810. Rebuilt. Destroyed by fire 1842.
Trinity House, Tower Hill, London, 1793–95. (*Country Life*, Jan 18, 1941.)
Penrhyn Castle, Caernarvonshire, with L. W. Wyatt, 1797. Rebuilt c. 1836.

Literature: J. M. Robinson, "The Evolution of the Wyatt Style," *Country Life*, Dec. 13–20, 1973.

WYATT, Thomas Henry (Loughlin, County Roscommon, 1807–London, 1880)

Brother of M. D. Wyatt, he had an extensive and varied practice, though his work is generally very coarse. He was a pupil of Philip Hardwick and was in partnership with David Brandon from 1838 to 1851. He specialized in Elizabethan-style country houses, but his most interesting work is the Italian Romanesque church at Wilton. He held numerous official architectural appointments and was president of the Royal Institute of British Architects in 1870.

Principal executed works:
Assize Court, Devizes, Wiltshire, 1835.
Llantarnam Abbey, Monmouthshire, 1835.
Malpas Court, Monmouthshire, 1838.
St. Mary and St. Nicholas, Wilton, Wiltshire, 1840–46.
St. Andrew, Bethnal Green, London, 1841.
Assize Courts, Cambridge, 1842. Demolished 1954.
Fonthill House, Wiltshire, 1848. Demolished.
Orchardleigh House, Somersetshire, 1855–58.
Carlet Park, Cheshire, 1859–60.
Capel Manor, Kent, 1859–62. Demolished.
St. George, Woolwich, London, 1863.
Exchange Buildings, Liverpool, 1865–69.
Holy Trinity, Fonthill Gifford, Wiltshire, 1866.
St. Peter, Wimblington, Cambridgeshire, 1874.
Nuneham Paddox, Warwickshire, 1875.
Barcote, Berkshire, 1876.
St. Andrew, Bredenbury, Herefordshire, 1877.
North Perrott Manor, Somersetshire, 1878.
Knightsbridge Barracks, London, 1878–79. Demolished 1963.
Brompton Hospital, London, southern part, 1879–82.

WYATVILLE, Sir Jeffry (Burton-on-Trent, 1766–London, 1840)

A pupil of his uncle Samuel Wyatt and then of his more famous uncle James Wyatt, he specialized in medieval and Elizabethan styles and carried out important alterations to such sixteenth-century houses as Longleat and Wollaton. The culmination of this aspect of his career was his spectacular remodeling of Windsor Castle, begun in 1824. Perhaps the most significant part of his work was his free Picturesque planning as, for example, at Endsleigh. His extensive alterations to Bretton Hall show that he was equally at home in a bold, late classical manner.

Principal executed works:
Longleat House, Wiltshire, alterations, 1806–13. (*Country Life*, Apr. 29, 1949.)
Endsleigh, Devonshire, 1810–11. (*Country Life* 130 [1961], pp. 246, 296.)
Ashridge, Hertfordshire, alterations and additions, c. 1814–17. (*Country Life* 50, pp. 160, 192.)
Bretton Hall, Yorkshire, alterations and additions, c. 1815. (*Country Life* 83 [1938], pp. 530, 554.)
Chatsworth House, Derbyshire, alterations and additions, 1818–41. (*Country Life* 143 [1968], pp. 146, 220, 280, 496, 552.)
Windsor Castle, Berkshire, alterations and additions, 1824–40.

Literature: D. Linstrum, *Sir Jeffry Wyatville: Architect to the King*, Oxford, 1972.

ZANOIA, Giuseppe (Genoa, 1752–Omegna [Novara], 1817)

He studied first in Piacenza, then at the Accademia di Brera, in Milan. He was a typical product of the school of Giuseppe Piermarini: an efficient administrator and a sound scholar rather than a designer. He taught throughout most of his later life at the Accademia di Brera and was a member of the Commissione d'Ornato, enjoying wide administrative powers. He dutifully completed the work on the Milan cathedral facade with Carlo Amati and built much else, but nothing of interest.

Principal executed works:
Chapel of S. Savina, S. Ambrogio, Milan, 1798.
Seminario della Canonica, Milan, 1798–1802.
Villa Annoni, Guggiono, 1809.
Palazzo Annoni, Porta Romana, Milan, extension on the Via Maddalena, 1810.
Porta Nuova, Milan, 1810–13.

Literature: G. Mezzanotte, *Architettura neoclassica in Lombardia*, Naples, 1966.

ZILLER, Ernst (Oberlassnitz, Austria, 1837–Athens, 1923)

His father, a master builder from Dresden, taught him initially, but he trained thereafter with T. E. Hansen, and was sent by him to Athens in 1861. There he supervised the building of the Academy and of the National Library. He took advantage of a break in the building activity to travel to Italy and to attend the Akademie der Bildenden Künste in Vienna, before returning in 1864 to Greece. There he married and remained for the rest of his life, building prolifically in a somewhat tawdry and mixed classical style, thereby prolonging the neoclassical movement in Greece but adding nothing of vigor or even novelty to it. He became professor of architecture at the Polytechnic in Athens.

Principal executed works:
Church, Oberlössnitz, 1865.
Theater, Zakynthos, 1871–72.
Municipal theater, Athenas Street, Athens, 1872. Demolished.
Katsandris House, Euripidou and Athenas streets, Athens, 1878.
A. Vottis and J. Sclivaniotis House, Nicodemou Street, Athens, 1880.
Lüders House, Solonos Street, Athens, 1884.
Ossios Loukas church, Patissiou Street, Athens.
German Archaeological Institute, 1 Pheidiou Street, Athens, 1887.
Theater, Patras, 1888.
Phaneromeni church, Aigion, 1890.
Schliemann House (now Supreme Court), Leoforos Venizelou, Athens, 1890.
Pezmazoglou House, Herodes Atticus Street, Athens, 1893.
Eisodia church, Aigion, 1893.
National Theater, Athens, 1894.
P. Patsiades House, Castella, Piraeus, 1894. Demolished 1973.
Stathatos House, Vassili Sofias and Herodotou streets, Athens, 1895.
J. N. Svorounos Villa, N. Phaleron, 1896.
Varvaressos House, Piraeus, 1897.
J. Vougas House, 5 Stadiou Street, Athens, 1898.
A. Coutozoudakis Villa, Kifisia, 1900.
Austrian Archaeological Institute, Athens, 1905.
Aiyos Athanasios, Pyrgos, 1911.
Hagia Triada, Piraeus Street, Athens, 1915–16.
    There are many more buildings by Ziller, as yet undated: New Palace, Athens; a wing of the Achilleion, Corfu; churches at Vello and Villia; church of the Hadjikonstas Orphanage, Athens; Archaeological Museum, Olympia; Town Hall, Hermoupolis, Syros; National Bank of Greece, Piraeus; Pezmazoglou and Kalamaras (Ziller) villas, Kifisia; and Embirikos, Kalligas, Deligeorgis, Kontostavlos, Plataniotis, Vasilakis, Melas (now post office), and Coupas houses, Athens.

Literature: Ernestos Ziller, exhib. cat., National Gallery, Athens, 1973.

SELECTED BIBLIOGRAPHY

A number of general reference books, as well as monographs and articles on individual architects and buildings, are included in the Biographies.

GENERAL

Arts Council of Great Britain. *The Age of Neo-Classicism.* Council of Europe exhibition catalogue. London, 1972.

BRAUDEL, F. *Capitalism and Material Life.* Translated by Miriam Kochan. London, 1973.

CASSIRER, E. *The Philosophy of the Enlightenment.* Princeton, N.J., 1951.

COLLINS, P. *Changing Ideals in Modern Architecture, 1750–1950.* London, 1965.

ERDBERG, E. VON. *Chinese Influences on European Garden Structures.* Cambridge, Mass., 1936.

FORSSMAN, E. *Dorisch, Ionisch, Korinthisch: Studien über den Gebrauch der Säulenordnungen in der Architektur des 16.–18. Jahrhunderts.* Stockholm, 1961.

FRANKL, P. *The Gothic: Literary Sources and Interpretations Through Eight Centuries.* Princeton, N.J., 1959.

GERMANN, G. *Gothic Revival in Europe and Britain: Sources, Influences and Ideas.* London, 1972.

GIEDION, S. *Mechanization Takes Command.* New York, 1948.

GUSDORF, G. *Naissance de la conscience romantique au siècle des lumières.* Paris, 1976.

HAUTECOEUR, L. *Rome et la renaissance de l'antiquité à la fin du XVIIIe siècle.* Paris, 1912.

HITCHCOCK, H. R. *Architecture: Nineteenth and Twentieth Centuries.* Rev. ed. Baltimore and Harmondsworth, 1971.

HONOUR, H. *Chinoiserie: The Vision of Cathay.* 1961. Reprint. London, 1973.

———. *Neo-Classicism.* Harmondsworth, 1968.

IMPEY, O. *Chinoiserie: The Impact of Oriental Style.* Oxford, 1977.

KAUFMANN, E. *Von Ledoux bis Le Corbusier: Ursprung und Entwicklung der autonomen Architektur.* Vienna, 1933.

LAVEDAN, P. *L'histoire de l'urbanisme: renaissance et temps modernes.* Paris, 1941.

MAINSTONE, R. J. *Developments in Structural Form.* London, 1974.

MEEKS, C. L. V. *The Railroad Station: An Architectural History.* New Haven, Conn., 1956.

MICHEL, A. *Histoire de l'art.* Vol. 7. Paris, 1926.

OMONT, H., ed. *Athènes au XVIIe siècle: dessins des sculptures du Parthénon.* Paris, 1898.

PEVSNER, N., ed. *The Picturesque Garden and Its Influence Outside the British Isles.* Washington, D.C., 1974.

PEVSNER, N., and LANG, S. "Apollo or Baboon." *Architectural Review* 104 (1943): 271–79. Reprinted as "The Doric Revival" in *Studies in Art, Architecture and Design,* by N. Pevsner, vol. 1, pp. 196–211. London and New York, 1968.

———. "The Egyptian Revival." *Architectural Review* 119 (1956): 243–54. Reprinted in *Studies in Art, Architecture and Design,* by N. Pevsner, vol. 1, pp. 212–35. London and New York, 1968.

PRAZ, M. *An Illustrated History of Interior Decoration.* London and New York (as *An Illustrated History of Furnishing*), 1964.

ROSENBLUM, R. *Transformations in Late Eighteenth-Century Art.* Princeton, N.J., 1967.

SELING, H. "The Genesis of the Museum." *Architectural Review* 141 (1967): 103–14.

SIRÉN, O. *China and Gardens of Europe of the Eighteenth Century.* New York, 1950.

VIERENDEEL, A. *L'architecture métallique au XIXe siècle.* Brussels, 1890.

———. *Esquisse d'une histoire de la technique.* 2 vols. Brussels, 1921.

ZEITLER, R. W. *Klassizismus und Utopia.* Stockholm, 1954.

———. *Die Kunst des 19. Jahrhunderts.* Berlin, 1966.

CONTEMPORARY SOURCES

ADAM, R. *The Works in Architecture of Robert and James Adam, Esquires.* 3 vols. 1773–1822. Reprint. London, 1931.

ALBERTOLLI, G. *Ornamenti diversi inventati.* Milan, 1782.

———. *Alcune decorazioni di nobili sale ed altri ornamenti.* Milan, 1787.

ALPHAND, A. *Les promenades de Paris.* Paris, 1867–73.

BARRY, A. *The Life and Works of Sir Charles Barry.* London, 1867.

BLONDEL, J.-F. *Cours d'architecture.* Paris, 1771–77.

BOILEAU, L.-A. *La nouvelle forme architecturale.* 1853.

———. *Histoire critique de l'invention en architecture.* Paris, 1886.

BUTTERFIELD, W. *Instrumenta ecclesiastica.* 1844–57.

CAMPBELL, C. *Vitruvius Britannicus; or, The British Architect.* 3 vols. London, 1715–25.

CARMONTELLE, L. C. de. *Jardin de Monceau.* 1779.

CHOISY, A. *Histoire de l'architecture.* 1903. Reprint. Paris, 1954.

CONSIDERANT, V. *Considérations sociales sur l'architecture.* 1834.

DRESSER, C. *Principles of Decorative Design.* London and New York, 1873.

DUMONT, G.-P.-M. *Recueil de plusieurs parties de l'architecture sacrée et profane de différents maîtres tant d'Italie que de France.* Paris, 1764–67.

DURAND, J. N. L. *Vues des plus beaux édifices publics et particuliers de la ville de Paris.* Paris, [1787?].

———. *Recueil et parallèle des édifices de tout genre anciens et modernes.* Paris, 1800.

———. *Précis des leçons d'architecture données à l'École royale polytechnique.* Paris, 1802–5.

EASTLAKE, C. L. *A History of the Gothic Revival.* 1872. Reprint. Leicester and New York, 1970.

FISCHER VON ERLACH, J. B. *Entwurff einer historischen Architektur.* Vienna, 1721.

GARNIER, C. *Le nouvel Opéra de Paris.* Paris, 1878–81.

GONDOIN, J. *Description des écoles de chirurgie.* Paris, 1780.

GOURLIER, C.-P. et al. *Choix d'édifices publics projetés et construits en France depuis le commencement du XIXe siècle.* Paris, 1825–50.

HITTORFF, J.-I. *Restitution du temple d'Empédocle à Selinonte; ou, l'architecture polychrome chez les grecs.* Paris, 1846–51.

HOPE, T. *Household Furniture and Interior Decoration.* 1807. Reprint. London, 1946.

[KENDALL, H. E.] *Modern Architecture.* [1856.]

KLENZE, L. von. *Sammlung architektonischer Entwürfe für die Ausführung bestimmt oder wirklich ausgeführt.* 10 pts. Munich, 1830–50.

KNIGHT, R. P. *An Analytical Inquiry into the Principles of Taste.* London, 1805.

KRAFFT, J. K. *Choix des maisons et d'édifices publics de Paris et de ses environs.* Paris, 1838.

KRAFFT, J. K., and RANSONNETTE, P. N. *Plans, coupes, élévations des plus belles maisons et des hôtels construits à Paris et dans les environs.* 1771–1802. Reprint. Paris, 1909.

LABORDE, A. de. *Description des nouveaux jardins de la France et de ses anciens châteaux.* Paris, 1808–15.

LANDON, C. P. *Annales du musée et de l'école moderne des beaux-arts.* 1803–22. Reprint. Paris, 1834.

[LAUGIER, M.-A.] *Essai sur l'architecture.* Paris, 1753.

LEDOUX, C.-N. *L'architecture considérée sous le rapport de l'art, des moeurs et de la législation.* Paris, 1804.

LEEDS, W. H. "An Essay on Modern English Architecture." In *The Travellers' Club House . . . and the Revival of the Italian Style,* by Charles Barry. London, 1839.

LE ROUGE, G.-L. *Description du Colisée élevé aux Champs Élysées.* Paris, 1771.

———. "Jardins anglo-chinois." *Cahiers* 13 (1785).

LE ROY, J.-D. *Les ruines des plus beaux monuments de la Grèce.* Paris, 1758.

MAROT, J. *Le temple de Balbec.* [c. 1680.]

NARJOUX, F. *Paris: monuments élevés par la ville, 1850–1880.* Paris, 1880–83.

NEUFFORGE, J.-F. de. *Recueil élémentaire d'architecture.* 9 vols. Paris, 1757–72.

DE L'ORME, P. *L'architecture de Philibert de l'Orme.* 1567. Reprint. Ridgewood, N. J., 1964.

PAINE, J. *Plans, Elevations and Sections of Noblemen's and Gentlemen's Houses Executed in the Counties of Derby, Durham, Middlesex, Northumberland, Nottingham and York.* 2 vols. London, 1767–83.

PATTE, P. *Monumens érigés en France à la gloire de Louis XV.* Paris, 1765.

PERCIER, C., and FONTAINE, P.-F.-L. *Journal des monuments de Paris.*

PERRAULT, C. *Les dix livres d'architecture de Vitruve.* Paris, 1673.

PETITOT, E.-A. *Mascarade à la grecque.* Parma, 1771.

PEYRE, M.-J. *Oeuvres d'architecture.* Paris, 1765. 2d ed. Paris, 1795.

PIRANESI, G. B. *Prima parte di architetture, e prospettive.* Rome, 1743.

———. *Le antichità romane.* 4 vols. Rome, 1756–.

———. *Parere su l'architettura.* Rome, 1765.

———. *Diverse maniere d'adornare i cammini.* Rome, 1769.

———. *Différentes vues de quelques restes de trois grands édifices qui subsistent encore dans le milieu de l'ancienne ville de Pesto.* Rome, 1778.

PUGIN, A. W. N. *Contrasts; or, A Parallel Between the Noble Edifices of the Fourteenth and Fifteenth Centuries, and Similar Buildings of the Present Day.* London, 1836.

———. *The True Principles of Pointed or Christian Architecture.* London, 1841.

———. *An Apology for the Revival of Christian Architecture in England.* London, 1843.

QUATREMÈRE DE QUINCY, A.-C. *Le Jupiter Olympien; ou, l'art de la sculpture antique considérée sous un nouveau point de vue.* Paris, 1815.

RONDELET, J. *Traité théorique et pratique de l'art de bâtir.* Paris, 1802–3.

RUSKIN, J. *The Seven Lamps of Architecture.* New York, 1849.

SCHINKEL, K. F. *Sammlung architektonischer Entwürfe.* 28 portfolios. Berlin, 1819–40.

———. *Werke der höheren Baukunst für die Ausführung erfunden.* 2 vols. 1842–48.

SCOTT, G. G. *Personal and Professional Recollections.* London, 1879.

SEMPER, G. *Der Stil in den technischen und tektonischen Kunsten.* Frankfurt-am-Main, 1860–63.

SOANE, J. *Plans, Elevations, and Sections of Buildings Erected in the Counties of Norfolk, Suffolk, Yorkshire, etcetera.* London, 1788.

———. *Sketches in Architecture.* London, 1798.

———. *Designs for Public and Private Buildings.* London, 1828.

———. *Description of the House and Museum on the North Side of Lincoln's Inn Fields, the Residence of John Soane.* London, 1835–36.

SPON, J. *Voyage d'Italie, de Dalmatie, de Grèce, et du Levant, fait aux années 1675 et 1676.* Lyons, 1676.

STUART, J., and REVETT, N. *The Antiquities of Athens.* 4 vols. London, 1762–1816.

TALLIS, J. *Tallis's History and Description of the Crystal Palace.* London and New York, 1852.

VIOLLET-LE-DUC, E.-E. *Dictionnaire raisonné de l'architecture française du XIe au XVIe siècle.* 10 vols. Paris, 1854–68.

———. *Entretiens sur l'architecture.* Paris, 1863–72.

FRANCE

BABEAU, A. A. *La ville sous l'Ancien Régime.* Paris, 1880.

BALLOT, M. J. *Le décor intérieur au XVIIIe siècle à Paris et dans la région parisienne.* Paris, 1930.

BELEVITCH-STANKEVITCH, H. *Le goût chinois en France au temps de Louis XIV.* 1910. Reprint. Geneva, 1970.

BENOIT, F. *L'art français sous la Révolution et l'Empire: les doctrines, les idées, les genres.* Paris, 1897.

BLOMFIELD, R. *A History of French Architecture from 1661 to 1774.* 2 vols. London, 1921.

BRAUNSCHWIG, M. *L'Abbé Dubos, renovateur de la critique au XVIIIe siècle.* Toulouse, 1904.

BRUNEL, G., ed. *Piranèse et les français, 1740–1790.* Rome, 1978.

CASSIRER, K. *Die ästhetischen Hauptbegriffe der französischen Architektur-Theoretiker von 1650–1780.* Berlin, [1909?].

CHANGNEAU, C. et al. *Jardins en France, 1760–1820.* Exhibition catalogue. Paris, 1977.

CHARVET, E.-L.-G. *Lyon artistique: architectes, notices biographiques et bibliographiques avec une petite note des édifices et la liste chronologique des noms.* Lyons, 1899.

CHOPPIN DE JANVRY, O. "Le Desert de Retz." *Bulletin de la Société de l'Histoire de l'Art Français,* Année 1970, pp. 125–48.

CLOZIER, R. *La Gare du Nord.* Paris, 1940.

CONTET, F. et al. *Les vieux hôtels de Paris.* 2 vols. Paris, 1908–37.

CORDIER, H. *Le Chine en France au XVIIIe siècle.* Paris, 1910.

COUSSILLAN, A. A. [HILLAIRET, J.]. *Dictionnaire historique des rues de Paris.* 2 vols. Paris, 1968.

DARTEIN, F. DE. *Études sur les ponts en pierre remarquables par leur décoration: Antérieurs au XIXe siècle.* 4 vols. Paris, 1907–12.

DELABORDE, H. *L'Académie des Beaux-Arts depuis la fondation de l'Institut de France.* Paris, 1891.

DESHAIRS, L. *Bordeaux, architecture et decoration au dix-huitième siècle.* Paris, 1907.

———. *Aix-en-Provence, architecture et décoration aux dix-septième et dix-huitième siècles.* Paris, 1909.

———. *Dijon, architecture et décoration au dix-septième et dix-huitième siècles.* Paris, 1909.

DREXLER, A., ed. *The Architecture of the École des Beaux-Arts.* New York, 1978.

ERIKSEN, S. *Early Neo-Classicism in France.* London, 1974.

D'ESPOUY, H., ed. *Les Grands Prix de Rome d'architecture: 1850–1900, 1900–1905.* 2 vols. Paris, n.d.

———. *Monuments antiques, relevés et restaurés par les architectes pensionnaires de l'Académie de France à Rome.* 2 vols. Paris, n.d.

GALLET, M. *Paris Domestic Architecture of the 18th Century.* London, 1972.

GANAY, E. DE. "Les jardins à l'anglaise en France." 1923. Ms. in 2 vols., Bibliothèque des Arts Décoratifs, Paris.

GIEDION, S. *Bauen in Frankreich, Eisen, Eisenbeton.* Leipzig, 1928.

GRUBER, A. C. *Les grandes fêtes et leurs décors à l'époque de Louis XVI.* Geneva, 1972.

HAUTECOEUR, L. *Histoire de l'architecture classique en France.* Vols. 3–4. Paris, 1950–57.

———. *Paris de 1715 à nos jours.* Paris, 1972.

———. "Les places en France au XVIIIe siècle." *Gazette des beaux-arts* 85 (1975): 89–116.

HÉLIOT, P. "La fin de l'architecture gothique dans le nord de la France aux XVIIe et XVIIIe siècles." *Bulletin de la Comm. Royale des Monuments et des Sites* 8 (1957).

HERMANN, W. *Laugier and 18th-Century French Theory.* London, 1962.

HUNT, H. J. *Le socialisme et le romantisme en France.* Oxford, 1935.

JARRY, P. *La guirlande de Paris; ou, maisons de plaisance des environs, au XVIIe et au XVIIIe siecle.* Paris, 1928–31.

KALNEIN, W. G., and Levey, M. *Art and Architecture of the Eighteenth Century in France.* Baltimore and Harmondsworth, 1972.

KIMBALL, S. F. *The Creation of the Rococo.* 1943. Reprint. New York, 1964.

LEITH, J. A. *The Idea of Art as Propaganda in France, 1750–1799.* Toronto, 1965.

LELIÈVRE, P. *L'urbanisme et l'architecture à Nantes au XVIIIe siècle.* Nantes, 1942.

LÉON, P. *La vie des monuments français: destruction, restauration.* Paris, 1951.

LEONARD, C. M. *Lyon Transformed: Public Works of the Second Empire, 1853–1864.* Berkeley and Los Angeles, 1961.

LOCQUIN, J. *La peinture d'histoire en France de 1747 à 1785.* Paris, 1912.

LUCAS, C. L. A. *Étude sur les habitations à bon marché en France et à l'étranger.* Paris, 1899.

MAGNE, L. *L'architecture française du siècle.* Paris, 1889.

MALLION, J. *Victor Hugo et l'art architectural.* Paris, 1962.

MARION, M. *Dictionnaire des institutions de la France aux XVIIe et XVIIIe siècles.* Rev. ed. Paris, 1968.

MAROT, P. *La Place Royale de Nancy.* Nancy, 1966.

MIDDLETON, R. D. "The Abbé de Cordemoy and the Graeco-Gothic Ideal: A Prelude to Romantic Classicism." *Journal of the Warburg and Courtauld Institutes* 25 (1962): 278–320; 26 (1963): 90–123.

MORNET, D. *Le sentiment de la nature en France de J.-J. Rousseau à Bernardin de Saint-Pierre.* Paris, 1907.

———. *Le romantisme en France au XVIIIe siècle.* Paris, 1912.

MORTIER, R. *La Poetique des ruines.* Geneva, 1974.

MOULIN, M. *L'architecture civile et militaire au XVIIIe siècle en Aunis et Saintonge.* La Rochelle, 1972.

MULLER, E., and CACHEUX, E. *Habitations ouvrières et agricoles.* Paris, 1855–56.

NIÈRES, C. *La reconstruction d'une ville au XVIIIe siècle: Rennes 1720–1760.* Paris, 1972.

NOLHAC, P. DE. *Hubert Robert.* Paris, 1910.

———. *Histoire du château de Versailles: Versailles au XVIIIe siècle.* Paris, 1918.

PARISET, F. G. *Histoire de Bordeaux, 1714–1814.* Vol. 5. Bordeaux, 1968.

PINKNEY, D. H. *Napoleon III and the Rebuilding of Paris.* Princeton, N.J., 1958.

SAISSELIN, R. G. *Taste in Eighteenth-Century France.* New York, 1965.

SCHNEIDER, R. *L'esthétique classique chez Quatremère de Quincy (1805–1825).* Paris, 1910.

————. *Quatremère de Quincy et son intervention dans les arts (1788–1830)*. Paris, 1910.

STAROBINSKI, J. *The Invention of Liberty, 1700–1789*. Geneva, 1964.

————. *1789: les emblèmes de la raison*. Paris, 1973.

STEINHAUSER, M. *Der Architektur der Pariser Oper*. Munich, 1969.

SUTCLIFFE, A. *The Autumn of Central Paris: The Defeat of Town Planning, 1850–1970*. London, 1970.

THIBERT, M. *Le rôle social de l'art d'après les Saint-Simoniens*. Paris, 1926.

TOURNIER, R. *Les églises comtoises: leur architecture des origines au XVIIIᵉ siècle*. Paris, 1954.

————. *Maisons et hôtels privés du XVIIIᵉ siècle à Besançon*. Paris, 1970.

VAUDOYER, A.-L.-T., and BALTARD, L. P., eds. *Grands Prix d'architecture, 1801–1831*. 3 vols. Paris, 1818–34.

VERLET, P. "Le mobilier de Louis XVI et de Marie-Antoinette à Compiegne." 1937. Ms., Louvre, Paris.

————. *French Furniture and Interior Decoration of the Eighteenth Century*. London, 1967.

GERMANY AND AUSTRIA

BEENKEN, H. *Schöpferische bauideen der deutschen romantik*. Mainz, 1952.

DU COLOMBIER, P. *L'architecture française en Allemagne au XVIIIᵉ siècle*. 2 vols. Paris, 1956.

GROTE, L., ed. *Die deutsche Stadt im 19. Jahrhundert*. Munich, 1974.

MANN, A. *Die Neuromanik: eine rheinische Komponente im Historismus des 19. Jahrhunderts*. Cologne, 1966.

MUTHESIUS, S. *Das englische Vorbild*. Munich, 1974.

PLAGEMANN, V. *Das deutsche Kunstmuseum, 1790–1870*. Munich, 1967.

ROBSON-SCOTT, W. D. *The Literary Background of the Gothic Revival in Germany*. Oxford, 1965.

VOGT, G. *Frankfurter Bürgerhäuser des Neunzehnten Jahrhundert*. Frankfurt, [1970?].

WAGNER-RIEGER, R. *Wiens Architektur im 19. Jahrhundert*. Vienna, 1970.

WAGNER-RIEGER, R., ed. *Die Wiener Ringstrasse: Bild einer Epoche*. Cologne, Graz, and Vienna, 1969–. (9 vols. to date.)

GREAT BRITAIN

ALLEN, B. S. *Tides in English Taste (1619–1800)*. 2 vols. 1937. Reprint. New York, 1969.

AMES, W. *Prince Albert and Victorian Taste*. London and New York, 1968.

ANSON, P. F. *Fashions in Church Furnishings, 1840–1940*. Rev. ed. London, 1965.

ARMYTAGE, W. H. G. *Heavens Below: Utopian Experiments in England, 1560–1960*. London, 1961.

BOASE, T. S. R. *English Art, 1800–1870*. Oxford, 1959.

BURKE, J. *English Art, 1714–1800*. Oxford, 1976.

CHADWICK, G. F. *The Park and the Town: Public Landscape in the 19th and 20th Centuries*. London and New York, 1966.

CLARK, K. *The Gothic Revival*. London, 1928. Reprint. New York, 1974.

CLARKE, B. F. L. *Church Builders of the 19th Century*. 1938. Reprint. Newton Abbot, Devon, 1969.

————. *Parish Churches of London*. London, 1966.

CLIFTON-TAYLOR, A. *The Pattern of English Building*. Rev. ed. London, 1972.

COLVIN, H. M. *A Biographical Dictionary of British Architects, 1600–1840*. London, 1978.

CRAIG, M. J. *Dublin, 1660–1860*. Rev. ed. London, 1969.

CROOK, J. M. *The Greek Revival: Neo-Classical Attitudes in British Architecture, 1760–1870*. Feltham, 1968.

————. *The British Museum*. London and New York, 1972.

CROOK, J. M., and PORT, M. H. *The History of the King's Works*. Vol. 6 (1782–1851). London, 1973.

DYOS, H. J. *Victorian Suburb: A Study of the Growth of Camberwell*. Leicester, 1966.

DYOS, H. J., and WOLFF, M., eds. *The Victorian City: Images and Reality*. 2 vols. London, 1973.

FAWCETT, J., ed. *Seven Victorian Architects*. London, 1976.

FERRIDAY, P., ed. *Victorian Architecture*. London, 1963.

FOWLER, J., and CORNFORTH, J. *English Decoration in the 18th Century*. London, 1974.

GARRIGAN, K. O. *Ruskin on Architecture: His Thought and Influence*. Madison, Wis., 1973.

GIROUARD, M. *The Victorian Country House*. Oxford, 1971.

————. *Sweetness and Light: The Queen Anne Movement, 1860–1900*. Oxford, 1977.

GOMME, A., and WALKER, D. *Architecture of Glasgow*. London, 1968.

GOODHART-RENDEL, H. S. *English Architecture Since the Regency*. London, 1953.

HITCHCOCK, H.-R. *Early Victorian Architecture in Britain*. 2 vols. 1954. Reprint. New Haven, Conn., 1972.

HOBHOUSE, H. *Lost London*. Boston and London, 1971.

HOPKINS, H. J. *A Span of Bridges*. New York and Newton Abbot, 1970.

HUNT, J. D., and WILLIS, P., eds. *The Genius of the Place: The English Landscape Garden, 1620–1820*. London, 1975.

HUSSEY, C. *The Picturesque*. 1927. Reprint. New York, 1967.

————. *English Country Houses: Late Georgian, 1800–1840*. London, 1958.

————. *English Country Houses: Mid-Georgian, 1760–1800*. Rev. ed. London, 1963.

JERVIS, S. *High Victorian Design*. Ottawa, 1974.

KELLET, J. R. *The Impact of Railways on Victorian Cities*. London, 1969.

London, County Council. *Survey of London*. London, 1896–. (39 vols. to date.)

MACAULAY, J. *The Gothic Revival, 1745–1845*. Glasgow and London, 1975.

MACLEOD, R. *Style and Society: Architectural Ideology in Britain, 1835–1914*. London, 1971.

MORRIS, W. *Collected Works of William Morris*. Edited by M. Morris. 24 vols. London, 1910–15.

MUTHESIUS, H. *Die neuere kirchliche Baukunst in England*. Berlin, 1901.

MUTHESIUS, S. "The 'Iron Problem' in the 1850's." *Architectural History* 13 (1970): 58–63.

————. *The High Victorian Movement in Architecture, 1850–1870*. London, 1971.

OLSEN, D. J. *Town Planning in London: The Eighteenth and Nineteenth Centuries*. New Haven, Conn., 1964.

————. *The Growth of Victorian London*. London, 1976.

PEVSNER, N. *The Buildings of England*. 46 vols. Harmondsworth, 1951–74.

————. *Some Architectural Writers of the 19th Century*. Oxford, 1972.

Port, M. H. *Six Hundred New Churches: A Study of the Church Building Commission, 1818–1856*. London, 1961.

PORT, M. H., ed. *The Houses of Parliament*. New Haven, Conn., 1976.

RICHARDSON, A. E. *Monumental Classic Architecture in Great Britain and Ireland During the Eighteenth and Nineteenth Centuries*. London, 1914.

Royal Institute of British Architects (RIBA). *Catalogue of the Drawings of the Royal Institute of British Architects*. London, 1969–. (17 vols. to date.)

RUSKIN, J. *The Works of John Ruskin*. Edited by E. T. Cook and A. Wedderburn. 39 vols. London, 1903–12.

SAXL, F., and WITTKOWER, R. *British Art and the Mediterranean*. London, 1948.

SHERBURNE, J. C. *John Ruskin; or, The Ambiguities of Abundance*. Cambridge, Mass., 1972.

STEEGMANN, J. *Consort of Taste, 1830–1870*. London, 1950.

SUMMERSON, J. *Heavenly Mansions, and Other Essays on Architecture*. 1949. Reprint. New York, 1963.

————. *Architecture in Britain, 1530–1830*. 5th ed. London, 1969.

————. *Georgian London*. Rev. ed. London, 1970.

————. *Victorian Architecture: Four Studies in Evaluation*. New York, 1970.

————. *The London Building World of the 1860s*. London, 1973.

————. *The Architecture of Victorian London*. Charlottesville, 1976.

WATKIN, D. J. *Morality and Architecture: The Development of a Theme in Architectural History and Theory from the Gothic Revival to the Modern Movement*. Oxford, 1977.

WHIFFEN, M. *Stuart and Georgian Churches: The Architecture of the Church of England Outside London, 1603–1837*. London and New York, 1948.

WHITE, J. F. *The Cambridge Movement: The Ecclesiologists and the Gothic Revival*. Cambridge, 1962.

WOODBRIDGE, K. *Landscape and Antiquity: Aspects of English Culture at Stourhead, 1718 to 1838*. London, 1970.

YOUNGSON, A. J. *The Making of Classical Edinburgh, 1750–1840*. Edinburgh, 1966.

GREECE

RUSSACK, H. H. *Deutsches Bauen in Athen*. Berlin, 1942.

SINOS, S. "Die Gründung der neuen Stadt Athen." *Architectura 1* (1974): 41–52.

TRAVLOS, J. *Architecture néoclassique en Grèce*. Athens, 1967.

ITALY

ANGELINI, L. *L'avvento dell'arte neoclassica in Bergamo*. Bergamo, 1966.

BASSI, E. *Architettura del sei e settecento a Venezia*. Naples, 1962.

BORSI, F. *La capitale a Firenze e l'opera de G. Poggi*. Rome, 1970.

BRUSATIN, M. *Illuminismo e architettura del '700 Veneto*. Castelfranco Veneto, 1969.

HASKELL, F. *Patrons and Painters: A Study in the Relations Between Italian Art and Society in the Age of the Baroque*. 1963. Reprint. New York, 1971.

LAVAGNINO, E. *L'arte moderna dai neoclassici ai contemporanei*. 2 vols. Turin, 1956.

MEZZANOTTE, G. *Architettura neoclassica in Lombardia*. Naples, 1966.

POMMER, R. *Eighteenth-Century Architecture in Piedmont:*

The Open Structures of Juvarra, Alfieri and Vittone. London and New York, 1967.

PROZZILLO, I. *Francesco Milizia, teorico e storico dell' architettura*. Naples, 1971.

VENDITTI, A. *Architettura neoclassica a Napoli*. Naples, 1961.

WITTKOWER, R. *Art and Architecture in Italy, 1600 to 1750*. 3d ed. Baltimore and Harmondsworth, 1973.

ZUCCA, L. T. *Architettura neoclassica a Trieste*. Trieste, 1974.

PORTUGAL

FRANCA, J. A. *Lisboa Pombalina, e o iluminismo*. Lisbon, 1965. (First published as *Une ville des lumières: la Lisbonne de Pombal*. Paris, 1965.)

RUSSIA

BATER, J. H. *St. Petersburg: Industrialization and Change*. London, 1976.

EGOROV, I. A. *The Architectural Planning of St. Petersburg*. Athens, Ohio, 1969.

HAMILTON, G. H. *The Art and Architecture of Russia*. Baltimore and Harmondsworth, 1954.

HAUTECOEUR, L. *L'architecture classique a Saint-Pétersbourg à la fin du XVIIIe siècle*. Paris, 1912.

ILYIN, M. *Moscow Monuments of Architecture: Eighteenth– the First Third of the Nineteenth Century*. 2 vols. Moscow, 1975.

KIRICHENKO, E. *Moscow Architectural Monuments of the 1830s–1910s*. Moscow, 1977.

SPAIN

CAREDA, J. *Memorias para la historia de la Real Academia de San Fernando y de las Bellas Artes en España*. 2 vols. Madrid, 1867.

GAYA NUÑO, J. A. *Arte del siglo XIX*. Ars Hispaniae, vol. 19. Madrid, 1966.

NAVASCUES PALACIO, P. *Arquitectura y arquitectos Madrileños del siglo XIX*. Madrid, 1973.

PARIS, P. "L'art en Espagne et en Portugal de la fin du XVIIIe siècle à nos jours." In *Histoire de l'art*, by A. Michel, vol. 8. Paris, 1926.

SWITZERLAND

CARL, B. *Die Architektur der Schweiz: Klassizismus 1770–1860*. Zurich, 1963.

CORBOZ, A. *Invention de Carouge, 1772–92*. Lausanne, [1968].

GERMANN, G. *Der protestantische Kirchenbau in der Schweiz*. Zurich, 1963.

UNITED STATES OF AMERICA

HAMLIN, T. *Greek Revival Architecture in America*. New York, 1944.

PIERSON, W. H. *American Buildings and Their Architects*. Vol. 1 (*The Colonial and Neo-Classical Styles*). New York, 1970.

STANTON, P. B. *The Gothic Revival and American Church Architecture*. Baltimore, 1968.

INDEX

LIST OF PLATES

457

PHOTOGRAPH CREDITS

Aerofilms, London: 43.

Wayne Andrews, Grosse Pointe, Michigan: 563.

Archives Municipales, Bordeaux: 176, 177.

Archives Photographiques, Paris: 166, 179, 225, 350, 352.

James Austin, London: 119, 136, 149, 150, 214, 215, 363, 391, 398, 401, 412.

Bruno Balestrini, Milan: 1, 8, 9, 11, 13, 15, 19–21, 29, 104, 113–115, 120, 127–133, 135, 155–158, 161, 167, 169, 178, 180, 182–185, 189, 198, 202, 205, 208, 211, 219, 236, 237, 295, 296, 299–301, 303, 309, 312, 346–349, 351, 356, 359–362, 364, 365, 367–370, 374, 375, 377–380, 382–384, 390, 392–395, 399, 400, 402–404, 408–411, 413–416, 418, 421, 424, 426, 428, 431–434, 477, 502–506, 509–516, 520–524, 526–528, 530–532, 534–536, 538, 542, 544–548, 550, 552, 553, 610–625, 629–637, 647, 649, 650, 654–656.

Bibliothèque Nationale, Paris: 137, 138, 143, 159, 206, 207, 282–290, 344, 345, 396.

Bulloz, Paris: 151, 305, 405.

J. Combier, Macon: 315.

Country Life, London: 32, 34, 35, 40, 42, 47, 52–56, 69, 95–98, 101, 103, 105, 106, 109, 153, 238–241, 244, 247, 251–259, 263, 265–269, 271, 272, 274, 275, 280, 281, 330, 437, 454, 455, 458–460, 463, 464, 574, 575, 577, 587, 589, 594, 598, 599.

Courtauld Institute of Art, London: 66, 67, 94, 246, 248, 249, 270, 334, 466, 592, 593, 600, 601.

Christopher Dalton, Daventry: 99, 100.

J. De Grivel, Besançon: 190–194.

Deutsche Fotothek Dresden, Dresden: 59–61.

Fitzwilliam Museum, Cambridge: 152.

Fotocielo, Rome: 539.

Jonathan M. Gibson, Guildford, Surrey: 68.

Giraudon, Paris: 4, 78, 174, 187, 201, 216, 217, 221, 223, 298, 317, 385–387, 397.

Greater London Council, Photographic Unit Department of Architecture and Civil Design, London: 435, 452, 453, 467, 469.

Irish National Trust Archive, Dublin: 573.

A. F. Kersting, London: 462, 603.

Landesbildstelle, Berlin: 107, 108, 470.

Leeds Art Galleries, Leeds: 262.

Library of Congress, Washington, D.C.: 557–562, 564–567.

Roland Liot, St.-Germain-en-Laye: 197.

Mensy, Besançon: 80.

Münchner Stadtmuseum, Munich: 478.

Musée de Strasbourg, Strasbourg: 186.

Musei Vaticani, Archivio Fotografico, Rome: 517–519.

National Monuments Record, London: 339.

National Museet, Copenhagen: 497, 498, 500.

National Trust, London: 41, 44, 62, 63, 572.

Sydney W. Newbert, London: 328.

Novosti Press, Rome: 482–491, 493–496.

Andrea Pagliarani, Verona: 507.

Fernand Perret, La Chaux-de-Fonds: 195, 196.

Photo Pierrain-Carnavalet, Paris: 79, 125, 134, 165, 203, 204.

G. B. Pineider, Florence: 525.

Reilly and Constantine Commercial, Birmingham: 639.

H. Roger-Viollet, Paris: 406, 407.

Royal Commission on Ancient Monuments (Scotland), Edinburgh: 111, 260, 264, 447, 448.

Royal Commission on Historical Monuments (England), London: 329, 338–340, 438, 440–442, 444–446, 457, 461, 576, 578, 580–585, 590, 591, 595–597, 609. All rights reserved.

Royal Library, Copenhagen: 499.

Tom Scott, Edinburgh: 45.

Semper-Archiv der ETH, Zurich: 662–664.

Service Photographique des Archives Nationales, Paris: 324.

Edwin Smith, London: 443.

Sir John Soane's Museum, London: 242, 243, 331, 335, 341–343.

Staatliche Landesbildstelle Südbayern, Munich: 480, 481.

Franz Stoedtner, Düsseldorf: 476.

TASS from SOVFOTO: 492.

Tate Gallery, London: 116.

Thorvaldsen Museum, Copenhagen: 501.

Topical Press, London: 327, 456. All rights reserved.

University Library, Warsaw: 154.

Jacques Verroust, Neuilly: 3.

Verwaltung der Staatlichen Schlösser, Gärten, und Seen, Munich: 479.

Wallace Collection, London: 144. All rights reserved.

Drawings by Studio Lodolo-Süss

c.1

NA
600
M513

CARLOW COLLEGE

Grace Library

Pittsburgh, PA   15213